SCHOOL PSYCHOLOGY

SCHOOL PSYCHOLOGY

A DEVELOPMENTAL AND
SOCIAL SYSTEMS APPROACH

ROBERT HENLEY WOODY

University of Nebraska at Omaha

JOSEPH C. LA VOIE

University of Nebraska at Omaha

SUSAN EPPS

University of Nebraska Medical Center

ALLYN AND BACON

Boston   London   Toronto   Sydney   Tokyo   Singapore

Series Editor: Ray Short
Series Editorial Assistant: Jo Ellen Caffrey
Production Coordinator: Holly Crawford
Editorial-Production Service: Lynda Griffiths, TKM Productions
Cover Administrator: Linda K. Dickinson
Cover Designer: Suzanne Harbison
Manufacturing Buyer: Megan Cochran

Copyright © 1992 by Allyn and Bacon
A Division of Simon & Schuster, Inc.
160 Gould Street
Needham Heights, MA 02194

Library of Congress Cataloging-in-Publication Data
Woody, Robert Henley.
    School psychology : a developmental and social systems approach /
Robert Henley Woody, Joseph C. LaVoie, Susan Epps.
        p.   cm.
    Includes bibliographical references and index.
    ISBN 0-205-13502-1
    1. School psychology – United States.   I. LaVoie, Joseph C.
II. Epps, Susan.   III. Title.
LB1027.55.W66   1992
370.15 – dc20   91-43932
                                                              CIP

Printed in the United States of America
10   9   8   7   6   5   4   3   2   1   97   96   95   94   93   92

To our parents:
Robert H. and Wilma R. Woody,
Oscar S. and Constance J. LaVoie,
and
Jones N. and Charlotte R. Epps

BRIEF CONTENTS

CONTENTS

PREFACE

It is time for an enhanced "New Age" school psychology. Having long been a mainstay of education, school psychology is now experiencing even greater importance for meeting educational and social problems associated with children and youth and their families. Through federal and state legislation, school psychologists are being asked to continue psychoeducational assessments and classroom-related consultations, and also to provide services for such critical problems as behavior disorders, emotional maladjustments, substance abuse, delinquency, unwanted pregnancies, sex education, teenage suicide, and chronic illness. Many of these problems necessitate the school's entering the family domain. Moreover, legislation mandates an ever-increasing age range. The concept of lifelong education supports the school extending its services from birth (e.g., to infants with developmental delays, health education for parents) throughout adulthood (e.g., education for senior citizens). The result is that the demand for school psychologists exceeds the number of candidates available. Stated simply, new competencies are required to meet the challenges of the abundant employment opportunities.

School Psychology: A Developmental and Social Systems Approach offers a new model for training and practice. In the past, school psychology adhered to a clinical model concerned with etiology and pathology, and more recently, a psychoeducational consultative model that facilitated growth and accomplishment through teacher intervention. Today, school psychology must accommodate the plethora of societal/school expectations, and it is clear that traditional clinical and consultative interventions will not suffice. What is needed is a model for training and practice that considers the developmental factors and conditions unique to each stage of life, and how they, in turn, interface with the social system(s) in which the child or youth lives. All school psychology services are influenced by numerous social systems, as reflected in the school's changing role in society, the policies of the board of education, and the particular student's familial values and characteristics. Consequently, the school and the school psychologist must reach beyond the confines of the classroom and into homes (e.g., family services) and the community (e.g., interagency coordination among health care, social, and legal services).

This book has been developed for graduate students preparing for careers in school psychology and related fields (e.g., special education, school and community counseling, and school social work). Practitioners will find the material useful for updating ideas and conduct to meet contemporary expectations and standards. The material is structured to provide authoritative academic information and practical guidelines suitable for all levels of training and experience. Each chapter covers relevant theories, analyzes conceptual issues, describes techniques, offers practical suggestions, and posits future trends in research, training, and practice.

Chapter 1, The Evolution of School Psychology, traces the steps of school psychology from the past to the present and reveals what may be expected in the future. The diminished dominance of professional associations in defining the discipline is matched to the present-day demand from public policy for accountability to governmental regulatory sources and courts of law. Using the scientist-practitioner model as a cornerstone and accepting the interface and link between school and clinical psychology, a model for training and practice is described according to behavioral science, and developmental, family, and social systems dimensions.

Chapter 2, Developmental and Social Systems, focuses on developmental factors associated with childhood and adolescence and how these factors interact with the various familial, social, and educational systems in which the child or youth functions. Major emphasis is given to a developmental perspective of human behavior and to the determinants of system performance, using the family and school as examples of systems.

Chapter 3, Research Methods, describes research strategies that fit a developmental and social systems approach to school psychology. Topics include a review of state-of-the-art in school psychology research, intra- and interindividual variation, a developmental function versus an individual differences approach, designs, observational methods, hypothesis testing, appropriate statistics, and ethics when conducting research.

Chapter 4, Learning Theories and Applications, underscores the notion that information exchange is a critical component in a developmental and social systems approach to school psychology. Within the framework of information processing, special attention is devoted to behavior theories (since they consider the interaction of the person and the environment). Cognitive strategies and their application to classroom learning, and as an intervention procedure for learning deficits, provide the major portion of the applied dimension.

Chapter 5, Behavior Analysis and Interventions, highlights the application of behavior analysis to childhood behavior problems and the interaction of the systems in which the child functions. Measurement and analysis of behavior change, methods for increasing and decreasing behavior, cognitive interventions, and ethical considerations in behavior analysis are discussed.

Chapter 6, Psychotherapeutic Interventions, adopts a general theory orientation and organizes psychodynamic, existential-humanistic, cognitive-behavioral, and systems theories into a unified approach. Concepts and techniques are discussed for the provision of therapeutic services to children and youth and the consultation process. Developmental issues relevant to counseling children and adolescents and the developmental tasks facing families also are addressed.

Chapter 7, School and Pediatric Consultation Theories and Techniques, provides an overview of major theoretical models for consultation, with emphasis on a six-stage model of consultation. Based on an ecobehavioral perspective, a preventive model is presented—one that prepares consultees to use skills proactively to analyze variables that may facilitate or interfere with children's learning and prosocial behavior. An empowerment philosophy is used to frame consultation.

Chapter 8, Psychoeducational Assessment I: Principles and Issues, retains some aspects of the traditional medical-diagnostic assessment model, but focuses on developing an individualized education program (IEP) and an individualized family service plan (IFSP). Along with definitions of key assessment terms, consideration is given to the essential nature of reliability and validity and meeting service delivery standards set forth by law and by professional associations. Guidance is given for establishing positive relations and communications with ancillary professions (e.g., classroom teachers, psychoeducational personnel, administrators, and community health-care and social service workers) and tailoring the psychoeducational report accordingly. The chapter includes discussion of the use of computerized assessment, such as for individualized adaptive testing, and the forensic role of the school psychologist in legal proceedings involving children and youth and their families.

Chapter 9, Psychoeducational Assessment II: Methods and Instruments, urges the use of a battery of data-collection strategies. Based on surveys of school psychologists' preferences for assessment approaches, detailed consideration is given to record analysis, interviewing, behavior rating scales, intelligence tests, achievement tests, perceptual tests, human figure drawings, personality and social/emotional methods, neuropsychological tests, and family evaluations. Guidelines are provided for preparing a meaningful psychoeducational assessment report.

Chapter 10, The School-Family-Community Interface, addresses unique service delivery issues that arise from contemporary public policy—namely, school psychology practice beyond the schoolhouse with community agencies and families. Emphasis is placed on two populations of high-risk children and adolescents: infants, toddlers, and preschoolers with developmental delays; and children and adolescents with chronic illness and special health-care needs. A multifaceted role is delineated for building effective partnerships among the school, family, and community. Specialized issues in family-centered assessment and intervention, contributions of psychology to the management of chronic illness, and practice in health-care settings also are addressed.

Chapter 11, Ethical Influences on School Psychology, considers ethical principles and standards for service delivery. It explains the importance of a code of ethics for professionalization, the structure of ethics, the benefits intended for the consumer and society, accountability through ethics, and the concept of self-regulation. Considering that ethical complaints are increasing, informal and formal resolution of ethical problems and possible sanctions for ethical violations are discussed.

Chapter 12, Legal Influences on School Psychology, explains the way that the legal system (e.g., through important legislation and critical cases) presents prescriptions and proscriptions in school psychology. Explanations are given for the relationship between law and education; the nature of criminal and civil law, statutory and common (case) law, jurisdiction, and the rules of civil and criminal procedure; and the school psychologist's role in expert testimony. An analysis is given of federal and state legislative dictates for educational programming for children with disabilities, as relevant to developing an individualized education program (IEP) and an individualized family service plan (IFSP) and honoring the family's educational and privacy rights (e.g., in school records). The legal tenets of confidentiality, privileged communication, and records are discussed, and exceptions due to a duty to warn (e.g., in child abuse and violent situations) are noted. Malpractice is explained, and guidelines are given for minimizing the risk of complaints (e.g., to the school administration, professional ethics committees, or state certification/licensing boards) and allegations of malpractice.

We believe that school psychology is at a critical juncture in its evolution. The contemporary demands posed by public policy present a challenge for school psychology to forsake tradition for tradition's sake, seek more integrated theories and techniques, and carve out a more useful role and set of functions. Any professional change must, of course, be predicated on behavioral science. Notwithstanding the economic vicissitudes that commonly plague education, standards for school psychology services must be elevated, not lowered. In the immediate future, the possibility of innovation is professionally exciting, the alternatives for new and expanded services are many, and the benefits to society from enhanced "New Age" school psychology are inspirational. In our opinion, the developmental and social systems approach is the compass for future directions of school psychology, research, and applications.

We wish to express our appreciation to the reviewers of our manuscript: John Brantley, University of North Carolina at Chapel Hill, and Steven Lee, University of Kansas. We also gratefully acknowledge the American Educational Research Association, the American Psychological Association, the National Association of School Psychologists, and the National Council on Measurement in Education.

R. H. W.
J. C. L.
S. E.

CHAPTER 1

THE EVOLUTION
OF SCHOOL PSYCHOLOGY

As the year 2000 approaches, there is growing recognition that Western civilization is at a transition point. The simplicity of the nineteenth century and the economic and social growth of the twentieth century will surely be replaced by an awesome complexity for living in the twenty-first century. With almost cyclic regularity, public attention is again turning to education to be the salvation from social problems (e.g., winning the war on drugs, increasing employability, counteracting the devastation of broken and abusive families, etc.). As a result, school psychology is receiving elevated public awareness and status, with professional predictions for greater employment opportunities and enhanced roles and functions.

RENOVATING PUBLIC EDUCATION

The public outcry for better education translates into a need for higher standards in the classroom, with a demand that educators guarantee that graduates, whether from elementary and secondary schools or from colleges and universities, be responsible and able contributors to society. As Phillips (1990) states, "The present crises in schools and schooling provide an opportunity for making innovations and infusing the field with new ideas, education and training models, and psychological service delivery structures" (p. 1); he adds, "Economic events have often stimulated criticisms of the public schools and demands for reforms" (p. 31).

Unfortunately, educational expectations and opportunism are constricted by an economic base that is withering under competitive expectations for stronger military defense, solutions to crime and other adverse social problems, and personal aggrandizement characteristic of the "me generation"—all of which receive quasi-leadership from politicians, as witnessed by rallying cries like "Read my lips; no new taxes!"

The National School Psychology Inservice Training Network (1984) has sounded the alarm that "America's public schools are in trouble" and "Help may be on the way, but it seems wise not to 'count on it' unless and until a coherent set of plans for improvement is persuasively advanced" (p. 5):

> The lives of many children are in disorder and significantly out of control. This is reflected by widespread slacking off in scholastic effort, decline in achievement, drops in school attendance, crime, and increases in precocious sexual behavior, drug use and alcoholism. (p. 5)

Over 1.5 million youngsters are arrested each year (Regnery, 1985). The criminal concomitant of school problems has led to increased involvement of school psychologists in forensic matters (Crespi, 1990).

The National School Psychology Inservice Training Network (1984) correctly asserts that all societal problems are evidenced in schools, and school personnel have responded with a nonsystem to low achievement, discipline problems, social/emotional problems, and the like. It should be noted that the problems cited impact on fundamental academic learning and reach into diverse spheres of personal, familial, and social behavior. London (1987) states, "Schools must lead the battle against the worst psychosocial epidemics that have ever plagued the children of our society" (p. 667). The premise is that schools must attain a transformation that will deliver educational excellence and, in the process, provide treatment to anyone who produces a problem in the life of a student. For example, Crespi (1990) states:

> Given the thousands of students entering psychiatric and correctional facilities, and given the age range of these clients, quality mental health and special education services are likely to become more available to incarcerated and hospitalized youth. There is a need for well-trained school psychologists who are knowledgeable in such traditional areas as assessment, counseling, consultation, and research and are equipped with the competence and ability to testify in court about intellectual, personality, and educational issues. (p. 87)

There is an inescapable connection between everyday conditions in the life of a child or youth and his or her schooling. Although the entire school system must make accommodations accordingly, school psychology in particular seems destined to be in the front line for planning, assessment, and intervention. Martin (1991) questions the responsiveness of school psychology to "the litany of problems" (p. 1), and urges more effectiveness in dealing with societal concerns, saying, "I fear we have missed this wave of public interest in education, and that another wave may be a long time coming" (p. 2).

Part of the concept of *institutionalization* is the wish to be free of blame. Too often no one accepts the responsibility necessary for effective action. A current public policy debate centers on whether it is the school or the student who is responsible for educational success or failure. If the answer lies with the student, the responsibility quickly reaches to nonschool sources, such as parents, public services, and society in general.

According to Keller (1989), there are critics who would use the educational shortcomings of the at-risk student as "an indictment of American democracy at large, not only of its schools" (p.

54), but he does not subscribe to the notion that individual students are blameless. He believes that schools and colleges need to be upgraded, but he notes that students "can be lazy, inattentive, or unable to see beyond immediate pleasure" (p. 54), and that greater importance should be placed on values, emotions, levels of self-control, and aspirations. In other words, social forces beyond the classroom, such as parental encouragement and familial/personal attitudes, contribute to the success or failure of formal learning. Therefore, the student must be able to engage in active learning, not just be a passive receptacle for force-fed information.

The classroom teacher is the chief engineer of constructive learning. Notwithstanding this primary role, the teacher will always need the wisdom and support of administrators and special services personnel. Of special importance to contemporary educational and social problems, psychoeducational personnel must be available and able to enter into the learning process of every child or youth. Psychoeducational personnel include curriculum consultants, resource teachers, speech and language therapists, special education teachers (for the mentally, behaviorally, emotionally, hearing, visually, and physically impaired), school nurses, and school psychologists. Of course, administrators (such as superintendents and principals) complement the efforts of the psychoeducational personnel and are, therefore, part of the psychoeducational team. The members of the school board and the parents are integral parts of the psychoeducational program. Note that the types of psychoeducational personnel will vary significantly in role definitions and duties, as influenced by federal and state laws, local school board policies, administrative priorities, and personal preferences expressed by the psychoeducational professional.

DEFINING *SCHOOL PSYCHOLOGY*

The definition of *school psychological services* is constantly changing. Barclay (1990) comments, "One of the incontrovertible conclusions that can be drawn from a review of the last decade in psychology, is that both the field and psychologists themselves have outgrown the classic definitions and parameters of our work" (p. 45). An appropriate opening definition is taken from the American Psychological Association's (1981) "Specialty Guidelines for the Delivery of Services by School Psychologists" (hereafter referred to as the "APA Guidelines"):

> *School psychological services* refers to one or more of the following services offered to clients involved in educational settings, from preschool through higher education, for the protection and promotion of mental health and the facilitation of learning:
>
> A. Psychological and psychoeducation evaluation and assessment of the school functioning of children and young persons. Procedures include screening, psychological and educational tests (particularly individual psychological tests of intellectual functioning, cognitive development, affective behavior, and neuropsychological status), interviews, observation, and behavioral evaluations, with explicit regard for the context and setting in which the professional judgments based on assessment, diagnosis, and evaluation will be used.
>
> B. Interventions to facilitate the functioning of individuals or groups, with concern for how schooling influences and is influenced by their cognitive, conative, affective, and social development. Such interventions may include, but are not limited to, recommending, planning, and evaluating special education services; psychoeducational therapy; counseling; affective educational programs; and training programs to improve coping skills.
>
> C. Interventions to facilitate the educational services and child care functions of school personnel, parents, and community agencies. Such interventions may include, but are not limited to, in-service school-personnel education programs, parent education programs, and parent counseling.
>
> D. Consultation and collaboration with school personnel and/or parents concerning specific school-related problems of students and the professional problems of staff. Such services may include, but are not limited to, assistance with the planning of educational programs from a psychological perspective; consultation with teachers and other school personnel to enhance their understanding of the needs of particular pupils; modification of classroom instructional programs to facilitate children's learning; promotion of a positive climate for learning and teaching; assistance to parents to enable them to contribute to their children's development and school adjustment; and other staff development activities.
>
> E. Program development services to individual schools, to school administrative systems, and to community agencies in such areas as needs assessment and evaluation of regular and special education programs; liaison with community, state, and federal agencies concerning the mental health and educational needs of children; coordination, administration, and planning of specialized educational programs; the generation, collection, organization, and dissemination of information from psychological research and theory to educate staff and parents.
>
> F. Supervision of school psychological services. (p. 672)

This is an important definition, and deserves careful analysis and consideration. Review supports an additional eight postulates:

> Postulate 1. The school psychologist shall serve persons at all stages of education. In the past, this has meant from preschool through higher education. It is a logical extension to provide services from birth to death. Public policy has recognized the rights of senior citizens, and promotes lifelong education. Although school psychology has yet to extensively serve persons in adult education programs, it is appropriate to do so.
>
> Postulate 2. The school psychologist shall provide comprehensive psychoeducational evaluations and assessments. This service involves far more than giving tests or determining IQ. The school psychologist must apply the assessment data for planning and decision making, be it for the student or the program.
>
> Postulate 3. The school psychologist shall provide interventions for education, emotional, behavioral, and familial problems.

Postulate 4. The school psychologist shall work with all material and relevant sources, particularly parents and other community services to children and youths, in order to maximize educational attainments and personal development.

Postulate 5. The school psychologist shall maintain an awareness of the developmental psychology of the learner, from infancy to senior age, and will promote lifelong education.

Postulate 6. The school psychologist shall assertively advocate program and resource development to meet the mental health and educational needs of all persons; this advocacy will, however, be predicated on academic and scientific information, as opposed to personal preferences.

Postulate 7. The school psychologist shall seek to be a creative leader among educators, students, families, and other public sources, such as through supervision for quality assurance of psychoeducational services or promotion of governmental policies and practices.

Postulate 8. The school psychologist shall conceptualize all professional ideas and services according to the interrelated sources that influence the student's development.

Clearly these postulates, derived from the APA Guidelines, buttress the developmental and social systems approach to school psychology.

THE BIRTH OF SCHOOL PSYCHOLOGY

Contrary to popular misconception, school psychology was not born in the 1960s. To be sure, the revolutionary legislation spearheaded by Presidents John F. Kennedy and Lyndon B. Johnson created great public concern about the handicapped and disenfranchised. Of importance, the Community Mental Health Centers Act was passed in 1963, and the resulting proliferation of mental-health services and the support by the public at large led Hobbs (1964) to refer to the community mental-health movement as the "Third Mental Health Revolution" (the first was the humane treatment of the insane and the second was Freud's contribution).

Numerous other legislative acts, at the federal and state levels, and hallmark judicial decisions highlighted the legal rights of persons with

adverse mental conditions (Woody, 1974). A great infusion of federal funds stimulated growth in mental-health services, which had a spillover effect for psychoeducational services in schools. The result was, in part, increased funding for mental-health and educational services. Psychoeducational services (including school psychology) increased rapidly and were accorded critical positioning in educational public policy.

Although the 1960s were surely the "glory days" of school psychology, school psychological services have, in fact, been a part of education for almost a century. In Philadelphia in 1896, Lightner Witmer established the first psychological clinic, and, in 1907, initiated the journal, *The Psychological Clinic* (Baker, 1988). Witmer is commonly credited with being the founder of clinical psychology and, since he established a hospital-based school (the Orogenic School, which investigated retardation, deviation, and restorative methods), he is also given parentage of school psychology.

Witmer endorsed an interdisciplinary team approach, with psychologists working closely with physicians, social workers, and teachers, as well as specialized clinics for speech and employment issues. The team involved the parents in the psychoeducational objectives. Witmer thought that it was especially important to have teachers remediating the children, and thus his "educational therapy" evolved. Diagnosis was the primary service of Witmer's clinic, but there were various treatment programs, including training for disciplinary and intellectual goals. Reinforcement techniques, especially social/emotional rewards from the trainer, were used. Witmer received professional criticism for his failure to pledge allegiance to Freudian principles (Shakow, 1968). Virtually no distinction was made between clinical and school psychology. Baker (1988) concludes:

> Although Witmer's contributions can be closely related to school psychology, he was a pioneer in the overall development of American applied psychology. Perhaps Witmer was too far ahead of his time. His desire to include a variety of disciplines in his brand of psychology may have proved too

threatening for the new American psychology, struggling to establish an identity of its own. It may be that the combination of his temperament and radical ideas led his contemporaries to regard him as an eccentric. Whatever the reasons for Witmer's obscurity, his legacy to modern psychology is clear. (p. 119)

It should be noted that clinical psychology and school psychology have always marched to essentially the same cadence, with only a few fanfares of exceptions. A counterpoint occurred just after World War II, when clinical psychology became more narrow in scope (i.e., it became part of the medically oriented mental-health movement). Consequently, "a clinical psychology rooted in child psychology no longer existed, and school psychology's capacity to prevent and repair school mental health problems of children was diminished" (Phillips, 1990, p. 9). Overall, however, school psychology and clinical psychology follow much the same orchestration for professional services.

Around the turn of the twentieth century, some psychologists became involved in what amounts to school psychology, but they carried titles and worked in settings that were not clearly aligned with schools. For example, French (1988) notes, "Between 1914 and 1925 research bureaus were established in about 50 schools across the country for the purpose of testing children and then solving the problems discovered through the testing" (p. 55). The personnel involved (about one-third of whom were women) were apparently psychologists, but specialized in what today might most aptly be termed *program evaluation* or *applied educational psychology*. French also cites the proliferation of child-guidance clinics, with their interdisciplinary emphases and their serving as referral sources for the schools, juvenile courts, and other agencies.

THE LINK BETWEEN CLINICAL PSYCHOLOGY AND SCHOOL PSYCHOLOGY

Clinical psychology and school psychology have long been banded together. In many ways, the specialty may be correctly thought of as "clinical child psychology in the schools." Consequently, some training programs have combined clinical psychology and school psychology (Vane, 1985). Modern school psychology retains its clinical psychology component (e.g., psychodiagnostics and therapy), but due to its broader scope, it will likely venture even further away from the clinical psychology formation. Certainly there are ties to prescriptive or psychoeducational services, educational programming, prevention, and systems engineering (Reynolds, Gutkin, Elliott, & Witt, 1984).

Historically, the link to clinical psychology was of great importance to school psychology training and practice. In the late 1940s, psychologists were concerned about the lack of scientifically based standards for clinical psychology. The American Psychological Association (APA) established a committee, chaired by David Shakow, that developed guidelines for clinical psychology training (Shakow, Hilgard, Kelly, Luckey, Sanford, & Shaffer, 1947). In 1949, the U.S. Public Health Service sponsored the historic Boulder Conference, at which a coterie of prominent psychologists concluded that the report from the Shakow committee should be implemented. With the intent of providing distinction and independence from psychiatrists (Frank, 1984), the Boulder Conference asserted the need for a *scientist-practitioner* training model (i.e., predicating clinical practice on systematic training in behavioral science) (Raimy, 1950). Competence for the practice of clinical psychology required knowledge of and research skills for behavioral science. The standards for training in and practice of clinical psychology were quickly embraced by school psychology.

To this day, the scientist-practitioner model reigns supreme in both clinical psychology and school psychology training and practice. Kanfer (1990) notes that, with the scientist-practitioner model, "the professional assists the client to assess a problematic situation, to define intervention goals, and to find ways that would remedy the client's distress by altering ineffective behavior, thoughts, emotional reactions, or environmental factors" (p. 265). The psychologist operates by three major cognitive components:

1. A *framework* for organizing knowledge about the relationships between psychological events, their settings, their correlates, and their antecedents (p. 265)
2. A *technology*—that is, a series of guidelines for action to achieve specific outcomes within the limits of the existing conditions and implements (p. 285)
3. A set of *guidelines* on how to relate the theoretical models and substantive knowledge about human behavior to decisions and actions in work with individual clients (p. 285)

To be sure that the scientist-practitioner model is maintained in practice, Kanfer suggests seven guidelines:

1. Obtain a statement of the current complaint and the factors that seem to contribute to it.
2. Translate this information into the language of psychological, biological, or social processes and structures.
3. Scan the field of principles, literature, and research relevant to the problem as it has been reformulated in the language of science. Examine the relevance of variables in adjacent data domains, such as those related to the social, cultural, or ethnic context and the biological or sociopolitical factors, as noted in the individual case.
4. Describe, at the conceptual level, the desired outcomes and the psychological processes that need to be influenced. Formulate an intervention strategy that is based on these considerations, defining the level (size of unit) of intervention.
5. Search for a technology and define specific parameters that may limit or enhance the feasibility and utility of the methods.
6. Apply the method. Monitor the effects and compare them against outcome criteria.
7. If desired effects are not obtained, recourse to Steps 1, 4, or 5, as needed. (pp. 266–267)

In February 1990, the National Conference on Scientist-Practitioner Training for the Profes-

sional Practice of Psychology met in Gainesville, Florida, and reaffirmed the importance of producing "a psychologist who is uniquely educated and trained to generate and integrate scientific and professional knowledge, attitudes, and skills so as to further psychological science, the professional practice of psychology, and human welfare" (Perry, 1990, p. 48).

The scientist-practitioner model holds that practice must be determined by academic and scholarly data; there is also reliance on the medical model (diagnosis, prescription). Since school psychology has evolved through trait-and-factor clinical notions to focus on psychoeducational, consultative, and systems notions, the traditional scientist-practitioner model does not assuredly accommodate contemporary needs in the field. Likewise, the developmental and social systems approach necessitates a flexibility in conceptualizations and actions (e.g., dealing with levels of systems that defy quantitative measurement) that may not always fit well with the traditional scientist-practitioner model. The model does, however, define the overall nature of school psychology practice, and remains the principal model that will shape ideas about role and functions. Nonetheless, the scientist-practitioner model probably needs to be altered toward open-mindedness to nontraditional strategies and pragmatism. Tenets of this nature can be found in the professional-practitioner model that emerged in the 1970s, which will be discussed shortly.

ORGANIZATIONAL INFLUENCES ON SCHOOL PSYCHOLOGY

Throughout the evolution of school psychology, professional associations have sought to influence the development of the specialty. These groups were ostensibly to promote the welfare of the public by improving the professionalization of the members or practitioners in the specialty, but, at times, they have seemed more bent on aggrandizement of the association and the industrialization, or marketing power, of the specialty.

Like clinical psychology, school psychology has had its own summit conferences. Essentially these meetings were aggregations of trainers, researchers, practitioners, and, to a limited extent, consumers who pooled their expertise, views, and aspirations relevant to school psychology for the purpose of shaping the specialty. From the onset of these comments about the school psychology conferences, the authors believe that (1) the conferences comprised a positive shaping force, (2) discussions were more theoretical (what should be) than action oriented (how progress can be made), and (3) conclusions were always subject to idiosyncratic filtering (as will be discussed later in the context of state and local home rule).

The Influence of the Thayer Conference

In response to receiving a grant from the National Institute of Mental Health (NIMH) and related governmental units, a conference on school psychology was held in 1954 at the Hotel Thayer in West Point, New York. The Thayer Conference was edited by Cutts (1955), who summarized the conference's agreed-upon definition, functions, qualifications, levels of positions, safeguards, and general principles of training for school psychology. The definition given was, "A school psychologist is a psychologist with training and experience in education" who uses "specialized knowledge of assessment, learning, and interpersonal relationships to assist school personnel to enrich the experience and growth of all children and to recognize and deal with exceptional children" (p. 174).

Functions included assessment, "facilitating the best *adjustment* of the largest possible number of children" (pp. 174–175), serving exceptional children of all types, remedial measures (usually through advising and planning with other personnel who will provide the direct remedial services), serving emotionally disturbed children (but there was disagreement, due to lack of training in intensive psychotherapy and other

role expectations, as to what extent this should be provided), and research (deemed "both a practical tool and a moral obligation of the school psychologist" [p. 175]). The conference also supported two levels of training (two-year subdoctoral and four-year doctoral programs).

For all intents and purposes, the Thayer Conference was the beginning of modern-day school psychology. As the school psychology training and employment boom of the 1960s arrived, the views expressed in Cutts's (1955) report on the Thayer Conference were held sacrosanct.

The Influence of Professional Associations

With the expansion of school psychology, professionals jockeyed for influence. The American Psychological Association created the Division of School Psychology in 1946, and seemed well on its way to dictating the standards for the specialty of school psychology (aided by its linkage to clinical psychology). Also, several other professional associations, most notably the American Association on Mental Deficiency (AAMD) and the Council for Exceptional Children (CEC), emerged as major influences on issues pertinent to school psychology.

While educational and mental-health professionals were involved with these two groups, there was commonly a consumer advocacy thrust, fashioned by handicapped persons and their families and by politicians. As one example of the blending of professional and consumer views, the AAMD promulgated terminology and operational definitions for *mental retardation;* throughout various revisions, the AAMD system shaped conceptualizations of mental retardation away from the simplistic notion of an "IQ deficit" toward recognition of the complex nexus between intelligence and adaptive behavior (with the latter emphasizing normalization).

In March 1968, a meeting was held in Columbus, Ohio. Primarily members of the Ohio School Psychologists Association, those present were concerned about the American Psychological Association's allegedly neglecting (some thought "discriminating against") the interests of subdoctoral school psychologists. It was concluded that school psychologists should

> establish a national effort which would develop a more adequate definition of the profession of school psychology, obtain a strong professional identity at the national level, provide more effective means of communication across the country, and establish clearly identifiable and strong representation for legislative action. (Farling & Agner, 1979, p. 141)

One year later (March 15, 1969), a convention in St. Louis led to the establishment of the National Association of School Psychologists (NASP), which gives emphasis to nondoctoral-level school psychology practitioners. It now has a major influence on the accreditation of school psychology training programs and, consequently, state certification requirements (NASP, 1986). Today, NASP has more than 16,000 members and is the largest professional organization representing school psychology (NASP, 1990–1991). A historical summary and analysis of the first 20 years of NASP has been provided by Fagan, Block, Dwyer, Petty, St. Cyr, and Telzrow (1989).

The coexistence of the APA's Division of School Psychology and the NASP is now politely referred to as engaging in complementary efforts, but there is doubt that unification has occurred. Genshaft and Wisniewski (1988) state,

> At the present time, disagreement exists as to who may legitimately use the title *school psychologist*. NASP defines *school psychologist* as a professional psychologist who has met all requirements for credentialing as stipulated by NASP (1984) standards. These standards currently advocate training at the specialist degree level. In contrast, APA defines a provider of school psychological services as either: (a) a professional school psychologist, who is trained at the doctoral level; or (b) a school psychological examiner (or a person

with a similar title), who is trained at the nondoctoral level and who must be supervised by a professional school psychologist. (p. 187)

With other organizational problems (e.g., trying to resolve the continuing clash about priority for research and practice), it may be summarized that the APA's Division of School Psychology tends to be dedicated to doctoral-level issues, whereas the NASP, with a membership comprised primarily of subdoctoral practitioners, tends to be dedicated to the pragmatics of school-based services (and, more recently, the school psychologist in private practice). Today, the APA's Division of School Psychology has 187 fellows, 1,597 members, and 498 associate members (APA, 1989).

The Influence of the Spring Hill and Olympia Conferences

The coexistence of the APA's Division of School Psychology and the NASP has been troubled enough to provoke sensible attempts at rapprochement. The National School Psychology Inservice Training Network, mentioned earlier, was formed because of a wish to have a cooperative conference on the future of school psychology. In 1980, the Spring Hill Symposium was held in Minnesota to analyze issues relevant to goals and roles for practice, ethical and legal issues, professionalization, training content, and accountability (Ysseldyke, 1982; Ysseldyke & Weinberg, 1981). In part because of the Spring Hill symposium, an ongoing NASP and APA task force was implemented.

From the issues-oriented Spring Hill Conference, the bipartisan effort moved to the action-oriented Olympia Conference, held in Wisconsin in 1981. This time, the sages of school psychology turned their attention to futurism, attempting to identify the internal and external forces that would impact on school psychology during the 1980s (Alpert, 1982).

The Influence of State and Local Home Rule

A major problem for all futuristic machinations for school psychology, no matter how astute, is that each state has great latitude for prioritizing conditions and services and setting forth definitive rules and regulations, all of which could be idiosyncratic and dissonant with what might be nomothetic notions. Similarly, school boards and their administrative personnel can cast a mold significantly different from what is masterminded at the state or federal level. Although governmental dictates, such as through legislation, must always be accommodated, the idea of *home rule* continues to thrive in educationally related service delivery. For example, local influences can prioritize the school psychologist's functions to some extent, such as whether the services shall be primarily clinical, educational, evaluative, instructional, consultative, psychotherapeutic, or whatever.

THE SCIENTIST-PRACTITIONER MODEL VERSUS THE PROFESSIONAL-PRACTITIONER MODEL

In 1973, the National Institute of Mental Health and the American Psychological Association held a meeting in Vail, Colorado, with the central theme being the schism that seemed to be developing between scientifically and academically oriented psychologists and practice-oriented psychologists (Korman, 1974). Some psychologists thought that the scientist-practitioner model had dropped the word *scientist* (Katkin, 1982). On the assumption that most psychological practitioners wanted to be viewed as doctor-practitioners rather than doctor-scientists, the Vail Conference supported a professional training model that would lessen emphasis on research and behavioral science and increase emphasis on practice or clinical skills. Instead of earning a Doctor of Philosophy (Ph.D.) degree, completion of the doctoral program would lead to a Doctor of Psychology (Psy.D.) degree. A significant

number of school psychology trainers and practitioners endorsed this model.

In the professional-practitioner approach, emphases include making research practical (e.g., being able to translate the research of others into practical solutions, as opposed to being able to conduct research); having course contents that are more technical than theoretical; seeking clinical acumen instead of academic wisdom; using practical settings to supplement classroom learning; and relying on faculty members who are, in fact, grounded in the reality of clinical practice and not isolated in an Ivory Tower (e.g., faculty members in Psy.D. programs are often part time, with part of their schedule being in services delivery in health-care facilities or private practice).

After considering the evidence, especially the views of Peterson (1985), Woody and Robertson (1988) state,

1. Graduates of scientist-practitioner programs and graduates of practitioner programs perform about equally well;
2. Curricula of professional schools and scientist-practitioner programs are more alike than different; and
3. The main differences between practitioner and scientist-practitioner programs lie in the attitudes and interests of faculty and students. (p. 40)

Although many of these ideas come from clinical psychology, the same conclusions seem applicable to school psychology.

School psychology training programs seem to favor the scientist-practitioner model, with the students being expected to understand, appreciate, and conduct problem-oriented research. Emphasis on technique is avoided; instead, preference is given to professionalism (a competency to approach the needs of children with a comprehensive and scholarly set) (Pryzwansky, Brantley, Wasik, Schulte, & Simeonsson, 1989). As mentioned earlier, the traditional scientist-practitioner model needs augmentation in order to accommodate pragmatic service thrusts unique to school psychology and to deal with developmental and social systems concerns. In other words, there should be an effective blending of the best aspects of both the scientist-practitioner and the professional-practice models.

THE INFLUENCE OF
FEDERAL LEGISLATION

Although the 1960s introduced legislation that boosted education and mental-health services, the support and endorsement were short-lived. In the 1970s, other priorities led to diminished federal funding for education and mental-health services. By the mid-1970s, legislative actions were creating a new set of commands for educators; however, federal funding was increasingly absent for fulfilling the orders.

In 1974, the Family Educational Rights and Privacy Act (FERPA) (34 C.F.R. 99) declared that parents and students could gain access to the student's educational records, they could (limitedly) control the disclosure of the records, and they were granted legal recourse for seeking corrections. In addition to bringing the parents and the school closer together, the legislation set guidelines relevant to psychoeducational records. For example, on the matter of parents having access to psychological test protocols, the legislative intent was for parents to have the right to have access to information about both the questions and the answers—at least in some manner—but the school need not actually show or provide a copy of the questions.

In 1975, the Education for All Handicapped Children Act (20 U.S.C., 1400), popularly known as Public Law 94-142, declared that all handicapped children had a right to a free and appropriate public education and set forth procedural protections (Stick, 1984). According to Schroeder, Schroeder, and Landesman (1987), there are six directives:

1. There must be a "free special education and related services for all handicapped children between 3 and 21 years, except in states that only serve children aged 5 to 18" (p. 805).

2. The child must receive "nondiscriminatory evaluation," that is, an interdisciplinary team assessment of the child's strengths and weaknesses.

3. Each child must have an "individualized education program" (IEP) that details "(a) *what* is to be taught, (b) *how* this is to be taught, and (c) the way *progress* will be measured" (p. 805).

4. Handicapped children must be taught in the "least restrictive environment" with nonhandicapped children to the maximum extent appropriate.

5. Educational decision making requires accountability and responsibility for both professionals and parents, and the principles of due process must prevail.

6. *"Parent participation* is a separate principle that recognizes that parents are among the most important teachers in a child's life and their involvement in their handicapped child's education can no longer be denied" (p. 806).

In 1986, the Education of the Handicapped Amendments (20 U.S.C. 1470), popularly known as Public Law 99-457, was passed. Short, Simeonsson, and Huntington (1990) declared it to be "a new national blueprint for expanding the opportunities and benefits of early intervention and preschool services to children and families" (p. 88). PL 94-457 mandates the extension of the right-to-education provisions to the 3- to 5-year-old group, and creates the new Handicapped Infants and Toddlers Program, with some financial assistance to states that provide services for the birth to 2-year-old group (Strein, 1989).

This legislation also focuses on the family and asserts that the intervention programs cannot be isolated to children: "Rather their needs can only be fully appreciated and understood within a family context. In turn, families must be seen as embedded within a larger social context" (Meisels, 1989, p. 452). Meisels points out that "the family focus suffuses all aspects of the early intervention service system—from prevention, to identification, to assessment, to service delivery"

(p. 452). Short, Simeonsson, and Huntington (1990) give emphasis to the early intervention aspects of PL 99-457, stating, "Implementation of the new law will result in a substantial increase in the demand for professionals who are knowledgeable about working with handicapped infants and their families" (p. 92).

In 1990, the Individuals with Disabilities Education Act (IDEA) was passed. PL 101-476 gives new impetus to the breadth and quality of services to children, youth, and adults with disabilities. These aspects are discussed in Chapter 12.

Note that although all of this legislation is at the federal level, each state has a certain degree of freedom for tailoring the rules and regulations that will implement the mandates. Whatever state-level adaptations are made, this line of legislation has sparked a fiery reentry of enthusiasm for psychoeducational services in public educational policy. It appears that these legislative commands will continue for decades to come, in some form or another. Unfortunately, funding to fuel the commanded efforts has not consistently or adequately materialized.

Of importance to this book, the tenets of Public Law 94-142 and its legislative progeny buttress a school psychology model that accommodates developmental stages, recognizes the social system in which the child develops and learns, and promotes optimal learning. Legislative mandates now cover birth to 21 years (with developmental consideration along the way), but it is anticipated that the upper age will be extended to more senior levels, which means more "adult school psychology." Also, it is clear that there must be more school-based services to families, and a systemic analysis and unification of resources, that will complement the individualized education program.

CURRENT AND FUTURE
SCHOOL PSYCHOLOGISTS

The recent line of federal legislation has piqued public and political interest in meeting the needs of exceptional children. Children with special needs constitute a significant portion of the popu-lation and therefore have a critical impact on our nation's welfare. According to Hodgkinson (1986), about 15 percent of children have mental and/or physical handicaps; similar (or higher) percentages suffer the consequences of living in a poverty-stricken family or with a parent or parents who provide minimal constructive influence. About 10 percent of children have poorly educated or illiterate parents. The American affinity for divorce leads to about half of our children being destined to live in a one-parent home prior to reaching age 18. Further, notwithstanding legal mandates for civil rights, racial and ethnic prejudice continues, imposing negative conditions (e.g., learned helplessness) on children. Even those children who are blessed with elevated intellect and talents require special help to maximize their potential.

To ignore the challenges, problems, and limitations created for children by mental, physical, and social factors represents a failure to cultivate the kind of human resources that contribute to the overall well-being and productivity of our society. Thus, it is an understatement to assert that the needs of all children, and particularly exceptional children, cannot go unattended.

The government recognizes the fragile balance of child development, as witnessed by the politically popular emphasis on the family. As the 1990s progress, there seems to be a governmental trend toward more services for all ages, including older persons. The present effort to promote lifelong education and counteract the negative aspects of aging with educational and cultural enrichment has implications for school psychology. The outcome may well be that school psychology will be made available to adults as well as children.

Of most importance, school psychology is now accorded a prominent role in the total educational system, and this role is likely to add new functions, duties, and services. As will be discussed, the services are already occurring outside of the confines of the school per se (i.e., private practice). Stated simply, the turn of the century finds school psychology being a growth industry, and employment opportunities and the concomitant benefits will increase accordingly. This section describes the primary conditions and influences relevant to school psychology in the present, and comments about what might be expected in the future.

School Psychology Credentials

Entry into the field of school psychology is controlled by credentialing. One form of credentialing is found in the awarding of graduate degrees; another form is gaining endorsement for employment by a school from the state department of education. On the latter, Brown and Horn (1980) report that in 1956 there were approximately 20 states that certified school psychologists, but by 1979, virtually all states had certification procedures.

Both the APA and the NASP accredit training programs in colleges and universities. The institutions must also have *regional* accreditation from a source recognized by the U.S. Office of Education. There are presently more than 200 graduate programs in school psychology with state-level certification or accreditation from the American Psychological Association and/or the National Council for Accreditation in Teacher Education (NCATE)/National Association of School Psychologists, and about 40 of the approximately 70 doctoral programs are accredited by APA (Phillips, 1988). McMaster, Reschly, and Peters (1989) provide a *Directory of School Psychology Graduate Programs.*

Each school psychology accreditation source has standards for training and field placement programs. These become quite detailed, such as the number of hours in a field placement, the experiences that should occur, and the nature of supervision that will be provided. Similarly, the qualifications for program faculty are prescribed, as well as admission and evaluation criteria for students in the program and the necessary institutional resources and facilities.

As might be expected, the accreditation sources also address the credentialing structure and requirements that they believe the state should maintain, even though each state is legally empowered to adapt and adopt its own credentialing standards. Relatedly, all relevant professional associations have a code of ethics, which either explicitly or implicitly address proscriptions and prescriptions for practice. Stated simply, entry into the field of school psychology is a highly institutionalized process, and with continuing education requirements necessary for certification for school employment or licensure for private practice, the credentialing process continues throughout the school psychologist's career.

Before leaving the topic concerning the influence that professional associations have on the credentialing of school psychologists, it should be noted that setting training and accreditation standards strengthens the association's control of the profession.

> Standards traditionally are considered to be criteria that are enforceable (e.g., eligibility for national certification is contingent on preparation consistent with NASP training standards). Principles and guidelines, on the other hand, describe expectations; they offer direction and provide recommendations. It clearly is in the best interests of a professional organization to develop or secure mechanisms through which it can enforce its standards. Without an enforcement mechanism, an organization's positions and policies, even if titled "standards," are in fact only guidelines. (Curtis & Zins, 1989, p. 182)

There have been instances when a professional association has set standards, which were then accommodated by state credentialing processes, that were, in fact, intended to enhance the association (e.g., requiring that an applicant for a credential have supervision only from a supervisor approved by the association). This sort of maneuver raises the ire of the Federal Trade Commission, namely because it seemingly promotes a monopoly. Consequently, it is common legislative practice to avoid citing an association's standards (e.g., ethics) per se in a state certification or licensing act. However, there can still be accommodation by requiring that statutory criteria (e.g., training necessary for eligibility for licensing) be "equivalent to" the training standards of a program accredited by a professional association.

A number of special credentials can be obtained by the school psychologist. Often freestanding "boards" award "diplomate" status in some specialized service. Since there is no quality control of these boards, many are allegedly comparable to a so-called degree mill. That is, their underlying purpose may be to generate income for the creator(s) of the boards, rather than to assert academic or practice excellence. The boards with dubious qualities have been known to "grandfather" or "grandmother" a candidate into diplomate status without requiring an examination.

Of honorable reputation, the American Board of Professional Psychology (ABPP) grants diplomate status, by careful examination, in the area of school psychology (as well as clinical psychology, counseling psychology, industrial-organizational psychology, clinical neuro-psychology, and forensic psychology; family psychology is soon to come). Diplomate status indicates that the school psychologist has received professional peer endorsement for his or her practice skills and related knowledge, and has established professional credibility. Being an ABPP Diplomate in School Psychology is a valuable and distinctive credential for one's career, but it does not eliminate the need for state certification or licensure.

Once school psychology credentials are obtained, professional training is not completed. The school psychologist must accept professional development as a career-long duty. Some credentials, such as for certification and licensure, require a certain number of continuing education units for renewal. Regardless, the concept of professionalism creates an obligation to continue to improve one's knowledge and competency, such as staying abreast of new ideas and methods. VandeCreek, Knapp, and Brace (1990) state:

> Professional psychology is a science-based practitioner profession. As such, professional psychology is committed to the continuing development of its knowledge base, and the practice of psychology should be guided not only by theory and previously established facts but also by any relevant more recent additions to what is known. Continuing learning is an essential part of the natural evolution of professions and professionals. (p. 135)

Thus, the student of school psychology should not view the award of a graduate degree as the final attainment. It is merely the demarcation of entry into the profession. The majority of academic learning and practice skills will presumably be obtained through postgraduate professional interactions (e.g., supervision), readings, seminars, workshops, and courses.

Personal Influences

Persons wishing to become school psychologists are known to be different from, say, those wishing to become clinical psychologists. For decades, there has been a quandary about whether school psychologists should be most closely aligned with education, and therefore recruited from among teachers and other educators, or with psychology, and therefore bypass or carefully screen teachers and other educators for meeting behavioral scientist standards. Current (and likely future) standards for school psychology training seem to be merging the two fields (education and psychology), but problems remain.

Since a significant number of school psychologists do come from the ranks of teachers, it is not surprising that they enter the program with several years of teaching (or other work-related) experience and are, thus, older than the typical college graduate. This means that they may have nonacademic responsibilities, such as families and a need to continue to work to be self-supporting.

Based on a national survey of first- and second-year school psychology doctoral students, Erchul, Scott, Dombalis, and Schulte (1989) found that the respondents had other duties (employment, family) that necessitated flexibility in course offerings (e.g., a preference for evening classes, part-time enrollment, extended internships), and a significant interest in clinical psychology, often equal to or greater than their interest in school psychology per se. (Nearly 20 percent of the respondents expected to do their predoctoral internship in a nonschool setting.) With the expected enhancement of career opportunities for school psychologists, it might be posited that the near future will see a shift toward more students pursuing graduate study of school psychology immediately following their receipt of an undergraduate degree (i.e., prior to work experience and acquisition of a family and employment duties).

A review of surveys concerning women's issues led Alpert, Genshaft, and Derevenco (1988) to conclude that (1) there is a trend for women to pursue graduate study, including school psychology; (2) women are underrepresented as trainers of school psychologists; (3) among faculty, women have lesser rank than men; (4) the salaries and incomes of female psychologists tend to be less than those received by their male counterparts; (5) women are underrepresented as editors of psychological journals (there has been, however, an increase in women being on editorial boards and serving as reviewers); and (6) female psychologists are authors of fewer journal articles than male psychologists. The researchers assert, "These trends raise the issue as to whether women have equal access to education and careers in psychology in general and school psychology in particular" (p. 9).

Russo, Olmedo, Stapp, and Fulcher (1981) report that 28.1 percent of school psychology faculty are women. There seems to be a trend toward more female clinical psychology faculty members (Klesges, Sanchez, & Stanton, 1982); if school psychology follows the pattern, more female school psychology faculty members may be expected.

Care must always be exercised to be sure that training and employment do not become tied to any form of discrimination, whether by gender, race, or age. It is known that the number of school psychologists and school psychology

trainers representing racial minorities are miniscule, and the enthusiasm for righting past wrongs against females and minorities can be a breeding ground for reverse discrimination against males, especially if they are older and Caucasian. A challenge facing school psychology—and all professions—is not to let "two wrongs make a right," and to move toward affirmative action that does not, in the process, wrongfully discriminate.

Functions in the Schools

Legislation (and the related rules and regulations) at the federal and state levels may create a framework for school psychology practice, but home rule allows specific definition for functions, duties, and services. Without doubt, assessment has been the primary service of most school psychologists. Early on, the press was for the school psychologist to administer standardized tests and, based on test scores, designate a child as being eligible or ineligible for a particular special education program. This approach was, of course, overly simplistic, and changes have been made. As might be deduced from the "test scores for labeling and categorization" approach, the focus was on pathology. That is, the school psychologist, relying on a clinical model, diagnosed problems and prescribed treatments (e.g., assignment to a special education classroom). Therefore, until about the early 1970s, the basic identity of school psychology was *clinical,* but as Bardon (1983) says, the specialty shifted its "priority from pathology (and its positive expression, mental health), to education (with its positive emphasis on human effectiveness)" (p. 191).

The identity passage reached educational programming, such as using ideas from school psychology to develop a preventive orientation in the minds of educators (e.g., the classroom teacher being prepared to stem problems before they materialize). Psychometrics, with an almost singular allegiance to intelligence testing, expanded to achievement, cognitive processes, perception, and other domains, with the goal being to foster a comprehensive psychoeducational communication channel to the teacher and the school system. The latter introduced systems-level actions, with school psychology inputs being used in organizational schema. These levels of functions still exist, but they do offer open-door acceptance to every school psychologist; access requires maturing and training, and entry must be gradual and progressive (Bardon, 1982).

As a preamble for the functions of school psychologists, the scientist-practitioner imposes a framework, yet there is a highly personal dimension, as reflected in Phillips's (1990) statement, "School psychology at its best is a science, a profession, and a calling." He indicates that the school psychologist is an applied scientist and interventionist for rational decision making; a descriptionist through ethnography, psychometry, and experimentation; a rational empiricist considering value, effects, costs, and morality; and a systems manager for planning, implementation, evaluation, and revision.

Five major functions for today's school psychologist are hierarchical in frequency or amount of time spent doing them (progressing from the most common to the least common): (1) assessment; (2) direct intervention (meaning some sort of remediation, instruction, guidance, counseling, or therapy with the student or others, such as parents, directly connected in the student's social system); (3) consultation (with teachers, other educators, and community health-care and agency personnel); (4) education (in-service training for school and community personnel, including perhaps parent-family life education); and (5) evaluation (program analysis and development) (Bardon, 1982).

These five functions may be sequential. That is, the school psychologist must be successful in assessment functions before moving into direct intervention. He or she must be successful in that function as a preface to moving into consultation, and so on to education and evaluation. It might be added that the repeatedly mentioned home-rule principle will determine greatly the functions and their frequency hierarchy and entry progression.

Functions are also shaped by legislative man-

dates, and due to these legal requirements, the future may bring on new roles, functions, duties, and services for school psychology. Meyers (1988) underscores how federal legislation mandates that psychoeducational services be for all children, their families, and their communities, and criticizes the all too common professional tendency to stress the needs of the discipline (school psychology's "guild interests") over the needs of the constituencies (children, parents, educators, and the community).

Relying on what seems to be a social systems approach and an analysis of research, Meyers (1988) delineates 16 "domains of competence" that are necessary for the practice of school psychology:

> Educational consultation
> Individualized assessment
> Environmental assessment and modification
> Stress reduction
> Individualized instruction
> Teaching basic academic and life skills
> Social, affective, and psychological education
> Group management
> Cooperative classroom social structure
> Parent involvement
> School-community relations
> Development and use of networks
> Public relations/political action
> Program evaluation and research
> Continuing professional development
> Law and education

Note that these domains are quite similar but more detailed than the five functions set forth by Bardon (1982).

The domains posited by Meyers may form a harbinger of what is to come in school psychology, namely that against a problematic organizational-societal backdrop, the school psychologist must advance from categorical functions to warding off detrimental conditions (e.g., ill-advised, political, self-serving pressures) to construct a developmental environment that will maximize learning and personal fulfillment. This will require academic astuteness, psychosocial advocacy, and professional leadership. The preceding ideas give impetus to the developmental and social systems approach embraced in this book.

Private Practice of School Psychology

Although most school psychology occurs and will continue to occur within the confines of a school system, there are school psychologists who work outside of the schools. This reference is to those who still identify themselves as school psychologists, not those with school psychology training, experiences, certification, or licensure who move to another specialty, such as marriage and family therapy, clinical psychology, or personnel management. The most thriving nonschool employment context for school psychologists is private practice, and employment in private school psychology practice seems to be increasing. Brown (1982) reported that about 6 percent of school psychologists were in some form of private practice, but five years later, Reschly, Genshaft, and Binder (1987) reported that about 17 percent of school psychologists engage in private practice on a part-time basis. As school psychology expands to include adult school psychology, as necessary to accommodate the public policy supporting lifelong education, it is likely that private practice of school psychology will become more prevalent.

To be in private practice, the school psychologist must commonly be licensed by a state agency (which is separate from the certification for employment in the schools). The use of licensure accomplishes a gatekeeping function; that is, it controls the persons who may practice to assure consumers of the competency of the service provider.

Although still too new to evaluate its total usefulness to credentialing (certification or licen-

sure), the National School Psychology Certification Board (affiliated with NASP) initiated a standardized (multiple-choice) examination in 1988 that is intended to become a nationwide mainstay. One of the problems facing any evaluation procedure, of course, is proving reliability and validity. Genshaft and Wisniewski (1988) point out that licensing criteria seem to reflect inherent face validity, but the diversity of and definitions for types of school psychological services and the differences between training programs may obfuscate any nexus between the selected criteria and the quality of the actual service in the field.

Private practice is greatly influenced by eligibility for reimbursement through health insurance. Since eligibility for third-party payment (from an insurance carrier) impacts on the incomes of other psychologists, there have been numerous clashes over the years between school psychologists and other types of psychologists, notably clinical psychologists. Their warfare has been clearly predicated on "economic turfsmanship," and has produced numerous unfortunate incidents, including legislative elimination of all licensing of psychologists until such time as the psychological specialties in the jurisdiction could gain some degree of professional compatibility.

Even with licensure, school psychologists in private practice have not received unlimited acceptance into third-party payment systems. Some states allow the insurance company to exercise discretion, and school psychologists in private practice may or may not be eligible for coverage (Genshaft & Wisniewski, 1988). An important support source for gaining third-party reimbursement is the National Register of Health Service Providers of Psychology, known popularly as the National Register. It has about 15,500 licensed or certified health-care psychologists enrolled, and will admit doctoral-level school psychologists because of its broad definition of a health service provider. However, the National Register's enrollment criteria are sometimes different from those maintained by school psychology sources (e.g., the required number of supervised internship hours and timeframe) and, thus, not all doctoral-level school psychologists may qualify (Genshaft & Wisniewski, 1988).

TOWARD A DEVELOPMENTAL AND SOCIAL SYSTEMS APPROACH

The specialty of school psychology has never had a shortage of ideas about what ought to be. Unfortunately, the reality of the world has often led to most or all of the pundits' sagacity being ignored, contradicted, short circuited, or rejected. The problem is, of course, connected to having to rely on hindsight. From looking at yesterday, insight can be gained about today, but tomorrow, as surely as it will dawn, can introduce unforeseen conditions. Therefore, the best that can be done is to apply the diagnostic *model* to the evolution of the professional specialty; that is, analyze today and yesterday, hypothesize about causative events and conditions, and prognosticate about what is needed, how it will be influenced, and what is apt to materialize tomorrow.

Modern school psychology must not let the past create a block to changes necessitated by contemporary conditions. In formulating the developmental and social systems approach for this book, the analysis relied, as much as possible, on objective and empirical data. However, by necessity this scientific set is blended with a reality set comprised of social values, public policies, and the strengths and frailties of the human condition. The remainder of the chapter will discuss the four essential dimensions of a developmental and social systems approach to school psychology.

The Behavior Science Dimension

School psychology has been plagued by conflicts, such as between school psychologists and clinical psychologists and between professional associations. Some of this dissonance may reflect a healthy effort to constructively influence the development of the specialty. Careful inspection of the differing views seems to reveal a professional push for greater specialization. Specialization helps delineate competencies but it carries the risk of reaching to overspecialization.

In examining the price that is extracted for specialization, Sarason (1987) notes that debate is necessary but he cautions against allowing it to be preempted by a "marketplace mentality." Sarason wisely asserts,

> The climate that provides no forum for serious and sustained discussion is one that encourages early and undue specialization. By undue I mean a degree of specialization that phenomenologically makes a part of psychology the whole of it, that makes the student an isolationist in the world of psychology. This happens unreflectively and with the best of intentions. (p. 37)

In school psychology, conflicts and competition between professional associations might contribute to overemphasis on specialization. Sechrest (1985) believes that specialties have been created at a "frightful rate," and states, "One suspects also that just sheer ego has something to do with the problem of specialization" (p. 1). Stated simply, school psychology cannot afford the risk that comes from a self-serving motive for specialization.

As a specialty, school psychology must be defined according to societal needs and preferences. Matarazzo (1987) believes "there is only one psychology," and asserts, "There is currently not even one specialty in psychology that meets the usual societal criteria utilized by significant others for the recognition of a specialty in the professions" (p. 893). Matarazzo's position is that psychology has different applications but they should not be transformed into being different specialties. Although school psychology may embrace particular proficiencies, there may be a lack of breadth for uniqueness, as would be necessary to merit specialty status (Sales, Bricklin, & Hall, 1983).

The proverbial bottom line is: The school psychologist, individually, must be an applied behavioral scientist first. With a broad base of academic training, cultivated skills for service, and identification as a member of the psychological profession generally, the school psychologist can tailor and develop proficiencies that will idiosyncratically attain service applications under the specialty banner of school psychology.

For training programs, this applied behavioral science posture should bring on a resource boon. Faculty and facilities for school psychology training can be drawn from virtually every other area of psychology training. Surely a professor in industrial-organizational psychology can provide school psychology students with information on personnel, leadership, and organizational theory issues useful in the school context. With the imperative need for understanding human development, the school psychologist cannot be kept away from professors aligned with developmental, child, learning, memory, physiological, and social psychology. School assessment and interventions can unquestionably be augmented with techniques from experimental behavioral analysis, counseling psychology, clinical psychology, special education, and on and on.

Although the developmental and social systems approach is compatible with the scientist-practitioner model, it need not reject the professional-practitioner model. Retaining a behavioral science basis for services allows a blending of the two models.

The Developmental Dimension

The school psychologist who is content to evaluate a child according to present functioning is not just shortsighted, he or she is blind to the axiom that behavior is a manifestation of developmental influences. School psychology and developmental psychology are interconnected. Developmental psychology is the study of intraindividual variability (Goulet & Baltes, 1970), which seeks to identify and explain individual changes from birth until death (Shaffer, 1985). The principal focus is on age-related changes in behavior and mental processes (McGraw, 1987). The same can be said about school psychology, but with the latter also including applications (e.g., treatments) aligned with developmental psychology and having a nexus to educational contexts and objectives.

According to John Dewey (1909), the school has endorsed the belief that social traits and values are connected to moral development, which passes through invariant qualitative stages; and moral development is based on the stimulation (in part, by the school) of thinking and problem solving in the child. Since the school psychologist is privileged to serve children at the behest of public policy (i.e., every person should be helped to make a positive contribution to society), moral development is a prerequisite for education: "We hold the schools accountable for transferring our values, attitudes, and cultural styles to our children" (Plas, 1986, p. 88).

Going beyond moral development per se, the research on child development is replete on stages occurring with everyone. Woody, Hansen, and Rossberg (1989) point out that, although Freud was

> one of the first to propose an orderly progression of human development based on the interactions between internal biological forces and the environmental forces of culture, the economy, and interpersonal relationships . . . many other psychologists have expanded upon his early observations and have proposed sequences of development through the lifespan with appropriate developmental tasks at each age. (p. 86)

For example, when the child enters school, he or she has already passed through a variety of stages, such as for attachment and bonding (which has its own stages or phases). Of proactive relevance, it is widely held that many, if not all, problems presented in school are linked to mental health in infancy. Consequently, there has been the emergence of developmental psychopathology (Kessler, 1988).

All problems encountered by the school psychologist should not, of course, be labeled *psychopathology*, but the developmental aspect is always present. For example, it is incontrovertible that the teenage years have innumerable developmental factors that influence the success or failure of coping behavior. The adolescent is particularly burdened by the developmental turmoil of the interrelationship between self-concept and sex-role orientation (Bryan & Petrangelo, 1989). Prior and subsequent to the teenage years, such concerns were unrecognized, inconsequential, or secondary to other developmental concerns. In other words, the developmental approach forecasts certain social, behavioral, emotional, and, thus, learning emphases according to the stage of the child or adolescent. School psychology interventions must be predicated on academically based awareness of the student's developmental psychology. In fact, even the interventions are commonly conceptualized according to an eclectic stage model that is systematic (Gilliland, James, & Bowman, 1989).

The Family Dimension

Going further and as a precursor to the discussion of the importance of the social and family systems of which the student is a part, all human organizations (e.g., the student's family) will also pass through stages. For example, if the student is the youngest and the last child in the family home, the parents may be at a stage of differentiation relevant to the older children's having "left the nest," and this will influence the remaining student. Or if the student's parents are retired (whereas his or her peers have parents who are mostly at the preretirement stage), he or she will have family developmental issues that will merit consideration in psychoeducation planning. There are, of course, countless other familial examples (e.g., death of a parent or sibling, divorce, unemployment, poverty, substance or drug abuse, etc.) that will cast the family into a developmental stage and that will, in turn, have an interactive developmental effect on the child or adolescent.

Cultural diversity is a backdrop for children in our schools. Each family has its unique characteristics, often derived from social, ethnic, and racial characteristics. For example, black families in the United States are so diverse that any stereotype will shortchange professional understanding, and contemporary social conditions are producing changes in the black family that require significant alterations in ideas about its constitution (Staples, 1986). School psychologists are called on to serve families *and* to promote benefits for children according to special cultural considerations. There can be no universal formula for school psychology services; that is, each child must be served according to the cultural set of his or her family. Promotion multiculturalism, which is fortified by cultural distinctions, is essential to modern school psychology. A school psychologist must oppose discrimination according to race, handicap, age, gender, socioeconomic and ethnic backgrounds, sexual preference, religion, or national origin, and seek to provide bias-free services.

As the preceding discussion of family development introduces, the family must be part of school psychology interventions. Phillips (1990) recognizes the needed commitment to family services and reminds us that "school and family partnerships cannot be built on yesterday's notion of the 'family' " (p. 33). As mentioned earlier, federal and state legislative acts mandate family involvement in educational planning, such as for the Individualized Family Service Plan (IFSP) required by PL 99-457 (Part H, Section 676).

Although the law is intended to interface the family and the school for the benefit of the handicapped child, the need for the family's involvement is much more fundamental—information from and cooperative efforts by family members are essential to high-quality school psychological services. For example, certain information is known only to parents, and unless they report it to the school psychologist, the psychoeducational report will be at risk for being inadequately documented. Or if school personnel implement an educational, remedial, developmental, or therapeutic plan, it will certainly be destined to less success than if it were implemented with parental approval, cooperation, and, indeed, active promotion. The school psychologist must support effective home-learning environments through working directly with families (Christenson, 1990).

The Social Systems Dimension

Human development is influenced by the interaction of biological, environmental, and social forces. This necessitates that school psychology accept a systems view:

> The systems view looks at the world in terms of relationships and integration. Systems are integrated wholes, whose properties cannot be reduced to those of smaller units. Instead of concentrating on basic building blocks or basic substances, the systems approach emphasizes basic principles of organization. (Capra, 1982, p. 266)

Drawing from Lewin's (1951) field theory, Plas (1986) considers a person's psychological movement through life space toward goals, and points out that traits result from the movement and are "as influenced by variables located outside the person as by those within the person" (p. 24). This means that understanding the person, such as for a school psychological assessment, is accomplished through thinking about the total social system in which the student exists. Phillips (1990) states, "A change in perspective is needed that draws attention to the child as an actor in a larger social system and to the institutional networks and resources in that larger environment" (p. 33).

Notions about social systems theory being applied to school psychology are not totally new to the specialty. School psychologists have long been associated with behavioral ideas, and Bandura (1978) has offered a behavioristic "reciprocal determinism" model that is clearly social systems in nature. Reynolds and colleagues (1984) endorse the reciprocal determinism model for school psychology, saying,

An ecologically-oriented model of behavior which also takes individuals' cognitions into consideration would be the most suitable model for analyzing the problems of all children, not just potentially abnormal children. . . . The reciprocal determinism model, deduced from social learning theory, conceptualizes human behavior as a continuous reciprocal interaction between an individual's thoughts, behaviors, and environmental factors. (p. 32)

The success or failure of the school's programs will be determined by the social system.

The future of education and the practice of psychology in education will be influenced dramatically by cultural, ethnic, and socioeconomic factors. Problems such as unemployment, inadequate housing, overcrowded conditions, social tension, and psychological stress, which characterize urban areas, have had a devastating influence on educational practice. . . . Because systemic factors contribute to bias in education, models of assessment and educational intervention must be broadened to focus on the environment in a systematic manner, and models of assessment must also be broadened to include intervention as part of the assessment process. (Meyers, 1988, pp. 168–169)

Meyers is especially concerned about the need for expanding novel approaches to service delivery, as might allow greater sensitivity to the needs of minority group members.

The systems point of view can accentuate the positive. By adopting a systemic approach to school psychology and giving emphasis to education (as opposed to pathology), Reynolds and Birch (1982) see positive criteria like human development, social competence, and achievement being promoted. Effective systemic analysis and intervention yields benefits to all persons, not just to those suffering problems at the moment.

Despite its critical relevancy to education and its appropriateness to school psychology, social systems theory (even under the guise of reciprocal determinism) will not assuredly receive ready acceptance in the schools: "All systems are resistant to change, and when pushed, tend to return to the status quo. Further parents and teachers may be reluctant to see themselves as contributing to a child's problems" (Fish & Jain, 1988, pp. 291–292). Fish and Jain recommend diverse strategies for unifying the family and the school.

Plas (1986) analyzes systems psychology in the schools and identifies parallels from the relatively extensive professional literature on family systemic therapy and the school system. She says, "The major difference between family and school systemic approaches lies in the inescapable fact that the most central school-based group (the classroom) is a clearly integral part of a larger system (the school), which in turn is part of another organizational structure (the school system)" (p. 90). This means that psychoeducational personnel, like the school psychologist, "will be relating to a system within a system (within a system)" (p. 90), which creates an additional set (or sets) of contingencies that must be acknowledged and responded to.

Conoley (1987) also sees functional and structural similarities between families and schools, mainly because they are both open systems: "All living or open systems survive by maintaining a delicate balance between import and export across system boundaries" (p. 193). In basic terms, this means that every person, including those in the family and in the school (at whatever level of analysis), is subject to influencing and being influenced by other sources. She proposes practical bridges between the family and the school for family, child, and school assessments, as well as interventions that will increase the "degrees of permeability across the school and family boundary" (p. 196). As might be predicted, Conoley calls for school psychologists to reach out to the student's family and help them function more adaptively.

This help may be in the form of brief family counseling, information sharing, collaboration on a behavioral plan, education, invitations to be meaningfully involved in the schooling process,

training of school personnel to deal more effectively with parents, and activity at administrative and governmental levels to monitor policies that affect children. (p. 199)

A school psychologist's effort to work with families may be impeded by institutional barriers. Since psychoeducational services are commonly funded according to eligibility criteria, there may be federal or state rules and regulations that preclude the school psychologist's providing certain services, such as family counseling. Indeed, certain school administrations are known to prohibit home visits by school psychologists, and to look with disfavor on any sort of family intervention, even if conducted in the school. When a barrier to effective school-family services is encountered, the school psychologist should seek to eliminate the opposition in the name of quality service and public policy.

SUMMARY

This chapter traces the steps of school psychology from the past to the present, and offers ideas about what can be expected in the future. There is no doubt that these are the best of times and the worst of times for America's children, and the school is expected to counteract the negative and enhance the positive at all age levels and in diverse areas. Consequently, school psychologists and other psychoeducational personnel have new, expanded, and more complex duties.

Despite changes in the prevailing service delivery model, school psychology continues to be linked to clinical psychology, yet has significantly different objectives and methods. The scientist-practitioner model is the cornerstone for structuring training and practice, but there is heightening interest in the professional-practitioner model.

As compared to past decades, professional associations have diminished in their dominance over (i.e., less self-regulation of) psychological practice. Instead, through certification and licensure, governmental sources have greater authority over the role and functions of school psychologists. Federal and state laws are defining the scope of service and enforcing standards, and have issued a mandate for appropriate education of all handicapped children and involvement of their families. It seems likely that school psychologists will eventually provide psychoeducational services to all persons, regardless of age. A developmental and social systems approach was presented, with discussion of the behavioral science, developmental, family, and social systems dimensions.

REFERENCES

Alpert, J. L. (1982). Synthesis at Olympia Conference. *School Psychology Review, 11,* 189–191.

Alpert, J. L., Genshaft, J., & Derevenco, M. (1988). Women and school psychology: Professional training, practice, and affiliation. *Professional School Psychology, 3*(1), 3–11.

American Psychological Association. (1981). Specialty guidelines for the delivery of services by school psychologists. *American Psychologist, 36*(6), 670–681.

American Psychological Association. (1989). *Directory of the American Psychological Association.* Washington, DC: Author.

Baker, D. B. (1988). The psychology of Lightner Witmer. *Professional School Psychology, 3*(2), 109–121.

Bandura, A. (1978). The self-system in reciprocal determinism. *American Psychologist, 33,* 344–358.

Barclay, A. G. (1990). The widening world of psychology. *Clinical Psychologist, 43*(3), 45–47.

Bardon, J. I. (1982). School psychology's dilemma: A proposal for its resolution. *Professional Psychology, 13,* 955–968.

Bardon, J. I. (1983). Psychology applied to education: A specialty in search of an identity. *American Psychologist, 38,* 185–196.

Bennis, W. (1989). *Why leaders can't lead: The unconscious conspiracy continues.* San Francisco: Jossey-Bass.

Block, P. (1988). *The empowered manager: Positive political skills at work.* San Francisco: Jossey-Bass.

Bolman, L. G., & Deal, T. E. (1984). *Modern approaches to understanding and managing organizations.* San Francisco: Jossey-Bass.

Brown, D. T. (1982). Issues in the development of professional school psychology. In C. R. Reynolds & T. G. Gutkin (Eds.), *The handbook of school psychology* (pp. 14–23). New York: Wiley.

Brown, D., & Horn, A. (1980). *Handbook of certification/licensure requirements for school psychologists* (3rd ed.). Washington, DC: National Association of School Psychologists.

Bryan, A. J., & Petrangelo, G. J. (1989). Self-concept and sex role orientation in adolescence. *Journal of Sex Education & Therapy, 15*(1), 17–29.

Capra, F. (1982). *The turning point: Science, society, and the rising culture.* New York: Simon & Schuster.

Christenson, S. L. (1990). Differences in students' home environments: The need to work with families. *School Psychology Review, 19*(4), 505–517.

Conoley, J. C. (1987). Schools and families: Theoretical and practical bridges. *Professional School Psychology, 2*(3), 191–203.

Crespi, T. D. (1990). School psychologists in forensic psychology: Converging and diverging issues. *Professional Psychology, 21*(2), 83–87.

Curtis, M. J., & Zins, J. E. (1989). Trends in training and accreditation. *School Psychology Review, 18*(2), 182–192.

Cutts, N. E. (Ed.). (1955). *School psychologists at mid-century.* Washington, DC: American Psychological Association.

Dewey, J. (1909). *Moral principles in education.* Boston: Houghton Mifflin.

Erchul, W. P., Scott, S. S., Dombalis, A. O., & Schulte, A. C. (1989). Characteristics and perceptions of beginning doctoral students in school psychology. *Professional School Psychology, 4*(2), 103–111.

Fagan, T. K., Block, N., Dwyer, K., Petty, S., St. Cyr, M., & Telzrow, C. (1989). Historical summary and analysis of the first 20 years of the National Association of School Psychologists. *School Psychology Review, 18*(2), 151–173.

Farling, W. H., & Agner, J. (1979). History of the National Association of School Psychologists: The first decade. *School Psychology Digest, 8,* 140–152.

Fish, M. C., & Jain, S. (1988). Using systems theory in school assessment and intervention: A structural model for school psychologists. *Professional School Psychology, 3*(4), 291–300.

Frank G. (1984). The Boulder model: History, rationale, and critique. *Professional Psychology, 15,* 417–435.

French, J. L. (1988). Grandmothers I wish I knew: Contributions of women to the history of school psychology. *Professional School Psychology, 3*(1), 51–68.

Garner, L. H., Jr. (1989). *Leadership in human services.* San Francisco: Jossey-Bass.

Genshaft, J. L., & Wisniewski, J. J. (1988). Present credentialing and prospects for the future. *Professional School Psychology, 3*(3), 187–194.

Gilliland, B. E., James, R. K., & Bowman, J. T. (1989). *Theories and strategies in counseling and psychotherapy* (2nd ed.). Englewood Cliffs, NJ: Prentice Hall.

Goulet, L. R., & Baltes, P. B. (Eds.). (1970). *Lifespan developmental psychology.* New York: Academic Press.

Hobbs, N. (1964). Mental health's third revolution. *American Journal of Orthopsychiatry, 34,* 822–833.

Hodgkinson, H. L. (1986). *Future search.* Washington, DC: National Education Association.

Horan, P. G., & Sherman, R. A. (1988). School psychologists and the AIDS epidemic. *Professional School Psychology, 3*(1), 33–49.

Kanfer, F. H. (1990). The scientist-practitioner connection: A bridge in need of constant attention. *Professional Psychology, 21*(4), 264–270.

Katkin, E. (1982). On reliable knowledge and the proliferation of professional schools of psychology. *Clinical Psychologist, 36*(1), 9–11.

Keller, G. (1989). Pavlov lives: Who's to blame for educational failures. *Change, 21*(3), 54.

Kessler, J. W. (1988). *Psychopathology of childhood* (2nd ed.). Englewood Cliffs, NJ: Prentice Hall.

Klesges, R. C., Sanchez, V. C., & Stanton, A. L. (1982). Obtaining employment in academia: The hiring process and characteristics of successful applicants. *Professional Psychology, 13,* 577–586.

Korman, M. (1974). National conference on levels and patterns of professional training in psychology. *American Psychologist, 29,* 441–449.

Lewin, K. (1951). *Field theory in social science.* New York: Harper & Row.

London, P. (1987). Character education and clinical intervention: A paradigm shift for U.S. schools. *Phi Delta Kappan, 68,* 667–673.

Martin, R. P. (1991). The school psychologist: Where's the psychology in school reform? *School Psychologist, 45*(1), 1–2.

Matarazzo, J. D. (1987). There is only one psychology, no specialties, but many applications. *American Psychologist, 42*(10), 893–903.

McGraw, K. O. (1987). *Developmental psychology.* San Diego: Harcourt, Brace Jovanovich.

McMaster, M. D., Reschly, D. J., & Peters, J. M. (1989). *Directory of school psychology graduate programs.* Washington, DC: National Association of School Psychologists.

Meisels, S. J. (1989). Meeting the mandate of Public Law 99-457: Early childhood intervention in the nineties. *American Journal of Orthopsychiatry, 59*(3), 451–460.

Meyers, J. (1988). School psychology: The current state of practice and future practice of the specialty. *Professional School Psychology, 3*(3), 165–176.

National Association of School Psychologists. (1986). *Standards for training and credentialing in school psychology.* Washington, DC: Author.

National Association of School Psychologists. (1990–91). *Membership directory.* Silver Spring, MD: Author.

National Coalition of Advocates for Students and the National Association of School Psychologists. (1990). Position statement: Advocacy for appropriate educational services for all children. *School Psychology Quarterly, 5*(3), 235–236.

National School Psychology Inservice Training Network. (1984). *School psychology: A blueprint for training and practice.* Minneapolis, MN: Author.

Oakland, T., & Cunningham, J. L. (1990). Advocates for educational services for all children need improved research and conceptual bases. *School Psychology Quarterly, 5*(1), 66–77.

Perry, N. W., Jr. (1990). Scientist-practitioner training. *Clinical Psychologist, 43*(3), 47–49.

Peterson, D. R. (1985). Twenty years of practitioner training in psychology. *American Psychologist, 40,* 441–451.

Phillips, B. N. (1988). Education, training, and evaluation of practitioners today and in the future. *Professional School Psychology, 3*(3), 177–186.

Phillips, B. N. (1990). *School psychology at a turning point.* San Francisco: Jossey-Bass.

Plas, J. M. (1986). *Systems psychology in the schools.* New York: Pergamon.

Poland, S. (1989). *Suicide intervention in the schools.* New York: Guilford.

Pryzwansky, W. B., Brantley, J. D., Wasik, B. H., Schulte, A. C., & Simeonsson, R. J. (1989). School psychology training at the University of North Carolina-Chapel Hill. *Professional School Psychology, 4*(2), 115–125.

Raimy, V. (Ed.). (1950). *Training in clinical psychology.* Englewood Cliffs, NJ: Prentice-Hall.

Regnery, A. S. (1985). Getting away with murder— Why the juvenile justice system needs an overhaul. *Policy Review, 32,* 65–68.

Reschly, D. J., Genshaft, J., & Binder, M. S. (1987). *The 1986 NASP survey: Comparison of practitioners, NASP, leadership, and university faculty members on key issues.* Washington, DC: National Association of School Psychologists.

Reynolds, C. R., Gutkin, T. B., Elliott, S. N., & Witt, J. D. (1984). *School psychology: Essentials of theory and practice.* New York: Wiley.

Reynolds, M. C., & Birch, J. W. (1982). *Teaching exceptional children in all America's schools* (2nd ed.). Reston, VA: The Council for Exceptional Children.

Russo, N. F., Olmedo, E. L., Stapp, J., & Fulcher, R. (1981). Women and minorities in psychology. *American Psychologist, 36,* 1315–1363.

Sales, B., Bricklin, P., & Hall, J. (1983). *Manual for the identification and continued recognition of proficiencies and new specialties in psychology.* Washington, DC: American Psychological Association.

Sarason, S. B. (1987). Is our field an inkblot? *American Psychological Association Monitor, 18*(1), 37.

Schroeder, S. R., Schroeder, C. S., & Landesman, S. (1987). Psychological services in educational settings to persons with mental retardation. *American Psychologist, 42*(8), 805–808.

Sechrest, L. B. (1985). Specialization. Who needs it. *Clinical Psychologist, 38*(1), 1–3.

Shaffer, D. R. (1985). *Developmental psychology.* Monterey, CA: Brooks/Cole.

Shakow, D. (1968). The development of orthopsychiatry: The contributions of Levy, Menninger, and Stevenson. *American Journal of Orthopsychiatry, 38,* 804–809.

Shakow, D., Hilgard, E. R., Kelly, E. L., Luckey, B., Sanford, R. N., & Shaffer, L. G. (1947). Recommended graduate training program in clinical psychology. *American Psychologist, 2,* 539–558.

Short, R. J., Simeonsson, R. J., & Huntington, G. S. (1990). Early intervention: Implications of Public Law 99-457 for professional child psychology. *Professional Psychology 21*(2), 88–93.

Slater, B. R. (1988a). School psychologists and abused children. *School Psychologist, 42*(5), 1, 3–4.

Slater, B. R. (1988b). Teen pregnancy and the schools. *School Psychologist, 42*(4), 1–2.

Staples, R. (1986). *The black family* (3rd ed.). Belmont, CA: Wadsworth.

Stick, R. S. (1984). Rights of handicapped children to an education. In R. H. Woody (Ed.), *The law and the practice of human services* (pp. 341–372). San Francisco: Jossey-Bass.

Strein, B. (1989). School psychologists and P. L. 99-457: Possibilities for nontraditional services to preschool children. *School Psychologist, 43*(5), 11.

VandeCreek, L., Knapp, S., & Brace, K. (1990). Mandatory continuing education for licensed psychologists: Its rationale and current implication. *Professional Psychology, 21*(2), 135–140.

Vane, J. R. (1985). School psychology: To be or not be. *Journal of School Psychology, 23,* 101–112.

Weinberg, R. B. (1990). Serving large numbers of adolescent victim-survivors: Group interventions following trauma at school. *Professional Psychology, 21*(4), 271–278.

Weithorn, L. A. (Ed.). (1987). *Psychology and child custody determinations.* Lincoln: University of Nebraska Press.

William T. Grant Foundation Commission on Work, Family and Citizenship. (1988). *The forgotten half: Non-college youth in America.* Washington, DC: Author.

Wilson, C. A., & Gettinger, M. (1989). Determinants of child-abuse reporting among Wisconsin school psychologists. *Professional School Psychology, 4*(2), 91–102.

Woody, R. H. (1974). *Legal aspects of mental retardation.* Springfield, IL: Thomas.

Woody, R. H., Hansen, J. C., & Rossberg, R. H. (1989). *Counseling psychology: Strategies and services.* Pacific Grove, CA: Brooks/Cole.

Woody, R. H., & Robertson, M. (1988). *Becoming a*

clinical psychologist. Madison, CT: International Universities Press.

Ysseldyke, J. E. (1982). The Spring Hill Symposium on the future of psychology in the schools. *American Psychologist, 37,* 547–552.

Ysseldyke, J. E., & Weinberg, R. (1981). Editorial comment: An introduction to the Spring Hill Symposium. *School Psychology Review, 10,* 116–120.

CHAPTER 2

DEVELOPMENTAL AND
SOCIAL SYSTEMS

Within the field of school psychology there is a perceived need to initiate a shift in training and orientation from the traditional models, with their focus on diagnosing deficiencies and prescribing treatment, to an approach that incorporates principles from both developmental psychology and systems theory. Over a decade ago, Carboy and Curley (1976) argued that school psychologists ought to be considered behavioral scientists and that they should be trained in child psychology. Their rationale for this change in identification is that the traditional approaches have not provided the needed information or modification expected by teachers and administrators, largely because ecological factors such as the family have been ignored, and the traditional methods assume linear causality rather than interactional or circular. A school psychologist with developmental training, on the other hand, would be concerned with the developmental processes and the contextual factors, especially the various systems, in the assessment and intervention of emotional and learning problems.

Over the years, school psychologists have adopted one of the traditional models. The *clinical model* assumes linear causality where the etiology of the academic problem is attributed to the child. The focus of this model is on diagnosis and treatment directed toward the child. The *psychoeducational model* is assessment oriented and prescriptive. It involves observation of the student and teacher input, with the emphasis on the remediation of the child's classroom behavior. According to the *behavioral model*, problem behaviors result from an interaction between the child and the environment. A problem exists when the child's behavior is less than or greater than some expected standard, and the intervention focuses on the environmental events associated with the problem. In the *consultation model*, attention is directed to problem solving between the school psychologist, who is the consultant, and the teacher who refers the problem and who is subsequently responsible for administering the treatment to the child. As described by Reynolds, Gutkin, Elliott, and Witt (1984), the consultation involves identifying and diagnosing the problem, followed by selecting and implementing the intervention strategy and specifying responsibilities. This model assumes that the child's behavior is a product of an interaction between the behavior cognitive factors, such as beliefs and attitudes of the child, and the environment.

Contrast these approaches with that taken by an integrative approach of developmental psychology and systems theory, which assumes that the child is continually developing in a system in which he or she interacts with the environment. Thus, the child's behavior in school frequently results from the child's interaction with the classroom, as suggested by Christensen, Avery, and Weinberg (1986). This contributing role of the child's developmental status and familial, cultural, and social systems factors is largely ignored in the traditional models. Even the introduction of nouveau approaches, such as family counseling and interdisciplinary teams, still focus on the child who has been referred, and thus reflect the traditional models. Christensen, Avery, and Weinberg (1986) contend that "school psychology has yet to reach its true potential" (p. 358). They assert that all we have done is to "transfer old wine into new bottles" (p. 358).

A more recent restructuring scheme for school psychology training has been advanced by Meyers (1988), in which he identifies the needs of children, parents, and teachers, and the necessity to integrate scientific knowledge and the practice of school psychology as the critical concerns. This plan fits nicely with Phillips's (1986) portrayal of the school psychologist as an applied scientist. According to this futuristic plan, school psychologists would shift their focus from a deficit model of pathology, necessitating remediation, to one emphasizing positive adjustment, social competence, and educational achievement.

Developmental psychology and systems theory have a central role in this plan because they provide a relevant research base and emphasize an interactional approach to behavior and development that incorporates familial, school, and societal influences. Because diagnosis cannot be separated from intervention, the diagnostic process needs to be interactional (Wendt & Zake, 1984). Most interventions will be directed at the child but the classroom and family may be involved. The interactional approach incorporates relevant developmental information with family systems interventions, of which there are three levels—parenting, communication skills training, and family therapy (Wendt & Zakes, 1984).

The viable alternative to the traditional models is to adopt a developmental approach that incorporates a systems perspective. (This integrated approach is discussed in Chapter 10.) According to this view, the child is seen as actively engaged in his or her development during the process of growth and maturation while interacting with the environment. Therefore the child is part of a social system that consists of the child, family, school, neighborhood, and community. An integrative developmental social systems orientation focuses on the developmental factors unique to the periods of childhood and adolescence, and how each of these developmental periods interfaces with the social/educational system in which the child or adolescent interacts.

The developmental/social systems orientation will be the focus of this chapter, the thrust of which is twofold. A developmental view of human behavior is discussed in the first half of the chapter. Two questions are of paramount importance: How does the child or adolescent change with development, and what are the determinants of these changes? The second half of the chapter, in which the systems approach is presented, will focus on the characteristics and the determinants of systems performance, using the school and the family as examples. In the final section of the chapter we will suggest an integrative developmental/social systems model for school psychology.

A DEVELOPMENTAL APPROACH

The developmental perspective examines those biological, cognitive, and social/emotional changes that occur in an individual across the life span. For those who take a dialectical view, the process is continual and it results from constant conflict. That is, imbalance or disequilibrium in development is necessary; therefore, stability is only temporary. The conflicts and challenges of one developmental period are resolved only to enter the next developmental period where other conflicts are experienced. A systems approach, as discussed earlier, examines the interaction between systems that impact on the individual. The various components of development become evident when one examines how it is defined.

What Is Development?

Although definitions of *human development* vary, there seems to be general agreement among writers (e.g., Clarke-Stewart, Perlmutter, & Friedman, 1988; Hoffman, Paris, Hall, & Schell, 1988; McCall, 1977; Papalia & Olds Wendkos, 1989; Santrock, 1989):

1. Development involves change that is systematic rather than random.
2. Change is permanent as opposed to temporary.
3. Change is cumulative because it adds to what occurred previously.
4. Change is organized, and this organization becomes more complex with advancing age.
5. Change is progressive and directional because it advances from infancy to the final period of later adulthood (old age) rather than declining or the converse.
6. All development is the result of an interaction involving the individual's genotype and the environment.

The type of change involved in development is different from that involved in such processes as learning. Developmental change is ontogenetic (Baltes, Reese, & Nesselroade, 1977), meaning that, with age, the individual undergoes a transformation resulting from complex interactions involving genes, environment, and culture. This age-related transformation occurs for biological, cognitive, social, and emotional processes.

How Is Developmental Change Characterized?

When developmental change occurs, is the change continuous over time so that one sees a pattern of a steady increase or decrease, or is the change discontinuous so that it appears to occur in spurts or stages? A related issue concerns stability/instability. Is the rate and pattern of developmental change similar across individuals or does it differ with respect to some reference group, such as a child's classmates? The stability/instability issue addresses a different question than the continuity/discontinuity issue. According to Lerner (1976), stability/instability refers to the relative functioning of a developing individual over time when compared to similar others, whereas continuity/discontinuity concerns the laws affecting development; that is, do these laws remain the same or change with time? For any

developmental change it is possible to find combinations of continuity and stability, continuity and instability, discontinuity and stability, and discontinuity and instability.

Continuity or Discontinuity?

If development is continuous, one ought to find, for example, that the pattern of physical growth is a positively accelerated function (i.e., it increases in a straight line across age). However, when the growth pattern of children is examined closely, one finds that growth does not proceed in this manner; rather, there is gappiness or unevenness. The confusion over this issue was clarified somewhat by Werner (1957) in his suggestion that developmental variation could occur through quantitative or qualitative change.

Quantitative change refers to how much, or a change in frequency or rate of some behavior. When the change is gradual, such as a gain in weight or height, quantitative continuity has resulted. If the change shows gappiness (i.e., is abrupt or sudden), it indicates quantitative discontinuity. This difference can be seen in Figure 2.1.

Qualitative change denotes whether some new behavior has emerged that previously was not present. If the newly emerged behavior was not present in any form before, and if its emergence was sudden or abrupt, then the change represents qualitative discontinuity. The appearance of principled moral reasoning, which is not present prior to puberty, is one example of this type of change. However, Werner (1957) contends, if the behavioral change was only abrupt or sudden, and did not involve a previously absent behavior, such as the growth spurt associated with puberty, quantitative discontinuity has occurred. The quantitative/qualitative distinction in continuity/discontinuity can also be seen in Figure 2.1.

One example of discontinuity in development is the assumption that human development proceeds in a sequence of stages. *Stage* usually refers to some grouping of behavior that is different from that observed at earlier or later periods in

(a) Quantitative Continuity

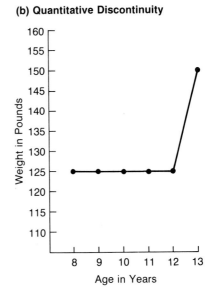

(b) Quantitative Discontinuity

(c) Qualitative Continuity

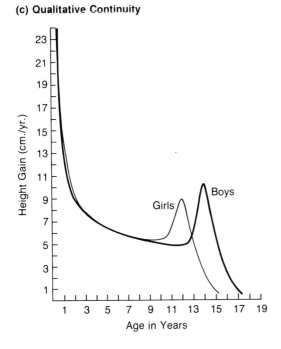

(d) Qualitative Discontinuity

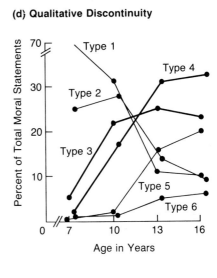

FIGURE 2.1 Examples of (a) quantitative continuity and (b) quantitative discontinuity and (c) qualitative continuity and (d) qualitative discontinuity

Source: Parts (a) and (b): Lerner, R. M. (1986). *Concepts and theories of human development* (2nd ed.). New York: McGraw-Hill. Reproduced with permission of McGraw-Hill, Inc. Part (c): Tanner, J. M., Whitehouse, R. H., & Takaishi, M. (1966). Standards from birth to maturity for height, weight, height velocity, and weight velocity: British children, 1965. *Archives of Diseases in Childhood, 41.* Reprinted by permission. Part (d): Adapted from Kohlberg, L. (1963). The development of children's orientations toward moral order. 1. Sequence in the development of moral thought. *Vita Humana, 6,* 11–33. Reproduced with permission of S. Karger, AG, Basel, Switzerland.

development. Stages are sequential; that is, they
display some type of order in their emergence.
Stages have other distinct properties as well.
Their appearance in development is abrupt or
sudden. They have structure, in that the skills or
abilities of each stage are interrelated in a pattern,
and these skills or abilities should develop or appear at about the same relative time (e.g., the
concept of concurrence). Finally, the changes
that occur are qualitative in that the abilities or
skills present at one stage are different from those
present at another stage or level (Flavell, 1985).
The stage approach is an attractive feature for development because it provides a convenient
method for describing the developmental phase
or period of a child. Although developmental
stages usually correspond to the child's chronological age, the level at which the child is functioning, not age, determines developmental stage
(Hoffman et al., 1988).

So which view—continuity or discontinuity—best describes developmental change?
Langer (1970) suggests that both views depict developmental change because discontinuity is
present when some general aspect of the
child's development becomes differentiated, but
gradually differentiation leads to continuity. By
focusing only on discontinuity, one perceives development as a disorderly process, whereas by
focusing on continuity, one fails to detect the
qualitative changes of the interactions associated
with the developing individual (Lerner, 1976).
Data on continuity and discontinuity in infant
emotionality reported by Belsky, Fish, and Isabella (1991) provide further support for exercising caution in viewing development as an
either/or phenomenon. Belsky, Fish, and Isabella
note that much of the existing literature indicates
that negative emotionality is continuous through
infancy and early childhood. However, their data
collected on infants at 3 months of age, and again
at 9 months, indicated that the pattern of emotionality was continuous for some infants but discontinuous for others, especially when negative
affect was involved. The change in negative affect
was attributed to parental factors, such as interpersonal affect, marital harmony, and parent-

infant interaction, with differential effects
associated for mothers and fathers. In this case,
qualitative changes were present.

Also the belief that intellectual development
is discontinuous may be incorrect. Early data
showed that correlations between infant tests of
intelligence and later scores were very low, but
more recent data cited by Weinberg (1989) suggests continuity across age rather than discontinuity. Further, certain skills that can be identified
early, such as coping with novelty or adjusting to
unfamiliar tasks, seem to continue into childhood.

The challenge facing the school psychologist
is to recognize continuity and discontinuity when
they are present. Because psychological maturation consists of changes in form, the school psychologist needs to be able to interpret the
meaning of behavior across a range of ages. For
example, does fear or frustration mean the same
to a preschool child as it may to an older child or
adolescent, even though the display of the behavior may be similar at the different ages (Clarke-
Stewart, Perlmutter, & Friedman, 1988)?

As Santrock (1989) notes, some psychologists view development as continuous, and
therefore interpret language and cognitive development as continuous processes, whereas
others focus on the discontinuous features of development by emphasizing critical stages or
periods, such as the terrible twos or the frightening threes. One's views on the continuity/discon-
tinuity matter also influences how one interprets
data. Carefully examine Figure 2.2, which shows
two approaches to analyzing data on aggression.
In part b the aggression score is plotted at each
age level, resulting in a plot that suggests discontinuity. However, if the data are plotted by age
range, such as occurs in part a, the aggressive behavior fits a continuous pattern; in this case the
scores decrease over age.

Stability or Instability?
This question can be considered another form of
the continuity/discontinuity issue (Santrock,
1989) but the latter terms do not describe what
transpires in the development of the child or ado-

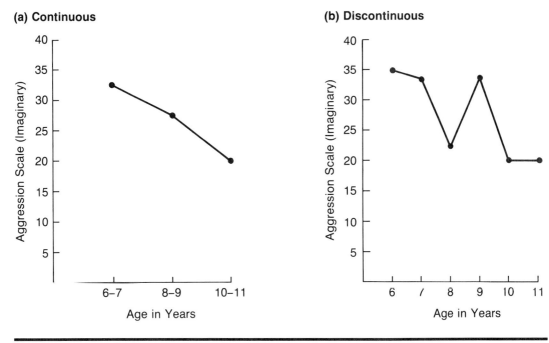

FIGURE 2.2   In these figures, one can interpret development as (a) continuous or (b) discontinuous

Source: R. M. Lerner (1976). *Concepts and theories of human development.* New York: McGraw-Hill. Reproduced with permission of McGraw-Hill, Inc.

lescent. Comparisons with agemates are necessary to determine if the relationship among important variables changes or remains constant. However, it is evident that whenever the continuity/discontinuity matter is addressed, the stability/instability question must also be considered. When a child's ranking on some behavior remains constant across time as compared to classmates, stability is present. If the child's ranking changes across time, instability is indicated. These two conditions are presented graphically in Figure 2.3. Note in this example that the child's behavioral score has increased from time 1 to time 2 in the stability as well as the instability case. Stability/instability is not concerned with absolute change but with reference to the child's classmates. Therefore, the child's achievement score may change, but if classmates' scores also change, the child's behavior is stable. On the other hand, if the child's achievement score remains the same across time, the child's behavior

would be stable if the score of agemates also did not change.

The stability/instability issue can be viewed from another perspective. Santrock (1989) suggests that the extent to which we remain constant across age in any behavior (e.g., aggressiveness, dependency, temperament, etc.) indicates stability, whereas any change in our behavior pattern denotes instability. For this reason, it was previously thought that most of the important behavioral changes occurred during childhood, and thus later periods of development were not very important.

What Causes Developmental Change?

Proponents of the nature position contend that development is largely the product of our heredity. That is, the genes that we receive from our parents form our *genotype* whose visible characteristics are expressed as our *phenotype.* The

(a) Stability   **(b) Instability**

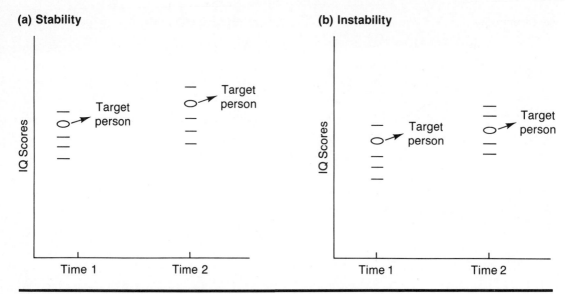

FIGURE 2.3   An illustration of (a) stability and (b) instability in development
Source: R. M. Lerner (1976). *Concepts and theories of human development.* New York:
McGraw-Hill. Reproduced with permission of McGraw-Hill, Inc.

environmental position claims that development
is largely the product of the experiences that have
been acquired, namely, socialization and its interaction with the culture. Stated somewhat differently, the issue is whether maturation, an innate
characteristic that is genetically determined, or
experience is more important. The position taken
on this issue will be determined by one's philosophy of science. The most widely held view today
is that we need to focus on the interaction between genes and environment rather than asking
which one.

This interaction effect is found in the reaction range model. A *reaction range* refers to the
variation in phenotype due to environmental effects permitted by the genotype. Similar environments lead to more similar phenotypes among
children who differ in genotype. This relationship can be seen in Figure 2.4. In this figure,
Alice and Laura are identical twins (i.e, they
have the same genotype) who are adopted by different parents and thus reared in different environments, the quality of which accounts for the
IQ difference between the twins. Paul's genotype

would indicate a higher IQ than Fred, but Fred is
reared in a more enriched environment, which
results in the same IQ for both. While a reaction
range may be present for some genotypic characteristics, others may be under more stringent genetic control, which is labeled *canalization*. In
this instance, environmental effects are not very
pervasive because the genetic control is so strong
that it almost totally directs development.

Not only does the environment influence genetic effects but genetic factors influence the environment that is experienced, which illustrates
further the complexity of the interaction between
genotype and the environment. According to
Scarr and McCartney (1983), our genotypes construct the environments that we encounter in
three different situations. Parents actively select
environments for their child(ren). For example, if
parents are physically active and are exercise en-
thusiasts, they will probably select activities for
their child(ren) that are physical, such as sports,
and they will actively encourage and structure the
situation so that the child(ren) participates. In
this instance, parents both contribute genes and

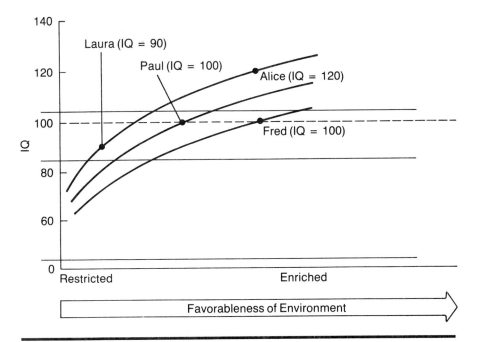

FIGURE 2.4   The environment-genotype relationship

Source: Clarke-Stewart, A., Perlmutter, M., & Friedman, S. (1988). *Lifelong human development.* New York: Wiley. Copyright © 1988 John Wiley & Sons, Inc. Reprinted by permission of John Wiley & Sons, Inc. Originally based on Gottesman (1963). Heritablity of personality: A demonstration. *Psychology Monographs, 77.* Copyright 1963 by the American Psychological Association. Adapted by permission.

select environments for the child, so the genetic effect on development has been doubled.

Second, because of their genotype, children elicit certain responses from the environment. Smiling babies will elicit more responses from others than nonsmiling babies. Attractive children of all ages will receive more social interaction than nonattractive children. Third, individuals of all ages seek out environments and experiences that are compatible with their genetic makeup. Children who are more creative will engage in activities that permit them to express their talent, such as art, music, or dance. Those with high verbal skills are more likely to select activities and fields of study where such skills can be used. These illustrations are examples of "niche-picking." Individuals select their own niches or environmental experiences that are suitable for their abilities, interests, and personality traits,

and this niche-picking appears to increase with age because the child is gradually acquiring more control over her or his environment (Clarke-Stewart, Perlmutter, & Friedman, 1988).

Heritability

The controversy over the relative effects of genetics and environment ultimately leads to attempts at estimating the contribution of genetics. This estimate is based on the assumption that any genetic trait will be more similar among identical twins than among fraternal twins or siblings. The rationale for the twin comparisons is that twins, regardless of relatedness, are socialized alike. Although there is some evidence that parents may respond to identical twins more similarly than fraternal twins, it appears that the parents are reacting to the degree of genetic similarity rather than creating differences between the sets of twins (Grusec & Lytton, 1988). Thus, it can be argued that individual differences in a trait are mostly the result of genetic factors.

Heritability (expressed as $[h^2 = [V(G)/V(P)]$, or variance due to genetics divided by phenotypic variance, which is the sum of genetic plus environmental variance) refers to the proportion of individual differences in a group or population for some trait, such as intelligence, that are attributable to genetic differences in that group or population (Grusec & Lytton, 1988; Lerner, 1976). Heritability in twin studies is calculated by multiplying the difference between the monozygotic (MZ/identical) and dizygotic (DZ/fraternal) intraclass correlation by 2. If the intraclass correlation for IQ in MZ twins is .81 and the correlation for DZ twins is .59, h^2 would equal .44 or 2(.81 − .59). The problem with this computation is that the difference score is quite unreliable (McCartney, Harris, & Bernieri, 1990). The heritability statistic ranges from 0.0 to 1.0, and it is an estimate of a group or population statistic. According to Plomin and Rende (1991), the heritability of IQ is about .50, a value that corresponds quite closely with the h^2 we calculated based on the MZ − DZ intraclass correlation.

Therefore, if the heritability estimate for intelligence is .50, one does not conclude that 50 percent of a child's IQ score is attributable to heredity, but only that 50 percent of the variability in intelligence in a specific population is attributable to genetic differences in children in that population. Any use of the term *heritability* requires an awareness that it does not imply fixed development; that is, heritability is not a measure of genetic determinacy.

Behavioral Genetics

In a recent review of genetics and environment as determinants of development, Plomin (1989) stated, "Genetic influence is so ubiquitous and pervasive in behavior that a shift in emphasis is warranted: Ask not what is heritable, ask what is not heritable" (p. 108). To justify this assertion, Plomin calls attention to the recent research in the area of behavioral genetics. The data from these studies indicate that genetic influences exert a substantial effect on IQ scores, specific cognitive abilities (e.g., tests of verbal and spatial abilities), perceptual speed and memory, academic achievement and reading disability, and recent evidence reviewed by Plomin and Rende (1991) suggest that information processing variables also are influenced by genetics. But development is an important factor in genetic influence. A meta-analysis reported by McCartney, Harris, and Bernieri (1990) on 103 studies describing IQ data on twins indicates that age may be a moderating variable on IQ. They found that twin correlations tended to decrease with age, especially those between dizygotic (fraternal) twins, and thus heritability increased. This heritability increase seems to be greatest in childhood. Interestingly, tests of creativity reveal less genetic influence than any other area within the cognitive domain. However, mild mental retardation seems to be due largely to polygenic (i.e., combinations of genes acting together) and environmental factors.

What is actually measured by an IQ test is debatable. Hebb (1949) contends that each of us is born with an intellectual potential, which Hebb labels intelligence A, but we have not developed instruments to assess this genotypic intelligence; rather, our IQ tests measure intelligence B, which is the product of our interactions with the environment, or our phenotypic intelligence. The problem is that the correlation between the two types of intelligence is unknown, so we cannot determine the location of our actual intellectual ability within the range of reaction because we do not know where the phenotypic intelligence score falls within this range.

With respect to personality traits, Grusec and Lytton (1988) conclude that genetic influences show less consistency across studies for personality traits than for cognitive variables. Data from a study by Tellegen, Lykken, Bouchard, Wilcox, Segal, and Rich (1988) of MZ (identical) and DZ (fraternal) twins reared together and apart showed that heritability for various personality traits ranged from .39 to .58, with an average of .48. There is also some evidence (e.g., McCartney, Harris, & Bernieri, 1990) that age may be a moderator factor for heritability in personality. Personality change in childhood seems to be influenced greatly by genetics (Plomin & Rende, 1991). Plomin's (1989) review reveals that the heritability estimate for introversion/extraversion to be about 50 percent. Genetic factors make a significant contribution to sociability, emotionality, and activity, as well as some attitudes and beliefs, such as traditionalism. Genetic factors also seem to contribute to dominance or assertive behavior in males, but not in females, which is an interesting finding, given that dominant behavior seems to be more evident in males than females (Grusec & Lytton, 1988).

The genetic research on psychopathology reveals a genetic influence for schizophrenia and for affective disorders, although manic-depressive disorders seem to be more greatly influenced by genes than unipolar depression. Autism also seems to have a genetic link (Plomin & Rende, 1991). Genetic factors are also related to alcoholism, and there is some evidence that delinquency has a genetic component (Plomin, 1989). Social maladjustment, when assessed as antisocial behavior or neurotic anxiety, has a genetic component as well (Grusec & Lytton, 1988). Overall, the preponderance of evidence suggests that genetics contribute to personality variables, although the effect is not as large as that found for cognitive factors. This conclusion has also been reported by Plomin (1989).

Environmental Influences
The apparent pervasiveness of genetic influences should not lead one to underestimate the potential effect of the environment. Plomin (1989) notes that nongenetic factors account for more than 50 percent of the variance for any complex behavior. The concordance rate for schizophrenia among identical twins, for example, is less than 40 percent. Environmental factors seem to operate in complex ways, which suggests that one needs to examine person-situation interactions (Grusec & Lytton, 1988). One potential environmental influence on IQ is the school experience. After reviewing the literature on this issue, Ceci (1991) concludes that "the processes associated with schooling influence performance on IQ tests through a combination of direct instruction and indirect inculcation of modes of cognizing and values associated with standard setting" (p. 711). One factor that seems to account for a significant portion of variance in children's IQ is attendance. The effect ranges from .25 to 6 IQ points per year of missed school (Ceci, 1991). Other factors identified by Ceci include late school start, early school drop out, achievement and aptitude test score equivalence, and years of school completed.

The family environment illustrates this principle quite conclusively. After reviewing the literature on the effects of family environment, Plomin (Plomin, 1989; Plomin & Rende, 1991) concludes that there is little similarity among siblings in the same family. Plomin (1989) reports that the correlations between children in the same family average around .40 for various cognitive measures, .20 for personality traits, and generally less than .10 for psychopathology concordance. Plomin further asserts that the similarities among children in these reported traits are attributable to their shared genes rather than being reared in the same family environment. Taking this position does not imply that environmental effects in general or family rearing specifically do not contribute to the child's phenotype.

The impact of environment operates specifically for each child, so that what is present is a "nonshared environment" (Plomin, 1989). To support this contention, Plomin refers to the data on adoptive siblings who share the same family environment. The data show an insignificant effect of this environment in terms of correlations approaching zero for behavioral traits among adopted siblings. A shared family environment exerts minimal influence on personality and psychopathology, therefore any environmental influence is nonshared, although a shared environment seems to influence aggressive behavior and delinquency (Plomin & Rende, 1991). IQ is greatly influenced by nonshared environments as well. As Plomin and Rende (1991) note, "Although shared environmental influences are important in childhood, their influence wanes to negligible levels during adolescence. In the long run, environmental effects on IQ are nonshared" (p. 181). The reality of nonshared environmental effects points to the need to shift from a focus on what McGraw (1987) has termed *between-family variance* to *within-family variance*. In the past, we have tended to concentrate on such differences between families as socioeconomic status, educational level of parents, family size, socialization practices, and family status. But as Plomin observes, if these factors do not differ among children in the same family, their effect on development is nonsignificant. If between-family differences are not important within the family, what are the sources of the within-family factors that result in nonshared environmental influences? Some of the sources identified by Rowe and Plomin (1981) appear in Table 2.1. In viewing these sources, one needs to realize that even small differences could have significant effects on the child, and further, children's perceptions of differences in the family may also play a role. McCartney, Harris, and Bernieri (1990) provide formulas for estimating environmental compo-nents of variance. Shared environmental effects can be estimated by the formula, MZ intraclass correlation minus h^2, whereas nonshared environmental effects are estimated by 1 minus the MZ intraclass correlation.

Some Conclusions about Nature and Nurture and Implications

Although we have discussed the effects of genetics and environment as though they were independent, development is the product of a very complex interaction between the two forces. Our purpose in examining each separately was to show that behavioral genetics is concerned with explaining individual differences between persons in their development, not their development per se. It is important to be aware that behavior is influenced by combinations of genes acting together (polygenic) and that these genetic effects are probabilistic rather than fixed or determined. With respect to environment, we need to be cognizant that environmental effects may differ across families, but within families they are specific to each child, and their impact will differ contingent on the child's genotype.

The implications for the school psychologist are that assessments must reflect an awareness of

TABLE 2.1   Specific Sources of Within-Family Environmental Variance

	SOURCES				
MEASUREMENT	*Accidental Factors*	*Sibling Interaction*	*Family Structure*	*Parental Treatment*	*Extrafamilial Networks*
Error of measurement	Teratogenic agents Physical illness Prenatal and postnatal trauma Separation	Differential treatment Deidentification	Birth order Sibling spacing	Differential treatment of children Interactions of parent and child characteristics	Peer-group members not shared by siblings Relatives Teachers Television

Source: Rowe, D. C., & Plomin, R. (1981). The importance of nonshared (E_1) environmental influences in behavioral development. *Developmental Psychology, 17,* 524. Copyright 1981 by the American Psychological Association. Reprinted by permission.

individual differences due to genetic and environmental factors, and the intervention plan must also incorporate this awareness. We now have a somewhat better understanding why two children in the same family may display totally different behavior patterns, and why an intervention plan for one child may not fit a sibling. Further, certain behaviors associated with a particular personality trait that is genetically influenced will be more resistant to change.

DEVELOPMENTAL THEORIES

Developmental theories are important because they provide a general framework for describing and explaining developmental change and they furnish a conceptual basis for framing questions and guiding research. It is not our purpose in this chapter to engage in a lengthy discourse on theories. Instead, we will group the major theories using descriptive labels, summarize their position on the critical issues of development, and then identify some current conceptual advances. A somewhat different discussion of developmental theories can be found in Tharinger and Lambert (1990).

Psychodynamic Theories

The two major theories to be discussed are those of Freud and Erikson. Both theories view development as proceeding in a series of sequential stages, during which one is faced with resolving conflicts; this resolution may contain some negative elements, but the positive elements still dominate. For example, the trust stage of Erikson's theory implies that basic trust is essential for psychological functioning; yet, as Santrock (1989) suggests, if you trust people under every condition, it is unlikely that you will survive. Both theories stress that personality is the product of current experiences as well as those from earlier ages. Developmental change is viewed as discontinuous between stages, but there is some continuity between early experiences and later development.

Psychoanalytic Theory

For Freud, development progressed in a series of stages associated with an erogenous or sexually sensitive zone. During the *oral stage* (from birth to 1 year), the infant experiences both pleasure and frustration resulting from the withholding of pleasurable activities. Anxiety, which has its origin in birth, will be reexperienced when excessive stimulation from the environment is encountered, or when objects of gratification are missing. The major acquisition during this period is the formation of an attachment to the caretaker initially and then to other meaningful persons. Freud was the earliest theorist to focus on the importance of the mother-infant relationship. The oral stage is assumed to be critical because the experiences acquired during this stage form the basis for adult personality. For example, the oral aggressive substage that appears during this period is a prototype for later aggressive behaviors.

The *anal stage* (from 1 to 3 years) presents the child with demands for control, which sets up a potential conflict with parents and conditions for anxiety. The outcome will determine whether the child is compulsive and overcontrolled or impulsive and undercontrolled. The most important development during the *phallic stage* (from 3 to 5 years) is the formation of a sex-role identity in which the child adopts the behaviors appropriate for his or her gender, identifies with an appropriate same-sex model, and acquires a conscience based on conceptions of right and wrong.

Latency (from 5 years to around 11 or 12 years) is the stage during which the child consolidates experiences, focuses on the acquisition of school-related skills, and interacts with peers of the same sex. The emergence of puberty marks the appearance of the *genital stage,* during which time the adolescent must cope with sexual urges and learn how to interact with a peer of the opposite sex (Clarke-Stewart, Perlmutter, & Friedman, 1988; Miller, 1989). Freud's main contributions to our understanding of development were those relating to attachment, anxiety and its sources, defense mechanisms, and his ideas about sex-role identity and moral development.

Erikson's Theory

Erikson, a so-called neo-Freudian, also viewed development as progressing through a series of stages, but rather than biologically based, these stages reflected a sociocultural influence in which conflict resolution enhanced future development. The *trust vs. mistrust stage* corresponds to Freud's oral stage and is the time during which nurturant, sensitive care giving by the parents will enhance the likelihood of a trusting relationship. *Autonomy vs. shame and doubt* corresponds to Freud's anal stage and is the time when the child learns to exercise control and develop a sense of autonomy. *Initiative vs. guilt,* corresponding to Freud's phallic stage, is a time for the child to explore, to engage in symbolic thought, and to engage in fantasy play. The *industry vs. inferiority* stage, corresponding to Freud's latency stage, is an important period for achievement and for understanding the rewards of effort. The value placed on school and the pleasure from learning new skills facilitate the child's valuing of the products obtained from work.

The emergence of adolescence marks the stage of *identity vs. role confusion,* corresponding to Freud's genital period. This is a time of role experimentation and the acquisition of a positive identity, which will be contingent on the valence of the accrued identities to this time as well as the adolescent's resolution of who, what, and why as they pertain to the adolescent. Erikson's main contributions are his focus on the central role of trust in development, the important role of achievement during middle childhood, and the adolescent's continuing search for an individual identity.

Cognitive Theories

Piagetian theory and information processing are the cognitive theories most often discussed. Both are concerned with mental processes and how the mind functions. The developing person is seen as using reasoning to interact with and exercise control over the environment.

Piagetian Theory

Piaget is a constructivist who contends that the human mind constructs new knowledge, as opposed to the nativistic position that knowledge is innate, or the empirical/behavioral position that knowledge is learned from the environment. According to Piaget, development progresses through a series of invariant, distinct stages in which we see the child changing from the infant who must motorically interact with the environment in a physical way to understand it, to an adolescent who can use scientific reasoning in problem solving, so that thought becomes logical, abstract, and hypothetical (Miller, 1989).

In the *sensorimotor period* (from birth to 2 years), the infant is engaged in constructing a knowledge base consisting of motoric intelligence by coordinating various sensory experiences (e.g., seeing, hearing, vocalizing) with motor actions, such as sucking and grasping. The motoric intelligence is the base for the changes in cognitive functioning that occur with development. At the end of the sensorimotor period, the child has the capability to mentally represent experiences and to use language. During the *preoperational period* (from 2 to 7 years), the child is using mental images and words to represent experiences with the real world. This use of symbolic thought or representational intelligence provides the child with greater cognitive skills for interacting with and understanding the world, but the child is not yet capable of performing mental operations, such as reversibility, in problem-solving situations.

With the onset of the *concrete operations period* (from 7 to 11 years), the child can reason about object and event through the application of various mental operations such as reversibility, classification, and seriation, or ordering of objects and events. The cognitive change that occurs during this period permits the child to shift from intuitive thought to logical thought, provided that the principles can be applied to specific events or objects. The child now has an operational intelligence but it is restricted to concrete objects or experiences. The final stage, *formal operations* (from around 11 to 15 years), is described as the period of hypothetico-deductive thought, or scientific intelligence, as the child shifts from descriptive reasoning to explanatory reasoning. What is acquired during this period is a set of problem-solving strategies. The adolescent has been transformed into a more abstract and logical thinker who can now consider all possibilities in a situation and can consider the future and what it might be like.

Several important educational applications emerge from Piaget's theorizing. Piagetian-based assessment is one such application. Some psychologists (e.g., DeVries, 1974) have suggested that assessment of children's cognitive level should be based on Piaget's stages and their contents (e.g., classification, seriation, conservation) instead of the content found in such tests as the Wechsler Intelligence Scale for Children III (WISC-III). DeVries's research reveals small positive correlations (rs mostly in the low 30s and 40s) between Piagetian measures, such as those just identified, and scores on the Stanford-Binet. Similar small correlations ($r = .20$) have been found between Piaget's number conservation and scores on the Metropolitan Arithmetic Achievement Test (DeVries, 1974).

The minimal association between Piagetian skills and standard IQ tests suggests that there is little overlap in their content assessment, and DeVries (1974) has argued that an instrument based on Piagetian skills would be a more valid assessment of a child's cognitive developmental level than psychometric measures. Further, DeVries proposes that learning disabilities and mental retardation ought to be viewed as reflecting developmental delay commensurate with Piagetian-based assessment, which suggests greater possibility for change, rather than some fixed ability level such as an IQ score, which tends to label individuals as having permanent mental retardation. Piaget has contributed greatly to our understanding of *readiness,* that is, the age

at which a child can acquire a concept as a result of training. It appears that the closer a child is to a particular stage, the more likely that child will benefit from training in concepts associated with that stage. But as Miller (1989) notes, assessing readiness among children of the same age may be a difficult task because we lack the methodology. Based on our discussion of genetics and environment, individual differences are expected among children.

Information Processing

These theories focus on how individuals encode, organize, store, transform, and retrieve information about the world, which can enable them to engage in such cognitive activities as reasoning and problem solving. A major developmental focus is on memory processes and the changes that occur with increasing age. The use of cognitive strategies in memory processing is seen as an important developmental change. Although stages are not used by information processors, one could construct a set of descriptive stages, based on strategy use, which are related to age.

During the preschool period, there is some evidence of primitive strategy use to remember, such as pointing and looking. Beginning with the primary grades, around 7 years of age, children start to use rehearsal as a memory strategy, and somewhat later, around 8 to 9 years of age, categorization is used. By 10 to 11 years of age, the child uses a combination of the two strategies and finds that this combination enhances memory in varied settings. Combining strategies in this way portrays the child as *general strategic* (using generalization of memory strategies). Later, around 15 years of age, some adolescents have added a third strategy, self-testing, to the combination, so that the adolescent practices retrieval before engaging in an actual retrieval task, such as a subject-matter test in school (Horras & LaVoie, 1986).

What are the processes that explain the memory changes that have just been identified? Information-processing theorists suggest several possibilities. The child's knowledge base increases with maturation, and this enlarged knowledge base enables the child to relate new information that increases retention in memory. Automatization is another factor. With increasing age, the child becomes more skillful at transforming certain processes, such as memory strategies, into automatic processes that are engaged when materials to be remembered are encountered.

Certainly experience is an important factor in memory development, and perhaps the major experience affecting memory is schooling. When a child enters school, he or she quickly learns that information has to be remembered and, furthermore, that this information is on tests. As a result, children begin to experiment with different methods for studying and remembering information and for taking tests (Kail, 1990). Of course, there are great individual differences in how schooling experiences benefit a child. A child's level of intelligence is one factor. Children of high intelligence are more likely to experiment with different study strategies and they are likely to be better test takers.

Among the major contributions of information-processing theory are those related to memory, language, and academic skills. Our discussion of memory strategies has shown how children develop these strategies and how developmental change occurs with increasing age. Language is closely tied to sensorimotor development in that the child's early vocabulary reflects the child's experiences during the sensorimotor period. Piaget has argued that language is mapped onto cognition. That is, thought emerges before language. Our understanding about the development of reading, writing, and arithmetic has been enhanced by information-processing theory.

As Siegler (1991) has noted, the methods that children use to secure information in school are quite similar to those that they use in settings out of school. Allocation of processing resources and use of strategies are important for becoming proficient in reading, writing, and arithmetic. The ability to estimate is an important skill in mathematics. Phonetic awareness, ability to identify individual words, automatization, reading potential (i.e., general IQ, knowledge base, motivation), as well as short-term memory are critical components for reading. Drafting and revising are important for writing (Siegler, 1991).

Behavioral and Social Learning Theories

According to these theoretical approaches, development is the product of environmental experiences. Behavioral theory assumes that all behavior is learned, either as the result of operant or Pavlovian (i.e., classical) conditioning. The major theme of operant conditioning is that behavior is contingent on the consequences that follow it. Reinforcement and punishment can be used to change behavior in varied settings. For example, a parent may foster helping behavior and cooperation by rewarding the child each time these behaviors are emitted. Aggressive behavior, on the other hand, can be decreased by sending the child to her or his room, which is a form of punishment. In Pavlovian conditioning, a previously neutral stimulus, when paired with a stimulus capable of eliciting some reflex or emotional behavior such as fear or happiness, can soon elicit that emotional behavior. For the young child, being left alone in a dark room can elicit fear, if on some previous occasion the child had become fearful of darkness.

Social learning theory added the process of observational learning, which assumes that behavior can be acquired merely through watching another perform the action. Reinforcement can occur vicariously; that is, observing the consequences of a behavior by another influences the likelihood of that behavior in the observer. Cognitive social learning theory emphasizes that behavior is the product of environment and cognition. Observation of another's behavior can be mentally represented and stored in memory for future occasions.

A more recent version of social learning theory, developed by Bandura (1986), incorporates the characteristics of the person, his or her behavior, and the environment in an interdependent, interactive model, which is shown in Figure 2.5. One can note from this model that the three factors reciprocally control and influence each other in a process that Bandura has labeled *reciprocal determinism*. This theoretical idea recognizes that the child's behavior influences, or actually constructs, the environment.

Miller (1989) illustrates this point by noting that children who are heavy television viewers subject themselves to a different set of models (e.g., aggressive models if violence is viewed) than children who choose to play with friends. But behavior can affect cognition as well as the environment. Certainly behavior can elicit certain experiences, which then influence how the child reasons and forms expectations, which then affect behavior (Miller, 1989). For example, if a child acquires some type of expertise or mastery of a skill, these acquisitions may earn him or her status in the peer group. This in turn may stimulate the child to think more positively of herself or himself.

If the contributions made by behavioral theory are considered, behavior modification immediately comes to mind. Operant learning procedures have been used in a wide variety of

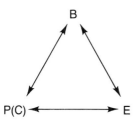

FIGURE 2.5 Bandura's model of reciprocal determinism, which illustrates the reciprocal influence of behavior, B, personal and cognitive factors, P(C), and environment, E.

Source: Albert Bandura, *Social foundations of thought and action: A social cognitive theory,* © 1986, p. 24. Adapted by permission of Prentice Hall, Englewood Cliffs, New Jersey.

settings to remediate such developmental problems as aggression, social isolation, noncompliance, enuresis, and language delays. Through the use of Pavlovian conditioning, children's fears, anxiety, and other emotional problems have been treated. (The application of operant and Pavlovian techniques will be discussed more extensively in Chapter 5.) Social learning theory has given us insight into the acquisition and maintenance of such maladaptive behaviors as aggression, by showing how reinforcement functions in social settings. The coercive cycle in families of aggressive children reported by Patterson and Reid (1984) is one example of how a network of behaviors can function as stimuli and reinforcement in an escalating cycle of aggression.

MARGINALITY

Although the term *marginality* has been in the developmental vocabulary for some time, it has been relatively ignored until recently. This situation is somewhat of a paradox, given the developmental importance of the concept. *Marginality* refers to multiple-group membership in which one alternates between the values and standards of the various groups to which he or she belongs (Sameroff, 1983). Two examples illustrate what is meant by marginality.

Adolescence can be considered a period of marginality because individuals in this developmental period appear to be continually shifting between the period of childhood and their present societal status as an adolescent (Sameroff, 1983). The mentally handicapped and the physically handicapped have also been marginalized (McGee, 1989). Although the physically handicapped are intellectually and emotionally normal, their physical anomalies make them "abnormal" in the eyes of society. Conversely, persons with mental handicaps may be physically normal, but their developmental cognitive delay makes them appear "abnormal." In both cases, society, and often parents, experience difficulty in coping with these conditions, and may treat the individual differently than a normal child or adolescent. Being marginalized compounds the problem of identification for the individual, and makes it more difficult for others to establish consistent patterns of interaction with the marginalized child or adolescent.

APPLIED DEVELOPMENTAL PSYCHOLOGY

Applied developmental psychology refers to the application of developmental theories, principles, and research to societal problems. Several factors have provided the impetus for this applied field. One is the recognition that the events that affect children are those associated with the social system in which the child is a member. Thus, children are influenced not only by their families but also by their school, neighborhood, community, and mass media (Zigler & Finn-Stevenson, 1988).

Another factor is the changes in family life that have occurred in the last 10 or more years. Among the most dramatic changes are the shift to two wage earners in the family; single-parent households, resulting mostly from divorce (in the United States at the present time about 20 percent of white children and 50 percent of black children live in single-parent households [Zigler & Finn-Stevenson, 1988]); and blended or reconstituted families.

These changes have generated questions that demand attention. Two such areas of concern are daycare and the effects of divorce on children. Availability of adequate daycare is one of the most pressing social issues facing our country today. The lack of adequate daycare may force the parent to leave children at home alone for a period of time, which presents the problem of latchkey children. Research on this problem suggests that such children are not only more fearful and anxious but they also are more likely to deviate from societal norms (Steinberg, 1986). Another issue relates to the quality of childcare, not only as it pertains to daycare centers but also to private homecare. The research literature suggests that the quality of care received by young children does affect development and well-being (Zigler & Finn-Stevenson, 1988).

The need for adequate childcare raises social policy issues. As Zigler and Finn-Stevenson (1988) note, satisfaction and work output are related to functioning within the family system; therefore, adequate childcare arrangements not only exert an effect on the workplace but also on the marital relationship. Given these associations, the policy issue then focuses on the responsibility of the workplace to provide childcare facilities and flexible work schedules. The school can assist by providing facilities for childcare, constructing school calendars that mesh with parent work schedules, and arranging sick-child policies that consider the work status of the parent.

The effects of divorce on children have social implications for the school as well as society in general. Overall, research on this issue indicates that divorce entails a major transition in the life of the child as well as among the spouses, and that major adjustments in living arrangements, finances, and socialization of the child are necessary. Most children still envision a reunion of their parents. Custody and visitation rights can produce legal conflicts that extract a substantial emotional cost from the child and the parents. It is quite apparent that a need exists for a support system not only for children and their families who are experiencing divorce but for all families who are encountering various stressors (Zigler & Finn-Stevenson, 1988).

Applied developmental psychology concerns have implications for the practice of school psychology. Childcare and its effects need to be understood by school psychologists because they are likely to have referrals of children whose primary caretaker is a parent surrogate. School psychologists must be knowledgeable about the effects of divorce so that they can be effective consultants with teachers who observe changes in the behavior of children whose parents are divorcing, and the school psychologist may need to consult with parents on ways to cope with the problem. Last, school psychologists have an obligation to be advocates for the child in matters of childcare, preschool education, and the impact of stressors such as divorce and family conflict.

IMPLICATIONS OF THE DEVELOPMENTAL MODEL FOR SCHOOL PSYCHOLOGY

Our review of the major concepts in developmental psychology illustrate the utility of the developmental model for psychological assessment, intervention, and planning educational outcomes. Psychological assessment differs from psychological testing, according to Sattler (1988), because this type of assessment considers the characteristics and the context of the child. Further, assessment interprets the data in terms of the systems and networks in which the child functions—namely, the child's situation and the family.

What child characteristics and context need to be considered? Certainly developmental change is important to understand if the school psychologist is to determine what is appropriate and inappropriate behavior at any age. The school psychologist should be able to determine when continuity/discontinuity is present. Will a defiant behavior continue in the child? What about the aggressiveness (a social behavior that seems to continue over time) that has been observed in the child? Within this context it is also necessary to understand stability/instability of a behavior or trait. When consulting with teachers or parents about a particular child, is it likely that some trait, skill, or behavior will change with respect to the child's classmates?

There is also the matter of the genetics-environment, or nature vs. nurture, issue. As Christensen, Avery, and Weinberg (1986) note, if such factors as IQ, cognitive skills, school achievement, certain personality traits, and other items are largely genetically determined, what effect can educational interventions have on the child's development? To compound the issue further, add the interacting effect of nonshared environments, which we discussed previously. Although genetics do not totally determine environments, we know that children with certain genotypes are

more likely to seek out specific kinds of experiences. It is also the case that environments (experiences) can modify genetic input, so there is some flexibility or plasticity in the relationship, in that genes set a range of possible experiences that environments can provide.

Some knowledge about developmental theories is important information for the school psychologist. If one takes a stage view of development, then the interpretation given to the child's behavior will follow from this theoretical approach. From a stage perspective, alienation during early adolescence, for example, is typical, *not* atypical, behavior. Knowledge of Piagetian theory can provide an alternative to accepted psychometric assessment and reveal the importance of readiness. From information-processing theories, we can obtain some insight into strategy use by the child and how study skills and information acquisition can be modified. Behavioral and social learning theories provide explanations for the acquisition and modification of behavior. If the school psychologist is to observe and interact with children in their natural environments, instead of just administering psychological tests, it is necessary to understand developmental processes to facilitate the child's learning, adjustment, and social adaptation.

A SYSTEMS APPROACH

Systems theory's focus on relationships, roles, functions, and principles of organization found a eager adherent among school psychologists who recently have become aware of the need to consider the system in which the child functions in her or his assessment, intervention, and educational plans. This discussion begins by first examining some general principles of systems.

What Are Systems?

A *system* is a organized arrangement of a set of component parts, called *subsystems*, that can achieve some specified goal or objective. Any system is part of another system; that is, any system can be recognized as a subsystem of another larger, inclusive system called a *suprasystem* (Curtis & Zins, 1986; M. Ford, 1986; D. Ford, 1987; Ford & Ford, 1987; Urban, 1978). A systems perspective considers the context in which individual behavior occurs. Therefore, the behavior of one system component influences and is influenced by the behavior of others (Dowling, 1985). The dynamics of a system are truly interactive.

Integration and differentiation are component parts of systems organization. The components are related; that is, they are not independent of each other, and therefore the organization is lost when a system is reduced to its components (M. Ford, 1986; D. Ford, 1987). Families are systems composed of parents, children, and relatives (Minuchin, 1985), but when the individual members of the family are separated out (i.e., differentiated), the family organization is no longer present. The advantage of organization is that it provides greater effectiveness in functioning when components are coordinated toward achieving a common goal. But organization extracts a cost in that each segment is limited in the way it functions by the other segments to which it is related. That is, organization decreases differentiation (M. Ford, 1986; D. Ford, 1987).

Using the family again as a example, family members are often constrained in their options by the family structure, but this structure enables members to achieve goals that they may be unable to attain individually. Consider this family situation. Jill, a 14-year-old, wants to take a separate vacation, but is considered too young to solo in this venture. However, she finds that by combining her money with that budgeted by the family, a longer vacation will result, and some decisions about family activities during the vacation can be made. Thus, Jill can vacation in a more desirable location and she can engage in some independent activities, but she will have to go with the family.

Developmental Systems Theory

There is an accommodation between the human and the environment in which the human func-

tions throughout the life span. To explain this process, Bronfenbrenner (1977) constructed four major systems. A *microsystem* refers to the relationship between an individual and the environment. A *mesosystem* examines the interactions between the individual and such settings as the family, peer group, and school. An extension of the mesosystem is the *exosystem,* which includes such entities as the world of work and the neighborhood. Finally, the *macrosystem* is a general prototype that encompasses such settings as the school classroom.

Bronfenbrenner contends that it is necessary to examine all possible subsystems such as the family, school, peer group, and, more importantly, the potential interactions between them. Further, second- and third-order effects have to be considered. The effects of marital satisfaction on parent-child interactions have to be considered as well as the effects of classroom climate or teacher attitudes about the school on teacher-child interactions. Not to be overlooked is the environmental or context effect and the changes over time that occur as the result of ecological transitions (e.g., child at home to student at school, husband to father, etc.).

Determinants of Systems Performance

A systems model can be more easily understood by examining several key concepts commonly associated with this approach.

Reciprocal Interaction

The tendency for a change in any system component to affect other components within the system, as well as the output, is a core concept of systems theory. Systems are either open or closed. Open systems can respond to external forces; they depend on exchanges with the environment for their survival and development. Closed systems (e.g., mechanical systems) exist independently of their environments (von Bertalanffy, 1981). Only open systems are capable of developing toward more complex states of organization.

All living systems (those involving people)

are open systems; they are flexible and have more degrees of freedom in how they will respond than mechanical systems. Living systems are in a state of continual dynamic change resulting from internal and external input that affect each other as well as the system. The family and the school are both open and living systems because people are involved and several subsystems are included in each (e.g., the family consists of subsystems that include spouse, parent, and child; the school has teachers, administrators, and service personnel such as school psychologists). Each of the subsystems is connected to the others for common objectives. The objectives of the family are to function as a unit to attain familial goals such as the socialization of children. The goal of the school is to educate children.

Circular Causality

Within systems, behavior is viewed in terms of cycles of interaction. Note in Figure 2.6 that the behavior of A is influencing and being influenced by B and C.

Problems experienced by the child in school can affect her or his behavior within the family, just as family problems can impact on the child's performance in school. Wendt and Zake (1984) note that the child's negative behavior seems to decrease following family therapy. Two other examples from Dowling (1985) may help to clarify this point. One spouse complains about the other's unwillingness to help care for their child, but it would be more productive to examine the sequences of interactions that are associated with

FIGURE 2.6 An illustration of circular causality

Source: Dowling, E. (1985). Theoretical framework – A joint systems approach to educational problems with children. In E. Dowling & E. Osborne (Eds.), *The family and the school*. London: Routledge & Kegan Paul. Reprinted with permission.

the problem. Similarly, in a school situation, a bossy teacher may complain about the lack of staff support, so this teacher continues to make decisions without consulting others, which are then seen by the staff as unwarranted, producing further distancing by the staff. In both cases, cycles of interactions that fit circular causality are operating. A cause-effect model would ask why? but a systems model focuses on the sequences of interactions and the repetitive behavior that are associated with an event (Dowling, 1985).

Punctuation

According to Dowling (1985), this concept is closely aligned with circular causality. *Punctuation* refers to that point at which some sequence of events is interrupted to give the sequence a specific meaning. Therefore, any interpretation of causal events depends on how reality is punctuated. Dowling notes that Bateson (1973) has taken the position that any behavior may be a stimulus or a response contingent on the punctuation of the sequence.

To illustrate this point, Dowling (1985) cites the case of a high school student who was seen as somewhat maladjusted. One day the student struck a boy who had bumped his lunch tray, spilling milk on the boy's jacket. The school principal attributed this behavior to the boy's maladjustment; that is, the principal punctuated the sequence of behavior as further evidence of the boy's maladjustment. Further examination of the event revealed that the boy's mother had threatened him with physical punishment if the jacket that she had saved money for was stained, and this was the first time that the boy had worn the jacket. It is evident from this example that context influences behavior. Punctuation is not correct or incorrect; rather, punctuation reveals our perception of reality. The lesson from this case is that the various contexts, such as school and family, need to be considered when the child has a problem in school.

Boundary Permeability

Boundaries bind together the segments of a system and keep them cohesive. They provide a barrier between the system and its environment, and thus provide protective and regulating functions (Goldenberg & Goldenberg, 1985). In families, there is a need for boundaries and rules of inter-action to readjust with developmental change (e.g., maturation of the child). This readjustment to developmental change becomes a problem for dysfunctional families (Minuchin, 1985). The degree to which any system permits external in-fluences to affect it and the degree to which it responds to these influences is determined by its permeability. If systems are separated by illusory boundaries, the functioning of each subsystem is determined by its boundary permeability. Curtis and Zins (1986) identify three levels of boundary permeability.

1. *Impermeable*. All external influences are re-jected. For example, a school refuses to acknowl-edge or consider any information or input from the outside, such as parental concerns about the school's operation.

2. *Dysfunctional*. In this situation, the system takes in all external influences irrespective of their importance and responds at the same level to each stimulus input. As a result, the system is overpowered and its functioning is severely dis-rupted. Consider the following examples: Family A has no rules, so every situation that occurs pro-duces a chaotic situation that further increases the inconsistency in the family. School B re-sponds to every comment made about it and is soon controlled by parents. Therefore a change occurs in the school's operation any time a re-mark is made.

3. *Dynamic equilibrium*. This condition repre-sents a midpoint between impermeable and dys-functional. Certain external stimuli are accepted while others are rejected; that is, the system se-lectively discriminates. The system is responsive to external influences and responds to this input according to its importance. Accepted informa-tion is used advantageously by the system and re-sponded to in a manner that permits the system to maintain its stability. Curtis and Zins (1986) con-

tend that this is the most desirable boundary state because it reflects the goal of any system's change. When a system reaches dynamic equilib-rium, it is said to be *self-renewing* (Curtis & Zins, 1986).

Equifinality

According to this property, different starting points and diverse developmental routes can be used by a system to reach the same goal, and the same outcome may result from different anteced-ents. For example, two families whose interac-tional styles differ significantly may both have children who are behavior problems in school or who are compliant (Christensen, Avery, & Wein-berg, 1986). The implications for intervention are that in working with problem children, the school psychologist can begin at the home or the school, provided that the context of both and their reciprocal influence on each other is considered (Dowling, 1985).

Rules

Rules organize interactions and help maintain stability within the system by communicating prescriptions and proscriptions for a individual's behavior. The utility of rules is that they provide expectations for behavior that serve as cues and therefore ensure environmental predictability. Children encounter difficulty if the rules in two ecosystems are not shared. When this occurs, parents are likely to misinterpret a teacher's disci-pline, and their response is likely to result in the teacher stereotyping the parents' attitudes toward the school.

Homeostasis

Homeostatic systems are in a balanced state as a result of feedback from the external environment. The self-regulating properties of a family system are a example of this property. Changes in a fam-ily may be resisted or resolved when a problem occurs in another family member, which then permits family equilibrium to continue. The same principle applies to the school when accept-able or unacceptable behavior of children in a classroom is at least partially maintained by the task and demands placed on the child. In this instance, antisocial behavior is reinforced by the consequences present in the classroom (Dowling, 1985).

Information and Feedback

Information exchange is a mutually influencing process between systems, where each system is modified through its interaction with another system in a circular process referred to as a *feedback loop*. The reciprocal influence results from the interaction cycle that governs the perceptions and expectations of systems toward each other. Figure 2.7 illustrates this point. Note from this example that the evaluation of a school is contingent on the perceptions of those who are being influenced (in this case, the parents) and by the school's attitudes toward them.

Characteristics of the Systems Approach

The power of systems theory is that it permits the examination of the interaction of an individual within the system in which he or she functions, as compared to traditional approaches in school psychology that focus only on the individual. When a problem behavior is detected in a child, the traditional approach has been to examine the child's role in the school, home, and perhaps peer group, neighborhood, or community in isolation without considering the network that involves all of these systems. That is, the mesosystem (namely, the interaction of culture and other contexts such as the home-school interaction), among others, is largely ignored (Power & Bartholomew, 1987).

To clarify further systems dynamics, the family and the school as systems will be examined individually, although there are certain simi-

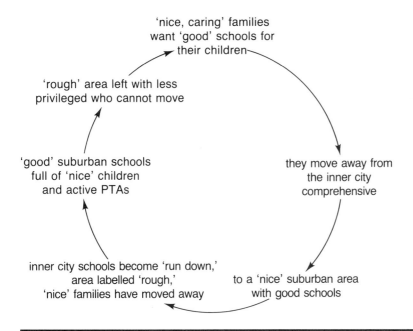

FIGURE 2.7   A model of reciprocal influence illustrating a feedback loop

Source: Dowling, E. (1985). Theoretical framework—A joint systems approach to the educational problems with children. In E. Dowling & E. Osborne (Eds.), *The family and the school.* London: Routledge & Kegan Paul. Reprinted with permission.

larities among the two (Wendt & Zake, 1984). Families and schools are open, living systems, and both are concerned with the socialization of children (Conoley, 1987).

THE FAMILY SYSTEM

Family systems theory views the individual as part of a larger system (namely, the family) and focuses on the reciprocal processes that occur between each of the interactional partners because these processes generate family structure, which organizes the dynamics of family interaction (Schwenk & Hughes, 1983). "A family is a rule-governed system; the interaction of family members follows organized established patterns" (Goldenberg & Goldenberg, 1985, p. 30). To understand the behavior of each family member, it is necessary to examine the rules of communication and interaction that regulate the family, and the reciprocal relations that exist among family members (Braden & Sherrard, 1987).

Because the family interacts in repetitive sequences, the system can be operated by a limited set of rules that control the specific relationships. These rules are not recorded and they are expressed covertly. Thus, children know which parent to approach when a problem has to be discussed, and the appropriate setting in which to make requests of parents. Parents acquire and follow rules about children, such as which child can follow directions and which family assignments are gender appropriate. Therefore, rules rather than individual traits regulate the pattern of interaction between individuals (Goldenberg & Goldenberg, 1985).

Rules are frequently the cause of family problems; dysfunctional rules characterize dysfunctional families. The family system strives for homeostasis or equilibrium. When this balance is threatened, measures are taken to restore equilibrium (Minuchin, 1985). For example, mechanisms within the family restrict the range of certain behaviors. Therefore, disputes between children do not exceed certain limits and become

physical (Goldenberg & Goldenberg, 1985). The regulation of autonomy in the child is an instance of homeostatic functioning in the family (Hinde, 1989; Minuchin, 1985). Homeostatic mechanisms also maintain equilibrium by reinstating the rules that govern the relationship. When children challenge rules, such as in adolescence, conflict and disequilibrium result until new interactional patterns with rules are established that restore the equilibrium (Goldenberg & Goldenberg, 1985). This is an instance of a developmental transition (i.e., the child entering adolescence), and as such, this transition affects the family system, necessitating a reorganization (Minuchin, 1985). Feedback and information processing are important for family system functioning. Negative feedback provides a corrective function by moving the system back to a balance state. Thus, feedback and information processing serve as self-regulating mechanisms for the family system (Ford & Ford, 1987).

Because the behavior of each individual influences and is influenced by the behavior of another, linear causality is irrelevant in this model. It is not the case that some behavior of A causes B to respond. New information is constantly being exchanged in the family system, and responses to the information are occurring because, as Bateson (1973) noted, information is something that makes a difference. Finally, the family system operates through various subsystems. Each family member is a component of several subsystems, so that wives are also mothers, sisters, and daughters, and as such, they engage in different relationships with other family members according to their role, with each relationship governed by a set of rules.

Within human relationships, there are two forces that act to counterbalance each other (Bowen, 1971): individuality (or autonomy) and togetherness (or fusion). The balance of these forces is never static, and each member of the relationship monitors the status of the balance. Each person has a capacity for intellectually determined functioning as well as emotional functioning. When these two systems remain functionally separate and operate harmoniously, the person can have a choice between functioning from either a emotional base or an intellectual base, and the system thrives because the individual can differentiate. But when the two systems are not separate, a person no longer has a choice, and thinking as well as behavior become emotionally determined, and the two systems tend to fuse, which produces relationship problems. What often happens when relationship problems arise, such as from fusion, is that one member tries to resolve the problem by moving toward a person who is outside the relationship, such as a child, which then produces a triangle with various outcomes, most often some type of child impairment (Kerr, 1981).

As Braden and Sherrard (1987) note, child behavior problems viewed within a family systems model are seen as a manifestation of family dysfunction. The child's problem behavior serves a particular function for the family system in that it may divert attention from a problem that the parental couple is facing, and what then occurs is that the child's problem actually maintains the family dysfunctioning. Family systems theory assumes that children's problem behavior in school settings is either the consequence of family dynamics or is reinforced by those dynamics (Braden & Sherrard, 1987). For example, an adolescent's truancy from school may reunite parents who are having marital problems. Thus, the cause of the truancy is placed within the family because the adolescent may be trying to keep the parental couple united by shifting the problem focus from the marriage to the truancy.

THE SCHOOL SYSTEM

Numerous examples and references to the school as a system have already made a case for the utility of applying systems theory to the school. Therefore, this discussion will mostly embellish the position that viewing the school as a system greatly enhances the school psychologist's effec-

tiveness as a change agent. The school has been identified as a open system that continually tries to maintain a balance between interchanges across system boundaries. Other system properties, such as punctuation, rules, equifinality, homeostasis, and information feedback, fit very well with the concept of the school as a system. Conoley (1987) argues that it is necessary to be as familiar with the characteristics of the school as it is to be familiar with the characteristics of the child. Schools, like families, have structure, reciprocal interaction among subsystems, and exchanges across boundaries.

For this book, the primary focus is on the classroom, which is actually a subsystem. Bardon (1986) contends that schools are also subsystems because the school district is the system. Within the classroom there exists a structure and a hierarchy, with the teacher having the control or power, although in some situations power may have to be shared with the parents of the children in the classroom. Rules are a integral part of the classroom, and a distinctive ethos can be found in most classrooms.

The pupils in the classroom form another distinct subsystem. Of course there are boundaries in the classroom, and the permeability of these boundaries will vary greatly from one classroom to another within the same school. Not to be overlooked are the various networks of relationships, including teacher and certain pupils, child-child, parent-teacher, and parent-child.

Modifying the School System

The discussion of the school as a system may give the impression that systems are experienced directly, and that they are easily repaired like replacing a broken glass in a window. This is not the case, however. Bardon (1986) holds that systems and relationships cannot be seen or heard; we can only observe behaviors from which we make various inferences about the system and relationship properties. Although systems per se are not modifiable, thinking and talking are, and it is through modification of these modes (i.e., the way we think and talk about a system and the manner in which we assist others to think and talk about the system) that we are able to modify a system (Bardon, 1986).

Maher (1981) has developed a behavioral systems approach (BSA) to intervention with school social systems that enables the practitioner to deal with school-related problems ranging from compliance with teacher requests to racial integration. Bardon (1986), on the other hand, argues that it is unlikely that school psychologists can effect any large-scale organizational change because they work through a central office that is a subsystem within the district or mesosystem. Bardon asserts that school psychologists may change teacher attitudes, modify team procedures, and perhaps organize special programs, but they are less likely to change or affect system organizational structure, attendance policies, or employment policies. According to Conoley (1987), however, comprehensive methods are available for assessing school systems. She lists four questions that need to be asked: (1) Is there any evidence of a emergency? (2) Are problem-solving procedures now occurring or have they been used in the past? (3) Who can be sought out to assist? (4) What is the status of communication patterns?

School Psychological Services

This element can also be viewed as a system, actually a subsystem, because psychological services are found within a school district or educational service unit (Curtis & Zins, 1986). Psychological service personnel, administrators, and clerical support are subsystems. Psychological services can also be characterized as a living, open system with reciprocal interaction because change within any subsystem has an effect. For example, a skilled staff member leaves and is replaced by a less skilled employee, or a change in psychological services can impact on the larger

system of the school, such as a reduction in funds for such services.

Boundary permeability is a significant factor in that the anticipation and responsiveness to change of school psychological service systems may vary greatly. Curtis and Zins (1986) cite the enactment of Public Law 94-142 (The Education for All Handicapped Children Act of 1975) as an example. Those psychological service systems that had anticipated passage of the act were prepared for its implementation, and therefore experienced few problems in making the adjustment, whereas other systems with impermeable boundaries experienced many problems in their attempts to comply with the act.

Curtis and Yager (1981) developed a systems model for use in supervising school psychological services. This model consists of a number of subsystems, beginning with the supervisor establishing some goals, the assessment of the supervisee's skill level, establishing learning needs and learning goals, followed by the necessary supervisory intervention and evaluation of the supervisee's progress. A critical feature in the model is the permeability of the supervisee's psychological boundaries. Consider the following three examples presented by Curtis and Yager (1981).

A person with an impermeable boundary rejects all advice and offers for help. Such persons are likely to claim that they already know everything that is needed for their job performance, and they therefore are unable to respond to any type of feedback. A person without a clearly defined boundary cannot discriminate the importance of feedback, and therefore responds similarly to all feedback, and soon becomes overwhelmed. A semi-permeable boundary permits the person to respond selectively to external forces according to their perceived importance. This type of person is open to feedback and new learning experiences. The advantage of this model is that it allows for the context of the setting and provides the supervisor with adequate flexibility to select the strategy that is most effective for each supervisory action.

A COMPARISON AND INTEGRATION OF FAMILY AND SCHOOL SYSTEMS

Although distinct differences exist between the functions of the two systems according to Conoley (1987), there are also some similarities. Families and schools have as a primary function the socialization of children. Their roles and functions pertain largely to that of interpersonal support among their members. Both teach, nurture, reward, and punish, but, unlike the school, the family does not directly evaluate children with formal testing procedures. However, families do attach various types of labels to children, such as stubborn or compliant (Conoley, 1987).

Three other elements are also common to families and the school. Both have some type of hierarchical organization or structure with different types of boundaries. Structure is necessary for families to function adequately, and structure is also probably necessary for schools. A set of rules specifying the manner in which individuals behave toward each other is critical to any social system, and some uniformity of rules between home and school is necessary (Dowling, 1985). When this rule congruence is absent, the child is faced with a different set of rules and compliance expectations from the home and school. These two systems are organized differently because the classroom is the major subsystem of the school, which is a subsystem of the school district. The family is not organized in this way (Plas, 1986).

Repeated interactional patterns between family and school produce various relationship patterns with specific boundaries. Power and Bartholomew (1987) identify the following five possible patterns:

1. An avoidant relationship has rigid boundaries between the two systems, which block the exchange of information.
2. A competitive relationship has a diffuse boundary between family and school, which results in intense conflict as each strives to influence the other.
3. A merged relationship has no clear boundary between family and school, thus creating a possible situation where parents and teacher merge and leave the child out, which may produce a behavior problem in the child.
4. A one-way relationship has one system communicating while the other ignores or avoids the attempt. The communicating system may confront or withdraw, resulting in the symmetrical escalation of the problem between the family and the school.
5. A collaborative relationship has a well-defined boundary where each system respects the rights of the other, and a reciprocal relationship evolves.

Several factors determine the pattern and form of the relationship: cultural patterns, developmental issues associated with the child, developmental within-system crises such as parental divorce or teacher stress, and system crises involving subsystems in the school (Power & Bartholomew, 1987).

When educational problems in children are detected, families and the school often view the problem differently (Dowling, 1985; Hughes, 1988), and the relationship between the systems becomes a factor. The family may deny that the problem is connected with the family in any way, and attribute the etiology of the problem to the school, who therefore has the responsibility to correct it. In a second scenario, the child's behavior problem appears in school, but the teacher attributes the problem to the home conditions, especially in those situations where some type of nonnormative developmental crisis, such as divorce, has occurred. The school staff argue that nothing can be done with the child, given the home situation. Distancing between the school and home may emerge as this view polarizes.

A third variation is where the school and family recognize that a problem exists with the child. Although they may not agree on the problem, they concur that the location of the problem is within the child, and suggest an etiology such

as personality or temperament. They may enlist
the services of a professional, such as the school
psychologist, who agrees with them and who
provides a label for the child such as *learning disorder, emotional disorder,* or *conduct disorder.*
The interaction context in which the problem occurs, and any differences between the school and
family, are ignored or not considered important.
The focus is on the diagnosis and how the child
behaves.

Contrast this view with the joint systems approach in which the dual context of the family
and the school and their relationship and reciprocal interaction are considered. In this type of setting, the school psychologist tries to enhance the
communication between the two parties, focuses
on how the problem occurs rather than why it occurs, negotiates some goals that can be agreed
upon, and explores some change strategies with
the two parties (Dowling, 1985).

Cultural Diversity in Social Systems

Various sociocultural factors influence the patterns of family-school interaction. Cultural patterns mold the values of the two systems (Power
& Bartholomew, 1987). Clearly defined differences between students in different cultures and
those required by the school are a factor in school
achievement. When instruction is compatible
with cultural patterns, there is an increase in
learning, which includes basic skills (Tharp,
1989).

Cultural factors have been deemed significant in the assessment of cognitive abilities. According to the arguments, performance in
cognitive tasks and the kinds of strategies children use are influenced by experiences in specific
sociocultural contexts, such as the home and the
neighborhood (Miller-Jones, 1989). Verbal skills
acquired by the child and used by the family are a
product of language socialization within the culture that may not fit with language use in the
school, even though the language acquired facilitates self-identity in the child (Heath, 1989).

Family structure ought to influence family-school interaction. The extended family, which
can be found in several cultures, but especially in
the black culture, is an example. Participation by
extended black family members (1) supports the
child's achievement and social adjustment, (2)
provides emotional support to the mother and facilitates the participation of the mother in self-improvement activities, and (3) increases the quality
of childcare and decreases the impact of single
parenting (Wilson, 1989). This brief discussion
cites a few ways in which culture relates to the
social system and to development, and highlights
the importance of recognizing cultural diversity
for the school psychologist.

Techniques for Effecting Change

From a systems perspective, many factors are
considered before intervention is enacted. The
existing hierarchies in the family and school must
be respected, and those who have control will
need to assist. Cultural diversity, when present in
the system, must be considered. At the outset
there is a need to define the problem in behavioral
terms and collect some baseline data on the frequency and other characteristics of the problem.
Next, the problem should be viewed from an interactional perspective by examining the context.
Plas (1986) notes that, unlike the traditional
models of school psychology, the person referring the problem is part of the focus of the system
intervention.

A systems-type approach is essential to formulate intervention goals and to decide on the
strategy that will be used. The most productive
strategies in a school context are those that result
in discontinuous change (Plas, 1986). For a more
extensive discussion of systems interventions, refer to Plas (1986). Wendt and Zake (1984) recommend that school psychologists receive
training in family therapy. This recommendation
is supported by Minuchin's (1985) observation
that psychologists tend to focus on developmental
antecedents of the child's behavior, such as as-

pects of parenting, whereas family therapists focus on "the function of the child's behavior in the family system" (p. 297).

One of the most effective strategies for producing change in family and school systems is *reframing* (Dowling, 1985; Hughes, 1988), which involves presenting a perception of a situation that differs from the view of those involved; that is, assigning a new meaning to the situation. For example, a parent who reacts with anger and blames the school for his or her child's problem is seen as being caring and concerned about his or her child rather than as defensive and hostile. Correspondingly, the school's action or teacher's behavior would be reframed to that of real concern for the child's welfare, and of acting in the best possible way to demonstrate this concern. As Hughes (1988) notes, "Truth is relative" (p. 99); the task facing the school psychologist is to determine which meaning of the situation will facilitate the desired change.

A caveat about intervening in a system is in order. Rutter (1982), quoting some thoughts about this matter from Lewis Thomas, states that Thomas noted:

> You cannot meddle with one part of a complex system from the outside without the most certain risk of setting off disastrous events you hadn't counted on in other, remote parts. If you want to fix something, you are first obliged to understand, in detail, the whole system. (cited in Rutter, 1982, p. 884)

A DEVELOPMENTAL/SYSTEMS APPROACH

Christensen, Avery, and Weinberg (1986) have proposed a model that provides a developmental perspective for service delivery based on the following considerations. School psychology must include psychosocial development of children, social interactive processes, and systems change in addition to teaching and learning. The school psychologist should be aware that the child brings all of his or her experiences to the classroom, and

that this classroom has a reciprocal shaping effect on the child.

The school psychologist also needs to be responsive to context effects, such as the community and the culture as well as the educational environment in the home. Certain identifiable characteristics are present in this developmental perspective. Development occurs from the interactions between the individual and experiences with the environment. Individual differences in development are the product of genotype-environment interactions. Two other important factors are the realization that individual behavior occurs within its environmental contexts (an ecological view), and the characteristics of both the child and the environment are continually changing (a transactional view).

Because the environment is critical to understanding developmental outcomes, consideration must be given to the four systems in which the child develops: the microsystem (the relationship between the person and the environment), the mesosystem (the interactions between the person and settings such as the family and school), the exosystem (the interactions involving such settings as the neighborhood), and the macrosystem (school classrooms).

To illustrate the implications of this developmental model for school psychology, consider two of its major characteristics: a transactional view and the genotype-environment interaction. From a transactional view, a child's problem behavior is not seen as a genetic trait or inability to respond appropriately in specific situations, but rather as the product of some maladaptive relationship between the child and a significant other(s), which prevents the child from adaptively coping. The focus of assessment now becomes the interactions between the child and the parents, teachers, peers, and so on. From this perspective, more attention must be given to individual differences. The nature-nurture controversy has shown that genes are not the sole determinant of ability or personality because environmental influences can modify genetic input. However, Scarr and McCartney (1983) have argued that genes can significantly influence the environments that are experienced. They contend that children with certain genotypes are more likely to experience certain environments.

Implications for Practice

The integrative developmental/systems approach provides a new direction for the practice of school psychology. The school psychologist must consider the child's behavior within its natural context rather than rely on tests. This means that the psychologist needs to understand the complex array of exosystems that influence the child and that are modified by the child. Further, the various systems need to be coordinated to facilitate the child's learning, adjustment, and social adaptation (Christensen, Avery, & Weinberg, 1986).

Conoley (1987) describes four levels of interventions that the school psychologist can use in working across boundaries between the family and the school. Level 1 interventions involve dissemination of information between parents and the school. Report cards and parent-teacher conferences are common methods at this level. To facilitate this exchange, school personnel need communication skill training and available methods for communication, and parents will need to be recognized as useful sources of information. At level 2, cooperative programs between home and school, such as skill teaching or implementation of reinforcement programs, are used. Each participant must understand what is expected and the designated change must be agreed on by all. Level 3 interventions necessitate active parent participation at school so that children can see their parents and the school as partners in the education process. This experience provides the parent with a better understanding of the teaching process, and enables teachers to use relevant information about children in the learning environment. Level 4 interventions incorporate a learning process whereby parents and teachers instruct each other. This educational experience can occur in various contexts, such as workshops, consultation, and more formal instruction.

The attractive features of Conoley's intervention approach is that it facilitates problem solving by bringing parents and school personnel into more structured contact settings that can enhance supportiveness.

SUMMARY

Throughout this chapter the virtues of an integrated model that incorporates principles from developmental psychology and general systems theory have been emphasized. It should now be evident that one cannot study or intervene with the child or adolescent without considering the system and the context in which the individual is an interacting part.

In our society there are regulating forces (two of which are the family and the school) that interact with the genetic blueprint to set the developmental pattern for the child to reach the desired role. Within each system there are self-correcting mechanisms that have become institutionalized. For example, school psychologists deal with children who have behavior problems in concert with the family. They also use assessment procedures that may lead to recommendations for remedial classes or special education. The family is charged with socializing the child to fit a expected societal role, and uses nurturance, rules, and discipline to reach this goal. When aberrations occur, the family uses various means, some of which may be pathological, to restore equilibrium.

Regardless of the mechanisms used, both systems have to continually consider the developmental stage of the child or adolescent and the context in which the behavior occurs. School psychology and developmental psychology are not separate entities. Behavior is always the product of developmental influences. Therefore, every assessment, intervention, and educational plan must involve developmental and systems considerations. Of the many contributions made by developmental psychology, the most widely used information in school psychology practice, according to Tharinger and Lambert (1990), is that applied to assessment.

REFERENCES

Baltes, P. B., Reese, H. W., & Nesselroade, J. R. (1977). *Lifespan developmental psychology: Introduction to research methods.* Monterey, CA: Brooks/Cole.

Bandura, A. (1986). *Social foundations of thought and action: A social cognitive theory.* Englewood Cliffs, NJ: Prentice-Hall.

Bardon, J. I. (1986). Psychology and schooling: The interrelationships among persons, processes, and products. In S. N. Elliott & J. C. Witt (Eds.), *The delivery of psychological services in schools* (pp. 53–79). Hillsdale, NJ: Erlbaum.

Bateson, G. (1973). *Steps to an ecology of mind.* St. Albans, England: Paladine.

Belsky, J., Fish, M., & Isabella, R. (1991). Continuity and discontinuity in infant negative and positive emotionality: Family antecedents and attachment consequences. *Developmental Psychology, 27,* 421–431.

Bowen, M. (1971). Family therapy and family group therapy. In H. Kaplan & B. Sadock (Eds.), *Comprehensive group psychotherapy* (pp. 384–421). Baltimore: Williams & Wilkins.

Braden, J. P., & Sherrard, P. A. D. (1987). Referring families to nonschool agencies: A family systems approach. *School Psychology Review, 16,* 513–518.

Bronfenbrenner, U. (1977). Toward an experimental ecology of human development. *American Psychologist, 32,* 513–530.

Carboy, J. J., & Curley, J. F. (1976). A new training model: Professional child psychology. *Psychology in the Schools, 13,* 152–155.

Ceci, S. J. (1991). How much does schooling influence general intelligence and its cognitive components? A reassessment of the evidence. *Developmental Psychology, 27,* 703–722.

Christensen, S., Avery, B., & Weinberg, R. A. (1986). An alternative model for the delivery of psychological services in the school community. In S. N. Elliott & J. C. Witt (Eds.), *The delivery of psychological services in schools* (pp. 349–392). Hillsdale, NJ: Erlbaum.

Clarke-Stewart, A., Perlmutter, M., & Friedman, S. (1988). *Life-long human development.* New York: Wiley.

Conoley, J. C. (1987). Schools and families: The theoretical and practical bridges. *Professional School Psychology, 2,* 191–203.

Curtis, M. J., & Yager, G. G. (1981). A systems model for the supervision of school psychological services. *School Psychology Review, 10,* 425–433.

Curtis, M. J., & Zins, J. E. (1986). The organization and structuring of psychological services within educational settings. In S. N. Elliott & J. C. Witt (Eds.), *The delivery of psychological services within schools* (pp. 109–138). Hillsdale, NJ: Erlbaum.

DeVries, R. L. (1974). Relationship among Piagetian, IQ, and achievement assessment. *Child Development, 45,* 746–756.

Dowling, E. (1985). Theoretical framework – A joint systems approach to educational problems with children. In E. Dowling & E. Osborne (Eds.), *The family and the school* (pp. 5–32). London: Routledge & Kegan Paul.

Flavell, J. (1985). *Cognitive development* (2nd ed.). Englewood Cliffs, NJ: Prentice-Hall.

Ford, D. H. (1987). *Humans as self-constructing living systems: A developmental perspective on behavior and personality.* Hillsdale, NJ: Erlbaum.

Ford, D. H., & Ford, M. E. (1987). Humans as self-constructing living systems: An overview. In M. E. Ford & D. H. Ford (Eds.), *Humans as self-constructing living systems; Putting the framework to work* (pp. 1–46). Hillsdale, NJ: Erlbaum.

Ford, M. E. (1986, April). *A systems approach to the study of social competence.* Paper presented at the American Educational Research Association, San Francisco.

Goldenberg, I., & Goldenberg, H. (1985). *Family therapy: An overview* (2nd ed.). Monterey, CA: Brooks/Cole.

Gottesman, I. I. (1963). Heritability of personality: A demonstration. *Psychology Monographs, 77.*

Grusec, J. E. & Lytton, H. (1988). *Social development: History, theory and research.* New York: Springer-Verlag.

Heath, S. B. (1989). Oral and literate traditions among Black Americans living in poverty. *American Psychologist, 44,* 367–373.

Hebb, D. O. (1949). *The organization of behavior.* New York: Wiley.

Hinde, R. A. (1989). Reconciling the family systems and the relationship approaches to child development. In K. Kreppner & R. M. Lerner (Eds.), *Family systems and life-span development* (pp. 149–164). Hillsdale, NJ: Erlbaum.

Hoffman, L., Paris, S., Hall, E., & Schell, R. (1988).

Developmental psychology today (5th ed.). New York: Random House.

Horras, G., & LaVoie, J. C. (1986). *Strategy selection and use: The metacognition-memory relationship in children.* Unpublished manuscript, University of Nebraska at Omaha.

Hughes, J. N. (1988). A joint systems approach to consulting with schools and families. *Journal of School Psychology, 26,* 97–101.

Kail, R. (1990). *The development of memory in children* (3rd ed.). New York: Freeman.

Kerr, M. E. (1981). Family systems theory and therapy. In A. S. Gurman & D. P. Knishkern (Eds.), *Handbook of family therapy* (pp. 226–264). New York: Brunner/Mazel.

Kohlberg, L. (1963). The development of children's orientations toward moral order. 1. Sequence in the development of moral thought. *Vita Humana, 6,* 11–33.

Langer, J. (1970). Werner's comparative organismic theory. In P. H. Mussen (Ed.), *Carmichael's manual of child psychology* (3rd ed., Vol. 1, pp. 733–771). New York: Wiley.

Lerner, R. M. (1976). *Concepts and theories of human development.* Reading, MA: Addison-Wesley.

Lerner, R. M. (1986). *Concepts and theories of human development* (2nd ed.). New York: McGraw-Hill.

Maher, C. A. (1981). Intervention with school social systems: A behavioral-systems approach. *School Psychology Review, 10,* 499–508.

McCall, R. B. (1977). Challenges to a science of developmental psychology. *Child Development, 48,* 333–344.

McCartney, K., Harris, M. J., & Bernieri, F. (1990). Growing up and growing apart: A developmental meta-analysis of twin studies. *Psychological Bulletin, 107,* 226–237.

McGee, J. J. (1989). *Being with others: Toward a psychology of interdependence.* Omaha, NE: Creighton University.

McGraw, K. O. (1987). *Developmental psychology.* New York: Harcourt Brace Jovanovich.

Meyers, J. (1988). School psychology: The current state of practice and future practice of the specialty. *Professional School Psychology, 3,* 165–176.

Miller, P. H. (1989). *Theories of developmental psychology* (2nd ed.). New York: Freeman.

Miller-Jones, D. (1989). Culture and testing. *American Psychologist, 44,* 360–366.

Minuchin, P. (1985). Families and individual develop-

ment: Provocations from the field of family therapy. *Child Development, 56,* 289–302.

Nagle, C. C., Wasik, B. H., & Schumacher, T. D. (1978). Use of the systems approach for successful token economies. *Journal of School Psychology, 16,* 245–252.

Papalia, D., & Olds Wendkos, S. (1989). *Human development* (4th ed.). New York: McGraw-Hill.

Patterson, G. R., & Reid, J. B. (1984). Social interactional processes within the family: The study of moment-by-moment family transactions in which human social development is embedded. *Journal of Applied Developmental Psychology, 5,* 237–262.

Phillips, B. N. (1986). The impact of education and training on school psychological services. In S. N. Elliott & J. C. Witt (Eds.), *The delivery of psychological services in schools: Concepts, processes and issues* (pp. 329–348). Hillsdale, NJ: Erlbaum.

Plas, J. N. (1986). *Systems psychology in the schools.* New York: Pergamon Press.

Plomin, R. (1989). Environment and genes: Determinants of behavior. *American Psychologist, 44,* 105–111.

Plomin, R., & Rende, R. (1991). Human behavioral genetics. *Annual Review of Psychology, 42,* 161–190.

Power, T. J. & Bartholomew, K. L. (1987). Family-school relationship patterns: An ecological assessment. *School Psychology Review, 16,* 498–512.

Reynolds, C. R., Gutkin, T. B., Elliott, S. N., & Witt, J. C. (1984). *School psychology: Essentials of theory and practice.* New York: Wiley.

Rowe, D. C., & Plomin, R. (1981). The importance of nonshared (E_1) environmental influences in behavioral development. *Developmental Psychology, 17,* 524.

Rutter, M. (1982). Prevention of children's psychosocial disorders: Myths and substance. *Pediatrics, 70,* 883–894.

Sameroff, A. J. (1983). Developmental systems: Contexts and evolution. In P. H. Mussen (Ed.), *Handbook of child psychology* (4th ed., Vol 1, pp. 237–294). New York: Wiley.

Santrock, J. (1989). *Life-span development* (3rd ed.). Dubuque, IA: Wm C. Brown.

Sattler, J. M. (1988). *Assessment of children* (3rd ed.). San Diego, CA: J. M. Sattler.

Scarr, S., & McCartney, K. (1983). How people make

their own environments: A theory of genotype-environmental effects. *Child Development, 54,* 424–435.

Schwenk, T. L., & Hughes, C. C. (1983). The family as a patient in family medicine: Rhetoric or reality? *Social Science and Medicine, 17,* 1–16.

Siegler, R. S. (1991). *Children's thinking* (2nd ed.). Englewood Cliffs, NJ: Prentice-Hall.

Steinberg, L. (1986). Latchkey children and susceptibility to peer pressure: An ecological analysis. *Developmental Psychology, 22,* 433–439.

Tanner, J. M., Whitehouse, R. H., & Takaishi, M. (1966). Standards from birth to maturity for height, weight, height velocity, and weight velocity: British children, 1965. *Archives of Diseases in Childhood, 41.*

Tellegen, A., Lykken, D. T., Bouchard, T. J. Jr., Wilcox, K. J., Segal, N. L., & Rich, S. (1988). Personality similarity in twins reared apart and together. *Journal of Personality and Social Psychology, 54,* 1031–1039.

Tharinger, D. J., & Lambert, N. M. (1990). The contributions of developmental psychology to school psychology. In T. B. Gutkin & C. R. Reynolds (Eds.), *The handbook of school psychology* (2nd ed., pp. 74–103). New York: Wiley.

Tharp, R. G. (1989). Psychocultural variables and constants: Effects on teaching and learning in schools. *American Psychologist, 44,* 349–359.

Urban, H. B. (1978). The concept of development from a systems perspective. In P. B. Baltes (Ed.), *Life-span development and behavior* (Vol 1). New York: Academic Press.

von Bertalanffy, L. (1981). *A systems view of man.* Boston: Houghton-Mifflin.

Weinberg, R. A. (1989). Intelligence and IQ: Landmark issues and great debates. *American Psychologist, 44,* 98–104.

Wendt, R. N., & Zake, J. (1984). Family systems theory and school psychology: Implications for training and practice. *Psychology in the Schools, 21,* 204–209.

Werner, H. (1957). The concept of development from a comparative and organismic point of view. In D. B. Harris (Ed.), *The concept of development.* Minneapolis: University of Minnesota Press.

Wilson, M. N. (1989). Child development in the context of the Black extended family. *American Psychologist, 44,* 380–385.

Zigler, E. F., & Finn-Stevenson, M. F. (1988). Applied developmental psychology. In M. H. Bornstein & M. E. Lamb (Eds.), *Developmental psychology; An advanced textbook* (2nd ed., pp. 595–634). Hillsdale, NJ: Erlbaum.

CHAPTER 3

RESEARCH METHODS

Research methods appropriate for a developmental/social systems orientation need to fit a dynamic framework where variability and change occur within contexts across time. Developmental psychology and social systems theory share a number of characteristics, perhaps the most important of which is their focus on change. Both development and social systems can be characterized by intraindividual variation as well as interindividual differences. Living systems such as the family and the school are open systems. Therefore, their functioning cannot be interpreted if separated from their context (Nesselroade & Ford, 1987). Because individuals function within their environment, it is necessary for the elements of individuals and environment to be organized, but both persons and environments are always changing (Nesselroade & Ford, 1987). However, this variability has limits, so that one sees some consistency or stability depicting this pattern of intraindividual variability.

Given this situation, one can observe continuity or discontinuity as well as stability or instability in the change occurring in individuals and systems. With these dynamics of change, the only method for discriminating change from stable intraindividual patterns of variability is to sample behavior across various occasions (i.e., contexts). The task at hand is to examine interindividual similarities and differences within intraindividual changes among persons and systems (Nesselroade & Ford, 1987).

Viewing persons as dynamic systems, and as behaving in order to control consequences, influences the understanding of change processes. This approach orients the researcher to a concern with the selection of persons, variables, and oc-

casions. Designs and methods based on models such as an analysis of variance are not very useful for systems research (Nesselroade & Ford, 1987). Rather, a multivariate approach is necessary to accommodate the selection of variables with multiple attributes that need to be made in developmental/social systems research. Some restriction on designs is also mandated. Cross-sectional designs, which are frequently used in developmental research, provide limited information about intraindividual variability because this design samples only one occasion. It is assumed that this sample is a valid measure of each individual's typical behavioral repertoire on all similar occasions or contexts. However, to obtain this variability information, it is necessary to sample across multiple variables and multiple contexts for each individual in the study (Nesselroade & Ford, 1987).

Applying a developmental/social systems orientation to research applications directs the investigator to think about the interaction between persons and the environment as it pertains to behavior, and to realize that the governing subsystems of the person are seeking to satisfy personal goals (Ford, 1982, 1989). Perhaps the major contribution of this integrated research approach is that it provides a conceptual framework for selecting the variables to study.

The research of Ford (e.g., Ford, 1982, 1989) on adolescent social competence illustrates this heuristic power. Ford chose a group of predictor variables consisting of such measures as goal directedness, goal capability, goal-improvement ideas, and means-end thinking to assess the social competence criterion obtained from self, peer, and teacher ratings. Subjects in grades 9 and 12 from two different schools were used to examine developmental change and generalizability from the two school contexts. Although this design is cross-sectional rather than longitudinal, the inclusion of grades 9 and 12 from each of two schools is a sequential feature that permits repeated measurements across grades and schools. A multiple regression analysis for each grade to detect developmental differences in the predictor-criterion relationships showed few such differences, but great developmental differences were found for performance on the predictor and criterion measures, and some differences in the overall magnitude of the predictor-criterion relationships were found between the two schools.

DEVELOPMENTAL DIFFERENCES VERSUS INDIVIDUAL DIFFERENCES RESEARCH

The study of developmental change focuses on the individual across time, and requires a decision about whether a developmental function or individual differences approach should be used. The study of systems, such the family or school system, examines systems across time. Both require designs using repeated measurement, such as longitudinal designs, and a multivariate approach. *Developmental* function refers to the frequency or amount of a specific behavior(s) over an age span for an individual or group of individuals, so the investigator is concerned with mean differences between ages. *Individual differences* refers to the relative rank ordering of individuals on some measure compared to their ranking on the same or a different measure at another age.

The point to remember is that the stability of individual differences across age is independent of the developmental function, which is expressed as a mean value for any age, because the correlation is independent of the means of the two distributions from which it is computed (McCall, 1977; Applebaum & McCall, 1983). Both developmental function and individual differences approaches are often couched in the research questions asked by school psychologists, so the

question to be studied will determine the approach.

Social Systems Research

The family system can be studied from one of three dimension perspectives—cohesion, adaptability, and communication (Olson & Lavee, 1989)—or from a level perspective (Schneewind, 1989). At the family system level, family *climate* needs to be examined because climate seems to be an important psychological indicator of the quality of intrafamilial interaction. The *marital relationship* is explored at the spousal subsystem level. *Parenting style,* consisting of patterns of behaviors, attitudes, and goals as experienced by parents and children, can be examined at the parent-child subsystem level (Schneewind, 1989).

One of the major methods for studying systems, and family systems in particular, is observation. Systematic observations are conducted on single family members, where each member, as well as subgroups, is observed on the relevant attributes within the same period of time. Data from member observations can be transformed into cross-classified frequency tables and analyzed with chi-square or log-linear models. The investigator needs to focus on the covariation pattern within a specific focus on the interaction of variables both within and between persons (von Eye & Kreppner, 1989).

Subgroup observations are necessary because these units will display variability that cannot be detected by constructing groups. That is, dyads will differ from the synthesis of two individuals, and triads will differ from grouping dyads plus another, such as a parent or child. Of course the entire family will exhibit variability that cannot be determined from examining only individuals or subgroups (von Eye & Kreppner, 1989).

Similarly, various systems within the school, such as the classroom, can be studied by observing children or the teacher within the classroom, or dyads or triads of children, or teacher and children, or the entire classroom. (The use of a systems model to supervise school psychological services was discussed in Chapter 2.) Nagle, Wasik, and Schumacher (1978) adapted a systems model for the implementation of a token economy in a classroom. They constructed a flowchart in which the various tasks, goals, and other criteria involving students and teachers within subsystems were identified and placed in a feedback loop for information exchange. In systems research, the investigator will need to make critical decisions about whether to examine individuals or constellations of individuals.

Appropriate Research Strategies

Certain research strategies are more appropriate than others for conducting research within a developmental/social systems framework. The topics to be discussed in this chapter fit within this framework and are intended to familiarize the reader with a research perspective that is congruent with this orientation. Therefore, the discussion will focus on the following areas: research design; descriptive research methods, including observations; subject selection, instruments and measures; an overview of certain qualitative and multivariate analyses; and research ethics. Topics pertaining to experimental approaches and linear analyses will not be discussed. The reader can consult other sources on research methods for information on these topics, such as Keith (1987). Before embarking on the discussion of research strategies, it seems appropriate to review the state of the art with respect to what has occurred in school psychology research.

RESEARCH AND THE PRACTICE OF SCHOOL PSYCHOLOGY

Scientist-Practitioner Model

In our opinion, the orientation that school psychologists should adopt is an empirical approach as espoused by the scientist-practitioner model.

This model is the most appropriate one because it directs school psychologists to "adopt a scientific attitude toward problems that they encounter in educational settings" (Gresham & Carey, 1988, p. 38). Gresham and Carey (1988) contend that practitioners (e.g., school psychologists) should be able to conduct research as well as be consumers and evaluators of research. According to the view of many writers (e.g., Bardon, 1987; Fagan, 1989; Phillips, 1982, 1987; Reynolds, Gutkin, Elliott, & Witt, 1984), school psychologists are scientist-practitioners and therefore they ought to be engaged in research activities and they ought to apply findings from research to their practice. Bardon (1987) maintains that the school psychologist has to be an "informed consumer of research" (p. 322).

A consumer needs to be more knowledgeable about research than having some familiarity with a particular research methodology, such as interviews or questionnaires. The school psychologist should have sufficient skills to frame a research question, design a study to answer the question, analyze the data and interpret the findings, use facts and principles from research, and know how to solve a problem that is research based. By performing these functions, school psychologists are engaging in research activities. For example, interventions, which involve identifying the target behavior, planning and carrying out a treatment, observing the results, and making changes in the design when necessary, can be considered research activity (Reynolds et al., 1984). Assessment activities are considered research projects to the extent that they provide information that can be used to formulate hypotheses about a child's problem. However, further data gathering, such as additional tests, behavioral observations, and teacher reports, are usually necessary to evaluate the hypotheses.

School psychologists who are trained in the scientist-practitioner model apply their methodological knowledge to referral problems, and therefore assessment and intervention are continually open to hypothesis testing and alternate explanations in seeking the most acceptable outcome. By so doing, there is a greater likelihood that the school psychologist can determine the factors that need to be modified to remediate the behavioral problem (Gresham & Carey, 1988).

If school psychologists are involved in the aforementioned research endeavors, what is the problem? According to Bardon (1987), the research methods training received by school psychologists does not transfer to their practice. One of his criticisms is that school psychologists do not keep abreast of the current research. The school psychologist has to use the information that can be gained from journal reading to evaluate the most effective intervention procedures in terms of cost (i.e., time and services to other children, the school psychologist's influence, etc). This cost-benefit analysis should also be extended to reading and evaluating the relevant research (Phillips, 1982). Reynolds and colleagues (1984) suggest generalizing the cost-benefit analysis to all aspects of the research-practice relationship, but in so doing, they argue for incorporating negative costs, such as those associated with errors in decision making that negatively affect children.

The emphasis on integrating research into practice is an important issue in school psychology. The question is: How does the school psychologist implement this integration? Bardon (1987) suggests that two components are probably involved. The first involves the application of research results to practice. What does the relevant research suggest about possible solutions for an identified problem? Of course, the school psychologist cannot be expected to know all the research literature pertaining to any problem. There is also the matter of interpreting the practical significance of research findings when the researcher is given statistical significance, and applying the findings. But research can serve as a basis for thinking about a problem and for deciding on an action.

Second, practice is a form of research because it pertains to the way in which the school psychologist thinks about her or his actions. Research in this context probably requires an ability to ask good questions and to be a scientific problem solver. Several processes are involved to think like a researcher, ranging from knowledge about the literature, to comparing inferences and conclusions with the literature, to replicating the study, and to implementing changes to fit new information.

Research Participation by School Psychologists

In reviewing studies of the activities of school psychologists, Shinn (1987) found that practicing school psychologists allocate less than 2 percent of their time to research and program evaluation, and of this total, research accounts for less than 1 percent. About 10 percent of the practicing NASP (National Association of School Psychology) members surveyed by Benson and Hughes (1985) reported engaging in any research activity, and their average length of time per day devoted to research and program evaluation was only eight minutes.

A further problem is evident from examining the school psychologist's contribution to the literature. A review of articles published in the *Journal of School Psychology* from 1983 to 1986, and *School Psychology Review* from 1982 to 1986 by Shinn (1987) revealed that contributions by practitioners accounted for only 15.65 percent of the articles in these journals. However, most of the articles were coauthored with university-based faculty, so that sole authorship by practitioners occurred in just 5.7 percent of the articles.

Shinn (1987) identifies five factors that have contributed to the poor publication record by psychologists in the schools.

1. They have limited understanding of research methodology.

2. Research methods are inappropriate, particularly the use of experimental methods, for applied research. Phillips (1987) notes that a treatment effect in an experimental study can be used to establish a cause-effect relationship, but this effect has occurred within the subject group. It is likely that the treatment was very effective with some subjects, had a minimal effect on another group, and no effect on a third group. Given this pattern, there is no constant effect for which the treatment is the cause. Therefore, it is necessary to examine individual differences among subjects to determine causal effects.

The most useful school-related research, according to Phillips (1987), is that which is done in natural contexts, such as the school classroom, where research methods other than experimentation are used. We need to realize that actual behavior occurs in specific contexts that cannot be explained by experimental research. Therefore, the strategies recommended by a developmental/ social systems approach are needed. A second problem has to do with statistical significance. Phillips contends that practitioners are not concerned with the probability of a chance result, which is statistical significance. The practitioner really cares about that point at which a difference is important, which is practical significance.

3. There is insufficient training of practitioners to conduct research. According to Shinn (1987), about 30 percent of the school psychology training programs have a research training emphasis. Most students receive information on research methods in various content courses, but their training does not seem to prepare them adequately to conduct a research program or to integrate information to solve a problem. Research and practice are reciprocal processes. One does not learn some research skills and then practice.

4. School psychologists have limited time and/ or interest. Because their role requires them to conduct assessments and classify students in terms of educability, school psychologists insist that sufficient time is not available for to conduct research. A survey of practicing school psychologists will likely show that their interest in conducting research is very low, due perhaps to the inadequacy of their research training. However, the role of research in practice is important, be-

cause research can effect educational change, and, to be an effective problem solver, the school psychologist must have research knowledge and skills.

Of course, school psychologists need other competencies as well, but research skills do enhance the practitioners' ability as change agents and do improve the school learning environment. Research activity is an important function for the school psychologist, although school administrators may not concur (Reynolds et al., 1984). However, once the school psychologist discovers that research findings can contribute to the solution of problems, he or she is then in a much stronger bargaining position with administrators with respect to the research role (Shinn, 1987).

5. Typically, there is little or no research funding available to practicing school psychologists. Local school districts usually do not have available funds, and monies at the state and federal levels are limited.

The Impact of Research on Practice

An even larger problem than insufficient research activity by school psychologists is the seeming lack of any impact by research on the practice of school psychology. Perhaps this is not so strange, given that many educators believe that research has little or no effect on educational practice (Fry, 1986). School psychologists have countered that much of the available research is not applicable to their practice. What explanations can be offered for this state of affairs? Fry (1986) suggests that most research does not ask important questions and that the quality of the research in general is very poor.

Has any research influenced the practice of school psychology? Yes, according to Fry, who cites some examples: Research based on Piaget's theory of cognitive development and Kohlberg's stage theory of moral development, research on the effects of school segregation, and the evaluation research from the Head Start programs. Assessment research that is focused on the use of nonbiased and competency-based assessment, as compared to norm-referenced assessment, has influenced school psychology practice. Research on learning and teaching has also influenced on the practice of school psychology, particularly the work on mastery learning, behavior modification, comprehension of text, and metacognition. In addition, research on the effect of schooling on the student and individual differences among teachers in classroom management has exerted some influence on school psychology.

RESEARCH PRINCIPLES FOR A DEVELOPMENTAL/SOCIAL SYSTEMS APPROACH TO SCHOOL PSYCHOLOGY

Research methods appropriate for a developmental/social systems approach have been identified. In the sections that follow, these methods will be discussed in greater detail. The first topic to be considered is problem identification.

Identify a Research Idea

Research starts with a question that needs to be answered. For the school psychologist, this question is likely to emerge from a problem encountered in working with children, teachers, or parents. For example, will a time-out procedure be effective for teachers or parents in controlling children who are identified as hyperactive? Can children who are identified as emotionally disturbed and retarded (EMR) be successfully integrated into the classroom? Although many such questions can be asked, the question must be answerable within an acceptable research methodology. The two questions just posed are potentially answerable under the constraints that have been set.

Questions such as What are the effects of informing children of their IQ? or Are classroom teaching methods more effective than letting children learn by themselves over the course of a year? are probably not answerable due to research ethics. A question such as How would

children's achievement of subject matter content be affected by an absolute tutorial method where all children in a school district were taught by individual tutors? is not answerable because of the cost and the logistics that would be involved. Once a general idea has been formulated, the relevant research literature can be consulted by referring to reviews of literature in the general area to obtain primary journal sources that appear to pertain to the idea, or through searching the relevant abstracts, such as *Psychological Abstracts* or *PsychSCAN: Developmental Psychology* for journal articles.

Knowledge of Previous Research

When a research question has been framed, the next step is to determine what studies have been done previously on the question or any related area. This task entails a search of the relevant journals and other literature sources, and it is a very critical component of any research endeavor. There are a number of benefits that emerge from a thorough review of the literature. Valuable ideas are often found that can contribute to the research methodology or the data analysis, and, as noted in the previous section, this task is a rich source of potential research ideas. Some useful literature sources are presented in Figure 3.1. This figure is organized so that it contains sources of journal abstracts, as well as major journals in school psychology, developmental psychology, and related areas in education and psychology. Each journal listing includes a brief description of the contents.

RESEARCH DESIGN

Research ideas are of little value if they cannot be phrased into the form of testable hypotheses (Miller, 1987). The research design has to permit the necessary hypothesis testing while also ensuring that internal, external, and ecological validity are present. Hypotheses are generally cast in the present tense and are directional. Rather than tak-

ABSTRACTS

Child Development Abstracts and Bibliography
Psychological Abstracts
PyschSCAN: Developmental Psychology

MAJOR JOURNALS IN SCHOOL PSYCHOLOGY

Journal of School Psychology
   Contains articles on research and practice in school psychology.
Professional School Psychology
   Contains articles on a wide range of topics pertaining to school psychology.
Psychology in the Schools
   Contains articles on application of school psychology, educational practices, and assessment and evaluation.
School Psychology Review
   Contains original research articles as well as reviews of applied topics, intervention techniques, and other
   related areas.

EDUCATION JOURNALS

American Educational Research Journal
   Contains theoretical and empirical articles on a wide range of educational questions.
American Journal of Mental Deficiency
   Contains articles on a wide range of topics relating to mental retardation.
Applied Psychological Measurement
   Contains empirical articles on applications of measurement to psychological problems.
Educational and Psychological Measurement
   Contains articles in the field of measurement as well as validity studies of tests.
Educational Research Quarterly
   Contains articles on research as well as educational design.
Educational Review
   Contains articles on such issues as teaching methods, tests and measurement, child development, and
   experimental education.
Elementary School Journal
   Contains articles in such areas as classroom practices, school and social change, and teacher training.
Exceptional Children
   Contains articles on various topics related to children with disabilities.
Journal of Educational Measurement
   Contains articles on measurement applications in educational settings as well as test reviews.
Journal of Educational Psychology
   Contains articles relating to development, teaching, learning, and other educational questions.
Journal of Educational Research
   Contains research articles relating to a variety of educational topics, such as teaching, tests and
   measurement, and curriculum.
Journal of Experimental Education
   Contains methodological articles on educational research.
Journal of Learning Disabilities
   Contains theoretical, applied, and research articles pertaining to learning disabilities.

FIGURE 3.1   Relevant journals for literature searches in school psychology

Journal of Psychoeducational Assessment
   Contains articles on a broad range of assessment issues and includes studies from various populations and subgroups.
Journal of Special Education
   Contains research and theoretical articles pertaining to special education as well as reviews.
Review of Educational Research
   Contains major reviews of relevant issues in the field of education, including methodology.
School Review
   Contains articles relating to education in all areas and from different perspectives.

DEVELOPMENTAL JOURNALS

Child Development
   Contains empirical articles and a few review pieces on all aspects of development in children and adolescents.
Developmental Psychology
   Contains empirical and review articles on development at all periods of the life span.
Developmental Review
   Contains major reviews of specific developmental issues.
International Journal of Behavioral Development
   Contains articles about developmental processes across the life span.
Journal of Applied Developmental Psychology
   Contains articles on application of empirical research from social and behavioral disciplines within the field of human development.
Journal of Early Adolescence
   Contains articles on development during the years of 11–14.
Journal of Research on Adolescence
   Contains articles about youth during the second decade of life from a variety of research perspectives.
Monographs of the Society for Research in Child Development
   Contains major reviews of developmental research that report new findings that are applied to relevant issues.

CLINICAL/BEHAVIORAL JOURNALS

Behavior Modification
   Contains research and clinical articles on behavioral therapies.
Family Therapy
   Contains articles relating to family processes and therapeutic approaches to dealing with family problems.
Journal of Abnormal Child Psychology
   Contains articles on psychopathology in children and adolescents.
Journal of Applied Behavior Analysis
   Contains research reports on the application of experimental analysis of behavior.
Journal of Clinical Child Psychology
   Contains articles that address a variety of issues related to the psychological health of children and youth.
Journal of Consulting and Clinical Psychology
   Contains articles on such areas as treatment, assessment, and development as they apply to clinical settings.
Journal of Counseling Psychology
   Contains articles largely focusing on the counseling process and its evaluation.

ing the null form, such as "There are no differences between males and females in verbal scores on the WISC-III," a directional hypothesis would state that "Females score higher than males on the vocabulary subtest of the WISC-III."

Internal validity refers to the extent to which the results in a study can be attributed to the variables under control of the investigator rather than some other explanation. If other plausible explanations can be offered for the results of a study, the investigator is severely limited in the inferences that can be made. Among those factors that can potentially influence internal validity are such matters as subject selection, loss of subjects, statistical regression, and the effect of repeated testing.

External validity refers to the extent to which the research findings are generalizable to other groups or similar conditions. This type of validity is especially important in terms of applications to practice. External validity, according to Keith (1988a), is contingent on the relationship of the study conditions to the real world and the appropriateness of the subjects, whereas internal validity is more closely aligned with the type of research.

Ecological validity implies that the environment experienced by a research participant contains the properties that have been expected by the investigator (Bronfenbrenner, 1977). This type of validity is especially critical for developmental/social systems research.

Every study ought to have internal, external, and ecological validity. However, increases in internal validity often result in subsequent decreases in external and ecological validity, in part because the researcher is moving away from a design that is more closely aligned with actual experiences and therefore the presumed context.

Basic Designs

If age comparisons are involved in the research question, a decision has to be made whether to compare the same group of subjects across subse-

quent ages, and thus use a longitudinal design, or compare different age groups of subjects to fit the age period in a cross-sectional design. Each design has specific advantages and disadvantages. Cross-sectional designs do not fit a systems approach to research because they use single-occasion measurements, which may or may not accurately represent the individual's typical behavior on similar occasions. But cross-sectional studies are frequently used in developmental research, and for that reason, they will be described in this section.

Longitudinal Designs

This design provides data on actual age change because the same subjects are followed over a designated time. A longitudinal design is necessary if the research objective is to trace the developmental course of some behavior, such as aggression, shyness, or hyperactivity, over a period of time. A major advantage for a developmental/social systems approach is that repeated testing of the same group of subjects results in a more representative measure of the person's typical behavior in similar contexts, as well as producing a smaller error variance, which therefore increases the likelihood of a significant effect.

However, there are some disadvantages to longitudinal research. Among the problems that are likely to occur are those of subject dropout or loss due to the extended period of time necessary for the study, the fit or usefulness of the instruments or measures used at the start of the study for later testing, and the confounding of the subjects and time of testing, which makes it difficult to determine whether an observed age change is due to the increase in age at the time of the testing or that the two tests were given at different times.

Nevertheless, longitudinal designs are an important tool in developmental/social systems research and should be used more extensively in school psychology research. They are necessary to answer such questions as the effects of school consolidation or matriculation from primary school to a middle or junior high school, the impact of AIDS education, or some intervention program to remediate a behavioral or learning problem.

Follow-Back and Follow-Up Designs

Both of these designs are subsets of a longitudinal design. In a follow-back design, the investigator selects a group of subjects that represents the end point of the study, perhaps seniors in high school or young adults who display the characteristics or traits to be examined, such as school dropout, school expulsion, or suicide attempt, and a second group of subjects who do not display the trait. The investigator then carefully examines all available school and other records to ascertain those earlier childhood behaviors or traits that were associated with the problem identified in the target population at the later age selected. There are several advantages of follow-back designs, such as ease of data collection and relative flexibility. However, they also have distinct disadvantages, such as reliance on earlier data that were not collected for the purpose of these later tests, and therefore may not be reliable or valid. Furthermore, they cannot be used to predict risk (Parker & Asher, 1987).

Follow-up designs use children who have been identified as differing on some trait, such as low frustration tolerance, and then compare each child's subsequent behavior at a later time. The advantage of this type of design is that it does permit the calculation of predictive risk; that is, the likelihood of later problems associated with an earlier identification of problematic behavior can be ascertained. This type of design was used by Breznitz and Teltsch (1989) to study the relation of age at school entry to achievement and social/emotional adjustment when the children were in fourth grade. They found that the younger children scored lower on achievement and social/emotional measures at first grade, and these profiles were also found at fourth grade. Although it is tempting to assume that follow-up studies will confirm follow-back studies, this is not always the case, as Parker and Asher (1987)

note. An identified population may not display a later expected behavior.

Cross-Sectional Designs

This design uses groups of individuals of different ages to span the age period under study, and thus provides data on age differences from which age change is usually inferred. Unlike the longitudinal design, which provides a direct measure of age change, the cross-sectional design gives only an indirect measure of age change. The main advantage of a cross-sectional design is that data on age differences for some behavior or measure under study can be obtained quickly, relatively easily, and with minimal cost, as compared to a longitudinal design.

One disadvantage is a possible selection bias due to the particular way in which age groups are selected that may make them different in ways other than that specified by the independent variable. Other disadvantages include selective dropout of subjects resulting in nonrepresentative groups, possible measurement problems resulting from the use of the same instrument with different age groups, the confounding of age of the subjects and the cohort or generation in which they were born, and the general unsuitability for social systems research. In spite of these problems, the cross-sectional design remains very popular, and it is the most frequently used design when age comparisons need to be made, such as in studies of different methods of teaching reading, social skills, and classroom adjustment, and the effects of TV on language use

Time-Series Designs

Time series is a type of quasi-experimental design in which the behavior of a single subject or group of subjects is recorded over a period of time through the use of repeated measurements. The repeated measures feature of these designs makes them especially useful for developmental/social systems research because this characteristic permits behavioral sampling across several occasions or contexts, which enables an assessment of intraindividual change. Some type of treatment is generally introduced after a baseline period of recording without the treatment. There are several variations on this basic design, the most common of which appear in Figure 3.2. Note from this figure that all of the design variations employ a baseline, and what differs are the treatment modes or the procedure that follows the treatment.

The most common variations are the A-B-A-B and the multiple baseline designs. Although the A-B design is no longer recommended, it is presented to show the basic building blocks in constructing time-series designs. The problem with the A-B design is that you cannot determine if a behavior change resulted from the treatment condition. This problem is corrected somewhat in the A-B-A design in which a second baseline condition follows the treatment. The example shows that the subject reverts back to the initial level of behavior. A stronger scheme is the A-B-A-B, or reversal, design, which shows stimulus control of

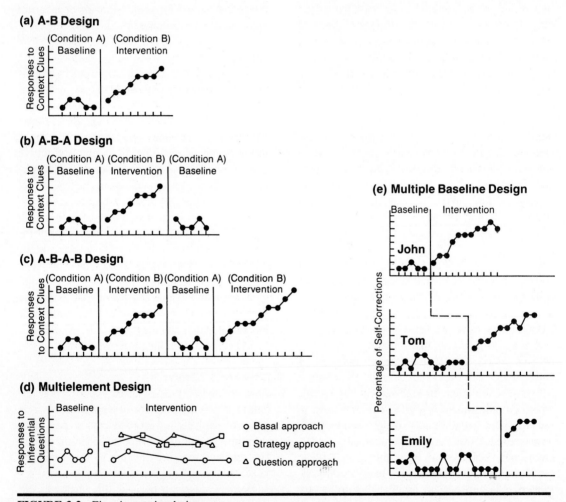

FIGURE 3.2 Five time-series designs

Source: McCormick, S. (1990). A case for the use of single-subject methodology in reading research. *Journal of Research in Reading, 13*, 77–79. Reprinted by permission.

behavior in that removal of the treatment results in the subject(s) returning to baseline, but the experimental effect can be reestablished through reintroduction of the treatment, thus demonstrating that the observed effects were the result of the treatment.

The multielement design, another variation of the basic time-series designs, has the advantage of controlling for sequence effects (McCormick, 1990), which makes it a very attractive scheme for educational research. It also samples different contexts, which increases its usefulness for developmental/social systems research. After an initial baseline, the investigator can introduce the various treatments randomly. The illustration shows the differential effects of three treatments, such as three strategies to increase classroom control. The multiple baseline design lets an investigator examine two or more behaviors in a single subject or group of subjects. In this latter setting, interindividual differences can be assessed, which is an important measure in developmental/social systems methodology.

First, a baseline is established, after which a treatment is applied to one of the behaviors or, in the case of the illustration in Figure 3.2, to one of the subjects. The expectation is that only the behavior or the subject to which the treatment is applied will show the expected change. When some type of stability is reached, the treatment is applied to the second behavior or subject, and this process continues until all behaviors or subjects have received the treatment. If each behavior or subject shows a change only when the treatment is administered, as can be seen in the figure, the intervention is deemed to be effective (Kratochwill, 1977, 1978). Notice that the multiple baseline design is really a series of A-B designs with a sequential introduction of the same treatment.

Time-series designs lend themselves nicely to educational applications, especially those associated with school psychology. Two examples should be sufficient to illustrate the utility of these designs for classroom use. McCormick (1990) describes one study in which a special education teacher developed an instructional pro-

gram for increasing semantic vocabularies in five selected students using an A-B-A-B design. Each student was charted separately, first with his or her baseline reading score and then after each training session, which was interspersed with another baseline measure.

A multiple baseline design was used by Mudre and McCormick (1989) to examine the outcome of parent teaching with children identified as low-achieving readers. After establishing a baseline, a teaching strategy was introduced, followed by a practice period and measurement, and then the next strategy was introduced. This procedure permitted a comparison of strategies.

Data from time-series designs are often not subjected to statistical analyses because the concern is with social significance, not statistical significance; therefore, one only needs to eyeball the data (Cooper, Heron, & Heward, 1987). Kratochwill (1978) discusses the matter of statistical analysis in some detail and makes a number of recommendations. The reader is directed to this source for a further discussion, as well as to Bass (1987), who compares the merits of a visual analysis of the data versus statistical analysis.

DESCRIPTIVE METHODS

School psychology research is similar to other fields in that a variety of research methods, designs, and strategies are used. A significant portion of the studies that could be classified as school psychology research are descriptive or what Keith (1988a) has labeled *nonexperimental;* that is, the investigator does not have direct control over the independent variables because their effect is assumed to have occurred. Control over variables, not data collection methods and analyses, distinguishes experimental research from nonexperimental. Therefore, use of such experimental techniques as random sampling, control for order effects of instrument presentation, and perhaps matching are as applicable to nonexperimental research as they are to experimental studies.

Descriptive research fills an important need

in school psychology, and providing standardization and norms for a psychometric instrument is an excellent example according to Reynolds and colleagues (1984). Descriptive research also fills a need for the developmental/social systems approach by providing information that can be used to make better reasoned decisions about variables and contexts to study. A discussion of the more common descriptive methods follows.

Case Studies

This approach uses a detailed examination of an individual, and is likely to include a personal history, psychometric data, input from teachers, and, in some instances, parental reports and information from school social workers, counselors, and others. Although clinical psychologists have been the most frequent users of this research method in the past, Reynolds and colleagues (1984) report that the procedure is gaining favor with school psychologists, and this interest has continued to the present time. Case studies serve an important function in the validation of treatment modalities and in understanding human behavior (Reynolds et al., 1984).

Standardized Tests

Providing psychometric data on various assessment measures comprises a significant portion of the relevant research in the school psychology area. Establishing norms for various populations is especially important, given the varied student clientele who are served by school psychologists. It is quite commonplace to find at least one such study published in a school psychology journal.

Questionnaires

Of all the research approaches, none is used more frequently than some type of questionnaire or rating scale. The popularity of this technique is obvious. Large amounts of data can be collected quite easily through the administration of questionnaires to complete classes or other larger groups. Responses can be standardized so that every subject has the same choice of possible responses, which is a definite advantage over the interview where responses are more open ended. Anonymity to the respondent can be assured. The responses can be tabulated easily, especially when computer-type answer sheets are used.

There are drawbacks, however. The questions have to be extremely well written to negate any problem of ambiguity or understanding. It is usually desirable to frame questions that can be answered with the limited number of responses that are provided. For example, identifying sources of children's fear of failure in the classroom requires questions that are phrased to ask this specific question, and the responses provided need to sample the universe of most likely answers.

Questionnaires are entirely dependent on reading ability, which rules out their use with nonreaders such as young children. The subject's level of reading ability is always of concern with this approach. One type of safeguard is to have teachers or reading experts review the questionnaire to determine its suitability for the population that is needed. Another potential problem is that subjects frequently give unexpected answers to questions that could provide some real insight into the research question, but with the anonymity of a questionnaire there is often no way to find this individual to follow up on the response. Of course, reliability and validity will be important. Finally, there is the problem of the accuracy of the data. Sometimes a lie scale (a scale that includes questions designed to assess false responding) can be built into questionnaires, but most studies do not include this precaution, so the data are always suspect. The best solution for this problem may be in the instructions where the need for accuracy and the guarantee of anonymity can be stressed.

Interviews

Although interviews are not used frequently, they do have some inherent advantages. Interviews are conducted face to face and they permit probing into unique responses (an option not available in questionnaires). However, skillfulness in interviewing is a necessary factor if accurate data are to be obtained. Social desirability is a problem, which means that the interviewer must be cognizant that the interviewee may not want to share all of the requested information. Such questions as conflicts in the family, use of punitive techniques, and controlled substance use are likely to elicit defensiveness in the subject.

As with questionnaires, accuracy of the report is always of concern. When using questionnaire or interview data, researchers often search for corroborative sources, such as parents, teachers, peers, or other instruments that tap questions similar to those used in the interview. Frequently, interviews and questionnaires are used to supplement each other, and thus the need for some form of corroboration is satisfied. Interview data also often present problems in scoring if it is necessary to quantify the data. Some form of content analysis is one option for analyzing these data.

Observations

A resurgence of observational methods has occurred in recent years, especially in developmental research, as concern over the artificialness of the laboratory study and ecological validity increased. Observational methods are one of the major procedures used in developmental/social systems research because they permit the study of interactions and behavioral variability between individuals and constellations of individuals such as groups.

The attractiveness of observational research lies in its simplicity of methodology, which basically requires that the investigator record the daily activities of the subject(s). The major advantage of this method of naturalistic observation is that the actual behavior of the subject is recorded in the subject's natural context. But, as Berk (1989) notes, it is not likely that similar opportunities will be present so that all children or adolescents emit a particular behavior in some setting. If this is an important requirement, the investigator can use a structured observation in which a situation is constructed so that an eliciting cue will be present for all subjects.

Suppose that a researcher is interested in how children react when a classmate is disciplined. Pairs of children could be brought into a classroom-like setting and engaged in some activity while an adult, acting as a teacher, scolds another child who has come to her or his desk. Reactions of the child pairs to the scolding would be recorded. The advantage of this observational method is that the researcher can exercise greater control over the situation, and it enables the study of behaviors that researchers often do not see in the daily activities of children.

What to Observe

One of the first questions facing the investigator is what to observe. Miller (1987) asserts that the type of behavior determines whether an observational method is feasible. Such overt behaviors as aggressiveness, shyness, and cooperation are more easily observable than anxiety, depression, or dreams. Next, it is impossible to record everything that can be observed. Therefore, a decision must be made on the level of specificity of the observed behavior. This question is usually phrased as the molar versus molecular issue (Miller, 1987). A *molar* approach is one in which more global observational units are observed, such as hitting or taunting to indicate aggressiveness. The *molecular* approach takes a more fine-grained analysis and focuses on greater detail in the behavior. In the case of aggressiveness, hitting could be broken down into slapping, striking with the fist, or the use of some object, whereas insults, teasing, and name calling could be used to describe forms of taunting. This contrast shows that the molar-molecular distinction is a continuum rather than a dichotomy.

How does the researcher determine which approach should be used? According to Miller (1987), the two major determinants are the research objective (i.e., a molar approach is satisfactory if the major goal is to observe instances of aggressive behavior, whereas a molecular approach is needed to specify the more exact forms of each type of aggression) and what can be observed. Ideally, the investigator may want to make a molecular recording, but the close proximity to the subjects or the available context could prevent this. Reliability of the recorded observations is another important consideration. Although a fine-grained analysis of some behavior may be desirable, if the observers cannot agree on categories because of the detail required, the observations are of little value. Similarly, making an interpretation about whether some observed behavior is really indicative of hyperactivity may have to be deleted in favor of recording the actual behavior or frequency of off-task behaviors.

These problems illustrate the importance of precision in writing the descriptions of the behavioral codes to be observed. Bird and LaVoie (1989) faced this problem in designing an observational study to examine differences between socially accepted and socially isolated/rejected preschoolers' social interactive behaviors in a peer context. Some of the behaviors selected to observe and their descriptions are shown in Figure 3.3. Note that the choice of behaviors taken from the literature on social skills deficits represent a midpoint on the molar-molecular continuum, and fits with the developmental/social systems objective to examine intraindividual and interindividual variability.

Observational Procedures

The nature of the research problem largely determines the procedure to be used, so procedures may vary from one study to the next. Three procedures are most often discussed in the literature on observational methods.

The *narrative record,* or specimen record, describes everything that is said or done by the subject(s) over some specific period of time. For example, an observation of a problem child in the classroom would include a complete description of his or her solitary behaviors as well as interactions with classmates and teachers. One of the strengths of this procedure is the detail that is

---

SOLITARY PLAY

1. Playing by Oneself—Any solitary activity that appears to be constructive.
2. Onlooker—Watching peers without any involvement in the ongoing activity.
3. Off-Task Behavior—Behaviors such as walking around aimlessly, sitting and doing nothing, and staring off into space.
4. No Play, but in Proximity of Peers—Child is in the proximity of peers but is not engaged in interactive play.

INTERACTIVE PLAY

5. Inappropriate Play—Behaviors such as destroying property, misuse of property, and disrupting other children's games or activities.
6. Aggressive Play—Rough and tumble activities not meant to harm other children. Includes such play activities as wrestling, playful shoving, and other general rough behavior.
7. Cooperative Play—Activities involving play with peer to include physical play, fantasy play, creative/constructive play, and games/competitive play.
8. Physical Play—Involves playing with peers in such activities as running, jumping, and climbing.

FIGURE 3.3 Examples of observational codes used for play behavior

Source: Bird, K., & LaVoie, J. C. (1989). *Sociometric status and play behavior in preschool children.* Unpublished manuscript, University of Nebraska at Omaha.

provided. Such information would be very important to the school psychologist in working with the teacher and the child's parents to design an intervention program. The disadvantages of this procedure are the time involved and the possibility of subjectivity and bias.

A second procedure is *time sampling,* in which a specific set of behaviors is selected for observation, and only these behaviors are recorded during a set unit of time. An observer might elect to record a specified behavior each 15-second period, or observe an ongoing stream of behavior for 15 seconds and record for 15 seconds. Although the observer is restricted to the set of selected behaviors, time sampling has an advantage in that frequencies of the selected behaviors can be determined. In time sampling, the behavioral definitions are present so it is not necessary to develop them (such as in a narrative record).

Time sampling has come under recent attack by Mann, Have, Plunkett, and Meisels (1991), who identify several problems based on their study comparing time sampling and continuous sampling procedures. The most serious problems seem to be the following:

1. Time sampling is not accurate when duration or frequency of a behavior are measured. Using time sampling intervals of 5, 15, 30, and 60 seconds, Mann and colleagues show that error rates are especially high when the behavior under observation is relatively brief and/or when long intervals are used. In these cases, frequency and duration of behavior are usually overestimated.
2. Both individual and group differences can vary depending on whether time sampling or continuous sampling is used.
3. Most behaviors occurring in observational contexts are not single behaviors, but rather sequential patterns. Time sampling does not enable this type of recording.

According to Mann and colleagues (1991), time sampling could be used in situations where

(1) stable durations of the observed behavior are present for each individual and across all individuals and (2) relatively long durations of behavior (greater than 10 seconds) are present, and the selected observation interval is nearly the same length as the duration of the behavior. Given the problems with time sampling, Mann and colleagues recommend the use of continuous recording.

Event sampling is a third observational procedure. Certain behaviors may be very infrequent, and thus narrative records and time sampling are not appropriate procedures. In event sampling, the unit of analysis is the specified behavior. The observer waits until this behavior occurs and then records the details, which may vary from a narrative type of report to a simple checklist. This procedure has been used to study such behaviors as children's quarrels and empathy, or to model appropriate behavior for a peer.

Observational Accuracy
Of course, observational methods are not without problems. One difficulty is observer influence. The presence of an observer and the child's awareness that she or he is being observed have the potential to alter the child's behavior in a way that is socially desirable. This observer effect may be less likely if some severe pattern of maladaptive behavior is present. The problem seems to be more acute for older children than for those under 7 or 8 years of age, who return to their usual behavior patterns after one or two sessions.

Berk (1989) suggests some techniques for minimizing the effects of observer bias. These include (1) use adaptation periods in which the subjects have an opportunity to acclimate; (2) use persons who are part of the child's environment, such as teachers or parents, and train them to act as observers (the use of parent diaries is one adaptation of this procedure); (3) have teachers prepare the children in their classroom for the appearance of visitors; and (4) use videotape and concealed cameras.

A second problem is observer bias. Expectations held by the observer can seriously distort what the observer sees and records because what is expected may be recorded rather than what was actually observed. The likelihood of observer bias can be reduced by constructing specific and objective scoring categories and behavioral codes, and by preventing the observer from knowing the objectives or hypotheses of the study, a technique known as *blinding* (Miller, 1987). Another problem is systematic subject-related differences due to such factors as sex of the subject and social class. Yarrow and Waxler (1979) report higher observer reliability for behaviors observed in boys than in girls. It appears that boys may be more reliably observed. Yarrow and Waxler also report extra or missed behaviors. Some observers apparently see more than others or they see in greater detail. Sometimes the differences appear to be due to narrative styles.

Reliability of Observations

It is often said that observers are made, not born (Boise, 1983). The key determinant of useful observational research is accuracy that will be reflected in the reliability ratings of the observers, expressed in terms of intrarater and interrater reliability. *Intrarater* reliability is not frequently reported in the literature, but it is an important determinant of observational accuracy because it gives some indication of the consistency of the observer.

Interrater consistency, or the agreement between two or more observers, is the usual reliability measure that is reported. The common rule of thumb is that at least 20 percent of the observations should be rated by a second observer, or, for intrarater reliability, the observer should rescore 20 percent of the observations. This leaves 80 percent of the observations with only a single observer, and should indicate to the reader the importance of having some information on each rater's internal consistency. Observer reliability can be expressed as a correlation coefficient, but the more common practice is to report percent agreement based on the following formula: reliability = number of agreements/number of agreements + number of disagreements.

At this point, it seems necessary to issue a caveat that reliability is necessary but not sufficient for validity. Incorrect observations can lead to high agreement but not to accuracy. Securing high reliability is rather straightforward. Observers need to be carefully trained, the observational codes and procedure must be very precise and clear, and a back-up system (e.g., videotape) is useful to check periodically on the observers, to keep them alert and to maintain their accuracy.

SUBJECT SELECTION

A critical design feature concerns the representativeness of the subjects that form the sample in the study. How similar or typical are they to other subjects? If other subjects were selected, would one find the same age pattern (Seitz, 1988)? This matter is especially important from a developmental/social systems perspective because the persons to be studied require a careful decision to ensure generalization. One way to check on representativeness is to replicate the study with a new subject group.

A related problem is that associated with the use of naturally formed groups (i.e., those categories where one cannot make random assignment such as age, gender, socioeconomic status, ethnicity, etc.). Use of intact classrooms prevents random sampling of subjects, and confronts us with a naturally formed group. Groups such as classrooms are not really comparable to the extent that randomly formed groups would be, and thus studies of these groups are always what Seitz (1988) has labeled "methodologically correlational" (p. 61). The objective in subject selection is to select randomly a sample of subjects from some existing population.

If age is one of the variables chosen for the design, subjects will need to be selected to fit the critical ages. In Chapter 2 we discussed how age selection influences the interpretation of data and how the researcher's philosophy of science influences age selection. The review of the previous literature relating to the question under study, along with the purpose of the study, should guide the age selection. One of the considerations in the age selection is whether age comparisons will be needed.

INSTRUMENTS AND MEASURES

The various tests, rating scales, questionnaires, and other similar measures that are used to obtain the desired data comprise a major design component. Selection of variables is a critical decision in a developmental/social systems approach to research where generalization plays such an important role. Major concerns with this component are the appropriateness of the instruments and measures for the subjects, their adequacy in terms of providing the data that are needed to test the hypotheses, and the reliability and validity of the measures.

Reliability of a measure refers to its consistency. At least three types of reliability will be reported for most instruments or measures. A *coefficient of internal consistency* is a measure of the consistency of response across items in the instrument. This coefficient is usually expressed as a K-R 20 correlation for instruments where items can be scored as right or wrong, or a coefficient alpha for items that cannot be scored right or wrong. A *coefficient of equivalence* is a measure of the relationship between two alternate forms of the same instrument and is expressed as a correlation. A *coefficient of stability* assesses the consistency of measurement of an instrument over some period of time, and is often referred to as *test-retest reliability.*

One of the results of poor reliability in an instrument is that on a second administration the scores may increase or decrease, but in general the scores will average out (i.e., regress toward the mean). Borg and Gall (1983) claim that the *standard error of measurement* (i.e., an estimate of the difference between an subject's actual score on a test and the true score) is a more functional gauge for interpreting a test score because it provides some information on the measurement error that is found within the particular test. The standard error of measurement is inversely re-lated to reliability in that as this error decreases, the reliability coefficient for the test increases.

Validity of a measure assesses whether the instrument measures what it claims to measure. For example, does an IQ test measure individual differences in intelligence? *Content* or *face validity* indicates the extent to which the items in an instrument sample some expected concept. Although predictive and construct validity have been used in the past, the current preference is to look for measures of discriminant and convergent validity.

Discriminant validity refers to the extent to which an instrument assesses the desired construct and not other related constructs. For example, an IQ measure has discriminant validity if it correlates highly with other IQ measures but not measures of creativity. *Convergent validity* assesses the extent to which the instrument correlates with other instruments that measure that construct. So, IQ tests should correlate highly with measures of critical thinking, problem solving, and memory.

Reliability alone does not ensure that an instrument will be valid, but for an instrument to be valid, it must be consistent. In evaluating instruments, the investigator needs to select those measures that have high reliability coefficients (e.g., .70 or greater), and discriminant and convergent validity, provided that the instrument is also appropriate for the task that has been chosen and that the subjects to be used are comparable with those for which the reliability and validity data were established.

PRELIMINARY EXAMINATION OF DATA

Before embarking on the actual data analyses, it is a good practice to perform a preliminary examination of the data. Several operations are useful for this initial inspection of the data set. Both Hartmann (1988) and Borg and Gall (1983) recommend inspecting the data for missing scores and *outliers* (a subject whose scores vary greatly from the pattern of other subjects in the study).

If data are missing, several options are available to the researcher. One option is to eliminate those subjects for which data are missing. Computer statistical packages, such as SPSSX, will allow the researcher to insert a missing data option that deletes missing data in the analyses that are performed. A second option is to estimate the missing values using the group mean for each cell or performing a regression analysis to determine the value. Kirk (1982) describes a method for estimating missing values using the group mean. Of course, the best method is to avoid missing data.

If outlier scores are detected, one likely cause is some type of data entry or calculation error. When this cause cannot be evoked, a decision has to be made about eliminating the score(s). Outliers can distort the data unless the sample size is quite large, but the investigator is not justified in eliminating these scores for that reason only. Other explanations for the distorted scores need to be examined. Some indication of the distortion resulting from the outliers can be obtained by using analyses of the data with the outliers and comparing the results (Borg & Gall, 1983).

Another preliminary operation is to examine the data distribution for skewness (i.e., a higher frequency of scores at one end of the distribution) by either plotting the data or inspecting a frequency analysis. Data that depart from normality may have to be analyzed with nonparametric statistical procedures if the planned parametric analyses assume a normal distribution. One other option is to use multivariate analyses if the data fit the required assumptions for these analyses. In addition to a visual examination of the data distribution resulting from the plot, the investigator should calculate the median, mean, variance, and standard deviation for the distribution. These descriptive statistics provide the researcher with additional information about the pattern of scores and their variability.

HYPOTHESIS TESTING

Traditionally, the null hypothesis is tested. By so doing, the investigator is comparing the observed score(s) to determine if the difference is large enough to exceed that which is expected by chance, and thus reject the null hypothesis of no difference. However, the usual practice is to state directional hypotheses (i.e., indicating where differences will be found), because the aim of most studies is to detect differences between groups or relationships, rather than to test the notion of no differences.

Before making a comparison, it is necessary to select a significance level commonly referred to as an *alpha* or *probability level* (*p* value). The most common alpha levels are .05 and .01, although .10 is sometimes selected for pilot or exploratory studies. In making this selection, Hartmannn (1988) contends that consideration must be given to the consequences of making a *Type I error* (rejecting the null hypothesis when there is not an adequate difference) as compared to the consequences of a *Type II error* (failing to reject the null hypothesis when the difference is adequate). It is quite clear that as the alpha level becomes smaller, the likelihood of a Type II error increases; conversely, an alpha level of .10 increases the possibility of a Type I error.

In exploratory research the increased risk of a Type I error may be more acceptable because the investigator wants to determine if an important effect occurred in the study, so the power of the test is increased to maximize the possibility of finding this effect. Frequently, investigators decide on a significance level after the analyses have been completed, but this is contrary to the logic of statistical inference, which assumes that this value is selected before any analyses are run (Borg & Gall, 1983). These investigators frequently report the actual *p* value of a test, such as $p = .03$, or they choose the smallest *p* value at which the test is significant, such as $p < .04$ or $p < .07$ rather than the traditional report of $p < .05$ or $p < .01$.

The *p* value has often been misinterpreted. According to Borg and Gall (1983), it is incorrect to say that: (1) the *p* value refers to the chance level of finding a difference, (2) 1 minus the *p* value indicates the probability that the hypothesis is correct, (3) the *p* value is the likelihood that repeating the study will produce the same result, and (4) the *p* value indicates the importance or theoretical value of the result. Rather, the *p* value indicates the probability that the reported difference in the subject sample(s) would also be found in the population from which the samples were drawn. The probability of finding support for the null hypothesis is 1.00 minus the alpha value that is selected, whereas the probability of rejecting a false null hypothesis (the power of the statistical test) is 1.00 minus the probability of a Type II error. (See Hartmann [1988] for the procedure in calculating test power.) What is an adequate power for a test? Hartmannn (1988) suggests that some value in excess of .80 would probably be acceptable.

ANALYSES FOR A DEVELOPMENTAL/SOCIAL SYSTEMS APPROACH

The need to examine behavioral change, and particularly intraindividual variability and interindividual differences, across contexts requires analyses that enable the examination of repeated measurements and multiple variables. Multivariate analyses appear to fit this need best. Social systems research, especially that involving families, and certain aspects of developmental research often require observational methodologies. Some of these data may need to be evaluated with qualitative procedures, such as contingency analyses. Given these needs, the discussion of statistical analyses will be restricted to contingency analyses and multivariate analyses with one exception. The versatility of meta-analyses for graduate students to embellish their research reports and convert them into potential manuscripts for publication submission seems to justify the inclusion of this procedure, which is not found in most chapters on research methods in school psychology texts.

Qualitative Analyses

Categorical data, such as the occurrence or non-occurrence of some event, numbers of males and females, or pass or fail on some test, are usually

evaluated with a chi-square analysis of some type. The more recent forms of chi-square analysis are called *contingency table analyses* or *log-linear models* (Applebaum & McCall, 1983). One variation of the latter form is a chi-square analysis of variance. Chi-square analyses have been used for such applications as testing differences between proportions or frequencies, determining correlations among categorical variables, and utilizing goodness-of-fit tests to determine certain assumptions like normality (Hartmann, 1988).

The chi-square analysis is generally used to test differences between group frequencies, most commonly in a four-cell table, such as the one illustrated in Table 3.1. Note that the data presented in this table show the frequencies of low- and high-test anxiety students whose grade point average (GPA) is above or below 2.00. The chi-square value indicates that more high GPA students are low in anxiety. Expected frequencies in each cell of a chi-square table must be 5.0 or larger, otherwise a correction will have to be made (Borg & Gall, 1983). Consult a statistical text such as Rosenthal and Rosnow (1991) for this correction procedure.

Contingency analysis tables have more than two groups, and the minimum expected frequency per cell must equal 10 or greater (Applebaum & McCall, 1983). An example of a contingency analysis table is shown in Table 3.2. The data in this table show the frequencies of so-

TABLE 3.1 Chi-Square Table of Frequencies for GPA by Test Anxiety

GPA	HIGH TEST ANXIETY		LOW TEST ANXIETY	
	Frequency	*%*	*Frequency*	*%*
Less than 2.00	19	29	2	7
Above 2.00	46	71	29	93

Source: From *Educational Research: An Introduction* by Walter R. Borg and Meredith D. Gall. Copyright © 1983 by Longman Publishing Group. Reprinted with permission from Longman Publishing Group.
Note: GPA = gradepoint average. $x^2(1) = 5.11, p < .03$.

TABLE 3.2   Contingency Analysis Table

		SOCIALLY ADEQUATE		SOCIALLY INADEQUATE		
		Intellectually Adequate	*Intellectually Inadequate*	*Intellectually Adequate*	*Intellectually Inadequate*	
INTERVENTION	Urban	n_{11}	n_{12}	n_{13}	n_{14}	$n_{1.}$
	Rural	n_{21}	n_{22}	n_{23}	n_{24}	$n_{2.}$
CONTROL	Urban	n_{31}	n_{32}	n_{33}	n_{34}	$n_{3.}$
	Rural	n_{41}	n_{42}	n_{43}	n_{44}	$n_{4.}$
		$n_{.1}$	$n_{.2}$	$n_{.3}$	$n_{.4}$	$n_{..}$

Source: Applebaum, M. I., & McCall, R. B. (1983). Design and analysis in developmental psychology. In P. H. Mussen (Ed.), *Handbook of child psychology* (4th ed.). New York: Wiley. Copyright © 1983 John Wiley & Sons, Inc. Reprinted by permission of John Wiley & Sons, Inc.

cially neglected and socially rejected children who scored above or below the mean on social competence, and whose GPA is above and below 2.00. These children were sampled from two different environments—urban and rural.

A significant chi-square value appeared for this table, but its meaning is unclear, because the groups that are significantly different cannot be determined from the overall chi-square value. It is necessary to compute one-way chi-squares using row and column variables to determine which groups differ. If rows are analyzed, it will be necessary to use the binomial test to determine whether GPA differs among the neglected or rejected children. Correlation coefficients can be calculated from contingency tables. A phi-coefficient is calculated from a four-cell chi-square table. If the table is more than four cells, a contingency coefficient is calculated. Both correlations give some indication of the magnitude of the relationship between the categorical variables.

Categorical data are usually discrete, meaning that the data can take on only a limited range of values, such as male/female for sex. Note that the examples in Tables 3.1 and 3.2 contained var-

iables that are continuous in nature. The anxiety score variable used in Table 3.1 and the social competence variable used in Table 3.2 were continuous variables because their scores could assume a large range of values. However, the scores were converted into categorical variables. This technique is often done with such nonparametric analyses as chi-square, and it illustrates the versatility of this analysis. If qualitative analyses are as multifaceted as they appear, then their misuse is highly likely, and this often occurs in chi-square analyses according to Hartmann (1988). The most frequent error concerns the assumption of independence of observations, which is violated when activities engaged in by subjects is used for the analysis rather than the subjects who are performing the activities. Other violations include such errors as ignoring the minimum expected frequencies per cell.

MULTIVARIATE RELATIONSHIPS

Many research questions arising from a developmental/social systems orientation are studied in a context of relationships involving several variables. All multivariate analyses share certain similarities and faults (Hartmann, 1988). They are similar in that all analyses multiply a subject's score by a weight to maximize a prediction or other function, but the problem with these analyses is that highly correlated variables cannot be used. The discussion that follows is intended only to introduce the student to some of the most common multivariate techniques. For a more detailed description and explanation of each of these procedures, the reader can consult such sources as Pedhazur (1982). Computer statistical packages, such as SPSSX, provide some conceptual information on each of the analyses and explain how to set up an analysis program for each of the procedures.

Multiple Regression

This procedure has been described as one of the most versatile and flexible statistical procedures available to the researcher because it can accommodate data at all levels of measurement. The basic form of multiple regression assesses the relationship between a set of predictor variables and some criterion variable. In many applications, however, the researcher is interested in the relationships among several independent and dependent variables. Perhaps the best way to explain multiple regression is through the use of an example.

Faulkner and LaVoie (1990) were interested in the power of various psychosocial variables to predict an index of drug use among adolescents. The regression analysis for this problem appears in Table 3.3. Note in this typical table that the first column contains the simple correlation coefficient (r) between each predictor variable and the criterion variable of drug use index. The multiple correlation (R) indicates the relationship between the predictor variables and the criterion. When this value is squared (R^2), the resulting value is the percent of variance accounted for by the correlation of the criterion and predictor variable(s).

The next value in the table is the R^2 change, which denotes the percent of variance increase resulting from the addition of each variable. Statistical tests are often performed in connection with multiple regression analyses to ascertain if the variance increment resulting from the addition of a variable is significantly different from the variance estimate without the addition. Note in Table 3.3 that the statistical test used in this analysis is the F test. The other value in the table is the beta weight (B), which is a standard score form of the regression weight. Summing the product of each subject's score on a predictor variable multiplied by its beta weight provides a good estimate of the subject's score on the criterion variable. Frequently, t-tests are used to denote significance of the beta weight.

TABLE 3.3   Multiple Regression Analysis of Drug Use Index Correlates

VARIABLE	r	MULTIPLE R	R^2	R^2 CHANGE	F	BETA
Social Avoidance	.51	.51	.26		69.97	$-.42$
Suicidal Ideation	.07	.58	.34	.08	50.01	$-.32$
Behavior	$-.43$	.61	.37	.03	38.08	$-.25$
Self-Worth	$-.26$	.64	.41	.04	33.24	.15
Ethnicity	.02	.66	.43	.02	29.64	.79
Year in School	.01	.67	.45	.02	25.98	.14
Loneliness	.27	.68	.46	.01	23.17	.22
Social Acceptance	$-.12$	.69	.47	.01	21.40	.14

Source: Faulkner, E., & LaVoie, J. C. (1990). *Psychosocial correlates of adolescent drug use.*
Unpublished manuscript, University of Nebraska at Omaha.

In a multiple regression analysis, the correlation between the best predictor and the criterion variable is usually computed first. Computer programs start the analysis with this computation unless the user specifies some other combination of variables to be entered. If an order of variables is not specified, most computer programs select the variable that increases the prediction of the first variable chosen by the largest amount. To increase the prediction equation substantially, the correlation between this variable and the first predictor should be minimal. The next variable entered is the one that would increase the predictability of the first two variables by the greatest amount. As predictors are added, they contribute less to the multiple correlation (R).

For most analyses, the researcher has some a priori conceptualization about the ordering of the predictors, and therefore will specify the order in which they are entered into the analysis. That is, a stepwise multiple regression analysis will be used. In other cases, the researcher may be interested in the prediction of a certain variable, and therefore will choose to enter this variable first. Two caveats need to be issued in regard to using multiple regression analyses. First, multiple regression analyses provide the researcher with information about the prediction of a criterion variable, not a causation or explanation. If the investigator is interested in causation, Borg and Gall (1983) recommend the use of path analysis. Second, sample size is an important consideration in this type of analysis. As a general rule, Borg and Gall (1983) recommend a minimum of 15 subjects per variable used in the analyses.

Canonical Correlations

This analysis is similar to multiple regression in that both predictor and criterion variables are used, but it differs from multiple regression in that sets of predictor and criterion variables are involved rather than the one criterion variable. Weighted combinations of each of the sets of variables are used to maximize the correlation between the sets. This analysis is often used to determine a set of predictor variables that maximizes the prediction of some set of criterion variables. For example, suppose that you wanted to examine the relationships among a selected group of social skills and perceptions of personal control in elementary school children and certain measures of cognitive ability as well as classroom performance. The canonical correlations would provide this information.

Discriminant Analysis

A single criterion variable and more than one predictor variable are also used in this analysis, but the purpose of discriminant analysis is to place subjects into certain groups (Hartmann, 1988). Weighted scores are also used for this analysis, but their function is to increase the differences between the groups to which the subjects have been assigned based on the weighted predictor variables. Classification into groups necessitates the formation of composite variables (i.e., discriminant functions), which equal one less than the number of groups formed. The usual output from this type of analysis gives the categories to which subjects are assigned, the proportion of subjects that can be correctly assigned based on the analysis, and the weights that have been used in forming the discriminant functions. Discriminant analysis could be used to assign children to reading levels based on their scores on certain reading tests, or to various categories based on their scores on certain behavior inventories, such as the Child Behavior Checklist (Achenbach & Edelbrock, 1981).

Path Analysis

This technique is similar in certain respects to the other multivariate analyses just discussed, but its purpose is to evaluate causal relations between variables rather than to examine their correlations. Keith (1988b) recommends the use of path analysis to test causation in nonexperimental data of the sort frequently collected by school psychologists. In path analysis, a model is constructed that graphically depicts relationships among the theoretically linked variables. The resulting correlations are placed in a formula that determines the various paths that best reflect the correlations. Figure 3.4 shows a simple path analysis for the links between family background, ability, and achievement.

Note that the correlations between these variables are indicated by the use of lower-case italic *r*s. The *p* values are the actual paths in the analysis, which are calculated using the correlations. Although the correlations between family background and achievement, and family background and ability, are very similar, the path analysis shows that the calculated paths of causation are

quite different. The higher *p* value for the family background to ability path indicates that the actual causal direction is family background-ability-achievement (i.e., the larger the *p* value, the greater the predicted effect). A path coefficient of .05 is usually used as the minimum value for a meaningful effect, according to Pedhazur (1982).

A somewhat more complex path analysis is shown in Figure 3.5, which depicts the correlations and causal paths for several variables associated with achievement. Keith, Harrison, and Ehly (1987), from whose study this path diagram was taken, were interested in the causal role of adaptive behavior with respect to achievement. School psychologists are frequently required to

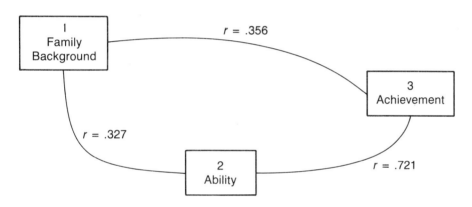

Paths are drawn from presumed "causes" to presumed "effects."

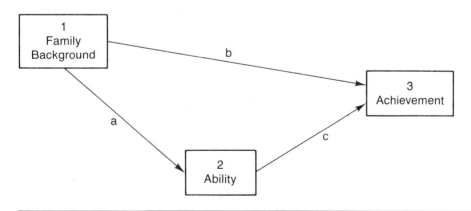

FIGURE 3.4   Path analysis showing the relationship among three variables

Source: Keith, T. Z. (1988). Research methods in school psychology: An overview. *School Psychology Review, 17,* 348. Reprinted by permission.

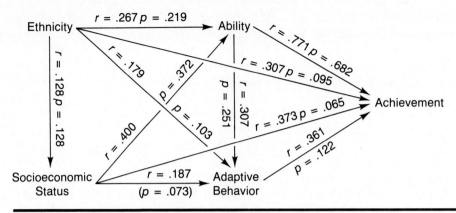

FIGURE 3.5   Path analysis model of factors influencing school achievement

Source: Keith, T. Z., Harrison, P. L., & Ehly, S. W. (1987). Effects of adaptive behavior on achievement. Path analysis of a national sample. *Professional School Psychology, 2,* 211. Reprinted by permission.

assess *adaptive behavior,* defined as how well an individual can cope with the demands of independence and social responsibility appropriate for the individual's age and group membership (Grossman, 1983).

According to this path model, adaptive behavior exerts a significant effect ($p = .122$) on achievement, and this effect is greater than that for socioeconomic status or ethnicity. What are the p values or path coefficients? Keith (1988b) describes these coefficients as indicating the amount of change in standard deviation units for the effect that would occur by changing each causal variable one standard deviation.

However, path analysis is no panacea for inferring causation from correlational data. At least three conditions must be met to assume causality, according to Keith (1988b): (1) it must be established that the assumed cause occurred before the effect, (2) the variables must be correlated, and (3) a legitimate relation among variables must be present. This condition can usually be met by the inclusion of common causal and effect variables. One way to estimate path coefficients is to use a multiple regression analysis. But in so doing, it is necessary to assume unidirectional causation. In certain cases where the researcher encounters

problems with reliability of measurement, reciprocal causal relations or, for longitudinal data, a computer program called LISREL should be used (Keith, 1988b). For a further discussion of this program, and path analysis in general, the reader can consult Keith (1988b).

Meta-Analysis

This research approach uses quantitative methods in a review of the literature on some specific topic and summarizes the results of the existing literature. Meta-analysis converts the results of studies into a common metric-effect size. One method for calculating effect size, Cohens' *d* statistic, uses the treatment group mean minus the control group mean divided by the standard deviation of the control group, so that a no effect treatment converts to an effect size of zero.

Keith (1988a) equates effect size with *Z* scores because they indicate the distance that some experimental condition moves a group from its control. A variety of different statistics can be converted to effect sizes. Literature reviews using a meta-analysis appear in research journals quite frequently. One such review was completed by Paschal, Weinstein, and Walberg (1984) in which they reviewed the literature relating the relationship between homework and achievement. Among the contrasts that could be made in this type of analysis were those that compared studies that examined the effect of graded homework versus those that examined the effects of ungraded homework. Literature analyses of this type are extremely helpful to the investigator in evaluating potential interactions and in designing future studies. Meta-analysis is a project that graduate students can undertake to enhance literature reviews that are often required in courses. A second application is to use a meta-analysis procedure in reviewing literature for thesis/dissertation or other research projects. Effect sizes can be used to identify factors under consideration for the planned study.

RESEARCH ETHICS

At all times the investigator must follow federal and state regulations as well as professional standards that specify the ethical requirements in conducting research. Numerous sources are available that detail the requirements for conducting ethical research with human subjects. The American Psychological Association has published *Ethical Principles in the Conduct of Research with Human Participants,* and the Society for Research in Child Development has also published a set of guidelines to follow in conducting research with children and adolescents. In addition, institutional review boards at universities have specific guidelines that must be followed. Today all research with human subjects needs to be evaluated by a peer review process. That means an independent group of competent individuals must pass judgment on whether one's research proposal meets the ethical standards that have been set.

What are the guidelines that need to be met for a study to be considered in compliance with ethical standards? The Committee for Ethical Conduct in Child Development Research of the Society for Research in Child Development has published the following revised guidelines in the *SRCD Newsletter* (Winter, 1990). These guidelines should meet the standards set by most institutional review boards.

1. *Informed consent.* Participation in research must be voluntary. The child or adolescent should be briefed on all aspects of the study that may affect him or her before the investigator seeks assent. This assent or consent is indicated by the child or adolescent signing a form that details the information that was presented verbally, including a statement that he or she is free to withdraw from the study at any time without prejudice. The consent form must be written at the reading level of the child.

Consent forms do not completely inform if some information is withheld from the child or adolescent as part of the study. But as Miller (1987) notes, there is a difference between incomplete disclosure of information and deception. In some cases it may be necessary to withhold some information, such as in an incidental memory study where the child or adolescent cannot be told that a test of memory will follow because this would seriously affect the incidental memory measures. Deception is another matter, however, and this issue will be discussed under a separate guideline.

Of course, there are instances where consent would bias the research or where it may not be necessary, such as field research in public places (e.g., playgrounds) where the subject's anonymity is absolutely protected. Judgments of this type are best made in consultation with research peers and the institutional review board (*SRCD Newsletter,* 1990).

2. *Parental consent.* Because children and adolescents are not legally competent to give informed consent, permission must be obtained from the legal parent, guardian, or other individual who can act in loco parentis. The consent must be in writing and the form should detail the procedures to be used, the risks and benefits associated with the research, the guarantee of anonymity, and the right to refuse consent as well as withdraw the child from the research at any time without prejudice. Although it may be ethically permissible to withhold some information from the child or adolescent due to the nature of the study, there is no need to withhold this information from the parent(s) unless they are involved in the research, and this condition would have been approved by the institutional review board.

3. *Additional consent.* Most of the time, research subjects will be drawn from schools, day-care centers, or other similar institutions. The consent of these institutions is also necessary, and the institutional review board will probably require a letter from the institution stating that you have permission to use the children or adolescents from the institution in your study.

4. *Anonymity/Confidentiality.* If information from institutional records is used in the study, the anonymity of this information must be maintained and used for only the purposes that it was obtained. This may mean that parent(s) would not have access to the information. The promise of confidentiality implies that all information obtained from the subject or parents will be concealed in such a way that it is not available. The method(s) for maintaining this confidentiality should be made known to the subject and parent(s). The use of subject numbers in place of names is one way of maintaining confidentiality of the information.

5. *Deception.* Whenever subjects are to be deliberately misled about some phase of the study, the researcher must satisfy his or her research colleagues and the institutional review board that the procedure is absolutely necessary and that the study cannot be conducted without this procedure. If deception is used, consent cannot be completely informed (Miller, 1987). One of the problems with the use of deception is that the researcher must ensure that the subjects will not be negatively affected and that they will be informed about the reasons for the deception at the end of the study.

Where might deception be used? Suppose that the subjects are told they will not be observed

as they play or perform any action, but in reality they are observed through a one-way mirror, or suppose the study is about cheating or some other moral virtue. This issue will be discussed further under the next guideline. In general, researchers are well advised to avoid the use of deception in studies involving children or adolescents.

6. *Nonharmful procedures.* The SRCD guidelines state that no research procedure should be used that could inflict either physical or psychological harm to the child or adolescent. In psychological research it is highly unlikely that some physical harm will be inflicted on the subject; therefore, the real danger comes from psychological harm. Although psychological harm may be difficult to define, it is the responsibility of the investigator to reduce it to the lowest level possible or eliminate it. If psychological harm is inevitable and of concern, then other methods should be found or the research should be abandoned (*SRCD Newsletter,* 1990).

What types of research manipulations are potentially harmful? Stress of any type is one problem. Procedures that produce negative feelings or negative self-images in the child or adolescent are another problem. Suppose a study uses a problem-solving paradigm where a failure experience is induced, and the child is told that the task assesses ability to obtain passing grades in school. Or perhaps the research involves cheating where subjects are placed in a situation in which the risk of detection of cheating is minimized. If the child believes that the transgression was not detected, he or she will still experience anxiety and guilt (Miller, 1987).

One obvious solution to these harmful effects is debriefing, where the real purposes of the study are clearly explained to the child and he or she is made to feel comfortable about the behavior in question. Debriefing is necessary if information is withheld from the subject. But is debriefing really the panacea for the problems resulting from psychological harm? Miller (1987) suggests that debriefing at times may create more problems than it solves.

Consider the problems associated with the cheating study. In the debriefing, the child is informed that she or he was observed cheating and that the purpose of the study was to find out when and why children cheat. Will a 6-year-old child understand this explanation? Might the child think that adults can actually see through mirrors? Suppose the child does not feel guilty or anxious about the cheating, but rather learns to cheat from participating in the study? And finally, there is the problem that the investigator actually lied to the child when he or she was told that "no one will know what you do." Perhaps the lesson learned by the child is not to trust researchers (Miller, 1987). The problems with withholding information and the potential psychological harm are quite evident. For a more detailed discussion of the problems, the reader is directed to Miller (1987).

Freedom from harm entails a careful risk-benefit assessment of the research procedures, and this type of assessment is likely to be a requirement of the institutional review board that evaluates the ethicality of the research project. A recent review of the issues associated with risk-benefit analyses of developmental research has been completed by Thompson (1990). In any research project, there are some risks to the subject, even though those risks may be very minimal.

Any risk-benefit analysis with children has to consider two additional factors. Because children are a heterogeneous population and because research risks do not decrease necessarily with age, but rather vary in more diverse ways, it is necessary to invoke a developmental perspective in the review of the risk-benefit analysis. Second, Thompson argues that research risk must focus on standards of treatment for children rather than just a consideration of minimal risk. The ethical basis for a risk-benefit analysis is based on the presumptions that harm is removed and positive benefits will result, as well as the belief "that it is wrong to intentionally inflict harm on another" (Thompson, 1990, p. 4).

The contention that developmental changes are associated with the effects of research participation implies that infants and young children are most susceptible to the risks associated with research procedures, whereas risk declines with increasing age of the child. However, it could also be argued that research risk increases with age, because, for example, young children may not be as harmed by insults to self-concept or other similar procedures. Further, the contention that risk be based on the real-world experiences of children, which change with age, disregards the dictum that children of all ages are entitled to considerate research treatment (Thompson, 1990).

Thompson offers some guidelines for assessing risk-benefit using an appropriate developmental model.

a. Infants and young children are at a greater risk for becoming stressed in psychological research. Movement away from laboratory settings to the home or daycare may decrease this stress, and the presence of parent(s) or other surrogates are very helpful as supportive agents.

b. Any threat to the child's self-concept will increase with age. The important transition in self-concept between 7 and 9 years of age suggests a particularly vulnerable period.

c. Performance comparisons with others may have a greater negative impact on older children.

d. Older children and adolescents are more sensitive to the cues and demands of others, and may be more likely to comply with the demands of others, but they also may be more suspicious about the purpose of the research.

e. Feelings of emotions such as embarrassment, shame, and guilt are more likely among older children.

f. Younger children are more susceptible to coercive procedures and deception than older children.

g. Younger children are more likely to divulge personal information, whereas older children and adolescents are likely to resist such intrusions into their private life, and they may consider any attempts at questions of privacy as invasive.

h. Given their less well-developed cognitive skills, debriefing may be less effective with younger children, but they may continue to trust investigators implicitly more than older children and adolescents.

i. As children age, they align with social groups, thus their sensitivity to research biases may increase.

It is clear that research risk in children is not solely a linear function of age. For some factors, the risk decreases with age, for other factors, there is an increase, and for yet other factors, the function is curvilinear (Thompson, 1990). As a result, the analysis of risk-benefit is a much more complex process for children. There is also the matter of individual differences in the heterogeneous population resulting from the diverse backgrounds of children at any age. To illustrate, take the ethical problems associated with conducting research with such populations as developmentally delayed, abused, chemically dependent, emotionally disturbed, and terminally ill children, to name but a few. Special consideration in all aspects of the procedure must be taken with such groups. Therefore, any risk-benefit analysis must also consider ethical principles of respect and empathic care for the child or adolescent subject, according to Thompson (1990).

7. *Unforeseen circumstances and jeopardy.* If the research procedures result in some unexpected consequences to the child or adolescent, the investigator is bound to initiate corrective action immediately and to make necessary changes in procedures for this and future studies. Further, if the investigator observes any behaviors on the part of the child or adolescent that threaten his or her well-being or any information that may have such an effect, the researcher needs to present this information to the parent(s), guardian, teacher, or others with expertise so that the necessary help may be obtained for the child.

8. *Informing participants.* Without question, the investigator has an obligation to report the general findings of the study to the subjects, their parents, and to the appropriate school or other institutional officials. The report must be written in a form that is understandable by the intended audience.

From this discussion of research ethics, it is evident that the investigator needs to be especially sensitive to a number of developmental considerations and ethical concerns in designing any study. It is clearly not the case that the ends necessarily justify the means. No study is worth conducting if it cannot meet the ethical requirements outlined.

SUMMARY

In their volume on school psychology, Reynolds and colleagues (1984) state, "Research must form the basis for change in the evolution of school psychology" (p. 302). They further note that little progress has been made toward this goal because there is not sufficient research to provide direction and guidance for change. The integrated developmental/social systems approach provides a framework for that evolutionary change in school psychology. The direction taken by this approach is to study human behavior within individuals and systems as they function within their environments and across varied contexts or occasions. The rationale for this departure from traditional methods is that school psychologists need to examine behavioral change and be able to separate actual change from stable patterns of variable behavior within the individual. We contend that school psychologists should adopt the scientist-practitioner model.

One of the major contributions of a developmental/social systems orientation is that it provides guidance in the selection of factors to investigate, and it directs the school psychologist to focus on persons, variables, and occasions in designs that incorporate repeated measures and multivariate applications. The availability of sophisticated computer programs facilitates the analysis of data from this type of research design.

Path analyses and multiple regression procedures offer a promising direction to take in identifying the contribution of factors that a developmental/ social systems orientation identifies as important in the behavioral repertoire of goal-seeking individuals.

REFERENCES

Achenbach, T. M., & Edelbrock, C. S. (1981). Behavioral problems and competence reported by parents of normal and disturbed children aged four through sixteen. *Monographs of the Society for Research in Child Development, 46*(188).

Applebaum, M. I., & McCall, R. B. (1983). Design and analysis in developmental psychology. In P. H. Mussen (Ed.), *Handbook of child psychology* (4th ed., pp. 415–476). New York: Wiley.

Bardon, J. I. (1987). The translation of research into practice in school psychology. *School Psychology Review, 10,* 317–328.

Bass, R. F. (1987). The generality, analysis, and assessment of single-subject data. *Psychology in the Schools, 24,* 97–104.

Benson, A. J., & Hughes, J. (1985). Perceptions of role definition processes in school psychology: A national survey. *School Psychology Review, 14,* 64–74.

Berk, L. C. (1989). *Child development.* Boston: Allyn and Bacon.

Bird, K., & LaVoie, J. C. (1989). *Sociometric status and play behavior in preschool children.* Paper presented at Society for Research in Child Development, Kansas City.

Boise, R. (1983). Observational skills. *Psychological Bulletin, 93,* 3–29.

Borg, W. R., & Gall, M. D. (1983). *Educational research: An introduction* (4th ed.). White Plains, NY: Longman.

Breznitz, Z., & Teltsch, T. (1989). The effect of school entrance age on academic achievement and social-emotional adjustment of children: Follow-up study of fourth graders. *Psychology in the Schools, 26,* 62–68.

Bronfenbrenner, U. (1977). Toward an experimental ecology of human development. *American Psychologist, 32,* 513–530.

Cooper, J. O., Heron, T. E., & Heward, W. L. (1987). *Applied behavior analysis.* Columbus, OH: Merrill.

Fagan, T. K. (1989). On science, mirrors, and lamps; A comment. *Professional School Psychology, 4,* 231–233.

Faulkner, E., & LaVoie, J. C. (1990). *Psychosocial correlates of adolescent drug use.* Unpublished manuscript, University of Nebraska at Omaha.

Ford, M. E. (1982). Social cognition and social competence in adolescence. *Developmental Psychology, 18,* 323–340.

Ford, M. E. (1989). Processes contributing to adolescent social competence. In M. E. Ford & D. H. Ford (Eds.), *Humans as self-constructing living systems: Putting the framework to work* (pp. 199–233). Hillsdale, NJ: Erlbaum.

Fry, M. A. (1986). The connections among educational and psychological research and the practice of school psychology. In S. N. Elliott & J. C. Witt (Eds.), *The delivery of psychological services in the schools* (pp. 305–327). Hillsdale, NJ: Erlbaum.

Gresham, F. M., & Carey, M. P. (1988). Research methodology and measurement. In J. C. Witt & F. M. Gresham (Eds.), *Handbook of behavior therapy in education* (pp. 37–65). New York: Plenum.

Grossman, H. (1983). *Manual on terminology and classification in mental retardation.* Washington, DC: American Association on Mental Deficiency.

Hartmann, D. P. (1988). Measurement and analysis. In M. H. Bornstein & M. L. Lamb (Eds.), *Developmental psychology: An advanced textbook* (2nd ed., pp. 85–147). Hillsdale, NJ: Erlbaum.

Keith, T. Z. (1987). Assessment research: An assessment and recommended interventions: *School Psychology Review, 16,* 276–289.

Keith, T. Z. (1988a). Research methods in school psychology; An overview. *School Psychology Review, 17,* 502–520.

Keith, T. Z. (1988b). Path analysis: An introduction for school psychologists. *School Psychology Review, 17,* 342–362.

Keith, T. Z., Harrison, P. L., & Ehly, S. W. (1987). Effects of adaptive behavior on achievement: Path analysis of a national sample. *Professional School Psychology, 2,* 205–215.

Kirk, R. E. (1982). *Experimental design* (2nd ed.). Monterey, CA: Brooks/Cole.

Kratochwill, T. R. (1977). N = 1: An alternative research for school psychologists. *Journal of School Psychology, 15,* 239–249.

Kratochwill, T. R. (1978). Foundations of time-series research. In T. R. Kratochwill (Ed.), *Single subject research.* New York: Academic Press.

Mann, J., Have, T. T., Plunkett, J. W., & Meisels, S. J. (1991). Time sampling: A methodological critique. *Child Development, 62,* 227–241.

McCall, R. B. (1977). Challenges to a science of developmental psychology. *Child Development, 48,* 333–344.

McCormick, S. (1990). A case for the use of single-subject methodology in reading research. *Journal of Research in Reading, 13,* 69–81.

Miller, S. A. (1987). *Developmental research methods.* Englewood Cliffs, NJ: Prentice-Hall.

Mudre, L. H., & McCormick, S. (1989). Effects of meaning-focused cues on underachieving readers' context use, self-corrections, and literal comprehension. *Reading Research Quarterly, 24.*

Nagle, C. C., Wasik, B. H., & Schumacher, T. D. (1978). Use of the systems approach for successful token economies. *Journal of School Psychology, 16,* 245–252.

Nesselroade, J. R., & Ford, D. H. (1987). Methodological considerations in modeling living systems. In M. E. Ford & D. H. Ford (Eds.), *Humans as self-constructing living systems: Putting the framework to work* (pp. 45–79). Hillsdale, NJ: Erlbaum.

Olson, D. H., & Lavee, Y. C. (1989). Family systems and family stress: A family life cycle perspective. In K. Kreppner & R. M. Lerner (Eds.), *Family systems and life-span development* (pp. 165–196). Hillsdale, NJ: Erlbaum.

Parker, J. G., & Asher, S. R. (1987). Peer relations and later personal adjustment: Are low-accepted children at risk? *Psychological Bulletin, 102,* 357–389.

Paschal, R. A., Weinstein, T., & Walberg, H. J. (1984). The effects of homework on learning: A quantitative synthesis. *Journal of Educational Research, 78,* 97–104.

Pedhazur, E. J. (1982). *Multiple regression in behavioral research* (2nd ed.). New York: Holt, Rinehart & Winston.

Phillips, B. N. (1982). Reading and evaluating research in school psychology. In C. R. Reynolds & T. R. Gutkin (Eds.), *The handbook of school psychology* (pp. 24–50). New York: Wiley.

Phillips, B. N. (1987). On science, mirrors, lamps, and professional practice. *Professional School Psychology, 4,* 221–229.

Reynolds, C. R., & Clark, J. H. (1984). Trends in school psychology research: 1974–1980. *Journal of School Psychology, 22,* 43–52.

Reynolds, C. R., Gutkin, T. R., Elliott, S. N., & Witt, J. S. (1984). *School psychology: Essentials of theory and practice.* New York: Wiley.

Rosenthal, R., & Rosnow, R. L. (1991). *Essentials of behavioral research: Methods and data analysis* (2nd ed.). New York: McGraw-Hill.

Schneewind, K. A. (1989). Contextual approaches to family systems research: The macro-micro puzzle. In K. Kreppner & R. M. Lerner (Eds.), *Family systems and life-span development* (pp. 197–222). Hillsdale, NJ: Erlbaum.

Seitz, V. (1988). Methodology. In M. H. Bornstein & M. L. Lamb (Eds.), *Developmental psychology: An advanced textbook* (2nd ed.). Hillsdale, NJ: Erlbaum.

Shinn, M. R. (1987). Research by practicing school psychologists: The need for fuel for the lamp. *Professional School Psychology, 4,* 235–243.

Society for Research in Child Development. (1990, Winter). Ethical standards for research with children. *SRCD Newsletter.*

Thompson, R. A. (1990). Vulnerability in research: A developmental perspective on research risk. *Child Development, 61,* 1–16.

von Eye, A., & Kreppner, K. (1989). Family systems and family development: The selection of units. In K. Kreppner & R. M. Lerner (Eds.), *Family systems and life-span development* (pp. 247–269). Hillsdale, NJ: Erlbaum.

Yarrow, M. R., & Waxler, C. Z. (1979). Observing interaction: A confrontation with methodology. In R. B. Cairns (Ed.), *The analysis of social interaction: Methods, issues, and illustrations* (pp. 37–65). Hillsdale, NJ: Erlbaum.

CHAPTER 4

LEARNING THEORIES
AND APPLICATIONS

Information exchange occurs between systems because each system is influenced by its interactions with others in a circular process analogous to a feedback loop. The focus of human information exchange within a systems framework is on "how people construct, organize, revise, store, and remember knowledge of themselves and the world" (Ford, 1987, p. 333). Information makes coordination of behavior-environment transactions possible. Human information mechanisms have to accommodate variability and are programmed to collect information from a variable environment. The information mechanism collects information as well as organizes and reduces information (Ford, 1987). These mechanisms are able to select relevant portions of information for the individual's needs and intentions.

There is also a concern with how information is used as a control system for direction (using thoughts to organize behavior), control (using information to organize a plan designed to produce a desired goal), and regulation (using thought to make one's behavior more effective). These processes, which are executive functions, are commonly included under the concept of metacognition (Ford, 1987). Motivation within a systems framework is interpreted as a directive function (i.e., personal goals and aspirations) and the associated self-evaluation (Ford, 1987). The integration of a developmental perspective within this systems framework adds the component of behavioral change across time. Therefore, each of the aforementioned information processes is expected to show certain changes with age (i.e., across time).

The primary focus of this chapter will be on a discussion of cognitive-based learning theories, especially information processing, to fit our emphasis on a developmental/social systems approach to school psychology. We will examine such processes as attention, encoding, retrieval, and memory stores, and specifically the developmental changes that occur within these processes and structures. Applications of information processing, particularly the teaching of cognitive strategies, will be considered. Some attention will be given to motivation, especially social-cognitive approaches, because of their relevance to a developmental/systems orientation. We will begin the discussion with a brief overview of some concepts associated with behavioral theories of learning that stress the interaction between the person and the environment.

BEHAVIORAL THEORIES OF LEARNING

Pavlovian Conditioning

In its most basic form, Pavlovian conditioning occurs when some neutral stimulus (NS) is paired with either an unconditioned reflex (US → UR: i.e., unconditioned stimulus → unconditioned response) or a conditioned reflex (CS → CR: i.e., conditioned stimulus → conditioned response), resulting in the NS becoming a CS capable of eliciting a conditioned response.

Test anxiety is one example of Pavlovian conditioning. Suppose a child has a history of feeling anxious when his or her parents are upset because the child does failing work in school or does not meet parental expectations for school performance. This situation causes the child to become very apprehensive in any evaluation setting and to feel nauseous. As a result, even the announcement of a test elicits anxiety and nausea in the child. Test anxiety may not appear immediately because it can require several experiences, but some behaviors, such as fear, may be acquired in one conditioning experience. This example illustrates the importance of becoming familiar with a child's past history.

Conditioned Emotional Responses

Perhaps the most important outcome of Pavlovian conditioning as it relates to human behavior is the role of CSs in the eliciting of conditioned emotional responses (CERs) such as happiness, affection, pleasure, sorrow, hate, anxiety, and especially fear. These responses are a product of Pavlovian conditioning. Because they occupy such an important function in our lives, it is important to understand their origin in order to acquire some control over them.

As we think about these emotions, it becomes obvious that the stimuli that elicit these responses were acquired through experience. Words as well as events and experiences can invoke emotional responses. Words become powerful CSs (e.g., consider the effect of such words as *love* or *hate*), which again illustrates the role that cognitive factors play in Pavlovian conditioning. In some cases, emotional responses, such as fear, are acquired in only one experience, and this setting may have occurred in very early childhood or very recently.

Emotional responses are continually occurring in our lives and in the lives of children and adolescents with whom we interact as school psychologists. But learning to identify and label emotions accurately is a difficult task for a child. Because parents do not have access to the child's mind, they cannot determine whether the child is correctly identifying any given emotion or discriminating between emotions; therefore, parents cannot provide feedback to the child. Although children may be somewhat aware of the causal stimuli associated with their behavior, they may

nevertheless make incorrect attributions based only on the timing of two events without considering their causal association. However, it is more often the case that children do not understand the causes of their behavior (Gage & Berliner, 1988).

The following example of a school experience described by Gage and Berliner (1988) exemplifies the conditioning of emotional responses. A 5-year-old goes to school on the first day and receives a friendly greeting following her name, and then a smile, a hug, and a positive comment about her appearance or behavior. In the days that follow, the child wants to go to school early and begins to talk about being a teacher. The teacher's responses can be considered unconditioned stimuli that elicit in the child the unconditioned emotional responses of positive affect and happiness. The teacher and school setting, which were initially neutral stimuli, also produce feelings of positive affect and excitement because of their association with the responses given by the teacher (i.e., they become CSs).

A child with this conditioning experience is less likely to have school-related problems that would demand our attention, and he or she will be a positive contributor in the classroom. Compare this situation with a child who comes to school and meets a threatening teacher, who finds the classroom experience to be dull and boring or the schedule very inflexible, and who sees the other children as mean. What is the outcome of this conditioning experience? A family experience can be substituted for these school experiences with similar emotional results. These examples highlight how a child's experience in school can influence subsequent behavior.

Extinction

Mazur (1990) notes that the length of time after acquisition has little effect on the strength of a conditioned response, but this does not mean that conditioned responses have permanency. Responses can be decreased and eventually removed through the process of extinction, during which the CS is presented in the absence of the US. Using the test-anxiety example, this negative emotion ought to decrease if fear of failure and negative feedback from parents and teachers are no longer experienced by the child. Childhood fears gradually disappear when they no longer are paired with aversive events, and this process can also occur for anxiety and other negative emotions. There are exceptions, however. Avoidance of the CS will impede extinction. If the child avoids tests by feigning illness, test anxiety will not extinguish because the child will be unaware that negative evaluations are no longer being given by parents and the teacher. This principle of avoidance explains why negative emotions such as fears are more difficult to extinguish than positive emotions. In the case of the former, the CS that elicits the fear is avoided, so extinction cannot occur.

A second factor that influences extinction is spontaneous recovery. During periods between extinction trials, the conditioned response regains some of its strength. In the case of a child with test anxiety, we should expect the test anxiety to recover somewhat during the intervals between tests when extinction is used. The concept of spontaneous recovery is not well understood, according to Benjamin, Hopkins, and Nation (1990), but it is important in such circumstances as treating phobias (i.e., irrational fears) because phobics who have had their fears extinguished find that they reappear for no apparent reason. Positive CERs can also extinguish over time if the stimuli eliciting them are not repaired at least occasionally with the original USs. Thus, positive affect and other similar responses need to recur in the original stimulus pairing from time to time. The 5-year-old's positive feelings about school will not continue indefinitely without reestablishment.

Operant Conditioning

The basic principle underlying this form of learning is that behavior is influenced by antecedent cues (i.e., those stimuli that precede the behavior) as well as the consequences (i.e., stimuli)

that occur after the behavior (Baldwin & Baldwin, 1986). Three postulates follow from this basic principle:

1. Behavior followed by a reinforcing stimulus will increase in frequency.
2. Behavior followed by a punishing stimulus will decrease in frequency.
3. Behavior followed by no stimulus will decrease or increase contingent on past conditioning history of the organism.

Both the antecedent cues and the consequences are stimuli that can consist of thoughts, words, actions, or emotions, to name but a few, and both antecedent cues and consequences influence the behavior that occurs.

Reinforcement

Stimuli that increase the frequency of a behavior that they follow are *reinforcers,* and they consist of two types—positive and negative. The critical difference between the two is that *positive* reinforcement occurs with the introduction of the stimulus, whereas the removal of an aversive stimulus results in *negative* reinforcement. There are many examples of both types of reinforcers that apply to educational settings. Praise and friendly greetings are positive reinforcers; removal of in-school suspension or cancellation of an unwanted test are negative reinforcers.

Negative reinforcement is an important concept because it is responsible for escape and avoidance behaviors, which have a daily impact on our lives and can create behavioral problems. Escape behaviors allow a person to get away from an aversive stimulus; they involve *reacting* after the aversive stimulus has occurred. Avoidance behavior enables the person to evade the experience of the aversive stimulus, and it involves *proacting* by taking a preventive action before the aversive stimulus occurs. For example, the child may use crying when punished in order to escape further punishment. Following rules could enable the child to avoid punishment.

An important feature of reinforcers is that

they are relative; that is, their ability to increase the behavior that they follow can be modified. Also, reinforcement is contingent on the situation, so that a stimulus may function as a reinforcer in one setting but as a punisher in another. Good grades in school may be a reinforcer for the child at home but a punisher in the peer-group setting if the child is rejected by peers because he or she is a "brain."

Reinforcement Schedules

Among the most powerful determinants of behavior are the reinforcement patterns called *schedules*. Baldwin and Baldwin (1986) contend that the effects of schedules are pervasive because of their involvement in every aspect of our daily lives.

Fixed ratio schedules are those in which a reinforcer is given after some set number of responses. An FR5 would be a schedule in which a reinforcer is given after each five responses. In school settings, children are often given stickers for each book they read, with a larger award for some designated number of books, or the reinforcer might be praise for cooperative behavior or on-task behavior. This type of schedule tends to produce high rates of responding with a pause, called a *scallop*, after each reinforcer.

Variable ratio schedules are more common where reinforcement is given over some range of behavior frequency. A VR7 would be a schedule where a behavior is reinforced on the average of about each seven times that it occurs. Gage and Berliner (1988) suggest that hand raising in the classroom commonly may be under this type of schedule. Behaviors on variable ratio schedules are not easily extinguished, but if the ratio becomes too high, so that children are not called on very often, they will stop raising their hands. This situation could be a very undesirable if a child then stops participating in class. In general, behaviors on this type of schedule are very persistent, which explains why certain annoying behaviors, such as interrupting, are so difficult to remove if the teacher responds only occasionally to the child.

Weekly science demonstrations in school are on a *fixed interval* schedule because they are held at the same day and time each week, so the reinforcement is determined by the passage of time. Exams are also on this schedule, which encourages a response pattern where activity increases near the time of reinforcement. This contingency explains why students often cram the night before a big exam. A limited hold (i.e., a behavior must occur within a fixed time to be reinforced) is often a component of fixed schedules, so that a behavior must occur within a specified time period. Teachers frequently specify a time period during which make-up work or exams will be accepted.

Variable interval schedules permit the reinforcement of an appropriate response after some average period of time has elapsed. Reinforcement on a VI6 schedule would be dispensed on the average of once every six time segments. In comparison with fixed interval schedules, variable interval schedules result in higher rates of responding but more variable behavior. A limited hold also may be a part of this schedule. Variable interval schedules are in effect when unannounced quizzes are given in the classroom or when unannounced visits of school psychologists are made by supervisors. In both cases the individuals affected are on constant alert, although some may try to anticipate the likelihood of the event occurring.

Extinction

Extinction involves the removal of reinforcement, which can decrease or remove a behavior. Extinction can also occur when there is less reinforcement for the target behavior than that which occurs for some desirable alternative (Baldwin & Baldwin, 1986). A person's prior history of reinforcement will determine the speed at which extinction takes place. Therefore, research shows that extinction will occur more slowly if a behavior is on a partial reinforcement schedule such as variable ratio or variable interval. Extinction of a negatively reinforced behavior also results in response decline, except in the case of avoidance behaviors, where the individual is not aware that the aversive stimulus is no longer present because he or she has constantly avoided any contact with that stimulus.

Punishment

A stimulus that suppresses the frequency of a response is a punisher. Both punishment and extinction cause a reduction in response frequency, but punishment is more rapid and complete in its effects. If a punisher is of sufficient intensity, it can totally remove a behavior. In most cases, however, punishment suppresses a behavior, it does not extinguish it. Punishment is most effective when it is sufficiently intense, immediate, and unopposed by reinforcement. If reinforcement is present, punishment effectiveness will be determined by the intensity and frequency of each. There is a cost-benefit ratio involving reinforcement and punishment that states that response suppression will be greatest when costs are high and benefits are low. But response suppression can result from low intensity or infrequent punishment if some alternative behavior with a better cost-benefit ratio is available (Baldwin & Baldwin, 1986).

Positive punishment occurs when an aversive stimulus is presented as a behavioral consequence. Natural consequences to careless acts, such as cutting oneself, are positive punishers. Reprimands and strong criticism are examples of social forms of positive punishment, as are school suspensions and failing grades. Social punishers often affect people differently because each person has a unique punishment history. Thus, a stare or an insensitive comment may be aversive to one person but not to another. *Negative punishment* results when a response brings about the loss of a positive reinforcer. Withdrawal of privileges and "grounding" are negative punishers. Time-out procedures, where students are removed from a classroom or denied the opportunity to attend a program, and response cost, where something of value (e.g., recess) is taken away are examples of negative punishers that are used in school settings.

Punishment presents a host of problems, including its ethical use. Among the undesirable features of punishment are that it often teaches aggression, it generally produces only temporary response suppression, it sometimes results in more intense responses, it leads to avoidance of the person who punishes, and it produces negative emotional conditioning of such behaviors as fear, shame, and guilt. These negative features have created a need for alternative procedures. The alternatives include differential reinforcement of alternative behavior (DRO), in which another behavior incompatible with the undesired behavior is reinforced. In some cases any behavior other than the undesired behavior is reinforced. DRO has been shown to be an effective behavior suppressant (Baldwin & Baldwin, 1986; Gage & Berliner, 1988).

Differential reinforcement of low rates of responding (DRL) is another alternative. This procedure could be used to reduce excessive talking in class by a student through reinforcing her or him when talking decreased. Extinction can be an effective alternative. Ignoring or removing attention is quite effective with children, but to increase the effectiveness of extinction, it is necessary to identify the reinforcers that are responsible for the undesirable behavior. Reasoning has also been shown to be an effective accompaniment of punished behavior, especially when the discussion focuses on the reasons for the misbehavior and explains why it is inappropriate (LaVoie, 1974; Walters & Grusec, 1977).

The Premack Principle

This principle becomes important when information about an individual's past reinforcement or punishment history is lacking, so that we have little or no idea about stimuli that could be effective reinforcers/punishers. The Premack Principle states that any high-probability behavior can function as a reinforcer for a low-probability behavior, and similarly a low-probability behavior can function as a punisher for a high-probability behavior. Many school applications can be found for this principle. Time with board games or in the science center can serve as a reinforcer for completing school assignments. Staying after school can be used as a punisher for being tardy to class. Notice that the Premack Principle supports the contention that a stimulus can be either a reinforcer, a punisher, or both, depending on the situation.

Shaping and Prompting

Shaping is a process for teaching a new behavior. It involves arranging a series of ordered steps for an individual to take, from the initial response to the final desired behavior. Each of the steps requires a refinement in the skill level of the previous behavior before a reinforcement is given. Differential reinforcement is a key component in the shaping process. When a specific behavior is reinforced and others are not, the reinforced behavior occurs more frequently. Shaping could be used by teachers in such settings as teaching printing or writing. The effective teacher carefully observes the student and gives positive reinforcement at the skill level that the child has attained, and then moves the child in a series of steps toward the desired goal. The school psychologist could use the same procedure in teaching a child a specific social skill, such as management of conflicts or group entry.

Shaping is concerned with response change, whereas *prompting* focuses on changes in the stimulus. In a task such as reading, prompting begins by showing the child a picture of an object, below which is printed the name. After the child repeats the name of the picture a number of times, the picture is gradually reduced in size or distinctiveness, so that over a period of time, only the word, which becomes an S^D, remains on the card. Reinforcement is given with each response. The process of gradually removing the picture is referred to as *fading*. Prompts are used in a variety of ways by teachers. Physical guidance in teaching various motor skills, pointers directed at the blackboard, use of diagrams, and various gestures are some common examples. Verbal prompts are often used to teach children words or to recall events. Both shaping and prompting can

be used to teach a new behavior. Mosk and Bucher (1984) found that shaping produced faster learning in retarded children and required less time than prompting.

Social Learning

Bandura (1977, 1986) contends that an individual's response to a stimulus is based on the cognitive representations of the consequences of the actions that are taken or contemplated. Therefore, reinforcement is a source of information about the effect that a person's behavior has on the environment. In essence, we learn a set of expectations about the relationship among events, and this learning occurs through observation as well as by direct experience and tuition. Bandura asserts that most of the behaviors that we acquire are the result of observational learning because it is much faster and relatively errorless, as compared to learning by means of shaping or the use of prompts.

Although Bandura agrees that the environment exercises control over behavior, the person's behavior and the characteristics of the person also influence behavior. These three factors are interdependent because they affect and exercise control over each other through the process of *reciprocal determinism*. (These ideas and an overview of Bandura's theory were discussed previously in Chapter 2.)

The influence of the environment and a person's characteristics have been recognized as influential determinants by other theories, but reciprocal determinism recognizes the environmental effect of the individual's behavior. Research indicates that persons do act on their environment and change it (Miller, 1989). Figure 4.1 depicts an example of a child influencing and being influenced by the environment. Reciprocal determinism further postulates that behavior affects thinking as well as the environment in that behavior elicits certain experiences that influence how the person thinks and what the person expects.

Child's Behavior   Social Environment

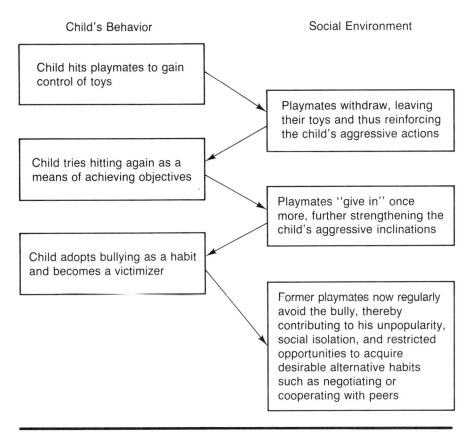

FIGURE 4.1   Example of reciprocal determinism

Source: From *Social and personality development,* 2nd ed., by D. Shaffer, p. 72. Copyright © 1988 by Wadsworth, Inc. Reprinted by permission of the publisher, Brooks/Cole Publishing Company, Pacific Grove, CA 93950.

Observational Learning

According to Bandura (1986), the observer acquires a symbolic representation of a model's behavior, which is then stored in memory and later retrieved when it is needed to guide the observer in a replication of the behavior. Four interrelated processes control the acquisition of modeled behavior: attention, retention, motoric reproduction, and motivation. Figure 4.2 shows these subprocesses.

The models that the person attends to and how effectively the model is attended to will be a function of the individual's ability to attend and his or her past experiences. The model's features

that are selected for processing are contingent on the person's cognitive ability to comprehend, his or her interests, and his or her expectations of what will occur. However, attention to the model is not sufficient for performance if the information is not stored for use when needed. The information is assumed to be stored in the form of retrieval sensory images to which verbal labels might be attached. There is a fair amount of evidence to suggest that symbolic coding of a model's actions does increase observational learning (Shaffer, 1988). Before the observer can imitate the model's behavior it is necessary to transform the symbolic representations into

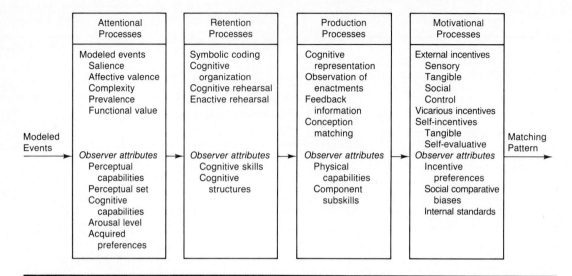

FIGURE 4.2   Subprocesses in observational learning

Source: Albert Bandura, *Social foundations of thought and action: A social cognitive theory,* ©
1986, p. 52. Reprinted by permission of Prentice Hall, Englewood Cliffs, New Jersey.

action. The ability to perform this action will be contingent on the observer's proficiency to enact the necessary components of the observed behavior.

The fourth component, motivational processes, focuses on the individual's tendency to produce behavior that is perceived as producing desirable outcomes. If an observer knows beforehand that she or he will be reinforced for imitating a model, this should motivate the individual to attend carefully to the model's actions and to exert effort to store the images of the observed act. Thus, anticipated incentives should enhance observational learning. If observational learning does not occur, the failure is attributed to one or more of the four component processes. That is, cognitive factors control what is observed, the perception of the event or person, organization of the information, whether observational learning has permanency, and the effect of observing (Miller, 1989; Shaffer, 1988).

What behaviors can be acquired through observational learning? According to Rosenthal and Zimmerman (1972, 1978) observational learning contributes extensively to the acquisition of cognitive skills. Their research shows that observational learning is involved in a child's acquisition of conservation (i.e., the understanding of invariance). If nothing is added to a substance and nothing is removed, the substance remains unchanged. Other studies have reported that children can acquire grammatical rules, problem-solving skills, and abstract concepts through observing a model (Rivera & Smith, 1987; Zimmerman & Blom, 1983). The acquisition of abstract concepts fits with Bandura's conception of abstract modeling, which assumes that a person can construct an abstract rule by combining relevant elements from several instances of observational learning (Miller, 1989).

Moral behavior and moral reasoning can be influenced by the behavior of models. A prime example is the effect that parental models have on children's moral behavior. It has been shown that young boys use moral reasoning that resembles that of their mothers (Leon, 1984). Bandura and McDonald (1963) reported that after a brief exposure to an adult model in a laboratory setting, children changed their level of moral reasoning. Those reasoning at a lower moral level shifted upward, whereas those reasoning at a higher level shifted downward. Both children and adults have been found to commit a rule or law infraction after observing an errant model (Lefkowitz, Blake, & Mouton, 1955; Walters, Leat, & Mezei, 1963), and children have been found to behave more altruistically after observing an altruistic model (Israely & Guttman, 1983). (Observational learning has also provided a pervasive tool for behavior intervention, which is discussed in Chapter 5.)

Television

Television is a potent source of observational learning. Observing violence on TV has been documented as a determinant of aggressive behavior in children (Parke & Slaby, 1983; Perry & Bussey, 1984), although the effect is not large, with most correlations in the 20s, and there is some question about the direction of causality (Grusec & Lytton, 1988). But there is evidence that young children can be inoculated against the effects of viewing violence on TV by changing their attitudes toward aggression as a means of conflict resolution (Huesmann, Eron, Klein, Brice, & Fischer, 1983). Television viewing has been shown to increase sex stereotypes in children as well as their beliefs about information in commercials (Perry & Bussey, 1984). It also seems to impair the level of moral reasoning, especially in kindergarten children who are heavy TV viewers (Rosenkoetter, Huston, & Wright, 1990).

However, television viewing does have some positive effects. Children's programs such as "Sesame Street" and "The Electric Company" have been found to improve children's performance on vocabulary, letter identification, and counting, as well as reading (Ball & Bogatz, 1972, 1973). Prosocial programs (e.g., "Mr. Rogers' Neighborhood") seem to increase sharing, cooperation, and an understanding of the feelings of others in those children who regularly view these programs.

Self-Reinforcement and Self-Efficacy

Bandura (1986) argues that human behavior is largely regulated by self-produced consequences (i.e., self-reinforcement), which are enacted as the result of self-monitoring. Performance standards for self-reinforcement are learned from parent teaching and observation of models. Individuals set standards of performance that are used to reward themselves for good performance or deny rewards for poor or mediocre performance.

Why are standards adhered to? Bandura contends that the motives for adhering to standards are internal. Once standards are set, their achievement becomes foremost in our behavioral objectives. We feel competent when we succeed in reaching our goals and incompetent when we fail. That is, we feel *efficacious* when we succeed. Self-efficacy, or a person's perception of competence emerging from interactions with the environment, is a cognitively based competence perception. It is important to the extent that it seems to influence our personal identity and our potential (Shaffer, 1988). (This matter will be considered again in this chapter during the discussion of motivation.)

INFORMATION-PROCESSING THEORY

Information processing is not a single theory but rather a conceptual approach to analyzing how the mind deals with the flow of information (Miller, 1989). The information flow begins with an input, consisting of some type of stimulus, such as visual or auditory, and ends with an output, which could be some type of action, a spoken word, or information stored in memory. Between the input and output stages, mental processes have been operational. These processes consist of operations such as pattern recognition, representation, organization, and memory or retrieval strategies.

One method for representing the information-processing concept is by means of a flow diagram, such as that shown in Figure 4.3, which is an information-processing model presented by Shiffrin and Atkinson (1969). Notice that this model consists of a sensory register, an executive control process, and memory stores. These components play a major role in information-processing theories, therefore we will examine each component briefly.

Registers

Apparently a register exists for each of the senses, and its function is to store incoming information for a brief period of time so that a decision can be made about recognizing the stimulus input and whether the information should be transferred to memory. Sensory registers have a limited capacity and they can hold information

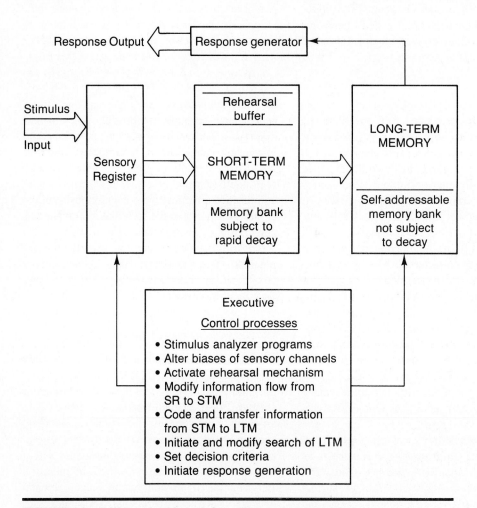

FIGURE 4.3   Shiffrin and Atkinson information-processing model

Source: Royer, J. M., & Feldman, R. S. (1984). *Educational psychology: Applications and theory.* New York: McGraw-Hill, p. 160. Reproduced with permission of McGraw-Hill, Inc. Shiffrin, R. M., & Atkinson, R. C. (1969). Storage and retrieval processes in long-term memory. *Psychological Review, 76.* Copyright 1969 by the American Psychological Association. Used with permission. Above adaptation from Royer & Feldman (1984), used courtesy of McGraw-Hill.

for a limited period of time. It is thought that the capacity of the auditory register may be larger than the visual register, and information can remain in the auditory register for a longer period of time (2 seconds or longer for auditory information; 1/4 second for visual information) to allow for recognition (Ellis & Hunt, 1989).

Because the visual register is especially important for reading, it was assumed that many reading problems were due to some dysfunctioning of the appearance of images on the register. But later research suggests that reading problems occur because of an inability to process information from the visual register (Ellis & Hunt, 1989). The auditory register is involved in speech perception (Seamon, 1980). Given these important functions of the registers, it is logical to assume that a person could be deficient in one and not in the other.

Attention

In information-processing models, attention has been assigned the role of an executive controller or processor, analogous to a programming language that controls the operation of a microcomputer. *Attention* is usually defined as "the process of allocating the resources or capacity to various inputs" (Ellis & Hunt, 1989, p. 52). Attention differs from *consciousness,* which refers to awareness or the realization that we can be cognizant only of a few things in any short period of time, and we cannot think about two things simultaneously.

Attention operates to select information for processing and to prevent other information from reaching awareness, because conscious capacity is limited. In this role, attention is functioning as a screen (Ellis & Hunt, 1989). There is disagreement about where in the information-processing sequence that attention is activated. Is attention present early to filter out information to be recognized, or does it engage after the information has been recognized, and thus select out certain aspects to be processed further? Both approaches seem to make some contribution to our under-

standing of attention. It appears that attention does not influence what we perceive, but rather selects the information that may become conscious. We probably can select out certain informational inputs that we attend to, but within that selection process some parts of the unattended information may be perceived (Ellis & Hunt, 1989).

Automaticity

The capacity allocation function of attention suggests that multiple tasks can be processed according to the demands of each task. Therefore, effort required for one task takes away from the effort that is available for other tasks. The more difficult the primary task, the less effort can be expended for other tasks. But some tasks seem to require no central processing capacity and are considered to be automatic, which means that these tasks should not affect the performance of a primary task.

The concept of automaticity is a major component in the capacity model of attention because it implies that central processing capacity is not needed in a particular task. Automaticity occupies a central position in discussions of attention. To be considered an automatic process, according to Posner and Snyder (1975), the following conditions are necessary:

1. The process occurs without a conscious decision. For example, the words that you are reading access their meaning in memory (this process is called *priming*) without your intention for this to happen (Ashcraft, 1988).
2. An automatic process occurs without conscious awareness. You are not aware that words are generating meanings.
3. Conscious resources are not needed.

The important role played by automaticity in our daily lives can be seen in the task of reading, which requires access to letter recognition and word meanings. The question that now arises is: How do tasks become automatic? The exact mechanism responsible for automaticity remains unknown, but a critical factor in its development is practice (Ellis & Hunt, 1989). Repetition and overlearning in a task seem to increase the likelihood that the task becomes automatic (Ashcraft, 1988), but some tasks may never become automatic. Nevertheless, practice still improves their performance. The more reading we do, the more proficient we should become. Practice in the use of various memory strategies, such as rehearsal and categorization, transform these strategies into automatic processes any time we encounter information that is to be recalled later.

Automaticity is one of the major changes in cognitive development. As children acquire more experience with the various mental processes, such as selective attention, their processing becomes more efficient, due to automaticity. This cognitive acquisition enables them to make associations between ideas, events, and other experiences that would not have occurred at an earlier age (Siegler, 1991). The claim that automaticity is one of the developmental changes occurring in a child's memorial ability is supported in studies reported by Guttentag (1984) and Kee and Davies (1988). In their studies with 7- to 12-year-olds, the child had to tap a telegraph key while rehearsing word lists. Tapping was slower at all ages while rehearsing the word lists, but the effect was greater for the 7- and 8-year-olds than for the older children.

Educational Implications of Attention

Understanding attention has important educational implications, two of which are reading and classroom management (Glover & Corkill, 1990). Word recognition is presumed to be an automatic process in fluent readers, which enables them to devote attention to comprehension. Less fluent readers, on the other hand, require more attentional capacity to recognize words, which leaves less attentional capacity for comprehension. The demands of classroom exercises vary; therefore, they will need to be adapted to the skill level of the students and the attentional resources that they require, which indicates that classroom management is important.

Studies of selective attention reveal that highly intelligent students are more capable of focusing their attention on relevant information instead of irrelevant information, when compared with students of average intelligence (Davidson & Sternberg, 1984), and intelligent students allot their time accordingly (Marr & Sternberg, 1986). What happens when selective attention breaks down? One condition associated with selective attention failure is petit mal epilepsy. In this condition, found primarily in children, there is a brief period of reduction in consciousness during which the child appears to be daydreaming, but interruption does not stop the daydream. Also, speech is characterized as repetitious and irrelevant to the situation (Seamon, 1980).

Short-Term Memory

This memory structure is characterized by its limited duration of about 30 seconds and its limited capacity of 5 to 9 chunks (i.e., units such as letters, numbers, words, or sentences) of information (Schweikert & Boruff, 1986). Because of these limitations, it becomes necessary to initiate control processes such as rehearsal (mentally repeating the information), chunking (grouping the information into larger units), and coding (attaching information from long term memory).

Capacity of short-term memory is thought to increase in children with age, but this developmental change is not independent of the types of processing that are used. An increase in the child's long-term memory knowledge base is probably the critical factor rather than size per se. Chi (1976) found no conclusive evidence that short-term memory capacity or rate of information loss varied as a function of age. However, short-term memory search rates do differ, with adults requiring about 38 msec (a millisecond is 1/1000 of a second) per digit, compared to 42 msec for twelfth-graders, and 238 msec for second-graders (Dugus & Kellas, 1974). Individual differences in short-term memory can be found in children. Brighter children apparently possess better short-term memories, in part because short-term memory is assessed in most IQ tests when the digit-span test is used. Mentally retarded children have a smaller capacity short-term memory, are slower in their manipulation of information, and have a more restricted access to long-term memory than normal children (Glover & Corkill, 1990).

Rehearsal

Information can be maintained in short-term memory and transferred to long-term memory by the use of rehearsal, which does not occur with any consistency in children until 7 years of age. With increases in age, children can rehearse larger numbers of words, and at adolescence a change in rehearsal flexibility emerges because adolescents can modify rehearsal procedures to fit the memory demands of the task. Although children below 7 years of age do not spontaneously rehearse information that is to be remembered, they can be trained to use rehearsal. Keeney, Cannizzo, and Flavell (1967) trained 6- and 7-year-old nonrehearsers to whisper names of words they were to remember over and over until they were asked to recall them. Children who received training used rehearsal for more than 75 percent of the test trials, and the training significantly increased recall.

Working Memory

Research on memory systems has not supported a separate short-term/long-term memory distinction, such as that proposed in a stage model, therefore an alternative *working memory* has been proposed. This memory structure includes a short-term store for information as well as an executive control system that is responsible for initiating the rehearsal process, making decisions (such as what to recall from long-term memory),

carrying out reasoning, and directing attention and mental resources. Since working memory does not include a two-system memory, all retention is determined by the type of processing used with the material.

Long-Term Memory

Information in the long-term memory store is considered to be relatively permanent, even though interference may occur and some memory may be lost through decay. Material stored in long-term memory is frequently divided into two classes: episodic and semantic. *Episodic* memory consists of knowledge about the specific events the individual has experienced. *Semantic* memory refers to the general knowledge base of the individual. Three long-term memory processes are most frequently discussed: encoding, organization, and retrieval.

Encoding

Encoding is a memory strategy that facilitates remembering. According to Gagne (1985), the methods that students use to encode information have a significant effect on remembering that information. What is remembered is likely to be the product of selective attention; that is, we seem to focus on certain aspects of an event and not on others. One important element of encoding is elaboration, in which information that is already known, and therefore stored in long-term memory, is added to incoming information. Semantic encoding, in which taxonomies are used (e.g., animals), has been found in children 6- to 12-years-old. Some evidence shows that 6-year-olds can use this form of encoding, but not more complex forms, such as shared characteristics (e.g., a coat and a sweater can be worn for warmth) or values. Use of these forms seems to appear at about 11 to 12 years of age (Hagen, Jongeward, & Kail, 1975). However, in studies of sentence memory, where semantic integration (i.e., encoding the meaning of the sentence) is necessary, children under 9 years of age do not seem to use relationships among sentences, but this encoding was evident among 11- to 12-year-olds (Paris, 1978).

Elaboration can also be used to form sentences, such as when word pairs are to be remembered. Rohwer (1973) reports that use of verbs is more effective than prepositions or conjunctions for children to use in connecting word pairs for later recall. Imagery is another form of encoding. When verbal elaboration (i.e., forming sentences) has been compared with the use of pictorial elaboration, verbal encoding is more effective in terms of later recall, but the converse effect has been reported in other studies (Rohwer, 1973). However, Pressley and Levin (1978), in their recall study of foreign words, reported that sixth-graders recalled twice as many words when they were told to create images for the words as they did with other encoding methods. Creating images as an encoding device may significantly increase recall; using pictorial encoding may not be as effective.

Mnemonics (memory cues that associate new information with something that is familiar) are another type of encoding strategy. Mnemonics such as the method of loci (associating items in lists by storing them as images along a walk through a familiar location such as a classroom) and the keyword method have been found to enhance various types of learning in children, such as vocabulary, foreign language, and fact learning (Pressley, Levin, & Delaney, 1982). The keyword method for vocabulary learning uses an acoustic link and an imagery link. If the task is to learn vocabulary words, the student is asked to find a keyword that sounds like part of the word to be remembered, and then to associate the word with an image; therefore, use of the keyword and the image elicits recall of the vocabulary word.

Other types of memory aides, such as adjunct aides (e.g., organizers, questions, and other mechanisms for helping students comprehend reading materials), have been found to enhance memory in children (Glover & Corkill,

1990). Use of advance organizers (i.e., materials that relate the reading to what the student knows and prepare the student for forthcoming reading) can increase children's prose learning (Dinnel & Glover, 1985). Prefacing a reading passage with appropriate questions increases intentional learning, but memory for overall content is higher when the questions focus on analysis of the content (Hamaker, 1986).

Spacing of the learning and self-generation of information are other factors that can be considered under the general heading of encoding. The classic studies comparing massed with spaced learning have consistently shown spaced learning to be more effective. Among the explanations for this effect are that the spacing of learning permits richer encoding of the material, and that more extensive processing can occur because previous encoding is not available. The generation effect, where students have to produce the information, seems to work only when the information is in semantic memory, and it seems best adapted for such applications as vocabulary and major points in a story (Glover & Corkill, 1990).

Organization

In this process, discrete items to be remembered are grouped into larger units according to a specific relationship existing among the items. Two forms of grouping, material-induced organization and subjective organization, have been the focus of study and seem to be the most effective in increasing retention, but any form of organization will improve memory when compared with no organization (Ellis & Hunt, 1989).

Material-induced organization refers to grouping items on the basis of some relationship or structure inherent in the items. Lists such as dog, horse, apple, bus, and train could be organized into groupings of animal, food, and transportation. If this regrouping appears in recall, clustering in recall is said to have occurred. *Subjective organization* refers to use of previous knowledge from long-term memory to group unrelated items. The presence of subjective organization is determined by consistency in recall order. Because subjective organization is the product of the learner's grouping efforts, rather than a grouping suggested by the material, subjective organization is a stronger indicator of organization in memory (Ellis & Hunt, 1989).

The findings from studies (e.g., Moely, Olson, Halwes, & Flavell, 1969) of children's use of organization, when presented with a series of pictures, reveal that organizational strategies (in this case, material-induced organization) are first used by children 10 to 11 years of age. This finding confirms that developmental differences that are present in children's use of memory strategies, and suggests that categorization is a more advanced strategy than rehearsal, which first appears consistently at 7 years of age (Kail, 1990).

Retrieval

Accessing information from long-term memory and transferring this information to working memory are retrieval processes. One of the critical elements in retrieval is the use of cues, which has prompted two proposals concerning how cues affect retrieval. The *associative strength theory* contends that effective retrieval cues are those that have occurred most frequently in the past with the event to be remembered. Thus, *sock* ought to be an effective cue for eliciting the word *foot*. It has been consistently shown in studies that strongly associated cues produce better memory than weakly associated cues (Ellis & Hunt, 1989).

A major element in the associative strength explanation is the notion of spreading activation. Information is stored in an associative network (a memory structure where information is grouped according to its association with a concept). When the cue activates the network, and as this activation spreads, each additional memory representation is activated, and those items closest to the cue are the most likely to be retrieved. The encoding specificity explanation states that the most effective retrieval cues are those that were encoded with the event to be remembered.

Associative strength and encoding specificity

imply that retrieval is a single process that occurs when the appropriate cue is present. It is largely automatic in that we do not think about it. Further, retrieval is the same in recall tasks as it is for recognition tasks. A *generation-recognition* model of retrieval argues that retrieval consists of at least two operations—generation and recognition. For recall tasks, it is necessary first to generate all the possible answers, and from them make a recognition decision concerning the correct answer. Recognition tasks, however, only require a recognition decision. In general, the research evidence seems to support both positions.

The other side of the retrieval coin is retrieval failure, which refers to the inability to access information that has been stored (i.e., forgetting). The two most common theories of forgetting are decay and interference. Although decay supposedly cannot occur in long-term memory because information is relatively permanent, it is probably the case that some decay of information does occur. Therefore, most attention has been given to interference, of which there are two sources: *retroactive,* where new information interferes with the retention of previous learned information, and *proactive,* where previously learned information interferes with newly learned information. Recently, alternative explanations for forgetting have been emerging. One of these explanations, cue-dependent forgetting, claims that failure to access information occurs because ineffective retrieval cues were used.

Use of retrieval strategies by children tends to parallel their use of other memory strategies. At 7 years of age, children seem to respond to a single cue associated with a recall item, whereas among children 10 years of age and older a cue activates an entire network of related concepts (Kail, 1990). For example, Ackerman (1988) found that 7-year-olds were more likely to recall a target word when three previously associated cue words were present than when only one of the key words was present. Recall of older children (10- to 18-year-olds) was very similar for both conditions. Kail (1990) suggests that this recall pattern resulted because young children search memory less extensively than older children. Also, recall for the younger group depended on the cue word directly retrieving the target word, thus, three words as cues increased the likelihood of this connection. For older children any of the three words was an effective cue because each activated the associative network in which the target word was imbedded.

Of course, a child's knowledge base cannot be separated from strategy use, because they are interactive (Chi & Ceci, 1987). The implication of this relationship is that a child may use an appropriate retrieval strategy but if his or her knowledge base is limited, poor memory performance will result (Kail, 1990).

Individual Differences

In their review of the literature, Glover and Corkill (1990) cite three possible sources for individual differences based on studies reported by Hunt (e.g., Hunt, 1978, 1988): (1) differences in a child's knowledge base as well as differences in the information-processing components, such as capacity and duration of the various memory stores; (2) long-term memory access and search speed; and (3) differences in the strategies that children possess. The comparison groups in which these differences have been found are usually developmentally delayed and normal children. The findings indicate differences in the duration of the visual store of the sensory registers; differences in working memory, such as speed of processing and capacity; and ease of access to long-term memory.

Educational Implications

Some of the applications that follow are adapted from the instructional implications suggested by Glover and Corkill (1990). To ensure that assignments given to students are properly spaced and make reasonable attentional demands, teachers need to consider students' attentional capacities and their ability to engage in automatization. Use of advance organizers and questions should facilitate encoding of material by students. Pacing and

spacing the presentation of instructional materials can enhance children's later recall of this information. Similarly, self-generation has been shown to be an exceptionally effective study strategy for mastering information in such subject areas as reading and spelling, where children are urged to generate major points from the reading or spelling words, instead of reading the material over a number of times (Glover & Corkill, 1990).

Organization in memory as well as retrieval, and to an extent, encoding, will be influenced by a child's knowledge about the way in which his or her memory works (i.e., metamemory). Children as young as 6 years of age know that familiar material can be remembered more easily, but it is not until 10 to 11 years of age that children understand the effect of immediate memory span on their ability to be able to recall varying numbers of items. Children below 9 to 10 years of age do not understand the usefulness of semantic relations in remembering word lists. When students do not spontaneously use organization, they benefit from material that is organized for them by the teacher.

Principles of encoding and retrieval apply directly to teacher-constructed tests. Effective test items need to provide cues that were present during encoding as well as fit the knowledge base of the child, represent a meaningful problem, and reflect the context in which the material was presented. Some understanding of the difference between recognition and recall tests seems to emerge around 6 years of age, but children do not know why recognition is easier. It is not until 10 years of age that children realize whether it would be easier to recall information verbatim or in paraphrase.

Associated with testing is the need to reduce forgetting. Ellis and Hunt (1989) suggest several practices that ought to enhance retention.

1. Pay attention in class. Concentrate on what the teacher is saying or what is being read.
2. Organize the material that is presented verbally as well as that presented in written form.
3. Use elaboration by relating new material to

other material to be learned as well as to what is already known. Make the material to be learned as distinctive as possible.

4. Concentrate on principles of retrieval. Develop good retrieval cues during study of the material.

5. Practice retrieval. Practicing retrieval will enhance retention more than additional study time.

These practices can help any student improve classroom performance, and for that reason, these study skills ought to be an integral part of classroom learning.

Memory Monitoring

The interaction of memory variables, such as difficulty and amount to remember, does not seem to be understood until adolescence (Kail, 1990). Judging when one has learned material so that it can be recalled (i.e., memory monitoring) is present to some extent in 6-year-olds and gradually improves through adolescence. Pressley, Levin, Ghatala, and Ahmad (1987) found that 10-year-olds' estimates of the number of words from a 30-word list that they could recall was more accurate than the judgments made by 7-year-olds.

Allocation of study time according to the difficulty of the task is another monitoring function that improves with age. Research (e.g., Dufresne & Kobasigawa, 1989) indicates that 10- and 12-year-olds understand the need to allocate more study time to difficult materials. This knowledge is not present at 6 years of age, and is just beginning to appear at 8 to 10 years of age.

COGNITIVE STRATEGIES

Strategies commonly refer to a plan or method for achieving a goal, most often directed toward enhancing one's academic performance. Cognitive strategies include such methods or techniques as rehearsal and organization in a memory task, or drafting and revising in a writing task. Metacognitive strategies are processes such as knowing when and where to use strategies, how

to engage a strategy, and how to select the appropriate strategy. All of these metacognitive processes require an understanding of strategies. Three prominent issues discussed in the literature on cognitive strategies are those relating to components of strategy use, individual differences in strategy use, and cognitive strategy instruction.

Components of Strategy Use

One of the most popular strategy models is Pressley's Good Strategy User Model (e.g., Pressley, 1986; Pressley, Borokowski, & Schneider, 1987). The components of this model include various cognitive strategies (task limited, goal limited, and general), metacognitive strategies, a knowledge base, and motivational beliefs and cognitive style (Symons, Snyder, Cariglia-Bull, & Pressley, 1989).

Individuals who are competent in information processing use task-limited strategies for enhancing performance on a specific task, such as remembering a collection of objects by using the first letter of each object to form a mnemonic. This strategy may be used across domains. Goal-limited strategies are used to reach specific objectives, such as using estimation in mathematics problem solving. Attention allocation, performance monitoring, and strategy modification are considered general strategies. *Metacognition* refers to the information held by the student about each strategy, particularly details about the appropriateness, usefulness, and timing for implementing the strategy (Symons et al., 1989).

Knowledge base, a central component in children's memory performance, also influences strategy use. Some strategies require an understanding of basic facts before the strategy can be implemented. At other times, knowledge of certain facts or other information negates the use of a strategy (Symons et al., 1989). Beliefs about self-efficacy influence the likelihood that strategies are used. This motivational factor is associated with cognitive style (i.e., the manner in which a student approaches a cognitive task) because self-efficacy modulates how the student thinks about the task (Symons et al., 1989).

Individual Differences in Strategy Use

This issue has focused on the comparison of skilled learners and learning-disabled (LD) children, although it is recognized that differences exist within the LD population. Some LD children may have structural deficits in memory, but the majority do not. Rather, most LD students do not process information strategically, and therefore they fail to use their memory capacity effectively (Short & Weissberg-Benchell, 1989).

Deficiencies in the use of cognitive strategies by LD students is only one aspect of their information-processing deficit. Students who are learning disabled are deficient in metacognitive strategies and motivational style. That is, LD students lack knowledge about how their information-processing system works and how strategies could increase performance. They are less able to monitor and evaluate their academic performance on a daily basis, and therefore they cannot make appropriate adjustments (Short & Weissberg-Benchell, 1989). When motivational factors are considered, LD students are often described as displaying "lack of effort, lack of persistence, . . . and task avoidance" (Short & Weissberg-Benchell, 1989, p. 45). In some respects, LD children resemble low-achieving students. Improving academic performance in this type of student will require training in metacognitive strategies and modifying motivational attributes in addition to teaching cognitive strategies.

Cognitive Strategy Instruction

Although strategy instruction is a popular educational research topic, strategy training is not commonly found in school curricula, according to Snyder and Pressley (1990). They surmise that this situation has occurred because teachers and others find it difficult at times to comprehend and integrate the instructional components. The major question confronting strategy instruction is how to identify those teaching methods that promote self-regulation so that the student engages strategies in a learning situation without prompts.

Several instructional models have been advanced, but they all share certain similarities according to Snyder and Pressley (1990). The common features are:

1. Instruction should include the most effective strategies for the task. This instruction needs to stress teaching a few strategies competently before adding new ones.
2. Student monitoring of strategy use must be part of the instructional program. This monitoring should include modification of strategies when problems arise.
3. Metacognitive information has to be a component of strategy instruction because this information tells students when and where to apply strategies.
4. The usefulness of strategies and their role in enhancing performance as compared to effort and ability should be explained.
5. The cognitive style adopted by the student should fit strategy use, and strategy instruction ought to encourage a compatible cognitive style.
6. Strategy instruction will be most influential when it is integrated into the entire curriculum that the student experiences.
7. An interaction between strategies and the student's knowledge base is necessary for successful academic performance. Therefore, instruction will have to focus on increasing student knowledge as well as adding to the student's repository of strategies.
8. The recommended form of instruction incorporates direct explanation of strategies and/ or modeling.

Evaluative feedback is provided to students as they practice strategies and are gradually given responsibility for strategy use. Encouraging students to apply strategies to other situations and prompting their use in different situations can facilitate generalization.

Each of the features of strategy instruction could be viewed as an intervention component for the school psychologist when confronted with learning problems experienced by students who seem to have the requisite cognitive ability. A general model for this type of strategy instruction proposed by Snyder and Pressley (1990) is presented in Figure 4.4. The components in this model are based on research in which methods of strategy instruction have been examined.

Peterson and Swing (1983) contend that four factors of individual differences ought to be considered when implementing strategy instruction in the classroom. Age of the student will influence training because younger children have difficulty in learning to use strategies, therefore they will require more training. Low-ability students seem to obtain greater benefits from strategy instruction than high-ability students because the

---

Teach a few strategies at a time, intensively and extensively, as part of the ongoing curriculum.

Model and explain new strategies.

Model again and re-explain strategies in ways that are sensitive to aspects of strategy use that are not well understood.

Explain to student where and when to use strategies.

Provide plenty of practice, using strategies for as many appropriate tasks as possible.

Encourage students to monitor how they are doing when they are using strategies.

Encourage continued use of and generalization of strategies.

Increase students' motivation to use strategies by heightening student awareness that they are acquiring valuable skills that are at the heart of competent functioning.

Emphasize reflective processing rather than speedy processing; do all possible to eliminate high anxiety in students; encourage students to shield themselves from distraction so they can attend to academic tasks.

FIGURE 4.4   General model for strategy instruction

Source: Pressley, M., & associates (1990). *Cognitive strategy instruction that really improves children's academic performance* (p. 18). Cambridge, MA: Brookline Books. Reprinted with permission.

latter group may already be using strategies. A third factor is prior knowledge. Without adequate verbal information and skills (or, in the case of mathematics, arithmetic skills), the student will not be able to use certain strategies. Lack of needed metacognitive knowledge will also limit strategy utilization. Selection of appropriate strategies and monitoring and evaluating their use are examples of metacognition that are necessary for strategy use.

Research on Strategy Use

Representative of research on strategy use is a classroom study of reading strategies cited by Duffy and Roehler (1989), in which those students who received explanations of reading skills as strategies and metacognitive information showed significant improvement in reading achievement. These direct-explanation students were more aware that reading involved strategy selection, processing of information, and self-direction. Palincsar (1987) found that students who were given responsibility for use of reading strategies, after receiving training and prompting by teachers, scored higher on measures of reading, as compared to children who did not receive strategy training.

Some of the most relevant information for school psychologists are the major findings from experimental studies across several areas reported by Symons and colleagues (1989).

1. One cannot generalize results from research on a specific strategy to some other strategy. Their developmental functions may be very different.
2. Strategy effects seem to be very specific in that there are probably many strategies rather than a few major ones that we might have expected from the research on children's memory (e.g., Kail, 1990). A strategy may influence one type of learning but not another.
3. Direct instruction of strategies as to time and context of their application can be incorpo-

rated into the instructional format, but the effectiveness of this instruction will vary among children.

4. Although young children are not effective monitors and are difficult to train to monitor, second-grade children can be trained to monitor strategy effectiveness, and this monitoring continues after the training has stopped (Ghatala, Levin, & Pressley, 1985).

Teaching children to use appropriate strategies does not guarantee that children will transfer this knowledge to other learning tasks. In one study, even fifth- and sixth-graders needed to be told that a mnemonic was appropriate for a new task (O'Sullivan & Pressley, 1984). Children need information about why strategies are effective and about their various uses so that they can make decisions about when strategy use would be effective, as well as when it would be ineffective, in a learning task (Kail, 1990; Pressley, Borkowski, & O'Sullivan, 1984).

Pressley, Levin, and Ghatala (1984) reported that children in grades 5 to 7 realized that associative elaboration was a more effective strategy for vocabulary learning than repetition with meanings, but experience in practice tests alone was not adequate. These children also needed explicit feedback on their performance from teachers. Methods for teaching strategies have been compared by Pressley, Snyder, and Cariglia-Bull (1987). Their analyses of strategies, ranging from discovery learning to direct explanation and modeling by teachers, with subsequent practice by students, showed that student understanding of strategies was highest in the direct teaching condition.

Several issues emerge when investigating strategy effectiveness: continued interaction between teacher and student, difficulty in controlling nuisance variables that may affect strategy use, and the short-term memory capacity problem arising from trying to process information in the classroom while simultaneously attempting to execute needed strategies (Symons et al., 1989).

Zone of Proximal Development

Belmont (1989) takes the position that strategy instruction ought to be the fundamental approach used to facilitate children's learning. His argument is based largely on the findings from the research on training children to use cognitive strategies as well as the work of Vygotsky and his ZPD (zone of proximal development) measure of learning potential. This is the child's present level of problem solving when working independently, and the higher level of responsibility attained by the child through acceptance of assistance from the teacher (Belmont, 1989). According to Belmont's interpretation of Vygotsky, "The child does not 'have' ZPD but, rather, 'shares' one with an instructor" (Belmont, 1989, p. 145), and it is specific to each domain.

Strategies can be transmitted from teacher to student by transferring responsibility for reaching the learning goal. This transfer takes place in the zone of proximal development. To achieve this transfer, according to Belmont, the teacher starts from that upper portion of the zone where the child can problem solve only with the aid of the teacher. With continued assistance and support from the teacher, as well as practice, the child should be able to automatize the chain of behaviors necessary for skill acquisition. Transfer of responsibility for performance takes place at this time, with the teacher gradually removing the prompts. The skill that results provides a base for a new ZPD. According to Vygotsky, "All uniquely human learning occurs as a transfer of responsibility" (Belmont, 1989, p. 145).

Our understanding of the problems associated with teaching strategies and their transfer is embellished by this explanation of ZPD. According to the zone of proximal development, children who are taught strategies but do not use them in appropriate settings without prompts were instructed in their use at the upper end of the child's zone (the child was not ready to use the strategy). The child who uses the strategy but fails to generalize it to other situations was apparently taught the strategy at the child's middle zone (the child is transitional with respect to strategy use). Those children who use the strategy and generalize appropriately were instructed at the lower end of their zone at a point where they were likely to use the strategy within a short time (Belmont, 1989).

If we apply this explanation to the teaching of mnemonics and other strategies, those children who failed to generalize the mnemonic were taught the memory aid at a ZPD well above their present developmental level. To support this explanation, Belmont cites an intervention study by Palincsar and Brown (1984) where they attempted to teach seventh-grade students, whose reading comprehension scores were more than two years below grade level, strategies for reading comprehension. They utilized principles that fit Vygotsky's instructional approach and the concept of ZPD. Those students who received instruction based on this approach showed an average reading score gain of 15 months after a training period of approximately 3 months. The lesson for the school psychologist and the teacher is that for any type of intervention to be successful and to generalize, it must be taught at the child's zone level where it might be expected to appear without instruction in the near future.

Curriculum Area Strategies

Pressley and associates (1990) describe strategies within several curriculum areas that elementary classroom teachers could use in a strategy instruction program. These strategies provide the school psychologist with another intervention tool when working with teachers on learning-deficit problems in children. Strategies for reading and mathematics have been selected to illustrate the types of strategies that can be used. A more detailed discussion of various curriculum strategies can be found in Pressley and associates (1990).

Reading Strategies
Decoding strategies focus on discriminating and identifying letters and clusters of letters, and how symbols are associated with sounds. Some strate-

gies suggested by Cariglia-Bull and Pressley (1990) are: (1) repeated readings where students read short selections until they achieve an acceptable level of fluency; (2) computer programs, such as Construct-a-Word, where students build words from strings of letters; (3) Integrated Picture Training, which uses pictures to teach letter-sound relations; and (4) Sound Categorization Training, which emphasizes categorizing words on the basis of sounds. However, decoding may not improve comprehension.

Comprehension strategies described by Symons, McGoldrick, Snyder, and Pressley (1990) offer these techniques: (1) summarization of the selected reading; (2) mental imagery in which the child is instructed to create images of what is read; (3) question generation where students are asked to think of questions that integrate the material that has been read; (4) question-answering strategies; (5) story grammar that focuses on the structure of the story; and (6) activating prior knowledge, which directs the reader to interpret the information using the experiences that have been encountered previously.

Mathematics Strategies
The first requirement is basic knowledge of arithmetic facts and operations. Among the strategies advanced by Burkell, Schneider, and Pressley (1990) are: reading the problem aloud, paraphrasing the problem, designating important information, drawing a diagram, checking work, and estimating an answer. These strategies fit well with the understanding, forming a plan, and looking back stages of problem solving. Burkell, Schneider, and Pressley conclude that strategy instruction increases performance on arithmetic tasks and problem solving, but some students will reap greater benefits than others because individual differences are always present.

Cognitive Strategies and Intervention

Weinstein and McDonald (1986) argue that knowledge of learning strategies are necessary because they can be used as a base for intervention programs. They define learning strategies as "any cognitive, affective or behavioral activity that facilitates encoding, storing, retrieving, or using knowledge" (p. 257). The learning strategies identified by Weinstein and McDonald as useful for the school psychologist consist of the following.

Knowledge acquisition strategies are methods for organizing and enhancing input to increase its meaning. They are used to associate present knowledge with incoming information. We know through experience that learning new information in an area where we have some familiarity will be easier than if the area is unfamiliar. A second knowledge acquisition strategy is elaboration, which enhances learning by attaching explicit information to the incoming information that we need to remember. Mnemonic devices function in a similar way when we are confronted with the task of remembering information that is unfamiliar. They enable us to find a way of making the information memorable, such as forming a nonsense word by using the first letters of words that we need to remember, but they do not make information more understandable.

How might the school psychologist use this type of strategy? Weinstein and McDonald (1986) suggest that children can be taught knowledge acquisition strategies to use with certain school tasks. For example, children can be taught mnemonic strategies to use in remembering sets of facts from reading or science. The child can be taught the use of analogies to understand science concepts. The key to ensuring effectiveness of the strategy intervention is to be familiar with the child's past history so that strategies that are meaningful to the child can be constructed. This strategy intervention then can be transferred to the teacher so that it will generalize to the classroom if the procedure is shown to be effective.

A second type of learning strategy is *comprehension monitoring,* which involves recognizing the attainment of learning objectives and the occurrence of comprehension. This type of knowing incorporates what Flavell (1985) has labeled metacognition or "knowing about knowing." Without this strategy knowledge, the child cannot

recognize or correct his or her failures in learning. Selection of remedial strategies for comprehension failure are also included in comprehension monitoring strategies. These include such techniques as the use of self-testing to determine reading comprehension and recall readiness, an inquiry approach to studying new material, class recitation, and homework problems.

The school psychologist can assess the use of comprehension monitoring in several ways. Weinstein and McDonald (1986) recommend asking the child about the schemes he or she uses when confronted with unfamiliar material or difficult tasks. Another method is to ask teachers about their observations of the child's use of strategies, and for reports on children's requests for help or further instructions on assignments. Various tests of self-monitoring could be used, such as asking the child to report on problems he or she detects when reading a test passage or working on problems that contain systematic errors.

Active study, another type of learning strategy, includes both knowledge acquisition and comprehension monitoring. Weinstein and McDonald (1986) use the term *active* to distinguish this category of strategy from the study skills, which emphasize procedures without considering how organizing, elaboration, and memory monitoring interact with study habits. Thus, study skills often emphasize such procedures as note taking and highlighting reading passages without stressing the need to input the information into organized networks of information that can be retrieved easily upon demand.

Integration of knowledge acquisition and comprehension strategies into the child's existing system of study skills will be needed for those children experiencing learning problems if they are to experience success in classroom measures of performance. This integration illustrates the complexity of academic difficulties involved when children experience failure in academic settings. Successful intervention requires a training program that contains strategy acquisition in addition to improving study skills.

The fourth category of learning skills is *sup-*

port strategies, including such techniques as coping with frustration and anxiety, time on task, selective attention, and classroom habits such as recording assignments, noting due dates for turning in assignments, and exam dates. One common source of learning and performance decrement identified by Weinstein and McDonald (1986) is anxiety. They attribute anxiety to maladaptive attention where the child focuses on fear of failure and perceived incompetencies rather than focusing on the academic tasks at hand, specifically information acquisition and study time.

Several techniques can be used with the child to redirect attention to the required task. These techniques include teaching students to monitor their thoughts during study periods or exam taking so that they can become aware when their cognitions are interfering with performance. This awareness will enable them to take the necessary corrective action by redirecting their attention to the demands of the task. Weinstein and McDonald recommend teaching students to "self coach"; that is, talk to themselves silently during their study periods, homework assignments, or test taking, and thereby providing reassurance that they can understand the material or that they can answer the questions if they try. The learning strategies approach is but one model of learning, but it serves to illustrate the utility of a learning approach to assessment and intervention, two of the major roles played by the school psychologist.

Transfer of Training

Transfer can be defined as the process by which previously learned responses occur in new situations. What factors seem to determine whether a child will transfer a previously learned response? Campione and Brown (1974) conducted a series of studies with children in kindergarten through fifth grade. Their findings enlighten us on several matters. First, there were no age differences in the children's ability to transfer learning in a discrimination task. When the transfer task used stimuli similar to those involved in training, transfer occurred. Further, transfer was found even when the task format changed if the training and transfer stimuli were the same, which highlights the importance of the context in which learning occurs.

According to Campione and Brown (1974), when a child is faced with a task, he or she retrieves a strategy that was learned in a similar task, and the success of this strategy selection will be contingent on the variety of situations in which training occurred. Positive transfer occurs in a variety of learning tasks. Transfer of motor skill learning has been reported in numerous studies, but the amount of this transfer depends on the similarity of the two tasks. Positive transfer seems to result when the two tasks require similar movements in similar situations, whereas negative transfer occurs when the task demands are in opposition to each other, such as pushing and pulling (Mazur, 1990).

Current research has focused on the differences in cognitive skills of those individuals who demonstrate transfer and those who do not (Gage & Berliner, 1988). One group of individual differences factors that has been examined is metacognitive skills, specifically those related to regulation of cognitions, such as self-monitoring, testing, evaluating, and self-regulation. Evidence indicates that these metacognitive skills will show improvement and transfer if they are taught to students (Belmont, Butterfield, & Ferretti, 1982).

The effect of teaching, in part, may be to correct a mediational deficiency of not using these skills. That is, teaching metacognitive skills serves a prompting function. Students have various memory strategies that are not activated because their knowledge of when, where, and how to use them is deficient (Borkowski, 1985). Children's achievement goals also seem to influence transfer. Farrell and Dweck, as cited in Dweck (1986), reported that children who had learning goals (seeking to understand or master material) demonstrated significantly greater transfer in a science class than those children who set performance goals (seeking a favorable evaluation of competence).

According to Gage and Berliner (1988),

teaching for transfer can occur in two ways. The objective in *substantive transfer* is to teach the content that you want the child to learn. But this type of teaching transfers only to other similar content areas. Teaching children specific problem-solving skills would be expected to transfer only to problems similar to those used in the teaching. In *procedural transfer,* the teaching objective is to provide broad training of various concepts, rules, and procedures. For example, teaching children how to represent a problem pictorially should transfer to several learning tasks, including solving story problems in math. The key to facilitating transfer is to teach general strategies and to have students practice. Note the similarity to problem-solving situations, which Campione and Brown (1974) claim are transfer tasks.

MOTIVATION

The motivational component in Ford's (1987) version of systems theory consists of a pattern of directive, arousal, and regulatory functions. It is assumed that individuals construct goals, purposes, or intentions that are used to produce some desired state or condition. That is, people are committed to pursuing goals or incentives.

To many of us, motivation is associated with such terms as *incentives, aspirations, goals, expectancies, performance,* and *effort.* These terms suggest that personal factors as well as environmental factors are components of motivation, a view consonant with Bandura's (1986) reciprocal determinism. Motivation is assumed to be a central factor in our behavior, and its role in education is paramount because achievement and performance are motivational correlates. The estimated mean correlation between various motivational measures and academic achievement is approximately .34, based on Uguroglu and Walberg's (1979) investigation. As further evidence for the assumed correlation between motivation and achievement, the relationship between time spent on a particular task and the motivational strength for that task is linear (Atkinson, 1980).

Motivation as a concept has made a major contribution to education by providing a mechanism for explaining differences in scholastic achievement in addition to those attributable to intelligence or aptitude. Intelligence, as typically assessed, and GPA correlate about .45, therefore we ought to find students who are high achievers (i.e., overachievers) but have low ability, as well as the converse (i.e., underachievers). The correlation suggests a tendency for high achievers to have high ability, but it is obvious that some over- and underachievers are also found in this group. There are behavioral differences between the two groups, as suggested in the literature (e.g., Mitchell & Piatkowska, 1974). Among the characteristics associated with underachievement are inadequate study skills, low academic goals, low academic performance, and minimal attention to academic matters.

We now turn to a brief overview of some approaches to motivation, specifically achievement motivation (i.e., the goal to succeed at something). A more extensive review of the literature can be found in Dweck and Leggett (1988), and in the *Journal of Educational Psychology* (1990).

Attributional Approaches to Motivation

This approach focuses on the beliefs about success and failure that influence persistence on achievement tasks. Characteristic of this approach is Weiner's (1979) model that assumes changes in expectancy as a result of success and failure experiences. According to the expectancy model, the causes of success and failure consist of ability and effort, which are internal to the person, and task difficulty and luck, which are external factors. Further, ability and task difficulty are relatively stable factors, whereas luck is variable, and effort may be increased or decreased.

The causal attributions that are made based on these factors guide subsequent behavior. If an individual attributes failure to lack of ability, performance expectancies will decrease more rapidly than if failure is attributed to lack of effort. Studies using the expectancy model have consistently showed that expectancies predict task persistence and performance, particularly on difficult tasks and when the individual is being evaluated (Dweck & Elliott, 1983). The problem with the attributional approach is that it has focused on why individuals expect to be successful, but not on why they want to be successful (Dweck, 1986).

A further problem with the attributional approach is that both knowledge and appraisal are involved, according to Lazarus (1991), and both need to be considered. Lazarus (1991) defines the two constructs in the following way: *"Knowledge* consists of what a person believes about the way that the world works in general and in a specific context. . . . *Appraisal,* on the other hand, is an evaluation of knowledge about what is happening for our personal well-being" (p. 354). From Lazarus's perspective, appraisal is the core component. Knowledge about task difficulty and ability are not sufficient to determine what an individual will do in an achievement situation. We also need to know how important what occurs in the situation is to the individual.

Learned Helplessness
One explanation for individual differences in thought patterns associated with performance changes accompanying failure is learned helplessness. Children who perceive no association between effort and performance are likely to see failure as a consequence of ability over which they have no control. The impairment resulting from this attribution leads to further decrease in performance (see Diener & Dweck, 1978, 1980; Dweck & Reppucci, 1973). A frequent precursor to learned helplessness is negative feedback from parents and teachers. Girls are more likely than boys to display the learned helplessness characteristics of ability attribution and low expectancy of success, which translates to decreased task persistence and poor performance following failure. This effect seems to occur because girls receive feedback from adults that credits their effort when they succeed but faults their ability when they fail (Dweck, Davidson, Nelson, & Enna, 1978).

Locus of Control
An individual's beliefs about control of reinforcement form the basis for this construct. Belief by the individual that an event is contingent on personal behavior is *internal* control. Belief that the event occurred as the result of luck or fate is *external* control. This internal-external control construct proposed by Rotter (1966) is assumed to influence a broad spectrum of behavior. Data on academic achievement (e.g., Phares, 1976) show that children who accept responsibility for success and failure have significantly higher grades than those children who are more externally controlled. In general, locus of control seems to be a better predictor of school grades than standardized measures of achievement or achievement motivation.

Intrinsic versus Extrinsic Motivation

At issue is the relative effect of motivation without apparent reward compared to the presence of a reward. The controversy arose with a now classic study by Lepper, Greene, and Nisbett (1973), in which preschool children who were told they would be given a reward for participating in an activity later spent less time in this activity than those children who unexpectedly received an award or those who did not receive a reward. This effect, labeled the *overjustification hypothesis,* had an impact on schooling because it suggested that the use of external rewards for participating in school activities would transform these activities into tasks that had little or no appeal (Lepper & Greene, 1975).

Later studies (e.g., Lepper & Greene, 1978; Lepper, 1981) have clarified this initial effect, and suggest that it may be more restrictive than originally thought. Adult observation of the activity combined with an expected reward results in a later decrease in activity interest, but if the reward is contingent on superior performance of the task, the usual decrease in interest does not occur (Lepper, 1981). Extrinsic rewards have been found to exert other effects, such as selective avoidance of difficult tasks (Condry, 1977).

Lepper (1981) suggests that to interpret the

effects of intrinsic rewards, you have to consider their multiple functions of incentive, evaluation, and social control (e.g., if activity is extrinsically motivated, then it is only of interest when rewards are present). Finally, the effects of extrinsic rewards will be determined by the form of the reward and in part by the characteristics of the child. Verbal rewards, such as praise, seem to impair interest less than rewards such as grades (Pittman, Boggiano, & Ruble, 1982). For some children, a reward might increase their interest if it was initially low, whereas the highly interested child will show decreased interest.

Social-Cognitive Approaches

This approach focuses on cognitive mediators, specifically how children perceive, interpret, and process information about a situation. One of the advantages of this approach is that it permits an examination of different patterns of achievement motivation, defined as goals involving competence. These goals consist of two types: *learning goals,* which are directed toward increasing competence and mastery, and *performance goals,*

which focus on obtaining positive evaluations and avoiding negative evaluations of performance.

According to Dweck (e.g., Dweck, 1986; Dweck & Leggett, 1988), achievement situations permit the child to choose among goals. The goal selected is based on the child's theory of intelligence (beliefs about or understanding of intelligence), which then determines the achievement pattern that is enacted. Belief in intelligence as an unchangeable element (an entity theory of intelligence) focuses the child on obtaining positive evaluations on that element (i.e., performance goals). Belief in intelligence as a changeable element (an incremental theory of intelligence) focuses the child on further development of this element (i.e., learning or mastery goals). The relationship between achievement goals and achievement behavior is presented in Table 4.1.

The two goals elicit different behavior patterns, as can be seen in the table. What are some of the effects that different goal selection can have on achievement behavior? One possible effect is on task choice. Performance goals seem to negate the selection of a challenging task because they require high-ability evaluations by the child,

TABLE 4.1 Dweck's Model of Achievement Goals and Achievement Behavior

THEORY OF INTELLIGENCE	GOAL ORIENTATION	CONFIDENCE IN PRESENT ABILITY	BEHAVIOR PATTERN
Entity theory ⟶ (Intelligence is fixed)	**Performance goal** (Goal is to gain positive judgments/avoid negative judgments of competence)	**If high** ⟶ **but**	**Mastery-oriented** Seek challenge High persistence
		If low ⟶	**Helpless** Avoid challenge Low persistence
Incremental theory → (Intelligence is malleable)	**Learning goal** (Goal is to increase competence)	**If high** ⟶ **or** **low**	**Master-oriented** Seek challenge (that fosters learning) High persistence

Source: Dweck, C. S. (1986). Motivational processes affecting learning. *American Psychologist, 41,* 1040–1048. Copyright 1986 by the American Psychological Association. Reprinted by permission.

which must remain high before a challenging task will be chosen. Children who give low evaluations of their ability frequently choose easy tasks where they know that they will succeed, or very difficult tasks for which failure would not indicate low ability. Learning goals tend to result in children selecting challenging tasks that enhance learning, even in those cases of low-ability assessment (Dweck, 1986; Dweck & Leggett, 1988).

Selection of achievement goals also affects task persistence. Those children who select performance goals perceive failure as lack of ability. Because this failure is a stable outcome, they stop trying and fail when faced with an obstacle. Children who select learning goals increase their effort when faced with an obstacle or they try different strategies, which result in increased performance (Dweck, 1986; Dweck & Leggett, 1988). But this relationship posits a result that is somewhat counterintuitive. Dweck and Leggett (1988) report that performance-goal children, in contrast to learning-goal children, view excessive effort as denoting low ability; thus, high effort may be viewed negatively by the performance-goal child.

Whether a performance goal or a mastery goal is chosen also influences behavior. Performance goals direct the child to make ability evaluations that result in avoidance of challenging tasks and increase the likelihood that the child will adopt maladaptive behavior patterns. Focusing on learning or mastery goals promotes challenge seeking (Dweck & Leggett, 1988). Selection of a performance or mastery goal produces different affective reactions to positive and negative outcomes. When failure is experienced or excessive effort is required to achieve a performance goal, low ability is assumed. Performance goals are associated with anxiety, negative affect, task devaluing, and boredom. Learning goal selection is associated with greater effort in achieving mastery, which produces positive affect for success and the intrinsic rewards of pleasure or pride (Dweck & Leggett, 1988).

There is also some evidence that mastery or

learning-goal children are more likely to express intentions of seeking help with school work than those children who are low achievers and who know they need help (Newman, 1990; Newman & Goldin, 1990). Further, assistance is more likely to be sought from adults than from peers because of the perception that this request of peers would portray the child as "dumb" (Newman & Goldin, 1990).

According to Dweck (1986), high-achieving children probably associate difficulty in overcoming an obstacle to lack of ability, and thereby prevent poor performance. Bright girls particularly seem prone to avoiding challenge, holding low expectancies, and attributing failure to ability (see Licht & Dweck, 1984). Dweck (1986) argues that these competent girls are aware of their ability, but this awareness does not seem to provide them with sufficient confidence when they encounter difficult tasks. Given these findings, one is left with the conclusion that bright children can possess maladaptive motivational patterns that we have usually assigned to the low achiever (Dweck, 1986).

Data from several recently published studies on motivation provide additional insight on how cognitive mediators may influence motivation. There is some evidence that children who pursue learning goals, as compared to those who pursue performance goals, make greater use of cognitive strategies and metacognitive strategies that are necessary for achieving instructional objectives (Pintrich & DeGroot, 1990). Gifted students display higher self-efficacy and make greater use of metacognitive strategies than regular students (Zimmerman & Martinez-Pons, 1990). Conversely, students who have less experience with a specific task, and perhaps those who are poor learners, use very specific strategies.

Children who report that they do not know what strategies would be effective show performance deficits on academic tasks (Skinner, Wellborn, & Connell, 1990). Strategy use is correlated with expectancy (Pokay & Blumenfeld, 1990). Berndt and Miller (1990) note that students' expectancies and values (e.g., values attached to success; beliefs about the usefulness of school learning) were positively correlated. These findings suggest that a child's theory of intelligence not only affects the achievement goal that is selected but the strategy as well.

Training in Achievement Motivation

One approach to motivation training, modeled after the work of McClelland (1969), stresses the training of achievement motives through encouraging students to use achievement concepts in planning ways to improve their performance and to experiment with new methods of thinking and behaving. Another method, expounded by De-Charms (1976), is the origin-pawn program. This program, based on a locus of control approach, stresses taking personal responsibility for action by such means as realistic goal choice, selection of actions to achieve goals, and evaluation. Evaluations of motivation training programs indicate that changes can occur; that is, the achievement motive is not a fixed trait. Improvements in goal setting, reduction in fear of failure, improved regard for personal competence, and more positive attitudes toward school have resulted from training (Heckhausen, Schmalt, & Schneider, 1985).

A second approach to motivation training is attribution training. Using Dweck's (1986) distinction between performance and learning goals, it follows that training should focus on enhancing learning goal orientation rather than a reliance on performance. However, many educational programs seem to focus on reinforcing performance goals by ensuring success and dispensing praise (Dweck, 1986). This practice, according to Dweck, has emerged from the assumption that positive reinforcement will create the wanted behavior, but this is not necessarily the case. A second factor is the impact of teacher expectancy, which shows the impairment resulting from teachers' awareness that a child has low ability.

Training that emphasizes success experiences on easy tasks with little challenge, or on more difficult tasks emphasizing performance, does not foster the desired qualities of task per-

sistence, preference for more effortful tasks, or strengthened confidence (Dweck, 1975, 1978), and in some cases it may reduce confidence in ability (e.g., Meyer, 1982). A more productive approach, according to Dweck, is to use learning goal orientation and modify children's perceptions of failure by teaching the children to attribute failure to effort or strategy choice rather than ability. The effectiveness of this type of intervention has been demonstrated in several studies (e.g., Dweck, 1975), including those that use modeling of self-effort statements (e.g., Schunk, Hanson, & Cox, 1987).

Use of attributional training with learning-disabled (LD) students presents other problems. In their review of this literature, Kamphaus, Yarbrough, and Johanson (1990) note that LD students often experience failure, for which they are less likely to make effort attributions. Further, they may fault teachers for a negative attitude if the teacher reprimands them for off-task or disruptive behavior. The problem is that LD students appear to have these types of problems, but we do not know whether their failure attributions focus on external factors or ability. The findings from the research are inconclusive. According to Kamphaus, Yarbrough, and Johanson (1990), care should be exercised in designing intervention programs, and these programs need to consider sex of the child, difficulty of the task, various external influences, and the attributions that are made.

SUMMARY

Throughout this chapter we have emphasized that information exchange is a critical component within a developmental/social systems approach to the practice of psychology within the school. The preceding discussion has indicated how information can be used to organize and regulate behavior and to provide meaning to the events that are experienced. Although the environment exercises control over behavior, it is also the case that stimulus events are a source of information about the effect of behavior on the environment.

From the discussion on information processing, we are made more aware of the role of attention in the learning process, and the importance of teaching for encoding the necessary information to enable students to succeed academically. Organization of content and test construction designed to ensure that the cues associated with classroom learning are incorporated in the mode of performance evaluation are important applications for classroom instruction and transfer of training.

Most of the learning that is acquired by the student seems to be mediated by the use of appropriate cognitive and metacognitive strategies. Therefore, strategy instruction becomes an important remedial tool for the classroom teacher as well as an intervention procedure for the school psychologist when confronted with the problem of learning deficits in children. Performance monitoring becomes a critical component in this intervention. The zone of proximal development suggests when strategy instruction is most effective. Based on the strategy research, the locus of the deficit in children with learning problems and low achievement appear to be in their metacognition, specifically their lack of metacognitive strategies rather than an absence of strategies per se.

The mediational effect of personal goals and aspirations, which provides a directive function within a systems framework, was examined. The selection of performance goals versus learning or mastery goals based on a student's theory of intelligence was shown to have effects ranging from a willingness to select challenging tasks to performance appraisal to affect. The implication of goal selection for fostering and academic achievement have important relevance for the school psychologist.

Bardon (1989) has argued that learning is a major component of school psychology. Given the information that is available on how students process information and how strategies, motivation, and cognitive style factors modulate learning, Bardon's argument receives strong support.

REFERENCES

Ackerman, B. P. (1988). Search set access problems in retrieving episodic information from memory in children and adults. *Journal of Experimental Child Psychology, 45,* 234–261.

Ashcraft, M. H. (1988). *Human memory and cognition.* Glenview, IL: Scott, Foresman.

Atkinson, J. W. (1980). Motivational effects in so-called tests of ability and educational achievement. In L. J. Fyons Jr. (Ed.), *Achievement motivation* (pp. 9–21). New York: Plenum Press.

Baldwin, J. D., & Baldwin, J. I. (1986). *Behavior principles in everyday life* (2nd ed.). Englewood Cliffs, NJ: Prentice-Hall.

Ball, S., & Bogatz, G. A. (1972). Summative research of Sesame Street: Implications for the study of preschool children. In A. D. Pick (Ed.), *Minnesota symposia on child psychology* (Vol. 6, pp. 3–18). Minneapolis: University of Minnesota Press.

Ball, S., & Bogatz, G. A. (1973). *Reading with television: An evaluation of the Electric Company.* Princeton, NJ: Educational Testing Service.

Bandura, A. (1977). *Social learning theory.* Englewood Cliffs, NJ: Prentice-Hall.

Bandura, A. (1986). *Social foundations of thought and action.* Englewood Cliffs, NJ: Prentice-Hall.

Bandura, A., & McDonald, F. J. (1963). Influence of social reinforcement and the behavior of models in shaping children's moral judgments. *Journal of Abnormal and Social Psychology, 67,* 174–281.

Bardon, J. I. (1989). The school psychologist as an applied educational psychologist. In R. C. D'Amato & R. S. Dean (Eds.), *The school psychologist in nontraditional settings* (pp. 1–32). Hillsdale, NJ: Erlbaum.

Belmont, J. M. (1989). Cognitive strategies and strategic learning: The socio-instructional approach. *American Psychologist, 44,* 142–148.

Belmont, J. M., Butterfield, E. C., & Ferretti, R. P. (1982). To secure transfer of training instruct self-management skills. In D. K. Detterman & R. J. Sternberg (Eds.), *How and how much can intelligence be increased* (pp. 147–154). Norwood, NJ: Ablex.

Benjamin, L. T., Jr., Hopkins, J. R., & Nation, J. R. (1990). *Psychology* (2nd ed.). New York: Macmillan.

Berndt, T. J., & Miller, K. E. (1990). Expectancies, values, and achievement in junior high school. *Journal of Educational Psychology, 82,* 319–326.

Borkowski, J. G. (1985). Signs of intelligence: Strategy generalization and metacognition. In S. R. Yussen (Ed.), *The growth of reflection in children* (pp. 105–144). New York: Academic Press.

Burkell, J., Schneider, B., & Pressley, M. (1990). Mathematics. In M. Pressley & associates, *Cognitive strategy instruction that really improves academic performance* (pp. 147–178). Cambridge, MA: Brookline Books.

Campione, J. C., & Brown, A. L. (1974). The effects of contextual changes and degree of component mastery on transfer of training. In H. W. Reese (Ed.), *Advances in child development and behavior* (Vol. 9, pp. 70–114). New York: Academic Press.

Cariglia-Bull, T. & Pressley, M. (1990). Decoding. In M. Pressley & associates, *Cognitive strategy instruction that really improves academic performance* (pp. 27–44). Cambridge, MA: Brookline Books.

Chi, M. T. H. (1976). Short-term memory limitations in children: Capacity or processing deficits? *Memory and Cognition, 4,* 559–572.

Chi, M. T. H., & Ceci, S. J. (1987). Content knowledge: Its role, representation and restructuring in memory development. In H. W. Reese (Ed.), *Advances in child development and behavior* (Vol. 20, pp. 91–142). New York: Academic Press.

Condry, J. C. (1977). Enemies of exploration: Self-initiated versus other-initiated learning. *Journal of Personality and Social Psychology, 35,* 459–477.

Davidson, J. E., & Sternberg, R. J. (1984). The role of insight in intellectual giftedness. *Gifted Child Quarterly, 28,* 58–64.

DeCharms, R. (1976). *Enhancing motivation.* New York: Irvington Press/Wiley.

Diener, C. I., & Dweck, C. S. (1978). An analysis of learned helplessness: Continuous changes in performance, strategy, and achievement cognitions following failure. *Journal of Personality and Social Psychology, 36,* 451–462.

Diener, C. I., & Dweck, C. S. (1980). An analysis of learned helplessness: II. The processing of success. *Journal of Personality and Social Psychology, 39,* 940–952.

Dinnel, D., & Glover, J. A. (1985). Advance organizers: Encoding manipulations. *Journal of Educational Psychology, 77,* 514–521.

Duffy, G. G., & Roehler, L. R. (1989). Why strategy instruction is so difficult and what we can do about it. In C. B. McCormick, G. E. Miller, & M. Pressley (Eds.), *Cognitive strategy research: From basic research to educational applications* (pp. 133–156). New York: Springer-Verlag.

Dufresne, A., & Kobasigawa, A. (1989). Children's spontaneous allocation of study time: Differential and sufficient aspects. *Journal of Experimental Child Psychology, 47,* 274–296.

Dugas, J. L., & Kellas, G. (1974). Encoding and retrieval processes in normal children and retarded adolescents. *Journal of Experimental Child Psychology, 17,* 177–185.

Dweck, C. S. (1975). The role of expectations and attributions in the alleviation of learned helplessness. *Journal of Personality and Social Psychology, 31,* 674–685.

Dweck, C. S. (1978). Achievement. In M. L. Lamb (Ed.), *Social and personality development* (pp. 114–130). New York: Holt, Rinehart, & Winston.

Dweck, C. S. (1986). Motivational processes affecting learning. *American Psychologist, 41,* 1040–1048.

Dweck, C. S., Davidson, W., Nelson, S., & Enna, B. (1978). Sex differences in learned helplessness II: The contingencies of evaluative feedback in the classroom and III: An experimental analysis. *Developmental Psychology, 14,* 268–276.

Dweck, C. S., & Elliott, E. S. (1983). Achievement motivation. In E. M. Hetherington (Ed.), *Handbook of child psychology* (Vol. 4, pp. 643–691). New York: Wiley.

Dweck, C. S., & Leggett, E. L. (1988). A social-cognitive approach to motivation and personality. *Psychological Review, 95,* 256–273.

Dweck, C. S., & Reppucci, N. D. (1973). Learned helplessness and reinforcement responsibility in children. *Journal of Personality and Social Psychology, 25,* 109–116.

Ellis, H. C., & Hunt, R. R. (1989). *Fundamentals of human memory and cognition* (4th ed.). Dubuque, IA: William C. Brown.

Flavell, J. H. (1985). *Cognitive development.* Englewood Cliffs, NJ: Prentice-Hall.

Ford, D. H. (1987). *Humans as self-constructing living systems.* Hillsdale, NJ: Erlbaum.

Gage, N. L., & Berliner, D. C. (1988). *Educational psychology* (4th ed.). Boston: Houghton Mifflin.

Gagne, E. (1985). *The cognitive psychology of school learning.* Boston: Little, Brown.

Ghatala, E. S., Levin, J. R., & Pressley, M. (1985). Training cognitive strategy-monitoring in children. *American Educational Research Journal, 22,* 199–215.

Glover, J. A., & Corkill, A. J. (1990). The implications of cognitive psychology for school psychology. In T. B. Gutkin & C. R. Reynolds (Eds.), *The handbook of school psychology* (2nd ed., pp. 104–125). New York: Wiley.

Grusec, J. E., & Lytton, H. (1988). *Social development: History, theory, and research.* New York: Springer-Verlag.

Guttentag, R. E. (1984). The mental effort requirement of cumulative rehearsal: A developmental study. *Journal of Experimental Child Psychology, 37,* 92–106.

Hagen, J. W., Jongeward, R. H., & Kail, R. V., Jr. (1975). Cognitive perspectives on the development of memory. In H. W. Reese (Ed.), *Advances in child development and behavior* (Vol. 10, pp. 57–101). New York: Academic Press.

Hamaker, C. (1986). The effects of adjunct questions on prose learning. *Review of Educational Research, 56,* 212–242.

Heckhausen, H., Schmalt, H-D, & Schneider, K. (1985). *Achievement motivation in perspective.* Orlando, FL: Academic Press.

Huesman, L. R., Eron, L. D., Klein, R., Brice, P., & Fischer, P. (1983). Mitigating the imitation of aggressive behaviors by changing children's attitudes about media violence. *Journal of Personality and Social Psychology, 44,* 899–910.

Hunt, E. (1978). Mechanics of verbal ability. *Psychological Review, 85,* 109–130.

Hunt, E. (1988). Science, technology, and intelligence. In R. R. Ronning, J. A. Glover, & J. Conoley (Eds.), *Cognitive psychology and measurement* (pp. 223–256). Hillsdale, NJ: Erlbaum.

Israely, Y., & Guttman, J. (1983). Children's sharing behavior as a function of exposure to puppet-show and story models. *Journal of Genetic Psychology, 142,* 311–312.

Kail, R. (1990). *The development of memory in children* (3rd ed.). New York: Freeman.

Kamphaus, R. W., Yarbrough, N. D., & Johanson, R. P. (1990). Contributions of instructional psychology to school psychology. In T. R. Gutkin & C. R. Reynolds (Eds.), *The handbook of school psychology* (2nd ed., pp. 143–174). New York: Wiley.

Kee, D. W., & Davies, L. (1988). Mental effort and elaboration: A developmental analysis. *Contemporary Educational Psychology, 13,* 221–228.

Keeney, T. J., Cannizzo, S. R., & Flavell, J. H. (1967). Spontaneous and induced verbal rehearsal in a recall task. *Child Development, 38,* 953–966.

LaVoie, J. C. (1974). Cognitive determinants of resistance to deviation in seven-, nine-, and eleven-year-old children of low and high maturity of moral judgment. *Developmental Psychology, 10,* 393–403.

Lazarus, R. S. (1991). Cognition and motivation in emotion. *American Psychologist, 46,* 352–367.

Lefkowitz, M., Blake, R. R., & Mouton, J. J. (1955). Status factors in pedestrian violations of traffic signals. *Journal of Abnormal and Social Psychology, 51,* 704–706.

Leon, M. (1984). Rules mothers and sons use to integrate intent and damage information in their moral judgments. *Child Development, 55,* 2106–2113.

Lepper, M. R. (1981). Intrinsic and extrinsic motivation in children: Detrimental effects of superfluous social controls. In W. A. Collins (Ed.), *Minnesota symposia on child psychology* (Vol. 14, pp. 155–214). Hillsdale, NJ: Erlbaum.

Lepper, M. R., & Greene, D. (1975). Turning play into work: Effects of adult surveillance and extrinsic rewards on children's intrinsic motivation. *Journal of Personality and Social Psychology, 31,* 479–486.

Lepper, M. R., & Greene, D. (1978). *The hidden cost of reward.* Hillsdale, NJ: Erlbaum.

Lepper, M. R., Greene, D., & Nisbett, R. E. (1973). Undermining children's intrinsic interest with extrinsic rewards: A test of the "overjustification hypothesis." *Journal of Personality and Social Psychology, 28,* 129–137.

Licht, B. G., & Dweck, C. S. (1984). Determinants of

academic achievement: The interaction of children's achievement orientations with skill area. *Developmental Psychology, 20,* 628–636.

Marr, D. B., & Sternberg, R. J. (1986). Analogical reasoning with novel concepts: Differential attention of intellectually gifted and non-gifted children to relevant and irrelevant stimuli. *Cognitive Development, 1,* 53–72.

Mazur, J. E. (1990). *Learning and behavior* (2nd ed.). Englewood Cliffs, NJ: Prentice-Hall.

McClelland, D. C. (1969). The role of educational technology in developing achievement motivation. *Educational technology, 9,* 7–16.

Meyer, W. U. (1982). Indirect communication about perceived ability estimates. *Journal of Educational Psychology, 74,* 888–897.

Miller, P. H. (1989). *Theories of developmental psychology* (2nd ed.). New York: Freeman.

Mitchell, R. R., & Piatkowska, O. E. (1974). Characteristics associated with underachievement: Targets for treatment. *Australian Psychologist, 21,* 55–73.

Moely, B. F., Olson, F. A., Halwes, T. G., & Flavell, J. H.(1969). Production deficiency in young children's clustered recall. *Developmental Psychology, 1,* 26–34.

Mosk, M. D., & Bucher, B. (1984). Prompting and stimulus shaping procedures for teaching visual motor skills to retarded children. *Journal of Applied Behavior Analysis, 17,* 23–34.

Newman, R. S. (1990). Children's help-seeking in the classroom: The role of motivational factors and attitudes. *Journal of Educational Psychology, 82,* 71–80.

Newman, R. S., & Goldin, L. (1990). Children's reluctance to seek help with schoolwork. *Journal of Educational Psychology, 82,* 92–100.

O'Sullivan, J. T., & Pressley, M. (1984). Completeness of instruction and strategy transfer. *Journal of Experimental Child Psychology, 38,* 275–288.

Palinscar, A. S. (1987). *An apprenticeship approach to the instruction of comprehension skill.* Paper presented at the annual meeting of the American Educational Association, Washington, DC.

Palinscar, A. S., & Brown, A. L. (1984). Reciprocal teaching of comprehension-fostering and comprehension-monitoring activities. *Cognition and Instruction, 1,* 117–175.

Paris, S. G. (1978). Coordination of means and goals

in the development of mnemonic skills. In P. A. Ornstein (Ed.), *Memory development in children* (pp. 129–156). Hillsdale, NJ: Erlbaum.

Parke, R. D., & Slaby, R. G. (1983). The development of aggression. In E. M. Hetherington (Ed.), *Handbook of child psychology* (4th ed., Vol. 4, pp. 547–641). New York: Wiley.

Perry, D. G., & Bussey, K. (1984). *Social development.* Englewood Cliffs, NJ: Prentice-Hall.

Peterson, P. L., & Swing, S. R. (1983). Problems in classroom implementation of cognitive strategy instruction. In M. Pressley & J. R. Levin (Eds.), *Cognitive strategy research: Educational applications* (pp. 267–287). New York: Springer-Verlag.

Phares, E. J. (1976). *Locus of control in personality.* Morristown, NJ: General Learning Press.

Pintrich, P. R., & DeGroot, E. V. (1990). Motivational and self-regulated learning components of classroom academic performance. *Journal of Educational Psychology, 82,* 33–40.

Pittman, T. S., Boggiano, A. K., & Ruble, D. N. (1982). Intrinsic and extrinsic motivational orientations: Interactive effects of reward competence, feedback, and task complexity. In J. M. Levine & W. C. Wang (Eds.), *Teacher and student perceptions.* Hillsdale, NJ: Erlbaum.

Pokay, P., & Blumenfeld, P. C. (1990). Predicting achievement early and late in the semester: The role of motivation and use of learning strategies. *Journal of Educational Psychology, 82,* 41–50.

Posner, M. I., & Snyder, C. R. R. (1975). Facilitation and inhibition in the processing of signals. In M. A. Rabbitt & S. Dornic (Eds.), *Attention and Performance* (pp. 669–682). New York: Academic Press.

Pressley, M. (1986). The relevance of the good strategy user model to the teaching of mathematics. *Educational Psychologist, 21,* 139–161.

Pressley, M., & associates (1990). *Cognitive strategy instruction that really improves academic performance.* Cambridge, MA: Brookline Books.

Pressley, M., Borkowski, J. G., & O'Sullivan, J. T. (1984). Memory strategy is made of this: Metamemory and desirable strategy use. *Educational Psychologist, 19,* 94–107.

Pressley, M., Borkowski, J. G., & Schneider, W. (1987). Cognitive strategies: Good strategy users coordinate metacognition and knowledge. In R. Vasta & G. Whitehurst (Eds.), *Annals of child de-*

velopment (Vol. 5, pp. 89–129). New York: JAI Press.

Pressley, M., & Levin, J. R. (1978). Developmental constraints associated with children's use of the keyword method of foreign language vocabulary learning. *Journal of Experimental Child Psychology, 26,* 359–372.

Pressley, M., Levin, J. R., & Delaney, D. H. (1982). The mnemonic keyword method. *Review of Educational Research, 52,* 61–92.

Pressley, M., Levin, J. R., & Ghatala, E. S. (1984). Memory strategy monitoring in adults and children. *Journal of Verbal Learning and Verbal Behavior, 23,* 270–288.

Pressley, M., Levin, J. R., Ghatala, E. S., & Ahmad, M. (1987). Test monitoring in young grade school children. *Journal of Experimental Child Psychology, 43,* 96–111.

Presslcy, M., Snyder, B., & Cariglia-Bull, T. (1987). How can good strategy use be taught to children? Evaluation of six alternate approaches. In S. Cormier & J. Hagman (Eds.), *Transfer of learning: Contemporary research and applications* (pp. 81–121). Orlando, FL: Academic Press.

Rivera, D. M., & Smith, D. D. (1987). Influence of modeling on acquisition and generalization of computational skills; A summary of research findings from three sites. *Learning Disability Quarterly, 10,* 69–80.

Rohwer, W. J., Jr. (1973). Elaboration and learning in childhood and adolescence. In H. W. Reese (Ed.), *Advances in child development and behavior* (Vol. 8, pp. 1–57). New York: Academic Press.

Rosenkoetter, L. I., Huston, A. C., & Wright, J. C. (1990). Television and the moral judgment of the young child. *Journal of Applied Developmental Psychology, 11,* 123–137.

Rosenthal, T. L., & Zimmerman, B. J. (1972). Modeling by exemplification and instruction in training conservation. *Developmental Psychology, 6,* 392–401.

Rosenthal, T. L., & Zimmerman, B. J. (1978). *Social learning and cognition.* New York: Academic Press.

Rotter, J. B. (1966). Generalized expectancies for internal versus external control of reinforcement. *Psychological Monographs, 80* (Whole No. 609).

Schunk, D. H., Hanson, A. R., & Cox, P. D. (1987). Peer-model attributes and children's achievement behaviors. *Journal of Educational Psychology, 79,* 54–61.

Schweikert, R., & Boruff, B. (1986). Short-term memory capacity: Magic number or magic spell? *Journal of Experimental Psychology: Learning, Memory, and Cognition, 12,* 419–425.

Seamon, J. G. (1980). *Memory and cognition.* New York: Oxford University Press.

Shaffer, D. R. (1988). *Social and personality development* (2nd ed.). Belmont, CA: Brooks/Cole.

Short, E. J., & Weissberg-Benchell, J. A. (1989). The triple alliance for learning: Cognition, metacognition, and motivation. In C. B. McCormick, G. E. Miller, & M. Pressley (Eds.), *Cognitive strategy research: From basic research to educational applications* (pp. 33–63). New York: Springer-Verlag.

Shiffrin, R. M., & Atkinson, R. C. (1969). Storage and retrieval processes in long-term memory. *Psychological Review, 76,* 179–193.

Siegler, R. S. (1991). *Children's thinking* (2nd ed.). Englewood Cliffs, NJ: Prentice-Hall.

Skinner, E. A., Wellborn, J. G., & Connell, J. P. (1990). What it takes to do well in school and whether I've got it: A process model of perceived control and children's engagement and achievement in school. *Journal of Educational Psychology, 82,* 22–32.

Snyder, B., & Pressley, M. (1990). Introduction to cognitive strategy instruction. In M. Pressley & associates, *Cognitive strategy instruction that really improves academic performance.* Cambridge, MA: Brookline Books.

Symons, S., McGoldrick, J. A., Snyder, B. L., & Pressley, M. (1990). Reading comprehension. In M. Pressley & associates, *Cognitive strategy instruction that really improves academic performance.* Cambridge, MA: Brookline Books.

Symons, S., Snyder, B., Cariglia-Bull, T., & Pressley, M. (1989). Why be optimistic about cognitive strategy instruction? In C. B. McCormick, G. Miller, & M. Pressley (Eds.), *Cognitive strategy research: From basic research to educational applications* (pp. 3–32). New York: Springer-Verlag.

Uguroglu, M., & Walberg, H. J. (1979). Motivation and achievement: A quantitative synthesis. *American Educational Research Journal, 16,* 375–389.

Walters, G. C., & Grusec, J. E. (1977). *Punishment.*

San Francisco: Freeman.

Walters, R. H., Leat, M., & Mezei, L. (1963). Inhibition and disinhibition of responses through empathetic learning. *Canadian Journal of Psychology, 17,* 235–243.

Weiner, B. J. (1979). A theory of motivation for some classroom experiences. *Journal of Educational Psychology, 71,* 3–25.

Weinstein, C. E., & McDonald, J. D. (1986). Why does a school psychologist need to know about learning strategies? *Journal of School Psychology, 24,* 257–265.

Zimmerman, B. J., & Blom, D. E. (1983). Toward an empirical test of the role of cognitive conflict in learning. *Developmental Review, 3,* 18–38.

Zimmerman, B. J., & Martinez-Pons, M. (1990). Student differences in self-regulated learning: Relating sex and giftedness to self-efficacy and strategies. *Journal of Educational Psychology, 82,* 51–59.

CHAPTER 5

BEHAVIOR ANALYSIS
AND INTERVENTIONS

As an intervention procedure, behavior analysis fits quite well within the developmental/social systems approach that we have proposed. Both orientations are concerned with the functional relationship between the child or adolescent's behavior and the environmental consequences. Social systems theory views the individual's behavior as goal directed to control the consequences. The developmental/social systems focus directs the school psychologist to view the child or adolescent within the context of his or her environment—that is, the transactions that occur in the system (e.g., family, school, peer group) in which the child functions. The developmental level of the student is an important factor. Therefore, the school psychologist must take into account what is normal at different ages, what is normal variation in behavior, and what is the family history/genetic background of the child or adolescent, as well as be sensitive to developmental delay (Harris & Ferrari, 1988).

Decisions about the intervention, such as goals and objectives, should fit the child's developmental level. The treatment modality will be influenced by the developmental capability of the child. For example, cognitive therapies may not be appropriate for young children or those who are low functioning. According to McConaughy and Achenbach (1990), "Interventions should be designed to facilitate mastery of important developmental tasks, especially the acquisition of academic and social skills needed for effective adaptation in later life" (p. 245).

The attractiveness of behavior analysis as an intervention procedure is partly due to its ease of use, although Reynolds, Gutkin, Elliott, and Witt (1984) claim that this advantage directly contradicts the reported failures, most of which occurred from incorrect use of the procedures. Nevertheless, the application of behavioral principles in the school has been successful for a wide range of behaviors and settings (Martens & Mellcr, 1990). The use of behavior analysis is usually associated with students who have some type of learning disability or behavior problem, but it has also been used with gifted students for such problem areas as underachievement, cultural differences, maladjustment, and behavior problems (Belcastro, 1985). Belcastro recommends a greater frequency of use of behavioral interventions and at a younger age for the gifted.

The focus of this chapter will be on behavioral approaches to problems in school settings, using principles from operant and Pavlovian conditioning, which we will refer to as *behavior analysis.* Because the concepts associated with Pavlovian and operant conditioning were explained in Chapter 4, we will restate briefly only the major terms that are necessary to clarify important ideas. Following an overview of the behavioral approach, the discussion will shift to the measurement and analysis of behavioral change. Increasing and decreasing behaviors, cognitive approaches to behavioral modification, generalization, and a discussion of ethics will comprise the remainder of the chapter. For a more extensive presentation of behavior analysis, the reader is directed to such sources as Cooper, Heron, and Heward (1987).

AN OVERVIEW OF THE
BEHAVIORAL APPROACH

The behavioral approach takes the position that behavior is learned; therefore, abnormal behavior does not differ from normal behavior because the social context is the critical factor. A behavior may be viewed as abnormal in one context but not in another. For example, talking to one's self may be perfectly normal for a child working on a difficult task but abnormal if the child is walking around the halls in the school. Abnormal behavior is based on social norms, which vary across cultures and groups within a culture. What is considered acceptable in one setting may be deviant in another. Therefore, an abnormal behavior may be learned, but the context or frequency determines whether this behavior is considered abnormal. Because abnormal behavior is the result of specific learning experiences, behavioral change can be effected through basic learning principles (Kazdin, 1980).

Behavior analysis provides this type of intervention. It stresses defining problems in behavior terms that can be measured and accepting change as the indicator that improvement is occurring (Martin & Pear, 1983). Most applications of behavioral analysis use principles from either operant or Pavlovian conditioning, although there are some offshoots of operant conditioning. Precision teaching, developed by Lindsley (1971), emphasizes the control of stimuli and curriculum to effect behavioral change. A second offshoot is social learning theory; its emphasis is on observational learning and reciprocal determinism. Cognitive behavior modification is a third derivative of operant conditioning. This approach focuses on cognitive mediation by means of self-instruction and the individual's interpretation of events. Both observational learning and cognitive approaches to behavioral intervention will be reviewed in our discussion of behavior analysis.

Self-Control

Self-control, the major objective in any behavioral intervention, can be defined as "those be-

haviors a person deliberately undertakes to achieve self-selected outcomes" (Kazdin, 1980, p. 248). Many instances of self-control may be observed in daily life. Some examples are deciding to study rather than attend a movie, dieting to wear a particular style of clothing, refraining from taunting a child even though one's peers did so, counting or walking away from a stimulus that elicits anger, and using self-statements to avoid a careless act. Perhaps you have noticed from these examples that the behaviors have conflicting consequences involving reinforcement and punishment, and further that the behaviors are relinquishing more immediate reinforcement for delayed reinforcement.

Self-control is learned through such procedures as stimulus control, self-reinforcement, self-observation, self-instructions, and self-punishment (Kazdin, 1980). Stimulus control promotes self-control through providing additional cues to elicit the desired behavior and by decreasing the likelihood of an undesirable behavior (Cooper, Heron, & Heward, 1987). If the problem is nail biting while reading, one could sit next to other children, place a picture of hands with healthy fingernails in front of the child, and perhaps use such procedures as pungent-tasting material on the fingers of chewed nails. Self-reinforcement enhances self-control not only by the delivery of a reward of some type but also by deciding on the magnitude of the reward. For fingernail biting, the reward could be TV time or some treat for each day that nail biting does not occur. The decision is left to the child.

Self-punishment can aid self-control through applying aversive consequences for undesirable behavior. In the case of nail biting, self-punishment might consist of removal of TV time or placing a very distasteful substance on the fingernails. Observation of one's behavior activates self-control by increasing awareness of inappropriate responses. Recording instances of thoughts of nail biting or actual placement of a finger in the mouth are examples of self-observation. Certainly statements by the individual can be important in the control of behavior, as evidenced by the work of Luria (1961). Self-instructional statements are important cues for children as they shift to internal direction of behavior. Such cues could be used to exert self-control of nail biting by such self-statements as "Don't bite your nails."

Why is self-control important? Cooper, Heron, and Heward (1987) offer a number of reasons. Self-control can increase generalization of a behavioral change by arranging consequences, such as the child with deficient study skills using self-praise each time an assignment is completed. Some types of behavior are not amenable to external control. Any type of behavior, such as nose picking, thumb sucking, or nail biting, that has to be monitored continually is a good candidate for self-control strategies.

Various classroom activities lend themselves to self-control procedures. For example, students can score their math seatwork or correct daily spelling tests. Interestingly, some children may work harder when they select the reinforcement contingencies. This finding does not hold across all situations, however, because children have also been found to set rather minimal standards (Cooper, Heron, & Heward, 1987). Finally, self-control can be viewed as an educational objective because the goal of education is to train the student to be self-directed and to be able to evaluate individual performance.

Stimulus Control

If self-control is an important objective in a behavioral intervention, stimulus control is the critical element. In Chapter 4, we defined *stimulus control* as occurring when a stimulus sets the occasion for a response. That stimulus is defined as an S^D, or discriminative stimulus. Most sources (e.g., Martin & Pear, 1983; Schreibman, Koegel, Charlop, & Egel, 1990) associate an S^D with an antecedent cue preceding a response that was reinforced. However, recall from our discussion in Chapter 4 that an S^D can also be associated with a response that receives more reinforcement than another response (Baldwin & Baldwin, 1986), so reinforcement per se is a necessary but not sufficient condition because the magnitude of the reinforcement must be considered. Discriminative

stimuli also can be associated with punishers, in which case the antecedent stimulus becomes an S^Δ (a discriminative stimulus for punishment), which indicates that the individual should not respond.

Different degrees of stimulus control of behavior may be present at any one time. Stimulus control is relatively loose when other similar stimuli can also elicit responses, such as in the case of stimulus generalization. If the child has received praise from the teacher for on-task behavior in the classroom, and the child remains on task when any adult is in the classroom, this would be considered rather loose stimulus control. Stimulus discrimination, on the other hand, denotes a more stringent degree of stimulus control. In the previous example, if the child remained on task only when the teacher is in the room, this would be considered discrimination. Ineffective stimulus control might be attributed to failure to discriminate, but failure of the S^D to generalize to other similar stimuli when this is desired would also be considered ineffective stimulus control (Martin & Pear, 1983).

Maladaptive Stimulus Control

Specific behavior problems result from ineffective control of behavior. Kazdin (1980) identifies three groups of behavioral problems. Certain behaviors may be controlled by stimuli that have been identified for modification. A disruptive student may be cued by several stimuli, including teacher attention, attention from classmates, and escape from difficult assignments. The intervention goal is to eliminate the control exercised by these stimuli. A second group of behaviors cannot be controlled by the restricted range of stimuli that are necessary. Students who are unable to work at their desks lack adequate cues associated with the completion of assignments, such as awareness of due date, free time, and availability of resource materials. The third group of behaviors is controlled by unsuitable stimuli which depart from acceptable social standards. Included in this category are such behaviors as sexual exposure and bullyism.

Identification and Transfer of Stimulus Control

One way to identify stimulus control is to locate the stimulus that precedes and best predicts the behavior (Baldwin & Baldwin, 1986). If the problem behavior is aggression, those events that seem to precede aggression must be identified. Once this stimulus event is identified, an intervention plan can be formulated because the controlling stimuli to be changed are known. A second method for identifying stimulus control, at least for problem behavior, is to use a scatterplot (Touchette, MacDonald, & Langer, 1985). This procedure uses a grid with time of day plotted on the Y axis and days of the week plotted on the X axis. Filled cells indicate the frequency of the behavior and present a visual pattern from which one can then identify times of highest occurrence and associate events with those times. Touchette, MacDonald, and Langer note that this plotting scheme provides the intervention agent with insights into the problem behavior that are not available from other types of graphs because behavior bursts are readily identifiable.

Fading is a technique that can be used for transferring stimulus control. In fading, the antecedent stimulus is gradually withdrawn. Numerous examples of fading procedures commonly occur in the classroom. In learning to write or print, teachers often use physical guidance to direct a child's hand and then gradually remove this guidance. Similar types of procedures are used in artwork and in arithmetic where the teacher solves sample problems and then sets up portions of other problems before letting the child work without help.

THE MEASUREMENT AND ANALYSIS OF BEHAVIORAL CHANGE

The focus of this section is on the selection, measurement, and analysis of behaviors targeted for change. Several topics that were addressed in Chapter 3 are relevant to the present discussion; you may want to review the sections on reliability, observational research, and time-series designs.

The discussion begins with an examination of some factors to consider in selecting and defining target behaviors.

Selecting and Defining Target Behaviors

Selecting Target Behavior

Kazdin (1980) cautions that although the intervention goal is to change a designated target behavior, the antecedent and consequent events associated with the behavior have to be considered. In other words, what are the necessary cues for the target behavior to be performed? Once those cues have been identified, the next step for the school psychologist is to determine the child's problem and how to remediate this problem; that is, to make a behavioral assessment. This assessment information can be obtained through interviewing the child, interviewing the teacher and parents, observing the child, administering tests to the child, roleplaying, and self-monitoring by the child (Martin & Pear, 1983).

The child interview is important because it helps to identify potential target behaviors for subsequent confirmation by means of observation. One of the advantages in interviewing teachers and parents is that you can determine their willingness to participate in the planned intervention. Observational data are especially useful in constructing a general pattern of the child's behavior. Tests contribute to behavioral assessment by providing information about the child's performance on the target behavior; of particular interest is information about the child's level of skill mastery. Roleplaying can substitute for actual observation of the child in a particular setting. If adequate training is provided and the right instruments for recording are used, self-monitoring can be another suitable substitute for direct observation.

Behavioral assessment is likely to reveal several behaviors that could be changed. The next question is: Which target behavior(s) have the most social significance? Several considerations are important in this regard based on the discussion by Cooper, Heron, and Heward (1987). The school psychologist needs to determine if changing the target behavior will improve the child. Target behaviors that benefit the teacher, or perhaps the parent, rather than the child per se are frequently selected for intervention programs. For example, the teacher may see the child's restlessness and excessive activity as needing correction, whereas greater benefit from intervention may be obtained by improving the child's reading because the child becomes restless when difficult reading is encountered.

A second consideration is whether the targeted behavior is appropriate for the child's age. The general rule seems to be that behaviors should be age appropriate (a developmental consideration discussed earlier) and functional within the demands of adult settings (Cooper, Heron, & Heward, 1987). The target behavior that is selected must be the actual behavior that needs to be changed. Although on-task behavior is targeted for change to improve school performance, it is possible for a student to be on task and yet not complete the necessary school assignments. If the intervention procedure involves the removal or reduction of a behavior, then it is necessary to replace it with some adaptive behavior. As Goldiamond (1974) has noted, the maladaptive behavior has served a purpose for the child in the past, and its removal does not provide the child with training about an alternative.

Defining Target Behaviors

One criterion for behavioral analysis is an accurate definition of the target behavior. General statements, such as learning deficits or hyperactivity, are not sufficiently precise for a behavioral analysis program. To be useful, the target behavior to be defined does not need to be named but it should meet these requirements, according to Hawkins and Dobes (1975): (1) An objective definition must specify a behavior that is observable, and the environment if necessary. (2) The definition must have sufficient clarity so that it can be read and explained by an observer. (3) The limiting conditions of the definition must specify the behaviors to be included and excluded. A written

definition of a target behavior might be similar to the following example for restlessness: Restlessness occurs when the child is observed to be moving around in her or his seat, glancing about the room, moving in and out of the seat, playing with hair or parts of clothing.

Behavioral Recording and Measurement

Once the target behavior has been defined, the next consideration is the behavior(s) to be recorded and the measure(s) to be used. At this juncture, measurement becomes a critical factor. An effective intervention program can answer the following questions: Is the desired change evident? Is the necessary skill level emerging or, if already present, is it showing improvement? The decision on effectiveness must be based on actual data, not subjective judgment. Hartman and Wood (1990) present an excellent summary of observation technology.

Two approaches can be taken to recording and measuring behavior—direct measurement of some product, such as exam scores or homework assignments, or observational recording (Hartman & Wood, 1990). Many behaviors of concern to school psychologists do not result in some type of score or grade; rather, the behaviors have social significance, so they have to be observed and recorded. Among the most common recordings are those involving frequency, duration, latency, and intervals (Kazdin, 1980; Martin & Pear, 1983).

Regardless of the recording measure chosen, information about antecedent and consequent events are likely to be deleted unless the school psychologist records this information with the data record. Antecedent events, such as a particular aspect of some setting, or the presence or absence or a particular individual, may be important indicators underlying stimulus control of the target behavior. Similarly, information about consequent events can provide the school psychologist with important insights. For instance, consistent performance of an undesirable behavior indicates that some stimulus is reinforcing it.

Inconsistent performance, on the other hand, may indicate the absence of reinforcement. Because recording measures are so important to the success of behavioral interventions, some discussion of each of the most common measures is needed. Table 5.1 lists some of the most frequently used observational measures and guidelines for their selection.

Frequency

This measure, which involves a count of the behavior(s) as they occur in a designated period of time, is often labeled *response rate* (Kazdin, 1980). Frequency can be used in a range of settings provided that the target response is discrete, with a definite start and ending so each response can be counted. Consideration also needs to be given to: Is the response rate reasonably constant across time and recorded for a constant amount of time to make the frequencies directly comparable? Very high rates of responding will be difficult to record, and frequency is not a recommended measure for behaviors that may occur for different amounts of time, such as out of seat, smiling, or talking to other children (Kazdin, 1980). Talking without raising a hand, late homework, and noncompliance to a teacher request are examples of behaviors that fit a frequency measure quite nicely. Figure 5.1 shows a sample data form that could be used for frequency recording. Note that this form contains spaces for the school psychologist to record relevant antecedent and consequent events associated with the target behavior.

Duration

This measure is appropriate for recording continuous responses; total time of high rate responses because of difficulty in accurately recording frequency; or behaviors that extend over long periods of time (Cooper, Heron, & Heward, 1987). In all of these instances, length of time is a major concern. Temper tantrums, sitting at a desk, and attention span are examples of behaviors that fit duration recording. Two forms of duration recording can be obtained—duration per

behavior occurrence or total duration. When compared with frequency, duration is the appropriate measure for off-task behavior, rather than frequency recording (Cooper, Heron, & Heward, 1987), because the child might be off task for 15 to 20 minutes duration, but only once in that period. Cooper, Heron, and Heward (1987) suggest that duration per occurrence is a better measure because it combines both duration and frequency.

In general, duration per occurrence is a better choice than total duration for the reason just given, but total duration may be the best measure if the major concern is length of time that the behavior persists. A sample data sheet for recording duration per occurrence of a behavior is detailed in Figure 5.2.

Latency

This measure assesses the length of time required for a response to occur; that is, the time between onset of a stimulus and a response. Latency is the most appropriate measure when length of time required to emit a behavior must be known (Cooper, Heron, & Heward, 1987). Length of time to respond may indicate impulsiveness on the part of the child if the latencies are too short. Following instructions is one common behavior for which latency could be an informative measure.

Interval

Interval recording is used to indicate the presence or absence of a specified behavior within some segment of time. Intervals are determined by dividing the total observation period into equal time segments. The usual length of intervals is 6 to 15 seconds, contingent on the target behavior (Cooper, Heron, & Heward, 1987). Several occurrences of the target behavior during any one interval are not recorded separately. However, talking to several children one at a time or the child leaving his or her desk several times would be recorded in each interval in which it occurs. Interval recording can be partial, where the observer records whether the response occurred

TABLE 5.1 Observational Measures and Guidelines

BEHAVIORAL CHARACTERISTICS	SOME CONSIDERATIONS	RECOMMENDED ASSESSMENT SYSTEM	SOME SAMPLE BEHAVIORS
Frequency	1 Responses are relatively discrete. 2 Successive responses are quite similar in duration. 3 Total number of responses is of concern. 4 An observer if available.	Continuous frequency	Cigarettes smoked, pinches, objects thrown, saying "ain't," reprimands, math problems completed, self-slaps, teacher attention to child, going to the bathroom
Stimulus control	Same as 1–4 plus: 5 Main concern is percentage of appropriate responses.	Continuous frequency per opportunity	Correct imitations, pictures identified, school attendance, spelling words correctly, compliance to requests (all these may be converted to percentage of total opportunities)
Quantity (frequency or duration)	Same as 4 and 5, above, plus: 6 Instances of behavior can be of long duration. 7 Successive responses can be of variable duration. 8 Precise duration is not of major concern.	Interval recording	Smiling, sitting, lying down, talking, social behavior, withdrawn behavior, TV watching, studying, on-task or off-task behavior (e.g., in a classroom)
Quantity (frequency or duration)	Same as 5–8 plus: 9 An observer is recording two or more behaviors of two or more students.	Combination of interval recording and time-sampling recording	Same as those listed for interval recording
Quantity (frequency or duration)	Same as 5–9 plus: 10 The behavior has a high	Time-sampling recording	Sitting, talking, walking, playing, working, rocking,

TABLE 5.1   (Continued)

BEHAVIORAL CHARACTERISTICS	SOME CONSIDERATIONS	RECOMMENDED ASSESSMENT SYSTEM	SOME SAMPLE BEHAVIORS
	frequency or duration throughout long periods (e.g., a morning or a day). 11 The observer has many other things to do and can devote only brief periods of time, which are separated from one another by long intervals.		being in a particular location
Timing	12 Precise duration is of major concern. 13 An observer is available.	Continuous duration recording	Sitting, social interaction, time to run errands, tantrums, practicing piano, task completion
Timing	Same as 12 plus: 14 Appropriate behavior occurs with some frequency. 15 Main concern is that the behavior occurs at the time specified for it.	Continuous latency recording	Same as those listed for stimulus control

Source: Garry Martin & Joseph Pear, *Behavior modification: What it is and how to do it,* 2nd ed., © 1983, pp. 325–326. Reprinted by permission of Prentice Hall, Englewood Cliffs, New Jersey.

anytime during the interval period, or whole, which requires that the response occur during the entire interval period (Cooper, Heron, & Heward, 1987).

Interval recordings are generally recorded as the percent of the total intervals in which the behavior occurred (Cooper, Heron, & Heward, 1987). This calculation is similar to the proce-

dure used to determine inter- or intraobserver agreement as discussed in Chapter 3.

Observational Methods

The basic procedures in observational methodology—specifically, selecting behaviors to observe, procedures, accuracy, and reliability—were dis-

Date: *January 1*		Observer: *John H.*	
Student: *Corrine*			
		Observation	
	Instances	Total	Time	Additional Comments

	Instances	Total	Time	Additional Comments
Slops:	LHT HHT //	12	20 min	*Evening meal, three other students at the table. Meal: soup, mashed potatoes, hamburger, veg., jello, milk.*
Eating With Hands	///	3	20 min	*Evening meal, three other students at the table. Meal: same as above.*

FIGURE 5.1   Data form for recording frequency

Source: Garry Martin & Joseph Pear, *Behavior modification: What it is and how to do it,* 2nd ed., ©
1983, p. 310. Reprinted by permission of Prentice Hall, Englewood Cliffs, New Jersey.

cussed in Chapter 3. Reviewing this material would be helpful to you in better understanding the various aspects of observational methodology.

One of the first decisions in observing behavior is to choose between continuous behavioral recording, in which the observer records all instances of the target behavior during the allotted time period (e.g., all occurrences where the child hits another child during a 30-minute period), or some part of the time period (i.e, a sampling of the total time, such as a 7-minute segment of the previous 30-minute period). Mann, Thomas, Plunkett, and Meisels (1991) recommend continuous sampling for behaviors with a brief on-time

Teacher: *Mary*				Student: *Agnes*				Date: *Jan. 5/82*		

Attention Span	0		1		2		3		4		5
1-2 sec	///		/								
3-4 sec		//	X	/	//						
5-6 sec					/	/	/	/			
7-8 sec						X	/	/	/	/	/
9-10 sec								/	/	X	X	//	/

Session (minutes)

FIGURE 5.2   Data form for recording duration per observation

Source: Garry Martin & Joseph Pear, *Behavior modification: What it is and how to do it,* 2nd ed., ©
1983, p. 317. Reprinted by permission of Prentice Hall, Englewood Cliffs, New Jersey.

or when long intervals are used because error rates from time sampling are high in these situations. If the sampling option is selected, it is preferable to collect several samples of behavior across time, which may provide information about the patterning of the behavior, rather than a single continuous recording (Cooper, Heron, & Heward, 1987).

Time and Sample Selection

If possible, observation should occur each day or each classroom period in which the target behavior occurs. Daily observation of behavior is less critical if the target behavior is stable across time, because every-other-day observation will be as accurate (Kazdin, 1980). However, it is necessary to standardize the time of data collection, so that the observations are made at the same time each observational period to ensure equal likelihood that a behavior can occur, and to provide consistency from period to period.

Variability of behavior is another factor influencing time of observation. One of the concerns is selection of observation times that will provide a representative sampling of the target behavior. The most conservative time for observation of the target behavior should be selected; that is, select the time the behavior is most likely to occur. If the objective is to decrease a behavior, the observations need to be conducted at the time of highest occurrence, whereas the time of lowest occurrence needs to be observed when the objective is to increase the behavior (Cooper, Heron, & Heward, 1987).

Duration of the observational period is another decision to be made. The length of the period will depend on the setting and other environmental factors, as well as the natural occurring frequency of the behavior. As a general rule, the duration should be of sufficient length to produce representative data. If the target behavior occurs only a few times a day, a duration of 5 to 15 minutes may not be sufficient, and it may be necessary to schedule an entire day for the recording. But large periods of observation time are not always necessary. A brief period of 1 to 2 minutes may be adequate for certain classroom

measures, such as arithmetic and reading (White & Haring, 1980). Shorter observational periods should be adequate for behaviors that occur at a high rate.

Interval recordings require other time considerations, the major one being the length of the interval within the observational period. Relatively short intervals (e.g., 7 to 15 seconds) will be sufficient for high-rate target behaviors, such as out-of-seat for the hyperactive child. A longer interval would prevent the recording of most of the responding because only one recording per interval is permitted. But very brief intervals (e.g., 5 seconds or less) can present problems for reliable scoring because the brevity makes it difficult to determine if the behavior occurred. Other problems with time sampling are discussed in Chapter 3.

Behavior Codes

Some type of behavioral code generally is used to denote the various behaviors of interest in order to simplify the recording. Various schemes have been used in the literature to represent behaviors. Figure 3.4 in Chapter 3 shows the coding scheme used in a study of play behavior of preschool children. In this study, a series of two-digit numbers was used to represent the various play behaviors in order that the behavioral codes could be recorded with a lap-top computer. Sometimes coding sheets use abbreviations for the behavior codes, and these abbreviations are placed in each interval so that the observer only has to circle the appropriate or inappropriate behavior that has occurred. Coding schemes are unique to the problem under investigation, so each intervention agent designs a coding form for the situation.

Observer Reliability

Both intraobserver and interobserver reliability were discussed in Chapter 3, and the reader is again encouraged to review that discussion. Behavior analysis views reliability somewhat differently than a typical research perspective. In behavior analysis, observer reliability is assessed during the actual data collection, as compared to the research practice of calculating reliability prior to and again at the end of the data collection. The description of the reliability assessment is usually reported in behavior analysis, and rather than a single correlation or percent, behavior analysis reports the repeated measures of reliability (Cooper, Heron, & Heward, 1987).

Why is reliability so important in behavior analysis? Kazdin (1980) suggests three reasons: Observational data is interpretable only if it is consistent. If frequency or duration scores differ among observers, the child's behavior cannot be evaluated. Second, with a single observer, any recorded change in behavior could be the result of a reinterpretation of the behavior by that observer. Finally, reliability indicates whether the definition of the target behavior is sufficiently precise for observers to agree on its appearance.

Reliability assessment ideally begins prior to collecting baseline data. Kazdin (1980) suggests a few periods of prebaseline data to test the observational plan and the behavioral coding scheme, and to correct any problems that result. The interobserver agreement for the prebaseline data ought to be at least 80 percent. A lower value indicates some amount of error in the recording. The accuracy of the observation (i.e., the concordance between the observer's recording and a recognized measure) is also important because it refers to the *validity* of the observed behavior. Observer *reliability* assesses consistency of the observed behavior, not accuracy. Validity or accuracy is more difficult to obtain. It has been assumed that observations are valid, but it certainly can be argued that data recorded by observers may not represent the actual event (Hartman & Wood, 1990). Behavioral data need to meet the test of content validity, discriminant validity, and convergent validity. These forms of validity are discussed in Chapter 3. A more extensive discussion of the validity issue can be found in Hartman and Wood (1990).

Frequency Reliability

Interobserver agreement for frequency is calculated by dividing the smaller total of the observed behaviors by the larger total and multiplying this result by 100. If observer A recorded 20 occur-

rences of the target behavior and observer B recorded 24 in a 20-minute period, the reliability would be 20/24 × 100, or 83.33% agreement. This reliability needs to be interpreted with caution, however, because agreement does not ensure that the two observers recorded the same behavior during the 20-minute period (Kazdin, 1980; Martin & Pear, 1983). Observer A may have recorded over half of the responses during the first 10-minute segment, whereas observer B recorded most of the responses the last half of time period. One way to resolve this problem is to divide the time period into smaller segments, such as 5-minute parts, and then calculate the reliability for each interval (Cooper, Heron, & Heward, 1987).

Duration and Latency Reliability

This reliability measure is determined in the same way as for frequency. The lower duration or latency is divided by the larger duration or latency, which is then multiplied by 100. Suppose observer A recorded durations of 60 and observer B recorded 75; the reliability would be 60/75 × 100, or 80% agreement. A few difficulties are encountered with duration/latency reliabilities, according to Kazdin (1980). Accurately discriminating onset and offset of the behavior or onset of the stimulus and the response may be difficult. The starting and ending of the observation period for both observers must be synchronized. The interpretation problem with duration/latency reliability is the same as that discussed for frequency; namely, you cannot determine if the two observers were recording the same durations (Kazdin, 1980).

Interval Reliability

Interobserver agreement is determined by counting the number of intervals in which the two observers agreed on the presence or absence of the target behavior, and dividing this sum by the number of agreements plus the number of disagreements (Cooper, Heron, & Heward, 1987). The product is multiplied by 100. If the two observers agreed on the presence of the behavior in 8 intervals and its absence in 2 intervals, and if they disagreed on 4 intervals, the reliability would be $10/(10 + 4) \times 100$, or 71.43%.

Two other procedures are recommended by Cooper, Heron, and Heward (1987) to control for the frequency of behavior influence on percent agreement. One procedure uses only the intervals in which the two observers agree on the presence of the target behavior. For the above problem, that reliability would be $8/(8 + 4) \times 100$, or 66.67%. A second procedure uses the intervals in which the observers agreed that the target behavior was absent. For the above problem this value would be $2/(2 + 4) \times 100$, or 33.33%. Both procedures result in a more rigorous test of agreement, and they usually produce a lower agreement. The first procedure is applicable for interobserver agreement where low-rate behaviors are involved. The second procedure is used with high-rate behavior (Cooper, Heron, & Heward, 1987).

Influences on Reliability and Some Comments
At this juncture some attention needs to be given to what can be considered reliability confounds. The knowledge that an observer is being monitored influences observation accuracy by increasing it (e.g., Reid, 1970). The condition has been termed the *reactivity effect*. Its impact can be reduced by unobtrusive checking or informing the observers that all of their recordings will be checked. A second effect, labeled *observer drift,* appears when observers change their interpretation of the target behavior definition during the course of observation. This confound can be reduced by continuous training of the observers.

Observer checks ideally should be made for each condition in the experimental design, such as baseline and treatment, but in reality such checks occur once per several sessions. It is preferable that observer reliability be reported on each target behavior for each subject. The acceptable standard for interobserver agreement seems to be 80 percent, although a somewhat lower value might be acceptable for more complex recordings, such as those involving several behaviors or different children.

DESIGN AND ANALYSIS

Single-subject designs have been used extensively in behavior analysis to evaluate the effects of various intervention procedures. This need to assess behavioral change underlies every intervention and transforms this intervention into a psychological experiment. To illustrate the critical role that experimental design plays in behavioral change, consider this situation.

Carrie's teacher observed that Carrie would complete her homework on time whenever the teacher looked at her and smiled. The teacher reasoned that this attention might be responsible for Carrie's improved work habits, so she observed Carrie's homework over the next five days without any attention, and found that the homework assignments were turned in late each day. On the sixth day, the teacher again looked at Carrie and smiled as she worked on her assignments, and found that they were now turned in on time. Given this scenario, is the teacher justified in concluding that the attention and smiling were reinforcing events responsible for Carrie's promptness in completing her homework? If we are provided with only these data, it is not possible to reach an unqualified conclusion. The improvement in Carrie's behavior may have been due to other factors of which the teacher was unaware.

To evaluate the functional relationship between the teacher's behavior and Carrie's response, it is necessary to apply an experimental design. Several single-subject designs were discussed in Chapter 3. For our present discussion, we will focus on the two designs most frequently used in behavioral analysis. A more extensive discussion of experimental designs can be found in such sources as Hersen and Barlow (1976), Kratochwill (1978), and Hersen (1990). We begin our discussion of designs by first considering baselines.

Baselines

The child's behavior in the naturalistic setting serves as a baseline for interpreting behavioral change. Establishing this baseline also provides the school psychologist with the opportunity to make note of those stimuli that precede and follow the behavior, in the event that this information could be used later. A typical baseline might be one where the child frequently leaves his or her seat when the teacher is not watching. This information can be used in designing an intervention program that uses contingent reinforcement for the child remaining at the seat.

Baselines provide two other important pieces of information. Guidelines for reinforcement can be set, and the severity of the problem can be determined. How many points are necessary to establish a baseline? According to Barlow and Hersen (1973), a minimum of three observational points are needed to reveal some type of data pattern. More observational points may be necessary if the baseline is unstable.

Of the many possible baseline patterns (Hersen & Barlow [1976] list eight patterns), the four most common patterns are: stable, ascending, descending, and variable (Hersen, 1990). These patterns are illustrated in Figure 5.3. Note in the stable baseline pattern there is little variability, which suggests that the child's behavior in the natural environment is fairly constant. Therefore, the planned intervention can be interpreted free of qualifications. The ascending and descending baseline patterns present problems in interpretation because they indicate that the target behavior is undergoing change. Introducing an interven-

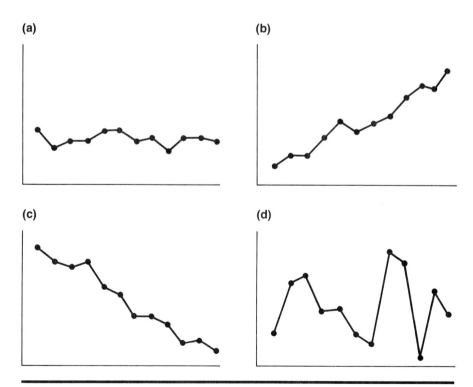

FIGURE 5.3   Four common baseline patterns: (a) stable baseline; (b) ascending baseline; (c) descending baseline; and (d) variable baseline

tion given these baseline patterns would preclude any interpretation because the causal variable could not be identified.

Cooper, Heron, and Heward (1987) recommend withholding treatment if either baseline is in the direction of the expected behavior change. Baseline should be continued until it stabilizes, but if the behavior continues to improve, an intervention may not be necessary. The variable baseline also presents a problem because a trend cannot be determined. It is likely that some unidentified stimulus is influencing the target behavior, and this stimulus would need to be identified. Any intervention in this situation would be difficult to interpret and should be withheld until a more stable baseline is observed. However, factors other than experimental rigor need to be considered. If the behavior is injurious, it may be necessary to intervene.

Reversal (A-B-A-B) Design

This design was explained briefly in Chapter 3, and the reader is directed to that discussion. A reversal design is used to show a functional relationship between the target behavior and the intervention plan (Kazdin, 1980). After a stable baseline is established (phase A), the treatment or intervention is introduced (phase B), and continued until the effect stabilizes or changes from the direction predicted. The treatment is then withdrawn and the baseline is reintroduced (phase A), in a procedure called a *reversal*, from which the design is named. The target behavior usually returns to baseline or almost to baseline. This reversal permits an examination of the change with respect to the baseline to determine whether the baseline occurrence of the behavior would have continued if the intervention had not been introduced.

The final phase is the reintroduction of the treatment (phase B), which occurs when the target behavior returns to baseline. If the behavior again returns to the previous treatment level, the functional relationship between the intervention and the target behavior has been established. The

number of replications that are necessary in a reversal design will vary. If the effect is highly salient and if it has been reported previously, one replication may be sufficient. Otherwise, several replications are needed to establish a reliable effect (Martin & Pear, 1983). A typical reversal design is presented in Figure 5.4.

For certain behaviors (e.g., headbanging, fighting, etc.), it may not be feasible to establish a baseline due to the urgency of some needed treatment. In this case, a modified reversal design, such as a B-A-B could be used. The reversal design can be modified in other ways. Rather than removing the treatment during the reversal phase, the reinforcer could be given noncontingently. That is, the reinforcer is given independent of the behavior, such as once per 10 to 15 minutes. The purpose of this procedure is to demonstrate that the reinforcer-behavior relationship was responsible for the change, not the reinforcer per se.

A second modification is to present a reinforcer for any behavior other than the targeted behavior during the treatment phase, which is a DRO schedule (discussed in Chapter 4). This procedure would show that behavioral change is contingent on the reinforcer following the target behavior. One of the advantages of using the DRO procedure is that behavior reverses more rapidly than when noncontingent reinforcement is given (Kazdin, 1980). The three reversal procedures we have discussed are designed to show that changing the contingency changes the target behavior.

Although the reversal design may be the most frequently used procedure in programs for behavioral change, it is not without its problems. One of the problems is that behavior does not always reverse when the treatment is removed. Some other unknown stimulus may be influencing the behavior. When a teacher withdraws supportive remarks that were earlier shown to increase a child's on-task behavior, the behavior may continue because classmates or some other factor is now supporting the behavior.

A second reason for nonreversal of behavior is that the intervention was not responsible for the

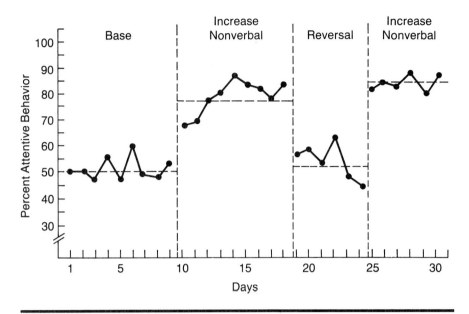

FIGURE 5.4 Reversal design showing rate of attentive behavior as a function of teacher use of nonverbal reinforcement

Source: Kazdin, A. E., & Klock, J. (1973). The effect of nonverbal teacher approval on student attentive behavior. *Journal of Applied Behavior Analysis, 6,* 643–654. Copyright © 1973, Journal of Applied Behavior Analysis.

behavioral change that was observed. A reversal design should not be used for certain situations. In the case where children are self-injurious, one would not want to return to baseline if the treatment had reduced the injurious behavior. Ethical issues also arise when children's behavior improves in some way, and one is faced with deciding whether to let the behavior return to its earlier state of unacceptability. These concerns about reversal designs have moved intervention agents to the use of multiple baseline designs.

Multiple Baseline Designs

Behavior change in these designs is confirmed by introducing the reinforcement contingency at differing points in time, by using one of the three designs. Multiple baseline designs are a series of A-B designs in which each phase A continues until the treatment has been introduced. The effects of a treatment are inferred from the un-

treated baselines; that is, behavior change should occur only when a treatment has been applied. In this respect the multiple baseline design provides less support for an observed effect than the ABAB reversal design where the effect of variables can be shown (Hersen, 1990).

Multiple Baseline across Behaviors

Baseline is recorded across two or more behaviors of an individual or several individuals until a stable rate is achieved. The treatment is then introduced for one of the behaviors while the other behaviors continue with baseline. A change is expected in the treated behavior only. When this behavior and the continuing baselines are stable, the second behavior is entered into the treatment. This procedure continues until all behaviors are treated. A major assumption of this design is that the target behaviors are independent of each other, which control the possibility that the treatment of one behavior would produce covariation in the second behavior. Each target behavior is expected to change only when the treatment is introduced. This design is especially well adapted to those cases where a child or group of children have several behaviors for which change is needed.

Figure 5.5 depicts a multiple baseline design across behaviors. Note in this example that baseline across three different academic skills has been recorded for this school-age child. The treatment consists of one extra minute of physical education class for each math problem, spelling word, or written sentence that is correct. Each of these behaviors is assumed to be independent of the others. The reinforcement for correctly solving math problems increased this behavior, but

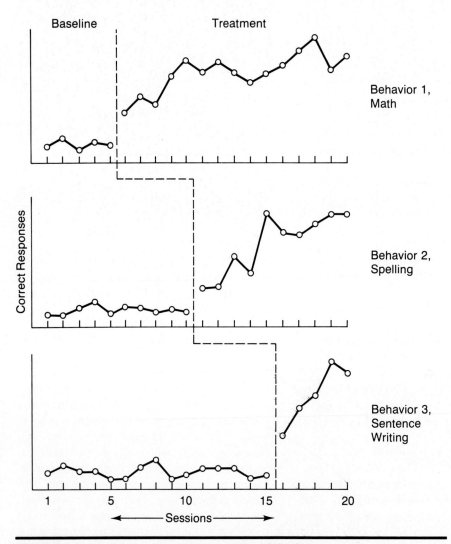

FIGURE 5.5   Multiple baseline design across three behaviors

Source: Garry Martin & Joseph Pear, *Behavior modification: What it is and how to do it,* 2nd ed., ©
1983, p. 339. Reprinted by permission of Prentice Hall, Englewood Cliffs, New Jersey.

did not affect spelling or sentence writing. Similarly, reinforcement for spelling did not affect sentence writing. Based on these data, the reinforcement contingency was responsible for the change in target behaviors.

Multiple Baseline across Settings

In this design, baseline data are recorded for one child or a group across two or more settings or situations. When stable baselines have been achieved for each situation, the treatment is introduced for the first situation, while baseline continues to be recorded for the other situations. This procedure continues until the treatment has been applied to all situations. The reinforcement contingency is demonstrated when a behavior changes only when the reinforcement is administered. This design is useful when an individual or groups of individuals enact or do not enact a specified behavior, such as cooperation, across situations (Hersen, 1990).

An example of this design can be found in Figure 5.6, which shows the frequency of bizarre vocalizations across various settings for a brain-damaged child. Baseline was collected for each setting in this camp situation, and the counselors were instructed to ignore all bizarre verbalizations as an extinction procedure. The effects of this procedure are evident from the figure. For each setting, when the ignoring treatment was introduced, the frequency of bizarre verbalizations decreased. The apparent conclusion from this intervention is that ignoring was an effective extinction mechanism for the strange verbalizations.

Multiple Baseline across Individuals

Baseline data are recorded across behaviors for two or more individuals. When a stable baseline is reached, the treatment is applied to the first individual, and baseline is continued for the others. The treatment introduction should produce a behavioral change for the target individual, but it should not affect the baselines of the others. The procedure is continued until all individuals have received the treatment. If a specific behavior needs to be changed across several individuals,

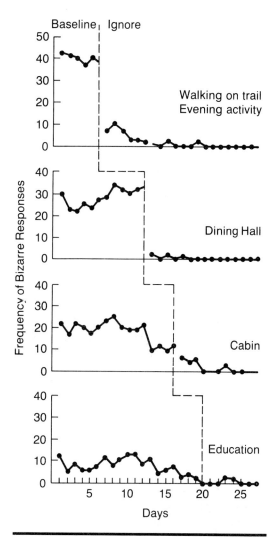

FIGURE 5.6 Multiple baseline design across situations

Source: Allen, G. J. (1973). Case study: Implementation of behavior modification techniques in summer camp settings. *Behavior Therapy, 4,* 573. Copyright 1973 by the Association for the Advancement of Behavior Therapy. Reprinted by permission of the publisher and the author.

this design is the best choice. Figure 5.7 shows the effects of training and a token reinforcement program on tooth-brushing behavior among a group of mentally retarded individuals. Note that for each of the individuals, tooth-brushing behavior increased with the introduction of the rein-

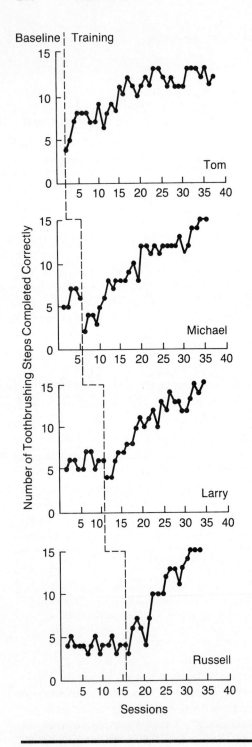

Baseline | Training

Number of Toothbrushing Steps Completed Correctly

Tom

Michael

Larry

Russell

Sessions

FIGURE 5.7   Multiple baseline across individuals

forcement contingency, demonstrating that the treatment was effective.

Some Concerns about Multiple Baseline Designs

The advantage of the multiple baseline design according to Kazdin (1980) is that the effects of the reinforcement/punishment contingency can be shown without using a reversal and removing the contingency for a time. The problem with this design is that an interpretable effect is demonstrated only when the behavior changes as a result of the application of the treatment. If a behavior change occurs at any other time, such as during baseline or in the second behavior before the treatment is applied, the specific effect of the contingency can not be ascertained. A multiple baseline design should not be chosen any time it appears that changes in one behavior may generalize to other behavior being measured (Kazdin, 1980).

METHODS FOR INCREASING ACCEPTABLE BEHAVIOR

During our discussion of operant conditioning in Chapter 4, we noted that both positive and negative reinforcement are consequences that increase the behavior that they follow. We also noted that the effectiveness of a reinforcer is related to an individual's past reinforcement history (i.e., the experiences of the individual with this reinforcer and the level of deprivation). Many of the interventions designed to improve school-related and social behaviors in the child have used some type of positive reinforcement. Those behaviors for which reinforcement has proven to be effective range from reading improvement and verbal communication to classroom disruption and school vandalism (Martens & Meller, 1990). Various types of reinforcers used for behavioral interven-

Source: Horner, R. D., & Kellitz, I. (1975). Training mentally retarded adolescents to brush their teeth. *Journal of Applied Behavior Analysis, 8,* 301–308. Copyright © 1973, Journal of Applied Behavior Analysis.

tion and some of the issues associated with reinforcement will be discussed in this section.

Reinforcer Functioning

The functional relationship between the reinforcer and the response is a critical matter. When a functional response-reinforcer relationship (e.g., teaching an autistic child to place hand out, palm up to receive a piece of candy) is compared with an arbitrary response-reinforcer relationship (e.g., same palm up behavior but the candy is placed in the child's mouth), the functional relationship produced very rapid learning, which, once acquired, was maintained with the arbitrary response-reinforcer condition (Williams, Koegel, & Egel, 1981).

Sometimes reinforcers function in ways other than expected. According to matching theory, as the amount of reinforcement for one behavior is increased, responding on concurrent alternatives will decrease regardless of whether alternative behaviors are aberrant or adaptive (Balsam & Bondy, 1983). Mace, McCurdy, and Quigley (1990) compared a continuous reinforcement schedule (CRF) with a variable ratio (VR2) using special education children who were solving arithmetic problems. They found that the children solved more problems when on the CRF schedule than the VR2 schedule.

Aberrant behaviors in autistic children have been shown to be more effective than food in training discriminations, answering questions, and telling time by the quarter hour (Charlap, Kurtz, & Greenberg Casey, 1990). This application of aberrant behavior demonstrates its saliency as a reinforcer, as well as illustrating the application of the Premack Principle. The Premack Principle, which states that any high-frequency behavior can function as a reinforcer for a low-frequency behavior, is one of the most powerful and flexible principles available to the intervention agent in selecting an effective reinforcer. Interestingly, in the study by Charlap, Kurtz, and Greenberg Casey, aberrant behaviors did not increase as a result of using them as reinforcers.

Types of Reinforcement

The reinforcers used in school-related settings have varied as widely as the behaviors for which reinforcement has been used. Both Forness (1973) and Christian (1983) have proposed a hierarchy of reinforcers ranging from more primitive consequences, such as physical contact and food, to more abstract consequences, such as competence and self-reinforcement. Forness used the following grouping of reinforcers: food, tangibles, tokens, contingent activities, social approval, feedback, and competence. The hierarchy proposed by Christian can be found in Table 5.2. This grouping includes the categories of physical contact, food, toys, school supplies, privileges, praise, and self-reinforcement. Christian recommends using the child's past reinforcement history as a basis for beginning, and then select the highest level of reinforcement that you predict will be effective in producing behavioral change.

Reinforcer Preference

One of the problems in using reinforcement is the satiation effect, especially with the use of food as a reinforcer. Other problems associated with the use of food include difficulty in dispensing in classrooms across time, the demands placed on teachers, possible allergic reactions, and parental disapproval of the foods chosen, such as candy (Martens & Meller, 1990). The manner in which food reinforcers are presented seems to influence their effectiveness. Egel (1981) compared the effect of using the same edible reinforcer for correct responses on a picture identification task to reach a criterion of 80 percent or better correct, versus changing the reinforcer after every third response. Performance decreased over trials with the constant food reinforcer, whereas correct responding increased over trials and reached asymptote when the varied reinforcer procedure was used. On-task behavior also showed improvement when the varied reinforcer was given.

Data from reinforcement preference studies (e.g., Mason, McGee, Farmer-Dougan, & Risely, 1989; Pace, Ivancic, Edwards, Iwata, &

TABLE 5.2   Reinforcement Hierarchy

	A	B	C	D	E	F	G
Consequence Level	*Infantile Physical Contact*	*Food*	*Toys*	*School Implements*	*Privileges*	*Praise*	*Internal Self-Reinforcement*
Examples	Hugs	Milk	Balloon	Eraser	Free Time	Verbal Comments	"I did well!"
	Pats	Raisins	Marble	Ruler	Errands	Grades	"My work's all complete."
	Physical Proximity	Crackers	Kite	Notepad	Collect Papers	Certificate	
		Gum	Clay	Crayon			
	< - - - - - - - Concreteness					Abstractness - - - - - >	

Source: Christian, B. T. (1983). A practical reinforcement hierarchy for classroom behavior modification. *Psychology in the Schools, 20,* 83–84. Reprinted by permission of Clinical Psychology Publishing Co., Inc., Brandon, VT 05733.

Page, 1985; Wacker, Berg, Wiggins, Muldoon, & Cavanaugh, 1985) with developmentally delayed children indicate that use of reinforcers that the children select in a preference test increases correct responding in various tasks, as well as decreases maladaptive behavior. The results of these studies show the greater effectiveness of subject-chosen reinforcers. But other reinforcers may be more effective than food. For autistic children, sensory reinforcement (i.e., such actions as tickling the child, clapping the child's hands, blowing bubbles for the child, and hair stroking) was more effective in increasing the learning of a visual discrimination task than a food reinforcer (Rencover & Newsome, 1985).

Social Reinforcers

Several types of social reinforcers are available in the classroom, such as verbal praise, positive strokes, peer approval, teacher attention, and smiles. This type of reinforcer is highly effective and perhaps more frequently used than any other, in part because it is easy to use and they are sufficiently powerful to alter the behavior that it follows. Teacher praise, a potent social reinforcer,

can be increased in the classroom by means of a rather simple procedure.

Gross and Ekstrand (1983) recorded baseline of teacher praise in preschool classroom for handicapped children, and then did a public posting of a graph showing the percent of 30-minute intervals in which praise occurred. The posting was followed by baseline, the reintroduction of posting, and feedback fading in an A-B-A-B-C-A design, which appears in Figure 5.8. Compared to baseline, teacher use of praise increased 16 percent, and, after dropping at the next baseline, continued at about the 35 percent level, as the figure shows. The public display of teacher practices, specifically use of praise, is a somewhat unique reinforcement contingency, but it illustrates the great variety of potential reinforcers.

Peers as Reinforcers and Models

It is well known that peers are effective reinforcers for inappropriate behavior but they can also be influential reinforcers for acceptable classroom behavior. Peers are especially useful in dispensing feedback and social reinforcement (Martens & Meller, 1990). "Normal" peers have

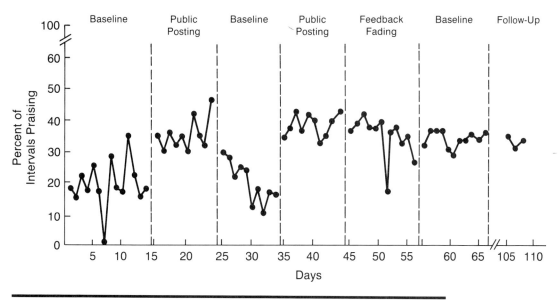

FIGURE 5.8   Effects of public posting on teacher use of classroom praise

Source: Gross, A. M., & Ekstrand, M. (1983). Increasing and maintaining rates of teacher praise. *Behavior Modification, 7,* 126–135, copyright © 1983 by Sage Publications. Reprinted by permission of Sage Publications, Inc.

been used to teach basic skills (e.g., crossing the street, buying a snack) to autistic children, and in this setting the peer tutors were more effective than adult models (Blew, Schwartz, & Lace, 1985). Accuracy of autistic children on discrimination tasks improved dramatically after these children saw peer models reinforced for correct responses (Egel, Richman, & Koegel, 1981).

Classwide peer tutoring, compared to teacher instruction, improved student performance in weekly spelling, arithmetic, and vocabulary tests, as well as scores on pre- and poststandardized achievement tests (Greenwood, Dinwiddie, Terry, Wade, Stanley, Thibadeau, & Delquadri, 1984). Further evidence of peer influence can be found in studies of peer-monitored token systems (e.g., Carden Smith & Fowler, 1984) for behavior control. Peer monitors are effective controllers of problem behavior in other children when the peer dispenses tokens for acceptable behavior.

Self-Reinforcement

One of the goals of many intervention programs is to design a program that will eventually guide the individual toward self-reinforcement for appropriate behavior. These programs often involve self-monitoring. Other's knowledge of the goal appears to be the critical factor influencing self-reinforcement effectiveness. That is, public goal setting is important. Self-reinforcement seems to acquire its effectiveness by setting a socially available standard so that performance can be evaluated (Hayes, Rosenfarb, Wulfert, Munt, Korn, & Zettle, 1985).

Group Contingencies

A group contingency occurs when reinforcement for an intact class is dependent on the performance of some part of the class. Overall, group contingencies appear to improve student performance (Martens & Meller, 1990), but there are some extenuating circumstances. In one study

(Pfeffner, Rosen, & O'Leary, 1985), an "all positive" approach, consisting primarily of praise used by teachers, was not effective in keeping children on task or in getting children to complete seatwork assignments. When an individualized reward system was used, both on-task behavior and academic performance increased.

A similar effect was reported by Dickerson and Creedon (1981), who compared teacher-selected standards on academic tasks with student-selected standards, when points were given for work completed. The group working under the condition of student-selected standards increased their correct responding by a significant amount compared to the teacher-selected standards group. However, no differences between an individualized contingency and a group contingency were found by Speltz, Wenters Shimamura, and McReynolds (1982) when the task was completion of daily worksheets. Social interaction within the groups increased as a result of the contingency application, but the greatest increase occurred when the comparison standard was that of a randomly selected student. According to these studies, individualized standards seem to result in the greatest academic gain.

Token Economies

A token economy is a reinforcement system based on items that can be exchanged for desired goods or activities. This system has been used widely in special education, remedial, and general classrooms. Among the major advantages of the token system for a school setting are its flexibility and the minimal time involved in administration. A token system also has the advantage that it provides a variety of reinforcers, which prevents satiation, and it allows for individual differences in reinforcer preference.

An example of a type of token program is a report card system developed by Dougherty and Dougherty (1977) in which children received a daily report card on their homework completion and raising their hand before talking. This report card was taken home each day for parent feedback. Within a 12-day period, failure to complete homework decreased by 17.7 percent, and mean talking rate decreased from 13.5 occurrences per hour to 2.3 occurrences.

However, there are some potential problems with token economies. Tokens may become S^Ds in that the desired behavior occurs only when tokens are dispensed, and therefore maintenance is a concern because tokens are not likely to be available in the real world. To counteract this effect, Kazdin (1980) recommends associating the tokens with a classroom consequence, such as free time or activity time.

One of the considerations with any intervention is its long-term effects. Overall, the data show that the effects of a token economy continue for a few years after the program has ended (Kazdin, 1982b). But there are some exceptions. Wasserman and Vogrin (1979) report that their token system, coupled with a response cost of token loss for inappropriate behavior, maintains such classroom behaviors as remaining seated, raising hands to talk, attending to instructions, and completing work over a 30-week period. However, the frequency of inappropriate behavior also increased across that time period even though this behavior resulted in a response cost.

Some further insight into this issue can be gained from a recent study (e.g., Sullivan & O'Leary, 1990) of a token program with a response cost component. The children were involved in a remedial program for reading and math that involved tokens for on-task behavior and token loss for off-task behavior. In a second phase of the study, both the response cost and the reward treatments were faded out by the teacher. Rates of on-task behavior were maintained by children in the faded response cost program, but only half of the children in the token program continued their on-task behavior. Those who did not continue had elevated scores on aggressiveness and hyperactivity. Thus, individual differences in treatment effects were clearly evident, and it appears that aggressive and hyperactive children may be poor candidates for token programs.

Individual Differences

Little or no mention is made of individual differences in reinforcer effectiveness in the literature on behavioral analysis. However, one should expect to find differences in reinforcement effectiveness among individuals given the premise that an individual's past experiences with reinforcers is a factor in their functioning as consequences. A careful perusal of the literature on reinforcement reveals a few studies in which individual differences are found. Two such studies are cited to illustrate this effect.

In their study of stimulus preference assessment and reinforcer value (described earlier), Pace and colleagues (1985) found some rather extensive individual differences in reinforcer effectiveness with their child subjects. For one boy, only juice and crackers were useful, whereas one girl responded only when crackers were given. None of the 16 reinforcers were uniformly effective for the six children in the study. Individual differences in the appearance of aberrant behavior used as reinforcers in the Charlap, Kurtz, and Greenberg Casey (1990) study influenced their use as consequences. Some of the children did not display certain of the aberrant behaviors, and other behaviors were not easily controlled by the therapist.

Some Concluding Comments on Reinforcers

Perhaps the most salient point in this discussion is the realization that the reinforcer must be matched to the individual. That is, the consequence has to be an element that will increase the target behavior. Therefore, the task facing the intervention agent is to find the effective reinforcer. One very powerful tool in this search is the Premack Principle, which was discussed earlier. This principle states that a high-probability behavior of the individual can be used to reinforce a low-probability behavior.

A second fact to consider is that contingent reinforcement does not have to follow the behavior immediately to be effective. The reinforcement can be delayed provided that the causal relationship between the behavior and the reinforcement is made known to the individual. Frequently this connection occurs through cognitive mediation (i.e, thinking about the behavior and its consequence), by establishing rules, or by the intervention agent explaining the relationship to the individual (Baldwin & Baldwin, 1986).

METHODS FOR DECREASING UNACCEPTABLE BEHAVIOR

Any type of maladaptive behavior is likely to be viewed negatively by the teacher because it interferes with classroom functioning. Therefore, the school psychologist should expect to receive a large number of referrals from teachers for disruptive behavior. Several intervention procedures have been used with disruptive behavior, and these procedures are frequently placed in the general category of punishment (Martens & Meller, 1990). In Chapter 4, we defined *punishment* as a stimulus that suppresses or decreases the frequency of a response. Two types of punishers—positive and negative—were identified in that discussion. *Positive punishers* were defined as adding an aversive event, such as a reprimand or criticism. *Negative punishers* were defined as taking away a positive event, such as response cost resulting from the removal of some privilege. Various procedures for modifying disruptive behavior will be discussed in this section.

Legal, Ethical, and Practical Matters Associated with Punishment

Legal proceedings have established rules for the use of punitive procedures in the school. In general, these rules specify that the least restrictive procedure that will likely provide a positive or acceptable end result should be used (Wherry, 1983). One interpretation of Public Law 94-142 is that the least restrictive rule should modulate the concerns for effective intervention with the rights of the child (Martens & Meller, 1990). According to Winett and Winkler, cited in Martens and Meller (1990), the major ethical consideration with respect to the use of punishment in the school ought to be whether its use enhances classroom learning.

There are several practical matters that need to be considered when the use of punishment is contemplated. Martens and Meller (1990) identify the following concerns:

1. Punishment provides information about an unacceptable way of responding but does not indicate what might be acceptable, so one unacceptable response could be replaced by another.
2. Teachers apparently prefer positive procedures rather than punitive procedures. However, this finding contradicts the data (e.g., Wyatt & Hawkins, 1987) on teachers' use of approval and disapproval, which reveal that teacher use of disapproval exceeds use of approval at every grade level except grades 9 and 12.
3. Use of punishment has a number of side effects, such as aggression, and when teachers use punishment they forfeit occasions for reinforcing acceptable behavior.
4. Punishment does seem to decrease disruptive behavior, so the teacher may rely on this procedure rather than seeking other forms of control.

Reprimands

Reprimands are frequently used to control disruptive behavior in the classroom because they represent a readily available method for teachers and they are effective. Wyatt and Hawkins (1987) report that teacher disapproval for conduct and academic behaviors occurs .28 times per minute across grades K through 4, 9 through 12, compared to .38 times per minute for praise. As expected, the use of reprimands decreases across grade level from K through 12. There is at least some evidence (e.g., Heller & White, 1975) to indicate that reprimands are more frequently

used for classroom control in low-ability classes than in high-ability classes, although this effect was not found when academic behaviors were examined.

Use of reprimands is not a function of such teacher characteristics as age, experience, or period when trained (Wyatt & Hawkins, 1987). One alternative to the high use of reprimands is to increase the academic engagement rate of students by means of teacher training and feedback (Leach & Dolan, 1985). Working on academic tasks is inversely related to disruptive behavior in the classroom.

The effectiveness of a reprimand is contingent on its administration. Delaying reprimands for two minutes decreases their effectiveness significantly in controlling interactive off-task behavior (e.g., physical and verbal exchanges involving another child) when compared with immediate reprimands. Noninteractive off-task behavior (e.g., out of seat, looking into space), on the other hand, does not seem to be affected by reprimands (Abramowitz & O'Leary, 1990), which suggests that this behavior is under control of another reinforcer. Eye contact seems to be a critical factor in obtaining compliance. Requiring students to make eye contact when using behavioral management can increase compliance by 200 to 300 percent (Hamlet, Axelrod, & Kuerschner, 1984). Combining verbal reprimands with eye contact and a firm grasp of the child's shoulder has been found to decrease disruptive behavior more extensively than a verbal reprimand alone (Van Houten, Nau, MacKenzie-Keating, Sameoto, & Colavecchia, 1982).

Van Houten and colleagues (1982) also observe that reprimands given from a distance of one meter are more effective than those given at a distance of seven meters, and that reprimands administered to one child of a pair seated together reduce disruptive behavior in the other child; that is, the reprimand generalizes. The reprimands were rotated on a VI 2-minute schedule, each 15 minutes after baseline was established. The variable interval schedule was chosen because it represented the teachers' natural reprimand rate.

Reprimands were delivered in a firm voice, within an arm's length of the student. The verbal reprimand only was given without eye contact, within two minutes of the disruptive behavior. The verbal reprimand plus grasp added teacher eye contact and a firm grasp of the child's shoulder. This finding illustrates the importance of attention and suggests that eye contact seems to function as an S^D.

Time-Out Procedures

According to our classification, time-out is a negative punisher because it involves removal of a positive event, reinforcement. Various forms of time-out procedures have been used. These include, from most to least restrictive, seclusion from others in a separate room, placed on a chair in the same room (usually in a corner), and ignoring the child (Martens & Meller, 1990). Isolating the child in a school setting presents several problems, such as providing an adequate room where the child can be protected but at the same time isolated; providing a staff member for time-out, although this procedure increases the probability of a confrontation, which can be reinforcing to the child; and avoiding abuse or misuse of time-outs, which has led to regulations on their use by review committees at each institution (Martens & Meller, 1990).

Although time-outs are usually understood to include exclusion from the classroom, they can be used without isolating the child from the classroom. Chair time-outs were employed by Roberts (1988) as an intervention measure with noncompliant preschool children. Mother-child pairs were placed in a compliance training program in which mothers made specific requests of their child. If the child complied, he or she was praised. Noncompliance was followed by a warning of chair time-out. If the child disobeyed, he or she was placed on a chair in the corner for a minimum of two minutes. Any disruption during this time extended the time-out. However, this type of contingent delay does not seem to be necessary for effective compliance because time-out without this delay has been found to be as effective (Mace, Page, Ivancic, & O'Brien, 1986). Efforts to escape from the chair were met with either a spanking by the mother or a one-minute room time-out. Both procedures controlled escape efforts and increased compliance to maternal requests.

Other types of time-outs include ignoring, restricting participation in activities, some designation that the child is in time-out, and facing the child away from the other students. Deciding to use time-out is only part of the decision process. One also needs to consider such matters as length of the time-out and conditions to be met for return to the class activities. Above all, ethical considerations must be foremost in the decision, and the procedure must adhere to the least restrictive rule for treatment (Martens & Meller, 1990). Because of these problems, other procedures are often recommended. Two of these procedures are differential reinforcement of other behavior and response cost, which will be discussed next.

Differential Reinforcement of Other Behavior

This procedure, which was also discussed in Chapter 3, specifies that any behavior other than the target behavior is reinforced. DRO is considered a behavioral suppressant because performing the disruptive behavior results in withholding reinforcement. Therefore, reinforcing helping behavior ought to decrease aggressive behavior because the two are incompatible. The greatest behavioral suppression occurs when the alternate behavior is incompatible with the disruptive behavior. A critical feature in the use of DRO is the selection of reinforcers that are significantly more powerful than the maladaptive behavior (Poleng & Ryan, 1982). Among the positive features associated with DRO is that it is relatively free of ethical issues and it does not involve aversive control. On the negative side, DRO necessitates monitoring and timing of intervals along with appropriate reinforcement (Poleng & Ryan, 1982).

Various methods for administering DRO

have been examined. Repp, Barton, and Brulle (1983) report that giving reinforcement for behavior at the end of the interval does not decrease disruptive behavior, but when the pattern is changed to reinforcement only if the target behavior does not occur, disruptive behavior decreases markedly. Further, dispensing reinforcement only when the target behavior does not occur anytime during the interval increases the effect of the momentary schedule (giving reinforcement if the target behavior is not present at the end of the interval) for DRO in maintaining the target behavior at a low level. Comparisons of DRO and time-out (e.g., Haring & Kennedy, 1990) show that the two suppressant procedures differ in the types of behavior that they control. DRO appears to produce greater suppression of problem behaviors when these behaviors occur within an academic or instructional setting. Time-out appears to be more effective when used to control problem behaviors that occur in other contexts.

Response Cost

Response cost requires the loss of positive reinforcement, whereas time-out removes the opportunity for reinforcement. Both procedures involve the removal of something. Examples of response cost are a penalty or a fine of some sort. One of the advantages of response cost is that its effect continues over time. A second advantage is that the procedure provides a context in which positive reinforcement can be given when the undesirable behavior is replaced with a acceptable behavior.

Response cost is frequently used with a token economy. This integrated intervention was used by Little and Kelley (1989) to assist parents in obtaining increased compliance behavior. Children were awarded free points at several intervals across the day. When an instruction was not followed by the child, the parent reprimanded in a calm manner and crossed off a point. With this procedure, noncompliance by the child decreased by over 50 percent from baseline, aversive child behavior decreased by over 20 percent, aversive

maternal behavior decreased by over 10 percent, and these effects continued to be present at the six-week follow-up.

However, removal of point loss can be viewed as negative reinforcement, thus leading to avoidance or escape contingencies to prevent this loss. There is some evidence (e.g., Cherek, Spega, Steinberg, & Kelly, 1990) that patterns of aggressive responding generated from these two contingencies differ. According to Cherek and colleagues, point loss seemed to function as an S^D for intervals that were free of point loss following a child's aggressive response. Point loss during avoidance contingencies did not exert this S^D control.

Response cost has been incorporated into a lottery procedure used by Proctor and Morgan (1991) to reduce disruptive classroom behavior in junior high school students diagnosed as disruptive. Each student may enter a lottery drawing at the end of dach day if his or her behavior is acceptable that day. This procedure resulted in a significant decrease in disruptive behavior.

Overcorrection

Overcorrection involves a consequence of the same general type as the problem behavior, whereas simple correction requires the return of a situation to its original condition. If a child throws paper on the floor, simple correction would require the child to pick up the paper, but overcorrection would have the child pick up that paper plus all other paper on the floor in the room. A simple correction procedure would not be used if a serious effect resulted from the behavior or if reparation could not occur (Cooper, Heron, & Heward, 1987). In using overcorrection, prompts of a directive type may be necessary, but this technique needs to be used with discretion and withdrawn quickly. Reinforcement of alternate behaviors seems to increase the effectiveness of overcorrection (Cooper, Heron, & Heward, 1987).

Restitutional consequences are those in which the child compensates for the undesirable behavior by upgrading the environment to a better quality than it was before the behavior. For example, a child may be required to clean and repaint a wall for writing on it.

Positive practice involves replacing the undesirable behavior with acceptable behavior. This response substitution could involve such behaviors as rewriting misspelled words or reworking incorrect math problems. Both of these procedures have as their aim the reduction of inappropriate behavior. Positive practice effects can be enhanced further by the use of positive reinforcement following the practice (Carey & Bucher, 1986). Positive practice, using error-correction procedures, is more effective than drill procedures in reducing oral reading errors and in increasing retention of passages for which positive practice was used (Singh & Singh, 1986). The effects of duration of the positive practice have also been examined. Both long and short practice periods seem to reduce off-task behavior and increase performance equally well. But over periods, less time is required for positive practice when short practice durations are used (Carey & Bucher, 1983).

There is some disagreement about what procedures constitute overcorrection. Overcorrection, according to Lenz, Singh, and Hewett (1991), is an intervention procedure for decreasing behavior that is considered to be excessive in individuals who have been diagnosed as mentally retarded. They contend that procedures such as rehearsal and attention directed to the learning task, which have been used to remediate academic problems, are not recognized methods of overcorrection.

Some Concluding Comments on Punishment

The use of punishment has several negative features associated with it, and although punishment appears to be effective, the negative aspects seem to outweigh the positive. Further, ethical issues are always present. Applying the rule of the least restrictive procedure to secure an effect may place the school psychologist in a very tenuous position. Fortunately, there are more acceptable alternatives. These include DRO; extinction (i.e., removing the reinforcers that maintain problem behaviors); observational learning, where models can provide information on acceptable behavior as well as reinforcement; and the use of rules and reasoning (Baldwin & Baldwin, 1986).

OBSERVATIONAL LEARNING

Many of the behaviors that we see performed by children have been acquired or modified as a result of observing others. Observation of a model by a child can result in: (1) the acquisition of a new response, (2) the performance or suppression of a previously acquired response, and (3) the provision of S^Ds that provide cues for a similar response from the observer. The various processes associated with observational learning were presented in Chapter 4. In this section we will explore briefly the use of observational learning as a method of behavioral intervention. A more detailed discussion can be found in Masters, Burish, Hollon, and Remm (1987). Some of our comments will be based on this source.

Observational learning, involving the use of models, has several advantages as an intervention procedure. In comparison to shaping and prompting (two methods for teaching a new behavior that were discussed in Chapter 4), observing a model can produce much faster behavioral change. All that is necessary is to say to the child, "Watch me" or "Watch that child." The procedure is nonintrusive, easy to administer, and a significant change in children's behavior can be obtained in about six to eight sessions (Gelfand, Jenson, & Drew, 1982).

Several types of modeling procedures are used in therapeutic settings. A few of the most common will be discussed. Graduated modeling and guided behavior with rehearsal are procedures for the acquisition of new behaviors. In *graduated modeling,* the child is helped by the intervention agent to produce the most accurate replication of the modeled act that is possible, which is then followed by reinforcement. This procedure has been used in such applications as treating test anxiety, where students modeled behavior that was incompatible with test anxiety. Students later reported feeling significantly less test anxious (Masters et al., 1987).

Graduated modeling has been used to cope with such behaviors as fears in much the same way that is done in systematic desensitization. Children who are fearful are exposed to models who display increasingly more threatening behaviors, such as gradually moving closer to a dog and finally petting the dog. Skill acquisition can be acquired through observing models. Social as well as problem-solving skills have been acquired as a result of observing models performing these behaviors (Masters et al., 1987). Covert modeling, which involves imaging or visualizing scenes described by the therapist, has also been used in such applications as fear reduction. Covert modeling seems to be most effective when the imagined models are similar to the child (Masters et al., 1987).

One area of modeling that has attracted a good deal of attention lately is self-modeling. This procedure produces behavioral change that results from observing videotapes of oneself that display the desired behavior only (Kehle, Owen, & Cressey, 1990). According to the limited published accounts, self-modeling is an effective intervention for various problem behaviors. When self-modeling was used with a small group of problem-behavior children who individually saw an edited videotape of their appropriate classroom behavior only, their misbehavior decreased 55 percent, and the occurrence of misbehavior remained at about 8 percent at a six-week follow-up (Kehle, Clark, Jenson, & Wampold, 1986).

Self-modeling has also been used to treat depression in children, by showing these children videotapes of such positive responses as supportive self-statements and smiling. The evaluation of this treatment revealed an absence of clinically defined depressive symptoms, and the treatment required less student time and was less restrictive

than the relaxation and cognitive treatments that were used with comparable groups (Kahn, Kehle, Jenson, & Clark, 1990). Another setting in which self-modeling has been effective is in treating children who choose not to talk in certain situations ("elective mutes"). Kehle, Owen, and Cressey (1990) treated one such child by showing videotapes that were edited to depict him talking in the classroom to the teacher. The treatment was so effective that the child freely interacted with the intervention agents on the second day of intervention, which used a modified tape showing him talking extensively to the teacher.

Modeling contexts have also been used to examine the effect of vicarious reinforcement (i.e., it has been shown that observing another receive reinforcement can be reinforcing to the observer). According to Ollendick, Dailey, and Shapiro (1983), when one child of a pair is praised for performance on a puzzle task on a continuous reinforcement schedule, the performance of the nonreinforced child also increases. But over time, the performance of the nonreinforced child begins to decrease to a point that is below baseline. Subsequent intermittent praise to this child increases the performance. The nonreinforced child may interpret the continued absence of praise for good performance as punishment. Several children in the study made comments that indicated that their efforts were not being recognized (Ollendick, Dailey, & Shapiro, 1983). Therefore, expected effects from modeling and vicarious reinforcement are contingent on the manner in which the child processes the information in the situation. (Refer to Chapter 4 for a further discussion of this issue.)

GENERALIZATION

For many interventions it is critically important that the treatment effects continue away from the treatment setting. This condition is known as *generalization*. When generalization occurs over time, it is referred to as *maintenance* (Edelstein, 1989; Stokes & Osnes, 1989). According to

Stokes and Baer (1977), generalization and maintenance must be explicitly programmed for their effects to occur. Stokes and Osnes (1989) propose several principles for programming generalization. Perhaps the most important goal is to train behaviors that have a high probability of encountering strong reinforcers that do not have to be programmed. Therefore, relevant behaviors need to be chosen that will come into contact with natural reinforcers. At times it may be necessary to recruit some strong consequences. For example, a child could be cued to obtain a response from the teacher for acceptable work by saying, "Did I do well?" Another guideline is to reinforce instances of generalization during training.

One of the most important guidelines is to program the treatment more flexibly through the use of multiple stimulus conditions, several trainers, and different settings. A final principle is to make the antecedent cues and the consequences less discriminable. Recall from our discussion of behavioral principles in Chapter 4 that discrimination is the opposite of generalization, and both are necessary in our learning environment. By introducing variations in training conditions, the child will be less likely to associate performance with any particular set of conditions. That is, the cues and the consequences become less predictable. One method for reducing the predictability of consequences is to use an intermittent or variable reinforcement schedule. Another mechanism is to delay reinforcement. Delay in offers of help by teachers has been found to generalize to other settings such as language use (Halle, Baer, & Spradlin, 1981). Peer-interaction behaviors, such as cooperation and sharing, have been found to generalize to other settings when reinforcement for such behaviors were given at the end of the day (Fowler & Baer, 1981).

Use of actual classroom activities and materials in training has also been shown to generalize to the child's performance in the classroom (Knapczyk, 1989; Wacker, Berg, Berrie, & Swatta, 1985). Social skills training with children who are deficient in this amenity has been found

to generalize when the intervention incorporated such naturalistic conditions as inclusion of "normal" peers and training in the classroom (Gaylord-Ross, Haring, Brien, & Pitts-Conway, 1984; Kohler & Fowler, 1985; Sisson, Babeo, & Van Hasselt, 1988). The importance of natural consequences in generalization is illustrated in a study by Fantuzzo and Clement (1981), who reported that improved performance in arithmetic, increases in attention span, and decreases in unacceptable behavior generalized from the training setting to the classroom when the token reinforcers were administered by the student, but not when they were administered by the teacher. What has actually generalized in all of these studies is the intervention procedures.

COGNITIVE BEHAVIOR THERAPY

As the name implies, cognitive behavioral therapy combines elements of both cognitive and behavioral psychology. According to cognitive behavior therapy, maladaptive behavior is the result of some cognitive deficiency. Therefore, the focus of the intervention is on modification of thinking and problems-solving processes in children to effect behavioral and cognitive changes (Craighead, 1982; Kazdin, 1982a). Two basic assumptions with respect to child development and intervention provide a conceptual framework for this approach. (1) The child is an active participant in the intervention, and the child's experiences can be interpreted only in the context of the child's cognitive abilities. (2) Interventions must be designed to fit the needs of the child's present level of cognitive ability, because age is an unreliable indicator of psychological functioning (Morris & Cohen, 1982). There are some data to support these assumptions. Bornstein (1985), in his review of self-instructional training, concludes that this form of intervention is more successful with children who have greater experience and who have higher intelligence.

The constructs underlying cognitive behavioral therapy differ from behavior analysis on at least two different dimensions. Behavioral therapy is based on operant learning principles. Cognitive behavioral therapy, on the other hand, integrates principles from cognitive development, information processing, and social learning. With this focus, the developmental status of the child is critically important in the assessment as well as the intervention program (Morris & Cohen, 1982). Therefore, when a first-grade child and a fifth-grade child are referred for some type of problem behavior, the intervention program must be designed to fit their developmental levels. (The conceptual basis for this decision was discussed in Chapter 2.)

Cognitive behavior interventions are not designed for low-cognitive functioning children and adolescents. Further, the child or adolescent's belief in self-efficacy may influence the intervention. There is some evidence to suggest that both cognitive and behavioral elements are necessary for certain intervention strategies. Jones, Ollendick, and Shinske (1989) report that children who both verbally rehearse fire emergency skills as well as practice them acquire a higher level of skill acquisition than those who only verbally rehearse the skills. Both groups scored higher on a knowledge test than did those children who only practiced the skills.

A second difference between the two types of intervention is their method of assessment. Behavior analysis tends to rely much more heavily on observation. Cognitive behavior therapy uses behavioral observations, but it also assesses the child's performance on the various types of problem-solving and perspective-taking tasks that are used. Self-report data are often collected, and attributional styles can contribute to the therapy because children's explanations for the behavior and events they observe seems to influence the treatment. One would expect that children who believe they are responsible for an improvement in their behavior to show more generalization than children who explain a behavioral change as a matter of luck (Kendall & Braswell, 1982). Private speech of the child can provide information about changes and their functioning, and children

can be asked about their thinking. Parent and teacher ratings are frequently used, and sociometrics contribute information about the child's social acceptance (Kendall & Braswell, 1982).

Cognitive behavioral therapy refers to several treatment approaches. A few of the more frequently used procedures will be described.

Self-Instructional Training

This technique, developed by Meichenbaum and Goodman (1971), teaches children to use overt instructions, which later become covert, to guide their behavior. Various combinations of modeling, overt and covert prompts, feedback, and social reinforcement are used in this intervention. The system developed by Meichenbaum and Goodman consists of the following segments: (1) The trainer uses cognitive modeling by performing the behavior while explaining each step. (2) The student performs the behavior with guidance from the trainer only when required, and this guidance is removed before the student (3) performs the behavior while talking about each step, with the trainer correcting errors. (4) The student performs the behavior while using verbal guidance in the form of whispering. (5) The student performs the behavior without overt verbal guidance. Meichenbaum (1985) provides suggestions for training children.

Self-instructional training has increased preschool children's accuracy in workbook exercises (Bryant & Budd, 1982; Guevremont, Osnes, & Stokes, 1988), but Guevremont, Osnes, and Stokes report great variability in performance accuracy among their subjects. Overt instruction training, but not covert training, showed generalization effects. Preschool subjects in the Billings and Wasik (1985) study showed no improvement in classroom behavior or in attending as a result of training. Use of self-instructional training with aggressive children has not been very effective. The focus of the training has been on reducing impulsivity through such strategies as teaching aggressive boys to use coping self-talk to deal with interpersonal problems. However, this training seems to be more effective with nonaggressive children (Hughes, 1988). Based on these findings, self-instructional training is not always effective.

Problem Solving

Problem solving focuses on training children to identify problems and to generate solutions to these problems. Problem solving, including self-instruction training, has been one of the components in treatment programs for aggressive children. Use of problem solving by children, which involved identifying situations that aroused their anger and then proposing ways to deal with this anger, such as telling oneself to "stop and think," produced significant decreases in rates of aggression based on observations and teacher reports (Dangel, Deschner, & Rasp, 1989), and increased on-task behavior in the classroom as well as self-esteem in the boys involved (Lochman & Curry, 1986).

Coaching

This intervention has been used mostly with older children, whereas modeling is more often used with preschool children. Coaching consists of processes such as instructions, structured practice opportunities, and feedback (Hughes, 1988). Interventions with socially incompetent students and those who are rejected and aggressive have included coaching procedures. Although the results of these interventions are mixed, there is some evidence of temporary increases in self-efficacy for social interaction, rate of social interaction, and peer acceptance, but peer-liking scores for the socially deficient students did not increase. That is, the students who received coaching were not liked better (Hughes, 1988).

Self-Monitoring

Self-monitoring refers to student self-observation of a designated target behavior and the self-re-

cording of this behavior. For example, a student may be asked to record frequency of out-of-seat behavior. Self-monitoring has a number of positive features: (1) student-collected data are easy to obtain; (2) data on covert target behaviors can be collected (e.g., reporting on the failure to ask questions in a class even when the student wanted to ask a question); (3) data can be collected about behavior occurrences across numerous occasions or settings; (4) the procedure can be used with behaviors that range from observable objective behaviors (e.g., on-task) to subjective personal behaviors (e.g., negative thoughts); and (5) the procedure can be used with students who range in ability from regular classes to special education classes (Gardner & Cole, 1988).

However, the developmental level of the student must be considered. The procedure will not be effective with children who are too young, who are low-cognitive functioning, or whose emotional status is not adequate (Gardener & Cole, 1988). In some cases, training may be required, and the procedure can be used with groups. The purpose of self-monitoring as an assessment procedure is to collect information on a target behavior or to evaluate the effectiveness of an intervention. The data from empirical studies indicate that motor responses and positive behaviors may be more accurately monitored than other behaviors (Gardener & Cole, 1988).

Self-monitoring can also function as a means for behavior change. When the student is directed to attend to a target behavior, the self-recording of that behavior may produce reactive effects—that is, changes in the strength of the target behavior may occur (Gardener & Cole, 1988). Dunlap and Dunlap (1989) trained learning-disabled students to use a checklist for monitoring their problem solutions in subtraction seatwork. They report that this procedure produced a gain of nearly 50 percent in correct problem solutions. Self-monitoring has also been shown to increase significantly attention and academic work in learning-disabled children, although the improvement on the academic task showed great variability (Harris, 1980). However, reactivity does not consistently result from self-monitoring. When behavior change occurs, positive behaviors increase in strength, whereas negative behaviors decrease (Gardener & Cole, 1988).

As a procedure for modifying behavior, self-monitoring appears to be most useful for establishing behaviors in students' repertoires that are within the existing skill level, and reactive effects are more likely to occur in students who are motivated to change a target behavior. Reinforcement for accuracy of self-monitoring can enhance reactive effects, and self-monitoring can facilitate generalization of acquired skills (Gardener & Cole, 1988).

Correspondence Training

The relationship between verbal statements and behavior is the focus of this procedure. The data show that behavioral changes can be made in mentally retarded children with such training. Positive correspondence occurs when the child says something will be or was done, and it is done. Negative correspondence occurs when the child says something will be done and it is not done, or when the child says and does nothing (Karlan & Rusch, 1982). Say-do correspondence training reduced out-of-seat behavior in special education students when they said they would stay in their seats, and it also improved sitting posture when the child made this statement, as well as increased the accuracy of the children's work (Whitman, Subak, Butler, Richter, & Johnson, 1982). Increased peer-directed talk has resulted from correspondence training with socially withdrawn children when they made a statement about talking with peers (Osnes, Guevremont, & Stokes, 1986).

Other Applications

Kane and Kendall (1989) successfully used cognitive behavioral therapy to treat anxiety disorders in children. Cognitive behavior therapy has also been used to modify negative body image cognitions in normal-weight females (Rosen, Saltzberg, & Srebnik, 1989), and it has been shown to be effective with those children for whom behavior analysis has not been successful (Lahey & Strauss, 1982).

SYSTEMATIC DESENSITIZATION

Although most of the discussion to this point has focused on operant procedures, Pavlovian conditioning has also contributed a very powerful set of intervention methods called *counterconditioning*. One of these procedures, systematic desensitization, has been used in school settings to treat such maladaptive behaviors as school phobia, test anxiety, and other school-related anxieties. In systematic desensitization, the conditioned stimuli that elicit the negative emotion are paired with those stimuli that elicit relaxation and comfortable feelings. This process is repeated continually by associating each successive stimulus with a higher level of fear and anxiety contingent on the child's feeling of security.

The following treatment example for school phobia, suggested by Prout and Harvey (1978), illustrates the procedure. The treatment usually starts with training in relaxation. During this time the child is not permitted to view TV or to experience any other rewarding events that might reinforce remaining at home during the school day. The schedule for the day should follow that which occurs in the school. When this phase has been established, the actual desensitization can begin. Various counterconditioning techniques can be used, such as imaging or visualizing events at school and rotating this with events that are enjoyed by the child. With the successful mastery of this phase, elements and objects associated with school can be introduced, such as some make-believe play involving school.

The next phase is further progress toward attending school, such as actually going to the school grounds. This latter phase should be supported by reinforcement. In their use of the treatment, Prout and Harvey (1978) found that the median length of time for remediation of school phobia was about 21 days. A common element in desensitization procedures is the incorporation of relaxation, so treatment for test and other anxieties would follow a similar procedure.

TEACHERS AS INTERVENTION AGENTS AND CHILDREN AS RECIPIENTS

In school settings it is highly likely that teachers will be the intervention agent, with the school psychologist acting as a consultant. Given this situation, it is often the case that the teacher will need to make some major changes in his or her interaction style with children. Therefore, it is important to know about teachers' acceptance of behavioral interventions and their skill as intervention agents. The findings from some of the earlier studies (e.g., Witt & Martens, 1983) on teacher acceptability of intervention methods suggest that the most acceptable methods are those needing minimal amounts of teacher time and used with relatively minor behavior problems. Methods requiring large amounts of time are rated least acceptable.

In their review of the literature, which included studies with parents and undergraduate students as well as teachers, Reimers, Wacker, and Koeppl (1987) identified several factors that appear to influence acceptability. Problem severity is one such factor. Behavioral treatments are more acceptable for severe problems. Parents judge all treatments to be more acceptable when they are used with severe behavioral problems. However, cost and side-effects of the treatment are two other factors that may influence acceptability. Very costly treatments are likely to receive lower ratings, and negative side-effects should decrease ratings in proportion to the severity of the effect. Time was also identified as a factor, with higher ratings given to those interventions that required less time. Positive treatments were rated more highly than those using some type of suppressant procedure.

Reimers, Wacker, and Koeppl (1987) propose some factors that may modify the acceptability of treatments. Treatments that are shown to be effective receive more acceptable ratings. Tingstrom (1990) found that teachers rated time-out more acceptable when it was used for severe behavior problems and when the intervention was effective. Another factor that fits intuitively, but for which there are little data, is treatment integrity; that is, the extent to which the intervention is performed as planned. Concern with this issue increases as control over the treatment moves away from the school psychologist.

Placing responsibility for treatment with the family entails a greater risk than having the teacher implement the intervention because the school psychologist has greater access to the teacher. As Reimer, Wacker, and Koeppl (1987) note, if the treatment is applied incorrectly, it cannot be considered an actual treatment. If the treatment is not effective, the school psychologist will experience difficulty in determining why the treatment failed if it was incorrectly applied. Finally, acceptability of any treatment is a function of how well teachers or parents understand it. The school psychologist should not assume that teachers or parents necessarily understand a treatment modality. However, this understanding can be enhanced through reading or training.

What information do we have about teachers as behavioral change agents in natural settings, such as the classroom? This question was addressed in an observational study of teachers in kindergarten through third grade by Strain, Lambert, Kerr, Stagg, and Lenkner (1983). They found great individual differences among the teachers in their use of commands, demands, and requests, with average rates ranging from .20 to 2.5 per minute, but the teachers did not discriminate in these behaviors among children who were high or low ability. High-ability children more frequently complied with command than low-ability children, and the teachers more often gave high-ability children positive feedback for compliance. Interestingly, teachers gave more positive feedback for noncompliance to low-ability children. That is, more misplaced positive commands, demands, or requests (e.g., "Be quiet") were directed toward these children, and these comments seemed to increase noncompliance. But teacher use of negative feedback did not differ between the two groups of children.

There is also some evidence to suggest that teachers may not take into consideration reward effectiveness when they select a reinforcer. Fantuzzo, Rohrbeck, Hightower, and Work (1991) found no relationship between the rewards that teachers used and the preference for rewards indicated by children in grades 1 through 5.

Given this information, the next question concerns the feasibility of training teachers as behavioral change agents, and the effect of this training. The rationale for training teachers is that they have control of contingencies affecting the child, and to be an effective change agent, one needs to have this control. Most of the studies on training teachers as intervention agents reviewed by Allen and Forman (1984) used direct instruction, but this form of didactic training did not seem to be effective as a training method. Use of cueing (telling the teacher in the classroom the response to direct to children) produces effects that are equivocal. With direct instruction, teachers used more praise and statements of contingencies than those who had received other training. Modeling and roleplaying appear to be an effective training procedure, at least for increasing the use of praise. Providing teacher trainees with feedback on their performance in using intervention procedures is also an effective training tactic, but some type of direct instruction may be needed to facilitate generalization (Allen & Forman, 1984).

However, training may not influence teachers' behavioral change strategies, at least with respect to the use of positive reinforcement. All teachers, regardless of their past training, preferred the use of positive comments and feedback to children for acceptable behavior, as shown in a study by Derevensky and Rose (1978). There is even less closure on the merits of training teachers, given the data reported by West and Sloane (1986), who found that teachers can decrease disruptive behavior in the classroom significantly by increasing their rate of presentation during instructional periods. Thus, better instructional methods frequently may supplant the need for classroom management procedures.

As yet, we have not considered the recipient of behavioral intervention, namely, the child. It is commonly reported that children who are referred for treatment do not want the treatment (Adelman & Taylor, 1986). When this occurs, there is a tendency to attribute this reluctance to such factors as lack of motivation, low ability, or maladjustment, without considering the likelihood that the child may be responding to perceived negative features of the intervention. One reason for the reluctance could be the child's perception of being forced into treatment. There is some evidence to suggest that this is the case (Adelman & Taylor, 1986).

Not to be overlooked is the realization that, as minors, children are referred for treatment by parents; they are not likely to refer themselves. Treatment acceptability is probably a contributing factor. According to Turco, Elliott, and Witt, cited in Adelman and Taylor (1986), children 10 years and older have definite views about the acceptability of various interventions, and they prefer negative sanctions or personal teacher-student remediation to reprimands and negative contingencies.

ETHICAL PRACTICES

Ethical issues in the practice of school psychology are discussed in Chapter 11, and ethical practices in the use of punishment were examined earlier in this chapter. In that discussion we subscribed to the principle that any intervention ought to follow the rule of being least restrictive and yet capable of eliciting positive effects (Feldman & Peay, 1982). Our present consideration will focus only on some of the major ethical concerns associated with behavioral interventions. More extensive accounts of ethical issues can be found in Gutkin and Reynolds (1990), Bellack, Hersen, and Kazdin (1990), and Stolz (1978).

Authority for professionals in school settings

to administer discipline is based on the principle of in loco parentis, which holds that because students are under control of the school, the educator assumes the role of a parent surrogate (Wherry, 1983). But as Wherry notes, this principle, by its very nature, places the school under the public eye, which means that certain principles may apply only to school settings. What kinds of rights do children have? Certainly they have a right to the most effective treatment available, and a treatment that considers, above all, their personal welfare (Van Houten, Axelrod, Bailey, Favell, Foxx, Iwata, & Lovaas, 1988). According to this position, the school psychologist is obligated to design, implement, and assess the treatment for each child so that it fits the child's emotional or academic needs.

To ensure that ethical principles are followed, the following guidelines recommended by Wherry (1983) should be given serious consideration:

1. Design and utilize individualized behavioral interventions.
2. Acquire the informed consent of the client and/or guardian.
3. Implement behavioral strategies before placing a student in a more restrictive environment.
4. Document student progress with careful attention to the redesigning of interventions found to be ineffective.
5. Limit the use of procedures employing punishment and timeout procedures. (p. 50)

If time-out procedures are deemed necessary because the behavior is highly disruptive, Wherry (1983) recommends that the time-out be one hour or less, with class materials provided for the student and close supervision of the student at all times. In all cases, other procedures, such as group- or home-based contingencies, ought to be exhausted first.

SUMMARY

An effective intervention program can be thought of as a well-designed psychological experiment.

Use of self-control is the main objective of behavioral interventions because it transfers the control of behavior from an external source to an internal source, thereby increasing the likelihood that the intervention effects will continue beyond the treatment setting. Self-control can be trained. Stimulus control of behavior is the central element because it provides information about reinforcement and punishment, the two major consequences of behavior. The intervention begins with the selection of a behavior that has been targeted for change, which is then explicitly defined, and decisions are then made about its measurement and recording. The selection of a design, which follows, may be the most critical feature of the intervention, because interpretation of the effect hinges on its adequacy.

Because teachers are the most likely intervention agents, consideration needs to be given to their preferences for intervention procedures. Reinforcement of some type is favored over suppressants unless the behavior is severe, in which case a suppressant procedure such as time-out will be considered if it is proven to be effective. The availability of a wide variety of reinforcers, given the Premack Principle, and the alternatives for punishment, such as DRO, provide the school psychologist with several procedures that do not have negative connotations.

Behavior analysis is a frequently used procedure in school settings, but this intervention approach has some inherent dangers, such as abuse and misuse of certain procedures. Also, the procedures are occasionally incorrectly used. Nevertheless, if the intervention is properly designed and correctly executed, it has the potential to make substantial behavioral changes. The emergence of cognitive behavior modification provides the school psychologist with another approach to behavior change. This approach may be especially useful in those situations where operant-based approaches have been ineffective. The overriding concern with the use of intervention procedures has to be the ethical considerations involving the rights of the child and the acceptability of the procedure. No method can be justified if it violates ethical principles.

REFERENCES

Abramowitz, A. J., & O'Leary, S. G. (1990). Effectiveness of delayed punishment in an applied setting. *Behavior Therapy, 21,* 231–239.

Adelman, H. S., & Taylor, L. (1986). Children's reluctance regarding treatment: Incompetence, resistance, or an appropriate response? *School Psychology Review, 15,* 91–99.

Allen, C. T., & Forman, S. G. (1984). Efficacy of methods of training teachers in behavior modification. *School Psychology Review, 13,* 26–32.

Baer, D. M., Wolf, M. M., & Risely, T. R. (1987). Some still current dimensions of applied behavior analysis. *Journal of Applied Behavior Analysis, 20,* 313–329.

Baldwin, J. D., & Baldwin, J. L. (1986). *Behavior principles in everyday life* (2nd ed.). Englewood Cliffs, NJ: Prentice-Hall.

Balsam, P. D., & Bondy, A. S. (1983). The negative side-effects of reward. *Journal of Applied Behavior Analysis, 16,* 283–296.

Barlow, D. H., & Hersen, M. (1973). Single-case experimental designs: Uses in applied clinical research. *Archives of General Psychiatry, 29,* 319–325.

Belcastro, F. P. (1985). Gifted students and behavior modification. *Behavior Modification, 9,* 155–164.

Bellack, A. S., Hersen, M., & Kazdin, A. E. (1990). *International handbook of behavior modification and therapy* (2nd ed.). New York: Plenum Press.

Billings, D. C., & Wasik, B. H. (1985). Self-instructional training with preschoolers: An attempt to replicate. *Journal of Applied Behavior Analysis, 18,* 61–67.

Blew, P. A., Schwartz, I. S., & Lace, S. C. (1985). Teaching functional community skills to autistic children using nonhandicapped peer tutors. *Journal of Applied Behavior Analysis, 18,* 337–342.

Bornstein, P. H. (1985). Self-instructional training: A commentary and state-of-the-art. *Journal of Applied Behavior Analysis, 18,* 69–72.

Bryant, L. E., & Budd, K. S. (1982). Self-instructional training to increase independent work performance in preschoolers. *Journal of Applied Behavior Analysis, 15,* 259–271.

Carden Smith, L. K., & Fowler, S. A. (1984). Positive peer pressure: The effects of peer monitoring on children's disruptive behavior. *Journal of Applied Behavior Analysis, 17,* 213–227.

Carey, R. G., & Bucher, B. (1983). Positive practice overcorrection: The effects of duration of positive practice on acquisition and response reduction. *Journal of Applied Behavior Analysis, 16,* 101–109.

Carey, R. G., & Bucher, B. D. (1986). Positive practice overcorrection. *Behavior Modification, 10,* 73–92.

Charlap, M. H., Kurtz, P. F., & Greenberg Casey, F. (1990). Using aberrant behaviors as reinforcers for autistic children. *Journal of Applied Behavior Analysis, 23,* 163–181.

Cherek, D. R., Spega, R., Steinberg, J. L., & Kelly, T. H. (1990). Human aggressive responses maintained by avoidance or escape from point loss. *Journal of Experimental Analysis of Behavior, 53,* 293–303.

Christian, B. T. (1983). A practical reinforcement hierarchy for classroom behavior modification. *Psychology in the Schools, 20,* 83–84.

Cooper, J. O., Heron, T. E., & Heward, W. L. (1987). *Applied behavior analysis.* Columbus, OH: Merrill.

Craighead, W. E. (1982). A brief clinical history of cognitive-behavior therapy with children. *School Psychology Review, 11,* 5–13.

Dangel, R. F., Deschner, J. P., & Rasp, R. R. (1989). Anger control training for adolescents in residential treatment. *Behavior Modification, 13,* 447–458.

Derevensky, J. L., & Rose, M. I. (1978). Teacher preference for various positive reinforcements. *Psychology in the Schools, 15,* 565–570.

Dickerson, E. A., & Creedon, C. F. (1981). Self-selection of standards by children: The relative effectiveness of pupil-selected and teacher-selected standards of performance. *Journal of Applied Behavior Analysis, 14,* 425–433.

Dougherty, B. S., Fowler, S. A., & Paine, S. C. (1985). The use of peer monitors to reduce negative interaction during recess. *Journal of Applied Behavior Analysis, 18,* 141–153.

Dougherty, E. H., & Dougherty, A. (1977). The daily report card: A simplified and flexible package for classroom behavioral management. *Psychology in the Schools, 14,* 191–195.

Dunlap, L. K., & Dunlap, G. (1989). A self-monitoring package for teaching subtraction with regrouping to students with learning disabilities.

Journal of Applied Behavior Analysis, 22, 309–314.

Edelstein, B. A. (1989). Generalization: Terminological, methodological and conceptual issues. *Behavior Therapy, 20,* 311–324.

Egel, A. L. (1981). Reinforcer variation: Implications for motivating developmentally disabled children. *Journal of Applied Behavior Analysis, 14,* 345–350.

Egel, A. L., Richman, G. S., & Koegel, R. L. (1981). Normal peer models and autistic children's learning. *Journal of Applied Behavior Analysis, 14,* 3–12.

Fantuzzo, J. W., & Clement, P. W. (1981). Generalization of the effects of teacher- and self-administered token reinforcers to nontreated students. *Journal of Applied Behavior Analysis, 14,* 435–447.

Fantuzzo, J. W., Rohrbeck, C. A., Hightower, A. D., & Work, W. C. (1991). Teachers' use and children's preference for rewards in elementary school. *Psychology in the Schools, 26,* 175–181.

Feldman, M. P., & Peay, J. (1982). Ethical and legal issues. In A. S. Bellack, M. Hersen, & A. E. Kazdin (Eds.), *International handbook of behavior modification and therapy* (pp. 231–261). New York: Plenum Press.

Forness, S. R. (1973). The reinforcement hierarchy. *Psychology in the Schools, 10,* 168–177.

Fowler, S. A., & Baer, D. M. (1981). "Do I have to be good all day?" The timing of delayed reinforcement as a factor in generalization. *Journal of Applied Behavior Analysis, 14,* 13–24.

Gardener, W. I., & Cole, C. L. (1988). Self-monitoring procedures. In E. S. Shapiro & T. R. Kratochwill (Eds.), *Behavioral assessment in the schools* (pp. 206–246). New York: Guilford.

Gaylord-Ross, R. J., Haring, T. G., Brien, C., & Pitts-Conway, V. (1984). The training and generalization of social interaction skills with autistic youth. *Journal of Applied Behavior Analysis, 17,* 229–247.

Gelfand, D. M., Jenson, W. R., & Drew, C. J. (1982). *Understanding childhood behavior disorders.* New York: Holt, Rinehart & Winston.

Goldiamond, I. (1974). Toward a constructional approach to social problems: Ethical constitutional issues raised by applied behavior analysis. *Behaviorism, 2,* 1–85.

Greenwood, C. R., Dinwiddie, G., Terry, B., Wade, L., Stanley, S. D., Thibadeau, S., & Delquadri,

J. C. (1984). Teacher versus peer-mediated instruction: An ecobehavioral analysis of achievement outcomes. *Journal of Applied Behavioral Analysis, 17,* 521–538.

Gross, A. M., & Ekstrand, M. (1983). Increasing and maintaining rates of teacher praise. *Behavior Modification, 7,* 126–135.

Guevremont, D. C., Osnes, P. G., & Stokes, T. F. (1988). The functional role of preschoolers verbalizations in the generalization of self-instructional training. *Journal of Applied Behavior Analysis, 21,* 45–55.

Gutkin, T. B., & Reynolds, C. R. (1990). *The handbook of school psychology* (2nd ed.). New York: Wiley & Sons.

Halle, J. W., Baer, D. M., & Spradlin, J. E. (1981). Teacher's generalized use of delay as a stimulus control procedure to increase language use in handicapped children. *Journal of Applied Behavior Analysis, 14,* 389–409.

Hamlet, C. C., Axelrod, S., & Kuerschner, S. (1984). Eye control as an antecedent to compliant behavior. *Journal of Applied Behavior Analysis, 17,* 553–557.

Haring, T. G., & Kennedy, C. H. (1990). Contextual control of problem behavior in students with severe disabilities. *Journal of Applied Behavior Analysis, 23,* 235–243.

Harris, K. R. (1980). Self-monitoring of attentional behavior versus self-monitoring of productivity: Effects on-task behavior and academic response rate among learning disabled children. *Journal of Applied Behavior Analysis, 19,* 417–423.

Harris, S. L., & Ferrari, M. (1988). Developmental factors and their relationship to the identification and treatment of behavior problems of children. In J. C. Witt & S. N. Elliott (Eds.), *Handbook of behavior therapy in education* (pp. 151–169). New York; Plenum Press.

Hartman, D. P., & Hall, R. V. (1976). The changing criterion design. *Journal of Applied Behavior Analysis, 9,* 527–532.

Hartman, D. P., & Wood, D. D. (1990). Observational methods. In A. S. Bellack, M. Hersen, & A. E. Kazdin (Eds.), *International handbook of behavior modification and therapy* (2nd ed., pp. 107–138). New York: Plenum Press.

Hawkins, R. P., & Dobes, R. W. (1975). Behavioral definitions in applied behavioral analysis: Explicit or implicit. In B. C. Etzel, J. M. LeBlanc, & D. M. Baer (Eds.), *New developments in behav-*

ioral research: Theory methods and applications. In honor of Sidney W. Bijou (pp. 167–188). Hillsdale, NJ: Erlbaum.

Hayes, S. C., Rosenfarb, I., Wulfert, E., Munt, E. D., Korn, Z., & Zettle, R. D. (1985). Self-reinforcement effects: An artifact of social standard setting? *Journal of Applied Analysis of Behavior, 18,* 201–214.

Heller, M. S., & White, M. A. (1975). Rates of teacher verbal approval and disapproval to higher and lower ability classes. *Journal of Educational Psychology, 67,* 796–800.

Hersen, M. (1990). Single-case experimental designs. In A. S. Bellack, M. Hersen, & A. E. Kazdin (Eds.), *International handbook of behavior modification and therapy* (2nd ed., pp. 175–210). New York: Plenum Press.

Hersen, M., & Barlow, D. H. (1976). *Single case experimental designs: Strategies for studying behavioral change.* Elmsford, NY: Pergamon Press.

Hughes, J. N. (1988). *Cognitive behavior therapy with children in schools.* New York: Pergamon Press.

Jones, R. T., Ollendick, T. H., Shinske, F. K. (1989). The role of behavioral versus cognitive variables in skill acquisition. *Behavior Therapy, 20,* 293–302.

Kahn, J. S., Kehle, T. J., Jenson, W. R., & Clark, E. (1990). Comparison of cognitive-behavioral, relaxation, and self-modeling interventions for depression among middle-school students. *School Psychology Review, 19,* 196–211.

Kane, M. T., & Kendall, P. C. (1989). Anxiety disorders in children: A multiple-baseline evaluation of a cognitive-behavioral treatment. *Behavior Therapy, 20,* 499–508.

Karlan, G. R., & Rusch, F. R. (1982). Correspondence between saying and doing: Some thoughts on defining correspondence and future directions for application. *Journal of Applied Behavior Analysis, 15,* 151–162.

Kaufman, K. F., & O'Leary, K. D. (1972). Reward, cost and self-evaluation procedures for disruptive adolescents in a psychiatric hospital school. *Journal of Applied Behavior Analysis, 5,* 293–309.

Kazdin, A. E. (1980) *Behavior modification in applied settings.* Homewood, IL: Dorsey Press.

Kazdin, A. E. (1982a). Current developments and research issues in cognitive-behavioral intervention: A commentary. *School Psychology Review, 11,* 75–82.

Kazdin, A. E. (1982b). The token economy: A decade later. *Journal of Applied Behavior Analysis, 15,* 431–445.

Kehle, T. J., Clark, E., Jenson, W. R., & Wampold, B. E. (1986). Effectiveness of self-observation with behavior disordered elementary school children. *School Psychology Review, 15,* 289–295.

Kehle, T. J., Owen, S. V., & Cressey, E. T. (1990). The use of self-modeling as an intervention in school psychology: A case study of an elective mute. *School Psychology Review, 19,* 115–121.

Kelley, M. L., & Stokes, T. F. (1982). Contingency contracting with disadvantaged youth: Improving classroom performance. *Journal of Applied Behavior Analysis, 15,* 447–454.

Kendall, P. C., & Braswell, L. (1982). Assessment for cognitive-behavioral interventions in the schools. *School Psychology Review, 11,* 21–31.

Kestner, J., Hammer, D., Wolfe, D., Rothblum, E., & Drabman, R. S. (1982). Teacher popularity and contrast effects in a classroom token economy. *Journal of Applied Behavior Analysis, 15,* 85–96.

Knapczyk, D. R. (1989). Generalization of student question asking from special class to regular class settings. *Journal of Applied Behavior Analysis, 22,* 77–83.

Kohler, F. W., & Fowler, S. A. (1985). Training prosocial behaviors to young children: An analysis of reciprocity with untrained peers. *Journal of Applied Analysis of Behavior, 18,* 187–200.

Kratochwill, T. R. (1978). *Single subject research.* New York: Academic Press.

Lahey, B. B., & Strauss, C. C. (1982). Some considerations in evaluating the clinical utility of cognitive behavior therapy with children. *School Psychology Review, 11,* 67–74.

Leach, D. J., & Dolan, N. K. (1985). Helping teachers increase student academic engagement rate. *Behavioral Modification, 9,* 55–71.

Lenz, M., Singh, N. N., & Hewett, A. E. (1991). Overcorrection as an academic remediation procedure. *Behavior Modificaion, 15,* 64–73.

Lindsley, O. R. (1971). An interview. *Teaching Exceptional Children, 3,* 114–119.

Little, L. M., & Kelley, M. L. (1989). The efficacy of response cost procedures for reducing children's noncompliance to parental instructions. *Behavior Therapy, 20,* 525–534.

Lochman, J. E., & Curry, J. F. (1986). Effects of social problem-solving training and self-instruction training with aggressive boys. *Journal of Clinical Child Psychology, 15,* 159–164.

Luria, A. (1961). *The role of speech in the regulation of normal and abnormal behavior.* New York: Liveright.

Mace, F. C., McCurdy, B., & Quigley, E. A. (1990). A collateral effect of reward predicted by matching theory. *Journal of Applied Behavior Analysis, 23,* 197–205.

Mace, F. C., Page, T. J., Ivancic, M. T., & O'Brien, S. (1986). Effectiveness of brief time-out with and without contingent delay: A comparative analysis. *Journal of Applied Behavior Analysis, 19,* 79–86.

Mann, J., Thomas, T. J., Plunkett, J. W., & Meisels, S. J. (1991). Time sampling: A methodological critique. *Child Development, 62,* 227–241.

Martens, B. K., & Meller, P. J. (1990). The application of behavioral principles to educational settings. In T. B. Gutkin & C. R. Reynolds (Eds.), *The handbook of school psychology* (2nd ed., pp. 612–634). New York: Wiley.

Martin, G., & Pear, J. (1983). *Behavior modification* (2nd ed.). Englewood Cliffs, NJ: Prentice-Hall.

Mason, S. A., McGee, G. G., Farmer-Dougan, V., & Risley, T. R. (1989). A practical strategy for ongoing reinforcer assessment. *Journal of Applied Behavior Analysis, 22,* 171–179.

Masters, J. C., Burish, T. G., Hollon, S. D., & Remm, D. C. (1957). *Behavior therapy.* New York: Harcourt Brace Jovanovich.

McConaughy, S. H., & Achenbach, T. M. (1990). Contributions of developmental psychopathology to school services. In T. B. Gutkin & C. R. Reynolds (Eds.), *The handbook of school psychology* (2nd ed., pp. 244–286). New York: Wiley.

Meichenbaum, D. (1977). *Cognitive behavior modification: An integrative approach.* New York: Plenum Press.

Meichenbaum, D. (1985). Cognitive behavioral theories. In S. Lynn & J. Garske (Eds.), *Contemporary psychotherapies: Methods and models* (pp. 261–286). Columbus, OH: Merrill.

Meichenbaum, D., & Goodman, J. (1971). Training impulsive children to talk to themselves: A means of developing self control. *Journal of Abnormal Psychology, 77,* 115–125.

More, F. C., McCurdy, B., & Quigley, E. A. (1990). A collateral effect of reward predicted by matching theory. *Journal of Applied Behavioral Analysis, 23,* 197–205.

More, F. C., Page, T. J., Ivancic, M. T., & O'Brien, S. (1986). Effectiveness of brief time-out with and without contingent delay: A comparative analysis.

Journal of Applied Behavior Analysis, 19, 79–86.

Morris, C. W., & Cohen, R. (1982). Cognitive considerations in cognitive behavior modification. *School Psychology Review, 11,* 14–20.

Ollendick, T. H., Dailey, D., & Shapiro, E. S. (1983). Vicarious reinforcement: Expected and unexpected results. *Journal of Applied Behavior Analysis, 16,* 485–491.

Osnes, P. G., Guevremont, D. C., & Stokes, T. F. (1986). If I say I'll talk more, then I will. *Behavior Modification, 10,* 287–299.

Pace, G. M., Ivancic, M. T., Edwards, G. L., Iwata, B. A., & Page, T. J. (1985). Assessment of stimulus preference and reinforcer value with profoundly retarded individuals. *Journal of Applied Behavior Analysis, 18,* 249–255.

Pfeffner, L. J., Rosen, L. A., & O'Leary, S. G. (1985). The efficacy of an all-positive approach to classroom management. *Journal of Applied Behavior Analysis, 18,* 257–261.

Poleng, A., & Ryan, C. (1982). Differential reinforcement of other-behavior schedules. *Behavior Modification, 6,* 3–21.

Proctor, M. A., & Morgan, D. (1991). Effectiveness of a response cost raffle procedure on the disruptive classroom behavior of adolescents with behavior problems. *School Psychology Review, 20,* 97–109.

Prout, H. T., & Harvey, J. R. (1978). Applications of desensitization procedures for school-related problems: A review. *Psychology in the Schools, 15,* 533–541.

Reid, J. B. (1970). Reliability assessment of observational data: A possible methodological problem. *Child Development, 41,* 1143–1150.

Reimers, T. M., Wacker, D. P., & Koeppl, G. (1987). Acceptability of behavioral interventions: A review of the literature. *School Psychology Review, 16,* 212–227.

Rencover, A., & Newsom, C. D. (1985). The relative motivational properties of sensory and edible reinforcers in teaching autistic children. *Journal of Applied Behavior Analysis, 18,* 237–248.

Repp, A. C., Barton, L. E., & Brulle, A. R. (1983). A comparison of two procedures for programming the differential reinforcement of other behaviors. *Journal of Applied Behavior Analysis, 16,* 435–445.

Reynolds, C. R., Gutkin, T. B., Elliott, S. H., & Witt, J. C. (1984). *School psychology: Essentials of theory and practice.* New York: Wiley.

Roberts, M. W. (1988). Enforcing chair timeouts with room timeouts. *Behavior Modification, 12,* 353–370.

Rosen, J. C., Saltzberg, E., & Srebnik, D. (1989). Cognitive behavior therapy for negative body image. *Behavior Therapy, 20,* 393–404.

Schreibman, L., Koegel, R. L., Charlop, M. H., & Egel, A. L. (1990). Infantile autism. In A. S. Bellack, M. Hersen, & A. E. Kazdin (Eds.), *International handbook of behavior modification and therapy* (2nd ed., pp. 763–789). New York: Plenum Press.

Semon, S. J., Ayllon, T., & Milan, M. A. (1982). Behavioral compensation. *Behavior Modification, 6,* 407–420.

Singh, N. N., & Singh, J. (1986). Increasing oral reading proficiency. *Behavior Modification, 10,* 115–130.

Sisson, L. A., Babeo, T. J., & Van Hasselt, V. B. (1988). Group training to increase social behaviors in young multi-handicapped children. *Behavior Modification, 12,* 497–524.

Speltz, M. L., Wenters Shimamura, J., & McReynolds, W. T. (1982). Procedural variations in group contingencies: Effects on children's academic and social behaviors. *Journal of Applied Behavior Analysis, 15,* 533–544.

Stokes, T. F., & Baer, D. M. (1977). An implicit technology of generalization. *Journal of Applied Behavior Analysis, 10,* 349–367.

Stokes, T. F., & Osnes, P. G. (1989). An operant pursuit of generalization. *Behavior Therapy, 20,* 337–355.

Stolz, S. B. (1978). *Ethical issues in behavior modification.* San Francisco: Jossey-Bass.

Strain, P. S., Lambert, D. L., Kerr, M. M., Stagg, V., & Lenkner, D. A. (1983). Naturalistic assessment of children's compliance to teachers' requests and consequences for compliance. *Journal of Applied Behavior Analysis, 16,* 243–249.

Sullivan, M. A., & O'Leary, G. G. (1990). Maintenance following reward and cost token programs. *Behavior Therapy, 21,* 139–149.

Thoresen, C. E., & Mahoney, M. J. (1974). *Behavioral self-control.* New York: Holt, Rinehart & Winston.

Tingstrom, D. H. (1990). Acceptability of time-out: The influence of problem behavior severity, interventionist, and reported effectiveness. *Journal of School Psychology, 28,* 165–169.

Touchette, P. E., MacDonald, R. F., & Langer, S. N. (1985). A scatterplot for identifying stimulus control of problem behavior. *Journal of Applied Behavior Analysis, 18,* 343–351.

Van Houten, R., Axelrod, S., Bailey, J. S., Favell, J. E., Foxx, R. M., Iwata, B. A., & Lovaas, O. I. (1988). The right to effective behavioral treatment. *Journal of Applied Behavior Analysis, 21,* 381–384.

Van Houten, P. A., Nau, P. A., MacKenzie-Keating, S. E., Sameoto, D., & Colavecchia, B. (1982). An analysis of some variables influencing the effectiveness of reprimands. *Journal of Applied Behavior Analysis, 15,* 65–83.

Wacker, D. P., Berg, W. K., Berrie, P., & Swatta, P. (1985). Generalization and maintenance of complex skills by severely handicapped adolescents following picture prompt training. *Journal of Applied Behavior Analysis, 18,* 329–336.

Wacker, D. P., Berg, W. K., Wiggins, B., Muldoon, M., & Cavanaugh, J. (1985). Evaluation of reinforcer preferences for profoundly handicapped students. *Journal of Applied Behavior Analysis, 18,* 173–178.

Wall, S. M., & Bryant, N. D. (1979). Behavioral self management of academic test performances in elementary classrooms. *Psychology in the Schools, 16,* 558–567.

Wasserman, T. H., & Vogrin, D. J. (1979). Long term effects of a token economy on target and off-task behaviors. *Psychology in the Schools, 16,* 551–557.

West, R. P., & Sloane, H. N. (1986). Teacher presentation rate and point delivery rate. *Behavior Modification, 10,* 267–286.

Wherry, J. N. (1983). Some legal considerations and implications for the use of behavior modification in the schools. *Psychology in the Schools, 20,* 46–51.

White, O. R., & Haring, N. G. (1980). *Exceptional teaching* (2nd ed.). Columbus, OH: Merrill.

Whitman, T. L., Subak, J. W., Butler, K. M., Richter, R., & Johnson, M. R. (1982). Improved classroom behavior in mentally retarded children through correspondence training. *Journal of Applied Behavior Analysis, 15,* 545–564.

Williams, J. A., Koegel, R. L., & Egel, A. L. (1981). Response-reinforcer relationships and improved learning in autistic children. *Journal of Applied Behavior Analysis, 14,* 53–60.

Witt, J. C., & Martens, B. K. (1983). Assessing the acceptability of behavioral interventions used in classrooms. *Psychology in the Schools, 20,* 510–517.

Wyatt, W. J., & Hawkins, R. P. (1987). Rates of teachers' verbal approval and disapproval. *Behavior Modification, 11,* 27–51.

CHAPTER 6

PSYCHOTHERAPEUTIC INTERVENTIONS

INTEGRATING THEORY AND SKILLS

General Theory and Cultural Intentionality

Theory provides organizing principles for counseling and therapy; practice refers to the integration of skills and theory. The task for the clinician is to exercise what he or she views as the most accurate concepts from each theory and to build his or her own theory about the world. The goal is to avoid a single-minded rigidity and to remain adaptable. Ivey, Ivey, and Simek-Downing (1987) advocate such a *general theory* orientation in which several different orientations are integrated into one unified approach. General theory, which can be described as a type of systematic eclecticism, aspires to organize components of a theory into a coherent and systematic framework. The culturally intentional counselor has knowledge of alternative theoretical approaches and treatment modalities and is competent in skills from diverse orientations so as to communicate with individuals from a variety of cultural and socioeconomic backgrounds. The greater number of responses professionals have in their repertoire, the more prospects there are for helping a client and the greater the opportunity for the client to develop.

It is possible to be committed to a single theoretical orientation and continue to be a general theorist. Consider a behavior therapist who could respect different theories and adapt segments of them into practice. For example, Albert Ellis has a central cognitive-behavioral theoretical commitment, but also draws on humanistic and psychodynamic frameworks to enrich his basic orientation. The purpose of this chapter is to describe psychodynamic, existential-humanistic, cognitive-behavioral, and systems theories, as well as particular concepts and techniques from each that are relevant for psychologists providing services to children and youth. Basic microskills of attending and influencing skills are discussed since they are common to all systems of counseling and since they substantially enhance the consultation process (see Chapter 7). An overview also is presented of developmental issues pertinent to counseling children and adolescents.

Definition of *Helping*

Helping is broadly defined as a general framework in which one person offers another person or group assistance, typically in the form of interviewing, counseling, and psychotherapy. Ivey, Ivey, and Simek-Downing (1987) define *interviewing* as a method of information gathering often done in a welfare office, career counseling, or consultation (see Chapter 7). *Counseling* is a more intensive process concerned with assisting typical people in realizing their goals or in functioning more effectively. *Psychotherapy* is a longer-term process concerned with reconstruction of the person and larger changes in personality structure. Although psychotherapy may be restricted conceptually to individuals with pathological problems, the distinction among these terms often is blurred in practice. *Therapy* is a word that has become increasingly popular and may develop into the generic, common description of both counseling and psychotherapy. Within this chapter, *counseling* and *therapy* are used interchangeably.

Skills of Intentional Interviewing

Skills form the foundation of effective theory and practice. There is a group of attending and influencing skills that provides a solid foundation for therapeutic techniques that can enhance client development. These basic microskills are invaluable regardless of one's theoretical orientation.

Nonverbal communication influences the content and process of counseling. Eye contact, appropriate body language, and vocal tone are the physical fundamentals of attending behavior. Listening (verbal following) also is necessary. In addition to attentive body postures, intentional therapists stay on the client's topic and infrequently change topics abruptly or interrupt. Cormier and Cormier (1979) discuss three dimensions of nonverbal behavior, which play an important role in communication and relationships with others. *Kinesics* are body motion, gestures, facial expressions, eye movements, and posture. *Paralinguistics* include vocal cues such as voice quality (level, pitch), fluency in speech (stuttering, hesitations, speech errors), rate of speech, silence, and autonomic responses such as clammy hands, shallow breathing, and blushing or paleness. *Proxemics* involve environmental and personal space such as seating arrangement, furniture array, and distance between counselor and client.

The Basic Listening Sequence

Specific types of verbal leads or counselor statements are termed *attending skills* or *listening skills*. These can be organized into the basic listening sequence, which is used to draw out information from the client. Most counselors and therapists use variations of this model as they become familiar with the client's life and concerns. The basic listening sequence also can be particularly valuable during the consultation process (discussed in Chapter 7). Following are descriptions and functions of attending skills within the interview.

Open questions are invitations for the client to talk. They often begin with *what, how, why, could,* or *would,* which usually require the client to provide an elaborated response.

Closed questions typically begin with the words *is, are, do,* or *did* and can be answered with a *yes* or *no* or in several words. They can be used to gather information, to clarify, to provide focus, and to narrow the area of discussion, or to prevent a client's meandering from the topic. If used excessively, they can deter conversation and obstruct the therapeutic relationship. *Why* questions can be especially problematic since they can engender client defensiveness, particularly with adolescents. The skills of encouraging, paraphrasing, and reflection of feeling can be less intrusive yet accomplish the same goals as questions. Some theories such as psychodynamic and rational-emotive may make extensive use of closed questions, whereas Rogerian and person-centered therapies often oppose the use of any questions at all.

Encouragers or *restatements* are a direct repetition of what the client has said, using such short comments as *uh-huh, so,* or *tell me more.* They are active ways for the counselor to indicate to clients that they are heard and can continue. Each leads the client into separate directions with more depth, which is a characteristic response of the effective use of encouragers and restatements. As Ivey, Ivey, and Simek-Downing (1987) emphasize, "Each minimal encourager can be considered a reinforcer to the client that will have influence on what the client will talk about next in more detail. Encouragers and restatements are by no means minimal in their impact on clients" (pp. 72–73).

Paraphrase occurs when the therapist repeats an encapsulated version of the client's main words or thoughts. The client's sometimes confused statements are distilled to their essence. Selective attention is given to objective content, with restating by the counselor to clarify and to merge recent comments or trends of discussion and to present ideas concisely.

Reflections of feelings often occur with paraphrase in practice. They are concerned with feelings associated with facts and afford the opportunity to ascertain where the client is emotionally on an issue. A reflection of feeling consists of three basic parts plus a fourth component that is a paraphrase: (1) the pronoun *you* or the client's name; (2) the emotional label such as *angry, fearful, ambivalent,* or *elated;* (3) a sentence stem (e.g., "You seem to feel . . ."); and (4) a context for the emotional experience (e.g., "You feel abandoned when your parents ignore you").

Reflection of meaning is another important microskill in which the deeper, underlying meaning of the client's statements is identified. They are closely associated with interpretations from the influencing skills. With the therapist providing the interpretation, the client has been assisted in finding a new interpretation or meaning in old information or situations. Rather than being included as part of the basic listening sequence, Ivey, Ivey, and Simek-Downing (1987) view it as a more interpretative, reflective skill that typically follows from effectual use of the basic listening sequence rather than being part of it.

Summarization reviews the content and main feelings communicated in the session, integrates common components, and clarifies. The client's verbalizations, facts, feelings, and meanings are profiled to the client. Summarization grants an opportunity for the counselor to check the accuracy of his or her thinking about the client's circumstance and also provides a break in the interview.

Influencing Skills

Although attending is important, client growth can be slow and difficult if used as the exclusive avenue for change. When counselors become active participants in the interview, influence and client change are accelerated. The counselor can use knowledge of theory and skills, personal life experience, and specific understanding of the particular client and culture to the benefit of the client. Influencing skills are complex and can be more effective if used sparingly and in conjunction with listening skills.

Interpretation is the central influencing skill. It offers the client an alternative view of issues

and can lead to a cognitive change in worldview. Such an alternate interpretation of life experience provides the groundwork for later change in client behavior. Because of the potential threat to a client's existing frame of reference, repercussions from overuse of interpretation can include a client's denying the therapist's judgment or leaving the interview.

Directive is the most influential of the influencing skills. It directs clients to do or to say something by guiding them through a fantasy (humanistic counseling), suggesting particular behavioral changes (assertiveness training), or making focused free-association suggestions (psychodynamic theory). Numerous directives are available once the basic listening skills and theoretical models are mastered. Examples include specific suggestions, paradoxical instructions, imagery, roleplay, Gestalt hot seat, relaxation, systematic desensitization, homework, and family therapy communications.

Advice/information includes suggestions or instructional information. Transactional analysis therapists or behavior therapists often teach the basics of their theories to their clients. And reality therapists may teach young people knowledge and skills they need to survive. Ivey, Ivey, and Simek-Downing (1987) caution against overuse of advice and instruction and suggest a change in style or use of an attending technique when the client responds with "yes, but. . . ."

Self-disclosure occurs when the counselor shares an experience with the client. In one type, the counselor emphasizes how he or she feels toward the client (e.g., I feel fortunate to know you). A second type includes relating a personal experience that relates to the client's topic (e.g., I can relate to that . . . ; I feel pulled in different directions when. . . .). Self-disclosure of feelings can be beneficial within a modern Rogerian theoretical paradigm. Its utility is enhanced if the self-disclosure is brief, if the counselor immediately shifts the focus back to the client, and when an open question is used to ascertain whether the self-disclosure was germane to the client's issues. Benjamin (1981) suggests that counselors "reveal

PSYCHOTHERAPEUTIC INTERVENTIONS **167**

everything that is absolutely necessary and absolutely nothing that is not" (p. 57). Self-disclosure
is not compatible with some theoretical frameworks and may not conform to a particular therapist's personal style.

Feedback helps clients see themselves as
others do. It is a major component of encounter
groups and may be an important skill of a family
therapy program when clients learn how other
family members view their behavior.

Logical consequences are used when clients
are led to understand the potential consequences
of their actions. The basic logic is that looking
ahead to the consequences of one's behavior will
help a client change current behavior. Rational-
emotive and cognitive-behavior therapies, Adlerian counseling, and reality therapy may use this
influencing skill, which can encounter client resistance and anger without a sufficient base of
rapport.

Influencing summary occurs when the therapist reviews what she or he said during the session. These often appear in concert with the
attending summarization in which the client's
verbalizations and feelings are summarized.

Confrontation

Confrontation, in which incongruities and discrepancies among attitudes, thoughts, or behaviors are pointed out, is a skill that balances both
attending and influencing skills. When framed in
the form of paraphrases, reflections of feeling, or
summarizations, confrontations render maximum opportunity for client growth. Clients often
give double messages in their verbal and/or nonverbal behavior, suggesting mixed thoughts and
feelings.

To assist the client in facing the issues, the
counselor identifies the mixed message. One
model of confrontation statements follows the
format: On one hand, you think/feel/be-
have . . . , but on the other hand, you think/feel/
behave. . . . While most persuasions of
psychotherapy attend to incongruities and discrepancies, each theory follows different avenues
toward resolving them. Ivey, Ivey, and Simek-

Downing (1987) suggest a careful balance of confrontation with supporting qualities of warmth,
positive regard, and respect.

Skill Patterns for Different Theories

The position of microskills theory is that all
models of counseling and therapy draw on attending and influencing skills. Since all systems use
the basic listening skills to some degree, the intentional counselor will find it easier to move
across paradigms. Figure 6.1 depicts the differential usage of microskills among diverse theoretical orientations. There is greater variation across
theories in influencing skills than in listening
skills. Differences in use of microskill leads also
are influenced by individual therapist style. In
addition to providing counseling services to different clients, the intentional professional with
competence in microskills can teach sensitive and
effective interview skills to others. Such skills
can improve role performance of virtually all professionals serving children and youth and their
families, including teachers and related-services
personnel.

**OVERVIEW TO COUNSELING AND THERAPY
WITH CHILDREN AND ADOLESCENTS**

The various models of psychotherapy essentially
are rooted in adult-based theories. Due to their
developmental stages, environments, and reasons
for entering therapy, children and adolescents
pose unique challenges. There are several issues
relevant to child mental-health service delivery
that are relevant to the various theoretical orientations: developmental issues, the adolescent
phase, unique aspects of counseling children and
adolescents, psychotherapy with adolescents,
multimodal perspective of treatment, and research and efficacy.

Developmental Issues

Many of the adult concerns about child behavior
may be normal developmental variation. There-

Microskill Lead	Nondirective	Modern Rogerian Encounter	Behavioral (Assertiveness Training)	Psychodynamic	Gestalt	Decisional Counseling	Rational-Emotive Therapy	Feminist Therapy	Business Problem Solving	Medical Diagnostic Interview	Traditional Teaching	Student-Centered Teaching	Eclectic/Metatheoretical
Attending Skills													
Open question	○	○	◐	◐	●	●	◐	◐	◐	◐	◐	●	◐
Closed question	○	○	●	○	◐	◐	◐	◐	◐	●	◐	◐	◐
Encourager	◐	◐	◐	◐	◐	◐	◐	◐	◐	◐	◐	●	◐
Paraphrase	●	●	◐	◐	○	◐	◐	◐	◐	◐	○	●	◐
Reflection of feeling	●	●	◐	◐	○	◐	◐	◐	◐	◐	○	●	◐
Reflection of meaning	◐	●	○	◐	○	◐	◐	●	○	○	○	◐	◐
Summarization	◐	◐	◐	◐	○	◐	◐	◐	◐	◐	◐	◐	◐
Influencing Skills													
Feedback	○	●	◐	○	◐	●	◐	◐	●	◐	◐	◐	◐
Advice/information/ and others	○	○	◐	○	○	◐	◐	●	●	●	●	◐	◐
Self-disclosure	○	●	○	○	○	○	◐	◐	○	○	○	◐	◐
Interpretation	○	○	○	●	●	◐	◐	◐	○	◐	○	○	◐
Logical consequences	○	○	◐	○	○	◐	●	◐	●	◐	◐	◐	◐
Directive	○	○	●	○	●	◐	◐	◐	●	●	●	◐	◐
Influ. summary	○	○	◐	○	○	◐	◐	◐	●	◐	◐	◐	◐
Confrontation (Combined Skill)	◐	◐	◐	◐	●	◐	◐	●	◐	◐	◐	◐	◐
Focus													
Client	●	●	●	●	●	●	◐	◐	◐	◐	◐	●	◐
Counselor, interviewer	○	◐	○	○	○	○	◐	◐	○	◐	○	◐	◐
Mutual/group/"We"	○	◐	○	○	○	○	○	◐	○	○	○	○	◐
Other people	○	○	◐	◐	◐	◐	◐	◐	◐	◐	○	◐	◐
Topic or problem	○	○	◐	○	○	●	●	◐	●	●	●	◐	◐
Cultural/ environmental context	○	○	◐	○	○	●	○	●	◐	○	○	◐	◐
Issue of Meaning (Topics, key words likely to be attended to and reinforced)	Feelings	Relationship	Behavior problem solving	Unconscious motivation	Here and now behavior	Problem solving	Irrational ideas/logic	Problem as a "women's issue"	Problem solving	Diagnosis of illness	Information/facts	Student ideas/info./facts	Varies
Amount of Interviewer Talk-Time	Low	Medium	High	Low	High	Medium	High	Medium	High	High	High	Medium	Varies

Legend

● Frequent use of skill   ◐ Common use of skill   ○ May use skill occasionally

FIGURE 6.1 Examples of microskill leads used by interviewers of differing theoretical orientations

Source: From Allen E. Ivey, Mary Bradford Ivey, & Lynn Simek-Downing, *Counseling and psychotherapy: Integrating skills, theory, and practice.* Copyright © 1987 by Allyn and Bacon. Reprinted with permission.

fore, "knowledge of development and the behavioral ranges that are considered normal at different ages is crucial to making the discrimination between truly deviant behavior and minor developmental crises" (Prout, 1983, p. 8). Behaviors can be normative at different age levels yet perceived as problematic to adults. Unless therapists understand what constitutes normal deviations in child behavior, it can be difficult to know when to intervene clinically (Harris & Ferrari, 1983). Indeed, one task of a consultant (discussed in Chapter 7) may be to clarify to teachers that a child's behavior may be quite typical of that particular age.

In addition, the child/adolescent therapist must set goals and intervention objectives (see Chapter 7) within a developmental framework in order to avoid setting expectations that exceed a child's developmental capacity. Developmental capability also influences treatment modality. For example, cognitive and insight-oriented therapies are not generally appropriate for young children. Professionals also must be sensitive to developmental delays in children and adolescents. Such delays may be contributing factors in the pathogenesis of emotional disturbances (e.g., depression in persons with mental retardation; see Epps, 1991). While considering developmental status, professionals must consider chronological age expectations as well (see Brown et al., 1979; Epps, 1983).

Developmental theory can be particularly relevant to the child/adolescent therapist. For example, Erikson's (1972) theory of psychosocial development characterizes adolescence as a moratorium from adult responsibilities. Yet some adolescents are faced with developmental tasks (see Havighurst, 1951) generally not encountered until adulthood, such as parenting a parent (e.g., one who is critically ill) or parenting a child (e.g., the adolescent's own child or a younger sibling when the natural parent is unavailable).

The Adolescent Phase

Adolescence is probably the single developmental period that creates the greatest bewilderment and trepidation for caregivers, teachers, and counselors (Prout, 1983). Physical development, changing sexual mores, emotional lability, peer and societal pressures, complex interpersonal relationships, family disorganization, alcohol and drugs, college and vocational pressures and decisions, and experimentation with different viewpoints and lifestyles can be vexing even for relatively well-adjusted adolescents. Prout identifies two important implications for adolescent psychotherapeutic work. First, the therapist must avoid overinterpreting typical and apparently peculiar behavior, thoughts, or feelings as indicative of severe disturbance. Second, the therapist must be alert to an unpredictable and exasperating progression of treatment.

Developmental Tasks

For the transition from childhood to adulthood, Havighurst's (1951) adolescent developmental tasks provide a useful framework for understanding the confusion adolescents often experience. Establishing multiple types of peer relationships and androgynous roles (rather than a traditional male-female association), realizing emotional and financial independence from parents, choosing among the vast array of occupation and higher-education opportunities, and synthesizing values that are compatible with one's learning and social history and anticipations of future career, family, and civic endeavors are monumental concerns facing today's adolescents. The problems associated with substance abuse and poverty also plague a growing number of our youth.

Characteristics of Thought, Affective States, and Behavior

Copeland (1974) and Prout (1983) describe several features of adolescent thought, affect, and behavior that influence the design and course of treatment plans. Several characteristics of adolescent thinking include the following:

1. *Preoccupation with self,* which may be narcissistic or combined with self-doubt
2. *Preoccupation with the struggle for self-expression,* with establishing a sense of iden-

tity a major hallmark of adolescence (Erikson, 1972)

3. *Conformism,* with role confusion not uncommon in adolescents (Erikson, 1972) as they adopt and conform to the values and behavior of a peer group

4. *Preoccupation with philosophical abstraction and ideals,* while formal operational thinking characterizes adolescence (Ginsburg & Opper, 1988), egocentrism (Elkind, 1967) is apparent in their difficulty differentiating between their own idealistic thought and the real world

5. *Preoccupation with sexuality,* which accompanies the torrent of physical development, with often intense and overidealized heterosexual relationships and substantial time in preening and concern about appearance

6. *Hedonism and/or asceticism,* an extreme reaction as the adolescent is largely compelled to respond to the fervor of drive states.

Several aspects of adolescent affect and behavior are:

1. *Heightened sensitivity,* with intense and fervid reactions as minor issues become major concerns

2. *Mood swings,* a form of labile emotionality

3. *Propensity to act out* in which impulsivity, rebelliousness, and, in extreme cases, delinquency and other antisocial behavior can occur

4. *Inhibition of behavior* and social withdrawal may arise.

Unique Aspects of Counseling Children and Adolescents

Differences exist between child/adolescent therapy and adult therapy. Clarizio and McCoy (1976) and Prout (1983) outline five distinctive features of the child/adolescent therapeutic relationship. First, the motivation for counseling is different. Often an adult decides that the child will enter treatment, with a varying degree of acceptance, compliance, and resistance from the child. This involuntariness may engender a motivational deficiency. Thus, the initial therapeutic tasks are to establish a relationship with the child and to develop motivation at least to consider the current situation.

Second, the child's lack of understanding of the therapeutic process and objectives is likely to interfere with motivation. The child may have an obscured view of therapy, ranging from complete misunderstanding to regarding the therapist as an agent of his or her parents, teachers, or professionals within the social services or judicial system. Children and adolescents also may have distorted or stereotyped notions of therapists. Their understanding may be particularly confused when treatment agents work in an out-of-the-ordinary setting such as a mental-health facility or hospital. Counselors within the education system, therefore, may have some advantage over clinic and community-based professionals. Hence, the counselor needs to educate the child about therapy, to demonstrate the potential benefit, and to negotiate the appropriate goals, objectives, and topics for counseling.

A third chief divergence from adult therapy is the child's more restricted language development, which relates to characteristics of cognitive development (addressed in Chapter 10). Children often have difficulty articulating their thoughts and emotions or they may use a word commonly expressed in their family. This author observed a 6-year-old girl use the term *nervous* in several therapy sessions. Upon further assessment, it became apparent that she was not anxious and that her mother (the only other member of her family) used this word nonchalantly on a regular basis. An additional consideration is the child's receptive vocabulary, which may be insufficient for understanding the interviewer's questions.

Regardless of theoretical paradigm, any clinician can be esoteric and use vernacular that is incomprehensible to children and adolescents and to the majority of adults as well. It is evident that "therapy must be geared at the appropriate developmental level for the child's . . . expressive and receptive language capabilities" (Prout, 1983, p. 18). In addition to play and other nonverbal techniques, counselors may teach the child labels (usually in his or her own terminology) and verbal mediators for emotional experiences, which in its own right may be a therapeutic goal for emotionally constricted children.

A fourth difference pertains to children's dependence on environmental factors. Typically, they react to rather than initiate change and have inconsequential resources to eliminate or to avert environmentally induced stressors such as divorce, family moves, abuse, or neglect. Problematic behaviors actually may be fairly typical reactions to environmental disturbances. Since the child's functioning is so dependent on environmental circumstances, it is especially crucial for persons in the child's world to be involved in the treatment program. When environmental changes are unlikely, therapy may focus on helping the child cope with a stressful situation. For example, the author provided child therapy to two siblings whose parents had psychiatric disorders involving generalized anxiety disorder and major depression. Since one or both parents were emotionally unavailable to the children on various occasions, the children were taught a variety of strategies to comfort themselves, such as listening to music, looking at a book, or playing quietly with each other.

A fifth variable contributing to the difference between child and adult therapy pertains to the child's less established and more malleable personality and behavioral style. Since defenses are less ingrained, the child can be more amenable to therapeutic influence. On the other hand, this greater range of normal emotional and behavioral responses can engender inconsistent responses in therapy, which should be anticipated.

Psychotherapy with Adolescents

Prout (1983) provides a fitting account of the impatience, intolerance, and uncommunicativeness that are characteristic of many adolescents in therapeutic contexts. They may deny any responsibility for difficulties and/or may have little insight into the reasons for their referral into treatment. A counselor skilled in microskills may become frustrated when reflective statements or discussion of nonthreatening and ordinary topics are met with limited responses and resistance.

In general, most adolescents are not prime candidates for insight-oriented therapy that involves the reworking of previous experiences. Weiner (1970) addresses the adolescent's unique perspective of treatment. Although many children initially are unaware of the implication of therapy, the adolescent typically is cognizant of the fact that he or she has been brought to counseling by those who can impose attendance. Unstructured probing, questioning about deep emotions and beliefs, or challenging the adolescent to explain the problematic behavior are likely to engender additional uncooperativeness. Prout (1983) suggests beginning with factual information in a nonjudgmental fashion and explaining how the therapeutic relationship will differ from those with parents, school personnel, and peers.

Consideration of developmental issues is germane throughout the course of treatment with adolescents. The counselor must deal with adolescents' concern about how counseling may affect their independence and be sensitive to regional adolescent values and styles and pressures related to their social and emotional developmental level. Consistent with Erikson's (1972) notion of a "moratorium," during which time adolescents are free of expectations and responsibilities of adulthood, the therapist strives to maintain a balance along the independence-dependence continuum. Adolescents are neither treated like a child nor given indications that they are unconstrained in making all their own life decisions.

Multimodal Perspective of Treatment

From the multimodal perspective, there are diverse forms of interventions and interactive modalities to serve children and youth. Lazarus (1976) introduced the BASIC ID acronym, which

Keat (1979) expanded to BASIC IDEAL. These components are: **B**ehavior, **A**ffect, **S**ensation, **I**magery, **C**ognition, **I**nterpersonal relationships, **D**rugs-diet, **E**ducational pursuits, **A**dults in the child's life, and **L**earn the child's culture.

Children and youth interact within larger systems, including family and school contexts. Hence, multifactorial treatment approaches typically are advised to provide comprehensive and effective therapeutic change. Thus, a variety of interventions might be used for a particular child such as individual therapy, casework assistance for the family, family therapy, group therapy for children or parents, behavior therapy, drug treatment, inpatient or outpatient treatment, educational approaches, speech therapy, or even separation from the current home situation (Barker, 1979). Within each alternative tactic, there is a range of possible services. For example, education strategies could include various combinations of remedial or special education services (see Coleman, 1986) or behavior management programs (see Jenson, Sloane, & Young, 1988).

Interventions with parents might involve parent education in developmentally and age-appropriate child activities, child behavior management, or communication styles. Prout (1983) cautions against adopting an overly and unnecessarily comprehensive approach and urges careful assessment of areas of difficulty for child and family (see Chapter 10), selection of suitable interventions that match the child's and family's needs, and coordination and communication across personnel, disciplines, and agencies (see Chapter 7).

Research and Efficacy

Systematic investigation of the efficacy of child psychotherapy is a complex process. Prout (1983) delineates a number of obstacles to efficacy research, which are expanded in this chapter.

1. Psychotherapy represents a conglomeration of techniques, which interferes with the develop-ment of a clear definition. While psychotherapy varies along several dimensions, such as therapist theoretical orientation and duration and format of treatment, Miller, Barrett, and Hampe (1974) (cited in Barrett, Hampe, & Miller, 1978) found a generic set of procedures. Such common components of child treatments could account in part for results in which no differential treatment effects are found since treatments are not unique. Child psychotherapy research needs to uncover and to characterize procedures common to most child treatments. Once the impact of these "G" variables is known, the field can examine whether techniques that are exclusive to one therapeutic mode contribute to outcome beyond these general strategies (Barrett, Hampe, & Miller, 1978).

2. The clinical definitions of childhood populations and disorders typically are ill defined. Symptomatology and characteristics can deviate across clinicians and settings. Additionally, subgroups of children (e.g., based on gender, ethnicity) may need to be examined separately (Prout, 1983). Barrett, Hampe, and Miller (1978) delineate at least four factors related to the child and the disorder that need to be controlled in research on child psychotherapy: (a) age, with a more sophisticated developmental assessment needed; (b) intelligence; (c) type of onset and chronicity of the condition, with a need to determine whether problems that occur, disappear, then resurface are acute or chronic; and (d) severity of disorder, with a need for a standard measurement practice. McConville and Purohit (1973) further suggest that severity subsumes another dimension, namely, community tolerance for the problem.

3. Therapeutic outcome could be affected by variation in counselor dimensions such as age, gender, training, theoretical orientation, competency, and style (e.g., use of a particular pattern of microskills) (Prout, 1983). Investigations of the relationship between therapist characteristics and the outcome of psychotherapy with adults suggest a reasonable consensus that warmth, genuineness, empathy, level of experience, and freedom from neurotic difficulties promote successful outcome. Research findings are not consistent with regard to the contributions of therapist's age, gender, race, religion, and social class, though there is an emerging view of a curvilinear relationship between these variables and outcome (Meltzoff & Kornreich, 1970). Therapeutic communication is more likely to occur between counselors and clients who are neither too much alike nor too different (Carson & Heine, 1962). While these generic variables are expected to apply to child clinicians in much the same manner as they pertain to adult therapists, the field does not yet know the distinct characteristics of a "supershrink" (Barrett, Hampe, & Miller, 1978).

4. Measurement of therapeutic change is challenging. Instrumentation issues pertain to what sorts of assessment scales are used. Technical adequacy concerns are relevant due to the necessity to evaluate change reliably and validly (see Nunnally, 1978). Strupp and Hadley (1977) further advocate a tripartite model in which different vantage points are considered to evaluate change: (a) society, including significant persons in the client's life (see the discussion of social validation in Chapter 7); (b) the individual client; and (c) the mental-health professional.

Following Eysenck's (1952) lead, Levitt and colleagues (1957, 1963; Levitt, Beiser, & Robertson, 1959) conducted a series of studies that evaluated the results of child psychotherapy and concluded that the effectiveness of child psychotherapy had not been demonstrated. Levitt (1957) further estimated a baserate of 72.5 percent improvement for "untreated" children, which Barrett, Hampe, and Miller (1978) regard as a "reasonable" estimate. Thus, with 100 treated clients, between 80 and 85 percent would have to be improved in order to exceed Levitt's baseline rate.

A focus on macrovariables (unanticipated variables that account for large amounts of variance) is likely to obscure results of studies comparing broad-based treatment paradigms. Heinicke and Strassman (1975) argue for abandoning pursuit of whether psychotherapy works.

Barrett, Hampe, and Miller (1978) advocate for a more productive line of research that investigates the complex questions of "Which set of procedures is effective when applied to what kind of patients with which sets of problems and practiced by which sort of therapists?" (p. 428).

Additionally, child psychotherapy research must take into account developmental level and the systems within which the child must interface. Child therapy cannot be evaluated independently of the family and the larger society, including child advocacy, parenting, development, education, and preparation for citizenship (Barrett, Hampe, & Miller, 1978). This shift in research focus is similar to Epps and Tindal's (1987) admonition of the limited utility of examining such a broad macrovariable as placement setting when investigating special-education efficacy. Rather than continuing with macrovariable research that merges diagnostic conditions and therapists with variation in their personal styles and assessing outcome using gross measurement, Barrett, Hampe, and Miller (1978) endorse a first step of refining measures in at least four critical areas: (a) the child and the disorder, (b) the therapist and her or his personality style, (c) intervention techniques, and (d) outcome measures.

Issues in Counseling Children and Adolescents with Disabilities

Matching therapeutic method and the specific issues while considering the implication of a disability is a challenging responsibility for the counselor. To enhance the relevance and sensitivity of counseling to children and youth with special needs, therapists must examine their own knowledge and attitudes toward handicapping conditions, provide information to the client and/or family about the disability, be aware of the possibility of social/emotional difficulties in concert with cognitive or physical impairments, and make accommodations in treatment techniques when necessary to enable developmentally appropriate services.

Therapist Attitudes

Children and adolescents with disabilities have special therapeutic needs. These youth must be appreciated as individuals, with their disability being only one facet of their behavioral repertoire. Cobb and Brown (1983) and Nathanson (1979) address several issues relevant to the child therapist who serves these children. First are the beliefs commonly held by professionals. The clinician must be cognizant of her or his own attitudes and feelings toward persons with disabilities because of the relationship between these attitudes and effectiveness with therapy (e.g., Cook, Kunce, & Getsinger, 1976; Greer, 1975).

Obstacles to fair and effective treatment may arise if the therapist views the child primarily in terms of the label for the handicapping condition and renders treatment based on preconceived beliefs about the label. For example, the counselor may appraise the child based on stereotypes or a salient, unitary dimension, such as lowered intelligence in persons with mental retardation, with a concomitant disregard for other child attributes such as social skills, adaptive behavior, and positive personality features (see Epps, 1991). As discussed in Chapter 10 regarding diversity within as well as across cultures, heterogeneity in behavioral and personality styles for a particular handicapping condition generally is evident.

A common feeling toward persons with disabilities is pity, and the counselor may see the child as a victim. Such a perception may deflect attention away from the child's strengths and capabilities. A therapist may inadvertently foster dependency by assuming that the child or adolescent is less capable of coping with difficulties and frustrations. Hence, therapeutic goals may be set too low. Counselors also may unintentionally reject children and adolescents with disabilities due to a sense of repugnance toward the handicap. Such a feeling may be manifested in avoidance or impatience. Anxiety and uncertainty also may be present.

Cobb and Brown (1983) recommend several steps for counselors to adopt when working with these youth: (1) examine one's own attitudes about persons with disabilities and alter them if necessary to be maximally respectful of human dignity and worth, (2) monitor one's behavior to prevent stereotyped beliefs from interfering with treatment, (3) acquire a working knowledge of various handicapping conditions and medical disorders (for example, see Batshaw & Perret, 1986), and (4) undergo peer review of one's therapeutic interventions.

Client Knowledge of Disability

Providing basic information about the disability to the child or adolescent may be the most significant aspect of the counseling process. The author has worked with young women with Turner's syndrome and youth with autosomal recessive microcephaly or fetal alcohol effects, the implications of which neither they nor their families fully understood. As these clients become older, the nature of the condition becomes increasingly salient in their lives. Cobb and Brown (1983) suggest saying to the client that other children with _____ often ask . . . , which assists the child in framing her or his thoughts and words and in expressing concerns and informs the child that such questions and apprehensions are similar to those of others.

The opinions a child or adolescent formulates about her/his condition, often based on parent, peer, teacher, and adult reactions, have a consequential bearing on self-concept. These youth may set impractical expectations, and it may be a slow and tedious process to support them in accepting any real limitations. In some children and youth with disabilities, emotional disorders or psychopathology may be apparent (see Epps, 1991; Matson & Frame, 1986; Sigman, 1985).

Historically, mental-health professionals have had numerous misconceptions about mental disorders in persons with mental retardation (Szymanski, 1985). Investigations of the prevalence of psychopathology in children with mental retardation consistently have shown rates much higher than in the general population (e.g., Chess

& Hassibi, 1980; Jacobson, 1982; Rutter, 1971; Rutter, Tizard, Yule, Graham, & Whitmore, 1976). In addition to higher rates of psychopathology, a variety of emotional disorders has been documented in children and youth with mental retardation, including depression (DeKrey & Ehly, 1981; Kelly, Koch, & Buegel, 1976), phobias (Matson, 1981), anxiety/withdrawal (Matson, Epstein, & Cullinan, 1984), and psychotic symptoms, neurotic symptoms, or personality disturbances (Phillips & Williams, 1975).

Although there is a trend toward attempts at greater understanding of childhood psychopathology and its potential overlap with mental retardation (Matson & Frame, 1986), a number of investigations has documented the presence of diagnostic overshadowing in which the salient feature of a handicapping condition (e.g., below cognitive functioning in mental retardation) overshadowed the presence of concurrent emotional disturbances (Epps, 1991; Levitan & Reiss, 1983; Reiss, Levitan, & Szyszko, 1982; Reiss & Szyszko, 1983).

Counselor Knowledge of Disability

Knowledge of the disability is necessary, but counselors also need to understand the particular learning, behavioral, and social/emotional characteristics accompanying the disability in addition to the child's distinctive attributes in order to provide therapeutic services. Awareness of normal development also is necessary coupled with therapeutic accommodations to the child's special needs. For example, Cobb and Brown (1983) submit that a more concrete approach may be required due to the more limited cognitive skills of youth with mental retardation. Since the overall maturity level and experiential background and vocabulary may be restricted, counselors must monitor the appropriateness of their expressive vocabulary.

While attending to their developmental level, counselors must attend to the chronological age appropriateness of their own language (e.g., avoid baby talk with an adolescent regardless of functioning level) and intervention techniques. A

shortened length of therapy sessions, increased frequency of sessions, and additional structure are advised if less sustained attention span and greater distractibility are apparent. For other conditions, physical stamina or neurological impairment (see Chapter 10) may be factors necessitating therapeutic accommodations. The acquisition of functional social skills may be the most consequential goal for children and adolescents with disabilities since the perception by others of their degree of impairment is largely influenced by their social skills. Hence, roleplaying and behavior rehearsal are often appropriate therapeutic techniques.

Special Needs of Children with Disabilities

Children with disabilities may be confronted with prejudice and stereotypes about their handicap; they also may be heckled by peers. Children in mainstreamed programs do not necessarily fare better than students in segregated programs (e.g., Gresham, 1982). Thus, the counselor must help the child develop coping mechanisms to deal with negative attitudes that may limit opportunities.

A principal therapeutic task is to help the child develop a healthy and positive self-concept, regarding herself or himself as a capable person. Focusing on competence can enhance self-esteem (e.g., Calsyn & Kenny, 1977; Kifer, 1975; Scheirer & Kraut, 1979). The therapist may need to involve family members to help them to accept the child's disability and to communicate their belief in the child's abilities. Group counseling can provide an appropriate context for helping the child acquire and refine interpersonal social skills as well as experiencing the feeling of not being alone. Participation of typical (i.e., nonhandicapped) peers in the group is recommended (Cobb & Brown, 1983).

Anxiety, frustration, lack of motivation, depression, and learned helplessness may be experienced by children and adolescents with handicapping conditions. These difficulties may result from feelings of inadequacy brought about by a history of repeated failure experiences. Worries about being accepted by others and doing well in school and community activities can be exacerbated for youth with disabilities. Sometimes frustration results from misinformation or lack of information from adults or from unrealistic expectations the child may have. It is within this context that the counselor may need to provide basic information about the handicap to the child and family. For example, human growth and development including sexuality and marriage may be issues that have been inadequately addressed for an adolescent.

Therapists also may need to help youth through the stages of grief when they have difficulty accepting any limitations imposed by the handicap. Once the adolescent has come to terms with her or his disability and developed appropriate interpersonal social skills, vocational counseling and teaching decision-making skills may be timely. The vocational domain is one of the specific functional, life skills curricula domains for learners with mental retardation (e.g., Wilcox & Bellamy, 1982).

PSYCHODYNAMIC THEORIES

More than any other theoretical perspective, psychodynamic formulations recognize the power of the past to shape the present. Contemporary psychodynamic theory is far from a unitary framework, although the original impetus for psychoanalysis came from the works of Sigmund Freud who conceptualized the emotional and irrational feelings underlying behavior. It is continually changing and adapting, with much of the practice in North America based on the work of ego psychologists (e.g., Erik Erikson) who believe that individuals can manage their own destiny and can adapt to the realities of the environment. Psychodynamic therapy may be practiced in a diverse fashion ranging from the orthodox, using only interpretation, to more humanistically oriented transactional analysis, which uses diverse techniques from other schools of counseling in addition to psychoanalysis (Ivey, Ivey, & Simek-Downing, 1987).

Central Theoretical Constructs

The concept of the unconscious is central to the psychodynamic worldview, with the premise that antecedents of daily behavior largely are beyond the realm of conscious awareness. The central goal of psychodynamic therapy is oriented toward uncovering and understanding the unconscious processes governing behavior as the therapist helps the client work through old unresolved developmental crises and tasks. It is argued by proponents of this perspective that the individual can reconstruct the personality once such unconscious forces are discovered (Weisz & Benoit, 1983).

Object relations is a technical term that refers to past interpersonal relationships. Object relations theory helps to identify how past childhood experience is reflected unconsciously in adult patterns of behavior. The therapeutic goal is to understand how such childhood patterns are repeated in a variety of forms in adult life. Thus, therapists are advised to search for consistent patterns of behavior and thinking in clients that are derived from earlier life events and to assist them in realizing how repetitive patterns are tied together and related affectively to childhood experiences (Ivey, Ivey, & Simek-Downing, 1987).

Defense Mechanisms

Emotions and thoughts underlying repeating patterns may be disguised through an assortment of defense mechanisms. For example, *denial* may be evident when an adolescent refuses to acknowledge that he or she has an eating disorder, with a health-threatening body weight. In *projection,* the individual fails to recognize a behavior or feeling in himself or herself and attributes (projects) it to others, as when an adolescent denies personal alcohol abuse yet sees the problem in others. Defense mechanisms typically are repetitive, stereotyped, automatic means used to deflect anxiety (Arlow, 1979). They represent varying degrees of psychological health, with extensive use of defense mechanisms potentially resulting in psychological disturbance. One goal in psychodynamic therapy is to learn how to investigate repeating patterns that may manifest themselves in a variety of defense mechanisms.

Basic Techniques

Most psychodynamic counselors use microskills such as minimal encouragers, directives, reflection of feeling and paraphrasing, feedback, self-statement, and summarization, which invariably are oriented toward interpretation from the psychodynamic perspective. Surface interpretations generally are appropriate early in therapy, with depth interpretations occurring after a relationship of trust has been established.

To accomplish the goal of client intentionality, psychodynamic therapists foster client skill in making his or her own interpretations. Although client insight into the origins of her or his problems is largely regarded as sufficient to effect client change (Weisz & Benoit, 1983), emphasis on verbally based insight has been criticized. A client who searches assiduously in the past while continuing to have difficulty in coping with current daily living may be ill served. Drawing on other therapeutic modalities (e.g., behavioral or cognitive-behavioral) may be necessary to enable lifestyle changes.

Just as the unconscious can be used to summarize Freudian theory, the technique of *free association* can be used to summarize the psychodynamic method. It forms the basis for all psychodynamic techniques, including *dream analysis*. Its use encourages the client to say anything that comes to mind regardless of how seemingly irrelevant. Out of the free associations, a pattern may emerge to explain the meaning of some behavior, thought, or feeling.

Free association may be coupled with the technique of *staying with the feeling* whereby the client is directed to stay with a certain positive or negative feeling and to use it as a base for free association. By staying with the feeling and free associating to a particular earlier experience, the client experiences a *focused-free association,* which can be enhanced further with *repetition* whereby the counselor relies on the microskill of directive-giving to have the client repeat the verbalization of the feeling (Ivey, Ivey, & Simek-Downing, 1987).

A major issue in psychodynamic approaches is *analysis of resistance.* Although other theoretical frameworks may ignore resistance or adopt another therapeutic technique, the psychodynamic counselor gives it prime attention. The view is that resistance manifests itself in a variety of ways, such as arriving late for a session, refusing to comply with therapist directives, or forgetting what was said, as the client unconsciously tries to sabotage the treatment process.

Analysis of transference is one of the cornerstones of psychoanalytic technique (Arlow, 1979). *Transference* refers to the repetition during therapy of earlier feelings or patterns of responding, which are directed toward the counselor. The transference phenomenon is regarded as a form of resistance that enables the therapist to observe the derivatives of the past conflict (Weisz & Benoit, 1983). Techniques of managing transference are similar to those for dealing with resistance. The transference is identified and labeled, and free association is used to elucidate meaning. Regardless of their theoretical orientation, many counselors observe transference in their client's comments. However, there is substantial variation among theories in the use of analysis of transference, with some disregarding this concept entirely.

To help counteract counselor blind spots, *analysis of countertransference* can be done by a supervisor much like a typical counselor-client session or in consultation with a colleague. Regardless of theoretical orientation, awareness of one's feelings toward the client and skill in coping with such feelings are essential to any therapist since countertransference feelings and feelings of resistance toward the client may obstruct effective treatment (Arlow, 1979).

Psychodynamic Therapy with Children and Adolescents

In general, it is the opinion of Freudian child analysts that psychoanalysis should be restricted to the severe forms of infantile neurosis, with manifestations including phobias, anxiety states, conversion hysteria, traumatic experiences, and obsessional behaviors. Often it is the parents' reaction to the symptom that leads to a request for treatment (Weisz & Benoit, 1983). General psychodynamic techniques with children include several features: (1) as few limitations as possible on the direction of treatment to allow free expression of thoughts and actions, (2) interpretation as the basic technique to deal with defenses, and (3) attempts to change the child's environment are restricted, with intervention only as necessary to maintain continuity of treatment (Sharfman, 1978).

Child Therapy

Disturbances in a child's capacity for developmentally appropriate play may be displayed in excessive and repetitive use of imaginary play; these are viewed as suggestive of neurotic conflict. The seriousness of dysfunction relates to the time period of the display of symptoms and the extent to which they restrict normal developmental processes (Weisz & Benoit, 1983).

Psychodynamic techniques vary as a function of the age of the child or adolescent, the nature of the symptoms, and the client's ability to respond to therapy. Since young children are incapable of free association, *play therapy* becomes relevant. It is based on the notion that play is the child's natural medium of self-expression, providing an opportunity for the child to "play out" her or his accumulated feelings of tension, frustration, insecurity, aggression, fear, bewilderment, and confusion, just as adults "talk out" their difficulties (Axline, 1969).

Excessive, repetitive, stereotyped play patterns and disturbances in constructive play are viewed as an indication of unconscious conflict. Hence, play is regarded as a source of information about the child, which provides the groundwork for interpretation. Interrupting a child's play for an interpretation or setting limits on the play, other than to circumvent destructive behavior, is viewed as counterproductive to the goal of discerning the meaning of the play. Play by itself does not resolve the neurosis, and some form of interpretation becomes necessary to uncover a connection for the child between past and present events, defenses and impulses, or fantasy and reality (Kessler, 1966). The timing of interpretation is a crucial factor.

Weisz and Benoit (1983) suggest that counselors provide a setting in which the child may express fantasies and unconscious conflicts. Some psychodynamic therapists champion a sparsely furnished room supplied only by a special collection of toys and materials that only the child will use. Other therapists endorse a well-equipped playroom (e.g., Axline, 1969) with such materials as dolls, puppets, and toy furniture, which the child can use to act out relationships with various family members; drawing and painting materials and a chalkboard for free expression of ideas; clay or plasticene, sand, and water; and various items or games for the expression of aggression. Most therapists allow the child to bring a preferred toy or object from home due to the belief that it is selected because of its significance to the child. Organized games or mechanical toys generally are less preferable since they tend to restrict self-expression (O'Connor, Lee, & Schaefer, 1983).

Adolescent Therapy

As with children, the symptoms for which psychoanalysis is held to be appropriate chiefly are psychoneurotic. It is important for the symptoms to be assessed against behaviors typical of adolescence and within the context of the obstacles they impose on normal development. The major defense mechanisms include regression, preoccupation with self, displacement, and withdrawal. Since adolescence spans a broad period of time from puberty to adulthood, psychodynamic techniques are varied. With younger and generally immature adolescents, play therapy may continue to be appropriate.

Although adolescents cognitively are capable of free association, they may be reluctant. Most therapists agree that treating adolescents requires modification of classical techniques (Weisz & Benoit, 1983). Laufer (1980) divides therapy material for adolescents into two categories: the immediate past reflecting the crises of puberty and adolescence and the preadolescent past of earlier stages of development. Emphasis is placed on helping the adolescent learn to test reality accurately, with less attention to analysis of the defensive structure.

Contraindications

Since a psychodynamic approach can be a time-consuming and expensive form of treatment, it is not indicated in situations in which client difficulties are relatively minor. Because much of psychodynamic technique depends on the analysis of transference, this paradigm is best suited to conditions in which transference attachments tend to be strong. If the individual's real-life circumstance is so adverse that there is nothing that he or she can realistically do about it, the insights gained from psychodynamic treatment will be of no benefit (Arlow, 1979).

The Ethical Principles of Psychologists (American Psychological Association [APA], 1990) provide clear guidance in such situations. Principle 6, Welfare of the Consumer, holds that psychologists "protect the welfare of the people and groups with whom they work" (p. 393). Principle 7, Professional Relationships, explicitly addresses the policy for psychologists to access a range of resources to best serve their clients:

> Psychologists understand the areas of competence of related professions. They make full use of all the professional, technical, and administrative resources that serve the best interests of consumers. The absence of formal relationships with other professional workers does not relieve psycholo-

gists of the responsibility of securing for their clients the best possible professional service, nor does it relieve them of the obligation to exercise foresight, diligence, and tact in obtaining the complementary or alternative assistance needed by clients. (p. 393)

These principles, of course, would apply to other schools of therapy as well.

Acosta, Yamamoto, Evans, and Wilcox (1982) maintain that many individuals who go to a public mental-health outpatient clinic are not suitable for insight-oriented therapy alone. They require a mixture of therapies to meet their "double neediness" due to emotional difficulties and problems of living. Hence, the mental-health professional also may serve as an adviser or advocate who assists clients in dealing with agencies and individuals, including paraprofessional staff who have been trained to help counselors deal with their clients' multiple living difficulties.

Therapists working with children and youth and their families must be ever attentive to their multiple needs, some of which may be far more pressing than counseling. For example, a pregnant adolescent may need housing, adequate nutrition, and prenatal care; an adolescent couple with an infant born preterm (who even at home must stay on an apnea and bradycardia monitor) may need financial counseling and a flexible education program and work schedule.

Laplanche and Pontalis (1973) caution against the use of "wild analysis" practiced by amateur or inexperienced therapists who apply only a few of the techniques without undergoing extensive theoretical and technical training. One of the primary problems of the psychodynamic approach has been the application of concepts and techniques by therapists with elementary understanding of psychodynamic constructs. Ivey, Ivey, and Simek-Downing (1987) regard psychodynamic training as requiring the most rigorous intellectual discipline of all methods. Nonetheless, they outline several implications of this approach that are useful for a general theory approach to counseling.

Implications

First is an awareness that what appears to be a surface problem may consist of underlying issues, which can be illuminated by psychodynamic techniques such as focused-free association or nondirective play. Second is the concept of transference in the therapeutic relationship in which clients transfer their past history of interpersonal relationships into sessions. Regardless of whether these issues become a focus of treatment, awareness of transference is essential across theoretical orientations.

Third, awareness of countertransference is important since clients' words and behaviors may represent issues in therapists' lives that have not been worked through. For example, an array of issues may arise in counseling sessions with adolescents such as unexpected pregnancy and abortion or parenthood, the search for independence and identity, isolation from family members, anger and confusion about parent divorce, or failure to meet parent and teacher expectations. Any of these issues could represent personal areas for the counselor.

EXISTENTIAL-HUMANISTIC THEORIES

Existential-humanistic theories have been termed the "third force" in counseling. Psychodynamic theory focuses on how history determines the present and behavior theory on how environmental contingencies shape the individual's learning. Existential-humanistic theory presents an alternative worldview in which the individual is the locus of control and decision rather than past history or the environment.

Existentialism is concerned with human existence, life's infinite possibilities, and the meaning of life. Humanism is a philosophy that dignifies humanity and considers people as making their own choices and decisions. Carl Rogers and his person-centered counseling have been most instrumental in popularizing this point of view. While Rogers has been described as an *attending or listening therapist,* Fritz Perls (Gestalt theory) is viewed as an *influencing therapist*

since the techniques are extremely directive. Viktor Frankl (logotherapy) balances Rogers and Perls and uses both attending and listening skills according to the diverse needs of the client (Ivey, Ivey, & Simek-Downing, 1987). This portion of the chapter focuses on person-centered counseling.

Person-Centered Therapy

Person-centered therapy developed out of the Rogerian revolution in the 1940s and 1950s and was America's first distinctly indigenous school of therapy (Belkin, 1987). This section reviews basic Rogerian constructs, conditions of therapeutic change, and stages of person-centered theory.

Basic Rogerian Constructs

The central issue in Rogerian and existential-humanistic counseling lies in how the individual perceives the world. Such a view emphasizes the individual and tends to devote less attention to person-environment transactions. A chief task of the counselor is to understand and to empathize with the client's unique experiential world. The therapist attempts to understand clients' perceptions in order to expose underlying positive traits. It is assumed then that a natural healing process will occur as individuals change their behavior in positive directions (Ivey, Ivey, & Simek-Downing, 1987).

Necessary Conditions of Therapeutic Change

The objective of therapy is to resolve discrepancies between ideal self and real self to eliminate tension and to substitute forward-moving self-actualization. Rogers (1957) proposed six basic conditions that will assist clients in progressing in positive directions, if these are adequately satisfied, regardless of the counselor's theoretical orientation. The conditions become a full circle, with client perception of the conditions only if a true relationship exists and positive regard and empathy are apparent.

1. A *relationship* must exist between two persons. According to Kanfer and Schefft (1988), an

effective therapeutic alliance permits the client to explore and to practice new behaviors, plans, and ideas in therapy sessions without fear of humiliation, but it is not a sufficient condition for change. Technical aspects of the treatment process also need to be applied within an atmosphere of encouragement and support.

2. The client is in a state of incongruity between the ideal self and the real self and is vulnerable and anxious. A task of the counselor is to assist the client in becoming aware of such incongruities and to work toward resolution.

3. It is essential that counselors be *genuine* and *authentic* as they listen to clients and open a dialogue of empathy. Genuineness, or congruence, is the basic ability of counselors to read their own inner experiencing and to allow it to be apparent in the therapeutic relationship (Meador & Rogers, 1979). Genuineness means being oneself without playing a role, being aware of one's feelings, and communicating verbal and nonverbal behaviors that are congruent (match) (Cormier & Cormier, 1979).

4. *Unconditional positive regard* for the client is present. The communication of warmth, respect, and caring is important in the development of positive regard. As Cormier and Cormier (1979) note, it is unrealistic to assume that counselors always have positive feelings for their clients. Counselors need to examine their feelings toward clients, which Rogers (1967) indicated often relate to counselors' own concerns and values. If negative feelings continue to block the relationship, the counselor may decide to discuss them with the client, colleague, or supervisor or refer the client to another professional.

5. The counselor experiences an *empathic* understanding of the client's internal frame of reference. Krumboltz and Thoresen (1976) suggest that one of the chief therapeutic functions of empathy is that it conveys that both the counselor and client are working on the same side. Empathy is communicated through the use of accurate attending skills of paraphrasing, reflection of feeling, and summarization. Ivey, Ivey, and Si-

mek-Downing (1987) discuss other constructs to help communicate understanding and empathy for the client, which include positive regard, respect and warmth, concreteness, immediacy, confrontation, congruence, genuineness, and authenticity.

6. *Communication* to the client of the counselor's empathic understanding and unconditional positive regard is realized.

In a series of studies, Fiedler (1950a, 1950b, 1951) examined the therapeutic relationship of psychoanalytic, Rogerian, and Adlerian persuasion and found that expert therapists across the three orientations were more similar to each other than to inexperienced therapists within their own theoretical perspective. In another important study, Barrett-Lennard (1962) investigated level of regard, empathy, congruence, unconditionality of regard, and willingness to be known and found higher levels of these facilitative conditions among experienced therapists than among those who were inexperienced.

Sloane, Staples, Cristol, Yorkston, and Whipple (1975) found that behavior therapists demonstrated higher levels of empathy, self-congruence, and interpersonal contact than psychotherapists, with approximately equal levels of warmth and regard. Nevertheless, there was no relationship between these measures and treatment efficacy, although clients with positive outcome in both therapies rated their personal interaction with the therapist as the single most important part of treatment. These facilitative conditions may be more important in some instances than the counselor's theoretical orientation.

However, the validity of these core conditions has been seriously questioned. The power and generalizability may not be as great as once thought (Mitchell, Bozarth, & Krauft, 1977); there may have been insufficient controls (Rachman & Wilson, 1980); and the methodology in empathy research may not always have been adequate (Lambert, DeJulio, & Stein, 1978). Hence, Rogerian theory may have a lesser influence on current practice (Ivey, Ivey, & Simek-Downing, 1987). An additional feature adding to the complexity of this process research relates to counselor synchrony with the client throughout the therapy session. Strupp (1977, 1984) suggests that simple application of empathic qualities is insufficient due to the necessity of judicious and sensitive applications of the various techniques at appropriate times.

Stages of Person-Centered Theory

Substantial change in person-centered therapy has occurred over the decades, with a basically listening approach to therapy transitioning to increased use of influencing skills. Three stages represent the development of person-centered theory (Moore, 1983).

> Stage 1, *Nondirective,* 1940–1950: Acceptance of the client, establishment of a positive nonjudgmental climate, trust in the client's wisdom, and permissiveness were highlighted.
>
> Stage 2, *Client-Centered,* 1950–1961: Personally threatening situations for the client were avoided, with reflection of feeling the main technique to resolve incongruities between the ideal self and the real self.
>
> Stage 3, *Experiential* (Hart & Tomlinson, 1979), since 1961: There is an emphasis on counselor attitudes and a more active (more questions and feedback) and self-disclosing role for the counselor. The concept of genuineness (congruence) assumed new significance, with therapists making themselves transparent to clients (Rogers, 1977), which is in stark contrast to psychodynamic therapy.

Child Therapy

Person-centered counselors in school settings more frequently may work with typical children to enhance their development and to assist them with developmental concerns. Children who require extensive or long-term help generally are referred to clinics or private clinicians. Person-

centered counselors who work with children provide a safe climate that encourages free and open expression of feelings and thoughts. The counselor believes in the child's capacity to move toward greater responsibility and socialization. Regardless of the deviance of the child's behavior, the counselor conveys empathy, respect, genuineness, and honesty. Moore (1983) addresses the challenge of such an approach, which respects the child's right to reject changing attitudes and behaviors. Reisman (1973) emphasizes the child's perception of the difficulty as most important because the child is the client.

In the counseling session, the counselor's first task is to build a relationship to establish an atmosphere in which the child feels no conditions for acceptance. The listening skills, discussed at the beginning of the chapter, can enhance the therapeutic relationship. Person-centered counselors try to be as open with children as possible and encourage parents and teachers to be open as well. With young children or those who have difficulty expressing themselves, counselors may invite them to draw, to respond to stimulus pictures, or to listen to a story designed to provide the child an opportunity to share feelings, thoughts, and experiences.

Due to time constraints, teacher concerns, accountability, and other pressures, person-centered counselors in school settings tend to be more action oriented. Within a warm and nonjudgmental context, the counselor may give the child honest feedback, but not in a threatening fashion, and delve into areas of goal setting, information giving, and decision making. Counselor statements that may increase child defensiveness or feelings of worthlessness as well as moralizing, judging, lecturing, and asking *why* questions are to be avoided. Indirect methods of getting at problem issues also are eschewed since these would violate the important attitude of counselor genuineness in the relationship.

As children begin to feel more secure with and accepted by the counselor, the view is that many will open up, expressing their frustrations and feelings. Experiences to enhance the child's positive feelings and strengths are incorporated into sessions. Children who externalize their difficulties as caused by others are confronted to further their proclivity toward responsibility and self-direction. Such confrontation is done with respect for the child's right to disagree with the counselor's assessment. As counseling progresses, person-centered counselors in the schools assist children in designing and implementing plans for addressing expressed concerns (Moore, 1983).

Person-centered therapy also can be applied to play as a therapeutic medium with children as the counselor accepts the child and allows him or her to select the direction of the sessions while the counselor tries to communicate an understanding of the child's actions and feelings. Person-centered therapy assumes that children can solve their own difficulties as they re-create their world in play. While early nondirective therapists championed freedom for children to select play materials, counselors may attempt to maximize therapy time by placing toys in view that have the potential to extract feelings and thoughts regarding areas of difficulty. Person-centered counselors may elect to use unstructured (e.g., puppets, art media) or more structured (e.g., games) means of promoting the counseling process as long as a climate of trust, acceptance, and empathy is applied unfailingly (Moore, 1983).

Adolescent Therapy

In a society with continually changing and often conflicting messages, adolescence has become a particularly tumultuous period. Adolescents have ample opportunity to doubt their competence and worth. Person-centered counselors convey their optimism to adolescents that they can become self-directing and competent in discovering viable coping strategies. Active listening is fundamental and cannot be accelerated. Adolescents themselves are viewed as the best judges of what they are experiencing, and they must be given sufficient opportunity to explore their identity and needs.

Neely (1982) points out the challenges to conveying warmth, congruence, unconditional

positive regard, and empathy in school settings when students are passing in the hall and asking for passes and the phone is ringing. Counselors must become adept at managing such interfering stimuli. The person-centered counselor helps students realize greater objectivity by gently confronting them. Despite time constraints, counselors refrain from succumbing to a pattern of advice giving (not to be confused with information giving, which often is desirable and necessary). Open-ended questions such as "What do you see as your options in this situation?" convey more respect than more directive statements such as "Here are your choices."

Depending on the adolescent's expressed needs and concerns, additional services may be used. These could include assessments of vocational interest as tools for self-exploration (Moore, 1983). Although counselors in school settings may not have the option of prolonged counseling, they must be knowledgeable of appropriate referral sources, consistent with APA (1990) ethical principles.

Limitations and Practical Implications

One concern about existential-humanistic therapies is the constant emphasis on individual growth and possibility. These theories tend to focus on the individual, with little consideration of relationships. Along with psychodynamic theory, the existential-humanistic approach tends to be highly verbal. Although the positive and accepting Rogerian philosophy appears to be welcomed by traditionally underrepresented groups, the techniques of slow reflection, lack of action, and failure to consider immediate problem solving seem largely inappropriate for individuals with pressing needs. For some clients, the tendency for existential-humanistic counseling to ignore person-environment transactions in daily practice is a notable limitation. Yet perhaps the principal contribution of Rogerian technique has been empathic and accurate listening along with warmth and respect.

Indeed, person-centered attitudes, skills, and emphasis on the counseling relationship have become incorporated into practice across theoretical orientations. Viktor Frankl's balanced listening and influencing approach may become increasingly prominent within existential-humanistic theory (Ivey, Ivey, & Simek-Downing, 1987), and a new blend of theory may be on the horizon that includes some components of cognitive-behavioral theory (Frankl, 1985).

COGNITIVE-BEHAVIORAL THEORIES

Three significant historical forces undergird the helping process: psychodynamic, existential-humanistic, and behavioral. Psychodynamic and existential-humanistic theory largely address cognitions, whereas behavioral psychology focuses on behavior. Cognitive-behavioral theories and methods have arisen to meet the need to integrate thought and action, meaning and doing. The cognitive-behavioral paradigm extracts from other theories and incorporates novel constructs to produce a new integration of theory and practice.

Cognitive-behavioral therapy comprises three tasks: (1) to examine how one thinks, and if necessary, to change cognition; (2) to insure that clients act on those cognitions through behavior in their daily life; and (3) to decide how one will act. This process of decision making at least partially connects the cognitive-behavioral framework to the existential-humanistic convention. Hence, to understand a client's problem, the counselor needs to understand both the cognitions and the behaviors (Ivey, Ivey, & Simek-Downing, 1987).

Cognitive behavior therapy encompasses an assortment of models and strategies for assessing and treating a person's behavior. Despite its diversity, three broad theoretical assumptions characterize the various clinical procedures subsumed under the term *cognitive behavior therapy*. First, an individual's thoughts, images, perceptions, and other cognitive mediating events affect behavior. A corollary postulate is that a particular focus on a person's cognitions is an effective strategy for changing behavior. Second is the presumption that individuals are active participants

in their own learning. A third assumption is the requirement that the utility of cognitive constructs in behavior-change endeavors must be demonstrated empirically.

Cognitive behavior therapy strives to sustain methodological behaviorism while accommodating modern developments in a number of spheres of experimental psychology particularly cognition, development, language, motivation, and learning (Hughes, 1988). Cognitive behavior therapy regards behavior as influenced by multiple and interactive determinants and contributes an extended scope of techniques for changing behavior (Wilson, 1978). There are a number of models within the cognitive-behavioral tradition. This section provides a brief overview of two approaches including that of Albert Ellis's rational-emotive therapy and Donald Meichenbaum's cognitive behavior therapy.

Rational-Emotive Therapy

Albert Ellis is considered the pioneer of cognitive-behavioral theory. Initially he practiced psychoanalysis and then was classified in the existential-humanistic tradition for many years. Gradually, he began adopting a more active role in therapy, attacking the client's logic and prescribing behavioral "homework" activities. Ellis's rational-emotive therapy (RET) is considered broader and more eclectic than some other cognitive-behavioral approaches. He uses techniques from diverse theoretical orientations to respond to the client's unique needs (Ellis, 1979). He emphasizes unconditional acceptance in a fashion similar to Carl Rogers, but may or may not devote time to developing a therapeutic alliance. Often the interview is started directly as the counselor moves rapidly into direct action. RET does not use behavioral strategies as fully as does Meichenbaum (Ivey, Ivey, & Simek-Downing, 1987).

Theoretical Constructs and Techniques
RET focuses more on thoughts than on feelings, with the view that irrational ideas (similar to Beck's [1972] "faulty reasonings") are the source

of client difficulty. Ellis has criticized humanistic approaches as being too gentle at times by failing to consider that people can self-destruct through irrational and confused thinking. The task of the RET therapist is to correct faulty thought patterns to relieve people of irrational ideas. The central proposition of RET is the A-B-C theory of personality (Grieger & Boyd, 1983; Ivey, Ivey, & Simek-Downing, 1987):

A The objective facts, events, and behaviors that a person encounters.

B The person's beliefs, ideas, or attitudes about *A*

C The emotional and/or behavioral consequence

Ellis challenged the *A* causes *C* equation as naive since it fails to consider that it is what people *think* about an event that determines how they feel. The therapeutic emphasis largely is on changing the way the client thinks about the behavior, rather than on altering the behavior itself. For example, an adolescent lives in a home in which he is verbally and emotionally abused by his parents (*A*, objective facts). His response would depend on his evaluative thoughts about the situation. He might think he was a "bad" person unworthy of kindness (*B*) and react with resignation or continued self-denigration (*C*). Or he might think his parents were unjustified in their treatment (*B*) and increase his efforts to distance himself from them (*C*). In this scenario, RET would focus on the irrational idea that he deserved such violations.

RET involves a comprehensive, multimodal, cognitive-emotive-behavioral array of therapeutic techniques (Ellis, 1979). First and foremost it is a highly cognitive therapy. In its emotive aspects, RET attempts to help clients change their irrational ideas by dramatizing these ideas by invoking humor, exaggerating the irrational beliefs to the point of absurdity, or using roleplay. The behavioral aspects of RET rest on the premise that an effective means of cognitive change is through

behavioral change. Compelling a client to behave in a manner that contradicts irrational ideas often serves to eliminate such ideas (Grieger & Boyd, 1983).

RET counselors may vary in their use of microskill, although Ellis uses a large number of open and closed questions, directives, interpretation, and advice and opinion. Basic to RET is confrontation as incongruent irrational thoughts are attacked. It is a fast-paced action therapy; the listening skills of paraphrasing and reflection of feeling do not play a prominent role. RET is psychoeducational for it demystifies the counseling process, shares important aspects openly with the client, and actively teaches clients how to think (Ivey, Ivey, & Simek-Downing, 1987).

Child Therapy

Rational-emotive techniques differ depending on age range. As emphasized throughout this chapter, children's developmental levels must be considered so that intervention is realistic for their level of maturation in cognitive, emotional, and behavioral domains. In the first stage of RET with children, the therapist attempts to overcome children's resistance and low verbal capacity. A situational assessment also is recommended to gather information about the context of the child's difficulties and the attitudes, expectations, and emotions of the child and significant others. Then the child's problems are categorized into a host of A-B-C sequences (Grieger & Boyd, 1980, 1983).

Children are not as intellectually and emotionally equipped as adults in gaining rational-emotive insight. Initially in the insight process, Grieger and Boyd (1983) recommend having children roleplay different emotional reactions to the distressing events in their lives. Then alternative responses to the event are demonstrated, which the children then practice. Next the counselor helps them explore the consequences of their behaviors and feelings. This activity, or other options such as observation of other children, puppet play, or games, is designed to enhance motivation for change.

Finally in the insight process, an attempt is

made to show the child that by thinking in certain ways, he or she is generating the disturbed feelings and behaviors. Once children gain these insights, they are ready for working through and skill training. Because of the nature of their cognitive processes, children require a concrete reeducation of their false assumptions, inferences, and evaluations. Hence, goals are to teach the child more rational attitudes, positive emotional responses, and constructive behaviors (Boyd, 1980).

A key feature of working through with children is the method of rational self-instruction and coping, which consists of constructing a rational self-talk dialogue that the child can practice and use when confronted with the problem situation. The rational beliefs are phrased in the child's language and rehearsed through imagery and role-playing (Grieger & Boyd, 1983). Meichenbaum's (1977) guidelines for teaching verbal self-instructions can enhance this practice.

Also during the working through stage, the RET therapist uses a number of strategies to eliminate the child's old irrationalities and to strengthen the new rational ideation. The goal then is to replace problematic A-B-Cs with a rational A-B-C sequence. Grieger and Boyd (1983) describe several such techniques including: (1) interpersonal skill training, (2) homework assignments to practice progressive gradations of rational responses, (3) structured (prearranged) situations, (4) written homework, (5) parents (who can be taught to teach and to help their children practice rational ideas, e.g., Waters, 1980), (6) rational-emotive imagery, (7) operant conditioning in which rational behavior is reinforced and maladaptive responses are placed on extinction, (8) roleplaying, and (9) evaluating success.

Adolescent Therapy

Grieger and Boyd (1983) caution the RET therapist about several adolescent issues that influence treatment. Establishing a therapeutic alliance is particularly crucial. They suggest allowing the adolescent initially to define the problem, even if there are other more troublesome issues, with-

holding a problem diagnosis and conceptualization to reduce defensiveness, and possibly temporarily going along with irrational beliefs and labile affect in order to avoid exacerbating adult power struggles. A standard motivational tactic is to help adolescents see that they can control their feelings and behave in a manner to obtain some of their desires.

The RET therapist appeals to adolescent concern of powerlessness and the drive toward autonomy, power, and independence. Once the adolescent learns to value self-change, a variety of learning aids such as readings, pictures and charts, and exercises, can be used to teach A-B-Cs and to identify irrational ideas. In contrast to younger children, adolescents can benefit from insights, and therapy dialogue is more interactional. Although elegant goals (a cognitive-emotive-behavioral reeducation in which irrational thinking is understood) may be achieved with adolescents, inelegant gains (symptom removal) may be more realistically obtainable for some adolescents.

Meichenbaum's Cognitive Behavior Therapy

Meichenbaum (1985) discusses several key components of his conceptualization of cognitive behavior therapy. In addition to cognitive behavioral theory previously presented, the following central constructs should be added.

The Importance of Behavior

In Beck's (1976) emphasis on cognition, and to some extent Ellis, the behavioral portion of cognitive behavioral can be lost. Meichenbaum (1985) terms Beck and Ellis "cognitive-semantic" therapists rather than actual cognitive-behaviorists. Techniques such as assertiveness training, social learning theory's modeling, and relapse prevention are key features.

Pinpointing Behavioral Targets

Centrally important to Meichenbaum's construction are applied behavior analysis, operationalization of behavior, and cognitive functional analysis (Meichenbaum, 1976). He underscores pinpointing behaviors and thoughts very specifically so that they are definable and measurable.

Stress Inoculation
Teaching clients how to manage stress can be useful (Meichenbaum, 1985; Meichenbaum & Jaremko, 1973). Such a training program involves three discrete phases: (1) helping the client develop a cognitive understanding of the role of stress in one's life, (2) teaching specific coping skills to deal effectively with stress (e.g., relaxation training, decision making to do fewer things, or social skills to learn alternatives), and (3) working with thoughts and feelings about stressful situations to enable the client to be motivated to act on the stress. According to Meichenbaum, the client must decide to act since neither cognitive awareness of stress nor skills are sufficient to effect change. *Skill training,* an increasingly important component of cognitive behavioral methods, itself is a significant theoretical and pragmatic form of treatment (Ivey, Ivey, & Simek-Downing, 1987).

Self-Instructional Training
In an attempt to combine the influences of developmental social learning literature and the work on mediational deficits and task analysis, Meichenbaum and Goodman (1971) developed a self-instructional training regimen composed of combinations of modeling, overt and covert rehearsal, prompts, feedback, and social reinforcement. Their five-step procedure consists of: (1) *cognitive modeling,* with teacher demonstration; (2) *overt external guidance,* with student performance and teacher prompts; (3) *overt self-guidance,* with the student talking himself or herself through the task out loud; (4) *faded overt self-guidance,* with the student whispering instructions to herself or himself; and (5) *covert self-instruction,* with student performance without talking out loud. The reader is referred to Meichenbaum (1977) for clinical suggestions as to how such training can be conducted with children.

Meichenbaum and Asarnow (1979) offer a general outline for conducting such think-aloud instruction programs in order to teach an assortment of performance-relevant skills: (1) problem identification and definition or self-interrogation skills ("What is it I have to do?"); (2) focusing attention and response guidance ("Now, carefully stop and repeat the instructions"); (3) self-reinforcement involving standard setting and self-evaluation ("Good, I'm doing well"); and (4) coping skills and error-correcting options ("That's all right, even if I make an error I can go slowly").

Such cognitive training is conducted across tasks, settings, and people in order to insure that children develop generalized tactics. An important consideration is that the training of cognitive strategies should focus directly and explicitly on the skills and tasks to be learned rather than on some presumed underlying deficit. Thus, instruction in skills that are unrelated to the ultimate goal of what is being taught, such as providing training in discriminating geometric shapes to a child who has difficulty in recognizing words, is academically irrelevant and unlikely to contribute to an intervention program.

Such self-instructional training may enable students to use their internal dialogue as a tool for facilitating reading comprehension, accelerating problem-solving ability, and fostering self-control (Meichenbaum & Asarnow, 1979). Meichenbaum (1974) views such self-instructions as a form of *cognitive prosthesis* that could be employed to help overcome inadequate performance.

Potential Limitations and Appealing Features
Cognitive behavior therapy offers an expanded behavioral paradigm that has substantial potential for helping children and youth. Yet like any theoretical perspective, it is not a cure-all approach for the complete range of child and adolescent difficulties, and it has certain pitfalls. First is the uncritical acceptance of any new technology. Other orientations including behavioral approaches may be a preferred treatment approach

in a number of situations. Hughes (1988) suggests that one of the greatest benefits of cognitive behavioral techniques is their combination with behavioral strategies. Collins, Rothblum, and Wilson (1986) contend that combined behavioral and cognitive behavioral approaches capitalize on the initial success derived from behavioral programs while increasing client self-efficacy, which in turn enhances maintenance of treatment gains.

A second concern is the overly broad and empirically unjustified assertion that cognitive behavior therapy effects augmented generalization. While there is some indication that cognitive behavior therapy promotes generalization and maintenance, the literature has been equivocal (Meichenbaum & Asarnow, 1979). As the behavioral paradigm has articulated the necessity of specific programming for generalization and maintenance (see Chapter 7), cognitive behaviorists have begun to examine variables that influence these processes (Wong, 1985).

A third concern about cognitive behavior therapy, particularly in school settings, is the cost effectiveness. Any superiority over behavioral approaches (if demonstrated) must be balanced against greater cost in terms of time, resources, effort expended, and efficiency (Wong, 1985). The necessity of evaluating cost efficiency relates to the need to ascertain the effective features in multicomponent interventions. Eliminating those features that do not augment treatment effectiveness will contribute to the development of more efficient programs, which in turn will increase treatment acceptability (see Chapter 7) and the likelihood that schools will allocate sufficient resources for the program (Hughes, 1988). Certain individual-subject experimental designs such as the multitreatment design (Birnbrauer, Peterson, & Solnick, 1974), alternating treatments design (Barlow & Hayes, 1979), or simultaneous treatment design (Kazdin, 1982) can assist in analyzing efficacy of treatment components.

Positive features of cognitive behavior therapy approaches are their congruence with a preventive orientation (see Chapter 7) to adjustment and learning. The emphasis on competence

rather than remediation of interfering behaviors and on self-control and problem-solving strategies versus external control are philosophically appealing (Hughes, 1988).

SYSTEMS THEORIES

This portion of the chapter provides a brief overview of systems theories, which attempt to treat individuals in relationships to others, to families, and to the organizations and communities within which they live and work. While individuals may make important gains after psychodynamic, existential-humanistic, cognitive behavioral, or behavior therapy, therapeutic changes may disappear over time as the person returns to the same family or community environment that contributed to the development of the original problem. Daily transactions can move the "improved" client back to her or his previous ineffective thinking and behaving.

Counseling has begun to devote increased attention to generalization from sessions to the client's natural environment and to prevention of relapse (maintenance) (see Chapter 7). Additionally, a group of therapies has sought to examine the person within the context of her or his environment and to provide counseling for both. Although systems theories work toward individual change, they explicitly strive to alter the individual's transactions with the environment. A systems worldview focuses on the interaction among individuals, families, and environments, with techniques that address the system of interaction directly rather than a single component of the system (Ivey, Ivey, & Simek-Downing, 1987).

Family Therapy

The field of family therapy is burgeoning with diverse methods and theories (see Nichols, 1984), although one unifying dimension is the conviction that individuals must be considered in relation to the family system, which is embedded within an assortment of neighborhood, cultural, and political systems. Within this systems framework, family therapists and family educators identify themselves as within the system they seek to restructure (Ivey, Ivey, & Simek-Downing, 1987).

Structural Family Therapy

Structural family therapy is a coherent approach identified with Salvador Minuchin. It offers a clear framework that brings order and meaning to the complex transactions that comprise family life. Family structure refers to the consistent, repetitive, organized, and predictable modes of family behavior. Nichols (1984) discusses three constructs that are essential components of structural family theory: structure, subsystems, and boundaries.

Family Structure. "Family structure is the invisible set of functional demands that organizes the ways in which family members interact" (Minuchin, 1974, p. 51). Repeated family transactions establish enduring patterns of how, when, and to whom to relate. Sometimes professional intervention adversely affects family structure. For example, multiple change agents (e.g., physical therapist, occupational therapist, speech clinician, early intervention special educator, and psychologist) recommend components of a home-based intervention program for a toddler with history of tonic-clonic seizures, gastroesophageal reflux, and failure to thrive.

These services are provided during daytime hours and require substantial time commitments from the parent at home whose role becomes one of intervention implementor. The other parent who works outside the home during the day begins to avoid participation in child-intervention activities since it is the other parent's "role." When this interactional pattern is repeated, it creates a structure in which the daytime parent assumes virtually all care-giving responsibilities for the child and the other parent becomes incom-

petent in specialized care giving. In addition, the marital subsystem may weaken.

Subsystems. Families are differentiated into subsystems of members who join together to carry out its functions. Individuals are subsystems as are dyads (e.g., husband-wife or parent-child) or larger groups formed by generation, gender, interest, or function. In different subsystems, a person can enter into different complementary relationships in which she or he has different levels of power and differentiated skills (Minuchin, 1974). A woman can be a professional, sister, daughter, mother, wife, and so on. If individuals are mature and flexible, they can vary their behavior to match the different subsystems in which they function. Obvious subsystems such as parents and children can be less significant than covert coalitions as when a parent and oldest child form such a tightly bonded system that others are excluded (Nichols, 1984).

Boundaries. The boundaries of a subsystem are the rules regulating the amount of contact with others. They serve to protect the differentiation of the system. The development of interpersonal skills realized in these subsystems is predicated on the subsystem's freedom from interference by other subsystems. The development of skills for negotiating and compromising with peers, learned among siblings, requires avoidance of interference from parents to settle all arguments. When young children are permitted to be noncompliant to parent requests, the boundary separating the parents from the children is minimal. The clarity of a family's boundaries is a useful parameter to evaluate family functioning. Rigid interpersonal boundaries are overly restrictive and allow little contact with outside systems, resulting in *disengagement*. When boundaries among subsystems are blurred, the differentiation of the family system diffuses, resulting in *enmeshment* (Minuchin, 1974; Nichols, 1984).

Family therapists seek to avoid the concept of

blame and do not accept one person as the problem (the identified patient). For example, the adolescent with anorexia nervosa or bulimia may have developed symptoms as a way of maintaining power and influence in the family, such as by keeping parents together for the sake of their "problem" child. In the structural approach, the therapeutic task is to restructure the power and rules of the family, with the goal of balancing disengagement and enmeshment through culturally appropriate boundaries between individuals. There is no single "appropriate" pattern since different cultures have various patterns of family hierarchy (Ivey, Ivey, & Simek-Downing, 1987). By far the strongest empirical support for structural family therapy comes from a series of studies with psychosomatic children and adult drug addicts (see Nichols, 1984).

Strategic Approaches

Adopting their starting point from the communications model of family systems, strategic therapists focus their attention on repeated sequences of behavior and patterns of communication. Strategic therapists take a systemic (circular) view of problem-maintenance and a strategic (planned) orientation to change. These approaches maintain extreme emphasis on the details of symptoms and symptom resolution, with little or no attempt to instill insight or to rearrange or to improve the family. Haley (1976) holds a minority position in suggesting that changing the structure of the family system in itself is an important goal. Hence, strategic therapists are interested more in change than in understanding.

Abnormal families are entangled in rigid repetitive sequences that permit only a narrow range of behavior. Their inflexibility limits the diversity of their responses, and they are particularly likely to get stuck at transitional points in the life cycle (Nichols, 1984). For example, families may have enormous difficulty in accepting and adapting to their child's disability, in enabling their child to participate in normal community activities, or in facilitating their child's interpersonal relationships. The efficacy of strategic ther-

apy rests largely on clinical case studies and anecdotal reports. Strategic family remains a promising, but unproven approach as are many other therapeutic paradigms (Nichols, 1984).

Family Therapy Techniques

Ivey, Ivey, and Simek-Downing (1987) outline some of the important techniques of family therapy. These can be added to microskills previously discussed to expand an intentional counselor's therapeutic repertoire.

Joining. The family therapist can join the family and metaphorically become a family member, which immediately changes the structure of the family and produces change on the spot. The definition of joining varies depending on one's orientation. It may mean becoming a family member, joining the language system, or listening to achieve empathic understanding.

Enactment. The therapist has the total family roleplay the problem situation so that the family interaction can be observed. Changes may be produced and suggested by the therapist, although structural therapists do not emphasize specific behavioral change as much as the behavioral or cognitive behavioral approaches.

Paradoxical Directive. The therapist instructs the family to continue what they already are doing or to exaggerate the behavior. Paradoxical instructions also may be used to antagonize the family in order to get them to work together against the therapist. The paradoxical directive may be extended into the following week as a homework assignment for the family.

Tracking. This technique involves listening carefully to conversational patterns such as who listens to whom and in what order. It may be followed by pointing out to the family what is happening, having them reenact, and then possibly joining the family in such a way that previous patterns of tracking are impossible.

Restructuring Techniques. These techniques concentrate on relabeling problem behavior, changing who makes decisions, suggesting alternative patterns of sitting at the dinner table, or changing the order of speaking.

Circular Questioning. Rather than asking individuals what they themselves think about problems and interactions, the therapist asks one family member what she or he believes someone else thinks. This technique can bring information out into the open that everyone "knows" but does not discuss and is not aware that others also know.

Reframing. This technique is directly parallel to the microskill of interpretation. The family problem is reframed or renamed, often from a more positive point of view. The very act of calling a problem a "family problem" rather than an "individual problem" itself is an important act of reframing.

Accommodation. Accommodation is analogous to empathy and is another word for acceptance of what is present in the family.

Mimesis. Mimesis refers to the direct mirroring of the body language of one or more family members plus observing which persons mirror each other's body language and in what sequence.

Strengths and Limitations of Family Therapy
One major contribution of the family therapy movement has been to make the field aware of how clients may be viewed from a systems or person-environment interactional perspective. As with all other methods, family therapy has its limitations. Ivey, Ivey, and Simek-Downing (1987) indicate that "wild analysis" is not restricted to those who employ analytic techniques. A limitation of the impact of family therapy may be individual therapists who resist change and avoid learning about family therapy theory and method.

Application of Family-Systems Theory to Special Education

The application of family-systems theory to special education identifies the entire family as the consumer of services (see Chapter 10). The central features of a family-systems model are the family's complexity and uniqueness. Turnbull, Summers, and Brotherson (1984) conceptualized four components of a family-systems framework and their interrelationships within the system: (1) family resources, (2) family interaction, (3) family functions, and (4) family life cycle.

Family Resources
Family resources consist of the descriptive characteristics of the family including characteristics of the child's exceptionality. They substantially influence the impact a child with a disability has on the family and the family's responses to the child's needs. Bronicki and Turnbull (1987) address three factors in understanding the diversity of a family's resources: (1) characteristics of child exceptionality, (2) family characteristics, and (3) personal characteristics of individual family members.

Characteristics of Child Exceptionality. For example, children with medically complex conditions (e.g., an infant on supplemental oxygen or an apnea and bradycardia monitor at home) can severely restrict a family's mobility and ability to participate in routine family and community activities (see Chapter 10). Although special education and related services have long appreciated the need for individualization in education programs, the fact that there is individualization in the way each child affects the family typically is overlooked.

Family Characteristics. Family characteristics vary in numerous ways including size, form (e.g., foster parents, blended family, single parents), cultural background (see Chapter 10), and socioeconomic status. The reader is referred to

Acosta, Yamamoto, and Evans (1982) for information about family characteristics of low-income and minority persons and to Morawetz and Walker (1984) for material about therapy with single-parent families.

Personal Characteristics of Individual Family Members. Individual family members have their own personal characteristics such as physical and mental health, intellectual faculties, and coping strategies, which Olson, McCubbin, Barnes, Larsen, Muxen, and Wilson (1983) categorize into five types: (1) passive appraisal such as ignoring, (2) reframing by changing the way one views the problem, (3) spiritual support, (4) social support from friends and family, and (5) professional support.

Family Interaction
Bronicki and Turnbull (1987) advise professionals to appreciate that any of their interactions with the child or family members can reverberate throughout the family. A home visit can induce family stress due to the need to change the family's routine, or the time of a parent conference can provoke a disagreement between two working parents about which one will take time off from employment. The impact of a child with a disability can vary across family subsystems by enhancing or encroaching upon marriages (Kazak & Marvin, 1984; Murphy, 1982), engendering greater sensitivity in siblings or contributing to adjustment difficulties (Vadasy, Fewell, Meyer, & Schell, 1984), and generating closer or more distant ties with the extended family (Vadasy, Fewell, & Meyer, 1986). Goals for the individualized family service plan (IFSP) and the individualized education program (IEP) should be designed to facilitate family interaction that considers the needs of all family members in addition to the exceptional child.

Family Functions
Turnbull and Turnbull (1990) identify seven family functions: (1) economic; (2) daily care; (3) recreation; (4) socialization; (5) self-definition

including self-identity, personal strengths and weakness, and feelings of belonging; (6) affection; and (7) educational/vocational. These functions are not independent, and one may facilitate or impede progress in another area. For example, economic hardship can substantially interfere with the other family functions. Bronicki and Turnbull (1987) advise professionals to examine all family functions, which must be systematically addressed given the tendency for educational personnel to concentrate on the educational/vocational function to the exclusion of the others.

Family Life Cycle
Families differ in resources, which influence interaction patterns that affect the ability of the family to meet its functional needs. Each distinctive family unit changes as it progresses through stages and transitions. The family life cycle is a series of developmental stages. Table 6.1 identifies four life cycle stages from early childhood to young adulthood and developmental tasks for each facing parents and siblings.

SUMMARY

The emphasis in this chapter has been on a general-theory approach to counseling in which therapeutic agents respect other theoretical perspectives beyond one's own conceptual view. To develop cultural intentionality, an integrated knowledge of theory and skills is essential in order to provide effective services for culturally diverse children and youth in developmental difficulty or emotional turmoil. Therapeutic knowledge and skills also can benefit the consultation process. An understanding of life-span developmental issues facing children and adolescents and their families is critical.

Due to the complexity of counseling and psychotherapy processes, helping professionals are urged to analyze which set of procedures (which may include components of several paradigms) are most appropriate for particular children with

TABLE 6.1 Possible Issues Encountered at Life-Cycle Stages

LIFE CYCLE STAGE	PARENTS	SIBLINGS
Early Childhood, ages 0–5	Obtaining an accurate diagnosis Informing siblings and relatives Locating services Seeking to find meaning in the exceptionality Clarifying a personal ideology to guide decisions Addressing issues of stigma Identifying positive contributions of exceptionality Setting great expectations	Less parental time and energy for sibling needs Feelings of jealousy over less attention Fears associated with misunderstandings of exceptionality
School Age, ages 6–12	Establishing routines to carry out family functions Adjusting emotionally to educational implications Clarifying issues of mainstreaming vs. special class placement Participating in IEP conferences Locating community resources Arranging for extracurricular activities	Division of responsibility for any physical care needs Oldest female sibling may be at risk Limited family resources for recreation and leisure Informing friends and teachers Possible concern over younger sibling surpassing older Issues of "mainstreaming" into same school Need for basic information on exceptionality
Adolescence, ages 13–21	Adjusting emotionally to possible chronicity of exceptionality Identifying issues of emerging sexuality Addressing possible peer isolation and rejection Planning for career/vocational development Arranging for leisure time activities Dealing with physical and emotional change of puberty Planning for postsecondary education	Overidentification with sibling Greater understanding of differences in people Influence of exceptionality on career choice Dealing with possible stigma and embarrassment Participation in sibling training programs Opportunity for sibling support groups
Adulthood, ages 21–	Planning for possible need for guardianship Addressing the need for appropriate adult residence Adjusting emotionally to any adult implications of dependency Addressing the need for socialization opportunities outside the family Initiating career choice or vocational program	Possible issues of responsibility for financial support Addressing concerns regarding genetic implications Introducing new in-laws to exceptionality Need for information on career/living options Clarify role of sibling advocacy Possible issues of guardianship

Source: Reprinted by permission of Merrill, an imprint of Macmillan Publishing Company from *Families, professionals, and exceptionality* (2nd ed.) by Ann P. Turnbull & H. Rutherford Turnbull III. Copyright © 1990, 1986 by Merrill Publishing.

194   CHAPTER 6

certain problems. Some areas of difficulty may need relatively benign intervention. A listening approach with a concerned adolescent in one session may be sufficient to assist her or him in feeling understood. More typically, counselors will need to draw from multiple therapeutic approaches in order to serve the variety of issues experienced by today's youth.

Each theory and technique have the potential to augment therapist skill and to enhance beneficial movement in clients. All children are influenced by their environmental situation and many live under daunting circumstances. Hence, a systems perspective is crucial in understanding the family ecology.

Psychotherapeutic interventions require vigilance. Helpers must be ever attentive to professional standards and ethics. Three guiding principles are the maintenance of confidentiality and recognition of any limits to confidences, appreciation of one's own therapeutic limitations and commitment to continuing education, and awareness of individual and cultural differences. Supervision of all aspects of the counseling process is essential particularly for the beginner. Quality assurance also dictates periodic peer review even for the advanced clinician. The challenge to the professional is great; the benefit to our youth can be substantive.

REFERENCES

Acosta, F. X., Yamamoto, J., & Evans, L. A. (Eds.). (1982). *Effective psychotherapy for low-income and minority patients*. New York: Plenum Press.

Acosta, F. X., Yamamoto, J., Evans, L. A., & Wilcox, S. A. (1982). Effective psychotherapy for low-income and minority patients. In F. X. Acosta, J. Yamamoto, & L. A. Evans (Eds.), *Effective psychotherapy for low-income and minority patients* (pp. 1–29). New York: Plenum Press.

American Psychological Association. (1990). Ethical principles of psychologists. *American Psychologist, 45,* 390–395.

Arlow, J. A. (1979). Psychoanalysis. In R. J. Corsini (Ed.), *Current psychotherapies* (2nd ed., pp. 1–43). Itasca, IL: F. E. Peacock.

Axline, V. M. (1969). *Play therapy* (rev. ed.). New York: Ballantine Books.

Barker, P. (1979). *Basic child psychiatry* (3rd ed.). Baltimore: University Park Press.

Barlow, D. H., & Hayes, S. C. (1979). Alternating treatments design: One strategy for comparing the effects of two treatments in a single subject. *Journal of Applied Behavior Analysis, 12,* 199–210.

Barrett, C. L., Hampe, I. E., & Miller, L. C. (1978). Research on child psychotherapy. In S. L. Garfield & A. E. Bergin (Eds.), *Handbook of psychotherapy and behavior change: An empirical analysis* (2nd ed., pp. 411–435). New York: Wiley.

Barrett-Lennard, G. T. (1962). Dimensions of thera-pist response as causal factors in therapeutic change. *Psychological Monographs, 76,* (43, whole No. 562).

Batshaw, M. L., & Perret, Y. M. (1986). *Children with handicaps: A medical primer* (2nd ed.). Baltimore: Paul H. Brookes.

Beck, A. (1972). *Depression: Causes and treatment*. Philadelphia: University of Pennsylvania Press.

Beck, A. (1976). *Cognitive therapy and the emotional disorders*. New York: International Universities Press.

Belkin, G. S. (1987). *Contemporary psychotherapies* (2nd ed.). Monterey, CA: Brooks/Cole.

Benjamin, A. (1981). *The helping interview* (3rd ed.). Boston: Houghton Mifflin.

Birnbrauer, J. S., Peterson, C. R., & Solnick, J. V. (1974). Design and interpretation of studies of single subjects. *American Journal of Mental Deficiency, 79,* 191–203.

Boyd, J. D., & Ramer, B. (1980). Teaching rational ideas: Rational-emotive education. *Middle School Journal, 11*(2), 18–20, 30.

Bronicki, G. J., & Turnbull, A. P. (1987). Family-professional interactions. In M. E. Snell (Ed.), *Systematic instruction of persons with severe handicaps* (3rd ed., pp. 9–35). Columbus, OH: Charles E. Merrill.

Brown, L., Branston, M. B., Hamre-Nietupski, S., Pumpian, I., Certo, N., & Gruenewald, L. (1979). A strategy for developing chronological-age-appropriate and functional curricular content for severely handicapped adolescents and young adults. *The Journal of Special Education, 13,* 81–90.

Calsyn, R. J., & Kenny, D. A. (1977). Self-concept of ability and perceived evaluation of others: Cause or effect of academic achievement? *Journal of Educational Psychology, 69,* 136–145.

Carson, R. C., & Heine, R. W. (1962). Similarity and success in therapeutic dyads. *Journal of Consulting Psychology, 26,* 38–43.

Chess, S., & Hassibi, M. (1980). Behavior deviations in mentally retarded children. *Journal of American Academy of Child Psychiatry, 23,* 122–130.

Clarizio, H. F., & McCoy, G. F. (1976). *Behavior disorders in children* (2nd ed.). New York: Thomas Y. Crowell.

Cobb, H. C., & Brown, D. T. (1983). Counseling and psychotherapy with handicapped children and adolescents. In H. T. Prout & D. T. Brown (Eds.), *Counseling and psychotherapy with children and adolescents: Theory and practice for school and clinic settings* (pp. 391–424). Brandon, VT: Clinical Psychology Publishing.

Coleman, M. C. (1986). *Behavior disorders: Theory and practice.* Englewood Cliffs, NJ: Prentice-Hall.

Collins, R. L., Rothblum, E. D., & Wilson, G. T. (1986). The comparative efficacy of cognitive and behavioral approaches to the treatment of obesity. *Cognitive Therapy and Research, 10,* 299–318.

Cook, P., Kunce, J., & Getsinger, S. (1976). Perception of the disabled and counseling effectiveness. *Rehabilitation Counseling Bulletin, 19,* 470–475.

Copeland, A. D. (1974). *Textbook of adolescent psychopathology and treatment.* Springfield, IL: Charles C. Thomas.

Cormier, W. H., & Cormier, L. S. (1979). *Interviewing strategies for helpers: A guide to assessment, treatment, and evaluation.* Monterey, CA: Brooks/Cole.

DeKrey, S. J., & Ehly, S. W. (1981). Factor/cluster classification of profiles from Personality Inventory for Children in a school setting. *Psychological Reports, 48,* 843–846.

Elkind, D. (1967). Egocentrism in adolescence. *Child Development, 38,* 1025–1034.

Ellis, A. (1979). Rational-emotive therapy. In R. J. Corsini (Ed.), *Current psychotherapies* (2nd ed., pp. 185–229). Itasca, IL: F. E. Peacock.

Epps, S. (1983). *Designing, implementing, and monitoring behavioral interventions with the severely and profoundly handicapped.* Des Moines, IA: Iowa Department of Public Instruction. (ERIC Document Reproduction Service No. ED 240 772).

Epps, S. (1991). *Depression and special education classification: Diagnostic overshadowing and school psychologists.* Manuscript submitted for publication.

Epps, S., & Tindal, G. (1987). The effectiveness of differential programming in serving students with mild handicaps: Placement options and instructional programming. In M. C. Wang, M. C. Reynolds, & H. J. Walberg (Eds.), *Handbook of special education: Research and practice* (pp. 213–248). New York: Pergamon Press.

Erikson, E. H. (1972). Eight ages of man. In C. S. Lavatelli & F. Stendler (Eds.), *Readings in child behavior and child development* (3rd ed., pp. 19–30). New York: Harcourt Brace Jovanovich.

Eysenck, H. J. (1952). The effects of psychotherapy: An evaluation. *Journal of Consulting Psychology, 16,* 319–324.

Fiedler, F. (1950a). A comparison of therapeutic relationships in psychoanalytic, nondirective, and Adlerian therapy. *Journal of Consulting Psychology, 14,* 435–436.

Fiedler, F. (1950b). The concept of an ideal therapeutic relationship. *Journal of Consulting Psychology, 14,* 239–245.

Fiedler, F. (1951). Factor analysis of psychoanalytic, nondirective, and Adlerian therapeutic relationships. *Journal of Consulting Psychology, 15,* 32–38.

Frankl, V. E. (1985). Logos, paradox, and the search for meaning. In M. J. Mahoney & A. Freeman (Eds.), *Cognition and psychotherapy* (pp. 259–275). New York: Plenum Press.

Ginsburg, H. P., & Opper, S. (1988). *Piaget's theory of intellectual development* (3rd ed.). Englewood Cliffs, NJ: Prentice-Hall.

Greer, B. G. (1975). Attitudes of special education personnel toward different types of deviant persons. *Rehabilitation Literature, 36,* 182–184.

Gresham, F. M. (1982). Misguided mainstreaming: The case for social skills training with handicapped children. *Exceptional Children, 48,* 422–433.

Grieger, R. M., & Boyd, J. D. (1980). *Rational-emo-*

tive therapy: A skills-based approach. New York: Van Nostrand Reinhold.

Grieger, R. M., & Boyd, J. D. (1983). Rational-emotive approaches. In H. T. Prout & D. T. Brown (Eds.), *Counseling and psychotherapy with children and adolescents: Theory and practice for school and clinic settings* (pp. 103–164). Brandon, VT: Clinical Psychology Publishing.

Haley, J. (1976). *Problem-solving therapy.* San Francisco: Jossey-Bass.

Harris, S. L., & Ferrari, M. (1983). Developmental factors in child behavior therapy. *Behavior Therapy, 14,* 54–72.

Hart, J. T., & Tomlinson, T. M. (Eds.) (1979). *New directions in client-centered therapy.* Boston: Houghton Mifflin.

Havighurst, R. J. (1951). *Developmental tasks and education.* New York: Longmans.

Heinicke, C. M., & Strassman, L. H. (1975). Toward more effective research on child psychotherapy. *Journal of the American Academy of Child Psychiatry, 14,* 561–588.

Hughes, J. N. (1988). *Cognitive behavior therapy with children in schools.* New York: Pergamon Press.

Ivey, A. E., Ivey, M. B., & Simek-Downing, L. (1987). *Counseling and psychotherapy: Integrating skills, theory, and practice* (2nd ed.). Englewood Cliffs, NJ: Prentice-Hall.

Jacobson, J. W. (1982). Problem behavior and psychiatric impairment within a developmentally disabled population: I. Behavior frequency. *Applied Research in Mental Retardation, 3,* 121–139.

Jenson, W. R., Sloane, H. N., & Young, K. R. (1988). *Applied behavior analysis in education: A structured teaching approach.* Englewood Cliffs, NJ: Prentice Hall.

Kanfer, F. H., & Schefft, B. K. (1988). *Guiding the process of therapeutic change.* Champaign, IL: Research Press.

Kazak, A. E., & Marvin, R. S. (1984). Differences, difficulties and adaptation: Stress and social networks in families with a handicapped child. *Family Relations, 33,* 67–77.

Kazdin, A. E. (1982). *Single-case research designs: Methods for clinical and applied settings.* New York: Oxford University Press.

Keat, D. B. (1979). *Multimodal therapy with children.* New York: Pergamon Press.

Kelly, J. T., Koch, M., & Buegel, D. (1976). Lithium carbonate in juvenile manic-depressive illness. *Diseases of the Nervous System, 37,* 90–92.

Kessler, J. (1966). *Psychopathology of childhood.* Englewood Cliffs, NJ: Prentice-Hall.

Kifer, E. (1975). Relationships between academic achievement and personality characteristics: A quasi-longitudinal study. *American Educational Research Journal, 12,* 191–210.

Krumboltz, J. D., & Thoresen, C. E. (Eds.). (1976). *Counseling methods.* New York: Holt, Rinehart & Winston.

Lambert, M., DeJulio, S., & Stein, D. (1978). Therapist interpersonal skills. *Psychological Bulletin, 85,* 467–489.

Laplanche, J., & Pontalis, J. (1973). *The language of psychoanalysis.* New York: Norton.

Laufer, M. (1980). On reconstruction in adolescent analysis. In S. C. Feinstein, P. L. Giovacchini, J. G. Looney, A. Z. Schwartzberg, & A. D. Sorosky (Eds.), *Adolescent psychiatry* (Vol. 8, pp. 460–468). Chicago: University of Chicago Press.

Lazarus, A. A. (1976). *Multimodal behavior therapy.* New York: Springer.

Levitan, G. W., & Reiss, S. (1983). Generality of diagnostic overshadowing across disciplines. *Applied Research in Mental Retardation, 4,* 59–64.

Levitt, E. E. (1957). The results of psychotherapy with children: An evaluation. *Journal of Consulting Psychology, 21,* 186–189.

Levitt, E. E. (1963). Psychotherapy with children: A further evaluation. *Behavior Research and Therapy, 60,* 326–329.

Levitt, E. E., Beiser, H. R., & Robertson, R. E. (1959). A follow-up evaluation of cases treated at a community child guidance clinic. *American Journal of Psychiatry, 29,* 337–347.

Matson, J. L. (1981). Assessment and treatment of clinical phobias in mentally retarded children. *Journal of Applied Behavior Analysis, 14,* 145–152.

Matson, J. L., Epstein, M. H., & Cullinan, D. (1984) A factor-analytic study of the Quay-Peterson scale with mentally retarded adolescents. *Education and Training of the Mentally Retarded, 19,* 150–154.

Matson, J. L., & Frame, C. L. (1986). *Psychopathology among mentally retarded children and adolescents.* Beverly Hills, CA: Sage Publications.

McConville, B. J., & Purohit, A. P. (1973). Classifying confusion: A study of results in a multidisciplinary children's center. *American Journal of Orthopsychiatry, 43,* 411–417.

Meador, B. D., & Rogers, C. R. (1979). Person-centered therapy. In R. J. Corsini (Ed.), *Current psychotherapies* (2nd ed., pp. 131–184). Itasca, IL: F. E. Peacock.

Meichenbaum, D. (1974). Self-instructional training: A cognitive prosthesis for the aged. *Human Development, 17,* 273–280.

Meichenbaum, D. (1976). Cognitive-functional approach to cognitive factors as determinants of learning disabilities. In R. M. Knights & D. J. Bakker (Eds.), *The neuropsychology of learning disorders: Theoretical approaches* (pp. 423–442). Baltimore: University Park Press.

Meichenbaum, D. (1977). *Cognitive-behavior modification: An integrative approach.* New York: Plenum Press.

Meichenbaum, D. (1985). Cognitive-behavioral therapies. In S. Lynn & J. Garske (Eds.), *Contemporary psychotherapies: Models and methods* (pp. 261–286). Columbus, OH: Merrill.

Meichenbaum, D., & Asarnow, J. (1979). Cognitive-behavioral modification and metacognitive development: Implications for the classroom. In P. C. Kendall & S. D. Hollon (Eds.), *Cognitive-behavioral interventions: Theory, research, and procedures* (pp. 11–35). New York: Academic Press.

Meichenbaum, D., & Goodman, J. (1971). Training impulsive children to talk to themselves: A means of developing self-control. *Journal of Abnormal Psychology, 77,* 115–126.

Meichenbaum, D., & Jaremko, M. (1973). *Stress reduction and prevention.* New York: Plenum Press.

Meltzoff, J., & Kornreich, M. (1970). *Research in psychotherapy.* New York: Atherton.

Minuchin, S. (1974). *Families and family therapy.* Cambridge, MA: Harvard University Press.

Mitchell, K., Bozarth, J., & Krauft, C. (1977). A reappraisal of the therapeutic effectiveness of accurate empathy, nonpossessive warmth and genuineness. In A. Gurman & A. Razin (Eds.), *Effective psychotherapy* (pp. 482–502). New York: Pergamon Press.

Moore, H. B. (1983). Person-centered approaches. In H. T. Prout & D. T. Brown (Eds.), *Counseling and psychotherapy with children and adolescents: Theory and practice for school and clinic settings* (pp. 225–286). Brandon, VT: Clinical Psychology Publishing.

Morawetz, A., & Walker, G. (1984). *Brief therapy with single-parent families.* New York: Brunner/Mazel.

Murphy, A. T. (1982). The family with a handicapped child: A review of the literature. *Developmental and Behavioral Pediatrics, 3*(2), 73–82.

Nathanson, R. (1979). Counseling persons with disabilities: Are the feelings, thoughts, and behaviors of helping professionals helpful? *The Personnel and Guidance Journal, 58,* 233–237.

Neely, M. A. (1982). *Counseling and guidance practices with special education students.* Homewood, IL: The Dorsey Press.

Nichols, M. P. (1984). *Family therapy: Concepts and methods.* New York: Gardner Press.

Nunnally, J. C. (1978). *Psychometric theory* (2nd ed.). New York: McGraw-Hill.

O'Connor, K., Lee, A. C., & Schaefer, C. E. (1983). Psychoanalytic psychotherapy with children. In M. Hersen, A. E. Kazdin, & A. S. Bellack (Eds.), *The clinical psychology handbook* (pp. 543–564). New York: Pergamon Press.

Olson, D. H., McCubbin, H. I., Barnes, H., Larsen, A., Muxen, M., & Wilson, M. (1983). *One thousand families: A national survey.* Beverly Hills, CA: Sage.

Phillips, I., & Williams, N. (1975). Psychopathology and mental retardation: I. Psychopathology. *American Journal of Psychiatry, 132,* 1265–1271.

Prout, H. T. (1983). Counseling and psychotherapy with children and adolescents: An overview. In H. T. Prout & D. T. Brown (Eds.), *Counseling and psychotherapy with children and adolescents: Theory and practice for school and clinic settings* (pp. 3–34). Brandon, VT: Clinical Psychology Publishing.

Rachman, S., & Wilson, G. (1980). *The effects of psychological therapy.* New York: Wiley.

Reisman, J. M. (1973). *Principles of psychotherapy with children.* New York: Wiley.

Reiss, S., Levitan, G. W., & Szyszko, J. (1982). Emotional disturbance and mental retardation: Diagnostic overshadowing. *American Journal of Mental Deficiency, 86,* 567–574.

Reiss, S., & Szyszko, J. (1983). Diagnostic overshadowing and professional experience with mentally retarded persons. *American Journal of Mental Deficiency, 87,* 396–402.

Rogers, C. R. (1957). The necessary and sufficient conditions of therapeutic personality change. *Journal of Consulting Psychology, 21,* 95–103.

Rogers, C. R. (Ed.). (1967). *The therapeutic relationship and its impact.* Madison, WI: University of Wisconsin Press.

Rogers, C. R. (1977). *Carl Rogers on personal power.* New York: Delacorte Press.

Rutter, M. (1971). Psychiatric disorder and intellectual retardation in childhood. In J. Wortis (Ed.), *Mental retardation: An annual review* (Vol. 3, pp. 186–221). New York: Grune & Stratton.

Rutter, M., Tizard, J., Yule, W., Graham, P., & Whitmore, K. (1976). Research report: Isle of Wight studies, 1964–1974. *Psychological Medicine, 6,* 313–332.

Scheirer, M. A., & Kraut, R. E. (1979). Increasing educational achievement via self-concept change. *Review of Educational Research, 49,* 131–150.

Sharfman, M. A. (1978). Psychoanalytic treatment. In B. B. Wolman, J. Egan, & A. O. Ross (Eds.), *Handbook of treatment of mental disorders in childhood and adolescence* (pp. 47–69). Englewood Cliffs, NJ: Prentice-Hall.

Sigman, M. (Ed.). (1985). *Children with emotional disorders and developmental disabilities: Assessment and treatment.* Orlando, FL: Grune & Stratton.

Sloane, R., Staples, F., Cristol, A., Yorkston, N., & Whipple, K. (1975). *Psychotherapy versus behavior therapy.* Cambridge, MA: Harvard University Press.

Strupp, H. (1977). A reformulation of the dynamics of the therapist's contribution. In A. Gurman & A. Razin (Eds.), *Effective psychotherapy* (pp. 1–22). Elmsford, NY: Pergamon Press.

Strupp, H. H. (1984). The Vanderbilt psychotherapy research project: Past, present, and future. In J. B. W. Williams & R. L. Spitzer (Eds.), *Psychotherapy research: Where are we and where should we go?* (pp. 235–246). New York: Guilford Press.

Strupp, H. H., & Hadley, S. W. (1977). A tripartite model of mental health and therapeutic outcomes: With special reference to negative effects in psychotherapy. *American Psychologist, 32,* 187–196.

Szymanski, L. S. (1985). Diagnosis of mental disorders in mentally retarded persons. In M. Sigman (Ed.), *Children with emotional disorders and developmental disabilities: Assessment and treatment* (pp. 249–258). Orlando, FL: Grune & Stratton.

Turnbull, A. P., Summers, J. A., & Brotherson, M. J. (1984). *Working with families with disabled members: A family systems approach.* Lawrence: University of Kansas, University Affiliated Facility.

Turnbull, A. P., & Turnbull, H. R. III. (1990). *Families, professionals, and exceptionality: A special partnership.* (2nd ed.). Columbus, OH: Merrill.

Vadasy, P. F., Fewell, R. R., & Meyer, D. J. (1986). Grandparents of children with special needs: Insights into their experiences and concerns. *Journal of the Division for Early Childhood, 10,* 65–72.

Vadasy, P. F., Fewell, R. R., Meyer, D. J., & Schell, G. (1984). Siblings of handicapped children: A developmental perspective on family interactions. *Family Relations, 33,* 155–167.

Waters, V. (1980). *RET parenting pamphlet series.* New York: Institute of Rational Emotive Therapy.

Weiner, I. B. (1970). *Psychological disturbance in adolescence.* New York: Wiley.

Weisz, F., & Benoit, C. (1983). Psychoanalytic approaches. In H. T. Prout & D. T. Brown (Eds.), *Counseling and psychotherapy with children and adolescents: Theory and practice for school and clinic settings* (pp. 331–388). Brandon, VT: Clinical Psychology Publishing.

Wilcox, B., & Bellamy, G. T. (Eds.). (1982). *Design of high school programs for severely handicapped students.* Baltimore: Paul H. Brookes.

Wilson, G. T. (1978). Cognitive behavior therapy: Paradigm shift or passing phase? In J. P. Foreyt & D. P. Rathjen (Eds.), *Cognitive behavior therapy: Research and applications* (pp. 7–32). New York: Plenum Press.

Wong, B. Y. L. (1985). Issues in cognitive-behavioral interventions in academic skill areas. *Journal of Abnormal Child Psychology, 13,* 425–442.

CHAPTER 7

SCHOOL AND PEDIATRIC CONSULTATION THEORIES AND TECHNIQUES

This chapter presents an overview to major theoretical models of school consultation and introduces pediatric psychology consultation as an emerging dimension resulting from the need to provide a liaison between psychology and pediatrics. Reversals in the typical consultative relationship are addressed in which school consultants function as consultees and neonatal and pediatric specialists serve as consultants. Defining features of consultation also are discussed. An alternative paradigm to case-centered consultation is highlighted in which a preventive model is adopted (drawing from systems theory and an ecobehavioral perspective) as consultees acquire and use skills proactively to analyze components of the instructional ecology that enhance and interfere with children's learning and prosocial behavior.

An empowerment philosophy also is encouraged whereby consultees become more effective in accessing available resources to address their own difficulties. A heuristic six-stage framework for consultation is integrated from the literature on mental health and behavioral consultation.

SCHOOL-BASED CONSULTATION

With the limitations of a direct-service model, consultation has become a major professional function and a highly preferred activity (cf. Curtis & Zins, 1980; Gutkin & Curtis, 1990; Meacham & Peckham, 1978). A plethora of articles on the topic has appeared. Pryzwansky (1986) reviewed the consultation literature from 1978 to 1985 and found 660 citations in *Psychological Abstracts* and 403 entries in *ERIC* (Educational Resources Information Centers). There is considerable empirical support for the efficacy of consultation as a form of service delivery.

Participation in the process of consultation has been found to have a number of desirable results, including changes in the frequency of requests for consultative services (Bergan & Tombari, 1976), in the behavioral precision of consultees' (student teachers) definitions of problem behavior (Conoley & Conoley, 1982a), in consultees' knowledge and professional skills (Gutkin, 1980; Martens, Lewandowski, & Houk, 1989), in consultees' and clients' behavior (Gutkin & Curtis, 1990), and in consultees' perceptions of the consultation process (Gutkin, 1986). Extensive reviews of research have concluded that consultation is an effective professional activity (Fullan, Miles, & Taylor, 1980; Mannino & Shore, 1975a, 1975b; Medway & Updyke, 1985). Curtis and Meyers (1985) also have discussed the preventive value of consultation.

In light of the benefits of school-based consultation, which originated in the 1960s based on dissatisfaction with the medical model (Curtis & Meyers, 1985; Meyers, Parsons, & Martin, 1979), heavy emphasis on this function would be expected within the profession. One problem that has plagued the field relates to the overuse of the generic (and meaningless) term *consultation,* which at one time referred to practically any form of contract or service in the schools and every interaction between two professionals (Reschly, 1976).

A second obstacle that interferes with the prominence that consultation should have in professional practice can be attributed to professional training programs (Curtis, 1983). A decade ago, Meyers, Wurtz, and Flanagan (1981) found only 40 percent of the responding programs offered coursework to provide training in consultation. A more recent survey is necessary to investigate whether there is a trend toward greater preservice training in this area.

Examination of national surveys provides some insight into participation in indirect service delivery. Results from Farling and Hoedt (1971) and Ramage (1979), with over three-fourths of respondents employed in school systems, indicated greater proportions of psychologists involved in direct services such as individual counseling (51 and 58 percent respectively) and individual evaluations (72 and 82 percent respectively) than in the more indirect services.

In more recent investigations (Benson & Hughes, 1985; Lacayo, Sherwood, & Morris, 1981; Smith, 1984), the time school psychologists devoted to various activities was examined. The proportion of time spent in assessment ranged from 21 to 48 percent and counseling from 5 to 9 percent. The proportion of time in consultation (teacher, parent, school staff/administrators) ranged from 18 to 25 percent. Although the majority of professional activity investigated in these studies was focused on direct assessment, the survey data suggest a trend in the provision of more consultative services.

Stewart (1986) interprets these survey data as suggesting that psychologists would prefer to devote more time to indirect services than they actually do. This view is consistent with the statement about the future of professional preparation and practice in school psychology provided by the National School Psychology Inservice Training Network in its document entitled *School Psychology: A Blueprint for Training and Practice* (1984). It emphasized the expanding role of school psychologists, with an increase in indirect service delivery including consultation.

Models of Consultation

Three major theoretical models of school consultation have been proposed (see Gutkin & Curtis, 1982; Meyers, Parsons, & Martin, 1979). They differ in the general problems they address and in the goals, techniques, and criteria for evaluation of outcome as well as on theoretical framework (Reschly, 1976). These three models are (1) mental-health consultation (e.g., Caplan, 1970; Meyers, Parsons, & Martin, 1979); (2) behavioral consultation (problem-centered and developmental) (Bergan, 1977; Bergan & Kratochwill, 1990), more recently referred to as ecological consultation (Gutkin & Curtis, 1990; Reynolds, Gutkin, Elliott, & Witt, 1984); and (3) organization development consultation (Schmuck & Runkel, 1985). A fourth model is instructional consultation (Rosenfield, 1987). The pediatric psychology literature also discusses three models of consultation: (1) resource consultation (Stabler, 1979, 1988) or independent functions consultation (Roberts & Wright, 1982), (2) indirect psychological consultation (Roberts, 1986; Roberts & Wright, 1982), and (3) collaborative team consultation (Roberts, 1986; Roberts & Wright, 1982).

Rather than adopting a narrow approach to consultation in which one model is regarded as more useful than another, a general theory orientation is advocated in which several models are integrated into one unified approach. Within this model, a consultant moves systematically and knowledgeably from theory to theory, using trans-theoretical concepts and skills to determine what treatment plan is most effective for a particular client and consultee for a certain goal under a particular set of circumstances (cf. Paul, 1969). This approach is consistent with the general theory approach to therapeutic practice with clients, discussed in Chapter 6, in which different theoretical paradigms are organized into a coherent and systematic framework (see Ivey, Ivey, & Simek-Downing, 1987).

One of the most influential figures in psychological consultation has been Gerald Caplan, a leader in the development of community psychiatry. His approach reflects both environmental and psychodynamic perspectives (Caplan, 1970, 1974). An environmental influence is found in his focus on helping social institutions (e.g., schools) function more effectively in dealing with clients' mental-health problems. His psychodynamic perspective is apparent in his attention to personality factors in consultees that interfere with their professional functioning and reduce their effectiveness with clients.

Caplan proposes four types of mental-health consultation: (1) client-centered case consultation, (2) consultee-centered case consultation, (3) program-centered administrative consultation, and (4) consultee-centered administrative consultation. His unique contribution has been consultee-centered case consultation in which consultees are assisted with their lack of knowledge, skill, self-confidence, or objectivity. The cornerstone of his theory is the nonhierarchical relationship between consultant and consultee. The reader is referred to Brown, Pryzwansky, and Schulte (1987), Meyers, Parsons, and Martin (1979), and Reynolds and colleagues (1984) for more detail about Caplan's model. Although his psychodynamic logic has been questioned in favor of situationally based explanations (such as the teacher's school environment) for most consultee behaviors, Caplan has made significant contributions to the development of consultation theory and technique and has had a major impact on the current defining characteristics of consultation.

Defining Characteristics

Although consultation theory and strategy mean assorted things to different professionals, there are a number of overlapping characteristics and assumptions that can be considered defining features of consultation. These include:

A problem-solving process (Bergan, 1977; Meyers, Parsons, & Martin, 1979)

An indirect service (Bergan, 1977; Curtis & Meyers, 1985)

A colleague and collaborative relationship (Bergan, 1977; Brown et al., 1987; Caplan, 1970; Curtis & Meyers, 1985; Lambert, 1974)

A work-related focus (Curtis & Meyers, 1985)

Shared responsibility for client (Curtis & Meyers, 1985)

Goals (Bergan, 1977; Curtis & Meyers, 1985)

Systems theory (Curtis & Meyers, 1985)

Behavioral psychology (Bergan, 1977)

Knowledge utilization (Bergan, 1977).

Problem Solving. The problem-solving undertaking is a fundamental component of consultation. Generally, consultation addresses an undesirable set of circumstances the consultee faces. The means to achieve a goal typically are unspecified at the initial stage. Through a process of information gathering and information sharing, the consultant and consultee determine the problem(s), goals, and strategies to ameliorate the problem. The consultant avoids assuming the role of exclusive problem solver.

Indirect Service. The consultant provides an indirect form of service delivery by working with the consultee, who in turn implements the intervention with the client(s). In this triadic relationship, the consultant has an indirect influence on the client. There are numerous advantages to this form of service delivery. It extends the purview of psychological services to a far greater number of individuals than could be served by direct services. Generally less time is necessary to provide consultative services than to render direct services to clients. Moreover, the consultee may acquire knowledge and skills during the span of consultation that can be used in other situations or for other clients (Bergan, 1977). Despite the plethora of overall advantages to a general consultation model, it does not obviate the need for direct services.

Collaborative Relationship. For the consultation process to occur, it is essential that there be a genuine, collaborative relationship among colleagues. In the reciprocal interaction, both the consultant and consultee contribute their expertise to the problem-solving activity, with both adopting an active role. With the increasing number of medically complex children in our education programs (see Chapter 10), there will be some reversal in the typical consultative relationship. School psychologists and other education professionals who traditionally have functioned as consultants will be the recipient of consultative services as infant-development specialists and psychologists in neonatal and pediatric intensive care units, wards, and clinics share their expertise about chronic illness and its psychosocial impact. (Functioning as a consultant and consultee within the realm of pediatric psychology is discussed later in this chapter.)

Curtis and Meyers (1985) outline several key components that influence the success of this colleague relationship. These are established as ground rules at the beginning of consultation. First, the consultant-consultee relationship is nonhierarchical. Second, the consultee is actively involved. A position of authority is avoided as both participants in consultation analyze the stimulus conditions associated with the problem, determine consultation goals, and generate problem-solving strategies. Through active participation, a sense of ownership in the intervention plan is engendered. This notion, referred to as treatment acceptability, is a subset of the larger domain of social validity (Wolf, 1978) and refers to "judgments by laypersons, clients, and others of whether treatment procedures are appropriate, fair, and reasonable for the problem or client" (Kazdin, 1981, p. 493).

It is a critical component of consultation efforts, considering the interrelationships among acceptability, use, integrity of the independent variable, and effectiveness of treatment (see Witt

& Elliott, 1985). Treatment acceptability may have direct implications for the success of interventions since strategies regarded as more acceptable are more likely to be used and implemented with greater fidelity (Kazdin, 1980, 1981). Indeed, nonacceptable perceptions of interventions may nullify their utility (Epps, Prescott, & Horner, 1990).

A third characteristic of the colleague relationship is the consultee's option to accept or to reject the intervention plan. This component dovetails with the first two features of collaboration. With a nonhierarchical arrangement, the consultant is not in an authoritative position to impose a particular strategy. Since the consultee assumes an active role in the development of the intervention, he or she ultimately accepts or rejects a collaborative plan. Since treatment acceptability is essential, explicit license to disagree with consultant suggestions and to repudiate treatment plans must be explained in the initial phase of consultation.

A fourth component is the consultee's voluntariness. It is preferable that the consultee self-initiate the consultation process. Creating an environment conducive to requests for consultative services is important and is regarded as the first stage of consultation, entry into the system.

A fifth feature of a colleague relationship is confidentiality. Open communication is facilitated when sensitive information (such as opinions about the school administration) is excluded from discussions outside the consultative relationship. Information about the treatment plan certainly should be shared with parents/legal guardians, principals, and possibly other professionals on an interdisciplinary team. Prior to employing intrusive, level-3 treatment procedures, such an exclusionary time-out, documenting systematic attempts at less intrusive strategies, and obtaining written permission from the agency's human rights committee, is very strongly advocated (see Epps, 1983; Foxx, 1982).

Confidentiality builds on an atmosphere of trust. However, confidentiality in consultation is unrelated to the legal status of confidential communication determined by state laws (Curtis & Meyers, 1985). It is incumbent on professionals to be knowledgeable about the status of privileged communication in their own states (see Dekarii & Sales, 1982).

Work-Related Focus. In an atmosphere of confidentiality and open communication, it is possible that the consultation process may become diverted as discussions begin to focus more on the consultee's areas of difficulty rather than the presenting issues with the client. It is important to differentiate consultation from adult therapy (Bergan, 1977; Caplan, 1970), which has a therapist-client rather than colleague relationship, and to avoid dual professional roles. While the consultant's repertoire includes such counseling skills as minimal encouragers, paraphrasing, and reflection of feeling (see Chapter 6), the consultant (even one with the necessary adult clinical expertise) should refer the consultee to another professional.

Responsibility for Client. Although the consultee has been regarded as the professional who assumes primary responsibility for the client, professional and ethical standards dictate shared responsibility by the consultant. Given the nature of interdisciplinary teams and the call for accountability, there is a trend toward consultants accepting a greater obligation for client welfare (Curtis & Meyers, 1985). Since consultants may have areas of specialization in such areas as behavior therapy, child development, or childhood psychopathology, they are in a position to recognize the need for additional services that may be necessary in the best interests of the client (cf. Epps, 1991).

Goals. There are several ways to conceptualize consultation goals. Parsons and Meyers (1984) discuss preventive goals, with three general types of prevention. Primary prevention postulates that a particular population should benefit from mental-health services. Rather than addressing a deficit issue, the goal is to promote growth, which

can be addressed via (1) analysis and modification of social environments, (2) development of competence and adaptive capacities, and (3) stress reduction. Secondary prevention concentrates on problems that already have begun to appear. With the goal of mitigating the impact of the problem by intervening prior to major escalation, early identification and treatment are emphasized. In tertiary prevention, the goal is to diminish the consequences of severe dysfunction after it has developed.

The model proposed by Meyers, Parsons, and Martin (1979) emphasizes primary and secondary prevention and defines four categories of consultation. Each is discussed as it relates to consultation goals. In level I, direct service to the client, the goal is to make changes in a client(s) who presents with a problem. The consultant directly collects the data about the client's behavioral repertoire. In level II, indirect service to the client, the goal of consultation is the same, but someone other than the consultant, such as the consultee, collects information about the client.

In level III, service to the consultee, known as consultee-centered case consultation in Caplan's (1970) model, the primary goal is to make some change in the consultee. For example, the general goal may be to assist the consultee in improving effectiveness with students by increasing knowledge or developing certain skills. A secondary goal is a concomitant change in the client's behavior. The ultimate goal at this level of consultation is to foster cultural intentionality (see Chapter 6) such that the consultee generates alternative behaviors for problem solving and intervention and responds to changing situations when necessary. The culturally intentional consultee has an increased behavioral repertoire (cf. Wolpe, 1973) and a sense of self-efficacy (cf. Bandura, 1982). Similarly, it is important for the consultant to develop cultural intentionality and to avoid sole reliance on consultation strategies tailored to the YAVIS consultee (young, attractive, verbal, intelligent, successful) (cf. Schofield, 1964).

The consultation goal is to improve the overall organizational functioning of the system in level IV, service to the system. Such a goal may be appropriate when the system does not permit certain interventions or when deterioration occurs in client or consultee behaviors because the desired behaviors are not supported by the system. The net effect of this level of consultation is improved mental health both for clients and consultees within the system.

These consultation goals are consistent with those outlined by Bergan (1977) to change client behavior, to effect change in consultee behavior, and to promote change in the social organization in which the client and consultee are operating. Additionally, Bergan (1977) discusses two types of consultative problem solving, each with somewhat different goals. In problem-centered consultation, the goal is to address the immediate presenting problem, such as severe aggression. In developmental consultation, there are reiterative applications of consultative problem solving in order to attain long-range developmental goals. For example, the goal for a toddler with bronchopulmonary dysplasia (a chronic lung disease) may be to improve eating skills. Due to the complexity of the pediatric feeding disorder associated with this iatrogenic illness, several areas would be targeted for treatment at varying points in time.

Since one of the benefits of adopting a consultation model is to provide more efficient and meaningful service delivery (as opposed to the diagnostic/gatekeeper role), the primary goal common to all models of consultation pertains to generalization. In providing consultative services, the ultimate goal is for the consultee to acquire a set of generalized responding that is useful in a variety of situations, with a variety of children, for an assortment of behavioral concerns. To achieve this goal, at a minimum, developmental consultative problem solving or several cases of problem-centered consultation with a consultee are necessary. (Consider the training sufficient exemplars approach outlined by Stokes & Baer, 1977, and general case programming discussed by Engelmann & Carnine, 1982). Pro-

gramming for generalization is a complex activity. The reader is referred to Epps, Thompson, and Lane (1985); Horner, Dunlap, and Koegel (1988); and Stokes and Baer (1977) for more in-depth coverage.

Systems Theory. Systems theory focuses on the operation of interrelated elements within an organized system (Bergan, 1977). System functioning is governed by feedback about system activities, which has been referred to as reciprocal interaction (Curtis & Meyers, 1985). A change in any part of a system effects change in other parts. The client, and similarly the consultee, are viewed as part of the system. Attention to systems theory facilitates an understanding of the process of consultation as it is affected by such variables as consultant and consultee characteristics and school district policy (Gallessich, 1973).

The systems approach implies the importance of various knowledge bases, particularly the social and biological sciences. Therefore, effective treatment often is interdisciplinary, requiring the consultant to be familiar with information that crosses disciplines (Kanfer & Schefft, 1988). As discussed in Chapter 10, intervention efforts also may be interagency, requiring consultant familiarity with policies of multiple agencies. Rather than regarding deviance as internal to the client, as in a person-centered perspective, a situation-centered approach is adopted whereby the environmental context is analyzed. This conceptualization is consistent with ecobehavioral analysis in which system-like interdependencies among environment, organism, and behavior are examined (Willems, 1974).

Rogers-Warren (1984) delineates several applications of ecobehavioral analysis strategies. First, it can be used in planning interventions by evaluating environmental contexts in order to anticipate impediments to behavior change and to identify naturally occurring support for the new behavior. A second application enables assessment of the effects of treatment on nontarget behavior of the client (collateral changes and side effects), behaviors of others, and the physical environment. Third, ecobehavioral assessment strategies can be employed to assess and to foster generalization and maintenance of newly acquired client or consultee behavior.

Behavioral Psychology. With the immense domain of behavioral research findings that draw on operant, respondent, social learning, and cognitive-behavioral strategies, there is a wealth of information that can be useful in designing an intervention plan. Whereas other theoretical orientations clearly contribute to the consultative process, the behavioral framework is particularly noteworthy for its effective methodology for evaluating treatment efficacy with individual or small groups of clients or consultees (e.g., Barlow & Hersen, 1984; Kazdin, 1982).

Social validation, with its attention to the social relevance of treatment goals, the acceptability of treatment procedures, consumer satisfaction with the effects of intervention (Wolf, 1978), and optimal levels for target behaviors (Van Houten, 1979), also substantially impacts the consultative process. The behavioral field also has brought attention to the importance of evaluating the integrity of the independent variable (Peterson, Homer, & Wonderlich, 1982) since fidelity of treatment is a critical factor in positive outcome of consultation.

Knowledge Utilization. One of the consultant's primary responsibilities is to access his or her own knowledge and expertise to provide relevant information to the consultee. Bergan (1977) outlines three consultant tasks in disseminating information. First, the consultant must be able to obtain the information, which comes largely from professional preparation in graduate school, internships, postdoctoral fellowships, supervised employment, and/or independent practice.

The consultant makes judgments on the basis of an amalgam of information derived from several sources: (1) the scientific data base, (2) the cumulative experiences and skills of the profession, and (3) the consultant's own personal and professional experiences (Kanfer & Schefft,

1988). With the exponential expansion in knowledge and the enormous quantity of professional journals, books, and intervention packages, it is unrealistic for a consultant to retain this level of information. Therefore, consultants need to be part of a system that accesses information (Bergan, 1977).

Second, principles and strategies from the psychological knowledge base must be made available to consultees. For instance, an ecobehavioral perspective may identify a repertoire problem in the client, instructional material inappropriate for the client's academic skill level, and an insufficiently structured and generally unsupportive classroom environment with little positive reinforcement. Such an analysis equips the consultant and consultee with information to develop an intervention plan.

A third task relates to effectively communicating the necessary information to consultees so that they may use it. Consultants need to convey conceptual and technical principles in a language understandable to their colleague in the consultation relationship. Such communication requires avoiding unnecessary jargon while also providing the logic behind employing various strategies in the intervention. This form of knowledge utilization facilitates active participation by the consultee and enhances treatment acceptability.

Similar to Bergan's (1977) conceptualization of knowledge utilization is *diffusion of innovations,* a term used by Meyers, Parsons, and Martin (1979) to refer to the process by which new information is disseminated to members of the system. The consultant's role is to expedite the diffusion of relevant knowledge to school personnel.

An Alternative Model to Case-Centered Consultation

Examination of the literature over the past 15 years reveals a substantial increase in the focus on consultation, with numerous articles and books devoted to the topic. As Meyers, Parsons, and Martin (1979) have noted, labeling oneself a consultant has become as fashionable as it previously was favored declaring oneself a therapist. We advocate a view of consultation in which a preventive model is adopted, with the general goal of engendering intentionality. In this model, consultees acquire skills and use them in a proactive manner to analyze variables that facilitate and interfere with children's learning and prosocial behavior. Although necessary in a variety of situations, too often a deficit model is the predominant perspective in which a crisis event draws attention to remediation (Parsons & Meyers, 1984).

The popularity of consultation has made it prone to problems that afflict other techniques popular at the time. With much of the literature illustrating a problem-solving approach applied on an individual case basis, a bandwagon effect has occurred such that the laudable goals of consultation are not accomplished. Indeed, this form of consultative problem solving has been sanctioned by social, political, and administrative structures (Witt & Martens, 1988).

Witt and Martens (1988) provide a cogent argument for a reexamination of the assumptions and goals of traditional case-centered consultation, which they maintain does little to foster independent functioning of teachers. Use of a conventional problem-solving approach in an attempt to address a client's interfering behaviors is viewed as a fragmentary approach because of its failure to consider the context within which the problem initially evolved. Since endurance of consultee behaviors and problem-solving skills is the key, a narrow and myopic approach to consultation would impose a behavioral or mental-health intervention strategy onto a classroom routine.

Such a tactic fails to consider systems theory and an ecobehavioral perspective and is likely to meet with failure eventually. Interfering variables that could mitigate behavior change, naturally occurring discriminative stimuli that cue appropriate behavior, and the natural community of reinforcement that could support client and consultee behaviors have not been analyzed (see

Rogers-Warren, 1984), thereby curtailing the ultimate effects of prevention of similar future problems.

Although consultation has provided a more positive approach than traditional diagnosis in which a child is identified as having some handicapping condition, it may still rely on a negative person-centered view, with the problem residing in the client. An alternative approach advocates an empowerment philosophy in which consultees become more effective in addressing their own difficulties by knowing how to access available resources (Dunst & Trivette, 1988). In this model, the role of the consultant is to assist consultees in indicating needs and pinpointing resources and in connecting them with the identified resources (Hobbs, Dokecki, Hoover-Dempsey, Moroney, Shayne, & Weeks, 1984). Consultation thus becomes a process that enhances consultee empowerment, with the goal of building a social structure within the system to support and to promote consultee learning and performance.

Witt and Martens (1988) maintain that school consultation is more hierarchical than truly collaborative in a case-centered approach given the differential salaries and formal education of psychologists and teachers. In some situations, a consultant's "help" by imposing an additional treatment for the referred client can have negative consequences by usurping consultees' independent problem solving and diluting their view of their own competence. Rather than a generally sole reliance on manipulation of consequences to correct a problem, a proactive approach to classroom management is advocated in which antecedent conditions are manipulated to prevent child misbehavior.

The large literature on effective teaching (e.g., Brophy & Good, 1986; Epps & Tindal, 1987; Good, 1983; Waxman & Walberg, 1982) makes an enormous contribution to this model. Ysseldyke and Christenson (1987) describe 12 components of the instructional environment that influence student achievement, but note that their collective effect is more important than a singular effect. This "multivariate world of the effective teacher" (Witt & Martens, 1988, p. 216) dictates a broad ecobehavioral perspective, with particular attention to antecedent events, and provides a catalyst for moving away from consequence based, client-centered problem solving.

Instructional Ecology

Competent teachers establish preventative routines and procedures whereas ineffective teachers may be inconsistent in contingency management and less skilled in curriculum deployment (McKee & Witt, 1990). With this scenario, Witt and Martens (1988) argue that it is ill advised to employ case-centered consultation in which a particular management technique is added to the classroom routine to modify client behavior. Such an approach fails to consider the factors that contributed to the client "problem" (the ecobehavioral analysis) and makes an additional demand on a teacher experiencing difficulty with classroom management. The reader is referred to Rosenfield (1987) for detailed information about instructional consultation and to Bergan, Feld, and Swarner (1988) for a description of macroconsultation to facilitate instructional management for large numbers of children.

Empowerment Model of Consultation

In the alternative approach to case-centered consultation, Witt and Martens (1988) propose an empowerment model of consultation in which efforts are directed at the antecedent conditions of effective teaching behaviors. The goal in this model is to assist consultees in skill development in proactive classroom management that endures over time. The logic for this model is based on several assumptions that are drawn from the literature about family empowerment (e.g., Dunst & Trivette, 1988), which is discussed in Chapter 10. This model contends that consultants should provide support for consultees while avoiding doing the task for them. As a result, improvements resulting from consultee implemented interventions can be ascribed to consultee skill and effort.

Build on Consultee Strengths. A beginning step for the consultant is to conduct an assessment of teacher strengths and classroom routines. One method of gaining this information is to use a combination interview-observe strategy as described in Epps, Thompson, and Lane's (1985) Common Stimuli Form, which was adapted from Miller's Environmental Analysis (Miller, Epp, & McGinnis, 1985). It is used as a guide to collect information about classroom rules, routines, and procedures, trapping behaviors and behaviors regarded as unacceptable by the teacher, reinforcement, reductive procedures, and instructional and evaluation strategies.

In the analysis of the current classroom management system, Witt and Martens (1988) suggest that attempts should be made to build on its positive features rather than supplanting it with the consultant's new plan. Such an approach enables fine tuning a program before any discussion of revamping, directs positive attention toward the consultee, and helps to build consultee self-esteem. These in turn contribute to treatment acceptability and successful consultation with enduring effects.

Use Existing Resources. Consultees are likely to have a lengthy history of managing their classrooms in particular ways. Therefore, the existing contingencies may not sustain a new intervention plan, which can be as obtrusive as "a foreign appendage" (Witt & Martens, 1988, p. 222). Rather than applying a supplemental treatment package, the consultant assists the consultee in activating currently existing resources. As a collaborative team, the consultant and consultee assess and use available resources. Within this model, the goal of consultation is for the consultee to develop self-sustaining skills in contacting and employing available resources.

One resource that may be available to consultees is a broad-scale, systemwide consultative service delivery known as *intervention assistance programs* (IAPs) (Ponti, Zins, & Graden, 1988; Zins, Curtis, Graden, & Ponti, 1988; Zins & Ponti, 1990). These programs operate within a prereferral consultation framework and are designed to address the needs of students via collaborative problem solving in the least restrictive environment prior to referral for consideration for a more restrictive form of service delivery. Consultees may request assistance from an individual IAP team member or from the entire team. Such a form of consultation requires administrative sanction.

Provide Support to Improve the Quality of Teacher Life. Witt and Martens (1988) maintain that enhancing the quality of teacher life would positively impact their students. Several possibilities include teacher networking to exchange ideas as well as resources and fund-raising activities. With the stress inherent in the teaching profession (Sarason, 1982), school psychologists would do well to draw on the industrial-organizational literature to provide support and stress-reducing activities.

Offer Proactive Consultation. Rather than waiting for a crisis to develop, which serves as the impetus for consultation, activities at the start of the school year can be designed to provide information about effective teaching and classroom management. School psychologists can assist in establishing school-based information exchanges among education personnel. From an organizational-development approach, consultants can facilitate problem solving (e.g., Curtis & Metz, 1986). Additionally, consultants can adopt a prevention focus and contact teachers early in the year to touch bases and to offer proactive support as the classroom contingencies are set into place.

Be Certain that Benefits Exceed the Costs of Consultation. In the cost-benefit analysis, effects on the consultee are no less important than client effects. The consultee must perceive that client behavior or overall classroom management has improved and that he or she was an active participant in the process (Dunst & Trivette, 1988). As previously discussed, teacher self-efficacy is likely to be diminished if the consultant is regarded as the agent responsible for improvement.

Witt and Martens (1988) provide a provocative analysis of the presumed decrease in referral rates following initiation of consultative services. It has been assumed that consultees can solve future difficulties, which results in less need for referral (e.g., Gutkin, Singer, & Brown, 1980). In their rival hypothesis, they maintain that school psychologists merely have instituted another time-consuming obstruction between teachers and their objective of having their more problematic students placed in special education.

Witt and Martens (1988) argue that teachers' requests for consultative services decrease because of the increased cost in their own time and energy. Such a situation attenuates the benefits of consultative services both to consultees and clients who are not necessarily better served by a special-education placement (see Epps & Tindal, 1987).

In summary, this proactive, empowering model of consultation strives to reestablish natural classroom operations in which consultees create a healthy ecology for student learning and welfare by exercising their duties in a supportive social system. Iatrogenic effects of traditional client-centered case consultation (e.g., limits to generalization and maintenance, undesirable side effects, consultee resistance) are viewed as resulting from infringement on the natural classroom ecology (Witt & Martens, 1988).

STAGES OF CONSULTATION

Regardless of theoretical model, consultation is a dynamic process as it moves through a series of stages. The stages do not always occur in the sequence presented in this chapter. A consultant may function simultaneously at several stages or move across stages. Portions of the mental-health and behavioral consultation literature are integrated to provide a heuristic six-stage framework for consultation.

Stage 1: Entry into the System

Consultants internal or external to the system initially will be viewed as an encroachment. Defensiveness may ensue since the initiation of consultation suggests that the system is not functioning effectively. Hence, the first item on the consultant's agenda is to gain acceptance by the system (Parsons & Meyers, 1984).

Entry into the Organization

Parsons and Meyers (1984) describe organizations as either proactive or reactive. In the proactive (anticipatory) system, the consultant's ease of entry depends on the skill in engendering a need for consultative services. With no readily apparent need, the preventive aspect of consultation can be emphasized. Since proactive systems rely on internal resources to address the challenges of future situations, the external consultant will need to explain that existing resources will be used and that the consultant's endeavors will be educative.

When consultative services are requested, it is more likely the case that the system is reactive to external forces demanding adaptation. For example, a mandate might require integrating students with severe disabilities into activities with their same-age peers without disabilities. Under conflict or crisis conditions, entry typically can occur more easily, although suspicion may be encountered from individuals experiencing a loss of autonomy or power. Whether the system is proactive or reactive, it is incumbent on the consultant to analyze and to diminish all possible sources of resistance. The reader is referred to Tables 3.1 and 3.2 in Sulzer-Azaroff and Mayer (1986) for guidelines for assessing environmental support and resources.

Organizational Resistance

Parsons and Meyers (1984) review four types of organizational resistance.

Resistance Due to Desire for System Maintenance. An entering consultant generates reverberations throughout the interdependent components of the organizational system. Any new addition that requires adaptation threatens system homeostasis with its added demands for change

in procedures and professional roles. Meyers, Parsons, and Martin (1979) emphasize the importance of a negotiation process that occurs in sufficient detail to permit possible objections and obstacles to emerge.

During the beginning meetings with organizational leaders, a clear precedent must be set for candid discussion of concerns and disparity between consultant and system views. Entry is facilitated when the consultant attempts to reduce the degree of demanded change. It is important for the consultant to identify means to reduce a variety of costs. Financial costs often can be controlled by using existing materials, space, and personnel. Circumventing the need for increases in human energy can be facilitated by relying on existing procedures, communications channels, chains of command, and network patterns.

A consultant must elevate the comfort level of persons within the organization. The consultant is well advised to analyze ways in which he or she may threaten or challenge existing roles. It clearly is necessary to emphasize the essential value of key individuals (e.g., administrators, lead teachers) and to help them feel some ownership of the consultative process. In this light, these persons can regard the consultant's involvement as an indication of his or her own competence without a sense of being threatened.

Another strategy for reducing resistance due to a desire to maintain the system is to be assimilated into the system as it currently operates. Entry will be less complicated with fewer demands for change in structure or process. Initially it may be better to adopt the institutional policy, with "plans to shape it slowly" rather than to attempt innovation too aggressively. A cardinal rule to be followed is to "do it their way." It is generally advisable to avoid introducing a new procedure initially even though it may have worked well in another system.

Resistance to the External Consultant. An external consultant is an unknown entity who may be regarded with distrust or provisional inclusion at best. Parsons and Meyers (1984) suggest that the consultant explore the organization's history, mission, philosophy, and procedures in order to acquire a common perspective. Increased knowledge about the system also augments the credibility of the consultant's recommendations. The consultant needs to attend to the discernible manifestations of outsider status. For example, being more or less formally dressed, using more or less official salutations, or wearing a pager when inside professionals do not could enhance or detract from the entry process.

Another recommended strategy to facilitate acceptance is to increase contact with persons within the system. Consultants can participate in routine activities such as staff meetings. It is helpful to ascertain the system's work schedule. For instance, if personnel congregate in a teacher's lounge or work area before school for informal conversation, there is an opportunity to increase referent power by participating in this unscheduled activity. Adopting a similar work style and mingling with staff may not be a simple matter given the substantial work load of school psychologists and a concomitant sense of need to "get caught up."

A determining factor in realizing entry is the relationship with the system's official and unofficial gatekeepers who oversee the consultant's entry (Parsons & Meyers, 1984). It is advisable that politicking (see Glidewell, 1959) be directed at persons regarded as the status leaders. In order to enhance the adoption of consultation, the consultants must focus their initiative on the opinion leaders in the social system (Meyers, Parsons, & Martin, 1984). Organizational sanction and some type of benefit to consultees can reduce resistance. The base of this relationship building should be broad enough to include persons not in administrative roles in order to avoid perception of a possibly alienating coalition.

Resistance Due to Rejecting the New as Nonnormative.   Although conforming to existing norms is contraindicated once a consultant has been sought, resistance may arise from the desire to maintain the status quo. Parsons and Meyers (1984) describe this form of intense resistance as an energy-depleting process, which results from concern that the consultant will intrude on time-honored programs and sacrosanct procedures. They recommend that the consultant become familiar with these areas and avoid interfering with such institutional practices while seeking entry and acceptance.

With a norm that consultation is unnecessary, Parsons and Meyers (1984) stipulate that the organizational leaders play a particularly important role in securing formal sanction for entry. Identifying the opinion leaders and institutional innovators (see Haveluck, 1973) can assist in furnishing the needed foundation of influence.

Resistance to Protect Vested Interest.   Members within the system may view the consultant as an encroachment on their particular interest, responsibility, or area of expertise. Resistance can be an attempt to preserve one's existing role and function. It is important for the consultant to work with such professionals to provide them opportunities for participation in the consultation process (Parsons & Meyers, 1984).

Entry with the Consultee

When consultation has been sanctioned at the organizational level, requests for consultative services will begin. For each consultee there are new demands for entry as the consultative relationship is established. The first task when seeking entry is to identify the consultee's motivations. Parsons and Meyers (1984) provide several examples: (1) reducing the emotional cost of a particular job-related task (e.g., removing the frustrations about a client), (2) avoiding the responsibility of managing a delicate situation, (3) having the consultant serve as a scapegoat, or (4) justifying the consultee's feelings of incompetence (e.g., a specialist had to be called because the problem was so overwhelming).

In addition, the consultant must illustrate that consultation is the most appealing resource available, with the highest possible payoff-to-cost ratio. Entry requires attention to several components including increasing the benefit, providing service as a problem solver and a source of support (or assistance in accessing sources of support), and reducing the costs of participating in consultation (Parsons & Meyers, 1984).

Consultee Resistance

Consultants frequently have encountered resistance to the consultation process (Abidin, 1975; Meyers, Parsons, & Martin, 1979; Piersel & Gutkin, 1983). There are a variety of manifestations of consultee resistance, which need to be anticipated and circumvented whenever possible. When resistance does occur, the consultant needs to analyze contributing factors. There are several conditions that may lead to resistance.

Consultee Unfamiliarity with Consultation. This form of resistance occurs with uncertainty about the consultation process. Consultees may be unfamiliar with any number of the features of consultation such as active participation or indirect service. Piersel (1985) refers to consultee uncertainty until the contingencies of reinforcement can be identified, and Parsons and Meyers (1984) discuss fear of the unknown. Questions about the unknown requirements or impact of the consultative relationship may be present. In the initial interview, the consultant must attempt to reduce this emotional cost to the consultee.

Several strategies include delineating the responsibilities and parameters of consultation, clarifying the nature of the consultant's role within the system, and assuring the consultee of confidentiality and his or her right to reject preventive or remedial management plans deemed unacceptable. Meyers, Parsons, and Martin (1979) further emphasize the need to clarify that indirect service is provided to the client and that both the consultee and consultant can renegotiate the informal consultation contract at any time, with no obligation for the consultee to continue if there are doubts about the consultation process.

Prior History with Consultation. This source of resistance may be difficult to discern, particu-

larly if the consultant is new to the system. Consultees may have known colleagues who had, or they themselves had, unpleasant experiences with previous consultative relationships for a variety of reasons. For example, former consultants may not have achieved entry, been supportive of the collaborative and voluntary nature of consultation, or devoted adequate attention to treatment acceptability. Or the organization may have required less effective teachers to become the first consultees, thus engendering negative reactions.

Zins and Ponti (1990) suggest identifying motivated consultees and situations with a likelihood of successful outcome. This approach can help to instill a sense of the effectiveness of consultation throughout a school. Piersel (1985) also identifies the role of unsuccessful outcomes with prior consultations and the sense of inadequacy at failing to solve a problem situation on one's own.

Fear of Being Evaluated. If consultees are unclear about the consultative relationship, they may be worried about a stigma associated with needing a consultant. They may view consultation as a service that highlights their failure or shortcoming. If requests for consultation are regarded as an indication of weakness, the consultant may be considered intimidating (Parsons & Meyers, 1984). Clarification of the consultation process as a nonevaluative, collaborative, problem-solving venture can reduce this apprehension.

Vacuum Cost. Parsons and Meyers (1984) indicate that consultees may solicit consultation only as a last recourse after repeated efforts to resolve the problem. They may anticipate that the consultant's attempts will be thwarted as well. Within this context, demands placed on the consultee are viewed as a cost without return, an exertion in a vacuum. To counter this presumption, Parsons and Meyers (1984) highlight the importance of demonstrating the consultant's value as a resource by "doing something." Consultants can demonstrate their value as they lessen the perceived costs of consultation by offering to complete a variety of tasks such as contacting a resource or completing certain paper work.

Stage 2: Goal Identification

The first session with a consultee defines the parameters of the consultative process and sets the stage for collaborative efforts. After the consultee indicates a desire to proceed, the process of goal identification can begin. Bergan (1977) refers to this phase as the problem-identification interview, consisting of five steps: (1) determine objectives, (2) develop measures for performance objectives, (3) design and implement data-collection procedures, (4) display data, and (5) define the problem by establishing a discrepancy between current client performance and desired performance. In this stage, the client's challenging behaviors are described and operationally defined. When preintervention baseline data document interfering behaviors, consultation proceeds with the next stage in which environmental variables that may influence client behavior and problem resolution are analyzed (Kratochwill, Elliott, & Rotto, 1990).

Witt and Elliott (1983b) draw on the work of Cormier and Cormier (1979) and expand Bergan's (1977) framework. They delineate the following nine components, which have been revised and expanded in this chapter, that facilitate the problem operationalization interview.

Explanation of Problem Definition

Witt and Elliott (1983b) discuss the importance of providing an overview of the task to be accomplished during the interview and the logic for identifying the problem. This point is necessary to help consultees avoid expecting quick and easy solutions to their concerns in lieu of their active participation in the problem-solving process. Explaining the role of the consultant can help to avert confusion with consultees who presume the consultant will provide a direct service such as assessment or counseling. Setting the tone for a situation-centered perspective can facilitate subsequent discussion of classroom and curricular

variables rather than exclusive attention to client behavior. In this initial stage, consultants are advised to avoid presenting themselves as experts in order to adopt the empowerment model.

Identification and Selection of Target Behaviors

Consultees without experience with consultation may have a general, emotionally laden impression of the client's difficulty (Sandoval, Lambert, & Davis, 1977). Therefore, the introduction to consultation and the nature of the consultant's questions should facilitate discussion of the area of concern in precise terms. Consultants need to be knowledgeable about the selection of socially valid target behaviors (see Epps, 1985, and the mini-series on target behavior selection in volume 7(1) of the journal, *Behavioral Assessment,* 1985, for a discussion).

In addition, particularly for special populations, the consultant needs to be acquainted with the current literature's influence on goal selection. For example, for learners with severe disabilities, functional, chronologically age-appropriate, life-skills activities and routines with community-transition value should be emphasized (see Browder, 1987; Brown et al., 1979; Epps, 1983; Wilcox & Bellamy, 1987).

Even if the consultee identifies only one problem behavior, the consultant must consider other relevant behaviors such as those that are part of a larger response class (e.g., hitting, kicking, and biting as aggression), those that are part of a separate response class (e.g., consider the distinct response classes of compliance to "do" and "don't" requests [Neef, Shafer, Egel, Cataldo, & Parrish, 1983]), or those untreated behaviors that covary with the target behavior (e.g., Russo, Cataldo, & Cushing, 1981).

Information about problematic areas initially is gathered via interview with the consultee. Behavioral observations and occasionally deliberate selection of instruments (e.g., behavior rating scales) to assess specific targets can supplement interview data and provide information that can be pursued further in interviews. Kanfer and

Schefft (1988) suggest a focused, pragmatic perspective rather than general interest to "understand the client" when considering the use of other measures. Attention should be focused on how such obtained information can assist in making a better decision with regard to treatment objectives and methods.

Identification of Behavioral Dimensions

In traditional client-centered case consultation with its remedial focus, a behavioral approach would require specification of the behavioral dimensions of the client's difficulty such as topography, rate, duration, intensity, accuracy, and latency (see Epps, 1985; Sulzer-Azaroff & Mayer, 1977). Since information obtained from the consultee via interview reflects *perception* of client problems, the consultant should attempt to understand the normative expectations that are the source of reference for the consultee (Witt & Elliott, 1983b).

In some situations, consultants may wish to supplement their interview with the use of behavior rating forms. Those that require ratings or rankings of other children in the classroom may be particularly suited to this purpose. Witt and Elliott (1983b) recommend clarifying the normal expectations for the behavioral concerns by sharing information with the consultee about developmental norms. A developmental perspective can help to determine what constitutes normal deviations in behavior (see Harris & Ferrari, 1983).

Identification of Stimulus Conditions

The factors that influence the behaviors of concern need to be examined since this information will influence the development of an intervention plan. The stimulus conditions associated with both the occurrence and *nonoccurrence* of problem behavior should be specified. This task is best accomplished by interview and systematic observation. A broader assessment of the classroom ecology can be done by using a guide such as the Common Stimuli Form (Epps, Thompson, & Lane, 1985). Conducting environmental observations has been found to assist consultants in

completing more efficient problem-identification interviews (Conoley & Conoley, 1982a).

Kanfer and Schefft (1988) describe a pyramid approach to behavior analysis for therapists that can be applied to the consultation process. Applying this model, the consultant completes an initial broad scanning of a wide range of events and activities then narrows the focus to increasingly smaller segments. They suggest that the broad scan enables the clinician to cultivate an unbiased perspective. The greatest attention is given to contextual factors that appear relevant to the presenting issues and to potential interventions. At this level of microanalysis, specific antecedents and consequences of appropriate and interfering behaviors are examined.

S-O-R-K-C Model. Kanfer (Kanfer, 1973; Kanfer & Phillips, 1970; Kanfer & Schefft, 1988) uses a S-O-R-K-C model for this micro-level of analysis of behavioral episodes, which summarizes the main components happening at the time of the response that affect the probability of the occurrence of the response. S represents the stimulus, O the biological state of the organism, R the response, K the ratio of consequence frequency to response, and C the consequence.

Setting Events. Some antecedent stimuli do not cue or reinforce specific responses, but may influence behavior in a more global way by altering broad patterns of responding. These setting events may facilitate or inhibit the occurrence of existing stimulus and response functions that follow the setting event (Wahler & Fox, 1981). (There has been debate in the literature regarding the appropriateness of the term *setting event*. Leigland (1984) argues that it may be too broadly defined and functionally unclear, with the possible effect of making it too easy to "explain" complex or obscure environment-behavior interactions.)

For example, Krantz and Risley (1977) found that kindergartners were more inattentive and disruptive during a story-reading activity following an antecedent period of vigorous activity (the setting event). Using this information, manipulation of the setting event by having a rest period before story time was an effective intervention. Sulzer-Azaroff & Mayer (1986) provide a number of examples of setting events such as an imminent vacation, the weather, or a satisfying or unpleasant experience earlier in the day.

The consultant may have specialized knowledge about certain populations, classes of behavior, or educational issues that helps identify potential setting events. For example, stereotypies have been shown to increase under at least three stimulus conditions: novelty, uncertainty, and conflict (see Cataldo & Harris, 1982; Epps, 1987). Therefore, when collaborating with a consultee, ecobehavioral assessment of the educational, home, vocational, and community environments of learners with severe mental retardation can be conducted to determine the extent to which these conditions are present.

Identification of the Required Level of Performance

It is important to obtain a description of the desired behavior. This expected level of performance serves as the goal. The consultant must consider the consultee's interpretation of the presenting problem, namely that a discrepancy exists between current client behavior and desired performance (Bergan, 1977). The focus of attention in case-centered consultation is the client's "problem," which can be addressed by altering the consultee's perception of current performance or expectation of preferred behavior or by ameliorating the client's behavior.

Witt and Elliott (1983b) suggest examining the appropriateness of the consultee's expectations, which provides an opportunity to comment on typical behaviors. Consideration of developmental principles (see Edelbrock, 1984) and two social validation methods (social comparison with normative peer data and subjective evaluation by persons with expertise, consensus, or familiarity with the client; see Kazdin, 1982) helps to evaluate the appropriateness of the consultee's perceptions and to specify levels of performance for the target behavior.

Parsons and Meyers (1984) suggest determining the consultee's general concerns in a relaxed atmosphere that enables discussion of perceived personal and institutional needs. They recommend use of the critical incident interview (Flanagan, 1954) in which the consultee describes in detail the previous occurrence of the problem. The consultant asks explicit questions to gather as much information as possible about the client's behavior, stimulus conditions, prior interventions, and general classroom routines. Within this framework, the consultee contributes as an active participant as interview data are gathered in narrative form.

The size of the instructional universe directly influences the objectives of consultation. It refers to the range of relevant stimulus and response variations, namely, all stimulus situations in which students are expected to produce a behavioral outcome and all behavior they should perform in order to achieve this outcome (Horner, Sprague, & Wilcox, 1982). The objective is for a student to respond appropriately (with varying topographies of the behavior as necessary) to a class of stimuli, not simply to one member of that class. (See Horner & Billingsley, 1988, for more detail about stimulus classes.)

As an illustration, consider Bergan's (1977) problem-centered versus developmental consultation previously described. If the presenting concern with a 17-month-old boy is developmentally inappropriate play with excessive mouthing of objects and restricted use of schemes, the instructional universe can vary in size depending on the objective. A range of toys can be included to reflect such schemes as shaking, pounding, pushing, and twisting (or more or less schemes). The stimulus class is the variety of toys; the response class of various topographies is the different ways to manipulate the toys. The objective for this toddler is for him to shake such toys as rattles or bells, to pound with such objects as a toy hammer, to push in order to get different geometric shapes into a box with corresponding holes, and to twist a dial in order to activate music or a moving picture show.

A small instructional universe can be related

to a problem-centered model since a limited number of behaviors of toy play are addressed in one consultative application. A developmental consultation model may be more appropriate for a larger instructional universe in which reiterative applications of consultation are more likely to enhance the toddler's acquisition of the generalized responding of developmentally appropriate toy engagement. This example depicts a multitheory approach to consultation in which Piagetian theory (e.g., Brainerd, 1978; Ginsburg & Opper, 1988) defined the objective and two models of behavioral consultation provided the approach.

Identification of Client Strengths

It is usually desirable to obtain information early about the client's behavioral, social, and educational strengths. Such a focus can help to set a positive tone about the client rather than drawing attention exclusively to difficult behavior as a confirmatory approach is adopted. Moreover, emphasis on client strengths can assist in identifying stimulus conditions associated with nonoccurrence of challenging behaviors and potential reinforcing events. For consultees who have negative impressions of a client, designing and implementing an intervention to expand client strengths can help engender more positive perceptions as desired behaviors are increased and maintained by the natural community of (classroom) reinforcement (cf. Stokes & Baer, 1977).

Identification of Behavioral Assessment Procedures

Having set the stage for consultation and identified areas of concern and objectives, attention is directed toward gathering data rather than immediate diagnosis and development of treatment plans. The behavioral consultation models advocate more direct baseline assessment in which in vivo systematic observations are conducted. Essentially, the consultant and consultee need to determine responses (or response classes) to be observed, conditions under which observations should be conducted (e.g., teacher, activity, location, time, number of other students present), who will be observed (which clients and social

comparisons), who will conduct the observations, when observations will be done, and the methods of data collection.

When such observations are conducted, the consultant is strongly advised against having tunnel vision and adopting a confirmatory approach in which the client "problem" merely is confirmed. Rather, a *disconfirmatory approach* (see Epps, 1985; Epps, Ysseldyke, & McGue, 1984) should be espoused. Observations conducted within such a framework seek to disconfirm client difficulties by searching for nonoccurrences of problematic behavior and occurrences of alternative appropriate (e.g., prosocial) behaviors. There is a plethora of references that can be reviewed for more in-depth analysis of strategies and validity issues in behavioral observation (e.g., Alberto & Troutman, 1990; Bakeman & Gottman, 1986; Barton & Ascione, 1984; Epps, 1985; Foster, Bell-Dolan, & Burge, 1988; Johnston & Pennypacker, 1980).

It is important for the consultant to explain the logic for baseline data collection, which helps to provide an objective assessment of the client's and peers' behavior. Baseline data also yield a level against which behavior during the intervention phase is compared to evaluate treatment efficacy. Under certain circumstances, information about behavioral assessment procedures might better be obtained in the second interview since primary attention in the first session is centered on entry with the consultee. As Witt and Elliott (1983b) note, securing a commitment from teachers to gather systematic data on their students, particularly if increased response and time demands are required, can be tedious. Negotiation about how such information will be gathered may result in observations conducted by the consultant, consultee, or other existing resources.

A major advantage of consultant observations is the opportunity for ecobehavioral assessment rather than a narrower focus on consultee-identified problems that may ensue from sole reliance on consultee observations. The consultant can observe the pattern of teacher-student interactions that most teachers cannot estimate on their own (Brophy & Good, 1974; Martin & Keller, 1976). Additionally, consultant contribution to the data-collection activity can enhance entry and consultee receptiveness to the consultation process. Consultant observations also can provide an index of agreement with consultee observations.

If untrained personnel are to conduct observations, considerable attention must be devoted to the accuracy of their data recordings and the feasibility of the observation system and schedule within their time constraints. The reader is referred to additional references for information about developing an observation code (Barton & Ascione, 1984; Hawkins, 1982) and observer training and maintenance of accurate recordings (Reid, 1982).

Identification of Consultee Effectiveness

Within the framework of the empowerment model of consultation and the goal of consultee intentionality, the consultee's problem solving and self-efficacy should be enhanced. The consultant can build on consultee strengths by assessing assets in several ways: (1) ascertain how the consultee has managed previous problems that were similar, (2) estimate the success of prior efforts at problem solving, (3) assess motivation by determining what proactive or remedial approaches have been applied, and (4) consider whether the consultee is "self-reliant or dependent on others for encouragement and reinforcement" (Meyer, Liddell, & Lyons, 1977).

When evaluating consultee support for the consultation process, both a consultee's skill level and degree of receptiveness need to be appraised. For example, effective teaching and proactive classroom management can be gauged via interview and direct observations. Consultees also may have varying degrees of skill in analyzing areas of classroom difficulty and operationalizing goals. To assess general consultee framework and support for consultation, several domains can be considered on a formative basis to provide ongoing feedback to the consultant.

First, the consultee's general orientation to client versus environmental influences on behav-

ior can be determined. Does the consultee predominantly make individual characteristics (adjectives) and background environment statements (suggesting a person-centered view to a problem) or behavior (behavioral dimensions) and behavior setting statements (suggesting a situation-centered perspective)? Similarly, is the consultee's verbal behavior largely objective and data based or inferential? Is the approach confirmatory, with a view that the problem resides within the client?

Second, the consultee's prior history and satisfaction with consultation can be considered. Has the consultee sought consultative services previously and has administrative support been present? Has the consultee assumed some ownership and actively contributed to the collaborative process?

Third, the consultee's motivation to participate in consultation and to continue with activities throughout the process must be evaluated continuously throughout the different phases of consultation. A school may have inadequate resources to assist a teacher in making environmental changes to support a consultation plan. Moreover, a negative reinforcement paradigm may be operating in which some teachers are more motivated to have a challenging student removed from their classroom than to participate in a problem-solving venture. Indeed, with traditional delivery of services, teachers' referrals may be negatively reinforced as students they regard as difficult are removed from their classroom.

Other process variables to consider are consultee resistance, defensiveness, openness to new ideas, and such feelings as frustration, anger, resentment, and enthusiasm. Abidin (1975) discusses "punishing internal events," which also need to be examined in order to understand resistance. These events, which are disruptive of work performance and are largely aversive in nature, include concerns about nontargeted children and teaching effectiveness. For continued participation throughout the duration of current and future consultations, consultees' attributions for success and failure also should be considered. Consistent with the empowerment model, consultees should develop a sense of self-efficacy as they problem solve in a proactive manner and attribute success largely to themselves rather than to an expert consultant.

Cherniss (1978) has formulated a five-level model to evaluate a consultee's readiness to participate in consultation. In level 1, no relationship, the consultee provides little information (by making short replies and failing to expand on responses) and denies the existence of a problem. At this level, the consultant must focus on entry issues with both the organization and consultee. In level 2, social only, the consultee discusses events unrelated to consultant questions or to client behavior. Entry may not have been achieved, or the consultee may be inexperienced in the consultation process. In level 3, limited work, the consultee provides information in response to specific consultee questions, with no expansion. For levels 1 through 3, it is particularly important for consultants to analyze the presence of resistance and to reexamine their own clarity in explaining key features of the consultation process.

In level 4, adequate work, the consultee expands and provides detail with minimal prompting. In level 5, informed work, the consultee describes the client's behavior as well as similar behaviors in others; previous interventions are delineated. This framework can assist the consultant in evaluating consultee readiness to collaborate actively with the consultant so that modifications in approach can be implemented as necessary.

Summarization and Identification of Future Contacts
The final component outlined by Witt and Elliott (1983b) includes a summarization of the key points discussed. The consultant should summarize periodically throughout the goal identification stage as well as at the end. The consultee also may be requested to provide summarizations. Bergan (1977) discusses three functions of summary verbalizations: (1) to serve as verbal rehearsal, (2) to establish focus in the interview,

and (3) to review information requiring agreement between the consultant and consultee. This last function relates to what Bergan (1977) identifies as a validation utterance, which helps to establish consensus between the consultant and consultee.

Summarizations and validations help keep the interview on track and ensure correct interpretations and agreement. Before the close of the goal identification interview, the consultant is well advised to review how the interview applied the principal features of consultation, to outline the goals of the next consultation session, and to arrange a time for the subsequent meeting.

Stage 3: Problem Analysis

This stage of consultation is an extension of the problem-identification stage, with an emphasis on identifying the factors related to the presenting issue. In this stage, all information is integrated as the definition of the problem is refined. With a disconfirmatory approach, attention is directed toward determining which behavior patterns are most appropriate for intervention targets, the controlling variables, and significant factors that need to be modified to rectify the situation (Kanfer & Schefft, 1988). Additionally, the best resources for change and problem resolution are reevaluated as an attempt is made to reestablish natural classroom operations.

Bergan (1977) describes two broad phases of the problem-analysis process. In the analysis phase, factors are analyzed that might influence the accomplishment of problem solutions in consultation. The second phase includes the design of the intervention.

Analysis Phase
In the analysis phase, conditions and/or skills can be examined. In the conditions analysis, environmental factors are considered that could affect goal acquisition. In the skills analysis, skills the client needs to realize consultation goals are appraised by identifying potential prerequisite skills and assessing skill mastery.

Wood, Duncan, and Hansell (1983) describe a procedure, called a *performance analysis,* that involves analyzing a behavior to determine if it results from a skill or a motivational deficiency. (The reader also is referred to Epps, Thompson, & Lane, 1985, for additional information.)

The performance analysis consists of four steps. The first step is a general statement of the client's problem and second is the specification of a measurable performance goal. In the third step, the behavior is pinpointed such that its behavioral dimensions are described as precisely as possible. The fourth step, determining whether the client's problem is due to a skill or a motivational deficiency, is most germane to our focus on problem analysis. Wood, Duncan, and Hansell (1983) discuss four questions that assist in differentiating skill (repertoire) and motivational (reinforcement) problems. Epps, Thompson, and Lane (1985) expanded the performance analysis to include the outline in Figure 7.1.

1. *Has the client performed the behavior in the past?* To answer this question, it may be beneficial to interview those who have had opportunities to observe the client. Additionally, two factors must be considered: (1) whether the student engages in the behavior independently or needs to be prompted to do so and (2) the level of environmental demands (Epps, Thompson, & Lane, 1985). In general, an assumption is made that there is a motivational problem only when the client has previously performed a behavior independently or in the presence of naturally occurring cues. For example, although students may have the skills to perform the behavior when special-education teachers prompt them, they may not have these skills in other situations (such as when they are in general-education classrooms). Thus, differentiating skill and motivational problems necessitates a consideration of the extent to which students need to be prompted.

A second factor to consider is the nature of the environmental demands placed on the client. Consider the example of resisting teasing. Roberto may demonstrate this skill under a low-

demand condition such as when one or two students call him a derisive name. However, when four or five students get together and repeatedly call him names and tease him, Roberto may not have the skills to resist teasing in this high-demand condition. It is possible that Roberto may have a motivational problem in the low-demand situation but a skill problem in the high-demand case.

2. *How complex is the task?* If the task is relatively simple, the client may have a motivational problem if the behavior is not performed. If the task is complex and consists of several steps, the client may have a repertoire deficiency. This question requires a subjective judgment. What may be considered simple may in fact be complex for the client. It can be useful to consider what most other students can do of the same age (or the same developmental or functioning level) or in the same classroom. Answering this question alone is insufficient to determine whether there is a skill or motivational deficit.

3. *Do temporary powerful reinforcement contingencies evoke the behavior?* If a temporary reinforcement program (after careful attention to the use of reinforcers tailored to the particular client and analysis of competing contingencies) does effect positive change in the client's behavior, a motivational problem is suggested. If no change occurs, a skill deficiency is more likely.

4. *Do current reinforcement contingencies, those presently being used, evoke the behavior of concern in the client's peers or evoke other appropriate behaviors by the client in other activities?* If the answer is yes to both questions, the client may have a repertoire problem. If the answer is no, particularly to item D.2 in Figure 7.1, a motivational issue is more likely. For instance, if a teacher's regular use of a point system leads to other students' seeking attention appropriately, but does not positively affect the student's behavior, he or she may have a skill deficiency and not know how to gain the teacher's attention. Similarly, if this point system is effective in getting the student to give and to accept compliments appropriately yet ineffective in seeking teacher attention appropriately, there is another suggestion that the student may have a repertoire problem.

Intervention Design

The second chief phase of problem analysis is more complex than is often apparent due to the multiple components that must be considered when developing a treatment plan. In determining factors that may facilitate problem resolution, resources must be identified. Zins and Ponti (1990) outline several possible resources, including student strengths, features of the system that foster client success in other situations, and available materials and human resources.

1. Identify target behavior: ______________________________
2. Performance goal: ______________________________
3. Is problem due to a skill or motivational deficiency?

A. Student has performed behavior in the past.		
1. Spontaneously (independently)		
a. under low level of environmental demands	YES	NO
b. under high level of environmental demands	YES	NO
2. With prompts		
a. under low level of environmental demands	YES	NO
b. under high level of environmental demands	YES	NO
B. Task is simple.	YES	NO
C. Temporary, powerful reinforcers evoke the behavior.	YES	NO
D. Reinforcement consequences already present in classroom.		
1. Evoke the behavior of concern in the student's peers.	NO	YES
2. Evoke other appropriate behaviors by the student in other classroom activities.	NO	YES
	MOTIVATION PROBLEM	SKILL PROBLEM

MOTIVATION PROBLEM → Train in single setting → Take generalization probes

SKILL PROBLEM → Train in several settings → Take generalization probes

FIGURE 7.1 Expanded performance analysis

Source: Epps, S., Thompson, B. J., & Lane, M. P. (1985). *Procedures for incorporating generalization and maintenance programming into interventions for special-education students.* Des Moines, IA: Department of Public Instruction. Reprinted with permission.

By this point in the consultation process, there is a clear understanding of the problem situation, and potential intervention plans can be specified. There are multiple solutions available for intervention as well as assorted goals that can be set (Kanfer & Schefft, 1988). Reynolds and colleagues (1984) (see also D'Zurilla & Goldfried, 1971, and Heppner, 1978) discuss four rules for brainstorming interventions: (1) produce as many ideas as possible, (2) let imagination freely generate options relevant to the problem, (3) suspend judgment of the quality of ideas, and (4) revise and synthesize ideas. Once a list of potential treatment plans has been identified, several variables need to be considered when selecting among the options.

First, the empirical literature must be examined to evaluate efficacy. The primary rationale for selecting a particular intervention strategy pertains to its effectiveness. This task is not straightforward due to the need to consider efficacy for particular clients, for certain behaviors, within various ecological contexts, and implemented by different change agents. Research results are not necessarily generalizable to the presenting consultation situation.

Second, treatment acceptability (addressed at the beginning of the chapter in the section on defining characteristics) must be assessed. A variety of scales has been developed to evaluate treatment acceptability such as the Treatment Evaluation Inventory (Kazdin, 1980) and the Intervention Rating Profile-20 (Witt & Martens, 1983). The Children's Intervention Rating Profile (Witt & Elliott, 1983a), which appears in Turco and Elliott (1986), was designed to measure children's judgments of treatment acceptability.

Elliott (1988) reviews a variety of variables that influence teacher preferences for treatments, including child variables, treatment characteristics, and teacher background variables. Other factors influencing acceptability include treatment efficacy and response effort in the form of time and resources expended (Witt & Elliott, 1985). Issues such as generalization, chronological age appropriateness, intrusiveness, and

trainer qualification may be particularly crucial for highly personal treatments with learners with mental retardation (Epps, Prescott, & Horner, 1990). The reader is referred to Lennox and Miltenberger (1990) for a discussion of 12 factors central to the conceptualization of treatment acceptability.

Additional factors that need to be considered when choosing among intervention alternatives are potential collateral and radiating effects (Kanfer, 1985; Schefft & Lehr, 1985), increased transitory distress or negative reactions from others and cost-benefit ratios (Kanfer & Schefft, 1988), cost-effectiveness analyses (Yates, 1985), and extent to which plan implementation is workable. Although the consultant actively participates in this portion of the problem-solving process and provides sufficient information about treatment options, the consultee ultimately selects the intervention plan (Zins & Ponti, 1990).

The ultimate outcome of the problem analysis stage is an intervention plan. Broad strategies and plan tactics are specified (Kratochwill, Elliott, & Rotto, 1990), and the level of intervention (e.g., preventive or remedial, individual or group, instructional or behavior management practices, classroom or districtwide) must be determined (Zins & Ponti, 1990). Although interventions that assist the development of socially appropriate behavior or reduce interfering behavior are laudable, the true significance of improved client functioning is not realized unless the improvement is apparent and continues to occur over time under nontreatment as well as treatment conditions.

Typically, improvements made in the treatment situation are not apparent in other situations where the controlling stimuli may be different. Thus, the "train and hope" method of intervening under one condition and hoping that improvements will occur elsewhere (see Stokes & Baer, 1977) constitutes a passive approach to comprehensive intervention design. It is in *this* stage (not in the plan evaluation stage) that generalization and maintenance enhancing techniques should be incorporated into treatment design prior to actual

implementation. *"If generalization and maintenance are to occur, they must be systematically
planned for within the intervention"* (Epps,
Thompson, & Lane, 1985, p. 2).

After a treatment plan has been selected, the
roles and responsibilities of participants in the
treatment process must be defined and agreed
upon. Zins and Ponti (1990) recommend that details of the plan be outlined in written form to ensure clarity of tasks and to serve an accountability
function.

Finally, performance and assessment objectives must be established. A model for data collection must be specified to evaluate progress
toward goal attainment, which includes generalized performance (Kratochwill, Elliott, & Rotto,
1990).

Stage 4: Plan Implementation

After careful attention to the first three stages of
consultation, the intervention can be implemented. Kratochwill, Elliott, and Rotto (1990)
outline three chief responsibilities of the consultant during this stage: (1) skill development in
consultee and resource personnel, (2) assessment
of treatment fidelity, and (3) plan revision.

Skill Development

Skill development may be necessary both for preventive and remedial approaches. The consultant
may provide the necessary guidance (e.g., via
modeling and supportive, constructive feedback)
or access the expertise of other professionals to
provide initial assistance. It is important to avoid
assuming that instruction in a small area of the
skill will ensure that the consultee develops skill
in the broader area (cf. Epps & Lane, 1987).
Hence, generalization programming for consultee skill development is as important as it is for
the intervention for the client.

Assessment of Treatment Fidelity

An informed observer (e.g., the consultant) may
report observing what the therapeutic agent (e.g.,
the consultee) was supposed to do rather that

what actually was done (Peterson, Homer, &
Wonderlich, 1982), and changes may develop between different treatment agents and within the
same agent across time (Hersen, 1981). Hence,
the integrity of the independent variable must be
evaluated as a critical component of evaluating
treatment effects. Such monitoring is particularly
critical for the generalization and maintenance
enhancing components of the intervention, which
are often neglected. Otherwise, participants in
the consultation process will be uncertain
whether the intervention was implemented as
prescribed.

If client goals are not reached, the question
will remain about whether the particular treatment was ineffective or whether it merely was not
implemented as intended. Peterson, Homer, and
Wonderlich (1982) recommend rigorously training treatment agents and periodically conducting
spot checks of the agent's service delivery. Additionally, naive observers can be trained to observe components of the intervention. Other
techniques for assessing treatment fidelity include examination of permanent products (e.g.,
lesson plans, client reinforcers such as points)
and informal queries about how the consultee is
implementing the treatment plan.

Plan Revision

With a thorough problem analysis, the stage is set
for a successful plan implementation. Yet revisions in the intervention may need to be made
once treatment is initiated due to unanticipated
events such as negative side effects or the view
that the intervention is too ecologically intrusive
and cannot be supported by the current system.
Additional information also may become available during plan implementation that was not apparent during problem identification and analysis
stages, thus, requiring modifications in the intervention.

As the treatment is implemented, ongoing
data collection should be examined to monitor
progress toward goal attainment, which, depending on the size of the instructional universe,
should include generalization objectives. Treat-

ment acceptability also needs to be monitored and consultee efforts reinforced throughout this stage.

Resistance

Resistance to consultation can vary from the over-cooperative, compliant consultee who participates in portions of the consultation process or concentrates on superficial issues to the consultee who refuses consultation. Several types of consultee resistance were discussed previously in Stage 1 of consultation in the section about entry with the consultee. During the plan implementation stage, resistance may be encountered for a variety of reasons: (1) substantial consultee effort and time, (2) contrasting perspectives of treatment outcomes, (3) lack of immediate problem resolution (Piersel & Gutkin, 1983), and (4) difficulty with implementation (Piersel, 1985). Munjack and Oziel (1978) suggest identifying the type of resistance in order to analyze its contributing factors and to intervene effectively.

Time and Energy Expenditure. Parsons and Meyers (1984) emphasize the importance of considering the limited time and energy that consultees, who also are involved with other work tasks and demands, have available to contribute to the consultation process. They recommend scheduling meetings that are convenient for the consultee and using data collection and intervention procedures that do not require extensive relearning. Furthermore, the consultant can perform much of the "busy work" such as organizing and accessing materials and resources.

Different Set of Expectations. Several authors have identified the congruence between the consultant and consultee as a significant variable in consultee participation (Berkowitz, 1975; Fine, Grantham, & Wright, 1979; King, Colter, & Patterson, 1975). For example, a teacher who expects the problem to be solved by having the student removed from the classroom may view the student's continued presence as a punishing situation and consultation as an additional de-

mand. Hence, the consultant can acquire aversive properties when there is no swift resolution of the problem (Piersel, 1985).

Difficulty with Implementation. Interventions that are ecologically intrusive are likely to be met with resistance. The consultant may not have adequately emphasized the option to reject the treatment plan in the entry stage or conducted a sufficient ecobehavioral analysis in the problem analysis stage. Piersel (1985) suggests that anger and frustration can result from punishing situations such as increased work demands, resulting in some pedagogical aspects being neglected, or incomplete treatment implementation, resulting in limited success. Additionally, the consultee may lack the necessary skills to implement procedures and may resent the perception that her or his skills are deficient.

Stage 5: Plan Evaluation

This stage has been defined as a formal plan evaluation interview to ascertain whether the intervention was effective and goals were attained (Bergan, 1977; Kratochwill, Elliott, & Rotto, 1990). In actuality, evaluation (both of client and consultee variables) occurs throughout the consultation process.

Evaluation of Client

Procedures for measuring client behavior were established in the problem-identification stage when baseline assessment was conducted. These pretreatment data are compared with posttreatment data using a variety of such individual-case designs as multiple baseline (e.g., Barlow & Hersen, 1984), AB with replication (e.g., Harris & Jenson, 1985), or mixed or combined designs (e.g., Wong & Liberman, 1981). One advantage of such designs is their utility in *formative* evaluation whereby continuous monitoring of treatment efficacy is possible throughout the plan implementation stage. Additionally, social validation criteria should be considered. For example, social-comparison data of other students within the classroom can be collected, or subjective evaluation by knowledgeable adults of appropriate levels of behavior can be done.

When an ecobehavioral perspective has been adopted and an instructional universe specified that includes generalized responding, evaluation of a sole target behavior is simplistic. Therefore, a comprehensive evaluation plan is necessary whereby multiple behaviors (i.e., the range of relevant response variation within each behavior) in a variety of contexts are evaluated. Although accurate, systematically collected observational data are necessary to facilitate objective plan evaluation, information collected from structured interviews or even from informal conversations should be used.

Epps, Thompson, and Lane (1985) have referred to this latter source of information as Informal Generalization (or Maintenance) Probes. When the consultee has informal contacts (e.g., in the hallway, lounge, playground) with other educators, natural opportunities arise for queries about client behavior in a variety of situations. One technique for recording this form of data is to use a grid that lists relevant client behaviors and several stimulus conditions. For example, Figure 7.2 illustrates a data sheet for recording interview data about the client's behavior. Epps, Thompson, and Lane (1985) suggest conducting formal observations in situations in which poor performance is reported.

Consultee Evaluation

Evaluation of the consultee's implementation of the intervention and opinion about treatment acceptability is done during the plan-implementation stage. Toward the end of consultation, particularly when an empowerment model has been adopted whereby consultee intentionality is a goal, the consultant will need to evaluate the extent to which the consultee can respond effectively to future challenging situations. Therefore, the consultant can raise hypothetical circumstances for discussion to assess the consultee's

proactive analysis of ecological variables and knowledge about accessing available resources. Such assessment will provide specific information about concepts or techniques that need to be clarified and reemphasized.

Consultants also need to evaluate their consumers' satisfaction with consultation. One such instrument is the Consultation Evaluation Form (Carlson & Tombari, 1986), which appears in Figure 7.3. It includes some original items from the Consultant Assessment Form (Conoley & Conoley, 1982b) and the Consultation Evaluation Survey (Gallessich, 1982).

Stage 6: Consultation Conclusion

The task of the final stage is to conclude the consultation relationship. Parsons and Meyers (1984) discuss the potential problem of consultee dependency on the consultant, which interferes with the educative and preventive goals of consultation. They recommend establishing a deliberate plan for terminating consultation and highlight the importance of consultant self-evaluation to assess self-serving intentions such as the need to be needed.

At the beginning of the consultation process, the consultant emphasizes the voluntary nature of participation and the option to discontinue services at any time. Yet some consultees may experience hesitation with termination. They may be concerned that they could offend the consultant or those within the system who sanctioned consultation. Furthermore, they may be apprehensive that future requests for consultation may be impeded (Parsons & Meyers, 1984). When an empowerment model of consultation has been adopted, these issues should be less salient as the consultant encourages the consultee to adopt a proactive approach.

Throughout consultation, the consultee may have had numerous opportunities to contact the consultant. By the end of consultation, the consultant needs to review a convenient and effective method for the consultee to contact the consultant

KEY: + Great (in top 3–5 students)*   – Poor (in bottom 3–5 students)*
        ✓ O.K. (any students between top   0 Not Applicable
          3–5 and bottom 3–5)

*''Top'' and ''bottom'' groups will vary depending on the class, setting, and activity.

Student's Name: _____

Settings:

Behaviors	Dates:															
Assignments completed																
Assignments accurate																
Follows rules/directions																
Needs few reminders to start work																
Seeks teacher attention appropriately and not too often																
Does not talk out																
Does not get out-of-seat often																
Does not bother other students verbally																
Does not bother other students physically																

FIGURE 7.2 Informal generalization probes

Source: Epps, S., Thompson, B. J., & Lane, M. P. (1985). *Procedures for incorporating generalization and maintenance programming into interventions for special-education students.* Des Moines, IA: Department of Public Instruction. Reprinted with permission.

1 = **Strongly Agree** 2 = **Somewhat Agree** 3 = **Neutral** 4 = **Somewhat Disagree** 5 = **Strongly Disagree**

1. I feel the consultant respects my ideas and solutions.	1	2	3	4	5
2. The consultant follows through with commitments she/he makes.	1	2	3	4	5
3. I feel the consultant does not understand my working environment.	1	2	3	4	5
4. The consultant is able to confront important issues.	1	2	3	4	5
5. The consultant tends to rely on only one approach to solving problems.	1	2	3	4	5
6. I feel that the consultant is sensitive to my feelings.	1	2	3	4	5
7. The consultant is able to summarize and facilitate problem solving.	1	2	3	4	5
8. I feel that the consultant is genuinely interested in me.	1	2	3	4	5
9. The consultant is careful to maintain confidentiality about my school-related concerns.	1	2	3	4	5
10. The consultant has difficulty understanding important aspects of the problems I bring up.	1	2	3	4	5
11. With the consultant I see complexities of the problem situation in greater depth and breadth.	1	2	3	4	5
12. The consultant offers advice that I do not think is relevant.	1	2	3	4	5
13. The consultant helps me see alternatives I haven't thought of before.	1	2	3	4	5
14. As a result of consultation, I find myself trying out some of my new ideas.	1	2	3	4	5
15. Solutions to problems are jointly arrived at by the consultant and myself.	1	2	3	4	5
16. I feel free to express my school-related concerns to the consultant.	1	2	3	4	5
17. As a result of consultation, my self-confidence in teaching has increased.	1	2	3	4	5
18. The consultant encourages communication between me and others with whom I work.	1	2	3	4	5
19. The consultant helps me to identify resources to use in problem solving.	1	2	3	4	5
20. The consultant does not explain his/her ideas clearly.	1	2	3	4	5
21. The consultant rushes into premature solutions.	1	2	3	4	5
22. The consultant helps me see my situation more objectively.	1	2	3	4	5
23. The consultant knows how and when to ask good questions.	1	2	3	4	5
24. I feel the consultant evaluates my performance.	1	2	3	4	5
25. The consultant plays a coordinate role.	1	2	3	4	5
26. I am satisfied with my consultant's services.	1	2	3	4	5
27. When I am a certified teacher, I plan to utilize a school psychologist/consultant's services.	1	2	3	4	5
28. If consultation were available again, I would encourage other student teachers to take advantage of the program.	1	2	3	4	5

FIGURE 7.3 Consultation evaluation form

Source: Carlson, C. I., & Tombari, M. L. (1986). *Professional School Psychology, 1,* 89–104. Reprinted with permission.

given a recurrence of problematic areas. In addition to telephone numbers, times to call and procedures for leaving messages should be addressed. A discussion of continued data collection and record keeping (long-term probes) is necessary to provide information about whether the consultant may need to be contacted.

Because of the variation among consultees, the consultant is advised against relying solely on consultee-initiated contact. Follow-up notes, telephone calls, or visits can serve to demonstrate one's continued availability (Parsons & Meyers, 1984). If a request for consultation ensues, the consultant should reinforce independence and self-reliance by redirecting the consultee to use skills previously acquired to analyze the problem and to access potential resources.

PEDIATRIC PSYCHOLOGY CONSULTATION

The development of a liaison relationship between psychology and pediatrics occurred as pediatricians begin to realize that patient problems included psychological components that extended beyond exclusive medical and physical interventions. Psychologists also began to recognize psychopathology related to organic illness and the utility of behavioral interventions for some pediatric concerns such as psychiatric, psychosomatic, developmental, learning, and other illness-related problems. Thus, applied child psychologists began to expand their skills and practice to health-related issues and to develop liaisons with medical professionals (Roberts & Wright, 1982). While the majority of pediatric psychologists are trained in clinical psychology, a significant number have backgrounds in school, educational, or developmental psychology (Stabler & Mesibov, 1984).

Considering the disparate training and orientation of psychology and medicine, the liaison at times is tenuous. Apprehension or resentment of encroachments onto professional practice (turf), differences in language and jargon, discrepancies in procedures, and distinct knowledge bases can obstruct productive collaboration (Roberts, 1986). As increasing numbers of health-impaired children join the ranks of students served by schools, particularly with the growing number of survivors of neonatal and pediatric intensive care units, there is an emerging need for school psychologists and other direct and related services personnel to understand medical psychology.

Neonatal and pediatric medicine (e.g., Avery & Taeusch, 1984; Behrman & Kliegman, 1990), behavioral medicine (e.g., Prokop & Bradley, 1981), pediatric psychology (e.g., Routh, 1988; Russo & Varni, 1982), chronic illness in children (e.g., Hobbs & Perrin, 1985), and health-care and psychoeducational intervention

(e.g., Ensher & Clark, 1986) are topics that need to be examined.

Models of Pediatric Consultation

Acceptance of the psychologist as a consultant to a medical specialist is dependent on the delivery of competent services, a particularly important consideration when beginning pediatric psychology consultation (Roberts, 1986). For psychologists working in hospitals, requests for a "psych consult" often require same-day action (Drotar, Benjamin, Chwast, Litt, & Vajner, 1982; Walker, Miller, & Smith, 1985). In outpatient activities, requests for consultation may be both for prompt intervention and for long-term strategies (Roberts & Wright, 1982). Consultation can require various levels of interaction, ranging from a short telephone call to longer "curbside" or hallway discussions to formal assessment workups and written reports.

The consulting psychologist may work directly with the child client or family in providing psychological intervention, although Salk (1970) and Stabler (1988) diminish the role of technician who performs extensive direct assessment and therapy. The consultant also may work through the pediatric staff to implement psychological services or with a team of professionals in which each discipline contributes to the overall treatment plan (e.g., a bone marrow transplant team). The pediatric psychologist, therefore, must have skills in forming flexible consultative relationships (Roberts, 1986).

Several conceptual models and approaches of pediatric psychology consultation to pediatricians have been developed. Pediatric consultation may involve any of the approaches individually or in combination. The consultant should move from one model to another depending on features of the case, functions of the consultation, service orientation of the referring physician, and demands of the setting (Roberts, 1986). This portion of the chapter briefly reviews three models of pediatric psychology consultation: (1) resource consultation (Stabler, 1979, 1988) or independent functions consultation (Roberts & Wright, 1982), (2) indirect psychological consultation (Roberts, 1986; Roberts & Wright, 1982), and (3) collaborative team consultation (Roberts, 1986; Roberts & Wright, 1982).

Independent Functions Consultation

Within this model, the psychologist functions as a specialist who independently provides diagnostic and/or treatment services to a patient referred by the physician. Except for information exchange (which could be as limited as a brief consult request in the patient's medical chart) before and possibly after referral, the physician and psychologist work noncollaboratively (Roberts & Wright, 1982). Although both professionals interact with the patient, there is minimal interaction between the two. It requires the exercise of technical skill and judgment (Stabler, 1988). This type of interaction has been referred to as *resource consultation* (Stabler, 1979) or *independent functions consultation* (Roberts, 1986; Roberts & Wright, 1982) because it requires sharing expert knowledge and skill.

This model has substantial merit in the diagnostic and information-gathering process and can provide an effective mechanism through which psychologists enter the health-care system (Stabler, 1988). Developmental, learning, and behavior issues are particularly well suited to psychologists' expertise. A potential problem is the possibility that the psychologist will lapse into a confirmatory approach to validate the physician's consultation question. While the diagnostic role of this approach can relegate the psychologist to the role of tester, roles have begun to expand to include treatment. Hence, the psychologist could assume primary responsibility for designing and implementing an intervention (Roberts, 1986). There are, however, several potential problems that can arise when independently intervening with patients referred by physicians.

First, the psychologist should avoid engulfing the patient and detaching the referring physician from participation and decision making. It is essential to keep open lines of communication such as succinct and informative progress notes, reports, letters, and/or telephone calls (Roberts, 1986).

"Turf" issues constitute a second area of potential problems. For example, considering psychologists' established success in treating encopresis (e.g., Christophersen & Rainey, 1976; Wright & Walker, 1977), the pediatric psychologist may assume treatment of both physical and behavioral components of an encopresis protocol. Although mineral oil and suppositories often used in treatment (e.g., Wright, 1975) do not require medical prescription and may be bought over the counter, physicians may view such recommendations from a psychologist as medical prescription, an infringement on their domain. Roberts (1986) recommends diplomatic education, such as by presenting psychology-based articles in the *medical* literature, to help avoid resistance to psychologists' practice.

The independent functions consultation has been the predominant form of consultation between pediatrician and psychologist largely due to the traditional independence each discipline adopts (Roberts & Wright, 1982). This model does have nontraditional applications, however. The pediatrician makes a referral and continues to provide medical treatment to the patient while the psychologist concurrently sees the patient and provides psychological services. Roberts (1986) provides the example of medical and behavioral management of juvenile diabetes in which compliance with medical regimen is necessary to avoid the toxic condition of diabetic acidosis.

Young children who have not yet attended public school typically are routinely seen by a pediatrician or the family physician. It is unlikely that many parents will have had any exposure to the mental-health community. Thus, there is a far greater likelihood that parents will talk first with their family physician about a psychologically related problem with their child. The physician may become aware of certain issues and request independent functions consultation. In such cases as psychometric assessment for special-education consideration and divorce counseling, little interactive collaboration may be required since the issue is outside the medical realm (Roberts, 1986). Psychologists just entering the pediatric healthcare system may use this form of consultation as a springboard for consultation opportunities at a more collaborative level (Stabler, 1988).

For psychologists interested in more expansive relationships with physicians, the resource consultation model has its drawbacks. The limited amount of interaction significantly handicaps the potential for further dialogue. A second limitation is the difficulty in adequately assessing what may be a complex case via single sessions (Stabler, 1988). An additional liability is the restrictive nature of the arrangement since the physician may consider only certain types of cases (e.g., those requiring assessment) to be appropriate for referral, with little realization of the value of referring patients whose behavioral difficulties are associated with medical conditions (Roberts, 1986). Stabler and Murray (1973) argue that physicians' stereotyped views of psychologists as diagnosticians and test specialists are reinforced when psychologists allow resource consultation to be the sole model. The psychologist may need to take the initiative to educate physicians about the broad array of psychological services and about appropriate referrals.

Indirect Psychological Consultation

Roberts and Wright (1982) and Roberts (1986) describe this second type of consultation as more collaborative than the independent functions model. In this arrangement, the physician retains the primary responsibility for patient management. It is the physician, with indirect input from the psychologist, who provides the psychosocial services. The psychologist has no or circumscribed contact with the client and typically examines only information gathered by the physician. This model often appears in medical center settings with a teaching role (e.g., a psychologist supervises a pediatric or family practice resident) because of an educative teacher-learner stance rather than a true egalitarian collaboration. This model has increased over the past decade given the emphasis for primary care physicians to provide some mental health-oriented services.

Roberts (1986) outlines a variety of forms this consultative arrangement can take. First, the physician may request a brief contact, such as by a telephone call or on-the-spot consultation, for particular information. Sample questions include (1) the developmental appropriateness of child behavior and possible treatments (e.g., nocturnal enuresis); (2) interpretation of test data, which could be from school assessments; (3) community or school resources (e.g., remedial tutoring, after-school activities); and (4) appropriateness of a referral. In response, the psychologist may provide a succinct reply or recommend more in-depth assessment.

A second type of indirect consultation can occur through seminars, conferences, pediatric section (e.g., nephrology) meetings, ground rounds, inservice training, or continuing education. Drotar (1982) found that many psychologists developing new consultation services in medical settings have found these activities worthwhile to announce their availability to provide basic psychosocial approaches. This indirect model, in which the psychologist may never see the actual recipients of this service, can augment the overall effectiveness of the physician and cultivate the psychosocial care of pediatric patients and their families.

A third approach to indirect patient treatment can occur when a mutual trust has developed about the other professional's competence. The physician would implement a particular intervention recommended by the psychologist-consultant. For example, behavioral pediatrics offers a number of standard protocols for certain types of behavioral disorders that regularly occur in pediatric practice. There are a variety of such treatment protocols:

Toilet training (Azrin & Foxx, 1974; Christophersen & Rapoff, 1983)

Encopresis (Christophersen & Rainey, 1976; Wright & Walker, 1977)

Urinary and fecal incontinence (Varni, 1983)

Child safety-seat use (Christophersen & Gyulay, 1981)

Bedtime problems (Christophersen, 1982)

Temper tantrums (Christophersen, 1982)

General child-behavior management (Forehand & McMahon, 1981)

Mealtime problems (Forehand & McMahon, 1981)

Pill swallowing (Funk, Mullins, & Olson, 1984)

Medical compliance (Jones, 1983).

The three types of indirect consultation have several constraints. The consulting psychologist must rely on information the physician obtains, which may not be entirely accurate. Roberts (1986) indicates that the psychologist may need to teach the physician (using substantial savoir-faire) some assessment skills and to provide suitable instruments. Such skills may include interviewing within the psychosocial domain. He recommends summarizing the relevant literature, diagnostic questions, and treatment recommendations in one- or two-page handouts that can be readily assimilated by both patient and physician. These can be furnished to the physician to give to the parent or adolescent and pediatric staff.

Resentment may develop in either the physician or the consulting psychologist (Roberts, 1986). The physician may perceive the role as consultee as subservient, or the psychologist may feel indignant about abdicating some psychological services and the physician's intrusion into the psychologist's domain. A final obstacle may occur within this model of consultation. The physician may neither be interested in providing the service nor have the time necessary to learn to implement the techniques. Hence, consultation and education to support staff (e.g, nurses, nurse practitioners, physician assistants) may be advised.

Collaborative Team Consultation

Genuine cooperation and collaboration is evident in the third major model of pediatric consultation, with shared responsibility and joint decision making. Each discipline contributes its own unique perspective to shared case management. This interdisciplinary approach is more frequently found in larger hospitals and medical teaching/research centers where teams of audiologists and speech pathologists, clergy, educational experts, nurses and physicians, psychologists, occupational and physical therapists, and social workers can collaborate (Roberts & Wright, 1982).

There is a myriad of problems amenable to this conjoint approach such as chronic illness and metabolic disorders. An independent functions approach would be contraindicated, although the indirect consultation approach may be possible for some cases. Roberts (1986) provides examples of obesity, anorexia nervosa, and juvenile diabetes that arc probably best treated within a collaborative team.

As an illustration of this model, consider a pediatric metabolic disorders specialty clinic that serves children with such conditions as phenylketonuria (PKU), an autosomal recessive condition that can result in mental retardation and other behavioral and physical anomalies. It results from a digestive enzyme deficiency (due to the absence of a particular gene) that produces an inability to metabolize phenylalanine, an amino acid present in dietary sources of protein such as milk. Damage occurs when phenylalanine accumulates in the brain. When diagnosed early, PKU can be treated effectively by eliminating foods high in phenylalanine from the child's diet (Weisfeld, 1982).

After diagnosis, a team including a physician, nurse, and nutritionist monitor the phenylalanine levels, explain the negative implications of toxicity (i.e., mental retardation), and provide specific dietary recommendations, which include formula intake and dietary restrictions. The psychologist on the team assesses numerous issues and can serve a variety of functions. At a minimum, the psychologist interviews the caregivers about the child's cooperation with the dietary regimen and their adherence to the treatment protocol. Information also must be obtained about the extent to which they have been able to explain the treatment package to other adults (e.g., school personnel, day care centers, babysitters, neighborhood parents, relatives). Often the psychologist develops a behavioral protocol for the parents to assist their efforts in fostering their child's compliance. These activities are performed within the team model so that all treatment components are mutually compatible.

Adjustment to the disorder also may be an issue for the child or adolescent and/or caregivers. Initially, some parents become highly anxious about the child's condition and their own ability to follow through with dietary management. Their concerns need to be allayed within a supportive framework that emphasizes their competence. As children begin to recognize their difference from other children and inability to participate in some activities with peers, such as hamburger and milkshake runs, social concerns may ensue. As part of general monitoring of children with PKU, behavioral and academic domains also can be explored. Additionally, standardized cognitive assessment is advised periodically as one measure of developmental status.

Although a pediatric psychologist serving such a specialty clinic is to be the primary psychologist for treatment of PKU, school psychologists also may become involved in portions of the intervention. Initially they may function more as consultees as they learn about the medical, developmental, social, and educational features of this metabolic disorder. Later they may assume more of a consultative role to other school personnel as they locate and coordinate various services. This role may become even more explicit as school psychologists contribute to the development and monitoring of Individualized Education Programs (IEPs) in which an identified need is to develop an adolescent's self-monitoring of a medical condition such as diabetes.

Developing New Pediatric Consultation Opportunities

A better understanding between pediatric psychologists and physicians must be developed in order to expand our clinical practices and professional relationships in nontraditional settings (Stabler & Whitt, 1980). If physicians tend to have stereotyped expectations about the role of psychology in medical care, it is incumbent on psychologists to clarify and to expand that role perception. To meet the challenge, the field needs a stronger emphasis on liaison. The pediatric psychologist's role would encompass clinical skills integrated with the skills of scientist-practitioner, educator, and consultant into the overall role. Contacts with physicians would be educative, thereby gradually altering the relationship from independent consultation to collaborative liaison. Such an association may range from sharing clinical responsibility to collective research and teaching activities (Stabler, 1988).

The integration of children with various medical conditions and chronic illness into public schools has posed substantive challenges to the educational system. These challenges will be met in part by consultation by pediatric psychologists. Since they are external to the system, they must gain entry and be particularly sensitive to issues of communication, hierarchy, ownership of the problem, professional role, and the natural ecology (Mesibov & Johnson, 1982). An emerging trend for school psychology is the increased responsibility to coordinate the multitude of services that are necessary for these children. Continuity of care will continue to be a complex, extraordinarily time-consuming activity that will require collaboration among school psychology, pediatric psychology, and the health-care field.

FUTURE ISSUES AND TRENDS

Standardization of Consultation

Bergan and Kratochwill (1990) advocate for standardized procedures and formats in future research. Such standardization would compel the development and use of formal interview guidelines, response protocols, and training manuals. One reported advantage is that standardization of consultation would enable replication of procedures to examine efficacy and generalizability of successful strategies across a variety of dimensions. Second, competency-based professional preparation in specific consultation skills would be possible. Prospective consultants could be trained to implement consultation procedures in a manner that would enable the integrity of consultation process to be monitored.

A third advantage is that practitioners may be more likely to use consultation once standardized approaches have been documented in the research literature. And fourth, procedurely standardized techniques with an empirical basis may set the stage for research to address current and emerging legal and ethical issues in the delivery of psychological services.

A Metatheory of Consultation

Despite the immense literature on consultation, Conoley and Conoley (1981) contend that there is a dearth of theory testing and research. Gallessich (1985) argues for a new paradigm, a consultation metatheory, to unify heterogeneous concepts, to identify their fundamental similarities and differences, and to guide consultation practice, research, and training. Competent practice depends on some unifying conceptual scheme. One impediment to the development of a cogent theory is an atheoretical attitude toward consultation. Additionally, its practices, principles, and concepts are spread across diverse professional groups and, therefore, are not easily organized. Another consideration is the rapid change in consulting practices, which respond quickly to social, political, and technological changes.

In constructing a metatheory of consultation, Gallessich (1985) suggests that three broad areas be considered. First, universal characteristics of consultation and its triadic structure would be explored. Second, parameters common to all consultation approaches would be surveyed. Knowledge and technique, content, goals, and role and relationship rules are some of these parameters. Additionally, processes such as gathering data, diagnosing problems, offering support

and encouragement, building rapport, and leading training are appraised. Ideologies and value systems are particularly important to investigate. While rarely explicated, they typically are determined by the consultant and govern consultation variables. Examples include scientific-technical values, management-supportive or worker-supportive ideologies, humanistic philosophy, consciousness-raising perspective (e.g., Jackson, 1975; Sue, 1981), feminist theory (e.g., Ballou & Gabalac, 1984), and professional elitism.

A third area to be considered pertains to the fundamental variants in the universe of consultation. In lieu of the traditional models of consultation, Gallessich (1985) suggests three new configurations, which differ along the value and ideological dimension: (1) scientific-technological consultation, (2) human-development consultation, and (3) social/political consultation. Bardon (1985) further suggests adding a medical/clinical model of consultation. In the first model, the scientific method is paramount. The consultant's primary role is technological or clinical expert, with the goal of providing the consultee with the necessary information and principles.

In the second model, the chief priority is human growth and development. The focus of consultation is conceptualized in terms of consultees' professional and personal developmental needs. There are two different assumptions about how best to assist this development. In the therapeutic approach, the consultant assumes the responsibility for assessing the work problem and determining intervention to enhance development. In the collaborative approach, the consultant and consultee work together to assess the situation and to generate alternative solutions. The consultant's role is primarily educative and facilitative in both approaches.

The value of the social/political model of consultation arises from a political or social perspective of the consultee's work and the organizational context. The consultant adopts a partisan role to alter organizations to make them more consistent with particular values. Examples include support for management interests, enhancement of quality of work life, and equalization of advancement opportunities for traditionally underrepresented groups.

Axioms derived from a metatheory could help formulate issues and research questions. Despite recurring conceptual and methodological difficulties, efforts to evaluate consultation process and outcome must continue. Evaluative models must evolve to match consultation's triadic structure, cyclical nature (consider reiterative applications of consultation), successive feedback loops, and changing goals. To date, a metatheory has yet to be formulated to examine the relationship between outcome and consultation components with precision (Alpert & Yammer, 1983). Both generic and specialized competencies, with collaboration across disciplines, need to be delineated to guide curricula for education and professional preparation (Gallessich, 1985).

REFERENCES

Abidin, R. R., Jr. (1975). Negative effects of behavioral consultation: "I know I ought to, but it hurts too much." *Journal of School Psychology, 13,* 51–57.

Alberto, P. A., & Troutman, A. C. (1990). *Applied behavior analysis for teachers* (3rd ed.). New York: Merrill.

Alpert, J. L., & Yammer, M. D. (1983). Research in school consultation: A content analysis of selected journals. *Professional Psychology: Research and Practice, 14,* 604–612.

Avery, M. E., & Taeusch, H. W. (Eds.). (1984). *Schaffer's diseases of the newborn* (5th ed.). Philadelphia: Saunders.

Azrin, N. H., & Foxx, R. M. (1974). *Toilet training in less than a day.* New York: Simon & Schuster.

Bakeman, R., & Gottman, J. M. (1986). *Observing interaction: An introduction to sequential analysis.* Cambridge: Cambridge University Press.

Ballou, M., & Gabalac, N. (1984). *A feminist position on mental health.* Springfield, IL: Thomas.

Bandura, A. (1982). Self-efficacy: Mechanism in human agency. *American Psychologist, 37,* 122–147.

Bardon, J. I. (1985). On the verge of a breakthrough. *The Counseling Psychologist, 13,* 355–362.

Barlow, D. H., & Hersen, M. (1984). *Single case experimental designs: Strategies for studying behavior change* (2nd ed.). New York: Pergamon Press.

Barton, E. J., & Ascione, F. R. (1984). Direct observation. In T. H. Ollendick & M. Hersen (Eds.), *Child behavioral assessment: Principles and procedures* (pp. 166–194). New York: Pergamon Press.

Behrman, R. E., & Kliegman, R. (Eds.). (1990). *Nelson essentials of pediatrics.* Philadelphia: Saunders.

Benson, A. J., & Hughes, J. (1985). Perceptions of role definition processes in school psychology: A national survey. *School Psychology Review, 14,* 64–74.

Bergan, J. R. (1977). *Behavioral consultation.* Columbus, OH: Merrill.

Bergan, J. R., Feld, J. K., & Swarner, J. C. (1988). Behavioral consultation: Macroconsultation for instructional management. In J. C. Witt, S. N. Elliott, & F. M. Gresham (Eds.), *Handbook of behavior therapy in education* (pp. 245–273). New York: Plenum Press.

Bergan, J. R., & Kratochwill, T. R. (1990). *Behavioral consultation and therapy.* New York: Plenum Press.

Bergan, J. R., & Tombari, M. L. (1976). Consultant skill and efficiency and the implementation and outcomes of consultation. *Journal of School Psychology, 14,* 3–14.

Berkowitz, M. I. (1975). *A primer on school mental health consultation.* Springfield, IL: Thomas.

Brainerd, C. J. (1978). *Piaget's theory of intelligence.* Englewood Cliffs, NJ: Prentice-Hall.

Brophy, J. E., & Good, T. L. (1974). *Teacher-student relationships: Causes and consequences.* New York: Holt, Rinehart and Winston.

Brophy, J. E., & Good, T. L. (1986). Teacher behavior and student achievement. In M. C. Wittrock (Ed.), *Handbook of research on teaching* (3rd ed., pp. 328–375). New York: Macmillan.

Browder, D. M. (1987). *Assessment of individuals with severe handicaps: An applied behavior ap-*

proach to life skills assessment. Baltimore: Paul H. Brookes.

Brown, L., Branston, M. B., Hamre-Nietupski, S., Pumpian, I., Certo, N., & Gruenewald, L. (1979). A strategy for developing chronological-age-appropriate and functional curricular content for severely handicapped adolescents and young adults. *The Journal of Special Education, 13,* 81–90.

Brown, D., Pryzwansky, W. B., & Schulte, A. C. (1987). *Psychological consultation: Introduction to theory and practice.* Boston: Allyn and Bacon.

Caplan, G. (1970). *The theory and practice of mental health consultation.* New York: Basic Books.

Caplan, G. (1974). *Support systems and community mental health.* New York: Behavioral Publications.

Carlson, C. I., & Tombari, M. L. (1986). Multilevel school consultation training: Preliminary program evaluation. *Professional School Psychology, 1,* 89–104.

Cataldo, M. F., & Harris, J. (1982). The biological basis for self-injury in the mentally retarded. *Analysis and Intervention in Developmental Disabilities, 2,* 21–39.

Cherniss, C. (1978). The Consultation Readiness Scale: An attempt to improve consultation practice. *American Journal of Community Psychology, 6,* 15–21.

Christophersen, E. R. (1982). Incorporating behavioral pediatrics into primary care. In E. R. Christophersen (Ed.), *Symposium on Behavioral Pediatrics: Pediatric Clinics of North America, 29*(2), 261–296.

Christophersen, E. R., & Gyulay, J. E. (1981). Parental compliance with car seat usage: A positive approach with long-term follow-up. *Journal of Pediatric Psychology, 6,* 301–312.

Christophersen, E. R., & Rainey, S. K. (1976). Management of encopresis through a pediatric outpatient clinic. *Journal of Pediatric Psychology, 1,* 38–41.

Christophersen, E. R., & Rapoff, M. A. (1983). Toileting problems in children. In C. E. Walker & M. C. Roberts (Eds.), *Handbook of clinical child psychology* (pp. 593–615). New York: Wiley-Interscience.

Conoley, J. C., & Conoley, C. W. (1981). Toward prescriptive consultation. In J. C. Conoley (Ed.), *Consultation in schools: Theory, research, and*

procedures (pp. 265–293). New York: Academic Press.

Conoley, J. C., & Conoley, C. W. (1982a). The effects of two conditions of client-centered consultation on student teacher problem descriptions and remedial plans. *Journal of School Psychology, 20,* 323–328.

Conoley, J. C., & Conoley, C. W. (1982b). *School consultation: A guide to practice and training.* New York: Pergamon Press.

Cormier, W. H., & Cormier, L. S. (1979). *Interviewing strategies for helpers: A guide to assessment, treatment, and evaluation.* Monterey, CA: Brooks/Cole.

Curtis, M. (1983). School psychology and consultation. *Communique, 9*(7), 9.

Curtis, M. J., & Metz, L. W. (1986). System level intervention in a school for handicapped children. *School Psychology Review, 15,* 510–518.

Curtis, M. J., & Meyers, J. (1985). Best practices in school-based consultation: Guidelines for effective practice. In A. Thomas & J. Grimes (Eds.), *Best practices in school psychology* (pp. 79–94). Kent, OH: National Association of School Psychologists.

Curtis, M. J., & Zins, J. (1980). *The theory and practice of school consultation.* Springfield, IL: Thomas.

Dekarii, M. B., & Sales, B. C. (1982). Privileged communications of psychologists. *Professional Psychology, 13,* 372–388.

Drotar, D. (1982). The child psychologist in the medical system. In P. Karoly, J. J. Steffen, & D. J. O'Grady (Eds.), *Child health psychology* (pp. 1–28). New York: Pergamon Press.

Drotar, D., Benjamin, P., Chwast, R., Litt, C., & Vajner, P. (1982). The role of the psychologist in pediatric outpatient and inpatient settings. In J. M. Tuma (Ed.), *Handbook for the practice of pediatric psychology* (pp. 228–250). New York: Wiley-Interscience.

Dunst, C. J., & Trivette, C. M. (1988). Helping, helplessness, and harm. In J. C. Witt, S. N. Elliott, & F. M. Gresham (Eds.), *Handbook of behavior therapy in education* (pp. 343–376). New York: Plenum Press.

D'Zurilla, T. J., & Goldfried, M. R. (1971). Problem solving and behavior modification. *Journal of Abnormal and Social Psychology, 78,* 107–126.

Edelbrock, C. (1984). Developmental considerations.

In T. H. Ollendick & M. Hersen (Eds.), *Child behavioral assessment: Principles and procedures* (pp. 20–37). New York: Pergamon Press.

Elliott, S. N. (1988). Acceptability of behavioral treatments in educational settings. In J. C. Witt, S. N. Elliott, & F. M. Gresham (Eds.), *Handbook of behavior therapy in education* (pp. 121–150). New York: Plenum Press.

Engelmann, S., & Carnine, D. (1982). *Theory of instruction: Principles and applications.* New York: Irvington Publishers.

Ensher, G. L., & Clark, D. A. (1986). *Newborns at risk: Medical care and psychoeducational intervention.* Rockville, MD: Aspen Publishers.

Epps, S. (1983). *Designing, implementing, and monitoring behavioral interventions with the severely and profoundly handicapped.* Des Moines: Iowa Department of Public Instruction. (ERIC Document Reproduction Service No. ED 240 772).

Epps, S. (1985). Best practices in behavioral observation. In A. Thomas & J. Grimes (Eds.), *Best practices in school psychology* (pp. 95–111). Kent, OH: National Association of School Psychologists.

Epps, S. (1987). Self-injurious and stereotypic behavior in children and adolescents. In J. Grimes & A. Thomas (Eds.), *Psychological approaches to problems of children and adolescents* (Vol. 3, pp. 207–241). Des Moines, IA: Department of Education.

Epps, S. (1991). *Depression and special-education classification: Diagnostic overshadowing and school psychologists.* Manuscript submitted for publication.

Epps, S., & Lane, M. P. (1987). Assessment and training of teacher interviewing skills to program common stimuli between special- and general-education environments. *School Psychology Review, 16,* 50–68.

Epps, S., Prescott, A. L., & Horner, R. H. (1990). Social acceptability of menstrual-care training methods for young women with developmental disabilities. *Education and Training in Mental Retardation, 25,* 33–44.

Epps, S., Thompson, B. J., & Lane, M. P. (1985). *Procedures for incorporating generalization and maintenance programming into interventions for special-education students.* Des Moines, IA: Department of Public Instruction.

Epps, S., & Tindal, G. (1987). The effectiveness of differential programming in serving students with mild handicaps: Placement options and instructional programming. In M. C. Wang, M. C. Reynolds, & H. J. Walberg (Eds.), *Handbook of special education: Research and practice* (Vol. 1, pp. 213–248). New York: Pergamon Press.

Epps, S., Ysseldyke, J. E., & McGue, M. (1984). "I know one when I see one"–Differentiating LD and non-LD students. *Learning Disability Quarterly, 7,* 89–101.

Farling, W. H., & Hoedt, K. C. (1971). *National survey of school psychologists.* Washington, D.C.: National Association of School Psychologists.

Fine, M. J., Grantham, V. L., & Wright, J. G. (1979). Personal variables that facilitate or impede consultation. *Psychology in the Schools, 16,* 533–539.

Flanagan, J. C. (1954). The critical incident technique. *Psychological Bulletin, 51,* 327–328.

Forehand, R. L., & McMahon, R. J. (1981). *Helping the noncompliant child: A clinician's guide to parent training.* New York: Guilford Press.

Foster, S. L., Bell-Dolan, D. J., & Burge, D. A. (1988). Behavioral observation. In A. S. Bellack & M. Hersen (Eds.), *Behavioral assessment: A practical handbook* (3rd ed., pp. 119–160). New York: Pergamon Press.

Foxx, R. M. (1982). *Decreasing behaviors of severely retarded and autistic persons.* Champaign, IL: Research Press.

Fullan, M., Miles, M. B., & Taylor, G. (1980). Organization development in schools: The state of the art. *Review of Educational Research, 50,* 121–183.

Funk, M. J., Mullins, L. L., & Olson, R. A. (1984). Teaching children to swallow pills: A case study. *Children's Health Care, 13,* 20–23.

Gallessich, J. (1973). Training the school psychologist for consultation. *Journal of School Psychology, 11,* 57–65.

Gallessich, J. (1982). *The profession and practice of consultation.* San Francisco: Jossey-Bass.

Gallessich, J. (1985). Toward a meta-theory of consultation. *The Counseling Psychologist, 13,* 336–354.

Ginsburg, H. P., & Opper, S. (1988). *Piaget's theory of intellectual development* (3rd ed.). Englewood Cliffs, NJ: Prentice Hall.

Glidewell, J. C. (1959). The entry problem in consultation. *Journal of Social Issues, 15,* 51–59.

Good, T. L. (1983). Classroom research: A decade of progress. *Educational Psychologist, 18,* 127–144.

Gutkin, T. B. (1980). Teacher perceptions of consultation services provided by school psychologists. *Professional Psychology, 11,* 637–642.

Gutkin, T. B. (1986). Consultees' perceptions of variables relating to the outcomes of school-based consultation interactions. *School Psychology Review, 15,* 375–382.

Gutkin, T. B., & Curtis, M. J. (1982). School-based consultation: Theory and techniques. In C. R. Reynolds & T. B. Gutkin (Eds.), *The handbook of school psychology* (pp. 796–828). New York: Wiley.

Gutkin, T. B., & Curtis, M. J. (1990). School-based consultation: Theory, techniques, and research. In T. B. Gutkin & C. R. Reynolds (Eds.), *The handbook of school psychology* (2nd ed., pp. 577–611). New York: Wiley.

Gutkin, T. B., Singer, J. H., & Brown, R. (1980). Teacher reactions to school-based consultation services: A multivariate analysis. *Journal of School Psychology, 18,* 126–134.

Harris, F. N., & Jenson, W. R. (1985). Comparisons of multiple-baseline across persons designs and AB designs with replication: Issues and confusions. *Behavioral Assessment, 7,* 121–127.

Harris, S. L., & Ferrari, M. (1983). Developmental factors in child behavior therapy. *Behavior Therapy, 14,* 54–72.

Haveluck, R. G. (1973). *The change agent's guide to innovation in education.* Englewood Cliffs, NJ: Educational Technology Publications.

Hawkins, R. P. (1982). Developing a behavior code. In D. P. Hartmann (Ed.), *Using observers to study behavior. New directions for methodology of social and behavioral science* (No. 14, pp. 21–35). San Francisco: Jossey-Bass.

Heppner, P. P. (1978). A review of the problem-solving literature and its relationship to counseling process. *Journal of Counseling Psychology, 25,* 366–375.

Hersen, M. (1981). Complex problems require complex solutions. *Behavior Therapy, 12,* 15–29.

Hobbs, N., Dokecki, P. R., Hoover-Dempsey, K. V., Moroney, R. M., Shayne, M. W., & Weeks, K. H. (1984). *Strengthening families.* San Francisco: Jossey-Bass.

Hobbs, N., & Perrin, J. M. (Eds.). (1985). *Issues in the care of children with chronic illness.* San Francisco: Jossey-Bass.

Horner, R. H., & Billingsley, F. F. (1988). The effect of competing behavior on the generalization and maintenance of adaptive behavior in applied settings. In R. H. Horner, G. Dunlap, & R. L. Koegel (Eds.), *Generalization and maintenance: Life-style changes in applied settings* (pp. 197–220). Baltimore: Paul H. Brookes.

Horner, R. H., Dunlap, G., & Koegel, R. L. (Eds.). (1988). *Generalization and maintenance: Life-style changes in applied settings.* Baltimore: Paul H. Brookes.

Horner, R. H., Sprague, J., & Wilcox, B. (1982). General case programming for community activities. In B. Wilcox & G. T. Bellamy (Eds.), *Design of high school programs for severely handicapped students* (pp. 61–98). Baltimore: Paul H. Brookes.

Ivey, A. E., Ivey, M. B., & Simek-Downing, L. (1987). *Counseling and psychotherapy: Integrating skills, theory, and practice* (2nd ed.). Englewood Cliffs, NJ: Prentice-Hall.

Jackson, B. (1975). Black identity development. *MEFORUM: Journal of Educational Diversity and Innovation, 2,* 19–25.

Johnston, J. M., & Pennypacker, H. S. (1980). *Strategies and tactics of human behavioral research.* Hillsdale, NJ: Erlbaum.

Jones, J. G. (1983). Compliance with pediatric therapy. *Clinical Pediatrics, 22,* 262–265.

Kanfer, F. H. (1973). Behavior modification—An overview. In C. E. Thoresen (Ed.), *Behavior modification in education* (pp. 3–40). Chicago: University of Chicago Press.

Kanfer, F. H. (1985). Target selection for clinical change programs. *Behavioral Assessment, 7,* 7–20.

Kanfer, F. H., & Phillips, J. S. (1970). *Learning foundations of behavior therapy.* New York: Wiley.

Kanfer, F. H., & Schefft, B. K. (1988). *Guiding the process of therapeutic change.* Champaign, IL: Research Press.

Kazdin, A. E. (1980). Acceptability of alternative treatments for deviant child behavior. *Journal of Applied Behavior Analysis, 13,* 259–273.

Kazdin, A. E. (1981). Acceptability of child treatment techniques: The influence of treatment efficacy and adverse side effects. *Behavior Therapy, 12,* 493–506.

Kazdin, A. E. (1982). *Single-case research designs: Methods for clinical and applied settings.* New York: Oxford University Press.

King, L. W., Colter, S. B., & Patterson, K. (1975). Behavior modification consultation in a Mexican-American school. *American Journal of Community Psychology, 3,* 229–235.

Krantz, P. J., & Risley, T. R. (1977). Behavioral ecology in the classroom. In K. D. O'Leary & S. G. O'Leary (Eds.), *Classroom management: The successful use of behavior modification* (2nd ed., pp. 349–366). New York: Pergamon Press.

Kratochwill, T. R., Elliott, S. N., & Rotto, P. C. (1990). Best practices in behavioral consultation. In A. Thomas & J. Grimes (Eds.), *Best practices in school psychology—II* (pp. 147–169). Washington, DC: National Association of School Psychologists.

Lacayo, N., Sherwood, G., & Morris, J. (1981). Daily activities of school psychologists: A national survey. *Psychology in the Schools, 18,* 184–190.

Lambert, N. M. (1974). A school-based consultation model. *Professional Psychology, 5,* 267–276.

Leigland, S. (1984). On "setting events" and related concepts. *The Behavior Analyst, 7,* 41–45.

Lennox, D. B., & Miltenberger, R. G. (1990). On the conceptualization of treatment acceptability. *Education and Treatment in Mental Retardation, 25,* 211–224.

Mannino, F. V., & Shore, M. F. (1975a). Effecting change through consultation. In F. V. Mannino, B. W. MacLennan, & M. F. Shore (Eds.), *The practice of mental health consultation* (pp. 25–46). New York: Gardner Press.

Mannino, F. V., & Shore, M. F. (1975b). The effects of consultation: A review of the literature. *American Journal of Community Psychology, 3,* 1–21.

Martens, B. K., Lewandowski, L. J., & Houk, J. L. (1989). The effects of entry information on the consultation process. *School Psychology Review, 18,* 225–234.

Martin, R., & Keller, A. (1976). Teacher awareness of classroom dyadic interactions. *Journal of School Psychology, 14,* 47–55.

McKee, W. T., & Witt, J. C. (1990). Effective teaching: A review of instructional and environmental variables. *The handbook of school psychology* (2nd ed., pp. 821–846). New York: Wiley.

Meacham, M. L., & Peckham, P. D. (1978). School psychologists at three-quarters century: Congruence between training, practice, preferred role and competence. *Journal of School Psychology, 16,* 195–206.

Medway, F. J., & Updyke, J. F. (1985). Meta-analysis of consultation outcome studies. *American Journal of Community Psychology, 13,* 489–505.

Mesibov, G. B., & Johnson, M. R. (1982). Intervention techniques in pediatric psychology. In J. M. Tuma (Ed.), *Handbook for the practice of pediatric psychology* (pp. 110–164). New York: Wiley.

Meyer, V., Liddell, A., & Lyons, M. (1977). Behavioral interviews. In A. R. Ciminero, K. S. Calhoun, & H. E. Adams (Eds.), *Handbook of behavioral assessment* (pp. 117–152). New York: Wiley.

Meyers, J., Parsons, R. D., & Martin, R. (1979). *Mental health consultation in the schools.* San Francisco: Jossey-Bass.

Meyers, J., Wurtz, R., & Flanagan, D. (1981). A national survey investigating consultation training occurring in school psychology programs. *Psychology in the Schools, 18,* 297–302.

Miller, L. E., Epp, J., & McGinnis, E. (1985). Setting analysis. In F. H. Wood, C. R. Smith, & J. Grimes (Eds.), *The Iowa assessment model in behavioral disorders: A training manual* (pp. 59–149). Des Moines, IA: Department of Public Instruction.

Munjack, D. J., & Oziel, R. J. (1978). Resistance in the behavioral treatment of sexual dysfunction. *Journal of Sex and Marital Therapy, 4,* 122–138.

National School Psychology Inservice Training Network. (1984). *School psychology: A blueprint for training and practice.* Minneapolis: Author.

Neef, N. A., Shafer, M. S., Egel, A. L., Cataldo, M. F., & Parrish, J. M. (1983). The class specific effects of compliance training with "do" and "don't" requests: Analogue analysis and classroom application. *Journal of Applied Behavior Analysis, 16,* 81–99.

Parsons, R. D., & Meyers, J. (1984). *Developing consultation skills: A guide to training, development, and assessment for human services professionals.* San Francisco: Jossey-Bass.

Paul, G. (1969). Strategy of outcome research in psychotherapy. *Journal of Consulting Psychology, 31,* 109–118.

Peterson, L., Homer, A. L., & Wonderlich, S. A. (1982). The integrity of independent variables in behavior analysis. *Journal of Applied Behavior Analysis, 15,* 477–492.

Piersel, W. C. (1985). Behavioral consultation: An approach to problem solving in educational settings. In J. R. Bergan, *School psychology in contemporary society: An introduction* (pp. 252–280). Columbus, OH: Merrill.

Piersel, W. C., & Gutkin, T. B. (1983). Resistance to school-based consultation: A behavioral analysis of the problem. *Psychology in the Schools, 20,* 311–320.

Ponti, C. R., Zins, J. E., & Graden, J. L. (1988). Implementing a consultation-based service delivery system to decrease referrals for special education: A case study of organizational considerations. *School Psychology Review, 17,* 89–100.

Prokop, C. K., & Bradley, L. A. (Eds.). (1981). *Medical psychology: Contributions to behavioral medicine.* New York: Academic Press.

Pryzwansky, W. B. (1986). Indirect service delivery: Considerations for future research in consultation. *School Psychology Review, 15,* 479–488.

Ramage, J. C. (1979). National survey of school psychologists: Update. *School Psychology Digest, 8,* 153–161.

Reid, J. B. (1982). Observer training in naturalistic research. In D. P. Hartmann (Ed.), *Using observers to study behavior. New directions for methodology of social and behavioral science* (No. 14, pp. 37–50). San Francisco: Jossey-Bass.

Reschly, D. J. (1976). School psychology consultation: "Frenzied, faddish, or fundamental." *Journal of School Psychology, 14,* 105–113.

Reynolds, C. R., Gutkin, T. B., Elliott, S. N., & Witt, J. C. (1984). *School psychology: Essentials of theory and practice.* New York: Wiley.

Roberts, M. C. (1986). *Pediatric psychology: Psychological interventions and strategies for pediatric problems.* New York: Pergamon Press.

Roberts, M. C., & Wright, L. (1982). The role of the pediatric psychologist as consultant to pediatricians. In J. M. Tuma (Ed.), *Handbook for the practice of pediatric psychology* (pp. 251–289). New York: Wiley.

Rogers-Warren, A. K. (1984). Ecobehavioral analysis. *Education and Treatment of Children, 7,* 283–303.

Rosenfield, S. A. (1987). *Instructional consultation.* Hillsdale, NJ: Erlbaum.

Routh, D. K. (Ed.). (1988). *Handbook of pediatric psychology.* New York: Guilford Press.

Russo, D. C., Cataldo, M. F., & Cushing, P. J. (1981). Compliance training and behavioral covariation in the treatment of multiple behavior problems. *Journal of Applied Behavior Analysis, 14,* 209–222.

Russo, D. C., & Varni, J. W. (Eds.). (1982). *Behavioral pediatrics: Research and practice.* New York: Plenum Press.

Salk, L. (1970). Psychologist in a pediatric setting. *Professional Psychology, 1,* 395–396.

Sandoval, J., Lambert, N. M., & Davis, J. M. (1977). Consultation from the consultee's perspective. *Journal of School Psychology, 15,* 239–243.

Sarason, S. B. (1982). *The culture of the school and the problem of change* (2nd ed.). Boston: Allyn and Bacon.

Schefft, B. K., & Lehr, B. K. (1985). A self-regulatory model of adjunctive behavior change. *Behavior Modification, 9,* 458–476.

Schmuck, R. A., & Runkel, P. J. (1985). *The handbook of organization development in schools* (3rd ed.). Palo Alto, CA: Mayfield Publishing.

Schofield, W. (1964). *Psychotherapy: The purchase of friendship.* Englewood Cliffs, NJ: Prentice-Hall.

Smith, D. K. (1984). Practicing school psychologists: Their characteristics, activities, and populations served. *Professional Psychology, 15,* 798–810.

Stabler, B. (1979). Emerging models of psychologist-pediatrician liaison. *Journal of Pediatric Psychology, 4,* 307–313.

Stabler, B. (1988). Pediatric consultation-liaison. In D. K. Routh (Ed.), *Handbook of pediatric psychology* (pp. 538–566). New York: Guilford Press.

Stabler, B., & Mesibov, G. B. (1984). Role functions of pediatric and health psychologists in health care settings. *Professional Psychology: Research and Practice, 15,* 142–151.

Stabler, B., & Murray, J. P. (1973). Pediatricians' perceptions of pediatric psychology. *Clinical Psychologist, 27,* 12–15.

Stabler, B., & Whitt, J. K. (1980). Pediatric psychology: Perspectives and training implications. *Journal of Pediatric Psychology, 5,* 245–251.

Stewart, K. J. (1986). Innovative practice of indirect service delivery: Realities and idealities. *School Psychology Review, 15,* 466–478.

Stokes, T. F., & Baer, D. M. (1977). An implicit technology of generalization. *Journal of Applied Behavior Analysis, 10,* 349–367.

Sue, D. (1981). *Counseling the culturally different.* New York: Wiley.

Sulzer-Azaroff, B., & Mayer, G. R. (1977). *Applying behavior-analysis procedures with children and youth.* New York: Holt, Rinehart and Winston.

Sulzer-Azaroff, B., & Mayer, G. R. (1986). *Achieving educational excellence: Using behavioral strategies.* New York: Holt, Rinehart and Winston.

Turco, T. L., & Elliott, S. N. (1986). Assessment of students' acceptability ratings of teacher-initiated interventions for classroom misbehavior. *Journal of School Psychology, 24,* 277–283.

Van Houten, R. (1979). Social validation: The evolution of standards of competency for target behaviors. *Journal of Applied Behavior Analysis, 12,* 581–591.

Varni, J. W. (1983). *Clinical behavioral pediatrics: An interdisciplinary biobehavioral approach.* New York: Pergamon Press.

Wahler, R. G., & Fox, J. J. (1981). Setting events in applied behavior analysis: Toward a conceptual and methodological expansion. *Journal of Applied Behavior Analysis, 14,* 327–338.

Walker, C. E., Miller, M., & Smith, R. (1985). An introduction to pediatric psychology. In P. A. Keller & L. G. Ritt (Eds.), *Innovations in clinical practice: A source book* (Vol. 4, pp. 415–434). Sarasota, FL: Professional Resource Exchange.

Waxman, H. C., & Walberg, H. J. (1982). The relation of teaching and learning: A review of reviews of process-product research. *Contemporary Education Review, 1,* 103–120.

Weisfeld, G. E. (1982). The nature-nurture issue and the integrating concept of function. In B. B. Wolman (Ed.), *Handbook of developmental psychology* (pp. 208–229). Englewood Cliffs, NJ: Prentice-Hall.

Wilcox, B., & Bellamy, G. T. (1987). *A comprehensive guide to The Activities Catalog: An alternative curriculum for youth and adults with severe disabilities.* Baltimore: Paul H. Brookes.

Willems, E. P. (1974). Behavioral technology and behavioral ecology. *Journal of Applied Behavior Analysis, 7,* 151–165.

Witt, J. C., & Elliott, S. N. (1983a, August). *Assessing the acceptability of behavioral interventions.* Paper presented at the annual meeting of the American Psychological Association, Anaheim, CA.

Witt, J. C., & Elliott, S. N. (1983b). Assessment in behavioral consultation: The initial interview. *School Psychology Review, 12,* 42–49.

Witt, J. C., & Elliott, S. N. (1985). Acceptability of classroom management strategies. In T. R. Kratochwill (Ed.), *Advances in school psychology* (Vol. 4, pp. 251–288). Hillsdale, NJ: Erlbaum.

Witt, J. C., & Martens, B. K. (1983). Assessing the acceptability of behavioral interventions used in classrooms. *Psychology in the Schools, 20,* 510–517.

Witt, J. C., & Martens, B. K. (1988). Problems with problem-solving consultation: A re-analysis of assumptions, methods, and goals. *School Psychology Review, 17,* 211–226.

Wolf, M. M. (1978). Social validity: The case for subjective measurement or how applied behavior analysis is finding its heart. *Journal of Applied Behavior Analysis, 11,* 203–214.

Wolpe, J. (1973). *Behavior therapy.* Elmsford, NY: Pergamon Press.

Wong, S. E., & Liberman, R. P. (1981). Mixed single-subject designs in clinical research: Variations of the multiple-baseline. *Behavioral Assessment, 3,* 297–306.

Wood, S., Duncan, P., & Hansell, P. (1983). *Performance analysis and the generalization problem.* Des Moines, IA: Department of Public Instruction. (ERIC Document Reproduction Service No. ED 240 773).

Wright, L., & Walker, C. E. (1977). Treating the encopretic child. *Clinical Pediatrics, 16,* 1042–1045.

Yates, B. T. (1985). Cost-effectiveness analysis and cost-benefit analysis: An introduction. *Behavioral Assessment, 7,* 207–234.

Ysseldyke, J. E., & Christenson, S. (1987). *The instructional environment scale.* Austin, TX: PRO-ED.

Zins, J. E., Curtis, M. J., Graden, J. L., & Ponti, C. R. (1988). *Helping students succeed in the regular classroom: A guide for developing intervention assistance programs.* San Francisco: Jossey-Bass.

Zins, J. E., & Ponti, C. R. (1990). Best practices in school-based consultation. In A. Thomas & J. Grimes (Eds.), *Best practices in school psychology—II* (pp. 673–693). Washington, DC: National Association of School Psychologists.

CHAPTER 8

PSYCHOEDUCATIONAL ASSESSMENT I: PRINCIPLES AND ISSUES

If a teacher or parent is asked to describe the services provided by a school psychologist, it is likely that "psychological testing" and "identifies children for placement in special education programs" will be the first descriptors. As school psychology has evolved, a primary service has been the provision of psychoeducational assessment. It should, however, be quickly pointed out that psychoeducational assessment involves much more than administering and scoring psychological tests (and a resulting "pinning on a label"). There are many assessment strategies. Psychological testing is but a small, albeit important, sector of psychoeducational assessment, and diagnosis is much more than labeling. Further, as federal legislation directs involvement with preschool children and families, the nature of assessment will embrace new and different strategies. The developmental and social systems approach certainly requires services other than administering tests per se and categorizing children for placement in programs—there must be psychoeducational assessment information to guide intervention and consultation efforts.

The school psychologist is typically the best trained, and often the only, professional within the school system to perform systematic psychoeducational assessment. To be sure, the entire educational process and every professional associated with it relies on evaluation and assessment, such as a principal's making a judgment about how a school situation should be handled and a teacher's grading classroom answers for correctness. The school psychologist, however, makes use of knowledge, skills, and techniques that are advanced in scientific bases and yield comprehensive diagnostic information.

Traditionally, the school psychologist has been distinguished among educational personnel by his or her capabilities in the assessment realm. For example, in earlier days, some states did not certify "school psychologists"; they certified "school diagnosticians." In other words, while the overall array of services were much the same then and now, the school psychologist was recognized as the professional within the school who was capable of and responsible for measuring, evaluating, assessing, and diagnosing.

Since these functions necessarily involve distinguishing a child, there is good reason to be concerned about *distinction* being transformed into a *stigma*. At all times, even when assigning a child to a particular diagnostic category (which might impose "labeling"), the school psychologist should be concerned about losing the uniqueness of the child to a conscious or unconscious discriminatory, deviancy, or stigmatizing notion. This risk of negative consequences for the child often creates a press on the school psychologist to denounce assessment in general and diagnosis in particular. In fact, the importance that effective assessment has for the child should propel the school psychologist toward advocacy of assessment. Granted, this advocacy should always be filtered through a concern for the best interests of the child. Incidentally, there is nothing to be ashamed of from being a "diagnostician." To the contrary, there is a European historical reason for conceptualizing the diagnostician as the super-grade professional—one who, in a sense, is the fail-safe checkpoint in the human service or educational system.

THE MEDICAL-DIAGNOSTIC ASSESSMENT MODEL

In mental-health services (including school psychology), the medical model has ruled and continues to rule supreme. With an emphasis on diagnosis, there is a connotation of "illness," that is, that the person being assessed is deviant, pathological, or abnormal. Arbuckle (1965) defines *diagnosis* as analysis of difficulties and their causes: "More clinically, it may be thought of as the determination of the nature, origin, precipitation, and maintenance of ineffective abnormal modes of behavior" (p. 22). The medical model assumes that emotional and behavioral problems reflect illness, makes use of diagnosis, prescribes a treatment to cure or remediate the adverse or abnormal condition, and uses classifications.

A *nosological system* is comprised of clinical categories, and assessment data are used to determine with which category the "patient" (which could be a child seen by a school psychologist) is most closely aligned. This categorization process is termed a *differential diagnosis,* meaning that the school psychologist collects, interprets (weighs), and judges assessment data to determine which criteria for each relevant category have been met by the child, as would lead to nosological assignment.

DIFFERENTIAL DIAGNOSIS

Aside from the questionable advisability of labeling a child, as would potentially produce stigmatizing effects, the process of differential diagnosis has its shortcomings. Martin (1988) points out that "such a system should include, among other information, a clear set of criteria for inclusion in the category, as well as statements about similar diagnostic categories and the critical factors that differentiate one from the other" (p. 74). Subjectivity often plagues assessment functions, and a

given school psychologist may find that he or she is inconsistent over time or between children (i.e., poor intrajudge reliability). Also, because of competency differences (perhaps rooted in conscious or unconscious discrimination or bias), his or her judgments about a particular set of assessment of data might be discordant with those judgments made of the same set of assessment data by another school psychologist (i.e., poor interjudge reliability).

No matter how well trained and clinically astute the school psychologist may be, his or her diagnoses are always dependent on the qualities of the relationship with the child:

> In the diagnosis of mental disorders the diagnostician, through the *medium of a personal relationship, elicits and observes* a range of *psychological functioning* which he considers *relevant on some theoretical grounds* for understanding the disorder so that he can make a *recommendation* which stands a good chance of being *acted on as a basis for dealing with the disorder.* (Shevrin & Shectman, 1973, p. 451)

The school psychologist must attain a relationship with the child (and others) that will reveal the child's developmental, social/emotional, and intellectual functioning, as well as the psychological influences from the child's educational, familial, and social systems. From this vantage point, the next step is to be able to gain "an appreciation of a patient's internal experience and understanding of it and the drawing of proper conclusions" (Shectman, 1973, p. 524).

The Elements of Diagnosis

The diagnostic process is more than labeling. Woody (1969) indicates that there are three components: "the present functioning or characteristics should be evaluated and described; possible causative factors or etiology should be posited; and a prognosis should be made and a treatment approach recommended" (p. 77). Beller (1962) sets forth six requirements: "observation, description, a delineation of causation or etiology, classification, prediction or prognosis, and control-modification or treatment plan" (p. 109). Focusing on the latter, Woody and Robertson (1988) state,

> Determining the recommended treatment approach necessitates, in effect, making a probability statement about how the patient will respond to the various treatment alternatives (recognizing that the availability of resources will enter into the considerations; e.g., it may be that the patient would respond better to intensive psychotherapy, but the financial picture leads to only occasional supportive counseling being available). (p. 228)

As noted in the earlier quotation from Shevrin and Schectman (1973), a goal is to "make a *recommendation* which stands a good chance of being *acted on as a basis for dealing with the disorder"* (p. 451). Thus, the Woody and Robertson (1988) caveat about the availability of resources entering into the considerations is underscored and has special relevance to school psychology. School administrators have diverse constituencies, each of which has its own pleadings for programmatic and funding priorities. Although the objectives of school psychology may be impeccable in logic and based on honorable intentions, it is unlikely that there will be unreserved endorsements for recommendations. Indeed, it is most likely that every ideal embraced by a diagnostic recommendation for intervention or treatment will have to be amended to accommodate other priorities maintained by the school, the family, or the community.

Nosological Systems

Returning to the issue of nosological categorization, there are two sources that mandate attention from the school psychologist: the American Psychiatric Association's (1980) *Diagnostic and Statistical Manual of Mental Disorders-Revised,* known as the DSM-III-R; and legislative categories.

The DSM-III-R Categories

The DSM-III system (which is revised periodically) was created by psychiatrists and other mental-health professionals to be responsive to the needs of institutions and health insurance companies for a standardized classification system (Miller, Bergstrom, Cross, & Grube, 1981). This volume contains numerous classifications that are relevant to children who receive school psychological services. Each category has certain criteria that rely on a subjective blending of psychiatric tradition and empirical research (Robins & Helzer, 1986).

Figure 8.1 contains selected categories that have special relevance to school psychology. Each of these categories defines, describes, and then sets forth agreed upon diagnostic criteria for the particular disorder. Although there are variations between the sections, the structure is generally predicated on a temporal factor (e.g., the duration of the problem) and specific observable behavioral conditions, with qualification for the particular diagnostic disorder depending, in part, on the number of observable behavioral conditions that are present with the child.

Figure 8.2 presents the diagnostic criteria for DSM-III-R 314.01 Attention-Deficit Hyperactive Disorder. Achenbach (1982) questions the clinical agreement that is possible for diagnoses of children and adolescents using the DSM-III-R, asserting the following impediments:

1. Imprecise criteria for determining which diagnosis a case warrants
2. Inadequate rules for deciding between diagnoses
3. Users' failure to master the criteria and rules
4. Problems in assessing the characteristics of individual cases needed to make the diagnosis
5. Mismatches between the taxonomy categories and the phenomena to be categorized (p. 550)

In the instance of Attention-Deficit Hyperactivity Disorder, Ostrom and Jenson (1988) point out that, notwithstanding the popularity of attention-deficit disorders, the conceptual research basis is ill formed (e.g., relevant to definition and

DIAGNOSTIC CRITERIA FOR 315.00 DEVELOPMENTAL READING DISORDER

A. Reading achievement, as measured by a standardized, individually administered test, is markedly below the expected level, given the person's schooling and intellectual capacity (as determined by an individually administered IQ test).

B. The disturbance in A significantly interferes with academic achievement or activities of daily living requiring reading skills.

C. Not due to a defect in visual or hearing acuity or a neurologic disorder.

DIAGNOSTIC CRITERIA FOR 315.10 DEVELOPMENTAL ARITHMETIC DISORDER

A. Arithmetic skills, as measured by a standardized, individually administered test, are markedly below the expected level, given the person's schooling and intellectual capacity (as determined by an individually administered IQ test).

B. The disturbance in A significantly interferes with academic achievement or activities of daily living requiring arithmetic skills.

C. Not due to a defect in visual or hearing acuity or a neurologic disorder.

DIAGNOSTIC CRITERIA FOR 315.31 DEVELOPMENTAL RECEPTIVE LANGUAGE DISORDER

A. The score obtained from a standardized measure of receptive language is substantially below that obtained from a standardized measure of nonverbal intellectual capacity (as determined by an individually administered IQ test).

B. The disturbance in A significantly interferes with academic achievement or activities of daily living requiring the comprehension of verbal (or sign) language. This may be manifested in more severe cases by an inability to understand simple words or sentences. In less severe cases, there may be difficulty in understanding only certain types of words, such as spatial terms, or an inability to comprehend longer or more complex statements.

C. Not due to a Pervasive Developmental Disorder, defect in hearing acuity, or a neurologic disorder (aphasia).

DIAGNOSTIC CRITERIA FOR 315.31 DEVELOPMENTAL EXPRESSIVE LANGUAGE DISORDER

A. The score obtained from a standardized measure of expressive language is substantially below that obtained from a standardized measure of nonverbal intellectual capacity (as determined by an individually administered IQ test).

B. The disturbance in A significantly interferes with academic achievement or activities of daily living requiring the expression of verbal (or sign) language. This may be evidenced in severe cases by use of a markedly limited vocabulary, by speaking only in simple sentences, or by speaking only in the present tense. In less severe cases, there may be hesitations or errors in recalling certain words, or errors in the production of long or complex sentences.

C. Not due to a Pervasive Developmental Disorder, defect in hearing acuity, or a neurologic disorder (aphasia).

FIGURE 8.1   Selected DSM-III-R categories relevant to school psychology

Source: Diagnostic and statistical manual of mental disorders (3rd ed.). Reprinted with permission of the American Psychiatric Association.

DIAGNOSTIC CRITERIA FOR 315.39 DEVELOPMENTAL ARTICULATION DISORDER

A. Consistent failure to use developmentally expected speech sounds. For example, in a three-year-old, failure to articulate p, b, and t, and in a six-year-old, failure to articulate r, sh, th, f, z, and l.

B. Not due to a Pervasive Developmental Disorder, Mental Retardation, defect in hearing acuity, disorders of the oral speech mechanism, or a neurologic disorder.

DIAGNOSTIC CRITERIA FOR 315.40 DEVELOPMENTAL COORDINATION DISORDER

A. The person's performance in daily activities requiring motor coordination is markedly below the expected level, given the person's chronological age and intellectual capacity. This may be manifested by marked delays in achieving motor milestones (walking, crawling, sitting), dropping things, "clumsiness," poor performance in sports, or poor handwriting.

B. The disturbance in A significantly interferes with academic achievement or activities of daily living.

C. Not due to a known physical disorder, such as cerebral palsy, hemiplegia, or muscular dystrophy.

DIAGNOSTIC CRITERIA FOR 315.80 DEVELOPMENTAL EXPRESSIVE WRITING DISORDER

A. Writing skills, as measured by a standardized, individually administered test, are markedly below the expected level, given the person's schooling and intellectual capacity (as determined by an individually administered IQ test).

B. The disturbance in A significantly interferes with academic achievement or activities of daily living requiring the composition of written texts (spelling words and expressing thoughts in grammatically correct sentences and organized paragraphs).

C. Not due to a defect in visual or hearing acuity or a neurologic disorder.

---

suitable objective measures, as relied upon by the DSM-III-R). They believe that before a category is accepted, a "multigating" should occur, which means that all data must pass through several "assessment gates" that screen for externalizing/excessive behaviors, resulting in only the most handicapped children reaching the final gate. The DSM-III-R is not infallible and can be problematic. Despite these problems, Martin (1988) concludes that the DSM-III-R categories have "real advantages in communication among clinicians and researchers" (p. 76), but warns, "It is important for the assessor to understand, however, that the imperfect state of our knowledge about diagnostic categories sets an upper limit on the accuracy and usefulness of differential diagnosis" (p. 76).

Legislative Categories
Federal legislation casts a powerful and controlling framework for school psychology and all psychoeducational services. Most notably, Public Laws 94-142, 99-457, and 101-476, now known as the Individuals with Disabilities Act, provide relevant legislation (and related rules and regulations) and "home rule" interpretations provide additional prescriptions and proscriptions. These legislative sources have definitional properties, including the assignment of students to a particular diagnostic category. It should be recognized that the legislative categories are intended to safeguard the rights of students (that is, assure that a student is not wrongfully included in a "handicapped" category) and to provide for financial accountability (that is, assure that a student will not

---

DIAGNOSTIC CRITERIA FOR 314.01 ATTENTION-DEFICIT HYPERACTIVITY DISORDER

Note: Consider a criterion met only if the behavior is considerably more frequent than that of most people of the same mental age.

A. A disturbance of at least six months during which at least eight of the following are present:

    (1) often fidgets with hands or feet or squirms in seat (in adolescents, may be limited to subjective feelings of restlessness)

    (2) has difficulty remaining seated when required to do so

    (3) is easily distracted by extraneous stimuli

    (4) has difficulty awaiting turn in games or group situations

    (5) often blurts out answers to questions before they have been completed

    (6) has difficulty following through on instructions from others (not due to oppositional behavior or failure of comprehension), e.g., fails to finish chores

    (7) has difficulty sustaining attention in tasks or play activities

    (8) often shifts from one uncompleted activity to another

    (9) has difficulty playing quietly

    (10) often talks excessively

    (11) often interrupts or intrudes on others, e.g., butts into other children's games

    (12) often does not seem to listen to what is being said to him or her

    (13) Often loses things necessary for tasks or activities at school or at home (e.g., toys, pencils, books, assignments)

    (14) often engages in physically dangerous activities without considering possible consequences (not for the purpose of thrill-seeking), e.g., runs into street without looking

Note: The above items are listed in descending order of discriminating power based on data from a national field trial of the DSM-III-R criteria for Disruptive Behavior Disorders.

B. Onset before the age of seven.

C. Does not meet the criteria for a Pervasive Developmental Disorder.

Criteria for severity of Attention-deficit Hyperactivity Disorder:

Mild: Few, if any, symptoms in excess of those required to make the diagnosis **and** only minimal or no impairment in school and social functioning.

Moderate: Symptoms or functional impairment intermediate between "mild" and "severe."

Severe: Many symptoms in excess of those required to make the diagnosis **and** significant and pervasive impairment in functioning at home and school and with peers.

FIGURE 8.2 DSM-III-R attention-deficit hyperactivity category
Source: Diagnostic and statistical manual of mental disorders (3rd ed.). Reprinted with permission of the American Psychiatric Association.

---

receive a special educational expenditure unless he or she legitimately qualifies for the program being funded).

In the past, certain legislative definitions, especially at the state level, have included rather exact text scores as criteria. For example, a state might require that to be placed in a special-education classroom for the mentally handicapped, the child must receive a test score of 75 or lower on an individual intelligence test, with the test having to be an approved instrument. This practice is so rigid that it may either deny services to children who, but for a test score, should receive a special-educational placement, or encourage devious means to circumvent the cutting-point issue.

To illustrate, one superintendent, wanting more state funding, sought to maximize the number of children placed in special-education programs by urging that the school psychologists use a particular verbally loaded intelligence test and disregard mitigating case information as a way of increasing the number of children who could be placed in classrooms for the mentally handicapped—"at least until the date upon which the state funding is determined."

To this day, having eligibility criteria that are predicated, either explicitly or implicitly, on test scores is commonplace. There is, however, a trend away from fixed scores, in part because it is recognized that test scores are not exact and seldom, if ever, is there a single test (or even a battery of tests) that will assuredly measure the criteria that indisputably constitute the essence of the category. Unfortunately, Frank (1975) was correct when he asserted, "We have never seemed to find a truly satisfactory system of classification of psychopathology" (p. 5). It can be added that a classification system for any sort of human development or behavior will never be perfect.

Accepting the Diagnostic Mandate

Being a school psychologist necessitates accepting a diagnostic mandate. Public policy undergirds the school psychologist's responsibility for assessment of children for psychoeducational purposes. Consequently, it is both essential and pragmatic to accept that clinical judgments must be made. As Thorne (1961) says, "Even in view of the admitted invalidity or relative inefficiency of many clinical decisions, society must depend upon clinical decisions because of the practical and economic limitations of life situations" (p. 23). School psychologists have been designated the guardians of standards for psychoeducational assessment, yet must also continually produce assessment data upon which life-influencing decisions will be made.

In school psychology, there has been a shift away from the medical model, with greater consideration being given to accentuating the positive while still eliminating the negative. As discussed, the medical model connotes a patho-

logical condition. This abnormal framework is somewhat ill-suited for the developmental framework that must be present in education. Terms like *mental illness, maladjustment, immaturity, deviance, psychopathology,* and *psychological disorder* justify consideration in school psychology. But the emphasis is better placed, at least for most children being served by school psychologists, on terms like *normality, mental or psychological health, psychological maturity, adjustment,* and *psychological competence.* Thus, while accommodation of pathology is made, hygiology is accentuated—that is, bringing out the optimal potential of every child (and those in his or her social system).

CRITICAL PSYCHOEDUCATIONAL ASSESSMENT TERMS

In accepting a developmental and social systems approach to psychoeducational assessment, it is necessary to recognize that (1) *measurement* is the assignment of numbers to assessment data; (2) *evaluation* is broad, but often connected to programmatic fulfillment of objectives (Woody & Robertson, 1988); and (3) *appraisal* is commonly defined in qualitative terms, such as for a selection process (Hamersma, 1972; Woody & Robertson, 1988). *Assessment* is a broad, encompassing term, but is distinguished by its focus on problem solving: "A simple definition for an extremely complex process is that *psychological assessment is a process of solving problems (answering questions)* in which psychological tests are often used as *one* of the methods of collecting data" (Maloney & Ward, 1976, p. 5). Kleinmuntz (1982) adds, "Assessment includes all systematic (or standardized) and objective procedures (or devices) for obtaining observations and scores reflecting samples of psychological behavior" (p. 6).

In addition to all types of psychological tests, Kleinmuntz endorses "systematically recording behavior observations and scoring and quantifying data gleaned from personal documents, case histories, interviewing, and behavior analysis" (pp. 6–7). To distinguish psychological assessment from psychological testing, Maloney and Ward (1976) state,

1. Psychometric testing is primarily measurement oriented, while psychological assessment is primarily problem oriented.
2. Psychometric testing is primarily concerned with describing and studying *groups* of people, while psychological assessment focuses on a description and an analysis of a particular *individual* in a problem situation.
3. Psychometric testing demands little if any clinical expertise other than that of a psychometrist, while the role of the clinical or expert is crucial and integral to the process of psychological assessment. (p. 38)

All of these terms and principles can be readily adapted to psychoeducational assessment.

THE CONCEPT OF RELIABILITY

The term *reliability* refers to consistency: "In everyday conversation, 'reliability' is a synonym for dependability or consistency—as in 'the reliable train that you can set your watch by' or 'the reliable friend who is always there if you are in need'" (Cohen, Montague, Nathanson, & Swerdlik, 1988, p. 99). If the term is applied to psychological testing, the framework is consistency in measurement:

> The concept of the *reliability* of a test refers to its relative freedom from unsystematic errors of measurement. A test is reliable if it measures consistently under varying conditions that can produce measurement errors. Unsystematic errors affecting test scores vary in a random, unpredictable manner from situation to situation; hence, they lower test reliability. On the other hand, systematic (constant) errors may inflate or deflate test scores, but they do so in a fixed way and hence do not affect the reliability of the test. Some of the variables on which unsystematic error depends are the particular sample of questions on the test, the conditions of administration, and the level of

motivation or attentiveness of the examinee at testing time. (Aiken, 1988, p. 95)

There is a professional duty to meet the qualities set forth in *Standards for Educational and Psychological Testing* prepared by the American Educational Research Association, American Psychological Association, and National Council on Measurement in Education (hereinafter referred to as the AERA/APA/NCME Standards, 1985). Therein, it is stated:

> *Reliability* refers to the degree to which test scores are free from errors of measurement. A test taker may perform differently on one occasion than on another for reasons that may or may not be related to the purpose of measurement. A person may try harder, be more fatigued or anxious, have greater familiarity with the content of questions on one test form than another, or simply guess correctly on more questions on one occasion than on another. For these and other reasons, a person's score will not be perfectly consistent from one occasion to the next. Indeed, an individual's scores will rarely be the same on two forms of a test that are intended to be interchangeable. (p. 19)

Therefore, even a psychological test with strong statistical properties (i.e., the test itself is relatively free from error) can produce results that will have poor reliability in practice, namely because of conditions imposed by the child (client) or professional (the school psychologist). A school psychologist's not being consistent (e.g., using differing test-data criteria for a given diagnosis, being prejudiced against or biased in favor of a child because of his or her personal characteristics) refers to *intrajudge* reliability. Similarly and for many of the same kinds of reasons, several school psychologists' interpreting the same test data differently refers to *interjudge* reliability.

When it comes time to select an assessment strategy, "reliability is a major consideration in evaluating the psychometric characteristics of a test or scale" (Salvia & Yesseldyke, 1988, p. 109). Reliability is important for fulfilling the goal of formulating a generalization about the child based on a sampling (a set of test data). If the test results would be different at a follow-up session or if another school psychologist would derive a different interpretation, generalization is contradicted. It is outside the scope of this discussion to go into great detail about statistical techniques for estimating the reliability of an assessment strategy, such as a psychological test. Additional information is available in Aiken (1989) and Anastasi (1988).

THE CONCEPT OF VALIDITY

In searching for high-quality assessment, validity is of foremost concern: "Undoubtedly the most important question to be asked about any psychological test concerns its validity, that is, the degree to which the test actually measures what it purports to measure" (Anastasi, 1988, p. 28). The AERA/APA/NCME (1985) Standards state:

> Validity is the most important consideration in test evaluation. The concept refers to the appropriateness, meaningfulness, and usefulness of the specific inferences made from test scores. Test validation is the process of accumulating evidence to support such inferences. A variety of inferences may be made from scores produced by a given test, and there are many ways of accumulating evidence to support any particular inference. Validity, however, is a unitary concept. Although evidence may be accumulated in many ways, validity always refers to the degree to which that evidence supports the inferences that are made from the scores. The inferences regarding specific uses of tests are validated, not the test itself. (p. 9)

Salvia and Yesseldyke (1988) add:

> *Validity* refers to the extent to which a test measures what its authors or users claim it measures. Specifically, test validity concerns the appropriateness of the inferences that can be made on the basis of test results. A test's validity is not measured; rather, a test's validity for various uses is judged on a wide array of information, including its reliability and adequacy of its norms. The process of gathering information about the appropriateness of test-based inferences is called *validation*. (p. 132)

Cohen and colleagues (1988) describe different forms of validity (e.g., face, content, criterion-related, and construct validity).

THE IDIOGRAPHIC AND NOMOTHETIC SETS

Before proceeding, it is important to recognize that there are two assessment vantage points: idiographic and nomothetic.

Idiographic assessment seeks to provide intrapersonal distinctions, whereas *nomothetic assessment* allows for interpersonal comparisons. McDermott (1988) states:

> Behavioral science and clinical convention have long appreciated both the idioigraphic and nomothetic aspects of human assessment. *Idiography* focuses on an individual child's unique developmental and social history and on those environmental and personal factors that help make each child special. Assessment is directed to a child's health, features of culture and language, family life, community environs, handicaps, talents, and educational background. One hopes to answer questions about individual pathogeneses, coping and adaptation, expectations and motivations, and likely prognosis. This is possible because we recognize that, as the course of child growth and development shapes individual characteristics, human differences become apparent only through comparison of children along certain common dimensions of functioning, for example ability and personality. The process of comparison across children is known as *nomothesis* (as in "normal" or "natural law"). (p. 226)

McDermott connects that degree of diagnostic agreement between school psychologists to the set, saying that without strong interjudge agreement, the assessment is restricted to the idiographic set.

Nomothetic judgments necessarily require points of comparison. Most tests used by school psychologists have been standardized on norm groups, and are, therefore, called *norm-referenced measures:*

> In norm-referenced testing an examinee's performance is compared with the performance of a specific group of subjects. A norm provides an indication of average or typical performance of the specified group. Norms are needed because the raw score in itself is not very meaningful. Knowing that a child scored 20 or answered correctly 70 percent of the items tells us very little unless we also know how other children performed on the same test; a relevant normative population is needed. (Sattler, 1982, p. 17)

Norm-referenced measures are used to make a comparative analysis of the child's functioning, using a sample of his or her seeming counterparts as the point of comparison. Of course, tests are established on nationwide samples, and the assumption must be made that the comparison group is, in fact, comparable to what the child is actually experiencing.

Giving more attention to data relevant to the child's development and social system lends support to the idiographic set. For example, Meyers (1988) alleges, "A dramatic shift is needed so that psychoeducational assessment will lead to intervention designed to facilitate learning and adjustment" (p. 123). Meyers believes that this can best be achieved by environmental assessment (e.g., assessing *how* children learn, as opposed to searching for products, like IQ scores, percentiles, and grade equivalent scores). To the contrary, Bergan (1988) defends norm-referenced data because of necessary societal needs and program placement decisions:

> Norm-referenced instruments serve a number of essential functions in the schools. They provide a global, relatively easy to interpret index of how well children are doing. Norm-referenced instruments also tell parents and teachers how well individual children are doing in relation to others.

Parents and teachers need this kind of information to make basic decisions about how to guide children's development. Finally, norm-referenced instruments offer information that is widely used in making program placement decisions. (p. 135)

He cautions, "Evaluations that focus on changes in the performance of isolated skills run the proverbial risk of overlooking the forest for the trees" (p. 137).

Strict adherence to either the idiographic or nomothetic assessment set is unwise. Alessi (1988), who supports systemic analysis, explains,

> The danger in child assessment is that we *punctuate* reality in different ways depending on where in the process we choose to end our evaluation. When we stop at the point where we have identified factors on the child's side of the equation, we create a reality that individual child factors are responsible for most problems. When we end evaluations at the point when we have identified factors on the environmental side of the equation, we create a reality that environmental factors are responsible for most problems. (p. 147)

For the developmental and social systems approach, it is advisable to avoid alignment with a singular assessment set. In fact, psychoeducational assessments do and should embrace both the idiographic and nomothetic sets. The important step is formulating concepts for services that integrate the two data sets, as will accord consideration to social systems and developmental factors.

PROBLEM SOLVING

As reflected in the definition of *psychological assessment,* the common denominator of psychoeducational assessments is problem solving. From the initial referral for psychological services, the school psychologist marches toward an answer according to the cadence of the referral question; that is, he or she takes steps to solve the problem that led the classroom teacher to initiate a referral. This does not mean that the quest to solve the initial problem will exclude attention being given to other problems. In fact, it is not unusual for the initial referral question to be attached to another problem, and for the school psychologist to eventually replace it with more critical questions that may have been overlooked or avoided by the referral person for defensive or competency reasons.

To find an answer to the referral questions, Bergan (1977) suggests that the school psychologist identify the problem, analyze it for significant components (facilitating a diagnosis and considering intervention alternatives), establish a plan to ameliorate the problem, and (after a period of time) evaluate the intervention (i.e., how well the plan has solved the problem, and, if needed, what modifications should be made in the intervention plan).

Similarly, Gutkin and Curtis (1982) have a seven-stage model, designed for consultation, that has usefulness for virtually any school psychology problem-solving effort:

1. Define and clarify the problem.
2. Analyze the forces that impinge on the problem.
3. Brainstorm for alternative strategies.
4. Evaluate and select a strategy from the available alternatives.
5. Specify the responsibilities for each professional involved.
6. Implement the chosen strategy.
7. Evaluate the effectiveness of the implemented strategy and make changes if necessary or desirable (which might mean reverting to one of the previous stages and progressing again through the sequence of stages).

STANDARDS FOR PSYCHOEDUCATIONAL ASSESSMENT

When making a decision about psychoeducational assessment, such as which data-collection strategies to use, the school psychologist must

constantly reckon with the differences between the "Ivory Tower" views of textbooks and mentors and the "Real World" views of parents, teachers, administrators, and others that are fashioned by legislation (and related rules and regulations), board of education policies, and community (and personal) preferences. There must be an allegiance to science, yet an accommodation of practical considerations.

Albee (1970) gave a useful credo when he said that science and professional practice "must exist in a mutually rewarding and symbiotic relationship" (p. 1080). It may be relatively easy for the school psychologist to accept this idea in theory, but the differing postures of colleagues and constituencies commonly make it difficult to obtain in day-to-day activities. Since there are few, if any, scientifically incontrovertible rules for practice, Phillips (1989) wisely notes that school psychologists must accept uncertainty:

> In accepting uncertainty, they accept not only the fact that they must learn from other practitioners, and from researchers and research findings, but also the fact that in accepting uncertainty, they also accept improvement of practice efforts as ways of exploring, rather than controlling, the unknown and realize that they therefore open themselves to risk and take ultimate responsibility for the results of their practice. (p. 6)

Selection of Assessment Strategies

The selection of an assessment strategy is restricted by knowledge of alternatives. Beyond fundamental training in a graduate program and the information gleaned directly from colleagues and practical experience, the school psychologist is blessed with numerous compendia of available tests, such as *The Mental Measurement Yearbook* (MMY) series (Buros, 1978; Mitchell, 1985; Conoley, Kramer, & Mitchell, 1988; Conoley & Kramer, 1989; Kramer & Conoley, 1990) and the *Tests in Print* series (Mitchell, 1983). Anastasi (1988, pp. 19–22) provides additional information and sources, and Kessler (1988, pp.

467–530) provides a useful guide to instruments for the assessment of children and childhood disorders.

The implementation of any psychoeducational assessment strategy requires five steps:

1. Determining the scope of the assessment
2. Determining the generalized purpose of the assessment
3. Evaluating the cost
4. Selecting the instrument
5. Maximizing the reliability of the assessment information (Martin, 1988, p. 69)

Throughout these steps, consideration must be given to the child's unique needs and characteristics (e.g., age, socioeconomic status, and subcultural values) and the characteristics of the assessment instruments or strategies. Martin warns, "Frequently, assessors of children must make difficult choices because available instruments may not meet the criteria for psychometric soundness and client appropriateness" (p. 83).

The issue of psychometric soundness connects to professional standards. Being a member of a profession, the school psychologist has an ethical obligation (and indirectly a legal duty) to fulfill disciplinary standards. Among many sources and standards, the AERA/APA/NCME (1985) have promulgated numerous standards that impact upon the selection of assessment strategies. Of special note, psychological tests must have proven qualities. For example, the AERA/APA/NCME Standards for validity require:

> Standard 1.1 Evidence of validity should be presented for the major types of inferences for which the use of a test is recommended. A rationale should be provided to support the particular mix of evidence presented for its intended uses. (p. 13)
>
> Standard 1.2 If validity for some common interpretation has not been investigated, that fact should be made clear, and potential users should be cautioned about making such interpretations.

Statements about validity should refer to the validity of particular interpretations or of particular types of decisions. (p. 13)

> Standard 1.3 Whenever interpretation of subscores, score differences, or profiles is suggested, the evidence justifying such interpretation should be made explicit. Where composite scores are developed, the basis and rationale for weighting the subscores should be given. (p. 14)
>
> Standards 1.4 Whenever it is suggested that the user consider an individual's responses to specific items as a basis for assessment, the test manual should either present evidence supporting this use or call attention to the absence of such evidence. (p. 14)

Note that these are but a few of the standards pertaining to validity, but they provide an illustration of the fact that a test or assessment strategy cannot be blindly accepted. There must be a scientific basis that meets the standards of the profession. In the developmental and social systems approach, the reliance on observational methods has the concomitant of poorly defined standards; thus, careful definition and planning for data collection strategies will be necessary.

As noted in the foregoing standards, a unique relationship exists between school psychologists and test publishers. With school psychologists, the objective is high-quality assessment, which requires academic and research bases, an expensive process to complete. With test publishers, the objective is financial profit. Of course, maximum profit cannot be achieved without credibility with the consumers (i.e., the school psychologists who will potentially purchase the test materials and scoring/interpretive services). As diverse and potentially conflicting as these objectives may be, there has been a seemingly conscientious effort by the two groups to merge their objectives in a complementary fashion. Fremer, Diamond, and Camara (1989) describe the efforts of the Joint Commission on Testing Practices (JCTP), which brings professional organizations and test publishers together, and its Code of Fair Testing Practices, which promotes understanding of testing issues in the minds of the general public and mental health and educational professionals.

Delivery of Assessment Services

The delivery of psychological services is influenced by myriad sources. Of relevance to this section on standards, several authoritative statements deserve consideration.

In the American Psychological Association's (1981b) "Specialty Guidelines for the Delivery of Services by School Psychologists," the first service defined involves assessment:

> A. Psychological and psychoeducational evaluation and assessment of the school functioning of children and young persons. Procedures include screening, psychological and educational tests (particularly individual psychological tests of intellectual functioning, cognitive development, affective behavior, and neuropsychological status), interviews, observation, and behavioral evaluations, with explicit regard for the context and setting in which the professional judgments based on assessment, diagnosis, and evaluation will be used. (p. 672)

The Guidelines go on to specify standards for: (1) *providers* (with training and in number enough to "assure the adequacy and quality of services offered" [p. 673]); *programs* (with "appropriate types of assessment materials and norm reference groups" [p. 675] and with personnel sufficient to "achieve its goals, objectives, and purposes," [p. 675] as well as certain types of quality assurance policies and practices); *accountability* (for the promotion of human welfare, school psychologists functioning as an autonomous profession of psychology, and evaluative safeguards); and *environment* (with a physical, organizational, and social conditions that facilitate optimal human functioning).

In the National Association of School Psychologists' (1984) "Standards for the Provision of School Psychological Services," there are numer-

ous assessment-related standards that lead to information for maximizing student achievement and educational success; autonomous decision-making responsibility by the school psychologist; use of assessment procedures (techniques and instruments) with established validity and reliability; multidisciplinary team involvement in assessment; and non-biased assessment techniques. There are five noteworthy standards for section 4.3.2. Psychological and Psychoeducational Assessment:

> 4.3.2.1 School psychologists conduct multifactored psychological and psychoeducational assessments of children and youth as appropriate.
> 4.3.2.2 Psychological and psychoeducational assessments include consideration as appropriate of the areas of personal-social adjustment, intelligence-scholastic aptitude, adaptive behavior, language and communication skills, academic achievement, sensory and perceptual-motor functioning, environmental-cultural influences, and vocational development, aptitude, and interests.
> 4.3.2.3 School psychologists utilize formal instruments, procedures, and techniques. Interviews, observations, and behavioral evaluations are included in these procedures.
> 4.3.2.4 When conducting psychological and psychoeducational assessments, school psychologists have explicit regard for the context and setting in which their assessments take place and will be used.
> 4.3.2.5 School psychologists adhere to the NASP resolutions regarding non-biased assessment and programming of all students (see Section 3.5.3). They are also familiar with and consider the *Standards for Educational and Psychological Tests* (developed by APA, AERA, and NCME) in the use of assessment techniques. (pp. 30–31)

The reference to nonbiased assessment connects to standards that will "maximize the student's opportunities to be successful in the general culture, while respecting the student's ethnic background" (p. 28), as well as other standards that will enhance the quality of assessment.

In the context of the delivery of assessment services, the AERA/APA/NCME (1985) Standards offer crucial guidance:

Standard 8.1   Those responsible for school testing programs should ensure that the individuals who administer the tests are properly instructed in the appropriate test administration procedures and that they understand the importance of adhering to the directions for administration that are provided by the test developer. (p. 52)

Standard 8.2   Those responsible for school testing programs should ensure that the individuals who use the test scores within the school context are properly instructed in the appropriate methods for interpreting test scores. (p. 52)

Standard 8.3   If test results are used in making statements about the differences between aptitude and achievement for an individual student, any educational decision based on these differences should take into account the overlap between the constructs and the reliability or standard error of the difference score. (p. 52)

Standard 8.4   When a test is to be used to certify the successful completion of a given level of education, either grade-to-grade promotion or high school graduation, both the test domain and the instructional domain at the given level of education should be described in sufficient detail, without compromising test security, so that the agreement between the test domain and the content domain can be evaluated. (p. 52)

Standard 8.5   When a test is developed by a state or local district to be used for student promotion, graduation, or classification decisions, user's guides or technical reports should be developed and disseminated. (p. 53)

Standard 8.6   Results from certification tests should be reported promptly to all appropriate parties, including students, parents, and teachers. The report should contain a description of the test, what is measured, the conclusions and decisions that are based on the test results, the obtained score, information on how to interpret the reported score, and any cut score used for classification. (p. 53)

Standard 8.7   When a test is used to make decisions about student promotion or graduation, there should be evidence that the test covers only the specific or generalized knowledge, skills, and abilities that students have had the opportunity to learn. (p. 53)

Standard 8.8   Students who must demonstrate mastery of certain skills or knowledge before being promoted or granted a diploma should have multiple opportunities to demonstrate the skills. (p. 53)

Standard 8.9   Relationships between predictors and criterion measures that are used in educational admissions should be described by regression equations and associated standard errors or estimate or by expectancy tables in addition to correlation coefficients. (p. 53)

Standard 8.10   The possibility that differential prediction exists in educational selection for selected groups should be investigated where there is prior evidence to suggest that positive results may be found and where sample sizes are adequate. (p. 53)

Standard 8.11   Test users should not imply that empirical evidence exists for a relationship among particular test results, prescribed educational plans, and desired student outcomes unless such evidence is available. (p. 54)

Standard 8.12   In elementary or secondary education, a decision or characterization that will have a major impact on a test taker should not automatically be made on the basis of a single test score. Other relevant information for the decision should also be taken into account by the professionals making the decision. (p. 54)

The latter standard has special relevance to minority groups. A given minority group may "form such a small fraction of the overall population that few schools can be expected to have enough students for an adequate differential prediction study" (p. 54), which means that there may need to be "cooperative efforts by many institutions that allow combining information across institutions" (p. 54). Other sections of the AERA/APA/NCME Standards deal with linguistic minorities and persons with handicapping conditions, as well as with general principles, clinical testing, use of tests in counseling, employment testing, licensure and certification, program evaluation, and other matters.

REPORTING ASSESSMENT RESULTS

From the vantage point of helping children, collecting psychoeducational assessment data is futile unless there will be an implementation of a service plan. To formulate organizational plans and interventions, the school psychologist is expected to communicate the results of psychoeducational assessment. There is no universal prescription for reporting assessment results; the medium, format, and contents must be idiosyncratically determined according to the developmental needs of the child and the conditions of the educational, familial, and social systems.

In addition to the obvious benefits that accrue to the school (and thus to the child) by collecting and acting on psychoeducational data, Public Law 94-142 contains a legal mandate for the reporting of assessment results (see Chapter 12). The Act calls for each handicapped child's receiving an Individualized Education Program (IEP):

> The term "individualized education program" means a written statement for each handicapped child developed in any meeting by a representative of the local educational agency or an intermediate educational unit who shall be qualified to provide, or supervise the provision of, specially designed instruction to meet the unique needs of handicapped children, the teacher, the parents or guardian of each child, and, whenever appropriate, such child, which statement shall include (A) A statement of the present levels of educational performance of such child, (B) a statement of annual goals, including short term instructional objectives, (C) a statement of the specific educational services to be provided to the child, and the extent to which such child will be able to participate in regular educational programs, (D) the projected date for initiation and the anticipated duration of such services, and (E) appropriate objective criteria and evaluation procedures and schedules for determining, on at least an annual basis, whether

instructional objectives are being achieved. (89 Stat. 776, section 4, paragraph 19)

This mandate is enlarged by Public Law 99-457, which requires an Individualized Family Service Plan (IFSP) for handicapped infants and toddlers and their families (see Chapter 12). All early intervention services must be provided in conformity with the IFSP, which shall include:

(1) a multidisciplinary assessment of unique needs and identification of services appropriate to meet such needs, and

(2) a written individualized family service plan developed by a multidisciplinary team, including the parent or guardian. (100 Stat. 1149)

The IFSP must be evaluated once a year and the family must receive a review at no less than six month intervals. The IFSP must contain:

(1) a statement of the infant's or toddler's present levels of physical development, cognitive development, language and speech development, psychosocial development, and self-help skills, based on acceptable objective criteria,

(2) a statement of the family's strengths and needs relating to enhancing the development of the family's handicapped infant or toddler,

(3) a statement of the major outcomes expected to be achieved for the infant or toddler and the family, and the criteria, procedures, and timelines used to determine the degree to which progress toward achieving the outcomes are being made and whether modifications or revisions of the outcomes or services are necessary,

(4) a statement of specific early intervention services necessary to meet the unique needs of the infant or toddler and the family, including the frequency, intensity, and the method of delivering services,

(5) the projected dates for initiation of services and the anticipated duration of such services,

(6) the name of the case manager from the profession most immediately relevant to the infant's or toddler's or family's needs who will be responsible for the implementation of the plan and coordination with other agencies and persons, and

(7) the steps to be taken supporting the transition of

the handicapped toddler to services provided under part B [the periodic review] to the extent such services are considered appropriate. (100 Stat. 1150)

These legislative directives constitute the end goal to which the school psychologist will direct psychoeducational assessment efforts. In other words, these legislative mandates cannot be fulfilled without careful compilation, analysis, and communication of psychoeducational assessment data. Consequently, the selection of assessment strategies and the fashioning and communication of conclusions will give consideration to the elements of the Public Law 94-142 and Public Law 99-457 prescriptions.

When the school reaches the point of constructing the IEP and IFSP, there will be informational inputs from diverse sources, and deliberations and decisions will be accomplished by committee. The school psychologist's report is not expected to be the final version of the IEP or IFSP; it will, however, make a substantial contribution to the contents. To attain this end, the school psychologist must be prepared for and able to transmit assessment-related communications that are clear, concise, and persuasive.

In reporting assessment data, the school psychologist must always pass the information through a filter determined by to whom the report is directed. At the same time, it must be remembered that often an unanticipated source (e.g., a court in a custody dispute between the parents) will also have access to the information. This means exercising prudence in: (1) interpretations—say nothing that is not data based and in accord with professional standards; (2) word choices and explanations—avoid unnecessary psychological jargon and pathological terms, and carefully define any technical matter; and (3) recommendations—tailor every suggestion to the sources receiving the information, with a blending of the ideal with the practical.

Be warned that there is neither a single formula for deciding what should be included in a psychoeducational assessment nor a universal

format for presenting psychoeducational assessment data. As a prefacing set for deciding what assessment information should be communicated, Sattler (1982) offers the following ideas about report writing (see also Sattler, 1988):

The writing of a report involves analyzing, synthesizing, and integrating numerous sources of data, including the child's test scores, previous test scores, teachers' reports, behavioral observations, interview material, social and family history, and medical findings. The report is one of the principal vehicles of communication, serving as a medium through which findings are described and impressions conveyed as clearly and as concisely as possible. Even before the report is begun, an attempt is made to make some kind of coherent whole of all of the available information. The report should clearly present findings, interpretations, and recommendations and should meet acceptable writing standards. (p. 491)

Ownby (1987) reviews research on psychological reports in school settings, and states,

(a) the report should be written with the needs of the referring person in mind,
(b) reports should provide information that is relevant to work with the client but may not have been requested,
(c) reports should communicate in a way that is appropriate to the report's intended recipient, and
(d) reports should affect the way the reader works with the client. (p. 14)

He clarifies,

The purposes of reports are:
(1) to answer referral questions as explicitly as possible, depending on how well defined the questions are;
(2) to provide the referring agent with additional information when it is relevant to his or her work with the client and when it is appropriate to the use the report will be put to (this includes providing a general description of the client);
(3) to make a record of the assessment activities for future use;

(4) to recommend a specific course of action for the report's recipient to follow in his or her work with the client. (p. 16)

This leads Sattler (1982) to suggest the following report outline: identifying data (e.g., name, date of birth, chronological age, date of examination, date of report, grade, test(s) administered); reason for referral; general observations; test results; recommendation(s); and summary. Similarly, Ownby (1987) suggests that the sections of the report include the following (*Note:* MLCs refer to middle-level constructs, which lie between low-level test scores or observation and high-level conclusions):

I. *Reason for Referral,* including:
   —data-based statement of the reason for referral
   —specific statement of questions to be answered
II. *Background Information,* including:
   —discussion of previous evaluation results
   —school or social history
   —other pertinent information obtained from other sources
III. *Observations,* including:
   —discussion of behavioral observations during testing
   —discussion of home, classroom, or playground behavior linked to MLC's
IV. *Assessment Results,* including:
   —list of assessment tools with referencing abbreviations
   —results in tabular or narrative form
V. *Summary and Recommendations,* including
   —statement integrating MLC's and providing conclusions drawn from them
   —statement linking conclusions to what follows, i.e., general instructional strategy recommendations and specific activity recommendations (p. 95)

In summary, any report of assessment results, whether in oral or written form, must be tailored to the case. For example, the terms and contents might be quite different according to whether the communication is directed to a parent, teacher, administrator, psychologist, pediatrician, or whomever, or is intended for educational, legal, or medical purposes. It is an understatement to assert that the overall success or failure of a school psychologist's service will be greatly influenced by the quality of assessment-related communications, whether they be in discussions with the child, parents, educators, or other professionals, or in written reports that will become a component of psychoeducational committee or administrative deliberations.

COMPUTERIZED ASSESSMENT

It will come as no surprise that computerization has become an integral part of psychoeducational assessment. Papert (1984) asserts that computerization "gives us the opportunity for making much more radical changes in the conditions of learning than any other means we have had in the past" (p. 424). There has been a rapid increase in assessment-related computer applications. Computerized services are now widely available for test administration, scanning, scoring, profiling, and interpretation, among other things. Also, the voluminous amount of psychoeducational assessment data that amasses can be stored, ordered, and retrieved readily by computer; in addition to improved client services, this availability of data accommodates much needed research.

McCullough and Wenck (1984) provide an overview of computer applications in school psychology:

In daily practice heavily influenced by the evaluation demands of PL 94-142, software that provides help with these tasks can increase (a) efficiency, (b) scoring accuracy, (c) standardization of test interpretation; and decrease (a) scoring errors, (b) scoring time, (c) report writing time, and (d) interpretive misjudgments. (p. 429)

Brantley (1984) describes various computerized school psychology techniques, and recommends that school psychology training embrace computers:

The microcomputer as "teaching-assistant" offers an important new opportunity for training to become competency-based through the unlimited systematic or randomized presentation of information, extended opportunities for practice, cueing, corrective feedback and reinforcement, and performance measured too specified criterion levels. (p. 452)

Moursund (1984) covers technical information relevant to school psychology.

Although computerization offers many advantages—namely, efficiency and economy—it is not free from problems. In computerized assessment, the use of clerks or technicians may relieve the press for professionals, and thus potentially be more economical. However, purchasing expensive equipment and services that are not used to their fullest can also be costly, and reliance on computerized assessment required caution, planning, and training.

A threshold question for the school psychologist is: Will computerization produce a negative effect in psychoeducational assessment? Bersoff (1983) believes that there is no apparent reason to expect harmful impact on validity or other constructs. This issue must be examined carefully: "It is important that comparisons be made between the computerized test results and conventional test results for a particular test when theory or previous research suggests that the validity of the two versions may differ" (Burke & Normand, 1987, p. 46). One thing that can be assumed, the computer-generated information will be reliable, since the program is steadfast (but will the information be valid?).

Computerized assessment can adjust the difficulty of a test to the ability of the subject being assessed. This is referred to as *computerized* or *individualized adaptive testing.* Niehaus (1979) explains,

> A computer-assisted or adaptive test uses a multi-stage process to estimate a person's ability several times during the course of testing, and the selection of successive test items based on those ability estimates. The person tested uses an interactive computer terminal to answer a test question. If the answer is correct, the next item will be more difficult; if not, an easier item follows. With each response, a revised and more reliable estimate is made of the person's ability. The test proceeds until the estimate reaches a specified level of reliability. Generally, the results both are more reliable and require fewer items than a paper and pencil test. (p. 222)

Anastasi (1988) offers a related definition:

> The individual's score is based, not on the number of items answered correctly, but on the difficulty level and other psychometric characteristics of those items. The total test score is derived from the ability estimates corresponding to each item passed. This ability estimate is readjusted and refined as each new item is added, until the predetermined measurement precision is reached. Such scores will be comparable for all persons examined with the item pool, regardless of the particular set of items given to each individual.
>
> In general, research by various methods indicates that individualized adaptive testing can achieve the same reliability and validity as conventional tests, with a much smaller number of items and less testing time. It also provides greater precision of measurement for individuals at the upper and lower extremes of the ability range covered by the test. (p. 316)

Since this is an emerging school psychology assessment strategy, professional competency must be assured. To search of quality control, the AERA/APA/NCME (1985) Standards state:

> Standard 2.11   In adaptive testing, estimates of the magnitude of errors of measurement, based on the analysis results from repeated administrations using different items should be provided. (p. 22)
> Standard 3.9   For adaptive tests, the rationale and supporting evidence for procedures used in selecting items for administration, in stopping the test, and in scoring the test should be described in the test manual. (p. 27)
> Standard 4.6   When scores earned on different forms of a test, including computer-presented or computerized adaptive tests, are intended to be

used interchangeably, data concerning the parallelism of the forms should be available. Details of the equivalence study should be available, including specific information about the method of equating: the administrative design and statistical procedures used, the characteristics of the anchor test, if any, and of the sampling procedures; information on the sample; and sample size. Periodic checks on the adequacy of the equating should be reported. (p. 34)

Standard 15.2 The testing environment should be one of reasonable comfort and with minimal distractions. Testing materials should be readable and understandable. In computerized testing, items displayed on a screen should be legible and free from glare, and the terminal should be properly positioned. (p. 83)

The utility of adaptive testing for exceptional children is easy to recognize. Individual differences that are manifested in giftedness or handicaps are accommodated. The technical and knowledge demands placed on the school psychologist cannot be circumvented, and the movement toward computerized adaptive testing will require considerable training. Given the progress of computer science, the cultivation of computerized skills will be ongoing.

Returning to the more conventional use of computerization in psychoeducational assessment, there are commercial services available to score, profile, and interpret innumerable educational and psychological tests, as well as present standardized interviews and interpret the responses. Indeed, computer programs can take the data from several tests and write a final report (Brown, 1984). These "canned" interpretations and reports have major drawbacks. The validity of the diagnostic opinions are, of course, only as astute as were programmed. Also, these computerized products do not integrate the child's unique personal and social system data (beyond a limited degree of plugging in delimited demographic or case data), which is essential to the developmental and social systems approach.

Despite its prominence, computerized assessment is relatively new. Consequently, certain issues relevant to ethics and standards are unresolved and require professional concern (Sampson & Pyle, 1988). As might be expected, professional ethics and standards are appearing that deal with the matter of computerization. The AERA/APA/NCME (1985) Standards for adaptive testing have already been presented. The APA's Ethical Principles for Psychologists (1981a, 1990) and the Specialty Guidelines for the Delivery of Services (1981b) and the NASP's Standards for the Provision of School Psychological Services (1984) have significant indirect relevance to computerized assessment. Of direct relevance, the American Psychological Association (1986) has proffered its *Guidelines for Computer-based Tests and Interpretations*. No doubt other ethical principles and standards for computerized assessment will be forthcoming.

FORENSIC SERVICES

Historically, the school system has kept a clear demarcation of its service responsibility. Among other limits, it has studiously avoided involvement with legal proceedings affecting children. To this day, a state may have statutes that provide exceptions for school-related information. Nonetheless, certain societal conditions—namely, the escalation of divorce (with the concomitant child custody and visitation determinations) and reported child neglect and abuse—have created a new demand for an interface between the school and the court.

Also, but more rare, school psychologists may be drawn into legal proceedings for a possible court-ordered commitment of a child to a mental-health or correctional facility. Because of the nature of the legal issues, forensic psychological assessment, in general, has become a mainstay of legal proceedings (Grisso, 1987). In specific, psychoeducational assessment data and information about a child's educational progress are considered to be virtually essential to any adjudication impacting on a child.

The potential number of children in need of legally related psychoeducational assessment services is huge in size. The National Center for Health Statistics (1985) reports that, in 1982, 1.17 million marriages ended in divorce, with 1.1 million children being affected. With child abuse, Slater (1988) cites estimates of approximately 50,000 children being abused in the United States during one year (since these data came from 1974, there is reason to believe, regrettably, that the number is now larger) and, in 1982, a total of 332,000 child abuse cases were reported:

> Child abuse is one of the major issues faced by school personnel and one which will not decrease for some time. The school psychologist is in an excellent position to assist in the identification of abuse victims, to ensure that abuse is reported appropriately, to provide some form of intervention within the constraints of an individual school system, and to serve as a consultant to school personnel. (p. 4)

It is readily apparent that children of divorce and neglected and abused children will be at high risk for a multitude of learning, emotional, and behavioral problems. Psychoeducational personnel must be willing and able to become involved with legal proceedings to minimize the negative effects.

When a legal judgment is to be made about a child, the standard legal test is the best interests of the child (as opposed, say, to parental preference). The Uniform Marriage and Divorce Act (Section 402, 9, *Uniform Laws Annotated* 35, 1970, as amended 1971, 1973) provides for considering the wishes of the child's parent(s), but also considers the custody wishes of the child (with the weight varying according to the maturity of the child); the interaction and interrelationship between the child and his or her parents, siblings, and other significant persons; the child's adjustment to home, school, and community; and the mental and physical health of all persons involved with the matter.

From this cornerstone law, each state has constructed its own custody and related laws, of-

ten relying on special educational, social, and psychological factors that necessitate expert evaluation and opinion. This would require, for example, a school psychologist's conducting a psychoeducational assessment and testifying about the results and their relevance to custody and visitation to the trier of fact (e.g., the judge). With neglect and abuse, the school psychologist may be expected to collect data from the child about the ultimate legal issue (i.e., did or did not the neglect or abuse occur and, if so, who was the perpetrator). Further discussion of child custody proceedings, determinations, and evaluations may be found in Melton, Petrila, Poythress, and Slobogin (1987), Weithorn (1987), and Woody (1977, 1978). Melton and colleagues (1987) also cover evaluations for abuse and neglect cases.

The purpose of this section is not to teach how to conduct forensic assessments (see Chapter 12), but to issue an alert that there is a new and increasing demand for school psychologists to provide forensic psychology services (Crespi, 1990). This demand will not be easily met. Consider the following eight reasons.

First, the school is reluctant to allow its personnel to get involved in legal proceedings, because it will: (1) void a right-to-privacy rationale that has long separated the school from family; (2) likely provoke controversy (among legalists, it is an axiom that it is impossible to please everyone in a neglect, abuse, custody, or visitation battle); (3) require scarce financial resources; and (4) expand the liability of the school (one regulatory agency reports that one of the most common reasons for a complaint is dissatisfaction with testimony in a child custody case).

To avoid involvement in legal cases, one school system has a policy to file a motion for a protective order any time that a subpoena is issued for a school psychologist to testify in court or his or her records to be produced for legal use; if the court would grant the motion, it would mean that the school would not have to fulfill the subpoena.

Second, school psychologists are not trained for legally oriented services. Any new training objective will tax already overloaded curricula and faculty. Even if the competing demands for inclusion in the curriculum could be satisfied, faculty members with training in forensic services are few and far between.

Third, professional associations and other sources have not adequately prepared the school psychologist for exemplary social-advocacy involvement in legal cases. Wilson and Gettinger (1989) conclude that it is timely and essential for school psychologists to develop a positive view toward and a cooperative relationship with child protective personnel in the community, which will require proper training.

Fourth, the very nature of these problems—negative acts against children—create an undesirable area to service. Numerous professionals from various disciplines have reported that they sense discomfort working with such hurtful conditions, and these depressing circumstances seem to outweigh their motivation to benefit the emotionally and physically battered child.

Fifth, the type of data relied on is often questionable at best. That is, expert testimony about neglect, abuse, custody, and visitation does not have adequate research available and is anything but an exact science. Any reliance on children's competency to provide information or testify about these emotionally charged issues is suspect: "Social scientists have not provided enough evidence to justify conclusive statements about children's competency to testify or about the most effective way of presenting their testimony in court" (Haugaard, 1988, p. 106).

Sixth, professionals often sense that legal expectations are counter to ethics, perhaps because of what Rogers (1987) describes as "a less-than-perfect match between professionals' competency and the legal needs" (p. 158). Further, the professional lacks adequate legally related ethical guidelines to resolve the dilemma (Rogers, 1987).

Seventh, the legal arena is not always a cordial setting, and an attorney's advocacy of his or her client's interests may mean attempted impeachment of well-intentioned testimony:

It is often disturbing for the professional who agrees to testify, thereby fulfilling a societal duty, to encounter a "hostile" attorney from the other side, who laces into the professional's testimony in a manner that creates a sense of personal attack and professional denigration. In point of fact, the party-opponent's attorney is making sure that justice is at work. (Woody & Mitchell, 1984, p. 17)

Ziskin and Faust (1989), both psychologists, believe that testimony by mental-health professionals should be challenged for the level and the quality of expertise within the discipline and the conduct of the evaluations (errors of omission or commission and conclusions unwarranted by the supporting data or the state of knowledge):

Psychiatry and psychology have been described as conglomerations of unvalidated theories, with many differing schools of thought, each having a substantial number of adherents (and a greater number of opponents), none of which has proved itself superior to the others and none of which can even be considered to be generally accepted within the professions. (p. 45)

Ziskin and Faust also give guidelines for impeaching the expert's testimony.

Given the previously mentioned dearth of research on child neglect, abuse, custody, and visitation, it is not difficult for an attorney to quickly penetrate a professional shield and reveal that the school psychologist's testimony is lacking in scientific basis.

Eighth, the philosophical underpinnings that shape education are quite different from the philosophical underpinnings that shape the law (Melton et al., 1987), and the "rules of the game" are discrepant. Slovenko (1973) points out some of the differences between mental health and the law: "Much evidence may be rejected in a court of law, even though in other disciplines it is considered substantial enough from which to draw inferences" (p. 8); and "the law's method of arriving at a result is often purposely nonscientific or dependent upon a nonprofessional assessment" (p. 9). Melton and colleagues (1987) refer to attempts by mental health and legal professionals to work together as an "uneasy alliance" (p. 3).

Notwithstanding the foregoing eight reasons for the school to attempt to be distanced from the court, the fact remains that public policy demands any and all relevant and material evidence be made available to legal proceedings. Consequently, the school and the school psychologist must arrange for accommodation of this mandate. The school psychologist can expect a continuing and even greater demand for involvement in legal matters relevant to children, and psychoeducational assessment will be accorded special significance.

SUMMARY

Psychoeducational assessment is the *sine qua non* of the school psychologist's role and functions. The medical-diagnostic assessment model remains the cornerstone for building an individualized education program (IEP) and the individualized family service plan (IFSP), but the developmental and social systems approach requires going further. Differential diagnosis accepts the uniqueness of each child through evaluation and analysis of past and present characteristics and needs, and recommendations posited for interventions.

Critical psychoeducational assessment terms (e.g., *measurement, evaluation,* and *appraisal*) distinguish foci. Reliability and validity must be established for any assessment strategy or method. Standards for psychoeducational assessment are set forth by professional associations and laws and must be met in daily practices. It is crucial that assessment results be properly and meaningfully communicated, especially in the psychoeducational report. Computerized assessment, which facilitates individualized adaptive testing, is increasingly relied on by school psychologists. Since public policy endorses psychoeducational assessment, school psychologists have a duty to provide forensic services to legal proceedings that involve children and their families.

REFERENCES

Achenbach, T. M. (1982). *Developmental psychopathology* (2nd ed.). New York: Wiley.

Aiken, L. R. (1988). *Psychological testing and assessment* (6th ed.). Boston: Allyn and Bacon.

Aiken, L. R. (1989). *Assessment of personality.* Boston: Allyn and Bacon.

Albee, G. W. (1970). The uncertain future of clinical psychology. *American Psychologist, 25,* 1071–1080.

Alessi, G. (1988). Diagnosis diagnosed: A systemic reaction. *Professional School Psychology, 3*(2), 145–151.

American Educational Research Association/American Psychological Association/National Council on Measurement in Education. (1985). *Standards for educational and psychological testing.* Washington, DC: American Psychological Association.

American Psychiatric Association. (1988). *Diagnostic and statistical manual of mental disorders* (3rd ed., rev.). Washington, DC: Author.

American Psychological Association. (1981a). Ethical principles for psychologists. *American Psychologist, 36,* 633–638.

American Psychological Association. (1981b). Specialty guidelines for the delivery of services by school psychologists. *American Psychologist, 36,* 670–681.

American Psychological Association. (1986). *Guidelines for computer-based tests and interpretations.* Washington, DC: Author.

American Psychological Association. (1990). Ethical principles for psychologists. *American Psychologist, 45*(3), 390–395.

Anastasi, A. (1988). *Psychological testing* (6th ed.). New York: Macmillan.

Arbuckle, D. S. (1965). *Counseling: Philosophy, theory, and practice.* Boston: Allyn and Bacon.

Beller, E. K. (1962). *Clinical process: The assessment of data in childhood personality disorders.* New York: Free Press.

Bergan, J. R. (1977). *Behavioral consultation.* Columbus, OH: Merrill.

Bergan, J. R. (1988). Diagnosis of diagnosis diagnosed. *Professional School Psychology, 3*(2), 135–140.

Bersoff, D. N. (1983). *A rationale and proposal regarding standards for the administration and interpretation of computerized psychological testing.* Report prepared for Psych Systems, Inc., Baltimore, MD.

Brantley, J. C. (1984). Computers and school psychology training. *School Psychology Review, 13*(4), 449–454.

Brown, D. T. (1984). Automated assessment systems in school and clinical psychology: Present status and future directions. *School Psychology Review, 13*(4), 455–460.

Burke, M. J., & Normand, J. (1987). Computerized psychological testing: Overview and critique. *Professional Psychology, 18,* 42–51.

Buros, O. K. (Ed.). (1978). *The eighth mental measurements yearbook.* Lincoln, NE: Buros Institute of Mental Measurements.

Cohen, R. J., Montague, P., Nathanson, L. S., & Swerdlik, M. E. (1988). *Psychological testing: An introduction to tests & measurements.* Mountain View, CA: Mayfield.

Conoley, J. C., & Kramer, J. C. (Eds.). (1989). *The tenth mental measurements yearbook.* Lincoln, NE: Buros Institute of Mental Measurements.

Conoley, J. C., Kramer, J. J., & Mitchell, J. V. (Eds.). (1988). *The supplement to the ninth mental measurements yearbook.* Lincoln, NE: Buros Institute of Mental Measurements.

Crespi, T. D. (1990). School psychologists in forensic psychology: Converging and diverging issues. *Professional Psychology, 21*(2), 83–87.

Frank, G. (1975). *Psychiatric diagnosis: A review of research.* New York: Pergamon.

Fremer, J., Diamond, E. E., & Camara, W. J. (1989). Developing a code of fair testing practices in education. *American Psychologist, 44*(7), 1062–1067.

Grisso, T. (1987). The economic and scientific future of forensic psychological assessment. *American Psychologist, 42*(9), 831–839.

Gutkin, T. B., & Curtis, M. J. (1982). School-based consultation: Theory and techniques. In C. R. Reynolds & T. B. Gutkin (Eds.), *The handbook of school psychology* (pp. 519–561). New York: Wiley.

Hamersma, R. J. (1972). *Educational and psychological tests and measures.* Dubuque, IA: Kendall/Hunt.

Haugaard, J. J. (1988). Judicial determination of children's competency to testify: Should it be abandoned? *Professional Psychology, 19*(1), 102–107.

Kessler, J. W. (1988). *Psychopathology of childhood* (2nd ed.). Englewood Cliffs, NJ: Prentice Hall.

Kleinmuntz, B. (1982). *Personality and psychological assessment.* New York: St. Martin's Press.

Kramer, J. J., & Conoley, J. C. (Eds.). (1990). *The supplement to the tenth mental measurements yearbook.* Lincoln, NE: Buros Institute of Mental Measurements.

Maloney, M. P., & Ward, M. P. (1976). *Psychological assessment: A conceptual approach.* New York: Oxford University Press.

Martin, R. P. (1988). *Assessment of personality and behavior problems: Infancy through adolescence.* New York: Guilford.

McCullough, C. S., & Wenck, L. S. (1984). Current microcomputer applications in school psychology. *School Psychology Review, 13*(4), 429–439.

McDermott, P. A. (1988). Agreement among diagnosticians or observers: Its importance and determination. *Professional School Psychology, 3*(4), 225–240.

Melton, G. B., Petrila, J., Poythress, N. G., & Slobogin, C. (1987). *Psychological evaluations for the courts.* New York: Guilford.

Meyers, J. (1988). Diagnosis diagnosed: Twenty years later. *Professional School Psychology, 3*(2), 123–134.

Miller, L. S., Bergstrom, D. A., Cross, H. J., & Grube, J. W. (1981). Opinions and use of the DSM system by practicing psychologists. *Professional Psychology, 12,* 385–390.

Mitchell, J. V. (Ed.). (1983). *Tests in print III.* Lincoln, NE: Buros Institute of Mental Measurements.

Mitchell, J. V. (Ed.). (1985). *The ninth mental measurements yearbook.* Lincoln, NE: Buros Institute of Mental Measurements.

Moursund, D. (1984). Microcomputer technical overview. *School Psychology Review, 13*(4), 440–448.

National Association of School Psychologists. (1984). Standards for the provision of school psychological services. In *Professional conduct manual* (pp. 19–33). Washington, DC: Author.

National Center for Health Statistics. (1985). *Advance report of final divorce statistics, 33,* 11. DHHS Publication No. PHS 85-1120. Washington, DC: United States Department of Health and Human Services.

Niehaus, R. J. (1979). *Computer-assisted human resources planning.* New York: Wiley.

Ostrom, N. N., & Jenson, W. R. (1988). Assessment of attention deficits in children. *Professional School Psychology 3*(4), 253–259.

Ownby, R. L. (1987). *Psychological reports: A guide to report writing in professional psychology.* Brandon, VT: Clinical Psychology Publishing.

Papert, S. (1984). New theories for new learnings. *School Psychology Review, 13*(4), 422–428.

Phillips, B. N. (1989). Role of the practitioner in applying science to practice. *Professional Psychology 20*(1), 3–8.

Robins, L. N., & Helzer, J. E. (1986). Diagnosis and clinical assessment: The current state of psychiatric diagnosis. *Annual Review of Psychology, 37,* 409–432.

Rogers, R. (1987). Ethical dilemmas in forensic evaluations. *Behavioral Sciences & the Law, 5*(2), 149–160.

Salvia, J., & Yssseldyke, J. E. (1988). *Assessment in special and remedial education* (4th ed.). Boston: Houghton Mifflin.

Sampson, J. P., Jr., & Pyle, K. R. (1988). Ethical issues involved with the use of computer-assisted counseling, testing, and guidance system. In W. C. Huey & T. P. Remley, Jr. (Eds.), *Ethical & legal issues in school counseling* (pp. 249–261). Alexandria, VA: American School Counselor Association.

Sattler, J. M. (1982). *Assessment of children's intelligence and special abilities* (2nd ed.). Boston: Allyn and Bacon.

Sattler, J. M. (1988). *Assessment of children* (3rd ed.). San Diego: Author.

Shectman, F. (1973). On being misinformed by misleading arguments. *Bulletin of the Menninger Clinic, 37,* 523–525.

Shevrin, H., & Shectman, F. (1973). The diagnostic process in psychiatric evaluations. *Bulletin of the Menninger Clinic, 37,* 451–494.

Slater, B. (1988). School psychologists and abused children. *School Psychologist 42*(5), 1 & 3–4.

Slovenko, R. (1973). *Psychiatry and law.* Boston: Little, Brown.

Thorne, F. C. (1961). *Clinical judgment: A study of clinical error.* Brandon, VT: Journal of Clinical Psychology.

Weithorn, L. A. (Ed.). (1987). *Psychology and child custody determinations.* Lincoln, NE: University of Nebraska Press.

Wilson, C. A., & Gettinger, M. (1989). Determinants of child-abuse reporting among Wisconsin school psychologists. *Professional School Psychology 4*(2), 91–102.

Woody, R. H. (1969). *Behavior problem children in the schools: Recognition, diagnosis, and behavioral modification.* New York: Appleton-Century-Crofts.

Woody, R. H. (1977). Behavioral science criteria in child custody determinations. *Journal of Marriage and Family Counseling 3*(1), 11–18.

Woody, R. H. (1978). *Getting custody: Winning the last battle of the marital war.* New York: Macmillan.

Woody, R. H., & Mitchell, R. E. (1984). Understanding the legal system and legal research. In R. H. Woody (Ed.), *The law and the practice of human services* (pp. 1–38). San Francisco: Jossey-Bass.

Woody, R. H., & Robertson, M. (1988). *Becoming a clinical psychologist.* Madison, CT: International Universities Press.

Ziskin, J., & Faust, D. (1989). Psychiatric and psychological evidence in child custody cases. *Trial, 25*(8), 44–49.

CHAPTER 9

PSYCHOEDUCATIONAL ASSESSMENT II: METHODS AND INSTRUMENTS

The preceding chapter discussed principles and issues important to psychoeducational assessment. In continuing the coverage of psychoeducational assessment, this chapter provides an overview of methods and instruments. For the beginning student, this information will be an orientation to alternatives for data collection. For the advanced student or practitioner in the field, this information will be an update. For all readers, the information will place psychoeducational assessment methods and instruments in the developmental and social systems framework.

A *method* is a means for collecting assessment information according to a system, strategy, or technique that is based on behavioral science, but may be lacking in psychometric properties. Information from an assessment method may or may not produce quantifiable data; some of the information may be impressionistic and thus be highly subjective in interpretation. An *instrument* is a technique or test that, presumably, meets psychometric standards, such as those promulgated by AERA/APA/NCME (1985).

No single psychological test is adequate for a comprehensive psychoeducational assessment. Several instruments should comprise a *battery* of tests, which will accommodate differential diagnosis (that is, considering, weighing, weeding out, and settling on alternative interpretations and conclusions according to the information and data unique to the client). Rapaport, Gill, and Schafer (1968) describe the benefits of a battery of tests:

> The advantages of such a battery of tests are that indicators that for some reason are absent from one or several of the tests are likely to present in others; that indicators in the different tests are likely to present in others; that indicators in the different tests are likely to support and supplement each other; and that the presence of indicators in some of the tests may call attention to more subtle indicators in others which might otherwise be overlooked. (p. 48)

There is no one prescribed or preferred battery of tests for any purpose or type of client. Comprehensive psychoeducational assessment typically requires selecting methods according to the unique needs of the client and collecting data by means other than tests per se.

In considering the construction of a psychoeducational assessment battery, it is useful to look to statements from the profession. In the NASP (1984a) "Principles for Professional Ethics," it is stated (Section IV, B):

> School psychologists strive to maintain the highest standard of service by an objective collecting of appropriate data and information necessary to effectively work with students. In conducting a psychoeducational evaluation or counseling/consultation services, due consideration is given to individual integrity and individual differences. School psychologists recognize differences in age, sex, socioeconomic and ethnic backgrounds and strive to select and use appropriate procedures, techniques and strategies relevant to such differences. (p. 8)
> School psychologists combine observations, background information, multi-disciplinary results and other pertinent data to present the most comprehensive and valid picture possible of the student. (p. 8)

In the NASP (1984b) "Standards for the Provision of School Psychological Services," it is stated:

> 4.3.2.1 School psychologists conduct multifactored psychological and psychoeducational assessments of children and youth as appropriate. (p. 30)
>
> 4.3.2.2 Psychological and psychoeducational assessments include consideration as appropriate of the areas of personal-social adjustment, intelligence-scholastic aptitude, adaptive behavior, language and communication skills, academic achievement, sensory and perceptual-motor functioning, environmental-cultural influences, and vocational development, aptitude, and interests. (p. 31)
>
> 4.3.2.3 School psychologists utilize formal instruments, procedures, and techniques. Interviews, observations, and behavioral evaluations are included in these procedures. (p. 31)

From these statements, it is obvious that psychoeducational assessment relies on both methods and instruments, and that there is great latitude for individual preferences held and judgments made by the school psychologist to emerge in the selection and usage.

PREFERENCES BY SCHOOL PSYCHOLOGISTS

Guidance for selection of psychoeducational assessment methods and instruments may be gained from the opinions held by school psychologists. In a survey of school psychology practitioners, Reschly, Genshaft, and Binder (1987) indicated importance for (not in any rank order): adaptive behavior measures; ability/intelligence instruments; achievement screening and diagnostic instruments; projective methods and figure drawings and objective and behavior checklists/rating scales for personality or social-emotional appraisal; perceptual/motor instruments; and informal measures (e.g., structured and unstructured interviews, structured [behavioral] and unstructured [anecdotal] classroom observation); and there were various other batteries and miscellaneous assessment procedures.

The rank order for methods and instruments were: (1) the Wechsler Intelligence scales; (2) unstructured interviewing; (3) the Bender Visual-Motor Gestalt Test (BVMGT); (4) the Draw-A-Person (DAP) Test; (5) unstructured classroom observation; (6) the Wide Range Achievement Test-Revised (WRAT-R); (7) structured classroom observation (behavioral); (8) the Woodcock-Johnson Achievement Test; (9) the House-Tree-Person (HTP) Test; and (10) kinetic family drawings.

When a referral has a specialized focus, it is logical that the assessment battery will be tailored accordingly. At the same time, there are many referral problems that require a foundation of general assessment before the specialized assessment can be meaningfully accomplished. For example, while an assessment may focus on, say, achievement difficulties or emotional-behavioral issues, it will still be essential and necessary to have information about the child's developmental, family, and social history and data about his or her intellectual and/or perceptual (and other) qualities.

When assessing hyperactive children, Rosenberg and Beck (1986) found that clinical child psychologists and school psychologists "appear to rely on a standard battery approach (interviews, behavioral observations, IQ tests, and projective tests" (p. 146). The school psychologists' rank order of methods and instruments included: (1) interviews, (2) behavioral observations, (3) IQ or achievement tests, (4) drawing tests, (5) rating scales, (6) projective tests, (7) neuropsychological tests, and (8) tests for attention and impulsivity.

Prout (1983) surveyed practicing school psychologists and found that the reported utilization of assessment approaches for social-emotional assessment were (in rank order): (1) behavioral observation, (2) clinical interview, (3) projective personality tests, (4) behavior rating scales, and (5) objective personality tests. As for frequency of use, the rankings were: (1) clinical interview; (2) informal classroom observation; (3) human figure drawings; (4) BVMGT (for emotional indicators); (5) incomplete sentence blank; (6)

structured classroom observation; (7) House-Tree-Person; (8) clinical analysis of intelligence test responses; (9) behavior rating scales; (10) kinetic family drawings; (11) Thematic Apperception Test (TAT); (12) Children's Apperception Test (CAT); (13) Rorschach ink-blots method; and (14) the Minnesota Multiphasic Personality Inventory (MMPI)—and there were others of lesser usage.

In conducting reading assessment, Fish and Margolis (1988) found that school psychologists reported that 77 percent of referrals involved reading problems (yet they had received limited training in reading). Their rank ordering of frequency of use of reading diagnostic procedures included: (1) tests of perception (e.g., visual, auditory); (2) individually administered norm-referenced tests; (3) classroom observations of the child's reading behavior; (4) criterion-referenced reading tests; and (5) diagnostic teaching of a lesson (trial learning lesson).

As a final point for the development of a psychoeducational assessment battery, the reason for the referral for school psychological services should be considered. Harris, Gray, Rees-McGee, Carroll, and Zaremba (1987) surveyed school psychologists serving public elementary and secondary schools, and found that "poor academic performance was of primary concern in 52% of referrals and social/emotional problems in 31%" (p. 343). Poor academics include the following: lacks prerequisite skills or abilities; lacks motivation; lacks motivation and prerequisite skills or abilities; and causal factors unclear. Social/emotional difficulties include social deficits (shy, overanxious, inhibited); social excesses (aggressive, defiant, disruptive); and bizarre or unusual behavior.

This chapter will not provide an exhaustive coverage of psychoeducational assessment methods and instruments. Instead, this chapter will cover record analysis and interviewing, behavior rating scales, intelligence tests, achievement tests, perceptual tests, human figure drawings, personality or social/emotional methods, neuropsychological tests, family evaluation, and the psychoeducational assessment report. (*Note:* Although this chapter limitedly covers informal and formal classroom observations and the assessment of infants and toddlers, these topics are dealt with at various points in this book.)

RECORD ANALYSIS AND INTERVIEWING

The assessment of a child's development requires information from collaterals (e.g., parents, teachers, health-care providers), and the assessment of social systems requires information that often defies quantification. Consequently, record analysis and interviewing of collaterals and the child are relied on for assessment. Observation of the child is also important. These informational sources contribute diagnostic and prescriptive ideas.

Before direct contact with anyone, the school psychologist will usually have educational, psychological, and medical records available. The school's cumulative record gives a longitudinal account of the child's school activities. School records are seldom enough for background information, and must be supplemented by obtaining other records and, of course, conducting interviews. Once the records have been obtained, the documents can be analyzed for:

1. An understanding of the influences (positive and negative) in the client's psychological makeup;
2. Identifying any special considerations;
3. Evaluating the findings of other assessment data sources;
4. Weighing the efficacy of past interventions (i.e., how successful or unsuccessful they have been); and
5. Formulating a psychodiagnostic preface for the client that will allow subsequent assessment strategies and other interventions to be optimally beneficial and efficient. (Woody & Robertson, 1988, p. 240)

If the records are meager and information scarce, the school psychologist may create new background records, such as by asking teachers to prepare statements about particular issues. It is common practice to have a so-called life history questionnaire available, individually tailored to the emphases and preferences of the program. The questionnaire can be mailed or given to, say, the parent(s), and returned to the school psychologist with the completed information; or the form may be used in a structured interview format (to be discussed shortly), with the parent(s) or multiple sources providing the information. In some ways, a life history questionnaire has kinship to a behavior rating or adaptive behavior scale (or checklist) completed by the parent or other responsible informant; each of these methods depends on impressions and reports from third parties.

The information gleaned from records should be accepted with reservations. Certain point-in-time reports may have little or no relevance for the present, whereas others may merit detailed and weighty consideration. In any case, the school psychologist must always recall that record analysis is highly subjective.

Regardless of format or context, interviewing is intended to accomplish more than information or data collection. Interviewing is important for rapport building; that is, engendering trust and opening communication channels. Relying on counseling strategies, the school psychologist purposefully seeks to promote "facilitative conditions," those interpersonal qualities that lead to openness, richness, and productivity. When the school psychologist speaks in an interview, there should be

> *owning of feeling* (identifying and disclosing their reactions to themselves and others), *commitment to change* (resolving to work at maintaining and improving communication), *differentiation of stimuli* (identifying and discriminating between various sources of affect and anxiety and the corresponding reactions they stimulate), and *internalization* (immediate awareness of their actions and feelings, with appropriate recognition of the effects and impacts of their behaviors).

And when the school psychologist listens to the child, parent, teacher, or whomever, there should be

> *empathic understanding* (responding clearly and directly to the speaker so as to demonstrate hearing and understanding of what the speaker is saying), *concreteness* (responding so as to aid speakers in identifying and discussing their most relevant concerns), *genuineness* (demonstrating spontaneous and congruent reactions in a constructive manner), *respect* (the communication of regard and caring for the speaker's worth as a person), *confrontation* (constructively confronting the speaker with inconsistencies or conflicts which the listener experiences in the interaction), and *immediacy* (the expression of an awareness of dynamics between speaker and listener at any point in the relationship). (Schauble, 1980, pp. 1035–1036)

Clearly the school psychologist's personal qualities will govern the success or failure of creating facilitative conditions in an interview or any other type of relationship situation. Consequently, an essential and necessary part of professional school psychology training involves development of facilitative skills and qualities.

Interviews may be *structured* to assure the gathering of information about specific topics. Although similar to a life history questionnaire in terms of targeting informational areas, an interview is distinguished by involving a direct encounter between the interviewer (the school psychologist) and the interviewee (the child, parent, teacher, administrator, etc.).

The direct contact will commonly be in person, but it might also be by telephone interview. An *unstructured* interview involves direct contact, but no preplanned areas to explore. Rather, the interviewer follows the leads of the interviewee, perhaps giving some direction to the interaction via making interpretations, probes, or queries due to what was said by the interviewee. In all interviews, professional standards require carefully recording the information.

There is no preordained set of areas that must or should be explored in interviews. An often-quoted set of categories is by Sundberg (1977) includes identifying data, reason for coming, present situation, family constellation, early recollections, birth and development, health, education and training, work record, recreation and interests, sexual development, marital and family data, self-description, choices and turning points in life, views of the future, and any further material.

Obviously the nature of the referral or the reason for seeking the intervention of a school psychologist will cast a framework around each interview. For example, Wise (1989) suggests that a parent interview should cover health history/developmental history, family background and status, and parental attitudes. Wise gives suggested topics for each of these areas, but the specific elements of each area will always be subject to the particular child and the professional set of the school psychologist. The classic text on clinical interviewing is by Harry Stack Sullivan (1954), and additional information on the essentials of interviewing may be found in Houck and Hansen (1972) and Kleinmuntz (1982).

Holding interviews with parents of children who are potentially handicapped or exceptional can bring on a problematic aura. These parents may be especially sensitive to nuances, and communications must be carefully formulated to be effective and helpful. Relevant to parent interviews about psychoeducational assessment, Sattler (1982) provides seven guidelines for interviewing the parents of exceptional/handicapped children (see also Sattler, 1988). Although Sattler does not identify it as such, his four-stage approach has striking parallels to the approach endorsed by Harry Stack Sullivan. Like Sattler, Sullivan (1954) conceptualizes the clinical interview into four stages: the *formal inception* (exchange of preliminary information); the *reconnaissance* (survey of contributing factors and tentative formulations about interventions); the *detailed inquiry* (interpersonal data analysis and validation of impressions); and the *termination* (explicit statements about interventions).

The rapport-building function of interviewing can have a marked impact on the child's and the parents' cooperation with the intervention, thereby enhancing the efficacy of the interven-

tion. For psychoeducational assessment purposes, the information obtained through interviews will not be conclusive, but it will certainly be complementary to other information and data sources. The record analysis and interviewing will be helpful for determining what should be included in the psychoeducational assessment (e.g., what tests should constitute the battery).

BEHAVIOR RATING SCALES

The classroom teacher is usually the source of a child's being referred to a school psychologist. Commonly the teacher completes a form that describes the reasons for the referral. Many school psychologists self-create a referral form (which must, of course, be approved by appropriate administrative sources), including items that ask teachers or parents to rate the presence (and possibly the frequency) of particular desirable or undesirable behaviors. Adjectives describing the child's behavior may be used. Behavior rating scales and checklists usually produce nominal or ordinal data, and have limited utility for psychometric purposes. Most behavior rating scales lack standardization and can be considered, at most, opinion or anecdotal information but not psychometric data. Although behavior rating scales and checklists are useful, their information must be cautiously considered. Nonetheless, opinions by a teacher or parent about a child's behavior are rich in assessment potential.

Self-created behavior rating scales or checklists abound, but there are also behavior rating scales that have some degree of standardization. Perhaps of most importance to school psychology, the Achenbach Child Behavior Checklist (ACBCL; Achenback & Edelbrock, 1983) can be used for children 4 through 16 years of age and involves a parent's rating social competence (activities, social participation, and school performance) and behavior problems (internalizing, externalizing, and mixed patterns). There are specific syndromes under each major heading, which vary with the age and sex of the child. The syndromes are rather clinical in nature (e.g., schizoid or anxious, depressed, uncommunicative, obsessive-compulsive, hyperactive, aggressive, delinquent, sex problems, cruel, and others).

Considerable research has been done on the ACBCL, which leads Martin (1988) to state, "From several points of view, the ACBCL is the most sophisticated parent rating questionnaire now available for assessment of pathology and social competence in children" (p. 199), and "The normative data provided for the scale are impressive" (p. 199).

Martin (1988) reviews numerous behavior rating scales and checklists that deserve use in psychoeducational assessment, but the fact remains that these methods are complementary to other assessment methods and instruments. They can, however, make an important contribution to virtually any psychoeducational assessment battery.

INTELLIGENCE TESTS

If there is a birthright for school psychology, it is the use of intelligence tests. Early on, school psychologists were asked to assess "feeblemindedness" and to identify children "afflicted" with mental deficiency. With a move toward normalization, nomenclature changed to "mental retardation" and then "mental handicap." Intellectual impairments troubled school administrators and teachers. They rationalized that the "backwards child," one with below-average intelligence compared to his or her age group, would hamper the learning efforts of other children. There were also discriminatory stereotypes, such as the mentally handicapped child's being prone to violence or disruptive behavior.

Of course a pragmatic motive for educators was that the special needs of the mentally handicapped child necessitated teaching skills and methods different from what was used with "normal" children; the requirement for additional competency and effort may have led some educators, consciously or unconsciously, to search for ways to relegate the mentally handicapped child

to a special education classroom, removed from the regular classroom. This sort of attitudinal set was so pronounced that it required federal and state legislation to regulate assessment and placement practices, such as the present mandate for mainstreaming to promote "normalization."

As the years passed, the use of intelligence tests became widespread. Today, virtually every child, mentally handicapped or otherwise, is expected to provide the school system with test data related to intelligence. Unfortunately, there is still abuse of intelligence test scores, as evidenced by the case of *Larry P.* v. *Riles* (283 F.Supp. 1306, 1972). *Larry P.* found that black students constituted a disproportionately large segment of the students in classes for the mentally retarded, which established a racial imbalance. (This case is discussed in more detail in Chapter 12.) The potential for abuse through intelligence testing has created much controversy, and legislatures and professional associations have joined forces to assure appropriate standards.

Throughout the history of school psychology, there has been a demand for intellectual assessment data for purposes of categorizing or classification. Most prominent has been the school psychologist's duty to certify that a particular child is eligible for, say, special education. Since federal and state funds commonly go to the local school system to provide special support for programs for handicapped children, there is a criterion that a qualified school psychologist must qualify the child by an educational certification test. An *educational certification test* may, however, be other than an intelligence test per se (e.g., an achievement test), and may be used for all sorts of classification purposes:

> "Educational certification test" is a generic term that applies to many different uses of test results and perhaps obscures the considerable diversity among programs. Students' scores on educational certification tests are used either alone or in conjunction with other criteria to make decisions concerning high school graduation or grade-to-grade promotion, to classify students for remediation, to evaluate the effectiveness of schools, to classify or

certify school districts, to allocate compensatory funds or other resources to districts, and to evaluate teachers. (AERA/APA/NCME, 1985, p. 49)

Although classification is and probably always will be an inextricable component of the accountability demanded of the educational system by public policy and laws, it behooves the school psychologist to assure that all test data are used appropriately.

Even back in the nineteenth century, a version of intelligence testing was being done in the form of measurement of sensory abilities and reaction time. These laboratory studies were noticed by professionals with clinical interests and responsibilities,and practical applications began. Alfred Binet (1857–1911), a French pediatrician, is credited as being the father of intelligence testing. From his articles (about 1895) on memory and social comprehension, Binet collaborated with Theodore Simon to create a 30-item scale of intelligence to identify mentally retarded Paris school children (Binet & Simon, 1905).

Cohen, Montague, Nathanson, and Swerdlik (1988) say, "A historically significant innovation was the grouping of items by the age when the majority of children of a given age in the standardization sample could pass the item" (p. 204). After several revisions, which eventuated in an "age scale" from 3 years to the adult level, translations and adaptions proliferated, with Lewis Madison Terman (1916) providing the first American revision. Since Terman's research was conducted at Stanford University, the test was named the Stanford-Binet, and its current progeny, the fourth edition (Thorndike, Hagen, & Sattler, 1986a, 1986b), remains a major intelligence test.

To capture the importance of the Binet-related work, Pintner (1931) credits the Binet scale with being one of the most potent factors in the development and expansion of clinical psychology, noting that the scale moved from institutions for the feebleminded to juvenile courts, reformatories, prisons, children's homes, and schools. Certainly school psychology was propelled for-

ward by professional and public acceptance of the Binet scales.

An early popular concept for intelligence testing was *mental age*. This concept refers to estimating the developmental age to which a person's intellectual capabilities are most closely related. Cohen and colleagues (1988) trace references to mental age, such as in psychiatric testimony and psychological classifications of idiocy, to as early as 1838:

> The first use of the mental-age concept in a test was in 1877 when S. E. Chaille published an infant test in the *New Orleans Medical and Surgical Journal*. This infant test included items arranged according to age level. The assignment of particular age levels was made by determining the levels at which the tests were commonly passed. It was Alfred Binet, however who refined the mental age concept—first referring to it as "mental level"—made it more concrete in definition, and popularized it. (p. 206)

The mental age concept was integral to early American intelligence tests, particularly the Stanford-Binet series.

The *intelligence quotient* (IQ) emerged from the Binet scales. It is basically a computation that depends on the relationship between the client's chronological age and mental age. The concept of an intelligence quotient was formulated by Wilhelm Stern (1914), with the point being that the ratio between chronological age and mental age was an index of intellectual functioning. Aiken (1988) describes it:

> An examinee's mental age (MA) and intelligence quotient on the Stanford-Binet depended on the number of subtests passed at successive age levels. The IQ was determined from the ratio of the examinee's mental age (MA)—the total number of months credit earned on the test—to his or her chronological age (CA) in months, multiplied by 100 to get rid of the decimal. (p. 157)

The intelligence quotient has prevailed. In addition to heavy reliance from untolled sources and for countless assessment reasons, the IQ has been used as a statistical point of reference, such as for validating other instruments. Since it is a crude index, the IQ can mask many nuances of mental ability, and must be guardedly and knowledgeably used in statistical analyses.

The Stanford-Binet Intelligence Scale

To acquire adequate understanding of the Stanford-Binet, it is necessary to study the evolution of the various versions. By recognizing the similarities and differences between the versions, the school psychologist can more fully appreciate the nature of intelligence, and the theories, research, and public policy changes that have led to today's acceptance of intelligence testing in general and the Stanford-Binet in particular. An in-depth study of the evolution and development belongs in a specialized course on individual testing; therefore, this section is restricted, generally, to the most recent version (the fourth edition) of the Stanford-Binet Intelligence Scale (Thorndike, Hagen, & Sattler, 1986a, 1986b).

The Stanford-Binet IV must be individually administered. It is considered to be a norm-referenced measure of general intelligence for persons between the ages of 2 and 23. Despite its evolutionary reliance on the concept of mental age, the Stanford-Binet IV eliminates age scores:

> Raw scores for each subtest are converted to Standard Age Scores (SAS). These scores have a mean of 50 and a standard deviation of 8. Subtest scores are combined into area scores and an overall composite score, each with a mean of 100 and a standard deviation of 16. (Salvia & Ysseldyke, 1988, p. 163)

The manual contains many tables to facilitate scoring and interpretation. (*Note:* As with most psychological tests, the manual is an essential ingredient in testing, regardless of how many times the same test has previously been administered and interpreted.) Fifteen subtests are grouped into four areas. *Verbal Reasoning* is comprised of the Vocabulary, Comprehension, Absurdities, and Verbal Relations subtest. *Quantitative Reasoning* consists of subtests titled Quantitative, Number Series, and Equation Building. *Abstract/ Visual Reasoning* has three subtests: Copying, Matrices, and Paper Folding and Cutting. Finally, *Short-Term Memory* contains Bead Memory, Memory for Sentences, Memory for Digits, and Memory for Objects. The titles of each subtest reveals a global definition of its purpose or mental ability.

The Stanford-Binet IV is predicated on a three-level hierarchical theoretical model:

> The model consists of a general intelligence factor (g) at the first level, three broad factors (crystallized abilities, fluid-analytic abilities, and short-term memory) at the second level, and three factors (verbal reasoning, quantitative reasoning, and abstract-visual reasoning) at the third level. The verbal and quantitative reasoning factors at the third level make up the crystallized abilities factor at the second level, and the abstract-visual factor at the third level makes up the fluid-analytic abilities factor at the second level. (Aiken, 1988, p. 159)

In her review, Anastasi (1989) cites respectable reliability and validity, but noted, "In general, all reliabilities tended to be slightly higher at the upper age levels" (p. 772). She concludes, "This basic restructuring of a well-established clinical instrument shows a high level of technical quality in its test construction procedures" (p. 772).

In his review, Cronbach (1989) considers the Stanford-Binet IV and comments, "My impression is that SB4 is less game-like than some other individual tests and will be less attractive to children" (p. 773). He is critical of the norming plan, such as using only children whose parents responded to a request to participate, which resulted in "Parents from high occupational and educational strata responded more often and are overrepresented" (p. 774). Overall, Cronbach questions the Stanford-Binet IV as being the "instrument of choice at early ages" (p. 775).

Psychometric properties aside, a substantial

benefit comes from the school psychologist's being able to make a profile analysis of the Stanford-Binet IV results. That is, early versions of the Stanford-Binet yielded an intelligence quotient, a mental age, and scores for the number of months of credit earned at different age levels. The Stanford-Binet IV, much like the Wechsler intelligence tests, now provides a profile of subtest and area scores. Granted, the newness of this version leaves the school psychologist with a void in research and reported experiences to facilitate astute profile analyses and interpretations, but a remedy should come with time.

The Wechsler Intelligence Tests

David Wechsler created the intelligence tests most used by psychologists in general and school psychologists in specific. In 1939, Wechsler published his first adult intelligence test, called the Wechsler Bellevue Intelligence Scale (WBIS), and in 1955, published a revised version, called the Wechsler Adult Intelligence Scale (WAIS); to complete its evolution, he published the Wechsler Adult Intelligence Scale-Revised (WAIS-R, 1981). He has also developed the Wechsler Intelligence Scale for Children-Revised (WISC-R, 1974) and Third Edition (WISC-III, 1991), and the Wechsler Preschool and Primary Scale of Intelligence (WPPSI, 1967), followed by the WPPSI-Revised (WPPSI-R, 1989).

Perhaps a paradoxical tribute to his genius, Wechsler developed his tests without a clear-cut theory of intelligence. Apparently Wechsler relied on logical reasoning, based on his clinical experience and interpretation of others' writings, and set out to construct a set of subtests that would measure what he considered to be intelligence. Of note, through the years, statistical analyses give support to Wechsler's composite of items and subtests (Kaufman, 1979; Sattler, 1982, 1988). Wechsler (1958) said, "Intelligence, operationally defined, is the aggregate or global capacity of the individual to act purposefully, to think rationally and to deal effectively with his environment" (p. 7). Later, Wechsler (1975) said,

What we measure with tests is not what tests measure—not information, not spatial perception, not reasoning ability. These are only means to an end. What intelligence tests measure, what we hope they measure, is something much more important: the capacity of an individual to understand the world about him and his resourcefulness to cope with its challenges. (p. 139)

In the WAIS-R *Manual,* Wechsler (1981) states,

Intelligence is multifaceted as well as multi-determined. What it always calls for is not a particular ability but an overall competency or global capacity, which in one way or another enables a sentient individual to comprehend the world and to deal effectively with its challenges. Intelligence is a function of the personality as a whole and is responsive to other factors besides those included under the concept of cognitive abilities. (p. 8)

Like the Stanford-Binet, the Wechsler tests must be individually administered. Unlike the Stanford-Binet, the Wechsler tests are point scales, meaning a certain number of points are earned by successfully answering a question or responding to a task, and these points are totaled to determine a raw score for a particular subtest. All three Wechsler tests have various subtests that are assigned to either a Verbal Scale or a Performance Scale; provide subtest scale scores for interpretation of individual mental abilities or profile analysis; and yield a Verbal Scale IQ, a Performance Scale IQ, and a Full Scale IQ.

The Wechsler Adult Intelligence Scale-Revised

The WAIS-R (Wechsler, 1981) is applicable to persons 16 years of age or older; the test was normed on subjects from 16 to 74 years, but it is generally accepted that older clients can be assessed as well. The mental abilities profile, composed of 11 subtests, goes beyond a global intelligence measure to specific intellectual strengths and weaknesses, cerebral dysfunction (Fogel, 1964; Wilson, Rosenbaum, Brown,

Rourke, Whitman, & Grisell, 1978), and emotional problems (Anastasi, 1988; Gregory, 1987).

The WAIS-R Verbal Scale includes the Information, Digit Span, Vocabulary, Arithmetic, Comprehension, and Similarities subtests. *Information* estimates general academic knowledge by questions of fact (e.g., social studies, geography, history). *Digit Span* involves the client's ability to recall orally presented serial numbers, and repeat them forward and backward, which taps concentration, immediate memory, and recall. *Vocabulary,* a set of words that must be defined, is considered to be the best subtest measure of general intelligence, and is connected to academic achievement. *Arithmetic* is an academic measure of ability or computation (addition, subtraction, division, multiplication, etc.). The nature of the subtest (e.g., being timed) brings in auditory concentration and freedom from distractibility.

Comprehension presents questions that reach the client's knowledge and acceptance of social and cultural convention, that is, social logical reasoning and judgment in problem-solving situations. The client must explain what he or she would do, make a conceptual analysis, and derive common sense solutions. *Similarities* consist of analogies, for which the client must distinguish essential from nonessential elements. The results rely on general intelligence and require verbal abstract reasoning. Thought disorders may be revealed.

The WAIS-R Performance Scale consists of the Picture Completion, Picture Arrangement, Block Design, Object Assembly, and Digit Symbol subtests. *Picture Completion* requires detecting parts missing in pictures of objects, people, or scenes. It measures the client's ability to differentiate essential from nonessential details, concentration, reasoning, attention to the environment, and remote memory. *Picture Arrangement* involves the task of correctly ordering pictures to form a story, a kind of planning ability that is related to social intelligence. *Block Design* necessitates the client's recreating geometric designs with colored blocks, and involves abstract reasoning, concentration, and problem solving.

Object Assembly has puzzle pieces of common objects that must be assembled, which requires concentration, motor activity, visual perception, and sensory-motor feedback. *Digit Symbol* is a code-substitution test, where a symbol must be associated with a digit, and requires concentration, rapid responding, and fine-motor control. Additional definitions of the subtests are available in Gregory (1987), House and Lewis (1985), and Ogdon (1982).

It should be noted that the foregoing subtests have been presented according to their being part of the Verbal or Performance Scale. In actual assessments, the subtests are not presented to the client in this same order. Further, the descriptions given are for the WAIS-R, but with only minor exceptions, they are applicable to the comparable subtests on the WISC-R and the WPPSI-R. Distinctions for the WISC-R and WPPSI-R will be noted later.

The Wechsler Intelligence Scale for Children-Revised

The WISC-R (Wechsler, 1974) is applicable to children between the ages of 5 years and 15 years and 11 months of age. The Verbal Scale consists of the Information, Comprehension, Similarities, Arithmetic, Vocabulary, and (as a supplemental subtest) Digit Span subtests. The Performance Scale consists of the Picture Completion, Picture Arrangement, Block Design, Object Assembly, Digit Symbol, and (as a supplemental subtest) Mazes subtests.

In 1991, the *Wechsler Intelligence Scale for Children-Third Edition* (WISC-III, 1991) was published; it is too new to critique. Most of the features of the WISC-R are retained, but the WISC-III has up-to-date norms (e.g., minority subjects were added to the standardization; a bias analysis was conducted to protect ethnic minority interests), outdated items are replaced with items with enhanced wording (e.g., ethnicity and gender references are balanced; item bias is minimized), modernized artwork is used, validity data are provided, and certain stimulus materials are different and improved. A computer-based interpretive program is being developed.

The Wechsler Preschool and Primary Scale of Intelligence-Revised

The WPPSI-R (Wechsler, 1989) is applicable to children between 3 and 7 years, 3 months of age. The Verbal Scale consists of the Information, Comprehension, Arithmetic, Vocabulary, Similarities, and (as a supplemental subtest) Sentences subtests. The Performance Scale consists of Object Assembly, Geometric Design, Block Design, Mazes, Picture Completion, and (as a supplemental subtest) Animal Pegs. Telzrow (1989) provides a useful overview, and Salvia and Ysseldyke (1988) describe the subtests.

Summary of the Wechsler Scales

For its respective age group, each Wechsler test has achieved widespread acceptance and is clearly the most preferred intelligence measure. Reliability and validity studies have consistently upheld the tests' psychometric stature. Kaufman (1975) conducted a factor analysis of the WISC-R and found the subtests comprised three factors: *Verbal Comprehension,* consisting of Information, Similarities, Vocabulary, and Comprehension; *Perceptual Organization,* consisting of Picture Completion, Picture Arrangement, Block Design, Object Assembly, and Mazes; and *Freedom from Distractibility,* consisting of Arithmetic, Digit Span, and Coding. Kaufman (1979) states:

> The Verbal Comprehension and Perceptual Organization factors bear a clear resemblance to Wechsler's Verbal and Performance Scales, respectively. Although the correspondence between the factors and scales is not identical, it is close enough to justify assigning a primary role in WISC-R interpretation to the Verbal and Performance IQs and to consider these IQs as good estimates of the child's Verbal Comprehension and Perceptual Organization abilities. As presently defined, the first two factors are in the cognitive domain, whereas the distractibility dimension is in the behavioral or affective domain. (pp. 22–23)

Sattler (1982, 1988) provides an authoritative textbook on the WISC-R and WPPSI, as well as on a wide variety of other topics relevant to the assessment of children's intelligence and special abilities.

Other Intelligence Tests

There are, of course, many intelligence tests besides the Stanford-Binet IV and the Wechsler tests; however, these are the most widely used. Other tests may be preferred because of a client's unique characteristics or the purpose for the assessment. With the psychoeducational assessment of exceptional children, the need to select intelligence tests according to the unique characteristics and purpose would certainly be essential.

Given the Public Law 99-457 mandate to serve toddlers and preschool children, assessment methods have to be selected to accommodate the young age group and the developmental issues that are of concern. The assessment strategies might be other than intelligence tests per se (e.g., developmental scales with parents serving as informants). Even in the tender years, intelligence is of interest. Among many possible methods, the McCarthy Scales of Children's Abilities (McCarthy, 1972) is a standardized approach for measuring cognitive ability of children from 2 1/2 to 8 1/2 years; it provides a general level of intellectual functioning, a General Cognitive Index, and a profile of abilities (18 subtests grouped into one or more of six scales, with profile measures of verbal ability, nonverbal reasoning ability, number aptitude, short-term memory, and coordination, along with other data).

The Bayley Scales of Infant Development (Bayley, 1969) may be used with children from 2 months to 2 1/2 years, with standard scores for a Mental Developmental Index and a Psychomotor Developmental Index; there is also a Behavior Record rating scale. Describing the Mental Scale, Sattler (1982) indicates that it "evaluates a variety of activities and processes including shape discrimination, sustained attention, purposeful manipulation of objects, imitation and comprehension, vocalization, memory, problem solving, and naming objects," while the Motor Scale covers "gross and fine motor abilities, such as sitting, standing, walking, and grasping"; the Infant Behavior Record allows "ratings of social orientation, cooperativeness, fearfulness, tension, general emotional tone, object orientation, goal directedness, attention span, endurance, activity, and reactivity" (p. 253). Danielson, Lynch, Moyano, Johnson, and Bettenburg (1988) describe specialized methods for the assessment of infants and toddlers, as per Public Law 99-457.

There is present interest in *dynamic assessment,* which refers to procedures, not specific tests or instruments, including:

(a) a "test-teach-test" or at least a "teach-test" sequence;
(b) emphasis on assessment of processes of perception, thinking, learning, and problem solving rather than on the products of past opportunities to learn;
(c) teaching/learning of generalizable cognitive processes;
(d) attempts to specify obstacles to more effective learning and performance;
(e) attempts to specify response to teaching of generalizable processes;
(f) attempts to specify conditions that will permit or encourage more effective performance;
(g) attempts to distinguish between performance and potential, or between ignorance and inability. (Haywood, Brown, & Wingenfeld, 1990, p. 411)

The focus is on changing events, with rejection of normative, standardized, or static assessment. Laughon (1990) describes approaches to the dynamic assessment of intelligence, noting potential usefulness with children for whom traditional measures are of limited appropriateness (e.g., due to cultural, language, or sensory barriers). To meet some of the needs served by dynamic assessment, there are also standardized tests that are structured for use with children who need special administrative accommodations, such as those with hearing (Sullivan & Burley,

1990) or visual impairment; see Reynolds and Kamphaus (1990) for a useful handbook on the assessment of intelligence and achievement.

ACHIEVEMENT TESTING

Nothing is more central to the purpose of education than academic achievement. Academic achievement is the learned product of the educational effort. An *achievement test* is "a test that measures the extent to which a person commands a certain body of information or possesses a certain skill, usually in a field where training or instruction has been received" (AERA/APA/NCME, 1985, p. 89). An *aptitude test* estimates future performance and readiness to learn in a particular area: "Aptitude tests sometimes do not differ in form or substance from achievement tests, but may differ in use and interpretation" (AERA/APA/NCME, 1985, p. 89).

Cohen and colleagues (1988) point out,

> The primary difference between tests that are referred to as "achievement tests" and those that are referred to as "aptitude tests" is that aptitude tests tend to focus more on informal learning or life experiences as their subject matter, while achievement tests tend to focus on the learning that has occurred as a result of relatively structured input (p. 470).... Predictions about future learning and behavior can be made from both kinds of tests, though predictions made on the basis of achievement tests are usually limited to the subject matter of the test. (p. 472)

School psychologists in the past tended, it seems, to use brief global measures of key achievement areas, such as reading and arithmetic. To serve as a screening for referral for a more detailed aptitudinal analysis, such as by a reading or learning specialist, the emergence of certain achievement tests have led to keen interest on the part of today's school psychologists.

As was evident from the descriptions of the Wechsler subtests, academic achievement has a definitional connection to intelligence. Consequently, Kaufman (1979), states, "Intelligence tests are good predictors of school achievement, providing one justification for using them in an academic setting" (p. 14). There are, however, many interdependent factors rooted in the child's cultural background, emotional/behavioral composite, and cognitive style that may impact on the connection between intelligence and achievement. In other words, it cannot be automatically assumed that high intelligence means good achievement and low intelligence means bad achievement.

The need to accommodate cultural distinctions has intensified concern about the fairness of all tests, but particularly intelligence and achievement tests. For example, the System of Multicultural Pluralistic Assessment (SOMPA; Mercer, 1979) purports to incorporate medical, social, and pluralistic information for the assessment of cognitive, perceptual-motor, and adaptive behavior of black, white, and Hispanic children (ages 5 years through 11 years and 11 months): "On the basis of information obtained from the varoius assessments a child's Estimated Learning Potential (ELP), which takes family background, socioeconomic status and other cultural factors into account, is determined" (Aiken, 1988, p. 162).

Although SOMPA is well intentioned, Sattler (1982) questions its success at obtaining "educational decisions that are not racially or culturally discriminatory" (p. 282). The proliferation of tests with cultural considerations in their norms and item content should be applauded, but concern about cultural fairness must continue and serve as a reason for close scrutiny for unfair discrimination.

The Wide Range Achievement Test-Revised (WRAT-R; Jastak & Wilkinson, 1984) has been heavily relied on by school psychologists. The norms include subjects from 5 years to 74 years and 11 months. The test has two levels: Level 1 is for children 5 years to 11 years and 11 months, and Level 2 is for persons over 12 years. The WRAT-R yields raw scores that can be converted to standard scores and grade equivalents for reading, spelling, and arithmetic.

Despite its popularity, Clark (1989) points to important unanswered questions about the standardization sample ("With the exception of age, no demographic characteristics of the sample are described in the manual" [p. 901]), reliability, and validity ("Content validity cannot be judged" [p. 389]). She connects the use of the WRAT-R to a major flaw in the test selection practices of school psychologists, namely that some tests are used, not because of their established psychometric properties or clinical utility but because "the fact that this test can be administered and scored quickly will continue to contribute to its popularity" (p. 903)

Harrison (1989) asserts that the WRAT-R fails to meet psychometric standards for an achievement test, and says there is no support for using the test for screening purposes. To illustrate one problem, she points out how the WRAT-R does not measure comprehension, and warns, "A child with comprehension problems could obtain high scores and, thus, not be identified as a child with special academic needs" (p. 905). Without belaboring the point, the WRAT-R is discussed here to give emphasis to the fact that, for the wrong reasons, some psychological and educational tests are widely used. School psychologists should avoid "celebrity tests" and favor tests that merit scholarly endorsement.

Another well-established achievement test is the Peabody Individual Achievement Test-Revised (PIAT-R; Markwardt, 1989). The PIAT-R is suitable for persons 5 years through 18 years and 11 months, and has six subtests: General Information, Reading Recognition, Reading Comprehension, Mathematics, Spelling, and Written Expression. Each subtest, except Written Expression, produces age- and grade-based standard scores, stanines, normal curve equivalents, percentiles, and age- and grade-equivalents. (Written Expression has two levels, with Level I having grade-based stanines, and Level II having grade-based stanines and developmental scaled scores.) Edwards (1989) concludes, "Overall, the PIAT-R appears to be a well-constructed norm-referenced achievement test" (p. 12).

The Kaufman Assessment Battery for Children (K-ABC; Kaufman & Kaufman, 1983a, 1983b) could be placed in either or both the Intelligence Tests section or the Achievement Tests section. It is for children 2 years and 6 months through 12 years and 6 months, and it has ten subtests: Magic Window, Face Recognition, Hand Movements, Gestalt Closure, Number Recall, Triangles, Word Order, Matrix Analogies, Spatial Memory, and Photo Series. Raw scores are converted to standard scores, but there are also tables for global scale standard scores; bands of errors; national percentile ranks; sociocultural percentile ranks; age equivalents; grade equivalents for Arithmetic, Reading/Decoding, and Reading/Understanding; out-of-level norms; prorating; global scale comparisons; and subtest strengths and weaknesses.

Kaufman, Kamphaus, and Kaufman (1985) purport that the K-ABC has strong theoretical support (e.g., construct validity), separate scales for making intelligence-achievement comparisons with other instruments, and a standardization that reflects the minority group population. They claim such benefits as: "A non-verbal Scale for use with children who cannot be administered many existing intelligence tests, such as hearing impaired or youngsters who do not speak or understand English" (p. 268); "Sociocultural norms for generating hypotheses about cultural influences on a black or white child's performance" (p. 268); and "Empirical documentation of smaller black-white, Hispanic-white, and native American-white differences on the K-ABC than on IQ tests" (p. 268).

Noteworthy is the Kaufman Test of Educational Achievement (K-TEA; Kaufman & Kaufman, 1985). It can be used with children from 6 to 18 years. There are two forms. The Comprehensive Form includes five subtests: Reading Decoding, Reading Comprehension, Mathematics Applications, Mathematics Computation, and Spelling. The Brief Form has three subtests: Reading, Mathematics, and Spelling. Subtest scores and the Battery Composite Score (possible for both forms) are converted into standard scores, age-equivalent, and grade-equivalent scores; there are norms for both age and grade. Doll (1989) states, "In summary, the K-TEA appears to be a well-standardized, reliable measure with some innovative features that may make it the measure of choice for analyzing academic strengths and weaknesses" (p. 412).

The list of achievement tests could go on and on. Perusal of a compendium of psychological and educational tests will reveal many specialized achievement tests, including such exotic areas as apparel and accessories achievement and small engine repair achievement.

PERCEPTUAL TESTS

Psychological assessment of perception was once greatly restricted. Although the psychological laboratory was deemed an appropriate place to study such things as visual and auditory responses to stimuli, certain sectors of the medical community admonished psychologists for dealing with the realm of neurology. Despite obvious connections between perception and learning, as needed to understand a child's strengths and weaknesses, school psychologists were reluctant to move directly toward assessment of perception. As a result of neuropsychological research, school psychologists (and the medical community) now consider assessment of perception and brain-related behavior to be a necessary assignment. This section will discuss perceptual testing, and a later section will cover neuropsychological testing.

The developmental influences on children make it imperative that school psychological assessments consider perception. At each stage, normal development introduces new higher cortical functions, and perception is altered (Majovski, 1989). Further, if there is an injury to the neurological system that results in impairment to perception, all sorts of negative effects are possible: "Clearly, there are mental, emotional, and behavioral sequelae for the child who has sustained brain damage or who shows an anomalous course of brain maturation" (Tramontana & Hooper, 1989, p. 87).

Perception influences a child's learning. School psychologists must assess perception; for example, "for children with specific learning disability, every learning activity, whether it be gross-motor or fine-motor in nature, or whether it be of a nature not usually seen as 'motor,' must be complementary to the psychomotor deficit or psychopathology observed in the child" (Hallahan & Cruickshank, 1973, p. 262). Perceptual assessment data, along with other psychological data, contribute to, among other things, visual-motor training programs: "One way or another, all such programs offer remedial exercises based on the theory that learning problems result from inadequate development of the neurophysiological substrates regulating perceptual and motor functions viewed as cornerstones for the evolution of high-level cognitive functions" (Kessler, 1988, p. 367).

As with all types of psychological and educational tests, there are many perceptual tests. Without doubt, the most popular perceptual test with school psychologists is the Bender Visual Motor Gestalt Test (BVMGT; Bender, 1938). This test consists of nine cards, each containing a geometric design. Given a pencil and piece of paper, the client is asked to draw each design. As simple and straightforward as the task of drawing designs may be, the responses reveal important information to the psychodiagnostician. The type of data used for clinical impressions include:

> Modifications in size (e.g., expanding or reducing the drawings from the size depicted on the standardized cards); the arrangement of the designs (e.g., rigid, methodical, confused, collisions, logical); unusual modes of reproduction (e.g., angulation changes, circles or dots modified, closure difficulties, overlapping, perseveration, reversals, sloping deviations, and so on). (Woody & Robertson, 1988, p. 261; see also Ogdon, 1982)

The initial purpose of the Bender Gestalt Test was to gain data on neurological functioning; it is still a common part of neuropsychological assessment. It has, however, been extended in its usage.

For school psychologists, the BVMGT gained special applicability from a scoring system developed by Koppitz (1963, 1975). The Koppitz scoring system has normative data and is used with children between 5 and 11 years. When applying the Koppitz system, the school psychologist records the number of errors contained in the nine drawings, such as distortion of shape (e.g., misshaping destroys the general configuration), perseveration (e.g., produces more drawing than contained in the actual design), integration (e.g., failure to properly juxtapose parts of the design), and rotation (e.g., the drawing reflecting a turn from what is depicted on the card). The Koppitz system yields a Developmental Score, and data for Emotional Indicators.

Although reliability and validity studies support the Koppitz system, concern must be expressed about her assertion that "the Bender Gestalt Test can be used with some degree of confidence as a short nonverbal intelligence test for young children, particularly for screening purposes" (Koppitz, 1963, p. 50). However, she does suggest that "the Bender Test should if possible be combined with a brief verbal test" (p. 47).

Salvia and Ysseldyke (1988) state, "The BVMGT is *not* an intelligence test but a measure of a child's skill in copying geometric designs" (p. 283), and "In our opinion, the BVMGT should never be used as, or substituted for a measure of intellectual functioning" (p. 283). Koppitz (1975) believes that the BVMGT can aid the diagnosis of minimal brain dysfunction and emotional problems in school children. Hutt (1977) has an adaptation of the BVMGT for persons over 15 years and has a system for evaluating the drawings that will lead to a measure of psychopathology. Salvia and Ysseldyke (1988) cover other perceptual tests relevant to school psychology.

Too often, a test is selected for its ease of administration, regardless of its proof of reliability or validity: "The more cumbersome or apparently cumbersome the method seems to be, the more likely the clinician is inclined not to use it" (Canter, 1985, p. 225). Unfortunately, this is often the reason that the BVMGT is used. In fact, it may be used primarily because it is simple to administer and can serve as a warm-up to the testing session for the child.

HUMAN FIGURE DRAWINGS

An artist projects personal qualities into an artistic production: "The creation of the artistic production involves the expression of the unconscious through symbolism as well as the expression of the artist's style and approach" (Handler, 1985, p. 166). Even if the goal is not art, a drawing ends up being a revelation of self: "The body image projected on the paper may refer to deep, unconscious wishes, to a frank acknowledgement of physical or psychological impairment, to conscious or unconscious compensation for a physical or a psychological defect, or to a combination of all these factors" (p. 177).

Ogdon (1982) states, "Although person drawings usually reflect one's body image and self-concept, situationally induced temporary changes in attitude and mood are also expressed" (p. 66). Consequently, the drawing of a human figure, generically referred to as the Draw-A-Person Test (DAP), is often used by psychologists as an assessment strategy. Since the DAP provides both developmental and social/emotional information, it is separated in this chapter from placement in the personality assessment section.

In school psychology, the use of human figure drawings is anchored in the work of Florence Goodenough (1926). She developed the Draw-A-Man Test, which was a system for giving points to details and deriving an estimate of intelligence. Other systems for analyzing the human figure drawings of children have been created by Koppitz (1968) and Machover (1949), with emphasis on emotional indicators. Another version of human figure drawings is the House-Tree-Person Test (HTP; Hammer, 1989).

Often the drawing is used as a stimulus for verbalizations; for example, Kissen (1981) has the client introspect about the drawing, which "al-lows the patient to become spontaneous and open to inner experiential states" (p. 44). Specific questions can also be asked of the client (Machover, 1949). There are numerous methods for scoring a human figure drawing, but it is most common that the school psychologist will use the drawing task as a warm-up for the testing, as will build rapport, and formulate subjective diagnostic impressions from the drawing, much like what is done with the BVMGT.

Before any interpretation can be made, there must be awareness of the client's developmental state. Siegel (1987) points out, "The evolution of human figure drawing begins in the second year of life" (p. 122), and she describes how maturation leads to progressive drawing abilities (e.g., geometric forms by the third or fourth year): "From a developmental perspective, the child's drawing gradually progresses from a loose assemblage of separate fragments to a unified body concept" (p. 123). Therefore, there must be age-appropriate expectations for human figure drawings. With understanding of what is "normal" for a particular developmental stage, the school psychologist inspects the human figure drawing for adherence to or deviation from age-appropriate expectations.

Ogdon (1982) offers a compendium of research sources for analyzing human figure drawings for, among other things, graphomotor factors (erasing, placement, pressure, size, stroke, line and shading); and general projective drawing factors (detailing, distortions, and omissions, edge of paper, ground line treatment, midline emphasis, symmetry, transparencies, and miscellaneous projective drawing factors). He also gives ideas for clinical interpretations of the client's drawing relevant to head characteristics; hair treatment; facial features; eye and eyebrow; ears and nose; mouth and chin; neck and Adam's apple; torso and body; anterior appendages (arms, hands, fingers); locomotor appendages and stance; posture, view perspective, and movement; clothing and other appurtenances; miscellaneous modes of drawing a person; and differential treatment of male and female drawings. Due to possible reliability problems, Ogdon cautions, "Interpretations based on a particular detail of projective drawings must be made with particular care" (p. 101).

Kessler (1988) urges, "If the child's productions are viewed as a reflection of how he or she feels about life, rather than for prediction or diagnostic categorization, the projective materials are for the school-age child what the play materials are for the pre-schooler" (p. 218).

The message is this: Do not demand too much of the cues in a human figure drawing. A similar axiom for all psychological and educational tests is: Do not go beyond the purpose of the test and the proven qualities of the data. Preparation for use of human figure drawings should include, among other things, review of objective methods (Handler & Reyher, 1965; Koppitz, 1968), as well as an in-depth study of how to formulate clinical hypotheses that can be cross-checked against other data sources (Hammer, 1958, 1989). The prudent school psychologist does not want to be a party to Kessler's (1988) cryptic comment, "Drawing tests remain popular, *for cost reasons if nothing else"* (emphasis added, p. 217).

PERSONALITY AND SOCIAL/EMOTIONAL BEHAVIOR METHODS

Psychology is the only discipline that includes training in standardized measures of personality (i.e., psychiatry and social work rely on clinical judgment, not measurements). University trainers and school psychologists may differ in their views about personality assessment. School psychologists favor pragmatism over idealism. Prout (1983) found that "practitioners could be characterized as only moderately pleased with their training in the area of social-emotional assessment" (p. 383), and he speculated that "training was more in the traditional testing model than the currently preferred behavioral orientation"

(p. 383). Given the expectations placed on the school psychology, training programs should embrace the fluid nature of personality or social/emotional behavior assessment, and methods and instruments that integrate theoretical approaches (Knoff, 1983).

Personality tests can be dichotomized as being objective or projective. The *objective* personality test is typically a set of questions or items to which the child can respond with a discrete answer. Woody and Robertson (1988) summarize,

An objective personality test: (1) has specific stimulus items (such as questions about the client); (2) requires the client to give a discrete response (such as true or false, or a rating, say on a 1 to 5 scale, or to choose which of X number of descriptors is preferred most and which is preferred least)—that is, the objectivity comes, in part, from the form of the responses; (3) obtains a codification (usually in writing) of the client's responses (such as a self-report); (4) yields numerical measurements; and (5) has a standardization (such as norms to assist in the interpretations. (pp. 267–268)

Note that the use of "objective" in this context does not refer to reliability and validity; "projective" tests also claim reliability and validity.

The *projective* personality test is typically a set of stimuli (e.g., inkblots, pictures depicting human interaction) to which the child creates an idiosyncratic response (e.g., a drawing or a perceived object or story). The projective principle is psychoanalytic in origin, and the projective method or instrument is "a method of studying personality by confronting the subject with a situation to which he will respond according to what the situation means to him and how he feels when so responding" (Frank, 1948, p. 46).

Lindzey (1961) states,

A projective technique is an instrument that is considered especially sensitive to covert or unconscious aspects of behavior, it permits or encourages a wide variety of subject responses, is highly multidimensional, and it evokes unusually rich or profuse response data with a minimum of subject awareness concerning the purpose of the test. (p. 45)

Obrzut and Cummings (1983) assert, "The most central assumption of projective techniques is that an individual will 'project' (or reflect) his or her inner needs, desires, and/or conflicts when asked to impose meaning or order to an ambiguous or unstructured stimulus" (p. 414).

Since there is dubious standardization for projective techniques, there are many critics. A high degree of clinical judgment or subjectivity enters into the results of a projective test, but Matarazzo (1972) wisely reminds that the interpretation of both objective and projective tests is subjective and training and experience are prerequisites for the proper use of any personality method or instrument.

In a survey of clinical psychologists, Wade and Baker (1977) identified the six most supported tests to be:

1. The Rorschach ink-blots method (projective)
2. The Thematic Apperception Test (TAT; projective)
3. The Wechsler Adult Intelligence Scale (WAIS; objective)
4. The Minnesota Multiphasic Personality Inventory (MMPI; objective)
5. The Bender Visual Motor Gestalt Test (BVMGT; projective)
6. The Wechsler Intelligence Scale for children (WISC; objective)

As a follow-up with psychologists from different specialties, Lubin, Larsen, and Matarazzo (1984) found the following order for usage:

1. The WAIS
2. The MMPI
3. The BVMGT
4. The Rorschach
5. The TAT
6. The WISC

It is evident that psychologists hold personality assessment to be important and they make use of both objective and projective tests.

In a survey of school psychologists, Reschly, Genshaft, and Binder (1987) found that the rank order for projectives/figure drawings was:

1. The Rorschach
2. Draw-A-Person (DAP)
3. The House-Tree-Person (HTP)
4. Kinetic family drawing
5. The TAT

Incidentally, other surveys of use of personality tests (within various psychological specialties) can be found in Piotrowski (1985), Piotrowski and Keller (1984, 1989), Piotrowski and Lubin (1990), Prout (1983), and Rosenberg and Beck (1986).

While Prout (1983) wonders about a possible schism between trainers and practitioners because of theoretical allegiance, there is reason to believe that personality assessment, including with projective techniques, is endorsed by practitioners of virtually every theoretical leaning. Piotrowski and Keller (1984) surveyed behavioral psychologists and found that nonbehavioral assessment was generally acceptable to behaviorists, with about half of the respondents believing that use of objective personality assessment would increase in the future.

Based on the Lubin, Larsen, and Matarazzo study (1984), this section will discuss the MMPI, the Personality Inventory for Children, the Rorschach ink-blots method, and thematic apperception methods. Given the preferences of school psychologists, special consideration will be given to the Personality Inventory for Children (PIC; Lachar, 1982) and the Roberts Apperception Test for Children (RATC; McArthur & Roberts, 1982). These are, of course, only a few of the many personality tests that have relevance to school psychology (for other methods and instruments, see Martin, 1988). The personality and social/emotional behavior methods and instruments presented herein do, however, provide useful examples.

The Minnesota Multiphasic Personality Inventory

The Minnesota Multiphasic Personality Inventory (MMPI) has seemingly become the premier personality assessment instrument. With over 40 years of extensive research, it has received widespread professional and public support. In 1989, a restandardized edition was released, referred to as the MMPI-2 (Hathaway & McKinley, 1989). The MMPI-2 is objective, requiring a true or false answer to 567 questionnaire items. For the first MMPI, there are also shorter versions (see Graham, 1987, and Helmes & McLaughlin, 1983). In all likelihood, abbreviated versions of the MMPI-2 will be proposed eventually.

Both editions of the MMPI are criterion keyed, meaning that clinical groups of patients provided the bases for each scale: "In this *criterion-keyed* or group-contrast approach to inventory construction items are given a numerical scoring weight (keyed) for a particular group variable if they discriminate between members of that group (the contrast group) and a control group" (Aiken, 1989, p. 229). Both editions of the MMPI have validity scales, intended to allow detection of subjects who are faking health or illness or in some other way failing to respond in a consistent, valid, and straightforward manner.

The 10 clinical scales are: (1) Hypochondriasis (preoccupation with body and fears of illness and disease); (2) Depression (hopelessness, dissatisfaction with life); (3) Hysteria (involuntary psychogenic loss or disorder of function); (4) Psychopathic Deviate (delinquent acts, dishonesty, sexual promiscuity, substance abuse); (4) Masculinity-Femininity (gender-based preferences); (6) Paranoia (ideas of reference, delusions, suspiciousness, grandiosity, rigid opinions); (7) Psychasthenia (excessive doubts, compulsions, obsessions, reasonable fears); (8) Schizophrenia (disturbances of thought,

mood, and behavior, misinterpretations of reality, delusions, hallucinations); (9) Hypomania (elevated mood, accelerated speech and motor activity); and (10) Social Introversion (withdrawal) (Graham, 1987). There are also numerous supplementary scales.

The first edition of the MMPI is generally thought of as being for adults (over the age of 16, and with at least six years of formal education). Adolescent norms are available. Newmark (1985) states, "Patients as young as thirteen years of age and with less education may be able to take the MMPI if their reading level is adequate and their IQ is above 80" (p. 14). For the MMPI-2, Graham (1990) states:

> The MMPI-2 can be used with subjects who are 13 years old or older and who have at least an eighth grade reading level. Subjects younger than 13 sometimes have the requisite reading ability, but they lack the experiences necessary to make the MMPI-2 meaningful for them. Separate, age-appropriate norms should be used for subjects younger than 18 years old. (p. 14)

Graham (1990) provides conversion tables for adolescents. Hathaway and McKinley (1989), however, report that adolescent data are being analyzed, and say, "Until adolescent norms are available, we recommend that you use the original MMPI for adolescents" (p. 15).

With both editions of the MMPI, high scores on each of the individual scales can be interpreted, but the chief approach to interpretation is a profile analysis, that is, the configuration of two or more scales in combination (Meyer, 1989). Of benefit, there are "cookbooks" that contain descriptions of the various combinations of scales (Gilberstadt & Duker, 1965; Graham, 1987; Lachar, 1974; Meyer, 1989; Webb, McNamara, & Rodgers, 1981), thereby promoting reliability for the interpretive process. Since the preceding interpretive guides are for the first edition, Butcher (1990) and Graham (1990) provide comparable guidance for the MMPI-2.

In service to interpretive reliability, the MMPI can be scored and interpreted by computer. Presumably the descriptions and interpretations contained in the cookbooks and computer programs have valid bases, but it is common for them to be dependent on the clinical acumen of the creator.

The Personality Inventory for Children

Often heralded as the "Kids' MMPI," the Personality Inventory for Children (PIC; Lachar, 1982; Wirt, Lachar, Klinedinst, & Seat, 1984) is a parent rating scale that estimates the extent and type of maladjusted behavior within a child (ages 3 through 16 years of age). The parent (or other adult caretaker) provides a true or false response to 600 questionnaire items (there are shorter versions) about the child's behavior. Like the MMPI, the PIC is a criterion-keyed instrument, but it is standardized on normal boys and girls: "Unlike the MMPI, however, the PIC is an inventory of observed behavior rather than self-report" (Aiken, 1989, p. 255).

There are validity scales (e.g., for the tendency to attribute virtuous behavior to the child or to exaggerate symptoms, self-defensiveness), and thirteen (narrow-band) content scales: General Adjustment, Achievement Screening, Intellectual Screening, Developmental Rate, Somatic Concern, Depression, Family Relations, Delinquency, Withdrawal, Anxiety, Psychosis, Hyperactivity, and Social Skills. Broad-band factors are Undisciplined/Poor Self-Control, Social Incompetence, Internalization/Somatic Symptoms, and Cognitive Development. There are also supplementary (experimental) scales.

Lachar and LaCombe (1983) justify the PIC, at least in part, by the shortcomings of projective methods, and assert that it has special usefulness in school psychology, citing its diagnostic accuracy and its "substantial potential" to separate children who do and do not need special education services and to classify the children in specific special education classes. Martin (1988) credits "the general care with which the research

on its development has been done" (p. 218), but is negative toward its length, complexity, and the fact that it is "an instrument that cannot be fully understood except by a few experts" (p. 219).

The Rorschach Ink-Blots Method

The Rorschach Ink-Blots Method involves 10 ink blots, created by the Swiss psychiatrist, Hermann Rorschach, in the 1920s. People see different things, and there are no right or wrong answers. By analysis of what the subject perceives, the psychologist can make interpretations about personality structure:

> A basic assumption underlying the Rorschach techniques is that there is a relationship between perception and personality. The way in which an individual organizes or "structures" the ink blots in forming his perceptions reflects fundamental aspects of his psychological functioning. Ink blots are suitable as stimuli because they are relatively ambiguous or "unstructured," i.e., they do not elicit particular learned responses, but permit a variety of possible responses. (Klopfer & Davidson, 1962, p. 14)

After the ink-blot cards are presented and the subject responds, the psychologist goes back through the ink blots and conducts an "inquiry" about the subject's responses, gathering details as to exactly what, where, why, and how the subject came to formulate each particular response; then the details are coded and calculations made.

The Rorschach method is applied to persons of all ages, from "children as young as five through aged adults" (Erdberg, 1985, p. 66). There are several scoring systems, designed to enhance objectivity and reliability. Each scoring system has its unique features, such as the factors, dimensions, or categories for which the response or concept is scored and interpreted. For example, the so-called "Klopfer System" has five major scoring categories: (1) Location (where on the card the concept was perceived); (2) Determinant (how and what qualities determined the concept); (3) Content (the subject matter of the concept); (4) Popularity-Originality (the commonality of the response); and (5) Form Level (the accuracy of concept or how well it fits the blot area). There are also other scoring considerations (Klopfer & Davidson, 1962). The scoring and interpretive systems differ substantially, leading Aiken (1989) to note, "This state of affairs led to much dissension among proponents of the major systems, and critics were quick to seize the opportunity to refer to the chaos and disunity as unscientific in merit" (p. 335).

Despite the longevity of usage and the mountains of research studies that have been amassed, negative criticism of the Rorschach abounds. Much of the criticism is directed at the rationale (see previous quote by Klopfer and Davidson), but much of the criticism centers on the lack of validation. For example, Lanyon (1984) opines, "Little that is encouraging can be said about projective techniques, the literature on which continues to reflect a lack of interest in the generally accepted standards of empirical validation" (p. 692). Note that Lanyon's criticism is apparently applicable to other projective methods as well. The negative view is contradicted by widespread professional endorsement of the Rorschach and other projective methods. The surveys of psychologists cited earlier routinely placed the Rorschach and the TAT in the top few psychological tests in general and usually in the top three (along with the MMPI) personality assessment methods and instruments: "Recent refinements in scoring and interpretive systems might account for the persistence of popularity for some of the projective techniques" (Lubin, Larsen, & Matarazzo, 1984, p. 452).

Regardless of the system used, the interpretation of Rorshach responses is complex and fraught with reliability and validity challenges. A fundamental is that no one type of response or sign is adequate for an interpretation: *"single signs are not conclusive evidence of anything, it is the configuration of signs that must be considered"* (Ogdon, 1982, p. 21). Even with configurative analysis, doubts remain about the validity.

In fairness to the Rorschach, there has been continuing research and, to the surprise of many actuarially oriented psychologists, empirical validity for certain Rorschach signs is solidifying (Exner, 1983; Ogdon, 1982) and the result seems to be "new credibility for the Rorschach technique" (Aiken, 1989, p. 357). The Rorschach has received important support from computerized scoring and interpretation.

The Thematic Apperception Methods

Thematic apperception methods are based on the idea that fantasy can reveal personality. There are numerous thematic apperception methods, each involving a series of pictures. Whatever the method, each picture is presented and the client is asked to create (fantasize) a story. The story is analyzed for such things as the motives and feelings of the hero(es) in the story, the environmental forces or presses on the hero(es), themes and outcomes of the stories, and possible psychodynamic factors (defense mechanisms, interpersonal relations) (Murray, 1943). The interpretation of thematic apperception responses is highly subjective. Aiken (1989) states,

> A basic ground rule in the clinical interpretation of the TAT stories is that the interpersonal scenario described by the examinee cannot be taken at face value as reflecting the examinee's actual current or former relationships. The analysis is an analysis of fantasy, and waking fantasy has about as much correlation with reality as dreams do. To understand, and therefore correctly interpret, the fantasies expressed in TAT stories the clinician must consider them against a background of psychiatric interview findings, the results of a mental status examination, observational and historical data, and other psychological test data. (p. 373)

He concludes, "The interpretations should be viewed as hypotheses, to be confirmed by other data rather than as final diagnoses" (p. 373).

Like the Rorschach, thematic apperception methods have been criticized extensively for their nebulous reliability and validity. Much of the problem seems to center on the fact that, unlike the Rorschach, the TAT does not have well-researched scoring or interpretation systems. Consequently, the interpretation of thematic apperception responses is highly dependent on the clinical acumen of the psychologist: "TAT interpretation has become a clinical art form" (Dana, 1985, p. 90). Even when one of the quasi-systems is applied, doubts about both reliability and (especially?) validity remain, and information from thematic apperception methods might best be viewed as being comparable to what is gained by a structured interview.

There are numerous thematic apperception methods. The most popular is the Thematic Apperception Test (TAT; Murray, 1943), which can be used with adults and children. There are "specialized" thematic methods, such as the Senior Apperception Technique (SAT; Bellak, 1987) for older persons.

In school psychology, the Children's Apperception Test (CAT), which has animal and human versions, is useful for young children (Bellak, 1987). The Roberts Apperception Test for Children (RATC; McArthur & Roberts, 1982) has earned a peerless place in school psychology. The RATC is designed for children 6 through 15 years of age, and depicts children on the stimulus cards:

> The RATC emphasizes everyday interpersonal events of contemporary life. It includes those situations commonly used in thematic projective tests (e.g., parent-child relationships, sibling relationships, aggression, and mastery) as well as new situations such as parental disagreement, parental affection, observation of nudity, school, and peer relationships. The test also emphasizes the child's ability to cope with situations requiring an appropriate aggressive response. (McArthur & Roberts, 1982, p. 1)

Besides the relevance of the scenes to school psychology, the forte of the RATC is that it has well-defined administration and a scoring system, and it yields scale scores and indicators for

areas as reliance on others, supportive and interpersonal relations, limit setting, problem identification, anxiety, aggression, depression, rejection, ego functioning, and others. While impressive standardization, reliability, and validity efforts have been made, there is, of course, a need for considerable additional research (Martin, 1988). At this point in time, the RATC has already earned a place in the psychoeducational assessment battery for many types of problems and children.

NEUROPSYCHOLOGICAL TESTS

Clinical child neuropsychology ranges from assessment to educative/rehabilitative interventions. The constantly changing developmental processes, especially neurological and higher cortical development, create problems for neuropsychological assessment. Since school psychologists have responsibility for differential diagnosis, it is essential that assessment methods and instruments differentiate reliably between brain-injured and neurologically intact individuals and separate brain-injured groups into subsamples according to particular factors (Golden, 1981a). Faulty psychometric properties still plague the technical aspects, standardization, and usage of certain clinical neuropsychological methods and instruments (Reynolds, 1989).

Clinical neuropsychology is useful for "diagnosis, patient care—including questions about treatment and planning, and research" (Lezak, 1983, p. 8), and affords important data for evaluating all sorts of treatments (such as neurosurgical procedures and drug therapy) and checking progress (such as medical, educational, and rehabilitative) (Walsh, 1978). Within school psychology, neuropsychology has application to learning disabilities (Geary, Jennings, Schultz, & Alper, 1984; Leong, 1989), remediation of educational deficits (Teeter, 1989), cognitive rehabilitation (Gray & Dean, 1989), and a host of other problems commonly dealt with in the school context.

Haak (1989) describes a school-based neuropsychological unit, and discusses problems in instituting neuropsychological testing in the public schools, cautioning, "To institute such a component into the public school's assessment system is somewhat to do the proverbial 'rushing in where angels fear to tread' " (p. 492). Nonetheless, she makes a strong case for school psychology embracing neuropsychology, offers guidelines for surmounting obstacles. Similarly, Leavell and Lewandowski (1988) found school psychologists supportive of and wanting more training in neuropsychology.

The evolution of neuropsychology within school psychology progressively led to heavy reliance on brain-related interpretations of data on mental abilities, such as a profile analysis of the subtests on one of the Wechsler scales. For example, "Verbal-Performance IQ discrepancies of 25 points and greater are suspiciously indicative of an underlying pathological process" (Gregory, 1987, p. 72). Of course, an intelligence test should never be used as the sole basis for a diagnosis of brain injury. On the latter point, Kaufman (1979) states categorically that discrepancies between Verbal and Performance IQs "should not be used to infer neurological dysfunction without convincing support from supplementary data and observations" (p. 25).

Still a bit new to the scene, there are now neuropsychological test batteries for children. Nussbaum and Bigler (1989) describe the Halstead-Reitan, applicable to children 9 through 14 years, and the Reitan-Indiana, applicable to children 5 through 8 years. These batteries have various components, such as might measure concept formation, tactual performance, fine motor speed and coordination, auditory discrimination and attention abilities, nonverbal perception and attention/concentration, visual perception (sequential skills, symbol recognition), simultaneous processing and cognitive flexibility, differential tactile and visual perception, and many other domains.

Another instrument is the Luria-Nebraska Neuropsychological Battery-Children's Revision (LNNB-CR; Golden, 1981b, 1989), which has motor, rhythm, tactile, visual, receptive, expressive, writing, reading, arithmetic, memory, and intelligence scales. The results can be used to ascertain "whether significant brain injury exists in a given child as a screening procedure to differentiate neuropsychological from other possible disorders" (Golden, 1989, p. 195), describe the child's brain-related behaviors, identify "the probable underlying causes of the child's overall behavior" (p. 196) (i.e., brain-behavior relationships), and integrate "all findings and conclusions into descriptions of how the brain of the individual is functioning" (p. 196). Geary and colleagues (1984) found the LNNB-CR useful for distinguishing learning disabled and "normal" children.

FAMILY EVALUATIONS

The developmental and social systems approach requires assessment of family influences on the child, and the resources that family members can offer to school interventions. In general, family evaluations tend to be highly subjective, relying on the school psychologist's impressions from observations, interviews, and records. The interpretation, however, is according to social systems theory, aligned with the notion that the child's problems are connected to the family's dynamics: "Adopting a family perspective, a member's dysfunctional behavior may represent a system that is in disequilibrium; he or she may simply be the 'identified patient,' a representative of a troubled family" (Goldenberg & Goldenberg, 1985, p. 25).

The complexity of family interactions can be simplified by a visual representation. From information obtained in an interview, a *genogram* (Bowen, 1978), a structural diagram of a family's multigenerational relationship system, or an *eco-map* (Hartman, 1975), an illustration of a family's connections to resources and stressors in the external environment, can be prepared. There are numerous structured family interview formats, family relations and environmental scales, and other family assessment techniques. Goldenberg and Goldenberg (1985) and Paget (1987) provide overviews.

With preschool evaluations, Wilson (1986) points out how family assessment must consider environmental determinism (or interactionism), but it does not "exclude the contribution of genetic, cognitive and physiological factors" (p. 168). The evaluation is at the individual level (the preschool child, siblings, adult family members), the family system level, and the community level. Assessment strategies include interviews; naturalistic, analogue, and participant observations; self-reports and reports by others (using self-monitoring and questionnaires, checklists, and rating scales); and data from standardized tests and other methods can be integrated. These principles and strategies are applicable at other ages as well.

THE PSYCHOEDUCATIONAL ASSESSMENT REPORT

For the school psychologist, the end product of the psychoeducational assessment is the creation of a report: "The writing of a report involves analyzing, synthesizing, and integrating numerous sources of data, including the child's test scores, previous test scores, teachers' reports, behavioral observations, interview material, social and family history, and medical findings" (Sattler, 1982, p. 491). Combined with the school psychologist's peerless role in psychoeducational decision making, the report is often the most powerful single informational source for the individualized educational program or the individualized family service plan. It is beyond the scope of this chapter to present sample reports for analysis; that sort of exercise is appropriate in more advanced courses on assessment. The time is ripe, however, to underscore the purpose and nature of the psychoeducational report.

As for the purpose, there is room to debate. For example, should the report be restricted to or primarily directed at the referral question(s), or

should it encompass any and all issues deemed by the school psychologist to be relevant and useful? The question of purpose of the report is often answered, all or in part, by school administrative policies. That is, while members of the psychoeducational team in general and the school psychologist in particular will have input to the policies and practices pertaining to reports, the school administration will have the last say about what will be adopted. Of course, the school psychologist can and should always be ready to confront and try to change administrative preferences and policies that fail to adequately (optimally?) provide for psychoeducational standards and objectives.

The standards for psychoeducational reports may be defined by the school administration and state-level rules (such as from the state department of education or public instruction), and influenced by disciplinary ethics (such as from the National Association of School Psychologists', 1984, Principles for Professional Ethics).

Assuming that administrative prescriptions and proscriptions have been accommodated, the school psychologist is faced with exercising self-determination for the format and contents. Settling on a purpose is the first step. Ownby (1987) postulates, "The primary purpose of psychological reports is to communicate to a referral agent or agents information about a client in a way which will result in changes in the referral agent's beliefs about or behavior toward the client" (p. xii); and he adds four specific purposes:

1. To answer referral questions as explicitly as possible, depending on how well defined the questions are;
2. To provide the referring agent with additional information when it is relevant to his or her work with the client and when it is appropriate to the use the report will be put to (this includes providing a general description of the client);
3. To make a record of the assessment activities for future use;
4. To recommend a specific course of action for the report's recipient to follow in his or her work with the client. (p. 16)

With the purposes clearly in mind, the school psychologist begins to sort through objectives, goals, and issues unique to the particular child. Anastasi (1988) supports having the report follow directly from the purpose (e.g., the reasons for the referral) and suggests,

> From the mass of data the clinician has gathered by both formal and informal methods, he or she should select whatever is relevant to answering the questions raised at the outset. The current trend, moreover, is to make reports action-oriented, that is, directed toward recommendations or decisions regarding instructional programs, therapy, occupational choice, or other appropriate actions. Diagnosis, etiology, personality description, and understanding of personality dynamics tend to be deemphasized. (p. 516)

(It should be noted that when the "questions raised at the outset" prove to be off target, the school psychologist has a professional duty to at least consider addressing other issues and diagnostic questions that have been revealed to be equally or more important.) Continuing on, Anastasi also asserts, "A test of the effectiveness of a report is to see whether it is unique to the individual or whether it applies equally well to other persons of the same age, sex, education, socioeconomic level, or other demographic variables" (p. 516).

When the contents of a report are applicable to other than the person who has been assessed, the report is considered to reflect the *Barnum effect*. This term comes from circus entrepreneur P. T. Barnum's statement that a "sucker is born every minute"; that is, a statement can be made that has no direct relevance but is still accepted foolishly. Unfortunately, some psychological reports, like astrological statements published in a newspaper, contain generalities that can apply to almost anyone.

For guidance about writing the report, Oster, Caro, Eagen, and Lillo (1988) suggest, in the context of assessing adolescents (but applicable otherwise), the following outline:

Clearly answer each referral question.

If the report is going to help in determining placement, then make recommendations that include the relevant data to support your conclusions.

Identify the factors that may be affecting the growth and development of this individual.

Eliminate psychological jargon. Write to your audience.

Describe the adolescent's performance in a manner relating to his or her general interpersonal and academic efficiency.

Include raw data or verbatim material only if you are trying to support your hypotheses.

Statements surrounding your degree of certainty about the test data should not be too tentative or overly generalized. If you have to doubt your own conclusions they will be of little benefit to other professionals. Any interpretive statements you make should stand up to peer review. Your recommendations should be comprehensive enough to ensure that the adolescent you have evaluated will receive all the possible services available. (p. 123)

Shellenberger (1982) believes that psychological reports are effective when they answer the referral question; describe behavior; are written in a clear, precise, straightforward manner; synthesize and integrate information; provide recommendations that are explicit, specific, and implementable; and are timely (see pp. 52–53).

There is no one format for a psychoeducational report. As with other issues, the format will often be determined administratively or by personal preference by the school psychologist. Oster and colleagues (1988) recommend that section headings include the following: identifying information; reasons for referral; previous evaluations; instruments included in the present examination; historical data and/or knowledge gained from interviewing the youth and family; behavioral observations; test results and interpretations; summary and conclusions; and recommendations (see pp. 122–129).

When deciding on the format and contents, the reasons for the assessment will merit consideration. For example, if the referral centers around social/emotional problems, the report might emphasize type and level of affect, organic involvement, thought processes, integration of personality functions, and so on (Meyer, 1989). Aligned with school psychology, Sattler (1982, 1988) suggests a report outline that contains identifying information (name, date of birth, chronological age, date of examination, date of report, grade, and tests administered); reason for referral; general observations (e.g., physical characteristics, atypical behaviors, attitudes, and feelings); test results (which might be quite specific, such as IQ, precision range, percentile rank, etc.); recommendations; and summary.

Although producing the psychological report is commonly perceived by a school psychologist as his or her most challenging, creative, and rewarding endeavor, the repeated use of the same assessment methods and instruments and dealing with the same sorts of clients and referral questions can breed a repetitive writing style. Indeed, there are computerized report-writing programs that allow the school psychologist simply to plug in certain information and data, and the computer then spews out "canned" interpretations and reports. And some school psychologists have printed forms for recording and reporting, say, test scores, and then write an abbreviated report

that contains interpretations and recommendations. Both computer- and form-based reports may have usefulness, albeit restricted to the boundaries of the programs or forms. The school psychologist is best advised to seize the moment and maintain that the production of the psychoeducational report is a matchless opportunity to demonstrate professionalism and benefit the client.

SUMMARY

For psychoeducational assessment, it is preferable to use a battery of methods and instruments. The results of any psychological test are less useful than when supplemented with information from other methods, instruments, or tests. Surveys have revealed school psychologists' preferences for assessment approaches, and the following are of primary importance: record analysis and interviewing, behavior rating scales, intelligence tests, achievement tests, perceptual tests, human figure drawings, personality and social/emotional methods, neuropsychological tests, and family evaluations. The psychoeducational assessment report is the hallmark of the school psychologist's services and requires careful attention to maximizing its efficacy.

REFERENCES

Achenbach, T. M., & Edelbrock, C. S. (1983). *Manual for the Child Behavior Checklist and Revised Child Behavior Profile*. Burlington, VT: Department of Psychiatry, University of Vermont.

Aiken, L. R. (1988). *Psychological testing and assessment* (6th ed.). Boston: Allyn and Bacon.

Aiken, L. R. (1989). *Assessment of personality*. Boston: Allyn and Bacon.

American Educational Research Association/American Psychological Association/National Council on Measurement in Education. (1985). *Standards for educational and psychological testing*. Washington, DC: American Psychological Association.

Anastasi, A. (1988). *Psychological testing* (6th ed.). New York: Macmillan.

Anastasi, A. (1989). Review of the Stanford-Binet Intelligence Scale, Fourth Edition. In J. C. Conoley & J. J. Kramer (Eds.), *The tenth mental measurement yearbook* (pp. 771–773). Lincoln, NE: University of Nebraska Press.

Barona, A., Reynolds, C. R., & Chastain, R. (1984). A demographically based index of premorbid intelligence for the WAIS-R. *Journal of Consulting and Clinical Psychology, 52*(5), 885–887.

Bayley, N. (1969). *Bayley Scales of Infant Development: Birth to two years*. New York: Psychological Corporation.

Bellak, L. (1987). *The TAT, the CAT, and the SAT in clinical use* (4th ed.). New York: Grune & Stratton.

Bender, L. (1938). *A visual motor gestalt test and its clinical use*. New York: American Orthopsychiatric Association.

Binet, A., & Simon, T. (1905). Methodes nouvelle pour le diagnostic du niveau intellectuel des anormaux. *L'Annee Psychologique, 11,* 191–244.

Bowen, M. (1978). *Family therapy in clinical practice.* New York: Jason Aronson.

Butcher, J. N. (1990). *MMPI-2 in psychological treatment.* New York: Oxford University Press.

Canter, A. (1985). The Bender-Gestalt Test. In C. S. Newmark (Ed.), *Major psychological assessment instruments* (pp. 217–248). Boston: Allyn and Bacon.

Clark, E. (1989). Review of the Wide Range Achievement Test-Revised. In J. C. Conoley & J. J. Kramer (Eds.), *The tenth mental measurement yearbook* (pp. 901–903). Lincoln, NE: University of Nebraska Press.

Cohen, R. J., Montague, P., Nathanson, L. E., & Swerdlik, M. E. (1988). *Psychological testing.* Mountain View, CA: Mayfield Publishing.

Cronbach, L. J. (1989). Review of the Stanford-Binet Intelligence Scale, Fourth Edition. In J. C. Conoley & J. J. Kramer (Eds.), *The tenth mental measurement yearbook* (pp. 773–775). Lincoln, NE: University of Nebraska Press.

Dana, R. H. (1985). Thematic Apperception Test (TAT). In C. S. Newmark (Ed.), *Major psychological assessment instruments* (pp. 89–134). Boston: Allyn and Bacon.

Danielson, E. B., Lynch, E. C., Moyano, A., Johnson, B., & Bettenburg, A. (1988). *Assessing young children.* Washington, DC: National Association of School Psychologists.

Doll, E. J. (1989). Review of the Kaufman Test of Educational Achievement. In J. C. Conoley & J. J. Kramer (Eds.), *The tenth mental measurement yearbook* (pp. 411–412). Lincoln, NE: University of Nebraska Press.

Edwards, J. (1989). Peabody Individual Achievement Test-Revised. *NASP Communique, 18*(3), 12.

Erdberg, P. (1985). The Rorschach. In C. S. Newmark (Ed.), *Major psychological assessment instruments* (pp. 65–88). Boston: Allyn and Bacon.

Exner, J. E. (1983). Rorschach assessment. In I. B. Weiner (Ed.), *Clinical methods in psychology* (2nd ed., pp. 58–59). New York: Wiley.

Fish, M. C., & Margolis, H. (1988). Training and practice of school psychologists in reading assessment and intervention. *Journal of School Psychology, 26*(4), 399–404.

Fogel, M. L. (1964). The intelligence quotient as an index of brain damage. *American Journal of Orthopsychiatry, 34*(3), 555–562.

Frank, L. K. (1948). *Projective methods.* Springfield, IL: Thomas.

Geary, D. C., Jennings, S. M., Schultz, D. D., & Alper, T. G. (1984). The diagnostic accuracy of the Luria-Nebraska Neuropsychological Battery-Children's Revision for 9 to 12 year old learning disabled children. *School Psychology Review, 13*(3), 375–380.

Gilberstadt, H., & Duker, J. (1965). *A handbook for clinical and actuarial MMPI interpretation.* Philadelphia: Saunders.

Golden, C. J. (1981a). *Diagnosis and rehabilitation in clinical neuropsychology* (2nd ed.). Springfield, IL: Thomas.

Golden, C. J. (1981b). The Luria-Nebraska Children's Battery: Theory and formulation. In G. W. Hynd & J. E. Obrzut (Eds.), *Neuropsychological assessment and the school-age child: Issues and procedures* (pp. 277–302). New York: Grune & Stratton.

Golden, C. J. (1989). The Nebraska Neuropsychological Children's Battery. In C. R. Reynolds & E. Fletcher-Janzen (Eds.), *Handbook of clinical child neuropsychology* (pp. 193–204). New York: Plenum.

Goldenberg, I., & Goldenberg, H. (1985). *Family therapy: An overview.* Monterey, CA: Brooks/Cole.

Goodenough, F. (1926). *Measurement of intelligence by drawings.* New York: World Book Company.

Graham, J. R. (1987). *The MMPI: A practical guide* (2nd ed.). New York: Oxford University Press.

Graham, J. R. (1990). *MMPI-2: Assessing personality and psychopathology.* New York: Oxford University Press.

Gray, J. W., & Dean, R. S. (1989). Approaches to the cognitive rehabilitation of children with neuropsychological impairment. In C. R. Reynolds & E. Fletcher-Janzen (Eds.), *Handbook of clinical child neuropsychology* (pp. 397–408). New York: Plenum.

Gregory, R. J. (1987). *Adult intellectual assessment.* Boston: Allyn and Bacon.

Haak, R. A. (1989). Establishing neuropsychology in

a school setting. In C. R. Reynolds & E. Fletcher-Janzen (Eds.), *Handbook of clinical child neuropsychology* (pp. 489–502). New York: Plenum.

Hallahan, D. P., & Cruickshank, W. M. (1973). *Psycho-educational foundations of learning disabilities.* Englewood Cliffs, NJ: Prentice-Hall.

Hammer, E. F. (Ed.). (1958). *The clinical application of projective drawings.* Springfield, IL: Thomas.

Hammer, E. F. (1989). The House-Tree-Person Test. In C. S. Newmark (Ed.), *Major psychological assessment instruments* (pp. 135–164). Boston: Allyn and Bacon.

Handler, L. (1985). The clinical use of the Draw-A-Person Test (DAP). In C. S. Newmark (Ed.), *Major psychological assessment instruments* (pp. 165–216). Boston: Allyn and Bacon.

Handler, L., & Reyher, J. (1965). Figure drawing anxiety indexes: A review of the literature. *Journal of Personality Assessment, 29,* 305–313.

Harris, J. D., Gray, B. A., Rees-McGee, S., Carroll, J. L., & Zaremba, E. T. (1987). Referrals to school psychologists: A national survey. *Journal of School Psychology, 25*(4), 343–354.

Harrison, P. L. (1989). Review of the Wide Range Achievement Test-Revised. In J. Conoley & J. J. Kramer (Eds.), *The tenth mental measurement yearbook* (pp. 903–905). Lincoln, NE: University of Nebraska Press.

Hartman, A. (1975). *Finding families: An ecological approach to family assessment in adoption.* Beverly Hills, CA: Sage.

Hathaway, S. R., & McKinley, J. C. (1989). *Manual for administration and scoring: Minnesota Multiphasic Personality Inventory-2.* Minneapolis, MN: University of Minnesota Press.

Haywood, H. C., Brown, A. L., & Wingenfeld, S. (1990). Dynamic approaches to psychoeducational assessment. *School Psychology Review, 18*(4), 411–422.

Helmes, E., & McLaughlin, J. D. (1983). A comparison of three MMPI short forms: Limited clinical utility in classification. *Journal of Consulting and Clinical Psychology, 52,* 786–787.

Houck, J. E., & Hansen, J. C. (1972). Diagnostic interviewing. In R. H. Woody & J. D. Woody (Eds.), *Clinical assessment in counseling and psychotherapy* (pp. 119–186). New York: Appleton-Century-Crofts.

House, A. E., & Lewis, M. L. (1985). Wechsler Adult Intelligence Scale-Revised. In C. S. Newmark (Ed.), *Major psychological assessment instruments* (pp. 323–379). Boston: Allyn and Bacon.

Hutt, M. L. (1977). *The Hutt adaptation of the Bender-Gestalt Test* (3rd ed.). New York: Grune & Stratton.

Jastak, S., & Wilkinson, G. (1984). *Wide Range Achievement Test-Revised.* Wilmington, DE: Guidance Associates.

Kaufman, A. S. (1975). Factor analysis of the WISC-R at eleven age levels between 6 1/2 and 16 1/2 years. *Journal of Consulting and Clinical Psychology, 43,* 135–147.

Kaufman, A. S. (1979). *Intelligent testing with the WISC-R.* New York: Wiley.

Kaufman, A. S., Kamphaus, R. W., & Kaufman, N. L. (1985). The Kaufman Assessment Battery for Children (K-ABC). In C. S. Newmark (Ed.), *Major psychological assessment instruments* (pp. 249–275). Boston: Allyn and Bacon.

Kaufman, A. S., & Kaufman, N. L. (1983a). *K-ABC administration and scoring manual.* Circle Pines, MN: American Guidance Service.

Kaufman, A. S., & Kaufman, N. L. (1983b). *K-ABC interpretive manual.* Circle Pines, MN: American Guidance Service.

Kessler, J. W. (1988). *Psychopathology of childhood* (2nd ed.). Englewood Cliffs, NJ: Prentice-Hall.

Kissen, M. (1981). Inferring object relations from human figure drawings. *Bulletin of the Menninger Clinic, 45,* 43–54.

Kleinmuntz, B. (1982). *Personality and psychological assessment.* New York: St. Martin's Press.

Klopfer, B., & Davidson, H. H. (1962). *The Rorschach technique.* New York: Harcourt Brace Jovanovich.

Knoff, H. M. (1983). Personality assessment in the schools: Issues and procedures for school psychologists. *School Psychology Review, 12*(4), 391–398.

Koppitz, E. M. (1963). *The Bender Gestalt Test for young children.* New York: Grune & Stratton.

Koppitz, E. M. (1968). *Psychological evaluation of children's human figure drawings.* New York: Grune & Stratton.

Koppitz, E. M. (1975). *The Bender Gestalt Test for young children: Volume II: Research and application, 1963–1975.* New York: Grune & Stratton.

Lachar, D. (1974). *The MMPI: Clinical assessment and automated interpretation.* Los Angeles: Western Psychological Services.

Lachar, D. (1982). *Personality Inventory for Children: Revised format manual supplement.* Los Angeles: Western Psychological Services.

Lachar, D., & LaCombe, J. A. (1983). Objective personality assessment: The Personality Inventory for Children and its applications in the school setting. *School Psychology Review 12*(4), 399–406.

Lanyon, R. I. (1984). Personality assessment. *Annual Review of Psychology, 35,* 667–701.

Laughon, P. (1990). The dynamic assessment of intelligence: A review of three approaches. *School Psychology Review 19*(4), 459–470.

Leavell, C., & Lewandowski, L. (1988). Neuropsychology in the schools: A survey report. *School Psychology Review, 17*(1), 147–155.

Leong, C. K. (1989). Neuropsychological models of learning disabilities. In C. R. Reynolds & E. Fletcher-Janzen (Eds.), *Handbook of clinical child neuropsychology* (pp. 335–355). New York: Plenum.

Lezak, M. D. (1983). *Neuropsychological assessment* (2nd ed.). New York: Oxford University Press.

Lindzey, G. (1961). *Projective techniques and cross-cultural research.* New York: Appleton-Century-Crofts.

Lubin, B., Larsen, R. M., & Matarazzo, J. D. (1984). Patterns of psychological test usage in the United States. *American Psychologist, 39,* 451–454.

Machover, K. (1949). *Personality projection in the drawing of the human figure.* Springfield, IL: Thomas.

Majovski, L. V. (1989). Higher cortical functions in children: A developmental perspective. In C. R. Reynolds & E. Fletcher-Janzen (Eds.), *Handbook of clinical child neuropsychology* (pp. 41–67). New York: Plenum.

Markwardt, F. C. (1989). *Peabody Individual Achievement Test-Revised.* Circle Pines, MN: American Guidance Service.

Martin, R. P. (1988). *Assessment of personality and behavior problems: Infancy through adolescence.* New York: Guilford.

Matarazzo, J. D. (1972). *Wechsler's measurement and appraisal of adult intelligence.* Baltimore: Williams & Wilkins.

McArthur, D. S., & Roberts, G. E. (1982). *Roberts Apperception Test for Children: Manual.* Los Angeles: Western Psychological Services.

McCarthy, D. A. (1972). *Manual: McCarthy Scales of Children's Abilities.* New York: Psychological Corporation.

Mercer, J. R. (1979). *System of Multicultural Pluralistic Assessment technical manual.* New York: Psychological Corporation.

Meyer, R. G. (1989). *The clinician's handbook* (2nd ed.). Boston: Allyn and Bacon.

Murray, H. A. (1943). *Thematic Apperception Test.* Cambridge, MA: Harvard University Press.

National Association of School Psychologists. (1984a). Principles for professional ethics. In *Professional Conduct Manual* (pp. 1–17). Stratford, CT: Author.

National Association of School Psychologists. (1984b). Standards for the provision of school psychology services. In *Professional Conduct Manual* (pp. 189–133). Stratford, CT: Author.

Newmark, C. S. (1985). The MMPI. In C. S. Newmark (Ed.), *Major psychological assessment instruments* (pp. 11–64). Boston: Allyn and Bacon.

Nussbaum, N. L., & Bigler, E. D. (1989). Halstead-Reitan neuropsychological test batteries for children. In C. R. Reynolds & E. Fletcher-Janzen (Eds.), *Handbook of clinical child neuropsychology* (pp. 181–191). New York: Plenum.

Obrzut, J. E., & Cummings, J. A. (1983). The projective approach to personality assessment: An analysis of thematic picture techniques. *School Psychology Review, 12*(4), 414–420.

Ogdon, D. P. (1982). *Psychodiagnostics and personality assessment: A handbook* (2nd ed.). Los Angeles: Western Psychological Services.

Oster, G. D., Carol, J. E., Eagen, D. R., & Lillo, M. A. (1988). *Assessing adolescents.* Elmsford, NY: Pergamon.

Ownby, R. L. (1987). *Psychological reports.* Brandon, VT: Clinical Psychology Publishing.

Paget, K. D. (1987). Systemic family assessment: Concepts and strategies for school psychologists. *School Psychology Review 16*(4), 429–442.

Pintner, R. (1931). *Intelligence testing.* New York: Holt.

Piotrowski, C. (1985). Clinical assessment: Attitudes of the Society for Personality Assessment. *Southern Psychologist, 2,* 80–83.

Piotrowski, C., & Keller, J. W. (1984). Attitudes toward clinical assessment by members of the AABT. *Psychological Reports, 55,* 831–838.

Piotrowski, C., & Keller, J. W. (1989). Psychological testing in outpatient mental health facilities: A national study. *Professional Psychology, 20*(6), 423–425.

Piotrowski, C., & Lubin, B. (1990). Assessment practices of health psychologists. *Professional Psychology, 21*(2), 99–106.

Prout, H. T. (1983). School psychologists and social-emotional assessment techniques: Patterns in training and use. *School Psychology Review, 12*(4), 377–383.

Rapaport, D., Gill, M. M., & Schafer, R. (1968). *Diagnostic psychological testing.* New York: International Universities Press.

Reschly, D. J., Genshaft, J., & Binder, M. A. (1987). *The 1986 NASP survey: Comparison of practitioners, NASP leadership, and university faculty on key issues.* Washington, DC: National Association of School Psychologists.

Reynolds, C. R. (1989). Measurement and statistical problems in neuropsychological assessment of children. In C. R. Reynolds & E. Fletcher-Janzen (Eds.), *Handbook of clinical child neuropsychology* (pp. 147–166). New York: Plenum.

Reynolds, C. R., & Kamphaus, R. W. (Eds.). (1990). *Handbook of psychological and educational assessment of children: Intelligence and achievement.* New York: Guilford.

Rosenberg, R. P., & Beck, S. (1986). Preferred assessment methods and treatment modalities for hyperactive children among clinical child and school psychologists. *Journal of Clinical Child Psychology, 15*(2), 142–147.

Salvia, J., & Ysseldyke, J. E. (1988). *Assessment in special and remedial education* (4th ed.). Boston: Houghton Mifflin.

Sattler, J. M. (1982). *Assessment of children's intelligence and special abilities* (2nd ed.). Boston: Allyn and Bacon.

Sattler, J. M. (1988). *Assessment of children* (3rd ed.). San Diego: Author.

Schauble, P. G. (1980). Facilitative conditions in communication. In R. H. Woody (Ed.), *The encyclopedia of clinical assessment, Volume 2* (pp. 1035–1041). San Francisco: Jossey-Bass.

Shellenberger, S. (1982). Presentation and interpretation of psychological data in educational settings. In C. R. Reynolds & T. B. Guthrie (Eds.), *The handbook of school psychology* (pp. 51–81). New York: Wiley.

Siegel, M. G. (1987). *Psychological testing from early childhood through adolescence: A developmental and psychodynamic approach.* Madison, CT: International Universities Press.

Stern, W. (1914). *The psychological method of testing intelligence.* Baltimore: Warwick & York.

Sullivan, H. S. (1954). *The psychiatric interview.* New York: Norton.

Sullivan, P. M., & Burley, S. K. (1990). Mental testing of the hearing-impaired child. In C. R. Reynolds & R. K. Kamphaus (Eds.), *Handbook of psychological and educational assessment of children: Intelligence and achievement* (pp. 761–788). New York: Guilford.

Sundberg, N. S. (1977). *Assessment of persons.* Englewood Cliffs, NJ: Prentice-Hall.

Teeter, P. A. (1989). Neuropsychological approaches to the remediation of educational deficits. In C. R. Reynolds & E. Fletcher-Janzen (Eds.), *Handbook of clinical child neuropsychology* (pp. 357–376). New York: Plenum.

Telzrow, C. (1989). WPPSI-R seen as improved assessment. *NASP Communique, 18*(2), 6.

Terman, L. M. (1916). *The measurement of intelligence.* Boston: Houghton Mifflin.

Thorndike, R. L., Hagen, E. P., & Sattler, J. M. (1986a). *Guide for administering and scoring the fourth edition: Stanford-Binet Intelligence Scale.* Chicago: Riverside.

Thorndike, R. L., Hagen, E. P., & Sattler, J. M. (1986b). *Technical manual: Stanford-Binet Intelligence Scale, Fourth Edition.* Chicago: Riverside.

Tramontana, M. G., & Hooper, S. R. (1989). Neuropsychology of child psychopathology. In C. R. Reynolds & E. Fletcher-Janzen (Eds.), *Handbook of clinical child neuropsychology* (pp. 87–196). New York: Plenum.

Wade, T. C., & Baker, T. B. (1977). Opinions and use of psychological tests. *American Psychologist, 32,* 874–882.

Walsh, K. W. (1978). *Neuropsychology: A clinical approach.* New York: Churchill Livingstone.

Webb, J., McNamara, K., & Rodgers, D. (1981). *Configural interpretations of the MMPI and CPI.* Columbus: Ohio Psychology Publishing.

Wechsler, D. (1958). *The measurement and appraisal of adult intelligence* (4th ed.). Baltimore: Williams & Wilkins.

Wechsler, D. (1967). *Manual: Wechsler Preschool and Primary Scale of Intelligence.* New York: Psychological Corporation.

Wechsler, D. (1974). *Manual: Wechsler Intelligence Scale for Children-Revised.* New York: Psychological Corporation.

Wechsler, D. (1975). Intelligence defined and undefined. *American Psychologist, 30,* 135–139.

Wechsler, D. (1981). *Manual: Wechsler Adult Intelligence Scale-Revised.* New York: Psychological Corporation.

Wechsler, D. (1989). *Manual: Wechsler Preschool and Primary Scale of Intelligence-Revised.* San Antonio: Psychological Corporation, Harcourt Brace Jovanovich.

Wechsler, D. (1991). *Manual: Wechsler Intelligence Scale for Children – Third Edition.* San Antonio: Psychological Corporation. Harcourt Brace Jovanovich.

Wilson, C. C. (1986). Family assessment in preschool evaluation. *School Psychology Review, 15*(2), 166–179.

Wilson, R. S., Rosenbaum, G., Brown, G., Rourke, D., Whitman, D., & Grisell, J. (1978). An index of premorbid intelligence. *Journal of Consulting and Clinical Psychology, 46*(6), 1154–1555.

Wirt, R. D., Lachar, D., Klinedinst, J. K., & Seat, P. D. (1984). *Multidimensional description of child personality: A manual for the Personality Inventory for Children* (rev. ed.). Los Angeles: Western Psychological Services.

Wise, P. S. (1989). *The use of assessment techniques by applied psychologists.* Belmont, CA: Wadsworth.

Woody, R. H., & Robertson, M. (1988). *Becoming a clinical psychologist.* Madison, CT: International Universities Press.

CHAPTER 10

THE SCHOOL-FAMILY-
COMMUNITY INTERFACE

This chapter describes less traditional aspects of school psychology service delivery, with particular focus on interventions with families. A developmental and social systems framework is applied to two populations of high-risk children and adolescents to illustrate the multifaceted role child psychologists can assume in providing services to children and families and in building effective school-family-community partnerships.

The major portion of the chapter is devoted to the implications of federal legislation and educational policy toward infants, toddlers, and preschoolers with developmental delays. Because of the extensive programmatic needs of this diverse early childhood population, specialized issues in family-centered assessment and intervention are discussed. The theme of family-centered service delivery beyond the confines of school buildings is highlighted. The second group discussed is children and adolescents with chronic illness and special health-care needs. The contribution of psychology to the management of chronic illness is discussed and the importance of the liaison role addressed. Administrative issues related to practice in health-care settings also are considered.

NATIONAL POLICY AGENDA FOR SERVING YOUNG CHILDREN

On October 8, 1986, President Reagan signed Public Law 99-457 (Ballard, Ramirez, & Zantal-Wiener, 1987). The Education of the Handicapped Act (EHA) Amendments of 1986 represent the most far-reaching federal policy ever implemented for early childhood intervention. It not only extended and reauthorized existing programs for children and youth (ages 3

through 21) with special needs, it also created new policy and programmatic opportunities for children with special needs (ages birth to 5 years). This law acknowledges the critical role families play in the development of their children with disabilities and the need for a partnership of citizens to provide leadership for change.

In its design, Congress made the realistic assumption that no single agency, advocacy group, parent organization, or discipline could accommodate all the needs of children with special needs and their families (Trohanis, 1989). This statute lowers the age range stipulated in Public Law 94-142, the Education for All Handicapped Children Act of 1975, from age 5 to age 3. Although the bill did not mandate universal services to children younger than 5 years of age, it strengthened incentives for states to serve preschoolers and established a new discretionary program for services to children with disabilities from birth to 3 years (Meisels, Harbin, Modigliani, & Olson, 1988; McNulty, 1989). There are two portions of PL 99-457 that are especially crucial to the expansion and improvement of comprehensive services to infants, toddlers, and preschoolers.

Title I, Programs for Infants and Toddlers with Disabilities

Title I (or Part H) is a new component of the Education of the Handicapped Act. It established a discretionary program to assist states in planning, developing, and implementing a statewide system of comprehensive, coordinated, interdisciplinary, interagency programs for all young children with handicaps who are 0 to 36 months of age. Effective October 1, 1990, the Individuals with Disabilities Act (PL 101-476) revised and extended EHA, with a specific call to facilitate and improve the early identification of infants and toddlers with disabilities or those at risk of having developmental disabilities. It also called for evaluation of progress being made toward providing early intervention services for infants and toddlers with disabilities. The statewide systems under PL 99-457 are aimed at the needs of infants and toddlers with developmental delays (criteria determined by each state) or a diagnosed physical or mental condition with a high probability of an associated developmental delay. At a state's discretion, children at-risk for substantial developmental delay also are included (Ballard, Ramirez, & Zantal-Wiener, 1989). Children meeting these criteria are eligible for early intervention services that are developmental in nature.

The language of Part H implies a focus on enhancing family functioning. Both family strengths and needs that relate to enhancing the development of the young child with a disability are to be specified as components of the *Individualized Family Service Plan* (IFSP) (Dokecki & Heflinger, 1989). Basic components of Part H and the IFSP are outlined in Chapter 12.

The IFSP is to specify all relevant services for the young child and the family without regard to the services available from existing programs. All early intervention services must be provided at no cost to parents except where federal or state law provides for a system of payments by parents, including arrangement for a schedule of sliding fees (Ballard, Ramirez, & Zantal-Wiener, 1989). Once the IFSP has been instituted, a reasonable estimate can be generated of the cost of each of the service components the child and family will receive. The plan would indicate service needs, outcome objectives, costs, and time frames, and could be used both for case management and allocation of fiscal responsibility to the assorted public and private payers, including parents.

As an illustration, Fox, Freedman, and Klepper (1989) indicate that on the basis of an IFSP, a private insurance carrier could be charged for health services (e.g., physical therapy) covered in the family's policy; Medicaid could be billed for the services it provides enrolled children; and the parents, if they had sufficient resources, could be required to finance services not covered by public or private insurance or the school system (e.g., physical accommodations within the home). IFSP review at 6-month intervals compel concomitant updates of the cost allocation procedure. The reader is referred to *Medicaid Financing for Early Intervention Services* (June 1987), *Private Health Insurance Financing for Early Intervention Services* (March 1988), and *Private Health Insurance Coverage of Chronically Ill Children* (March 1986) for reviews of financing opportunities of health care for children with special needs.

Required services such as case management and individualized family service plans are based on the premise of a coordinated and comprehensive service system. Service providers will need to reorient themselves toward a more global systems view as they broaden their vision beyond their own discipline and programs to meet the multifaceted needs of families through interdisciplinary and interagency programs (McNulty, 1989).

While providing new federal appropriations for direct service to early childhood populations, the law significantly challenges a complex and fragmented service delivery system. In a 1985–1986 survey of current state policies, Meisels and colleagues (1988) found an exceptionally wide variety of ways in which birth-to-6 services were administered. For birth-to-3 services, Public Health ($N = 28$, 54.9%) was the most frequently named lead administering state agency, followed by the State Education Agency and State Human or Social Service Agency ($N = 23$, 45.1% for each). Other agencies listed were private ones such as Easter Seals, United Cerebral Palsy, Catholic Charities, and Association for Retarded Citizens ($N = 18$, 35.3%). For 3- to 5-year-olds, a different pattern of lead administration was found. The most frequent lead agency was the State Education Agency ($N = 37$, 72.6%), followed by the Local Education Agency ($N = 29$, 56.7%) and Public Health ($N = 18$, 35.3%).

With the passage of PL 99-457, a law encourages mandated services in a collaborative, interagency-administered environment (Meisels et al., 1989). To address the problem of less than optimal interagency cooperation, the statute requires the creation of a state interagency coordinating council composed of parents, public and private providers, a state legislator, and higher education and state agency representation appointed by the governor. Its function is to advise and to assist the state's lead agency in planning and operating the comprehensive system. While the council is required only for the infant and toddler program, McNulty (1989) advocates for its use to provide guidance to the entire birth-to-5 initiative. In some states, the lead agency for service delivery to infants and toddlers with disabilities is the Department of Health, whereas for preschoolers it is the Department of Education. PL 101-476 recognizes the difficulty with interagency coordination and highlights the importance of facilitating the transition from early intervention services for infants and toddlers to preschool special education or general education.

Title II, Preschool Grants Program

Title II of PL 99-457 amended Section 619 of PL 94-142, the prior Preschool Incentive Grant program. It extended the rights and protections of PL 94-142 (EHA, Part B) and authorized a dramatic increase in the federal fiscal contribution for all eligible children (3 through 5 years) with disabilities. States are not required to report these children by disability category. In 1987, the U.S. Department of Education made the first grants to state education agencies (SEAs) to implement the preschool initiative. The SEAs disbursed the funds to local education agencies (LEAs), intermediate education units, and other contracted service agencies. By the 1990–1991 school year, SEAs must have made amendments in their Part B state plans to incorporate policies and procedures to ensure the availability of a free appropriate public education (FAPE) for all children with disabilities ages 3 through 5 (Trohanis, 1989).

Community services to provide provisions of FAPE (individualized education program [IEP], due process, confidentiality, and least restrictive environment) can be implemented in several ways. Directly or indirectly through contracts with other qualified service agencies, the SEA/LEA may administer home- or center-based programs, with diversity in the acceptable length of the service day and type of program (e.g., part-day home based or part- or full-day center based). Family services assume an important role in preschool programs, with parent instruction included in the preschooler's IEP whenever appropriate and to the extent the parents prefer (Ballard, Ramirez, & Zantal-Wiener, 1987). PL 101-476 encourages family education.

Challenges for Policy Implementation

Public and private participation in planning, implementing, monitoring, and evaluating PL 99-457 is underway. Translating policy statements into motion requires cooperation across all government levels and between public and private sectors. Trohanis (1989) poses challenges to improving and expanding services for young children with special needs and their families.

1. Theoretically, Titles I and II are intended to be interrelated rather than distinct state programs. Coordinating the substance of the separate but related portions of the law needs to be done in a coherent fashion.
2. General designs, responsibilities, and activities—including other federal and state early childhood initiatives such as child care, early education, adolescent pregnancy, child abuse, mental health, Head Start, maternal and child health, and Even Start, along with best practices—must be coordinated.
3. Eligibility requirements—including definitions of developmental delay and at-risk, as well as the special needs of minority, migrant, rural, native, and Pacific-Basin Americans—should be addressed.
4. A comprehensive and community-based mixture of early intervention and preschool services—including FAPE, IFSP, child identification and placement, case management, developmental and family assessment, parent

training, health-care services, and procedural safeguards—must be enacted.

5. Transitions from critical care facilities—such as the neonatal intensive care unit, to early intervention, to preschool, to kindergarten programs—must be coordinated. PL 101-457 emphasizes the need for transition planning from medical care to early intervention services.

6. A comprehensive system of professional preparation must be formulated to address such issues as qualification, preservice and inservice training, and licensure/certification.

7. Parents must genuinely be integrated into the planning, development, and implementation stages within communities and at the state level through Interagency Coordinating Councils.

IMPLICATIONS FOR CHILD PSYCHOLOGY

Short, Simeonsson, and Huntington (1990) discuss a number of service domains highlighted in PL 99-457 in which psychology can make a contribution. This chapter expands the discussion of two of these areas: (1) assessment and diagnosis and (2) intervention.

Assessment and Diagnosis

As a result of this legislation, assessment activities will differ from traditional models. Infants, toddlers, and preschoolers pose significant challenges to assessment. Thus, a reconceptualization of practice is necessary due to special characteristics of this population and a variety of measurement issues (see Epps & Jackson, 1991).

Child Characteristics
Behavioral States. In infant assessment, behavioral states are a crucial consideration. They reflect the maturity, status, and organization of the central nervous system (CNS) and provide a context for understanding the infant's behavior. Sleep states may be quiet or active; awake states include alert, active/fussy, or crying. Drowsiness typi-

cally is regarded as an awake but transitional state. State may serve as an obstacle during the assessment process (Korner, 1972). For example, fussy infants will not attend optimally. Since CNS dysfunction is a common feature of at-risk and handicapped infants, consideration of the clarity, lability, and rhythmicity of behavioral states is especially important in assessment and intervention because they mediate behavior and influence the infant's ability to respond to various forms of stimulation (Helm & Simeonsson, 1989).

Temperament. There are several different theoretical perspectives of individual differences in behavioral style or temperament. Measuring temperament in young children with developmental delays provides an avenue for considering characteristics of the child as they are viewed by or influence the caregiver. Thomas, Chess, and Birch (1968) have done much of the early work on temperament. They demonstrated the concurrent and predictive validity of nine categories of temperament: activity, rhythmicity, adaptability, approach, mood, intensity, distractibility, persistence, and threshold. The three personality clusters derived from these categories were difficult, easy, and slow-to-warm up. In later research, the difficult infant was described as fussy, hard-to-soothe, and labile (Bates, Freeland, & Lounsbury, 1979).

However, the notion of a "difficult" child has been criticized on the basis that difficultness does not reside within the child, but rather is evident in the interactions between particular temperament characteristics and certain environmental demands. As such, any child characteristic can appear to be difficult if it violates the caregiver's expectations of appropriate behavior. Since caregiver perceptions of the easiness or difficultness of their child will have a transactional effect on the family interactions, and consequently on the child's development, caregiver impressions of their child's temperament must be included in a complete assessment (Huntington, 1989).

Clearly, infant assessment is not merely a downward extrapolation of child assessment (Ulrey, 1982a). Similarly, assessment of toddlers and preschoolers requires specialized knowledge and skills due to their cognitive and behavioral differences from older children. Ulrey (1982b) discusses the impact of emerging developmental skills in cognition and behavioral controls on assessment results.

Preoperational Thinking.   Piagetian theory provides a framework for understanding cognitive differences between preschoolers and school-age children. Piaget has described young children's thinking as preoperational, which applies to the nominal age range of 2 to 7 years. Piaget (1967) and Piaget and Inhelder (1969) discuss preoperational cognitive contents as a distinct stage of cognitive development; Piaget (1973) seems to consider them as the preparatory phase of the concrete-operational stage. In either case, this stage is characterized by the absence of certain abilities.

One feature chiefly illustrative of the preoperational stage is egocentrism, introduced in Piaget's first book on children's language (Piaget, 1926). Egocentrism is a dimension related to the degree to which children view themselves as the center of reality. Behaviors that suggest that children are preoccupied with themselves and/or unconcerned with events around them or that indicate that the child has difficulty relating to other's feelings are termed *egocentric*.

According to Piagetian theory, preoperational children are unaware of points of view other than their own since they think that everyone experiences the world in the same manner they do (Brainerd, 1978). This egocentric thinking has significant implications throughout the assessment process. The preoperational child has minimal regard for ensuring that the examiner understands an explanation (Ulrey 1982b). With the inability to deal with several aspects of a situation concurrently, the young child cannot consider both the other's point of view and her or his own simultaneously. The child, therefore, centers solely on her or his own point of view (Ginsburg & Opper, 1988).

Behavioral Controls.   Toddlers' nonverbal behavior also signifies the limited dimension and egocentricism of preoperational thinking. They often seek to test behavioral limits and may refuse items or be easily distracted by more interesting items. Resistance and independence during assessment are related to the child's emerging sense of autonomy and initiative (consider Erikson's Theory of Psychosocial Development, Erikson, 1972). For slightly older children, the child's behavior becomes less of a struggle with limits. The child uses manipulation or appeal to adults to gain some control. To ensure adult attention and approval, various social behaviors such as eye contact, smiling, and physical proximity are seen. While these behaviors are a way of gaining attention, the 3- to 6-year-old remains cognitively egocentric with little concern for correctness in responding. The challenge for the examiner is to structure and to restructure tasks to maximize attention to task (Ulrey, 1982b).

Assessment Issues
Abuse in Assessment.   Psychometric theory details the logic of technically adequate assessment instruments (e.g., Nunnally, 1978). For early childhood populations, there are few psychometrically sound and developmentally appropriate assessment tools (Lehr, Ysseldyke, & Thurlow, 1987). Bias in assessment can occur when instruments normed on children without disabilities are used to derive norm-referenced scores for children with disabilities. Some instruments even enable the user to generate developmental age scores when the instrument never was standardized on a representative sample of children (Bailey, 1989).

In addition, stimulus characteristics and response demands of test items may penalize many children with impairments. For example, a preschooler with hemiparesis is at a distinct disadvantage when performing tasks such as puzzles that require use of hands. Infants with sensory impairment cannot perform many items on the Bayley Scales of Infant Development (Bayley,

1969) such as tasks involving the red ring and/or rattle. Hence, assessment for the purpose of diagnosis and classification is fraught with difficulties.

Although there are numerous measures used with early childhood populations (see Bailey, 1989; Meisels & Provence, 1989), they are not valid for all purposes of assessment. There is abuse in assessment when practitioners use an instrument such as the Denver Developmental Screening Test (Frankenburg & Dodds, 1969) to make an eligibility decision or the Mental Development Index of the Bayley Scales of Infant Development (Bayley, 1969) to plan a developmental intervention.

Family Assessment. PL 99-457 is family-centered legislation. Hence, professionals must involve the family at all levels of assessment and intervention. For example, to screen a child for psychosocial risk, the stress endured by the child's caregivers and the supports available to buffer and to alleviate that stress must be considered (Meisels & Provence, 1989). To follow the intent of this federal policy, family strengths and needs must be identified in order to individualize family support and services. Therefore, the purview of assessment must be expanded beyond a sole child focus as professionals regard the family as a system and assess various factors influencing it (see Ostfeld & Gibbs, 1990).

Bailey (1988) discusses at least five reasons for conducting comprehensive family assessment: (1) to meet legal mandates, (2) to understand a child as part of a family system, (3) to identify families' needs for services, (4) to identify families' strengths that promote family adaptation, and (5) to expand the base for evaluating services.

1. *Legal basis.* With the passage of PL 99-457 came the provision that instruction for parents should be included in the IEP for preschoolers when appropriate and desired by parents. In addition, parents of infants and toddlers should assist

in developing their own IFSP with the support of an interdisciplinary team. Since the law emphasizes *individualized,* an appraisal of individual family needs is necessary.

2. *Child within the family system.* Bronfenbrenner (1977) emphasized the significance of an ecological view of development with the child nested within a family, which in turn is nested within a broader community system. The bidirectional nature of adult-child interactions (Bell, 1968) and transactional theory (Sameroff & Chandler, 1975) in which children and caregivers affect one another in interactions over time highlight the notion of the child-family interface. The child both affects and is affected by family system. Bailey (1988) outlines several implications of this child-family interaction for assessment and intervention.

First, child intervention will likely influence the family. Treatment effects may be beneficial for the family such as when a child becomes more independent in a personal-management routine or when the child participates more fully in family activities in the community. On the other hand, intervention may be stressful (or even change family structure, as discussed in Chapter 6) such as when multiple disciplines dictate time-consuming parent-implemented treatment protocols. Family assessment will help the professional to appraise the family's needs and preferences for intervention foci and procedures (consider the discussion of social validity in Chapter 7).

Second, family assessment can help determine the effect of interventions with one family member on other members in the family system. For example, home-based intervention services provided only in the early afternoon may involve only one parent to the consistent exclusion of the other parent. Interventionists, therefore, may inadvertently be reinforcing an enmeshed relationship between the child and one parent who works with the child during the therapist's home visits and continues with the treatment program throughout the week. This form of intervention also could serve to enhance a disengaged stance of the other parent who becomes less involved with the spouse whose major responsibility is to implement developmental interventions with the child. These concepts in structural family therapy (Minuchin, 1974) are discussed in greater detail in Chapter 6.

Third, family assessment elucidates systems influences on families such as how they view the services available to them.

3. *Family needs for services.* Many families of young children with disabilities have special needs. They may need information about the disability or assistance in locating child-care or respite services. They may experience stress for a variety of reasons such as the demands of caregiving and difficulty managing a combination of home-based and center-based services in addition to family routines. Considering that much of the literature tends to emphasize negative feelings experienced by siblings of children with developmental delays (Johnson & Murphy, 1990), families also may need support in helping their other children. While many have or develop natural support systems, as a group, families with children with delays have needs beyond those associated with caring for children without disabilities (Gallagher, Beckman, & Cross, 1983; Murphy, 1982).

4. *Family strengths.* Dunst (1985) and Turnbull and Turnbull (1986) have indicated that a deficit model traditionally has been promulgated that assumes that all families with children with disabilities have problems. There has been a tendency to apply negative generalizations and to diminish positive influences of a child with delays on family members. Alternatively, family assessment can be used to identify and to augment family strengths and resources (Bailey, 1988). A proactive empowerment approach focuses on family strengths and resources and is discussed in the following section about intervention.

5. *Evaluation of services.* A fifth rationale for family assessment pertains to the ultimate goals of early intervention since family outcomes may

be as significant as child outcomes (Bailey & Simeonsson, 1984; Bailey et al., 1986). Throughout the course of service delivery, data should be collected to provide ongoing assessment of family needs and strengths to determine when interventions and services are effective and satisfactory and when they may need to be altered (Bailey, 1988).

Characteristics of Effective Assessment

Best practice assessment of young children with disabilities and their families incorporates the following guidelines (Bailey, 1988, 1989):

> Socially valid developmental, behavioral, and family domains
>
> Recognition of the importance of family values and traditions
>
> Family priorities for goals and services
>
> Multiple sources and measures
>
> Interdisciplinary assessment
>
> Ecologically valid assessment
>
> Nondiscriminatory and culturally sensitive assessment
>
> Variation to match program type and demands
>
> Formative evaluation

Socially Valid Domains. Assessment must be comprehensive, addressing relevant developmental domains such as sensorimotor and cognitive skills, motor skills (including positioning and use of adaptive equipment), communication skills (including augmentative), play and social-interaction skills, and personal-management skills related to daily living. Behaviors such as alertness, consolability, endurance, goal-directedness, attention to task, and interfering behaviors such as resistance, noncompliance, stereotypy, and aggression also should be assessed (Bailey, 1989).

A large number of family dimensions could be assessed such as parent-child interactions, parent teaching behaviors and child behavior management, and family stress, coping, support, grief, and structure. Focal points of family assessment are relevant in that they influence subsequent decisions about service delivery. Assessment in each of these areas is not recommended since it would be intrusive and unnecessary (Bailey, 1988). Rather, plans for family assessment must have a clear purpose and be tailored to a particular family.

Family Values and Traditions. Serving culturally diverse populations of young children with disabilities and their families requires cultural sensitivity. If cultural and situational influences are ignored, even the best intentioned programs for culturally diverse young children and their families could be doomed for failure (Anderson & Fenichel, 1989).

Family Priorities for Goals and Services. Participation of family members in decision making can be enhanced by planned assessment of family needs and face-to-face interviews. Bailey (1987) advocates using parents' priorities as the primary basis for ascertaining goals and services and addressing these first since asking parents to pursue goals they regard as inappropriate is likely to be counterproductive. (The reader is referred to Chapter 7 for a discussion on the relationship between the acceptability of intervention targets and procedures and efficacious outcome.) Sole reliance on professional-determined goals usurps family decision making and can begin to foster in parents a sense of helplessness and powerlessness (Dunst, 1985).

In a related investigation, Brinckerhoff and Vincent (1986) found that parents involved in assessing their child's developmental status and in presenting their goals and concerns in the IEP meeting were more likely to make independent decisions and to contribute to programmatic decisions. In a review of 24 studies of parental congruency with professionals' assessment ratings, Sheehan (1988) found a fairly systematic pattern of parental estimates higher than test performance determined by diagnosticians. These find-

ings suggest that parents should be involved in the assessment process.

Multiple Sources and Measures. PL 99-457 mandates "a multidisciplinary assessment of unique needs and the identification of services appropriate to meet such needs" (p. 1149). PL 101-476 addresses "interdisciplinary models and practices." Thus, it has been asserted that a comprehensive, multidimensional assessment procedure be used to gather information across multiple domains from various sources using diverse measurement strategies (Brooks-Gunn & Lewis, 1981; Mott, Fewell, Lewis, Meisels, Shonkoff, & Simeonsson, 1986; Neisworth & Bagnato, 1986; Odom & Schuster, 1986; Paget & Nagle, 1986).

One type of assessment is *direct testing* of the child using norm-referenced, criterion-referenced, or curriculum-based assessment. Piagetian measures to assessment can be used as well. For information about specific instruments, the reader is referred to Langley (1989), Meisels and Provence (1989), and Paget (1989). Standardized inventories also can be used with parents and families to assess numerous variables (see Bailey & Simeonsson, 1988; Grotevant & Carlson, 1989; Simeonsson, 1986). Testing of early childhood populations is a highly specialized professional activity that is often misused. It is incumbent on practitioners to adhere to professional standards of test use and interpretation. For comprehensive guidelines, see the *Standards for Educational and Psychological Testing* (American Educational Research Association, American Psychological Association, & National Council on Measurement in Education, 1985). Ostfeld and Gibbs (1990) recommend a literature search to obtain current information about technical adequacy and target populations.

A second major mode of assessment is *direct observation.* Issues related to observation are discussed in Chapter 7. Systematic observations are a critical component of all assessment procedures and can provide enhanced information about a child's or parent's behavioral repertoire. There are certain domains, such as play skills, that can be assessed in a meaningful fashion only via observations within the natural ecology of typical play situations (Bailey, 1989; Wolery & Bailey, 1989). It is important to note, however, that interpretations of observations can be biased by information given to observers. For example, Epps (1991a, 1991b) found that a description of a premature infant's health status (no major medical complications vs. lung damage) significantly influenced nurses' and parents' ratings of the infant's behavior.

A third means of gathering information is by *interviewing* parents. The family-centered interview can serve the dual purposes of (1) assessment of family characteristics, family strengths, and family perceptions of situations, events, goals, or services; and (2) collaborative goal setting (Winton, 1988). A limitation of unstructured interviews is their inefficiency for gathering large amounts of information. The lack of standardization also can interfere with research and program evaluation (Ostfeld & Gibbs, 1990). *Rating scales or checklists* (see Meisels & Provence, 1989) also can be used, although a number of parents may regard some items as invasive and extending beyond the purview of the early intervention. For interpretation of some sensitive areas, a professional with clinical training in mental-health issues is advised (see Chapter 6).

Interdisciplinary Assessment. Federal policy dictates assessment by a team of professionals. Considering the diverse genotypes and phenotypes of young children with developmental delays, assessment for diagnosing needs is complex. It is improbable that one discipline will have sufficient breadth of expertise to design and to implement an appropriate program. Therefore, a team of professionals representing diverse disciplines and orientations is the preferred assessment model for a number of reasons (Ohio Department of Education [ODE], 1989):

1. It provides a mechanism for testing hypotheses across several data sources.
2. It promotes problem identification and development of approaches to intervention.

3. It contributes to total care and continuity of services for young children and their families by including professionals across agencies and settings.
4. It involves individuals sensitive to and knowledgeable about the culture of the child and family.
5. It provides a comprehensive description of the child's and family's strengths and areas of need.

For information about assessments conducted by other disciplines, the reader is referred to several sources: motor skills (Gallagher & Cech, 1988; Smith, 1989) and communication skills (Olswang & Bain, 1988; Roberts & Crais, 1989).

These interdisciplinary groups can consist of core teams and support teams whose membership can vary. One suggested composition of the core team includes early childhood education, speech and language, and school psychology (ODE, 1989). Members of the support team, who may represent other school professionals and agencies, contribute to assessment and program planning for individual cases. Figure 10.1 depicts the relationship between the core team and support team. The parent is an integral part of the assessment process and interfaces with both teams (Sexton, Miller, & Murdock, 1984).

The manner in which teams function can vary. Fordyce (1981) classifies three teams of multiple professionals. The *multidisciplinary team* consists of individuals from multiple disciplines who are largely autonomous and unaffected by the actions of other team members. The *interdisciplinary team* has expanded interactions among team members, with each team participant depending on other disciplines for significant input. The outcome is a comprehensive and integrated service plan that is accomplished by an interactive effort from the disciplines involved. In the *transdisciplinary team,* multiple disciplines function together in the initial assessment, but one or two team members provide services.

Within this framework, professionals relinquish their roles to the one or two direct service providers and instruct them in performing their

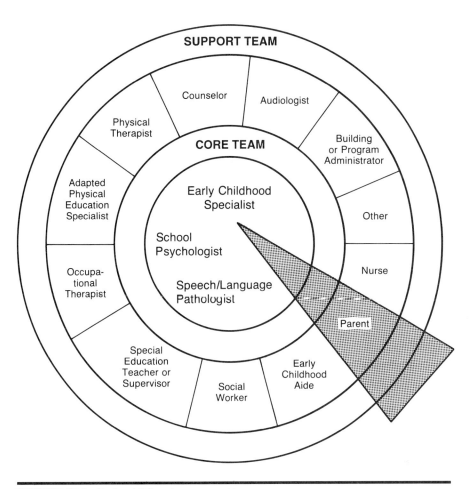

FIGURE 10.1   Early childhood assessment team

Source: From Ohio Department of Education, Division of Early Childhood Education (1990). *The early childhood identification process: A manual for screening and assessment.* Columbus, OH, p. 24. Reprinted with permission.

responsibilities (Lyon & Lyon, 1980). While the interdisciplinary team generally is regarded as superior to the multidisciplinary team, research articles and position papers have addressed numerous problems with the interdisciplinary team process (see Bailey, 1984). Disputes remain about the relative advantages and disadvantages of the transdisciplinary team (Bailey, 1989).

Bailey (1989) advocates interdisciplinary collaboration during the early stages of the assessment process. One possible tactic is for team members to use components of the same assess-

ment instrument that consists of various domains (e.g., communication, motor skills). Another approach is *arena assessment* in which the primary assessor begins the assessment with other team members and parents recording their observations and scoring segments of their assessment protocols from a distance. As the session continues, team participants may direct the primary assessor to administer certain tasks pertinent to the observer's discipline. Periodically an observer may assist or administer items directly.

The rationale for arena assessment lies in the

relatively undifferentiated state of the infant, which questions the logic of discrete assessments. This method creates a new unity among professionals as it aims to preserve the expertise of interdisciplinary specialization (Foley, 1990). Wolery and Dyk (1984) compared arena assessment with more traditional interdisciplinary assessment of young children and found that both parents and participating professionals preferred the arena procedure.

Ecologically Valid Assessment. Bailey (1989) outlines three components of ecologically valid assessment. First, parents are included as significant participants in the assessment process, which enables consideration of the home ecology to ensure socially valid target areas. Second, in vivo observations are conducted within the context of naturally occurring routines to assess the child's functional use of skills. And third, transition plans for future environments are incorporated into the assessment process. For example, assessment strategies must address the extent to which a toddler currently displays the skills needed in the anticipated preschool environment. Assessments performed by strangers, using irrelevant tasks in artificial settings and situations are antithetical to ecologically valid (and hence useful) approaches. (The reader is referred to Chapter 7 for more discussion of ecobehavioral analysis strategies.)

Nondiscriminatory and Culturally Sensitive Assessment. Given the heterogeneity of the early childhood special education population, there are formidable challenges to nondiscriminatory assessment. The stimulus characteristics and response demands of test items may be biased against children with developmental delays. The reader is referred to additional sources for more information about children with visual impairments (Orlansky, 1988), deafness (Hoffmeister, 1988), and motor impairments (Robinson & Fieber, 1988). In addition, some of the young children assessed may not be represented in various normative groups of diverse instruments.

To the greatest extent possible, professionals should consider a child's cultural background, economic background, and family value system when planning and performing assessments. Short, Simeonsson, and Huntington (1990) recommend devoting special attention to families who historically have been underserved or unsocialized about the systems of service delivery such as very poor families, parents with restricted educational backgrounds, and adolescent parents. Cultural sensitivity will help insure that intervention targets are important to individual families and do not conflict with family values (Bailey, 1989).

Anderson and Fenichel (1989) provide an excellent foundation for serving culturally diverse families of young children with disabilities. Cultural sensitivity presupposes knowledge that cultural differences as well as similarities exist. For instance, there is no generic entity of "the Southeast Asian family" or "the Native American family." Rather, each of these encompasses numerous cultures, with individual members sharing proclivities in some areas but not in others. Individuals and families lie along various points of their cultural continua (e.g., from traditional to fully bicultural). The early interventionist must be aware that cultural diversity affects families' participation in treatment programs. Therefore, professionals should assist family members in taking the lead in revealing their own position within their cultural paradigm.

The term *family* has permeated our discussion of early intervention. Yet the concept of what constitutes a family varies from culture to culture. In a number of cultures, the *extended family* takes a variety of forms. Family structures and relationships expected between family members may differ considerably across cultures. Children in many cultures may be cared for by siblings, grandparents, other relatives, neighbors, and entire families or communities as well as by their parents.

If early-intervention professionals wish to alleviate rather than to exacerbate family stress resulting from a young child with a disability, they need to understand the particular culture's manner of seeking and using help. To begin with, Anderson and Fenichel (1989) advise practitioners and program developers to realize the difficulty in explaining "early intervention" since specialized teachers appear in most cultures. It is members of the extended family who may serve as "case managers" or "home visitors" who give childrearing advice. Moreover, basic definitions of disabilities are cultural constructs influencing beliefs and practices. Different disabilities may generate various levels of concern in different cultures. For example, congenital hip dislocation may cause little concern in traditional Navajos, whereas epilepsy may be viewed with apprehension.

Developing cultural intentionality (Ivey, Ivey, & Simek-Downing, 1987; see Chapter 7) and working within and respecting a family's and community's cultural paradigm can significantly enhance the likelihood of success of an early intervention program. For instance, Native American parents tend to judge professionals slowly. If service providers change frequently, there may be no one able to establish sufficient trust to work effectively with the families (Anderson & Fenichel, 1989). The Education for Parents of Indian Children with Special Needs (cited in Anderson & Fenichel, 1989) further recommends that professionals allow adequate time with Native American families so that family members do not feel rushed and therefore feel open to voice their concerns.

To provide nondiscriminatory assessment to multicultural populations of infants, toddlers, and preschoolers, there should be an individual on the assessment team who is bicultural/bilingual. This person can be a key resource to assist in the development of nonethnocentric IFSPs and IEPs that address each family's cultural and situational goals. If comprehensive family-centered, community-based early intervention for young children with disabilities is to be realized, awareness and sensitivity to specific cultural, familial, and individual diversity must be declared as a priority at the outset (Anderson & Fenichel, 1989). To

work effectively with culturally diverse populations, these authors contend that

> family members must not be put into a position of choosing between traditional healing and helping practices and mainstream programs which they may or may not understand, agree with or value. Rather, efforts should be made to integrate mainstream and traditional approaches when a family so desires. (p. 12)

Variation to Match Program Type and Demands. Another characteristic of effective family assessment is tied to tailoring program type to unique family needs. Such programs as home based and center based provide very different types of services, resulting in assorted issues. As an example, consider home-based programs, which provide no respite for parents. Since the caregiver is the child's primary teacher, these programs emphasize parent teaching skills and parent-child interactions. Therefore, assessment of parent teaching and interaction skills, along with locating respite services, may be of primary importance. With respite and intervention provided directly to the child in center-based programs, family assessments may need to concentrate on facilitating generalization and maintenance (see Chapter 7) or other family issues (Bailey & Simeonsson, 1988).

Diverse family assessment also may be needed to examine family needs associated with mainstreamed versus self-contained programs. Families with children in mainstreamed programs have greater exposure to typical children without disabilities and interaction with their families. Feelings of exclusion or isolation may be engendered. Bailey and Winton (1987) describe an assessment to address individual family issues to gather information useful in providing services. Their rating scale is used to ascertain the hopes and concerns of parents of children with and without disabilities in mainstreamed programs.

Formative Evaluation. Effective child and family assessment must be conducted on a formative basis rather than once at the eligibility stage. Assessment also is needed to evaluate (1) the changing needs of the child and family, including specific cultural needs; (2) child progress; (3) family skills and issues; (4) consumer satisfaction and fidelity of the early intervention (see Chapter 7); and (5) program efficacy for the child and family members. Simeonsson (1988) provides more detail about evaluation of family-centered intervention. See also Bronfenbrenner (1979) and Dunst (1985) for suggestions of broad-based measures of program effectiveness and ecologically relevant outcome measures.

Intervention

Considerable attention was devoted to early intervention activities in the preceding discussion on assessment since the assessment-intervention process is intertwined (see Gradel, 1988; Wachs & Sheehan, 1988). Defining the client, the setting, and the disposition of intervention activities can become complex with early childhood populations. The young child, a parent-child dyad, and/or the family may be the appropriate focus of services at various times, and the context of service delivery may entail home- and center-based programs and school linkages (Short, Simeonsson, & Huntington, 1990; Widerstrom, Mowder, & Sandall, 1991). It is critical that a goodness-of-fit model be adopted in which intervention goals and services match parents' preferences for such services (Bailey & Simeonsson, 1988).

Professional Preparation in Family Services

Given the broad perspective of early intervention to include family services, the adequacy of professional preparation becomes a central issue. Bagnato, Neisworth, Paget, and Kovaleski (1987) found that most school and child psychologists have had little supervised preservice training and experience in family dynamics, assessment, and service delivery within the context of early childhood practice. In a national survey, Epps and Nelson (1991) found that approximately half of the doctoral-level school psychologists had university coursework (48 percent) and supervised

experience (57 percent) in family assessment; 28 percent indicated a preference for additional training. In counseling parents, 52 percent had university coursework and 70 percent had supervised experience. Only 7 percent desired additional training in counseling parents, although 25 percent wanted further training in grief counseling.

For those trained in individual therapy models, "untraining" may be necessary (Margolin, 1982). Involvement in marital and family therapy requires special learning about family therapy (e.g., through readings, seminars, observation) and learning to do family therapy via supervised practice and experience (Gurman & Kniskern, 1981). Substantive areas particularly relevant to school psychology include the study of healthy families, contemporary theories of the family, and parenthood (Winkle, Piercy, & Hovestadt, 1981). Margolin (1982) champions knowledgeable clinicians who are cognizant of the limits of their own competence and who confer with colleagues.

Social Systems Approach

Rather than promulgating an approach to early intervention that adopts a deficit perspective of the child and family (see Foster, Berger, & McLean, 1981, and Zigler & Berman, 1983), Dunst (1985) proposes a model that uses social systems theory as a framework to expand the definition of early intervention and to delineate a set of decision rules regarding the types of interventions likely to affect child, parent, and family functioning. The objective of a social systems approach is not merely to ameliorate child deficits, but to make the system work by strengthening normal socializing agencies (e.g., the family, school, church, neighborhood), not by replacing them (Hobbs, 1975). Rather than striving to "fix kids," the liaison professional endeavors to create relationships that are more responsive to the needs of the total ecology (Plas, 1986). Conoley (1987b) further highlights the utility of general systems theory to build positive interdependence between family and school systems.

Dunst (1985) describes a social systems approach to early intervention that highlights a *proactive* model, an *empowerment* philosophy (see Chapter 7), and *partnerships* between families and professionals. Features of this model are contrasted with the more traditional approach to early intervention in Table 10.1.

The proactive model focuses on a family's strengths rather than weaknesses (Dunst, 1985; Hobbs, 1975; Zigler & Berman, 1983), with primary emphasis on strengthening and supporting families (Hobbs et al., 1984). Empowerment rather than usurpation of control over decision making for families is fundamental to a proactive approach to intervention. Unfortunately, it is a common occurrence for parents to be told what is wrong with their child and family, when and how interventions should be conducted, and how long services should be provided, with the repercussion being a sense of helplessness, limited paren-

tal self-efficacy, and powerlessness in the caregivers (Dunst, 1985).

In the traditional approach to early intervention, the client seeks the expertise of the professional who designs treatment to alleviate problematic areas. Both the deficit (rather than proactive) model and the usurpation (rather than empowerment) paradigm are represented in the paternalism of numerous early intervention programs. However, in the proactive method, empowerment eventuates within the framework of partnerships between families and professionals, which circumvents the paternalism in the traditional client-professional paradigm. Dunst (1985) describes partnerships as individuals working together to attain designated objectives by exchanging skills, knowledge, and competencies.

A traditional view of early intervention presumes that program services are the primary vari-

TABLE 10.1 Two Contrasting Models of Early Intervention

TRADITIONAL MODEL		SOCIAL SYSTEMS MODEL	
Components	*Characteristics*	*Components*	*Characteristics*
Deficit approach	Differences in behavior are viewed as deficits and weaknesses inherent in the child, family, and their culture. Intervention focuses on the remediation of deficits.	Proactive approach	Differences are viewed as variations in behavior resulting from ecological forces that affect child, parent, and family functioning. Intervention focuses on strengthening families.
Usurpation	Locus of decision-making is with the professionals. Interventionists usurp decision-making by deciding for families what is wrong, what course of action needs to be taken, when and how often interventions ought to be done, and so on.	Empowerment	Locus of decision-making is with the family. Interventions empower families with skills, knowledge, and competencies that allow them access and control over resources that can be used to meet family needs.
Paternalism	The client (child, parents, family) is seen as having some sickness or pathology who seeks the expert advice of the professional who prescribes a treatment to alleviate the illness.	Partnerships	Families and professionals work hand-in-hand, on an equal basis, pooling their mutual strengths in order to devise courses of action that can be taken to meet family identified needs.

Source: Reprinted with permission from *Analysis and Intervention in Development Disabilities, 5,* by C. J. Dunst, Rethinking early intervention, Copyright 1985, Pergamon Press, Inc.

ables that effect change in outcome measures. Dunst, Jenkins, and Trivette (1984) tested this assumption by having 137 parents of preschool children with mental retardation or physical impairments or at-risk for developmental delay complete the Family Support Scale (FSS). This instrument includes 18 potential sources of support, which the parents rated on a 5-point scale in terms of how helpful each support source had been in the care of their preschooler. Six factors were retained in a varimax-rotated factor analysis. Factor scores were computed for each participant in the study and correlated with a number of outcome variables that were expected to be influenced by early intervention services.

The authors found that early intervention accounted for a significant ($p < .05$) proportion of variance in only one dependent measure (family opportunities). However, nuclear family support and informal kinship support accounted for significant amounts of variance beyond that accounted for by the early intervention factor in four and eight dependent measures respectively. Dunst, Jenkins, and Trivette (1984) interpret these results as failing to support the traditional position on early intervention (i.e., that services provided by a structured program are the principal factors leading to change) and propose that a broader-based conceptualization of early intervention is needed. Considering these data, Dunst (1985) defines early intervention as the

> provision of support to families of infants and young children from members of informal and formal social support networks that impact both *directly* and *indirectly* upon parental, family, and child functioning. . . . [It] can be conceptualized as an aggregation of the many different types of help, assistance, and services that are provided to families by individuals and groups. (p. 179)

He continues with the example of home-based or center-based services as one form of early intervention, then further describes empathy from a friend, suggestions from a developmental pediatrician, child care by a neighbor, participation in a parent-to-parent support group, and role shar-

ing between the child's parents as additional types of early intervention. Clearly, the nature of support systems a family has will vary, particularly when considering cultural diversity. Dunst (1985) maintains that quantifying this informal support provides a basis for judging the impact of the diverse interventions.

Behavioral States, Styles, and Characteristics

Variation in the stability, patterns, and clarity of behavioral states needs to be documented systematically and considered when individualizing intervention for young children. Clearly, the quality of a baby's alertness and sleep patterns influences care-giving patterns, a particularly critical variable with home-based services. Since quiet alertness provides the context for a child to learn many skills, the better that the factors affecting it are understood, the more likely it is that interventionists can help facilitate this state. Intervention, thus, is directed toward helping infants organize and control states (Helm & Simeonsson, 1989).

Documentation of behavioral styles (temperament) and behavioral characteristics (e.g., social and object orientation, attention span, reactivity) also may facilitate the provision of individualized intervention services. For example, knowing the child's preferred interaction style can influence the manner in which adults attempt to interact and the way in which various stimuli are presented. The child's preferred interaction strategies also are relevant for care-giving routines since a child perceived as difficult can increase caregiving demands and family stress (Huntington, 1989).

School Psychology as a Community/Family Service Provider

Historically, school psychologists have confined their practice to individual children in public school buildings. Recently, school psychologists have expanded their professional repertoire to include family services including family consultation, parent education, and brief family therapy. These activities are integral features of services in community mental health centers and social service agencies as well as in schools. This endeavor into family-centered treatment outside of and away from education agencies represents an emerging trend toward nontraditional practice (Conoley, 1989; Kramer & Epps, 1991), which has been supported by the passage of PL 101-476 that refers to instruction in the home, hospital, and other settings.

Community Forces

The diverse needs of children and families are becoming increasingly apparent. The effects of divorce, poverty, neglect and abuse, substance abuse, adolescent pregnancy, suicide, delinquency, and learning problems are widespread and increasingly considered suggestions of family dysfunction (Moynihan, 1986; Yogman & Brazelton, 1986). Conoley (1989) discusses an expanded role for school psychology to provide preventive (e.g., parent education) and remedial and crisis interventions (e.g., child protective services and family therapy) as a vital component of community health. As previously addressed, psychologists with specialization largely in individual diagnostics will need new information and supervision prior to adopting family-centered service delivery.

PSYCHOSOCIAL AND EDUCATIONAL IMPACT OF HOSPITALIZATION AND CHRONIC ILLNESS

There has been a surge of attention to the psychological and behavioral characteristics of children in pediatric settings in recent years (see Chapter 7), which has led to the growing clinical and empirical literature in behavioral and developmental pediatrics in such journals as the *Journal of Pediatric Psychology* and the *Journal of Developmental and Behavioral Pediatrics*. The complex needs of chronically ill children require comprehensive medical procedures and innovative and specialized psychological service delivery.

There are two major groups of children with special health-care needs. One group consists of children hospitalized for a variety of reasons ranging from acute conditions (e.g., appendicitis)

to nonacute circumstances (e.g., diagnostic workups or elective surgery). Those children who may need some form of psychological services are victims of accidents or other trauma (especially those involving the head) and children with diagnosed or suspected psychosomatic conditions. Traumatic brain injury is a new disability in PL 101-476 eligible for special education and related services. Children with chronic illness comprise the second group (Stabler & Simeonsson, 1986).

Developmental Implications of Chronic Illness

For the healthy teenager, adolescence can be a period of trials and tribulations in part due to their uneven development in competencies (Atwater, 1988). For the critically ill adolescent, this period can be extremely debilitating, resulting in frustration in the individual and family and obstacles to service providers. The adolescent, who has experienced tremendous physical, cognitive, and social/emotional changes, is particularly vulnerable when a prolonged illness intrudes upon her or his life. The impact of an illness on the adolescent's development often can outweigh the biological effects of the illness itself. An additional complicating factor is the families of these children who are prone to feelings of guilt, anger, and frustration, which may contribute to the high divorce rates of parents in this group (Neinstein, 1984).

Definition

Infants with chronic illness are especially vulnerable, although medical advances in technology (e.g., extracorporeal membrane oxygenation [ECMO], surfactant, high frequency ventilators) have substantially increased survival rate. Those born with myelomeningocele (spina bifida) or serious cardiac anomalies, for example, previously were unable to survive. Longitudinal investigations are only just beginning with some populations (e.g., ECMO survivors) due to the newness of the procedures. While many may develop normally, others may remain impaired and face potentially life-long chronic illness (Kleinberg, 1982).

Perrin (cited in Brandon, Frauman, Huber, Lucas, & Levine, 1989) has defined chronic illness as

> serious, ongoing health problems which last (or are expected to last) for at least three months and are likely to produce long term sequelae. Long term sequelae may include shortened life expectation, disability, disfigurement, limitation of function or activity in comparison to healthy persons, more medical or related services than usual for chronological age, special ongoing treatment at home and/or school, dependence on medication or special diet for normal function, and/or dependence on technology for normal function. (p. 1)

It is generally regarded in the literature that 7 to 10 percent of all children have some form of chronic illness (Mattson, 1972; Neinstein, 1984; Pless, Satterwhite, & Van Vechten, 1976).

Brandon and colleagues (1989) draw from the literature (Behrman, Vaughn & Nelson, 1987; Dimond & Jones, 1983; Kempe, Silver, & O'Brien, 1982; Mott, Fazekas, & James, 1985) and describe selected chronic illnesses affecting the respiratory system (asthma, cystic fibrosis, bronchopulmonary dysplasia), the hematological system (sickle cell disease and sickle cell trait, hemophilia), the circulatory system (congenital heart disease), the gastrointestinal system (short bowel syndrome), the renal system (chronic renal failure), the endocrine system (juvenile diabetes mellitus), the immune system (juvenile rheumatoid arthritis, leukemia, acquired immune deficiency syndrome [AIDS]), and the neurologic system (epilepsy).

For each condition, they present characteristics, likely treatments and rationale for treatment, and examples of possible influences on development. For example, cystic fibrosis may have a number of potential influences on development:

1. Fatigue resulting from efforts to breathe
2. Damage to the acoustic nerve due to antibiotics

3. Dependence on caregivers, who often have difficulty in knowing when to encourage independence
4. Limits placed on community involvement due to concern that the child will be exposed to respiratory illness
5. Adult fear about allowing child to explore opportunities, which may lead to restrictions that curtail exposure to new skills
6. Frequent hospitalization limits opportunities for normal social experiences
7. Self-consciousness due to awareness of small and somewhat fragile appearance, odor of bowel movements, and frequency of cough
8. Societal treatment of child as someone with an infectious disease, with restrictions on social interactions
9. Altered family function due to substantial financial and emotional toll

A basic understanding of such conditions is necessary given the increasing numbers of chronically ill children being served by interagency collaboration including education units (see Chapter 7). Psychologists need to understand the concomitant developmental ramifications of such illnesses for the child and her or his family in order to provide sensitive, realistic, and appropriate related services to assist in the transition from medical care to special education as outlined in PL 101-476.

Constraints to Developmental Progress

For many children with chronic illness, developmental potential may be normal since brain damage has not been found to be an element of most chronic conditions. However, developmental capacity may be upset by the illness due to its effects on normal childhood experiences (Drotar, 1981). Recurrent episodes of pain, limited strength, immobility, and separation from family and routine school, peer, and community activities inflict developmental restraints. Other risk factors include fatigue, dependency, altered body image, side effects of medications and treatments, altered nutrition and eating patterns, and societal prejudice (Brandon et al., 1989). Children may experience repeated failures and setbacks.

Requirements of medical treatment may be intrusive and interfere with acquisition of age-appropriate skills, and parents may be averse to setting appropriate limits (Perrin & Gerrity, 1984). Grupe, Greifer, Greenspan, Leavitt, and Wolff (1986) propose that it is the emerging developmental and behavioral capabilities during intervals when chronic illness compels significant medical treatment and follow-up that are most susceptible to delay.

Effects on Family Function

The fundamental resistance and resiliency of a chronically ill child is severely tested, and both child and family resources are drained over an indefinite (perhaps lengthy) period of time. Research findings suggest that these children often are depressed, anxious, lonely, and withdrawn (Stabler & Simeonsson, 1986). Numerous references can be consulted for more information about the psychological consequences of cancer (e.g., Adams, 1980; Spinetta, 1974), cystic fibrosis (e.g., Gayton, Friedman, Tavormina, & Tucker, 1977), genetic disorders (e.g., Leddet-Chevallier & Funderburk, 1983), hematology and oncology illnesses (e.g., Lindamood & Wiley, 1983), myelomeningocele (e.g., Whiteman & Feldman, 1983), and Duchenne's muscular dystrophy (Gilgoff, 1983).

Another risk factor is altered family function. Chronic illness has substantial effects on the child's family. If family function is notably changed after the child's diagnosis, there may be negative repercussions for the development of the child and siblings. Brandon and colleagues (1989) delineate various influences that contribute to altered family function including societal prejudice, strained family relationships, and pervasive cultural values of society. These are diagrammed in Figure 10.2.

Contribution of Psychology to Management of Chronic Illness in Adolescents

The challenge of health-care providers is to be aware of the tremendous emotional and social stresses associated with physical aspects of the illness as well as the biomedical vicissitudes. To address this approach to total-child health care, there is an emerging need for psychologists to recognize the interface between medical and psychological practices in the assessment and management of children with chronic illnesses. The role of psychological assessment is expected to expand significantly beyond attention to intellectual level, although neuropsychological testing to examine specific cognitive functions may continue to be relevant.

Stabler and Simeonsson (1986) describe several other appropriate areas of assessment, including (1) children's understanding of illness and health; (2) their understanding and adjustment to hospitalization and treatment; (3) emotional, behavioral, and academic adjustment to chronic illness; and (4) family adjustment including parental expectations, sibling attitude and adjustment, and parental reaction to child hospitalization (Chan & Heff, 1982). These areas represent an area in which professional psychology can make a unique contribution to interdisciplinary and interagency treatment teams. It behooves the psychologist to be cognizant of the complex child and family needs, to be acquainted with innovative and specialized psychological measures and techniques, and to be experienced in liaison activities between medical and behavioral fields.

Neinstein (1984) outlines 13 general guidelines for managing chronic illness in the adolescent. Implications for child psychologists are expanded in this chapter.

1. *Education.* The educational process includes a discussion of the nature of the illness and limitations of treatment. Psychologists with clinical skills can be particularly valuable in insuring that nonesoteric language is used and that both child and family education is addressed.

2. *Ventilation.* Some children, adolescents, and families may need opportunities to express their feelings, fears, and hopes. The nature of this ventilation is expected to change over the course of the illness.

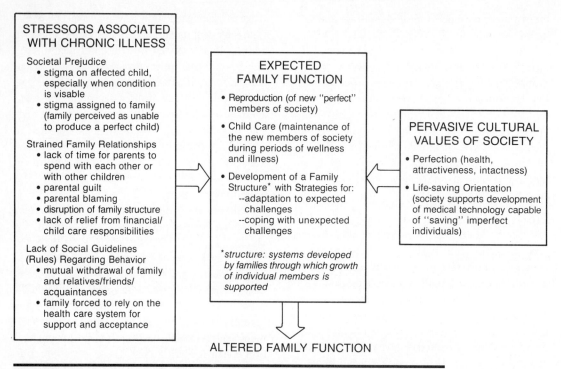

FIGURE 10.2   Influences contributing to altered family function
Source: Brandon, D. H., Frauman, A. C., Huber, C. J., Lucas, T. L., & Levine, M. D. (1990). *Toll control system manual.* Chapel Hill, NC: The Clinical Center for the Study of Development and Learning, University of North Carolina at Chapel Hill, p. 17. Reprinted with permission.

3. *Social skills.* If illness has been prolonged, children may have underdeveloped social skills. They also may have a history with social isolation and prejudice and have a number of areas needing intervention, particularly those associated with age-appropriate peer group involvement.

4. *Occupational goals.* Chronic illness may pose restrictions on vocational and educational plans and career options. If there are repeated treatments and hospitalizations, a slowing in educational progress may ensue, with interruptions in school attendance and participation in normal school activities. Underachievement can develop into an issue that jeopardizes self-esteem (Leddet-Chevallier & Funderburk, 1983). Prospects for future independent living situations also may be an issue.

5. *Continuity of care.* Continuity of care is a critical issue for medically complex populations particularly when multiple agencies (e.g., hospital, outpatient clinic, school) are involved. As discussed in Chapter 7, psychologists can play an important role in serving as a liaison between medical and educational settings.

6. *Patient involvement.* An adolescent with a chronic illness may remain in a passive, dependent relationship with her or his parents who tend to be overprotective (Leddet-Chevallier & Funderburk, 1983). Psychologists can work with the family to help the adolescent foster autonomy, independence, and increased participation in her or his own health care, thus resulting in a greater sense of self-control.

7. *Involvement in peer support groups.* Due to

the possible isolation from normalized activities with peers, integration into typical peer-group endeavors as well as participation in peer support groups may be needed. When assessing the psychological functioning of a chronically ill child, there is a tendency to focus on the deviation or maladjustment associated with the condition. The psychologist can serve to direct the team's attention to community resources such as church, scouts, 4-H, YWCA or YMCA, etc. (Stabler & Simeonsson, 1986).

8. *Self-help techniques*. Training in the self-regulation of pain perception, consisting of progressive muscle relaxation exercises, meditative breathing, and guided imagery techniques, has been used for arthritic pain perception by hemophiliacs (Varni, 1981a, 1981b; Varni, Gilbert, & Dietrich, 1981). Techniques of pain perception regulation and pain behavior regulation can be applied to a number of chronic pain syndromes (see Varni, Katz, & Dash, 1982).

9. *Interdisciplinary team*. The significance of interdisciplinary and interagency service delivery has been emphasized throughout this chapter. Effective team functioning is particularly critical considering continuity of care issues across agencies. Stabler and Simeonsson (1986) discuss the taxing demands placed on chronic-care teams who must support families through innumerable crises of medical management, coordinate multiple community service agencies, and face the omnipresent threat of death. The psychologist on such a team should be active in encouraging discussion of extended care plans, helping maintain community liaisons with schools and social service agencies, and evaluating child and family strengths, coping mechanisms, and needs.

10. *Consideration of sexual development*. Normal adolescent development is characterized by physical and sexual maturation. In some instances, adolescents experiencing early or late maturation may perceive themselves as members of a deviant group, which can generate considerable stress (Atwater, 1988). Adolescents with chronic illness generally have fewer opportunities for exploring their sexuality within the context of daily interactions with their peers. They may feel asexual secondary to delayed development, protective parents, and avoidance of discussion by family and physicians (Neinstein, 1984).

11. *Limit setting*. If age-appropriate behavior is deficient, pediatric consultation as discussed in Chapter 7 may be in order to assist health-care professionals and parents in understanding factors that influence the occurrence of the interfering behaviors and in implementing ecobehavior management strategies.

12. *Family involvement*. Family support and guidance as well as ongoing assessment of their strengths and needs are crucial. Neinstein (1984) recommends advising families to avoid the "overs"—overprotection, over-anxiety, and overattention.

13. *Inpatient care*. Hospitalization that provides an environment and staff oriented toward the developmental needs of the adolescent is most facilitative of normalized routines. Psychologists with understanding of adolescent psychosocial development and their emerging struggle for independence and identity can provide substantial assistance in this area.

Psychology in Health-Care Facilities

Wodrich and Pfeiffer (1989) discuss the superficial logic that questions the appropriateness of school psychology practice in medical settings. "School" has been construed as designating the location in which service delivery occurs, whereas clinical and counseling psychology suggest little about the location of practice. They maintain that it is the skills and competencies of all types of psychologists that should be examined when ascertaining who can most appropriately practice where. To further confuse matters, "clinical" psychology and professional psychology often are used interchangeably, which is inaccurate (Fox, Barclay & Rodgers, 1982).

For doctoral-level psychologists, a minimum requirement for the practice of psychology in medical facilities generally is a state license or certification for independent practice. An acceptable score on the Examination for Practice in Professional Psychology typically is required as well. An internship and/or supervised postdoctoral experience also may be necessary. Further criteria may be required to obtain hospital privileges. Thus, administratively and legally, school psychologists can practice in medical settings provided that they practice in a manner consistent with their training.

Wodrich and Pfeiffer (1989) emphasize that the bottom line should be competency in rendering services professionally, effectively, and ethically in medical settings. Therefore, expertise in performing necessary tasks is maximized while a priori assumptions about the unvarying suitability of any branch of psychology for a particular setting are minimized. *Clinical, counseling,* and *school* psychology titles, thus, have diminished pertinence since they fail to predict with precision preparedness to perform the expected tasks. It is the match between training and job demands that is the relevant issue.

School psychologists are well qualified to address numerous pediatric issues (see Chapter 7). Yet frequently, more specialized training is required (e.g., as with neuropsychological assessment). For those school psychologists without prior exposure to medically involved conditions and health-care facilities, supplemental professional preparation and supervision are necessary. Knowledge and experience related to the culture of hospitals also are needed (see American Psychological Association, 1985). Such experiences often are available at university medical centers, which sanction education and research activities.

Psychologists with school specialization are particularly encouraged to acquaint themselves with pediatric and family practice specialties since physicians in these areas provide primary health care to children and families. Pediatricians are frequently called upon to address issues of infant/toddler diagnosis and triage of children with disabilities, diagnosis and guidance about school learning and behavior problems (consider the ubiquitous diagnosis of attention deficit hyperactivity disorder), beginning school and grade retention, remedial child-management strategies and anticipatory guidance, enuresis and encopresis, sibling rivalry and difficulties with peers, and divorce issues (Pfeiffer, Dean, & Shellenberger, 1986). School psychologists, especially those with experience in behavioral pediatrics, are eminently suited to provide many of these services.

As nontraditional service delivery becomes increasingly realized, the issue of specialty title must be explored. Wodrich and Pfeiffer (1989) alert us to the possibility that the title *school psychology* could obstruct progress toward more diversified options for service delivery. An additional challenge is the longstanding dispute between NASP and Division 16 of APA regarding entry level to the practice of school psychology (Conoley, 1987a). The recent and substantial advances made in graduate training, specialty guidelines, and service delivery in family-centered, community-based efforts should launch the field into diverse opportunities.

SUMMARY

This chapter highlighted less traditional aspects of school psychology in terms of populations served, settings for service delivery, and foci of intervention. With an emerging trend toward school-family-community liaisons due to federal legislation and theoretical and research bases for broader partnerships, professional preparation in early intervention, special health-care needs, and families assumes significant importance.

University programs must accelerate their efforts to train psychologists with a broader range of skills by altering both the content and process of didactic and supervised activities (see Kramer & Epps, 1991). Practicing psychologists must be committed to continuing education to keep abreast of the conceptual knowledge and skills necessary to serve at-risk children and youth within a broader ecological context than the confines of school buildings. Interdisciplinary (e.g., psychology, public health, early childhood special education) and interagency (e.g., State Departments of Health, Education, and Social Services) education, training, and collaboration can enhance both the quality of service providers and the therapeutic outcome to consumers (Epps & Jackson, 1991; Epps & Nelson, 1991).

Following an empowerment model, a reconceptualization is necessary of the role parents play in decision making about child and family assessment and treatment. An expanded therapeutic goal also is needed that adopts a social systems approach designed to strengthen normal socializing agencies. Considering parents' socialization to be deferential towards professionals and professionals' training to impart their expertise, the goal of developing effective partnerships may require bold initiatives to "reeducate" each party.

Specialized issues in family-centered assessment and intervention have been addressed in this chapter. As programs expand their services to families, sensitive issues may arise that require professionals trained in the use of basic microskills (see Chapter 6) and clinically skilled in more complex issues such as coping with a special-needs child, marital relationship, family interaction, and adult forms of dysfunction (e.g., anxiety, depression). Such a mental-health professional also can assist in monitoring whether family assessment and services become intrusive. As an active member of interdisciplinary/interagency teams or as a consultant, clinically trained professionals are valuable assets.

With the increasing numbers of chronically ill children and youth being served by interagency collaboration (including education units), there is a significant need for professionals who understand the developmental ramifications of chronic illness and who can contribute to a medicine-education liaison. The complex and multidimensional needs of these children, their families, and education personnel who serve them require innovative psychological service delivery. The challenges before the field are to synthesize developmental and systems theories, research, and practice in order to enhance the multifaceted role of child psychologists in building effective partnerships with school, family, and community ecologies to serve our children and youth.

REFERENCES

Adams, D. W. (1980). *Childhood malignancy: The psychosocial care of the child and his family.* Springfield, IL: Thomas.

American Educational Research Association, American Psychological Association, & National Council on Measurement in Education. (1985). *Standards for educational and psychological testing.* Washington, DC: American Psychological Association.

American Psychological Association. (1985). *A hospital practice primer for psychologists.* Washington, DC: Author.

Anderson, P. P., & Fenichel, E. S. (1989). *Serving culturally diverse families of infants and toddlers with disabilities.* Washington, DC: National Center for Clinical Infant Programs.

Atwater, E. (1988). *Adolescence* (2nd ed.). Englewood Cliffs, NJ: Prentice Hall.

Bagnato, S. J., Neisworth, J. T., Paget, K. D., & Kovaleski, J. (1987). The developmental school psychologist: Professional profile of an emerging early childhood specialist. *Topics in Early Childhood Special Education, 7*(3), 75–89.

Bailey, D. B., Jr. (1984). A triaxial model of the interdisciplinary team and group process. *Exceptional Children, 51,* 17–25.

Bailey, D. B., Jr. (1987). Collaborative goal-setting with families: Resolving differences in values and priorities for services. *Topics in Early Childhood Special Education, 7*(2), 59–71.

Bailey, D. B., Jr. (1988). Rationale and model for family assessment in early intervention. In D. B. Bailey, Jr. & R. J. Simeonsson, *Family assessment in early intervention* (pp. 1–26). Columbus, OH: Merrill.

Bailey, D. B., Jr. (1989). Assessment and its importance in early intervention. In D. B. Bailey, Jr. & M. Wolery, *Assessing infants and preschoolers with handicaps* (pp. 1–21). Columbus, OH: Merrill.

Bailey, D. B., Jr., & Simeonsson, R. J. (1984). Critical issues underlying research and intervention with families of young handicapped children. *Journal of the Division for Early Childhood, 9,* 38–48.

Bailey, D. B., Jr., & Simeonsson, R. J. (1988). *Family assessment in early intervention.* Columbus, OH: Merrill.

Bailey, D. B., Jr., Simeonsson, R. J., Winton, P. J., Huntington, G. S., Comfort, M., Isbell, P., O'Donnell, K. J., & Helm, J. M. (1986). Family-focused intervention: A functional model for planning, implementing, and evaluating individualized family services in early intervention. *Journal of the Division for Early Childhood, 10,* 156–171.

Bailey, D. B., Jr., & Winton, P. J. (1987). Stability and change in parents' expectations about mainstreaming. *Topics in Early Childhood Special Education, 7*(1), 73–88.

Ballard, J., Ramirez, B., & Zantal-Wiener, K. (1987). *Public Law 94–142, Section 504, and Public Law 99–457: Understanding what they are and are not.* Reston, VA: Council for Exceptional Children.

Bates, J. E., Freeland, C. A. B., & Lounsbury, M. L. (1979). Measurement of infant difficultness. *Child Development, 50,* 794–803.

Bayley, N. (1969). *Bayley Scales of Infant Development.* New York: Psychological Corporation.

Behrman, R. E., Vaughn, V. C., & Nelson, W. F. (Eds.). (1987). *Nelson textbook of pediatrics* (13th ed.). Philadelphia: Saunders.

Bell, R. Q. (1968). A reinterpretation of the direction of effects in studies of socialization. *Psychological Review, 75,* 81–95.

Brainerd, C. J. (1978). *Piaget's theory of intelligence.* Englewood Cliffs, NJ: Prentice-Hall.

Brandon, D. H., Frauman, A. C., Huber, C. J., Lucas, T. L., & Levine, M. D. (1989). *Toll control system manual.* Chapel Hill, NC: The Clinical Center for the Study of Development and Learning, University of North Carolina at Chapel Hill.

Brinckerhoff, J. L., & Vincent, L. J. (1986). Increasing parental decision-making at the individualized educational program meeting. *Journal of the Division for Early Childhood, 11,* 46–58.

Bronfenbrenner, U. (1977). Toward an experimental ecology of human development. *American Psychologist, 32,* 513–531.

Bronfenbrenner, U. (1979). *The ecology of human development.* Cambridge, MA: Harvard University Press.

Brooks-Gunn, J., & Lewis, M. (1981). Assessing young handicapped children: Issues and solutions. *Journal of the Division for Early Childhood, 6,* 84–95.

Chan, J. M., & Heff, P. T. (1982). Parenting the chronically ill child in the hospital: Issues and concerns. *Children's Health Care, 11,* 9–16.

Conoley, J. C. (1987a). "Dr. Future, we presume," said school psychology. *Professional School Psychology, 2,* 173–180.

Conoley, J. C. (1987b). Schools and families: Theoretical and practical bridges. *Professional School Psychology, 2,* 191–203.

Conoley, J. C. (1989). The school psychologist as a community/family service provider. In R. C. D'Amato & R. S. Dean (Eds.), *The school psychologist in nontraditional settings: Integrating clients, services, and settings* (pp. 33–65). Hillsdale, NJ: Erlbaum.

Dimond, M., & Jones, S. L. (1983). *Chronic illness across the life span.* Norwalk, CN: Appleton, Century, Crofts.

Dokecki, P. R., & Heflinger, C. A. (1989). Strengthening families of young children with handicapping conditions: Mapping backward from the "street level." In J. J. Gallagher, P. L. Trohanis, & R. M. Clifford (Eds.), *Policy implementation and PL 99-457: Planning for young children with special needs* (pp. 59–84). Baltimore: Paul H. Brookes.

Drotar, D. (1981). Psychological perspective in chronic childhood illness. *Journal of Pediatric Psychology, 6,* 211–228.

Dunst, C. J. (1985). Rethinking early intervention. *Analysis and Intervention in Developmental Disabilities, 5,* 165–201.

Dunst, C. J., Jenkins, V., & Trivette, C. M. (1984). Family Support Scale: Reliability and validity. *Journal of Individual, Family, and Community Wellness, 1*(4), 45–52.

"Education for All Handicapped Children Act of 1975" (PL 94-142, 29 Nov. 1975), *United States Statutes at Large*.

"Education of the Handicapped Act Amendments of 1986" (PL 99-457, 8 Oct. 1986), *United States Statutes at Large* 100, pp. 1145–1177.

Epps, S. (1991a). *Nurse ratings of preterm infant behavior as a function of infant health status and parent demographics*. Manuscript submitted for publication.

Epps, S. (1991b). *Parent ratings of preterm infant characteristics as a function of degree of infant illness*. Manuscript submitted for publication.

Epps, S., & Jackson, B. J. (1991). Professional preparation of psychologists for family-centered service delivery to at-risk infants and toddlers. *School Psychology Review, 20,* 495–506.

Epps, S., & Nelson, T. (1991). *Analysis of professional preparation of psychologists and special educators in early intervention*. Manuscript submitted for publication.

Erikson, E. H. (1972). Eight ages of man. In C. S. Lavatelli & F. Stendler (Eds.), *Readings in child behavior and child development* (3rd ed., pp. 19–30). New York: Harcourt Brace Jovanovich.

Foley, G. M. (1990). Portrait of the arena evaluation: Assessment in the transdisciplinary approach. In E. D. Gibbs & D. M. Teti (Eds.), *Interdisciplinary assessment of infants: A guide for early intervention professionals* (pp. 271–286). Baltimore: Paul H. Brookes.

Fordyce, W. (1981). On interdisciplinary peers. *Archives of Physical Medicine, 62*(2), 51–53.

Foster, M., Berger, M., & McLean, M. (1981). Rethinking a good idea: A reassessment of parent involvement. *Topics in Early Childhood Special Education, 1*(3), 55–65.

Fox, H. B., Freedman, S. A., & Klepper, B. R. (1989). Financing programs for young children with handicaps. In J. J. Gallagher, P. L. Trohanis, & R. M. Clifford (Eds.), *Policy implementation and PL 99-457: Planning for young children with special needs* (pp. 169–182). Baltimore: Paul H. Brookes.

Fox, R. E., Barclay, A. G., & Rodgers, D. A. (1982). The foundations of professional psychology. *American Psychologist, 37,* 306–312.

Frankenburg, W. K., & Dodds, J. B. (1969). *Denver Developmental Screening Test*. Denver: University of Colorado Medical Center.

Gallagher, J. J., Beckman, P., & Cross, A. H. (1983). Families of handicapped children: Sources of stress and its amelioration. *Exceptional Children, 50,* 10–19.

Gallagher, R. J., & Cech, D. (1988). Motor assessment. In T. D. Wachs & R. Sheehan (Eds.), *Assessment of young developmentally disabled children* (pp. 241–254). New York: Plenum Press.

Gayton, W. F., Friedman, S. B., Tavormina, J. F., & Tucker, F. (1977). Children with cystic fibrosis: I. Psychological test findings of patients, siblings and parents. *Pediatrics, 59,* 888–894.

Gilgoff, I. S. (1983). The psychological effects of Duchenne's muscular dystrophy on children and their families. In C. E. Hollingsworth (Ed.), *Coping with pediatric illness* (pp. 229–242). New York: SP Medical & Scientific Books.

Ginsburg, H. P., & Opper, S. (1988). *Piaget's theory of intellectual development* (3rd ed.). Englewood Cliffs, NJ: Prentice-Hall.

Gradel, K. (1988). Interface between assessment and intervention for infants and preschoolers with disabilities. In T. D. Wachs & R. Sheehan (Eds.), *Assessment of young developmentally disabled children* (pp. 373–395). New York: Plenum Press.

Grotevant, H. D., & Carlson, C. I. (1989). *Family assessment: A guide to methods and measures*. New York: The Guilford Press.

Grupe, W. E., Greifer, I., Greenspan, S. I., Leavitt, L. A., & Wolff, G. (1986). Psychosocial development in children with chronic renal insufficiency. *American Journal of Kidney Diseases, 11,* 324–328.

Gurman, A. S., & Kniskern, D. P. (1981). Research on marital and family therapy: Progress, perspective, and prospect. In S. L. & A. E. Bergin (Eds.), *Handbook of psychotherapy and behavior change: An empirical analysis* (2nd ed., pp. 817–901). New York: Wiley & Sons.

Helm, J. M., & Simeonsson, R. J. (1989). Assessment of behavioral state organization. In D. B. Bailey, Jr. & M. Wolery, *Assessing infants and preschoolers with handicaps* (pp. 202–224). Columbus, OH: Merrill.

Hobbs, N. (1975). *The future of children*. San Francisco: Jossey-Bass.

Hobbs, N., Dokecki, P., Hoover-Dempsey, K., Moroney, R., Shayne, M., & Weeks, K. (1984).

Strengthening families. San Francisco: Jossey-Bass.

Hoffmeister, R. J. (1988). Cognitive assessment in deaf preschoolers. In T. D. Wachs & R. Sheehan (Eds.), *Assessment of young developmentally disabled children* (pp. 109–126). New York: Plenum Press.

Huntington, G. S. (1989). Assessing behavioral characteristics. In D. B. Bailey, Jr. & M. Wolery, *Assessing infants and preschoolers with handicaps* (pp. 225–248). Columbus, OH: Merrill.

"Individuals with Disabilities Education Act of 1990" (PL 101-476, 1 Oct. 1990), *United States Statutes at Large*.

Ivey, A. E., Ivey, M. B., & Simek-Downing, L. (1987). *Counseling and psychotherapy: Integrating skills, theory, and practice* (2nd ed.). Englewood Cliffs, NJ: Prentice-Hall.

Johnson, L., & Murphy, M. A. (1990). Siblings of children with handicapping conditions. *DEC Communicator, 16*(4), 3.

Kempe, C. H., Silver, H. K., & O'Brien, D. (Eds.) (1982). *Current pediatric diagnosis and treatment* (7th ed.). Los Alpos, CA: Lange Medical Publications.

Kleinberg, S. B. (1982). *Educating the chronically ill child*. Rockville, MD: Aspen Systems Corporation.

Korner, A. F. (1972). State as variable, as obstacle, and as mediator of stimulation in infant research. *Merrill-Palmer, 18,* 77–94.

Kramer, J. J., & Epps, S. (1991). Expanding professional opportunities and improving the quality of training: A look towards the next generation of school psychologists. *School Psychology Review, 20,* 449–458.

Langley, M. B. (1989). Assessing infant cognitive development. In D. B. Bailey, Jr. & M. Wolery, *Assessing infants and preschoolers with handicaps* (pp. 249–274). Columbus, OH: Merrill.

Leddet-Chevallier, I., & Funderburk, S. (1983). The psychological effects of genetic disorders in children and their parents. In C. E. Hollingsworth (Ed.), *Coping with pediatric illness* (pp. 173–188). New York: SP Medical & Scientific Books.

Lehr, C. A., Ysseldyke, J. E., & Thurlow, M. L. (1987). Assessment practices in model early childhood special education programs. *Psychology in the Schools, 24,* 390–399.

Lindamood, S., & Wiley, F. (1983). Emotional impact

of hematology and oncology illnesses on the child and family. In C. E. Hollingsworth (Ed.), *Coping with pediatric illness* (pp. 189–196). New York: SP Medical & Scientific Books.

Lyon, S., & Lyon, G. (1980). Team functioning and staff development: A role release approach to providing integrated educational services for severely handicapped students. *The Journal of the Association for the Severely Handicapped, 5,* 250–263.

Margolin, G. (1982). Ethical and legal considerations in marital and family therapy. *American Psychologist, 37,* 788–801.

Mattson, A. (1972). Long-term physical illness in childhood: A challenge to psychosocial adaptation. *Pediatrics, 50,* 801–811.

McNulty, B. A. (1989). Leadership and policy strategies for interagency planning: Meeting the early childhood mandate. In J. J. Gallagher, P. L. Trohanis, & R. M. Clifford (Eds.), *Policy implementation and PL 99-457: Planning for young children with special needs* (pp. 147–167). Baltimore: Paul H. Brookes.

Meisels, S. J., Harbin, G., Modigliani, K., & Olson, K. (1988). Formulating optimal state early childhood intervention policies. *Exceptional Children, 55,* 159–165.

Meisels, S. J., & Provence, S. (1989). *Screening and assessment: Guidelines for identifying young disabled and developmentally vulnerable children and their families*. Washington, DC: National Center for Clinical Infant Programs.

Minuchin, S. (1974). *Families and family therapy*. Cambridge, MA: Harvard University Press.

Mott, S. E., Fewell, R. R., Lewis, M., Meisels, S. J., Shonkoff, J. P., & Simeonsson, R. J. (1986). Methods for assessing child and family outcomes in early childhood special education programs: Some views from the field. *Topics in Early Childhood Special Education, 6*(2), 1–15.

Mott, S. R., Fazekas, N. E., & James, S. R. (1985). *Nursing care of children and families: A holistic approach*. Menlo Park, CA: Addison-Wesley.

Moynihan, D. (1986). *Family and nation*. San Diego, CA: Harcourt Brace Jovanovich.

Murphy, M. A. (1982). The family with a handicapped child: A review of the literature. *Journal of Developmental and Behavioral Pediatrics, 3,* 73–82.

Neinstein, L. S. (1984). *Adolescent health care: A practical guide*. Baltimore: Urban & Schwarzenberg.

Neisworth, J. T., & Bagnato, S. J. (1986). Curriculum-based developmental assessment: Congruence of testing and teaching. *School Psychology Review, 15,* 180–199.

Nunnally, J. C. (1978). *Psychometric theory* (2nd ed.). New York: McGraw-Hill.

Odom, S. L., & Schuster, S. K. (1986). Naturalistic inquiry and the assessment of young handicapped children and their families. *Topics in Early Childhood Special Education, 6*(2), 68–82.

Ohio Department of Education. (1989). *The early childhood identification process: A manual for screening and assessment.* Columbus, OH: Author. (A document in the National Association of School Psychologists Acquisition Series)

Olswang, L. B., & Bain, B. A. (1988). Assessment of language in developmentally disabled infants and preschoolers. In T. D. Wachs & R. Sheehan (Eds.), *Assessment of young developmentally disabled children* (pp. 285–320). New York: Plenum Press.

Orlansky, M. D. (1988). Assessment of visually impaired infants and preschool children. In T. D. Wachs & R. Sheehan (Eds.), *Assessment of young developmentally disabled children* (pp. 93–107). New York: Plenum Press.

Ostfeld, B. M., & Gibbs, E. D. (1990). Use of family assessment in early intervention. In E. D. Gibbs & D. M. Teti (Eds.), *Interdisciplinary assessment of infants: A guide for early intervention professionals* (pp. 249–267). Baltimore: Paul H. Brookes.

Paget, K. D. (1989). Assessment of cognitive skills in the preschool-aged child. In D. B. Bailey, Jr. & M. Wolery, *Assessing infants and preschoolers with handicaps* (pp. 275–300). Columbus, OH: Merrill.

Paget, K. D., & Nagle, R. J. (1986). A conceptual model of preschool assessment. *School Psychology Review, 15,* 154–165.

Perrin, E. C., & Gerrity, S. (1984). Development of children with a chronic illness. *Pediatric Clinics of North America, 31,* 19–31.

Pfeiffer, S. I., Dean, R. S., & Shellenberger, S. (1986). The school psychologist in medical settings. In T. R. Kratochwill (Ed.), *Advances in school psychology* (Vol. 5, pp. 177–202). Hillsdale, NJ: Erlbaum.

Piaget, J. (1926). *The language and thought of the child.* London: Kegan Paul.

Piaget, J. (1967). *Six psychological studies.* New York: Random House.

Piaget, J. (1973). *The child and reality.* New York: Grossman.

Piaget, J., & Inhelder, B. (1969). *The psychology of the child.* New York: Basic Books.

Plas, J. M. (1986). *Systems psychology in the schools.* New York: Pergamon Press.

Pless, I., Satterwhite, B., & Van Vechten, D. (1976). Chronic illness in childhood: A regional survey of care. *Pediatrics, 58,* 37–46.

Roberts, J. E., & Crais, E. R. (1989). Assessing communication skills. In D. B. Bailey, Jr. & M. Wolery, *Assessing infants and preschoolers with handicaps* (pp. 339–389). Columbus, OH: Merrill.

Robinson, C., & Fieber, N. (1988). Cognitive assessment of motorically impaired infants and preschoolers. In T. D. Wachs & R. Sheehan (Eds.), *Assessment of young developmentally disabled children* (pp. 127–161). New York: Plenum Press.

Sameroff, A. J., & Chandler, M. J. (1975). Reproductive risk and the continuum of caretaking causality. In F. D. Horowitz, M. Hetherington, S. Scarr-Salapatek, & G. Siegel (Eds.), *Review of child development research* (Vol. 4, pp. 187–244). Chicago: University of Chicago Press.

Sexton, D., Miller, J. H., & Murdock, J. Y. (1984). Correlates of parental-professional congruency scores in the assessment of young handicapped children. *Journal of the Division for Early Childhood, 8,* 99–106.

Sheehan, R. (1988). Involvement of parents in early childhood assessment. In T. D. Wachs & R. Sheehan (Eds.), *Assessment of young developmentally disabled children* (pp. 75–90). New York: Plenum Press.

Short, R. J., Simeonsson, R. J., & Huntington, G. S. (1990). Early intervention: Implications of Public Law 99-457 for professional child psychology. *Professional Psychology: Research and Practice, 21,* 88–93.

Simeonsson, R. J. (1986). Assessment of the family context. In R. J. Simeonsson, *Psychological and developmental assessment of special children* (pp. 179–192). Boston: Allyn and Bacon.

Simeonsson, R. J. (1988). Evaluating the effects of family-focused intervention. In D. B. Bailey, Jr. & R. J. Simeonsson, *Family assessment in early intervention* (pp. 251–267). Columbus, OH: Merrill.

Smith, P. D. (1989). Assessing motor skills. In D. B.

Bailey, Jr. & M. Wolery, *Assessing infants and preschoolers with handicaps* (pp. 301–338). Columbus, OH: Merrill.

Spinetta, J. (1974). The dying child's awareness of death. *Psychological Bulletin, 81,* 256–260.

Stabler, B., & Simeonsson, R. J. (1986). Assessment of hospitalized and chronically ill children. In R. J. Simeonsson, *Psychological and developmental assessment of special children* (pp. 305–335). Boston: Allyn and Bacon.

Thomas, A., Chess, S., & Birch, H. G. (1968). *Temperament and behavior disorders in children.* New York: University Press.

Trohanis, P. L. (1989). An introduction to PL 99-457 and the national policy agenda for serving young children with special needs and their families. In J. J. Gallagher, P. L. Trohanis, & R. M. Clifford (Eds.), *Policy implementation and PL 99-457: Planning for young children with special needs* (pp. 1–17). Baltimore: Paul H. Brookes.

Turnbull, A. P., & Turnbull, H. R., III. (1986). Stepping back from early intervention: An ethical perspective. *Journal of the Division for Early Childhood, 10,* 106–117.

Ulrey, G. (1982a). Influences of infant behavior on assessment. In G. Ulrey & S. J. Rogers, *Psychological assessment of handicapped infants and young children* (pp. 14–24). New York: Thieme-Stratton.

Ulrey, G. (1982b). Influences of preschoolers' behavior on assessment. In G. Ulrey & S. J. Rogers, *Psychological assessment of handicapped infants and young children* (pp. 25–34). New York: Thieme-Stratton.

Varni, J. W. (1981a). Behavioral medicine in hemophilia arthritic pain management: Two case studies. *Archives of Physical Medicine and Rehabilitation, 62,* 183–187.

Varni, J. W. (1981b). Self-regulation techniques in the management of chronic arthritic pain in hemophilia. *Behavior Therapy, 12,* 185–194.

Varni, J. W., Gilbert, A., & Dietrich, S. L. (1981). Behavioral medicine in pain and analgesia management for the hemophilic child with Factor VIII Inhibitor. *Pain, 11,* 121–126.

Varni, J. W., Katz, E. R., & Dash, J. (1982). Behavioral and neurochemical aspects of pediatric pain.

In D. C. Russo & J. W. Varni (Eds.), *Behavioral pediatrics: Research and practice* (pp. 177–224). New York: Plenum Press.

Wachs, T. D., & Sheehan, R. (1988). Issues in the linkage of assessment to intervention. In T. D. Wachs & R. Sheehan (Eds.), *Assessment of young developmentally disabled children* (pp. 397–406). New York: Plenum Press.

Whiteman, S. T., & Feldman, W. S. (1983). Psychological considerations in the spinal defects and meningomyelocele clinic. In C. E. Hollingsworth (Ed.), *Coping with pediatric illness* (pp. 209–227). New York: SP Medical & Scientific Books.

Widerstrom, A. H., Mowder, B. A., & Sandall, S. R. (1991). *At-risk and handicapped newborns and infants: Development, assessment, and intervention.* Englewood Cliffs, NJ: Prentice Hall.

Winkle, C. W., Piercy, F. P., & Hovestadt, A. J. (1981). A curriculum for graduate level marriage and family therapy education. *Journal of Marital and Family Therapy, 7,* 201–210.

Winton, P. J. (1988). The family-focused interview: An assessment measure and goal-setting mechanism. In D. B. Bailey, Jr. & R. J. Simeonsson, *Family assessment in early intervention* (pp. 185–205). Columbus, OH: Merrill.

Wodrich, D. L., & Pfeiffer, S. I. (1989). School psychology in medical settings. In R. C. D'Amato & R. S. Dean (Eds.), *The school psychologist in nontraditional settings: Integrating clients, services, and settings* (pp. 87–105). Hillsdale, NJ: Erlbaum.

Wolery, M., & Bailey, D. B., Jr. (1989). Assessing play skills. In D. B. Bailey, Jr. & M. Wolery, *Assessing infants and preschoolers with handicaps* (pp. 428–446). Columbus, OH: Merrill.

Wolery, M., & Dyk, L. (1984). Arena assessment: Description and preliminary social validity data. *The Journal of the Association for the Severely Handicapped, 3,* 231–235.

Yogman, M. W., & Brazelton, T. B. (Eds.). (1986). *In support of families.* Cambridge, MA: Harvard University Press.

Zigler, E., & Berman, W. (1983). Discerning the future of early childhood intervention. *American Psychologist, 38,* 894–906.

CHAPTER 11

ETHICAL INFLUENCES
ON SCHOOL PSYCHOLOGY

As might be deduced from the material in the other chapters, there are many sources that influence school psychology practice. Reduced to its most basic state, the school psychologist is not free to be self-determining in what and how services are provided. Certainly the preferences put forward by all human sources (e.g., children, parents, educators, administrators, and so on) are highly influential on, and often determinative of, school psychology practices. Because of these expressed preferences, institutionalized governmental sources promulgate mandatory directives (e.g., through federal and state laws, board of education policies). Somewhere in the chain of influences, lying between the human and governmental sources, is the professional association.

School psychology has, of course, major alignment with the National Association of School Psychologists (NASP) and the American Psychological Association (APA, especially its Division of School Psychology). There are also numerous other professional associations working on behalf of children or education that are influential on school psychology practice—among many, the Council for Exceptional Children, the American Association for Counseling and Development, the American Association for Mental Retardation, the Association for Behavior Analysis, the Association for the Advancement of Behavior Therapy, and the Association for the Severely Handicapped seem noteworthy. Each professional association relevant to school psychology espouses the goal of enhancing the quality of service, as would benefit both the profession and the consumer (e.g., the society, the school, the child).

This chapter explores ethical principles and standards for service delivery (as pertain to ethics). Rather than methodically dissect a code of ethics and to accommodate space limitations, the appendices contain several important documents, namely: the APA (1990a) Ethical Principles of Psychologists (see Appendix A); the APA (1987) General Guidelines for Providers of Psychological Services (see Appendix B); the APA (1981b) Specialty Guidelines for the Delivery of Services by School Psychologists (see Appendix C); the NASP (1984a) Principles for Professional Ethics (see Appendix D); and the NASP (1984b) Standards for the Provision of School Psychological Services (see Appendix E).

Although not included as indices, the reader should also be familiar with the NASP (1986a) Standards for the Credentialing of School Psychologists and the NASP (1986b) Standards for Training and Field Placement Programs in School Psychology. Each of these documents should be studied carefully. Familiarity with their contents and Chapter 12 will enhance the usefulness of the information in this chapter.

THE PROFESSIONAL CODE OF ETHICS

Although a code of ethics may emanate from a professional association and be a statement of disciplinary objectives and preferences, it is rooted in society's framework for professionalism in general:

> Professionalism is a product of society. Society recognizes that it needs services of a prescribed quality and cannot tolerate behaviors of a certain

type. To attain these ends, it uses university degrees and licenses to anoint certain persons with "professional" status. This status, however, is neither fixed in definition nor permanent to the holder. Professionals must maintain standards promulgated by public policy. The cornerstone is ethics (Woody, Hansen, & Rossberg, 1989, p. 237)

It is sometimes difficult for the practitioner to accept that it is society, not the professional association, to which there must be unreserved allegiance. Too often, especially in the early stages of one's career, it is tempting to enjoy the identification that comes from membership in a professional association, and in the process mistakenly believe that the association is the discipline and should determine all that is to be done in the name of professionalism. In fact, the professional association, although a valuable component of the overall discipline, is merely one voice in the shaping of services, and must amplify public policy needs and expectations. The true discipline is determined by the public policies of society.

A code of ethics supports maturity for a discipline in search of professional identity (Mabe & Rollins, 1986). Stated differently, "Sound ethical reflection is an essential component of professional development and practice" (Jordan & Meara, 1990, p. 107).

It must be underscored that professional ethics, regardless of source, are not of the same authority as the law. The law establishes the prescriptions and proscriptions implemented by influential governmental sources, whereas disciplinary interests propagate the codes of ethics for the influential professional association sources. All school psychologists are subject to the laws of the jurisdiction in which they practice, but only the members of the professional association are subject to the particular code of ethics.

A professional code of ethics is often an ideal. As Haas and Malouf (1989) state,

Although each set of standards is in some respects the consensus of society or culture that promotes

it, moral frameworks are (or should be) developed largely through rational processes; legal standards, on the other hand, are primarily developed through political processes; while norms of etiquette are developed, for the most part, by historical precedent (p. 1). . . . In the view of many moral philosophers, ethics is distinguished by three main features: (a) it is based on *principles;* (b) the principles have *universality* (i.e., could be applied universally); and (c) proper behavior may be deduced from the principles by *reasoning* (p. 2). [They believe that] professional ethics in psychology is not pure ethics, but rather a combination of ethics, law, and etiquette. (p. 2)

THE FOUNDATION OF PROFESSIONAL ETHICS

Practitioners are prone to believe that professional ethics come from a learned analysis of what the discipline can offer, and that this scholarship is objective. In fact, professional ethics commonly allow the objectivity of scholarship to be secondary to the subjectivity of morality. Ethics deal with the morality of the society (Taylor, 1978; DeGeorge, 1982). As Dyer (1988) puts it, "Matters of personal ethics very quickly get translated into matters of public policy" (p. 7).

As principles of ethics develop, the morality of the society becomes a requirement for professionalism, and determines the acceptability of particular professional behavior:

Traditionally, ethics has been a branch of study in philosophy concerning how people ought to act toward each other, pronouncing judgments of value about those actions, e.g., deciding whether in a just society people ought to act in a certain way, and developing rules of ethical justification (e.g., asking how we can justify holding one set of values over another). (Kitchener, 1984, p. 16)

DeGeorge (1982) adds, *"Ethics* in general can be defined as a systematic attempt through the use of reason to make sense of our individual and social moral experience in such a way as to determine the rules which ought to govern human conduct and the values worth pursuing in life" (p. 12).

Therefore, codes of ethics applied to school psychology should be thought of as rules of morality for application of disciplinary-related skills and services.

Professional associations rely on principle ethics; that is, specific statements (usually "thou shalts") that the practitioner is supposed to interpret and apply in day-to-day interactions with consumers. Jordan and Meara (1990) discuss *"principle ethics* (i.e., approaches that emphasize the use of rational, objective, universal, and impartial principles in the ethical analysis of dilemmas) and *virtue ethics* (i.e., characterized by an emphasis on historical virtues)" (p. 107). They point out that the principles approach evaluates "competing prima facie valid principles in the context of significant quandaries or dilemmas" (p. 108) and typically cover justice, autonomy, nonmaleficence, and beneficence, albeit that one or another of the principles may be elevated over others. Stated simply, "Principle ethics attempt to tie together cognitive analysis and behavioral responses" (p. 108).

All of these intentions are well and good, but problems remain. As will be discussed later, making decisions relevant to ethics is no easy matter. Van Hoose and Kottler (1985) state,

> It is difficult enough for a profession to establish a code of ethical practice to regulate individual behavior when the practitioner's duties can be systematically delineated and scientifically validated. The problem is even more difficult when ambiguities and differences of opinion prevail and when the practitioner's role is not generally understood. The type of service provided by helping professionals, as well as the way they provide it, sets them apart from other professionals. (pp. 12–13)

School psychology is certainly an amorphous discipline, and there are many divergent influences. The result is that any attempt to codify ethics will surely be lacking is universality and specificity. Consequently, the school psychologist must remain the decision-making source for translating morality into practice, which means there will be a personal filter through which professional judgments must pass.

THE PRIMARY BENEFICIARY

In accord with the societal control of access to professionalism, it is incontrovertible that professional ethics codes must be primarily directed at benefiting the consumer and society. On occasion, public policy has seemed to be contradicted by ethics that are too aggrandizing for the discipline, and governmental sources of accountability have intervened. That is, all professional ethics do not receive endorsement by public policy, and in those situations there is a possible revocation of support from public policy by its regulatory agencies. For example, the Federal Trade Commission has long been concerned about professional associations: "The rising tide of consumerism in America during the 1960s and 1970s was an important factor in the decision of the Federal Trade Commission and the U.S. Department of Justice to instigate changes in the ways professional associations attempted to regulate their members" (Keith-Spiegel & Koocher, 1985, p. 176).

Fortified by rulings in legal cases, the Federal Trade Commission did not want ethics used to eliminate competition in the professional services marketplace, and it honed in on ethics that prohibited: "(1) soliciting business by advertising or other means; (2) engaging in price competition; and (3) otherwise engaging in competitive practices" (Keith-Spiegel & Koocher, 1985, p. 177). In July 1986, the Federal Trade Commission, on behalf of public welfare, initiated an investigation and eventually charged that certain of the APA (1981a) ethical principles were a disservice (i.e., violation of the federal antitrust laws) (Bales, 1988). The Ethics Committee of the APA (1990b) reported, "The APA voluntarily placed a moratorium on the adjudication of complaints of unethical conduct under the challenged principles" (p. 874). The Committee noted,

> The federal and state antitrust laws are intended to protect the public by increasing consumer options by preventing, among other things, restrictions on access to service providers and various forms of nondeceptive advertising. The FTC has a long his-

tory of examining and challenging the ethical codes of various health professions. (p. 874)

There was a prompt revision of the ethics code (APA, 1990a), and "the documents have been submitted to the FTC for approval, and the matter is now in their hands" (APA, 1990b, p. 874).

The honorable intent of benefit for all concerned, but primarily the consumer and society, is reflected in the NASP (1984a) introduction to its "Principles of Professional Ethics":

> Standards for professional conduct, usually referred to as ethics, recognize the obligation of professional persons to provide services and to conduct themselves so as to place the highest esteem on human rights and individual dignity. A code of ethics is an additional professional technique which seeks to ensure that each person served will receive the highest quality of service. (p. 4)

The preamble to the APA's (1990a) "Ethical Principles of Psychologists" is in a similar vein:

> Psychologists respect the dignity and work of the individual and strive for the preservation and protection of fundamental human rights. They are committed to increasing knowledge of human behavior and of people's understanding of themselves and others and to the utilization of such knowledge for the promotion of human welfare. While pursuing these objectives, they make every effort to protect the welfare of those who seek their services and of the research participants that may be the object of study. They use their skills only for purposes consistent with these values and do not knowingly permit their misuse by others. While demanding for themselves freedom of inquiry and communication, psychologists accept the responsibility this freedom requires: competence, objectivity in the application of skills, and concern for the best interests of clients, colleagues, students, research participants, and society. (p. 390)

It is from this societal-consumer stance that ethical principles for school psychologists move into actual practice.

ASPIRATION VERSUS MANDATE

As might be expected, ideals or general ethical intentions may be beneficial for motivation for excellence, but may lend little, if any, definitive guidance for practice. Ethics are aspirational, and it would be rare, and perhaps impossible, for the school psychologist to practice with a 100 percent concordance with all possible ethical principles: "If one believes that aspirational obligations are in fact mandatory (i.e., mistakes the ceiling of ethics for the floor), one runs the risk of feeling hopelessly inadequate as an ethical practitioner" (Haas & Maulof, 1989, p. 4).

At the same time, there are certain ethical principles that are mandatory, namely those that failure to uphold leads to violation and discipline. Further, certain ethical principles are embraced by law, such as in certification and licensure rules, and a violation could lead to legal process and sanctions. Haas and Maulof (1989) distinguish, "Mandatory obligations can be thought of as 'thou shalt nots,' while aspirational obligations can be thought of as 'thou shalts' " (p. 3).

While ethics, in general, are aspirational, they represent a discipline's statement on standard of care. (*Note:* The code of ethics may, of course, be only a partial statement of the overall standard of care.) Levy (1974) states,

> Codes of ethics are once the highest and lowest standards of practice expected of the practitioner, the awesome statement of rigid requirements, and the promotional materials issued primarily for public relations purposes. They embody the gradually evolved essence of moral expectations, as well as the arbitrarily prepared shortcut to professional prestige and status. At the same time, they are handy guides to the legal enforcement of ethical conduct and to punishment of unethical conduct. They are also the unrealistic, unimpressive, and widely unknown or ignored guides to wishful thinking. The motivation to create a code of ethics may be zeal for respectability. However, occupational groups are most often moved by a genuine need for guides to action in situations of agonizing conflict and by sincere aspirations to deal justly with clients, colleagues, and society. (p. 207)

Keith-Spiegel and Koocher (1985) provide this pithy comment: "It is easy to find fault with a code that attempts to do so much" (p. 2). Given this potpourri of purposes, it is no wonder that the aspirational nature of ethics leads to ambiguity that may thwart effective decision making in real-life situations.

ACCOUNTABILITY THROUGH ETHICS

An ethics code prescribes that the practitioner answer to an external authority (Tennyson & Strom, 1986): "Ethics is usually concerned with *justifying* controlling practices rather than merely describing them" (Skinner, 1953, p. 328). Vande-Creek, Knapp, and Brace (1990) state, "The American public has a right to expect practicing psychologists to be accountable for their professional actions and to deliver high-quality psychological services" (p. 135). While the monitoring of this accountability starts with consumers and moves (sometimes through other practitioners in the community) to the members of the ethics committee for the professional association, the accountability extends on to myriad governmental sources on behalf of society, including the legal system. The external authority requires that the school psychologist act with responsibility, with the moral consciousness imposing responsibleness (Tennyson & Strom, 1986; Wilcoxon, 1987).

Since ethics are interwoven into the fabric of professionalism, any alleged transgression may trigger problematic emotional responses. Rogers (1987) describes it:

> While colleagues are willing to tolerate, and perhaps even welcome, negative comments regarding their professional practice, introduction of a description such as *unethical* is likely to have an inflammatory effect on the ensuing debate. At worst, professional ethics becomes a moral sledgehammer for pounding deviationalists into submission. To make matters worse, ethical proceedings may emanate a sense of righteousness in reviewing other professionals' shortcomings or have a decidedly inquisitional flavor. Because of

the emotionality surrounding professional ethics, a strong need exists for well-reasoned standards based on solid empirical research. (p. 149)

Rogers quickly acknowledges, however, that "professional ethics have eluded empirical investigation, based in part on their loosely constructed constellation of principles which appear to be deliberately vague" (p. 149).

SELF-REGULATION

Given the accountability, regulation, and potential discipline, it seems essential that professional ethics, notwithstanding the vagueness mentioned by Rogers, be translated into clear-cut guidelines for practice. Unfortunately, such is not the case. To date, there is a dearth of practical guidelines that would assist decision making in actual ethical dilemmas (Green & Hansen, 1986). Holding true to the scientist-practitioner model, what is needed is a set of guidelines that clearly connect theory to practice, with the goal being to determine "*which* minitheory, *what* body of scientific knowledge, and *which* treatment method are relevant to the problem at hand? What data domain and which level of analysis should be selected for the client's presenting problem?" (Kanfer, 1990, p. 265).

The lack of adequate guidelines for practice certainly plagues school psychology. Consequently, it will remain for the school psychologist to continue to seek effective self-regulation: "What appears to be necessary is a membership capable of making sophisticated judgments about which course of action may be ethical in situations in which no one behavior seems entirely ethical or unethical" (Welfel & Lipsitz, 1984, p. 31).

Making ethics-related judgments requires informed and cautious processing of the unique aspects of the particular situation. Haas and Malouf (1989) state,

> Briefly, the clinician must identify three elements before being able to make an ethical decision: (a)

the nature of the problem; (b) the identities and preferences of those persons who have a legitimate stake in the outcome of the problem (the "stake-holders"); and (c) the relevant professional and legal standards (if any) that bear on the case at hand. (p. 6)

They lament that "there is no way to eliminate completely the possibility of self-serving rationalization" (p. 14), and caution that legal considerations must be taken into full account.

DEALING WITH A POSSIBLE ETHICAL VIOLATION

There is no way to identify all ethical problems that do or could occur in school psychology. Usually the problem derives from a unique set of circumstances. That is, under one set of circumstances, a particular act might be appropriate ethically, whereas under another set of circumstances it might be inappropriate ethically. Further, a problem has to be under the rubric of a code of ethics that, in fact, apply to the particular school psychologist. That is, for an ethics committee to process an alleged violation in the context of a specific case, the potentially errant school psychologist must be a dues-paying member of the professional association that maintains the ethics committee, and a complainant would have to step forward and file a complaint.

Informal Resolution of a Possible Ethical Violation

On occasion, the problem may be resolved informally, and thus never be reported or subject to identification. The APA (1990a) ethics code (Principle 7, section g) states,

> When psychologists know of an ethical violation by another psychologist, and it seems appropriate, they informally attempt to resolve the issue by bringing the behavior to the attention of the psychologist. If the misconduct is of a minor nature and/or appears to be due to a lack of sensitivity, knowledge, or experience, such an informal solution is usually appropriate. Such informal correc-

tive efforts are made with sensitivity to any rights to confidentiality involved. If the violation does not seem amenable to an informal solution, or is of a more serious nature, psychologists bring it to the attention of the appropriate local, state, and/or national committee on professional ethics and conduct. (p. 394)

At first blush, this sort of informal resolution between colleagues seems appealing. It can, however, lead to problems for the would-be monitor of ethics. Consider two issues.

First, there is no clear definition of what is "misconduct of a *minor* nature" (emphasis added) versus "of a *more serious* nature" (emphasis added). In other words, the monitor must make a value judgment without the benefit of clear-cut criteria. In so doing, it is feasible that the monitor will incur the wrath of the alleged wrongdoer.

For example, one clinical psychologist received an announcement of a school psychologist's offering "clinical psychology services" through a local hospital. Concerned about the possibility of the school psychologist's misrepresenting competency and possibly being in violation of both ethics and laws, the clinical psychologist wrote a polite letter to the school psychologist, simply inquiring about whether the latter had verified the appropriateness of the announcement. The school psychologist sent back a brusque, hostile reply, making all sorts of allegations against the clinical psychologist and ending with a threat of legal action for defamation against the clinical psychologist.

Although it would be easy to chalk this situation up to a character disorder on the part of the school psychologist, it illustrates how honorable intentions, even when coupled with tact, may produce negative results for the monitor of ethics. Some of the same factors reflected in the foregoing situation, especially the specter of legal liability, have contributed to certain professional associations' avoiding adjudication of ethical complaints. For example, some state psychological associations no longer have ethical committees, except perhaps to provide education about ethics (APA, 1987b).

Second and related to the "minor" versus "major" nature of the situation, the monitor of ethics must make a decision about whether or not the violation seems "amenable to an informal solution" versus requiring that it be brought "to the attention of the appropriate local, state, and/or national committee on professional ethics and conduct." Not only is there a dearth of criteria for determining if the situation is "amenable" to informal efforts, there is no definitive guidelines for determining the "appropriate" committee source to contact.

It should be added that the NASP (1984a) ethics code is much like the APA (1990a) ethics code on the matter of dealing with potential violators of ethics. The NASP ethics code (Section III, subsection G, paragraph 3) states,

> When school psychologists are aware of a possible ethical violation by another school psychologist, they attempt to resolve the issue on an informal level. If such informal efforts are not productive and a violation appears to be enacted, steps for filing an ethical complaint as outlined by the appropriate association are followed. (p. 7)

Unfortunately, many of the same hazards discussed for the APA ethics code are present with the NASP ethics code. Therefore, the well-intended monitor of school psychology practices by others is left with considerable responsibility and risk.

It should be emphasized that ethics are not superior to law. The NASP (1984a) ethics code (Section III, subsection E, paragraph 5) makes this clear:

> School psychologists in public and private practice have the responsibility of adhering to federal, state and local laws and ordinances governing their practice. If such laws are in conflict with existing ethical guidelines, school psychologists proceed toward resolution of such conflict through positive, respected and legal channels. (p. 7)

Similarly, the APA (1990a) ethics code (Principle 3, paragraph d) states,

> When federal, state, provincial, organizational, or institutional laws, regulations, or practices are in conflict with Association standards and guidelines, psychologists make known their commitment to Association standards and guidelines and, wherever possible, work toward a resolution of the conflict. (p. 391)

Let there be no misunderstanding: If there is a conflict between ethics and law, the law is supreme, albeit that efforts can and should be made to bring about a resolution.

The Increase in Ethical Complaints

Notwithstanding the difficulties, the APA (1988) reports: "There has been a striking increase in the number of people who contact the Ethics Office expressing an intent to file a complaint," and "in the space of two years, there has been an increase of 76%, with an increment in the rate of increase" (p. 564). According to this report, the actual number of complaints continues to rise.

There are several interesting figures pertaining to gender. Relevant to who files a complaint:

> About three fourths of those who file complaints are female. The percentage of male complainants has declined from 54% in 1983 to 29% in 1987. The number of male complainants has remained stable during these five years; the number of female complainants has more than doubled. (p. 564)

The reasons for this substantial difference according to gender remain for conjecture. Is it because females are more sensitive to and/or concerned about ethics, less able to resolve ethical dilemmas informally, more willing to submit a complaint, or what? Relevant to the gender of the alleged wrongdoing psychologist, "in 1987, 80% of the psychologists against whom ethical complaints were filed were male. This figure is disproportionately higher than that of the male membership of that same year (64%)" (p. 565).

Although California is the home base for only 14 percent of the APA membership, "In

1987, almost one third (31%) of the complainees were residents of California" (p. 565).

REASONS FOR A FORMAL ETHICAL COMPLAINT

Given that professional ethics are stated as principles, it is up to the complainant to interpret a principle as being applicable to a particular action. Of course, the ethics review source, such as the APA Ethics Committee, could presumably realign the allegedly unethical conduct with ethical principles that were to be at issue. In terms of reasons for a complaint to the APA:

> In 1987, the highest number of alleged violations involved either Principle 1 (Responsibility) or Principle 6 (Welfare of the Consumer). Each accounted for approximately 22% of the 251 alleged violations. In descending order of frequency, the remaining Principles were Principle 3 (Moral and Legal Standards), accounting for 16%; Principle 2 (Competence), accounting for 12%; Principle 7 (Professional Relationships), accounting for 11%; Principle 5 (Confidentiality), accounting for 8%; Principle 8 (Assessment Techniques), accounting for 6%; Principle 4 (Public Statements) accounting for 5%; and Principles 9 (Research and Human Participants) and 10 (Care and Use of Animals), accounting for 0%. (Percentages fail to sum to 100 due to rounding). (APA, 1988, p. 564)

For 1988, the APA (1990b) Ethics Committee reported the issues involved in cases that were opened, and are presented in Table 11.1. These data are self-explanatory. While a wide variety of issues are involved, certainly "cases adjudicated in other jurisdictions" and "dual relationships" are substantial.

PROCESSING A FORMAL ETHICAL COMPLAINT

When a formal complaint is submitted to a professional association, it is processed through a system that assures due process and equal protection. Appeal procedures are included. The NASP

TABLE 11.1 Issues Involved in APA Ethics Cases Opened in 1988

TYPE OF CASE	NO. OF CASES
Cases adjudicated in other jurisdictions	
Conviction of felony	3
Loss of license	13
Expulsion from state association	3
Sexual intimacy with client, dual relationship, or exploitation and/or sexual harassment	23
Inappropriate professional practice	
Child custody abuses	9
Practicing outside area of competence	8
Inappropriate response to crisis	2
Breach of confidentiality	7
Lack of follow-up or desertion of client	1
Testing abuse	2
Fraudulent insurance claims/absence of advance notice of fee structure	8
Failure to respect other professionals	1
Inappropriate teaching, research, or administration	
Authorship controversies	1
Plagiarism	1
Lack of due-process firing or lack of adequate supervision	1
Discrimination	1
Public statements	
Misuse of media	1
False, fraudulent, misleading statements	3
Public allegations about colleague	1
Total	89

Source: Report of the Ethics Committee: 1986. *American Psychologist, 45*(7), 873–874. Copyright 1990 by the American Psychological Association. Reprinted by permission.

(1984b) has "Procedural Guidelines for the Adjudication of Ethical Complaints," and the APA (1985) has "Rules and Procedures." These documents set forth the objectives, authority, and procedures that will be applied to members against whom an ethical complaint has been filed. Since space restricts covering these procedures in detail, suffice it to say that it is a quasi-legal situation.

Even though the processing of an ethical complaint is supposedly between colleagues and is not in a court of law, the respondent (i.e., the school psychologist faced with a complaint) would be well advised to have legal counsel. Why go to the expense? Because any professional discipline for unethical conduct can have severe consequences.

Regardless of any immediate penalty for an ethical violation, the long-term penalty is likely to be greater. That is, having an ethical violation can tarnish one's professional record forever, and can potentially impact negatively on employment opportunities and other career issues. For example, applying for licensing or certification at some point in the future might require admission of past ethical violations, and thus jeopardize the application and, consequently, employment. Also, applications for professional malpractice insurance typically require reporting of ethical violations, and could lead to denial of insurance or a different insurance fee.

SANCTIONS FOR ETHICAL VIOLATIONS

There are various sanctions available against a violator of professional ethics. With NASP (1984a), the Hearing Committee can recommend that the respondent be expelled or dropped from membership or allowed to resign, and: "Other disciplinary measures may be recommended by a simple majority and would be decided upon per individual case" (p. 16). With APA (1990b),

> The sanctions available to the Ethics Committee are (a) cease and desist order, (b) reprimand, (c) censure, (d) supervision requirement, (e) rehabilitation requirement, (f) probation, (g) stipulated resignation, (h) recommendation to the Board of Directors that the individual be dropped from membership in the Association, and (i) recommendation to the Board of Directors that the individual be expelled from the membership in the Association. (p. 873)

To clarify APA's meanings of "dropped" versus "expelled":

> Cases that are opened secondary to a member being convicted of felonies or disciplined in other tribunals may result in a recommendation of the Board of Directors that the member be expelled from the Association and cases that are initiated by a complainant or *sua sponte* (but are not secondary to a serious action taken by another body) may result in a recommendation to the Board of Directors that the member be dropped from the Association. (p. 873)

Given the commitment that professional associations have to public welfare, it is commonplace to link legal actions, such as legal complaints to state regulatory agencies (e.g., licensing boards), with ethical complaints. The APA (1988) reports,

> In 42 instances over the past five years, APA Ethics Committee cases were based on actions taken by other adjudicative bodies. In 19 cases, the psychologist had been convicted of a felony. In 18 cases, the psychologist's license had been revoked by a state board. In 5 cases, the psychologist had been expelled by a state psychological association. (p. 564)

As for crime, "When APA members are convicted by the criminal courts, the Ethics Committee typically becomes aware of the action when a local psychologist or consumer sends a copy of the newspaper account" (p. 564), and the ethics investigation relies "heavily on court documents" (p. 564).

The notification of other adjudicative sources is embraced by the rules and procedures of the professional association. The NASP (1984a) states,

> In severe cases and when the welfare of the public is at stake, and when the Ethics and Professional Conduct Committee deems it necessary to maintain the principles of the Association and the profession, it may also notify affiliated state and

regional associations and state and local licensing and certification boards of the final disposition of the case. Other interested parties may be notified of the final action when, in the opinion of the Ethics and Professional Conduct Committee, notification is necessary for the protection of the public. (p. 17)

In a similar vein, the APA (1985) provides:

The Board of Directors shall notify affiliated state and regional associations, the American Board of Professional Psychology (ABPP), state and local licensing and certification boards, the American Association of State Psychology Boards (AASPB), and the Council for the National Register of Health Service Providers in Psychology (CNRHSPP), or other appropriate parties of its final action subsequent to adjudication of a formal charge when the Board deems it necessary for the protection of the public or to maintain the standards of the Association. (p. 694)

To illustrate how the net is spread: A psychologist had a problem with an application for licensure in State A. The problem led to State A's imposing discipline (the psychologist's not being eligible to apply for licensure for one year), and notifying a national professional psychological association (of which the psychologist was a member) and the licensing board for State B (another state in which the psychologist was licensed). Because of the disciplinary action by the licensing board in State A, a two-year-plus investigation was conducted by the licensing board in State B, apparently trying to detect other wrongdoing by the psychologist. None was found, but the psychologist experienced emotional distress and financial costs for legal representation throughout that extended period of time. Using solely the problem in State A (for which the psychologist acknowledged and apologized), the professional association found an ethical violation, and sanctioned the psychologist by requiring that, to maintain his or her membership, he or she had to complete several graduate courses on ethics for credit and to do so within a limited period of time.

Since the negative impact of an ethics violation has become so far-reaching and costly (in many ways), some psychologists are avoiding membership in professional associations. Said one psychologist, "It's just not worth the risk of some borderline patient filing a false and malicious complaint against me—I'll just subscribe to the journals."

It should be noted that school psychologists are being drawn more and more into situations that seem to elevate the risk of ethical, regulatory, or legal complaints. For example, Crespi (1990) describes school psychologists working in forensic psychology, which includes custody disputes and alleged abuse and neglect of children. From the senior author's work as an attorney for mental-health professionals, it is known that parents, disappointed over a custody, visitation, abuse, or neglect rulings, are relying on ethical and regulatory complaints to salve their feelings. Thus, the school psychologist who gives testimony in this sort of case is especially vulnerable to emotionally motivated allegations.

INSULATING AGAINST AN ETHICS COMPLAINT

Needless to say, there is no foolproof system for avoiding an ethics complaint. Logically, the safest route is through training in ethics and meeting standards for the professional service. Even then, however, the unique nature of each situation requires that impromptu and idiosyncratic judgments to be made. Inevitably, the human condition leads to certain judgments that seemed to be right at the moment, but prove to be less than perfect in the long run.

Training in Ethics

The NASP (1986b) "Standards for Training and Field Placement Programs in School Psychology" specify that the content of the school psychology program shall contain substantial preparation in legal and ethical issues, as well as professional issues and standards. Likewise, it is

"Standards for the Credentialing of School Psychologists," NASP (1986a) delineates legal and ethical issues, as well as professional issues and standards, as being essential to meeting the educational qualifications.

Given the connection between ethics and standards, it would seem preordained that ethics would assuredly be included in training. From a review of surveys of training in ethics provided to psychologists, Nagel (1987) notes, "There is considerable variation in the format and content of ethics courses, and to date, there is little empirical evidence of the relative efficacy of formal courses versus training by supervision" (p. 164). He adds that, while ethics training occurs in the large majority of master's psychology programs (in general), "there are no comparable data on school psychology training programs at the doctoral or subdoctoral level, although surveys indicate that professional seminars dealing in part with ethical and legal issues are important curricular components" (p. 164).

Nagel (1987) advocates more formalized ethics courses, but cautions that this does not necessarily mean a deemphasis on informal ethics training. Of special concern: "Given some of the inherent shortcomings of ethical codes, students need a greater understanding of the philosophical foundations of ethical principles and should be provided with models and strategies for making and justifying ethical decisions" (p. 169).

From a survey of a sample of NASP psychologists, Basel and Woody (1991) express concern about the respondents' lack of familiarity with the APA and NASP ethics codes (which might mean that they overrely on internal belief systems or personal values), and general denial of having encountered many ethical dilemmas in the past two years (which might mean that they are unable to recognize ethical dilemmas). Although the large majority of these respondents had completed formal courses and engaged in other means to obtain training in ethics, their limited recognition of ethical dilemmas led Basel and Woody to wonder if the respondents' training did, in fact, prepare them to adequately engage in ethical problem solving. In general, the respondents did, however, believe that they were prepared to solve an ethical dilemma.

Standards for Service Delivery

Avoiding an ethical problem is contingent on quality care. Stated differently, the school psychologist must meet the standard of care supported by the professional discipline. Nonetheless, it requires judgments being made: "There are two components necessary for the practitioner to provide effective services to patients: knowing what the most effective treatment consists of, and having the judgment to know *when* to use these effective techniques" (Haas & Malouf, 1989, p. 134). Presumably professional standards would determine what constitutes "the most effective treatment" and how to determine "when" the techniques are to be implemented. Unfortunately and as discussed earlier in this chapter, the guidelines are not specific enough to eliminate or replace individual judgments.

Recalling the earlier discussion of the aspirational nature of ethics, it should be noted that standards, if defined at all by a professional association, are also aspirational. For example, the APA (1987a) "General Guidelines for Providers of Psychological Services" state, "These General Guidelines are a set of aspirational statements for psychologists that encourage continual improvements in the quality of practice and service" (p. 712); and "Providers of psychological services have the same responsibility to uphold these specific General Guidelines as they would the corresponding Ethical Principles" (p. 712). Relatedly, the NASP (1984b) "Standards for the Provision of School Psychological Services" are "intended to serve as a guide" (p. 21) and "delineate what services might reasonably be expected to be available from most school psychologists" (p. 21).

If there is an ethical complaint subject to adjudication by a professional association, it is logical that the association's standards will be relied on for determining the appropriateness of the conduct, be it by omission or commission. Indeed, the link is specific in the NASP (1984b) standards (Section 4.9): "Each school psychologist practices in full accordance with the NASP *Principles for Professional Ethics,* and these *Standards"* (p. 33). Going even further, the APA (1981b) "Specialty Guidelines for the Delivery of Services by School Psychologists" (Guideline 2, subsection 2.2.3) state,

> All providers within a school psychological service unit are familiar with and adhere to the American Psychological Association's Standards for Providers of Psychological Services, Ethical Principles of Psychologists, Standards for Educational and Psychological Tests, Ethical Principles in the Conduct of Research With Human Participants, and other official policy statements relevant to standards for professional services issued by the Association. (p. 676)

As a specific interpretation of this standard: "A copy of each of these documents is maintained by providers of school psychological services and is available upon request to all school personnel and officials, parents, members of the community, and where applicable, students and other sanctioners" (p. 676).

By gaining insulation from an ethics complaint, the consumer (e.g., the student and his or her family, the school, the community) benefits, and the school psychologist, in turn, receives deserved protection against ethical complaints (and regulatory and legal complaints as well). If ethical problems are reduced to their most common denominator, it is a matter of achieving professional competence: "Indeed, it may be asserted that *all* ethical principles can be derived from the principles of competence" (Haas & Malouf, 1989, p. 16).

Every school psychologist, even he or she who is not a member of any of the major psychological associations, is wise to be well versed in the ethics and standards relevant to the practice of psychology in general and school psychology in particular. Further, the school psychologist must have knowledge of relevant legal principles; as stated earlier from the NASP (1984a) ethics code (Section III, subsection e, paragraph 5): "School psychologists in public and private practice have the responsibility of adhering to federal, state and local laws and ordinances governing their practice" (p. 7).

If university-based training deals minimally with ethics and law, the school psychology trainee should seek training from other sources, such as in the contexts of supervision and specialized seminars. Individually determined reading of ethics and the law should be a lifelong endeavor.

SUMMARY

This chapter considers ethical principles and standards for service delivery (as pertain to ethics), and explains the importance of a code of ethics for professionalization, the structure of ethics, the intention to primarily benefit the consumer and society (with only a secondary benefit to the discipline), accountability through ethics, and the concept of self-regulation. Ethical complaints are increasing. If a possible ethical violation cannot be resolved informally, a formal complaint can be made (with due process and equal protection for the respondent). There are numerous possible sanctions for an ethical violation, with each potentially having a significant negative impact on career. Training in ethical decision making is essential.

REFERENCES

American Psychological Association. (1981a). Ethical principles of psychologists. *American Psychologist, 36*(6), 633–638.

American Psychological Association. (1981b). Specialty guidelines for the delivery of services by school psychologists. *American Psychologist, 36*(6), 670–681.

American Psychological Association. (1985). Rules and procedures. *American Psychologist, 40*(6), 685–694.

American Psychological Association. (1987a). General guidelines for providers of psychological services. *American Psychologist, 42*(7), 712–723.

American Psychological Association. (1987b). Report of the Ethics Committee: 1986. *American Psychologist, 42*(7), 730–734.

American Psychological Association. (1988). Trends in ethics cases, common pitfalls and published resources. *American Psychologist, 43*(7), 564–572.

American Psychological Association. (1990a). Ethical principles of psychologists (Amended June 2, 1989). *American Psychologist, 45*(3), 390–395.

American Psychological Association. (1990b). Report of the Ethics Committee: 1988. *American Psychologist, 45*(7), 873–874.

Bales, J. (1988). FTC demands end to ad, fee-splitting restrictions. *APA Monitor, 19*(3), 19.

Basel, K., & Woody, R. H. (1991). *Ethical dilemmas confronting school psychologists.* Unpublished manuscript, University of Nebraska at Omaha.

Crespi, T. D. (1990). School psychologists in forensic psychology: Converging and diverging issues. *Professional Psychology, 21*(2), 83–87.

DeGeorge, R. T (1982). *Business ethics.* New York: Macmillan.

Dyer, A. R. (1988). *Ethics and psychiatry: Toward professional definition.* Washington, DC: American Psychiatric Press.

Green, S. L., & Hansen, J. C. (1986). Ethical dilemmas in family therapy. *Journal of Marital and Family Therapy, 12,* 225–230.

Haas, L. J., & Malouf, J. L. (1989). *Keeping up the good work: A practitioner's guide to mental health ethics.* Sarasota, FL: Professional Resource Exchange.

Jordan, A. E., & Meara, N. M. (1990). Ethics and the professional practice of psychologists: The role of virtues and principles. *Professional Psychology, 21*(2), 107–114.

Kanfer, F. H. (1990). The scientist-practitioner connection: A bridge in need of constant attention. *Professional Psychology, 21*(4), 264–270.

Keith-Spiegel, P., & Koocher, G. P. (1985). *Ethics in psychology: Professional standards and cases.* New York: Random House.

Kitchener, K. S. (1984). Ethics and counseling psychology: Distinctions and directions. *Counseling Psychologist, 12*(3), 15–18.

Levy, C. S. (1974). On the development of a code of ethics. *Social Work, 19,* 207–216.

Mabe, A. R., & Rollins, S. A. (1986). The role of a code of ethical standards in counseling. *Journal of Counseling and Development, 64,* 294–297.

Nagle, R. J. (1987). Ethics training in school psychology. *Professional School Psychology, 2*(3), 163–171.

National Association of School Psychologists. (1984a). Principles for professional ethics. In *Professional Conduct Manual* (pp. 1–17). Stanford, CT: Author.

National Association of School Psychologists. (1984b). Standards for the provision of school psychological services. In *Professional Conduct Manual* (pp. 19–33). Stanford, CT: Author.

National Association of School Psychologists. (1986a). Standards for the credentialing of school psychologists. In *Standards* (pp. 23–36). Washington, DC: Author.

National Association of School Psychologists. (1986b). Standards for training and field placement programs in school psychology. In *Standards* (pp. 5–22). Washington, DC: Author.

Rogers, R. (1987). Ethical dilemmas in forensic evaluations. *Behavioral Sciences & the Law, 5*(2), 149–160.

Skinner, B. F. (1953). *Science and human behavior.* New York: Free Press.

Taylor, P. W. (1978). *Problems of moral philosophy.* Belmont, CA: Wadsworth.

Tennyson, W. W., & Strom, S. M. (1986). Beyond professional standards: Developing responsibleness. *Journal of Counseling and Development, 64,* 298–302.

VandeCreek, L., Knapp, S., & Brace, K. (1990). Mandatory continuing education for licensed psychologists: Its rationale and current implementation. *Professional Psychology, 21*(2), 135–140.

Van Hoose, W. H., & Kottler, J. A. (1985). *Ethical and legal issues in counseling and psychotherapy* (2nd ed.). San Francisco: Jossey-Bass.

Welfel, E. R., & Lipsitz, N. E. (1984). The ethical behavior of professional psychologists: A critical analysis of research. *Counseling Psychologist, 12*(3), 31–42.

Wilcoxon, S. A. (1987). Ethical standards: A study of application and utility. *Journal of Counseling and Development, 65,* 510–511.

Woody, R. H., Hansen, J. C., & Rossberg, R. H. (1989). *Counseling psychology: Strategies and services.* Pacific Grove, CA: Brooks/Cole.

CHAPTER 12

LEGAL INFLUENCES
ON SCHOOL PSYCHOLOGY

As a preface to the legal framework for school psychology, there is a definite affirmative duty for the school psychologist to give attention to and advocate the law. From the American Psychological Association's (1981b) "Specialty Guidelines for the Delivery of Services by School Psychologists":

2.2.2 All providers within a school psychological service unit support the legal and civil rights of the users. (p. 676)
2.2.4 All providers within a school psychological service unit conform to relevant statutes established by federal, state, and local governments. (p. 676)

Turning to the National Association of School Psychologists' (1984b) "Standards for the Provision of School Psychological Services," there is guidance to federal and state level administrative agencies regarding administrative organization, laws, and regulations for school psychological services. At the federal level:

2.1.2.1 The Congress of the United States should ensure that the rights of all parents and children are protected by the creation and modification of laws which provide for the services of school psychologists. These services includes, but are not limited to, consultation, assessment, and intervention for individuals, groups, and systems. These services are available to all children, their families, and school personnel.
2.1.2.2 The Congress should ensure that school psychological services are provided in a free and appropriate manner to all children, their families, and school personnel in need of such services.
2.1.2.3 The Congress should ensure that federal

laws recognize the appropriate involvement of school psychologists in educational programs and that adequate federal funding is made available for the education, training, services, and continuing professional development of school psychologists in order to guarantee appropriate and effective services.
2.1.2.4 The Congress should create no laws which effectively prohibit the credentialed school psychologist from the ethical and legal practice of his/her profession in the public or private sector, or which would be in violation of these standards. (p. 24)

The four federal standards are, in essence, translated into five standards for state level administrative agencies, plus:

2.2.2.5 The state legislature should ensure that state laws provide for the credentialing of school psychologists consistent with NASP standards. (p. 25)
2.2.2.7 The state legislature should ensure that there are sufficient numbers of adequately prepared and credentialed school psychologists to provide services consistent with these *Standards*. [And this standard continues on to specify, with possible exceptions, a minimum ratio of a full-time school psychologist per 1,000 students.] (p. 25)

Incidentally, the foregoing direct reference to "consistent with NASP standards" is the sort of proclamation that some lawmakers might view as constituting a self-serving benefit, as opposed to promoting standards for the public (regardless of source). These quotations from the APA and the NASP exemplify the honorable intention of the professional associations to establish for their members an affirmative duty to give attention to and advocate the law.

Federal legislation has been enacted that creates prescriptions and proscriptions for the education of handicapped children and youth, and the trend seems to be toward casting the protective legal net over persons of all ages (as might spawn adult school psychological services). In turn, each state makes statutory adoptions and adaptations of the federal mandates, and passes rules and regulations that will allow legally acceptable implementation at the local level. Legislation or statutes (and their rules and regulations) seldom receive universal endorsement, and cases abound that define and interpret (e.g., what is an appropriate education and what is the proper usage of psychological tests).

Beyond legislation, there are many legal principles that shape school psychology. For example, the nature of school psychology dictates that confidentiality occurs at all times; however, there are situations in which the confidentiality cannot be allowed and exceptions must be made. This leads to a body of law that deals with the right of privacy and privileged communication, such as would be applied to the release of records and test data. Although federal legislation provides a cornerstone for confidentiality of school records (see next paragraph), other state statutes or common (case) law for the jurisdiction come into play. This chapter will provide an overview of legal fundamentals that have special relevance to school psychology.

This chapter will highlight four legislative acts that are critical to school psychology: Public Law 94-142, the Education for All Handicapped Children Act of 1975 (89 Stat. 773, November 29, 1975, referred to hereinafter as PL 94-142); Public Law 99-457, the Education of the Handicapped Act Amendments of 1986 (100 Stat. 1145, October 8, 1986, referred to hereinafter as PL 99-457); Public Law 101-476, the Individuals with Disabilities Education Act of 1990 (101 Stat. 1103, October 30, 1990, referred to hereinafter as PL 101-476); and Public Law 90-247,

the Family Educational Rights and Privacy Act of 1974 (34 CFR 99, amendments May 9, 1980, hereinafter referred to as FERPA; see also Public Law 93-380). To repeat, each state typically makes an idiosyncratic statutory codification, and the rules and regulations promulgated are of paramount importance for the day-to-day operations of the school psychologist. Since it would be impossible to include or review all state statutes relevant to these federal mandates, the reader is urged to gain familiarity with the state laws that are applicable to the jurisdiction in which he or she practices or intends to practice as a school psychologist.

Since the school psychologist has a profound impact on the rights and welfare of children and youth (and their families and society), the role carries a heavy duty to perform in an acceptable manner. Good intentions are not enough; there must be conduct and services that are compatible with a standard of care prescribed by public policy. This chapter will provide an analysis of the professional liability associated with being a school psychologist, and will explore specific problem areas, such as malpractice (e.g., misdiagnosis, faulty treatment). The chapter will conclude with comments about the school psychologist's providing expert testimony in legal proceedings (e.g., cases of child custody and abuse), and safeguarding suggestions for being an expert witness (see also Chapter 8 for information on forensic psychology).

FUNDAMENTALS OF THE LAW

In society, the law is intended to control all personal and professional conduct. As obvious as this axiom may be, many educators and mental-health professionals, including school psychologists, hold the erroneous notion that the discipline can define professional functions. It can, but only to the extent accepted by public policy and sanctioned by law.

Being a professional is a privilege (e.g., being granted certification or licensure), not a right. Indeed, holding a certificate or license is primarily for accountability, with the regulation being maintained by the public through its designated governmental unit (e.g., the state department of education and state department of professional regulation). Although the discipline will certainly have an important voice in decision making, it will not be the sole voice and is seldom the determinative voice. For example, even when the discipline has a representative on, say, a licensing board, there are other board members who are not part of the discipline (e.g., consumer advocates), and all board members have a first-order duty to protect the rights and welfare of the public. Likewise, a board of education will receive information from professionals, such as the superintendent and other administrators, but it, too, is the guardian of public rights and welfare. That is, it is not an advocacy source for professionals employed in the system (however, the board will certainly be cognizant of furthering professionalism, but only as it will be of public service).

After being schooled in academics and logical reasoning, the school psychologist may find it difficult to accept the way that the law is created and applied. Whether in the form of professional liability, federal mandates for education of the handicapped, or whatever, the law is the product of a nebulous entity known as public policy:

> Public policy is an amorphous body of ideas, attitudes, preferences, and behaviors, all assimilated into values that must interface with ethics. Societal values and ethics are manifested in law, as interpreted, implemented, monitored, and enforced by the legal system, and governmental units. The values and ethics applied to education, health, and social welfare shift with social evolution, especially financial conditions. A translation from public priorities into governance or regulation is accomplished by legislation, agency rules, and case law. (Woody, 1989, p. 76)

Thus, public policy is a purposeful course of action for dealing with a problem or matter of concern (Anderson, 1979). This course leads to the passing and implementation of laws.

School psychology relies on the collection and usage of psychoeducational data, but the law has a quite different thrust. Saks (1989) asserts that "law tends to be policy analysis without benefit of data" (p. 1110), and that "the law is an extremely important practical activity that typically is informed by little more than guesswork" (p. 1110). He points out that the legal process for receiving and using information is steeped in ceremony and ritual.

Similarly, Slovenko (1973) points to gross differences between legal and scientific inquiries, such as: "A lawsuit is not an abstract search for truth, but a proceeding to settle a controversy" (p. 8). The behavioral scientist seeks an objective test of a hypothesis. The attorney is a partisan, unabashedly advocating a single party's interests: "Loyalty to client becomes loyalty to truth" (p. 8); "The law's method of arriving at a result is often purposefully nonscientific or dependent upon a nonprofessional assessment" (p. 9). Behavioral science relies on measurement: "Results in law, on the other hand, are influenced but not ruled by hard data or hard facts" (p. 9); and "Justice incorporates social needs as well as scientific accuracy, but neither to the exclusion of the other" (p. 9). According to Meyer, Landis, and Hays (1988), "Because of the clash of perspectives between psychotherapy and the law, mental health professionals often find their interactions with legal systems confusing, frustrating, or even frightening" (p. 3).

Education and the law need not be in conflict; in fact, they are intended to be mutually facilitative. Dewey (1922) urged that the law not be given a straitjacket quality, that it be viewed as an interactive, social-human process that will be revised, expanded, and altered for societal and, therefore, educational vitality. There is no doubt that legal vitality fuels the educational fire, as witnessed by how federal legislation leads to changes in education policies, objectives, emphases, programs, and services.

The United States Constitution does not mention education per se. This means that education, unless specified by federal legislation (and/

or a related case ruling in a federal court) will be, for the most part, under the control of the state. Of course, educational procedures and services must be compatible with federal and state laws; for example, a school system must operate in a manner that assures every student of due process and equal protection (see Fischer & Sorenson, 1985).

Laws are criminal or civil in nature. *Criminal law* covers offenses against the state or society, whereas *civil law* deals with disputes between individuals (e.g., a student's believing that the school has failed to provide legally required services or that he or she has been injured by a breach of the standard of care by an educator or psychologist). *Statutory law* is created by lawmaking bodies, such as Congress, a state legislature, or city council. All statutes must be consonant with federal and state constitutions. *Common* or *case law* is a body of legal decisions, applicable to the jurisdiction, that yields legal rules for decision making. In other words, case decisions are "judge-made law," and can be looked to for guidance about how statutory laws or legal principles must, may, or can be manifested. A law is restricted to a particular *jurisdiction.*

> Jurisdiction is a critical concept. It involves two questions: (1) Which court, federal or state, should receive the case? (2) Once that determination has been made, which court (such as a specialty versus a general court) should hear the case? In other words, which court has the power or authority to act on the merits of the case—to resolve the dispute or to grant relief (or a remedy)? A court must have jurisdiction over both the subject matter (the type of case) and the person. (Woody & Mitchell, 1984, pp. 6–7)

Thus, a teenager accused of a criminal act might be under the jurisdiction of the juvenile court, a contract dispute between a teachers' union and the school might be under the jurisdiction of a specialty court of industrial relations, and a school psychologist alleged to have committed malprac-

tice might wind up in a general state trial court (however, if the parties were from different states, the diversity of citizenship might lead to the case's being under the jurisdiction of a federal court).

It should be noted that all legal matters are dealt with *rules of evidence* and *rules of civil or criminal procedure.* These rules govern what, how, and when events occur in a legal proceeding. For example, if a school psychologist were to be testifying in, say, a child custody or abuse case, the rules would provide the judge with the bases for what could be stated, the foundation and form of the opinions, and so on. Although the courts of each state will have unique rules (as will federal courts), the rules are generally similar.

When testifying, a professional, such as school psychologist, can expect respect, but there will not necessarily be unrestricted deference. For example, any testimony will be subject to *cross-examination* under oath: "For two centuries, common law judges and lawyers have regarded the opportunity to cross-examination as an essential safeguard of the accuracy and completeness of testimony, and they have insisted that the opportunity is a right, and not a mere privilege" (Cleary, 1972, p. 43). If the school psychologist, under cross-examination, cannot convincingly defend the scientific/professional quality of his or her testimony (or opinions stated in a psychological report), *impeachment* (a lessening of credibility, and diminished weight accorded to the testimony or opinion) will likely occur. (More will be said about expert testimony later in this chapter.)

When a child or adolescent is involved in a legal proceeding, the expertise of the school psychologist can be a double-edged sword. On one side, the school psychologist has peerless knowledge for human behavior and can offer invaluable information to assist the trier-of-fact (the judge or jury). On the other side, the ultimate legal question (e.g., guilt or innocence, which parent should have custody, what educational program is appropriate and necessary) remains for the trier-of-fact, not the school psychologist, to answer. The school psychologist must resist the seductive appeal of trying to determine the ultimate legal issue. By law, only the trier-of-fact can render that determination. A surefire way to court impeachment and possibly even malpractice is to go beyond one's professional competency.

Expert testimony must be based on facts or data of a type that would be reasonably relied upon by other experts in the field, and the opinions must present scientific, technical, or other specialized knowledge-based information that will assist the trier-of-fact in understanding the evidence or in determining a fact in issue. Heed the caveat: A school psychologist has a duty to be a participant in legal proceedings, but must not allow his or her role, knowledge, or skill to be perverted from that which is truly based on academic training. (Guidelines will be offered later in this chapter.)

A final legal principle comes from the application of tort law to personal injury. (Later this chapter will deal with professional liability, namely a school psychologist's being potentially liable for conduct, by omission or commission, that results in injury to another person, such as a student.) Professional liability is in the realm of *tort law:*

> Tort law represents our legal system's recognition that society functions best when individuals are safe from indiscriminate harm. It is a complex system for compensating a person who sustains a loss as a result of another's behavior. It then aims to place the cost of such compensation on those and only those who ought to bear it. (Palagi & Springer, 1984, p. 155)

The term *tort* refers to a civil wrong that produces compensable injury to the person, property, or recognized interest of another, and a civil remedy is sought (Kionka, 1977). Commonly encountered torts include assault, battery, false imprisonment, intentional infliction of mental distress, negligence, malpractice, breach of contract, personal injury, wrongful death, violation of civil liberties, and a host of others. (Causes of action based on tort law will be discussed in detail later in this chapter.) At this point, it is important to realize that the practice of school psychology carries liability for conduct, be it by omission or commission.

FEDERAL AND STATE LEGISLATION

There was a time when handicapped children were excluded from education. In *Beattie v. Board of Education of City of Antigo* (169 Wis. 231, 172 N.W. 158, 1919), the court upheld exclusion of a child with cerebral palsy, even though he was academically able, citing the "depressing" and "nauseating" effect on teachers and students, and saying that the right of a child to attend the public school "must be subordinated to the general welfare" (p. 233) (i.e., the best interests of the school). More insidious, the day is not long passed when educators would separate handicapped children from other students, such as placing special-education classrooms in an isolated facility. Clearly this sort of exclusionary and discriminatory stance is inappropriate to modern thinking, and legislation has brought about overdue change.

Probably nothing has had such a positive and profound impact on school psychology as PL 94-142, the Education of All Handicapped Children Act of 1975. It and its progeny, particularly PL 99-457, the Education of the Handicapped Act Amendments of 1986, PL 101-476, the Individuals with Disabilities Education Act of 1990, and PL 90-247 (and PL 93-380), the Family Educational Rights and Privacy Act of 1974 (34 CFR 99, 1980), have mandated services *and* standards that have greatly benefited handicapped children and youth, and in the process, promoted the professional development of the educational and mental-health disciplines that are designed critical to the fulfillment of the legal objectives.

This surge of support for services for the handicapped is a paradox. The 1960s introduced an unprecedented degree of public policy support and funding for general education, special education, and mental-health services; the period was deemed a mental-health "revolution" (Hobbs, 1964). Unfortunately, the "Great Society" years of the Kennedy and Johnson administrations passed away, and an era of dwindling public and political support and cutbacks in funding relegated education and human services to diminished priority. Notwithstanding the diminution, PL 94-142, almost miraculously, received legislative enactment, and like Phoenix—a centuries-old bird that, after being burned to death, rose from the ashes as a born-again fledgling—soared to new heights in public policy and service.

PL 94-142, the Education for All Handicapped Children Act of 1975

Before discussing PL 94-142, it should be recalled that this federal law preordains the essence of state law, but each state must, nonetheless, enact statutes and promulgate rules and regulations for the legal mandate to be transformed into practical services. Further, state and local home rule can have a distinct influence on the federal intentions and mandates.

The Act, which amends other general education legislation, establishes entitlement to education for all handicapped children aged 3 to 21, inclusive. Critical definitions for handicapped children in Public Law 93-380, the Educational Amendments of 1974 (Section 602, 20 U.S.C 1402), are incorporated and amended in PL 94-142. They cast the mold for definitions that will be adopted at the state level. For example, Nebraska (92 Nebraska Administrative Code 51, 1987) states that handicapped children will be those who, after a multidisciplinary team evaluation, are "behaviorally disordered, deaf-blind, hearing impaired, mentally handicapped, multihandicapped, orthopedically impaired, other health impaired, specific learning disabled, speech-language impaired or visually handicapped who, because of these impairments need special education and related services" (003.14); each category of handicap is defined in specific

terms. In PL 94-142, an important definition of "specific learning disabilities" is given:

> The term "children with specific learning disabilities" means those children who have a disorder in one or more of the basic psychological processes involved in understanding or in using language, spoken or written, which disorder may manifest itself in imperfect ability to listen, think, speak, read, write, spell, or do mathematical calculations. Such disorders include such conditions as perceptual handicaps, brain injury, minimal brain dysfunction, dyslexia, and developmental aphasia. Such term does not include children who have learning problems which are primarily the result of visual, hearing, or other handicaps, of mental retardation, of emotional disturbance, or environmental, cultural, or economic disadvantage. (89 Stat. 794)

Other noteworthy definitions include:

> The term "special education" means specially designed instruction, at no cost to parents or guardians, to meet the unique needs of a handicapped child, including classroom instruction, instruction in physical education, home instruction, and instruction in hospitals and institutions (89 Stat. 775) [and] The term "related services" means transportation, and such developmental, corrective, or other supportive services (including speech pathology and audiology, psychological services, physical and occupational therapy, recreation, and medical and counseling services, except that such medical services shall be for diagnostic and evaluation purposes only) as may be required to assist a handicapped child to benefit from special education, and includes the early identification and assessment of handicapping conditions in children. (89 Stat. 775)

PL 94-142 specifies allocations that will be made for exceptional pupil expenditures. Formulas are given for determining the allotment for a state. There are eligibility criteria for qualifying for federal assistance, including the state's assuring that:

(A) there is established (i) a goal of providing full educational opportunity to all handicapped children, (ii) a detailed timetable for accomplishing such a goal, and (iii) a description of the kind and number of facilities, personnel, and services necessary throughout the State to meet such a goal (89 Stat. 780) [and there be a] free appropriate public education available [and] all children residing in the State who are handicapped, regardless of the severity of their handicap, and who are in need of special education and related services are identified, located, and evaluated, and that a practical method is developed and implemented to determine which children are currently receiving needed special education and related services and which children are not currently receiving needed special education and related services. (89 Stat. 781)

Other plans, policies, and procedures (including safeguard for legal rights) must be created.

More will be said later about the problematic nature of determining an "appropriate" public education. At this point, it should be underscored that PL 94-142 mandates responsibility for the appropriate education of all eligible handicapped children to the local school district (including those handicapped children in private schools and facilities) at no cost to the parents or guardian. This means that, even if not in accord with home rule preference, priority and funding locally must occur, albeit that federal and state financial supplements are available.

Once the state has qualified, certain quality assurance methods are required. Perhaps of greatest significance, services to each child must be in accord with an individualized education program, commonly referred to as an IEP. (Chapter 1 contains a definition of the IEP and its designated contents.) Relevant to participating in regular educational programs, also known as *mainstreaming,* it is stated that there must be

procedures to assure that, to the maximum extent appropriate, handicapped children, including children in public or private institutions or other care facilities, are educated with children who are

not handicapped, and that special classes, separate schooling, or other removal of handicapped children from the regular educational environment occurs only when the nature or severity of the handicap is such that education in regular classes with the use of supplementary aids and services cannot be achieved satisfactorily. (89 Stat. 782.) [And it is necessary that] Each local educational agency in the State will maintain records of the individualized education program for each handicapped child and such program shall be established, reviewed, and revised. (89 Stat. 781)

To give emphasis to crucial points, PL 94-142 requires: (1) multisource and interdisciplinary inputs, including from parents or guardians (and possibly the child); (2) mainstreaming (integrating the child into the regular school curriculum as much as possible); and (3) careful, detailed, and monitored individualized educational programming.

Mentioned briefly before, various protections of legal rights must be in place. For assessment, there will be

procedures to assure that testing and evaluation materials and procedures utilized for the purposes of evaluation and placement of handicapped children will be selected and administered so as not to be racially or culturally discriminatory. Such materials or procedures shall be provided and administered in the child's native language or mode of communication, unless it clearly is not feasible to do so, and no single procedure shall be the sole criterion for determining an appropriate educational program for a child. (89 Stat. 781)

To dissect this statement, it is clear that the standardization of a test must accommodate the child's racial or cultural distinctions and communication qualities (e.g., use primary language for the non-English-speaking child and sign language for a deaf child), and that the assessment must be multifaceted. More will be said later about legal cases dealing with assessment issues, particularly disclosure of test materials and racial bias.

The Act also specifies that facilities and programs for and personnel dealing with handicapped children meet the educational standards of the state educational agency. If a state educational agency finds that a local educational agency or an intermediate educational unit fails to comply with any requirement, the state educational agency, after appropriate notice, shall be able to stop funding.

PL 99-457, the Education of the Handicapped Act Amendments of 1986

The enactment of PL 99-457, the Education of the Handicapped Act Amendments of 1986 (100 Stat. 1145), gave additional and amended life to the psychoeducational Phoenix—it spread its ever-more powerful wings over a broader scene. After hearing testimony and receiving evidence, the Congress declared [in Title I: Handicapped Infants and Toddlers] that there was an "urgent and substantial need" for four things:

1. To enhance the development of handicapped infants and toddlers and to minimize their potential for developmental delay,
2. To reduce the educational costs to our society, including our Nation's schools, by minimizing the need for special education and related services after handicapped infants and toddlers reach school age,
3. To minimize the likelihood of institutionalization of handicapped individuals and maximize the potential for their independent living in society, and
4. To enhance the capacity of families to meet the special needs of their infants and toddlers with handicaps. (100 Stat. 1145)

Therefore, the basis was economic (reduced spending) via early intervention, with a commitment to deinstitutionalization and normalization and bringing families into the programs. This was to be accomplished by "a statewide, comprehensive, coordinated, multidisciplinary, interagency program of early intervention services for handicapped infants and toddlers and their families" (100 Stat. 1145). Note that, in keeping with the developmental and social systems approach of this book, minimization of potential for developmental delay and the provision of services to families were specified.

Key terms are defined in Section 672. Consider the following:

1. The term "handicapped infants and toddlers" means individuals from birth to age 2, inclusive, who need early intervention services because they—
   (A) are experiencing developmental delays, as measured by appropriate diagnostic instruments and procedures in one or more of the following areas: Cognitive development, physical development, language and speech development, psychosocial development, or self-help skills, or
   (B) have a diagnosed physical or mental condition which has a high probability of resulting in developmental delay. (100 Stat. 1146)

In addition to early intervention services designed to meet a handicapped infant's or toddler's developmental needs, it is required that the following services be provided:

   (i) family training, counseling and home visits,
   (ii) special instruction,
   (iii) speech pathology and audiology,
   (iv) occupational therapy,
   (v) physical therapy,
   (vi) psychological services,
   (vii) case management services,
   (viii) medical services only for diagnostic or evaluation purposes,
   (ix) early identification, screening, and assessment services, and
   (x) health services necessary to enable the infant or toddler to benefit from the other early intervention services. (100 Stat. 1146)

Qualified multidisciplinary professionals are required. If eligibility requirements are met, federal grants in aid are available.

All early intervention services must be provided in conformity with an individualized family service plan, commonly referred to as the IFSP. (Chapter 1 presents a definition of the IFSP and its designated contents.) It should be noted how virtually every mention of intervention with the infant or toddler connects to mention of intervention with the family.

Like PL 94-142, PL 99-457 contains numerous funding criteria, procedural safeguards (such as the right to confidentiality of personally identifiable information and a parent's right to examine records, written prior notice of program changes), and establishment of a state interagency coordinating council (which creates a mandate for public agency cooperation in meeting the needs of the handicapped).

In Title II: Handicapped Children Aged 3 to 5, preschool grants are made available, with a cost-sharing formula for providing free appropriate public education to handicapped children in this age group. Title III: Discretionary Programs provides for grants to establish regional resource and federal centers (e.g., as might offer consultation, technical assistance, and training to promote education of the handicapped), as well as other services for deaf-blind children and youth, early education programs, programs for severely handicapped children, postsecondary education programs, and secondary education and transitional services for handicapped youth. Provisions are made for grants for personnel training and traineeships, research and demonstration projects in education of handicapped children, panels of experts, captioned films, and technology, educational media, and materials. Title IV: Miscellaneous calls for the removal of architectural barriers and assistance for the education of Indian children in schools operated by the Department of Interior.

PL 101-476, the Individuals with Disabilities Education Act of 1990

The most recent legislation that is important to school psychology is PL 101-476, the Individuals with Disabilities Education Act of 1990 (104 Stat. 1103). While regulations will be developed that refine the legislation, major changes can be set forth.

Autism and traumatic brain injury are added as separate categories for eligibility for services, and rehabilitation counseling and social work services are defined as "related services."

"Transition services" receive inclusion, and are defined as "a coordinated set of activities for a student, designed within an outcome-oriented process, which promotes movement from school to post-school activities, including post-secondary education, vocational training, integrated employment (including supported employment), continuing and adult education, adult services, independent living, or community participation" (Sec. 602(a)(19)). For assessments and other evaluative determinations, the law states, "The coordinated set of activities shall be based upon the individual student's needs, taking into account the student's preferences and interests, and shall include instruction, community experiences, the development of employment and other post-school adult living objectives, and, when appropriate, acquisition of daily living skills and functional occupational evaluation" (Sec. 602(a)(19)).

PL 101-476 adds two new requirements for the IEP, namely: "A statement of the needed transition services for students beginning at no later than age 16 and annually thereafter (and, when determined appropriate for the individual, beginning at age 14 or younger), including, when appropriate, a statement of the interagency responsibilities or linkages (or both) before the student leaves the school setting"; and "in the case where a participating agency, other than the educational agency, fails to provide agreed upon services, the educational agency shall reconvene the IEP team to identify alternative strategies to meet the transition objectives" (Sec. 602(a)(20)).

Note the emphases that PL 101-476 places on postsecondary education, employment, and adult education and services. Therefore, PL 101-476 buttresses the assertions that (1) school psychologists must be prepared to service adults as well as children and youth; and (2) eventually public education will quite likely have a legislative mandate to serve all persons, particularly those with disabilities, throughout the life span.

PL 101-476 contains a number of revised or new provisions relevant to administration, programs, services, and funding opportunities. The following eight areas are of special relevance to school psychologists:

1. A required Comprehensive System of Personnel Development (CSPD), as will "ensure an adequate supply of qualified special education and related services personnel" (Sec. 613(a)(3)): The CSPD, which must accommodate the newly mandated programs and persons eligible for services, should stimulate the employment marketplace for school psychologists, and certainly benefit persons with disabilities via the quality assurance dimension.
2. Evaluation and program information, as will "improve programs and foster systems change" (Sec. 618): The requirement for improvement and change means that school psychologists must be academically prepared and personally able to adopt new ideas about services delivery.
3. Services for deaf-blind children and youth for "expanding the program focus to include infants and toddlers who are deaf-blind, and emphasizing the need to increase the ability of school districts to serve children with deaf-blindness" (Sec. 622): School psychologists should advocate the needs of deaf-blind children to administrators, teachers, and other educational personnel (e.g., through in-service training), as well as to parents and the community.
4. Expanding early education for handicapped children (Sec. 623) and children with severe disability (Sec. 624): School psychologists will need to design and engage in early identification programs and be able to serve children with greater degrees of disability.
5. Secondary education and transitional services for youth with disabilities (Sec. 626): School psychologists will need to be prepared for new areas (e.g., vocational assessment and placement considerations), and to

serve older youths and adults (e.g., interagency/community-centered actions).
6. Programs for children and youth with serious emotional disturbances (Sec. 627): School psychologists must be able to offer services to the array of emotional disturbances, which will likely require greater knowledge of psychopathology and new assessment and intervention skills.
7. Early intervention services for infants and toddlers, to assure that "primary referral sources, such as hospitals and physicians, provide parents of infants and toddlers with disabilities with information about the availability of early intervention services" (Sec. 676): School psychologists must possess specialized knowledge of and skills with infants and toddlers, and be ready to work aggressively in the community, such as with health-care institutions and social agencies and the professional personnel therein.
8. Centers designed "to organize, synthesize, and disseminate current knowledge relating to children with attention deficit disorder": The establishment of one or more of these centers will likely stimulate both public and professional interest in attention deficit disorder, which will mean school psychologists working more in this area.

If anything, the components of PL 101-476 pose a challenge to school psychologists, university training programs, and school systems. Stated bluntly, school psychologists must be academically prepared and personally able to offer new services, university training programs must be modified to include new academic content areas, and school systems must make major shifts in policies, such as redefining the duties of school psychologists to accommodate these new programs and emphases. To say the least, PL 101-476 appears to have the potential for ushering in a challenging and dynamic era for school psychologists, with many new benefits accruing to children, youth, and adults with disabilities.

PL 90-245, the Family Educational Rights and Privacy Act of 1974

PL 90-245, the Family Educational Rights and Privacy Act of 1974 (FERPA) (20 USC 1232g, regulations at 34 CFR 99, amended at 45 FR 309.11, May 9, 1990; see PL 93-380), is for the protection of privacy rights of parents and students relevant to the students' educational records. As with many federal laws, FERPA is commonly adopted and adapted in state statutes, rules, and regulations, and the school psychologist needs to be familiar with the legal uniqueness of the jurisdiction in which he or she practices (e.g., what shall be contained in a student's cumulative record and procedures for disclosure of records).

FERPA applies to an educational institution or agency, including all components therein. To understand the information governed, consider the following excerpts:

"Educational records" (a) means those records which: (1) Are directly related to a student, and (2) are maintained by an educational agency or institution or by a party acting for the agency or institution. (b) The term does not include:

(1) Records of instructional, supervisor, and administrative personnel and educational personnel ancillary thereto which:

(i) Are in the sole possession of the maker thereof, and

(ii) Are not accessible or revealed to any other individual except a substitute [a definition of a "substitute" is given].

(2) Records of a law enforcement unit of an educational agency or institution which are [specifics are given].

(3) (i) Records relating to an individual who is employed by an educational agency or institution [specifics are given].

(4) Records relating to an eligible student which are:

(i) Created or maintained by a physician, psychiatrist, psychologist, or other recognized professional or paraprofessional acting in his or her professional or paraprofessional capacity, or assisting in that capacity;

(ii) Created, maintained, or used only in connection with the provision of treatment to the student, and

(iii) Not disclosed to anyone other than individuals providing the treatment; *Provided,* That the records can be personally reviewed by a physician or other appropriate professional of the student's choice. For the purpose of this definition, "treatment" does not include remedial educational activities or activities which are part of the program of instruction at the educational agency or institution. (p. 284)

At first, the foregoing might sound like the records of a school psychologist would be excepted from the control of FERPA, but as will unfold, such is not the case.

In brief, the school must provide parents or the student (who meets eligibility requirements) access to educational records that are directly related to the student. According to Subpart B, Section 99.11, the school, with some limitations (see Section 99.12), must permit the parents or eligible student to inspect and review the educational records of the student (and do so no more than 45 days after the request is made), with a right to a response from the school for explanations and interpretations of the records and the right to obtain copies of the records. Also, the school must allow the parents or eligible student an opportunity to seek correction of records that the parents or eligible student believe to be inaccurate, misleading, or in violation of the student's rights (see Section 99.20, through 99.22).

With a few exceptions, information contained in records cannot be disclosed without the written consent of the parents or the student. The school is required to formulate and adopt a policy that will inform parents of students or eligible students of their rights under FERPA (see Section 99.5), and give them annual notice by such means as are reasonably likely to inform them of their rights (see Section 99.6).

Of special relevance to school psychology, Ballinger (1986), on behalf of the FERPA Office of the United States Department of Education, addresses the question of whether the "sole possession" exclusion (cited earlier; see Section 99.3) allows psychological test protocols to be kept from parental review. She states,

> Generally, protocols cannot be excluded from parental review. This Office has found that information contained in the protocols is most likely discussed with school personnel in staffing meetings for the purpose of determining educational placement and/or programming of the student. Thus, even though the protocol may remain in the sole possession of the maker of the record, information contained in the protocol is revealed to other persons. As such, it then loses its exclusionary status, and becomes an educational record subject to inspection by the parent. (p. 1)

In deducing a legal principle it would appear that the Office's interpretation is that any material about a student that is created and held by a school psychologist must be accessible to the student's parents or the eligible student if such material was used for information that was shared with or revealed to (in any manner?) another professional.

Turning to the issue of providing copies of test protocols to the parents, Ballinger (1986) reiterates the rights of parents to records, and states, "In general, the FERPA does not require an agency to provide parents a copy of their child's education records, except when failure to do so would effectively deny access" (p. 2) (see Section 99.11 (b) (2)). She goes on to say,

> The FERPA requires an agency to give parents access to their child's educational records. If the test questions and answers are both personally identifiable to the student (that is, if the answers appear on the same sheet as the questions, and are identified by the student's name) the parents have the right to inspect both the questions and answers. If the questions are separate from the answers and only the answers are personally identifiable to the student, the parent has the right of access to the answers only. However, since the regulations require an agency to respond to a reasonable request for an explanation or interpretation of the record, the agency would have to inform the parent of the

questions, if so requested, in order to explain the answers to the questions. The FERPA would not require the agency to actually show the questions nor would it require the agency to provide a copy of the questions. (p. 2)

Note, however, that if there were litigation underway, discovery procedures (e.g., a subpoena duces tecum) might well, depending upon the law of the jurisdiction, require production of copies of any and all relevant and material documents or information.

FERPA still has inconsistent interpretations. Referring to FERPA and PL 94-142, Bersoff (1983) indicates that "whether test protocols are accessible under these laws is not altogether clear" (p. 79), and in view of the nature of special-education decision making (i.e., a team approach) concludes that "psychologists' tests and test results are almost always used in this process and could be considered accessible" (p. 80). In *Lora* v. *Board of Education* (456 F.Supp. 1211, E.D.N.Y. 1979, vacated and remanded on other grounds, 623 F.2d 248, 2d Cir. 1980) held that failure to provide parents with the "clinical records" upon which special education placements were made would violate due process (i.e., the parents would be unable to adequately contest placements).

LEGAL CASES ON APPROPRIATENESS OF EDUCATION

To fully understand legislation like PL 94-142 and PL 99-459, it is necessary to consider certain legal cases. There are two landmark cases that contributed impetus to the passage of legislation for the Education of All Handicapped Children.

First, *Pennsylvania Association for Retarded Citizens* v. *Pennsylvania* (343 F. Supp. 279, E.D. Pa., 1972), commonly referred to as PARC, challenged, among other things, a Pennsylvania state statute that denied public education to children certified as being uneducable or untrainable or those who had not attained a mental age of 5 and could not profit from school attendance:

In PARC the important point made by the plaintiffs in advancing their equal protection argument was that handicapped children *could* be educated—even though the expectation level for them was different from that of normal children. PARC was a landmark case because it introduced a massive amount of incontrovertible expert testimony showing that handicapped children could learn and benefit from a publicly funded education. Moreover, for such children a formalized education was even more critical to their learning progress than it was to the progress of a normal child. (Stick, 1984, p. 347)

PARC also attacked an alleged lack of due process, such as a parent's having a right to input on the appropriateness of an educational placement and how labeling a child *handicapped* had a stigmatizing effect and produced a deprivation of rights allowed to nonhandicapped peers. Based on a consent decree (an agreement entered into between the parties), PARC held exclusion of handicapped children from public education was unconstitutional (*Note:* Being a consent decree, the precedent value of the case was negated.)

In *Mills* v. *Board of Education* (348 F. Supp. 866, D.D.C., 1972), the plaintiffs represented all children excluded from public education because of mental, behavioral, emotional, and/or physical handicaps. The defendant school district asserted that, because of finances, it could not adequately serve the potential influx of students and that normal children would suffer. Based on a due process rationale, the court ruled that an exceptional child could not be excluded from public education, while affording such a benefit to other children. The claim of insufficient funds was rebuked, saying that the school's

interest in educating the excluded children clearly must outweigh its interest in preserving its financial resources. If sufficient funds are not available to finance all of the services and programs that are needed and desirable in the system then the available funds must be expended equitably in such a manner that no child is entirely excluded from a publicly-supported education consistent with his needs and abilities to benefit therefrom. (p. 876)

The foregoing two cases spawned numerous other cases that raised many of the same legal issues, relying particularly on constitutional arguments.

After PL 94-142 became law, the focus shifted to what constituted an *appropriate education*. The concept of appropriate education means that the special education and related services provided to the student must conform to an acceptable IEP. For example, the unique needs of a student might require related transportation, developmental, or corrective services; or multiagency involvement might be necessary. Court cases relevant to determining the criteria for an "appropriate" education emerged. As might be expected, parents do not always agree with the school about what is appropriate for the child. Parents want the best for their child, whereas the school will often decide by pragmatics (e.g., financial considerations).

In the *Board of Education of the Hendrick Hudson Central School District* v. *Rowley* (458 U.S. 176, 102 S. Ct. 3034, 1982), the school refused to fund a sign-language interpreter for an 8-year-old deaf child. The trial court ruled for the parents, stating that despite the child's performing better than the average child in her class and advancing in grade, she was understanding less in class than she would if she were not deaf. Thus, the court ruled that she was not receiving an appropriate education, which would have meant "an opportunity to achieve [her] full potential commensurate with the opportunity provided to other children" (p. 3040).

This ruling was affirmed by the U.S. Court of Appeals, but the U.S. Supreme Court reversed, saying the Act requires a handicapped student to receive an education that will allow him or her to succeed at a level comparable to nonhandicapped peers. The Act does not require that a handicapped child be provided an education to meet his or her full potential; it requires only an education substantially equal to that of nonhandicapped students in the same class, as would allow the handicapped child to receive an equal educational opportunity. The Court stated that available funds for use in the education of handicapped children must be divided equitably among all handicapped students; a disproportionately large allocation cannot be required to maximize the potential of a particular handicapped child.

In the *Irving Independent School District* v. *Tatro* (468 U.S. 883, 104 S. Ct. 3371, 1984), the parents of a 5-year-old girl born with spina bifida, which caused a bladder condition requiring catheterization every three or four hours, wanted the school to provide the catheterization process as a "related service," but the school refused. Relying on *Rowley,* the U.S. Supreme Court believed that supplying this service allowed the child to remain at school during the day; without the service, the girl would be denied "meaningful access to education" (p. 3376).

In *A. W.* v. *Northwest R-1 School District* (813 F.2d 158, 8th Cir., 1987), parents wanted their mentally retarded son placed in a regular elementary classroom rather than a state school which enrolled only handicapped children. While acknowledging that the child would receive only minimal benefit from placement in a school with nonhandicapped students, the court held that the requested placement was not possible (e.g., the school did not employ a teacher certified to work with severely retarded children). As per *Rowley,* the court indicated that the Act does not require states to provide each handicapped child with the best possible education, and that principles of equitable distribution of financial resources were necessary; that is, it would be inequitable to use limited funds to hire a certified teacher for the benefit of a few severely retarded children.

In *Springdale School District #50 of Washington County* v. *Grace* (693 F.2d 41, 1982), the court ruled that a hearing-handicapped child was not entitled to placement in a school for the deaf at the school district's expense. On remand, the Court of Appeals for the Eighth Circuit affirmed the decision that the girl was appropriately placed in the local school. Citing *Rowley,* the court stated that, although the girl might learn more quickly at the school for the deaf, the Act does not require the state to provide the best possible

education and that the public school was able to provide an appropriate education by employing a certified teacher of the deaf. The court also pointed out that this decision was supportive of the mainstreaming goals of the Act.

In *Yaris* v. *Special School District of St. Louis County* (558 F.Supp. 545, 1983), the school district provided educational services for severely handicapped children for only the traditional nine-month school year. Parents wanted a summer school program for their severely handicapped boy. The court ruled for the parents, because severely handicapped children received fewer services than nonhandicapped children. Although the court accepted the principle of equitable distribution of funds, it noted that the scarcity of funding weighed more heavily on severely handicapped children, thereby making the school district noncompliant with the Act.

As with the interpretation of FERPA, there are inconsistent interpretations about what constitutes an appropriate education and a related service. Often the conflicting interpretations, such as by the school versus by the parents, result in disputes and litigation (Gallant, 1982). Stick (1984) warns,

> Parents and advocacy groups must be constantly vigilant. They must police the educational system to be sure that handicapped children are being provided with an appropriate education. It is unfortunate that they are thrust into the role of enforcers, since they must also work with those whom they police—namely, the school personnel. To handle this difficult situation, tolerance and understanding are required on both sides. (p. 353)

Clearly there is no surety that every handicapped child will, in fact, receive the appropriate education to which he or she is legally entitled. This advocacy is, of course, appropriate for the school psychologist to undertake.

The foregoing cases are but a few of many cases that define PL 94-142 and PL 99-457. Additional case analyses and legislative interpretations, with application to everyday psychoeducational problems, may be found in Downey (1989), Martin (1979), Meisels (1989), Schroeder, Schroeder, and Landesman (1987), Sido and King (1989), Stick (1984), Woody, Yeager, and Woody (1990), and Woody, Woody, and Greenberg (1991). The selected cases discussed herein exemplify that courts: (1) oppose functional exclusion and prefer, to the maximum extent possible, that the handicapped child be placed with nonhandicapped children (i.e., there is emphasis on mainstreaming and using the least restrictive alternative); (2) support that while a school district is not required to maximize the potential of each handicapped student, it must provide reasonable learning opportunities; and (3) recognize that scarcity of funds is commonplace and problematic, and require that the funds that are available should be distributed equitably among the handicapped population.

LEGAL CASES ON PSYCHOEDUCATIONAL TESTING

The role of the school psychologist places great emphasis on psychoeducational assessment, especially with intelligence tests. Casting a spotlight on selective administration of tests, which could carry the potential for discrimination, noted intelligence test pundit Arthur Jensen (1980) states, "I can see little justification for routinely administering intelligence (or IQ) tests or scholastic aptitude tests to *all* of the school population" (p. 716). The risk of selective administration of tests is that there will be an unlawful disproportionate impact, such as on exceptional children or a racial group.

In *Hobson* v. *Hansen* (269 F.Supp. 401, D.D.C. 1967), a "tracking system" in the District of Columbia public schools was struck down because placement was determined by an assessment (i.e., teachers' observations and evaluations and standardized testing) that was based on the erroneous assumption "that school personnel can with reasonable accuracy ascertain the maximum potential of each student and fix the content and pace of his education accordingly. If this premise

proves false, the theory of the track system collapses" (p. 474).

With emphasis on the socioeconomic and racial bias on intelligence tests, the court stated that such tests were

> completely inappropriate for use with a large segment of the student body. Because these tests are standardized primarily on and are relevant to a white middle class group of students, they produce inaccurate and misleading test scores when given to lower class and Negro students. As a result, rather than being classified according to their ability to learn, these students are in reality being classified according to their socioeconomic or racial status, or—more precisely—according to environmental and psychological facts which have nothing to do with innate ability. (p. 514)

A later appellate court decision limited the applicability of the lower court's *Hobson* order, and permitted certain types of "full scope" ability groupings.

As might be surmised, pre-PL 94-142 judicial decisions were not uniform. Some judicial views tended toward leniency on the use of psychoeducational testing, notwithstanding a disproportionate impact. For example, in *Morales* v. *Shannon* (516 F.2d 411, 5th Cir., 1975), the school used standardized test scores and grades in a manner that led to disproportionate representation of Mexican-American students in less advanced group. The court stated, "The record shows no more than the use of a non-discriminatory teaching practice or technique, a matter which is reserved to educators under our system of government" (p. 414). At about this time, "our system of government" was undergoing change.

Perhaps most noteworthy and deserving of special mention is the case of the *Larry P.* v. *Riles* (343 F.Supp. 1306, 1972), wherein the plaintiffs sought to restrain the school district from administering intelligence tests for the purposes of placing black students in classes for the educable mentally retarded. The evidence indicated that blacks constituted 28.5 percent of all students in the school district, yet 66 percent of all students in classes for the educable mentally retarded were black, thereby creating a racial imbalance in classes where intelligence test scores were the most important consideration in making the assignments to the classes. Note that this case was prior to the enactment of PL 94-142, but it illustrates the sort of psychoeducational situation that influenced the passage of PL 94-142. In *Larry P. v. Riles,* the court adopted the view that students who are wrongfully placed in classes for the educable mentally retarded (also known as an EMR class) suffer irreparable harm:

> For even if a student remains in an EMR class for only one month, that placement is noted on his permanent record, his education is retarded to some degree, and he is subjected to whatever humiliation students are exposed to for being separated into classes for the educable mentally retarded. (p. 1308)

After considering the evidence, the court ruled:

> Accordingly, it is hereby ORDERED that defendants be restrained from placing black students in classes for the educable mentally retarded on the basis of criteria which place primary reliance on the results of I.Q. tests as they are currently administered, if the consequence of use of such criteria is racial imbalance in the composition of such classes. (p. 1315)

These words should be considered carefully. First, the order is applicable to only that case, and is restricted to the jurisdiction of the United States District Court for the Northern District of California, which is in the Ninth Federal Judicial Circuit. Second, if narrowly construed, the ruling addresses only the placement of black students in classes for the educable mentally retarded, and only restricts the use of an IQ score as the primary criterion. This restriction operates only if primary reliance on an IQ score fosters a racial imbalance in the composition of the class. Third, even if the ruling is used for a legal principle in other jurisdictions, it does not, contrary to popular misconception, ban the use of intelligence tests. What it does accomplish, quite logically, is a proscriptive warning about the

shortcomings of single-factor assessment. Fourth, this case (and others) was a harbinger of a problem that could best be solved by legislation, and supports the thrust of PL 94-142. (See Bersoff, 1980, for another legal perspective on *Larry P. v. Riles.*) Carpignano (1987) describes actions in San Francisco subsequent to the *Larry P.* case, and highlights administrative decisions that considered "legal, political, social and economic pressures from a number of sources" (p. 1), but seemed to give limited weight to professional standards and ethical practices.

CONFIDENTIALITY AND PRIVILEGED COMMUNICATION

Regardless of professional discipline or employment context, the helping relationship is founded on confidentiality. In response, legislatures have enacted statutes to assure that communications in a helping relationship will be sacrosanct, with strict limitations placed on legal processes that would seek access to the information. For example, there are federal laws that create special protections for information about persons receiving treatment for alcoholism or drug abuse, with requirements for strict confidentiality being established (Roach, Chernoff, & Esley, 1985).

To the contrary, where there is no clear-cut protective legislation, the modern trend seems to be toward allowing the confidential relationship to be penetrated by legal process. For example, if a school psychologist files a motion for a protective order to prevent having to provide information in response to a subpoena, the public policy supporting that all information that is relevant and material to litigation should be received as evidence may lead the judge to rule that protection for confidentiality and privileged communication does not apply.

The Legal Theory of Confidentiality

To better understand the public policy basis, consider the common law criteria that justify confidentiality:

(1) the communications must originate in a confidence that they will not be disclosed; (2) this element of confidentiality must be essential to the full and satisfactory maintenance of the relation between the parties; (3) the relation must be one which in the opinion of the community must be sedulously fostered; and (4) the injury that would inure to the relation by disclosure of the communications must be greater than the benefit thereby gained for the correct disposal of the litigation. (Wigmore [1913] 1940, vol. 8, p. 531)

As should be quickly evident, what the "in the opinion of the community must be sedulously fostered" could easily change with the times. For example, social attitudes and the resulting laws have been in a state of flux relevant to using drugs, informing parents of a teenage girl's seeking an abortion, child abuse, and so on. In these kinds of situations, what might win preference from the professional discipline might generate opposition in the community, and the school psychologist is left to grapple with the alternatives. It is often a situation where simplistic ethics are inadequate for resolving the dilemma, and even the advice of legal counsel, which the school should always readily afford to the school psychologist, may not be able to produce an incontrovertible answer.

State statutes that create mandatory reporting of child abuse unquestionably affront the notion of confidentiality and privileged communication. The mandate must, however, be honored by the school psychologist, even if the reporting jeopardizes a therapeutic relationship. Child abuse statutes connect to the need to protect the resources of the state; it is axiomatic that children are our most valuable resource.

The Duty to Warn

The duty to warn, while relevant to the idea of reporting child abuse, has broad coverage. The need to protect others from danger has been imposed, more or less, on mental-health professionals for several decades (e.g., *Merchants National Bank and Trust Co. of Fargo* v. *United States* [272 F. Supp. 409, D.N.D. 1967], wherein the court

held a Veterans Administration hospital mental-health team tortiously negligent for their failure to diagnose the dangerousness of a patient who killed his wife. The hallmark case was *Tarasoff* v. *Regents of the University of California* (17 Cal. 3d 425, 551 P.2d 334, 131 Cal Rptr. 14, 1976), wherein a university psychologist was told by a client that he planned to harm a girlfriend and then killed her. The California Supreme Court stated,

Once a therapist does in fact determine, or under applicable professional standards reasonably should have determined, that a patient poses a serious danger of violence to others, he bears a duty to exercise reasonable care to protect the foreseeable victim of that danger. While the discharge of this duty of due care will necessarily vary with the facts of each case, in each instance the adequacy of the therapist's conduct must be measured against the traditional negligence standard of this rendition of reasonable care under the circumstances. (p. 44)

Since *Tarasoff,* there have been many cases, in virtually every state, and numerous twists to the law have occurred. For example, in *Lipari* v. *Sears, Roebuck* (497 F. Supp. 185, D. Neb. 1980), a mental patient at a Veterans Administration hospital shot and killed one person and wounded others. Even though he had not designated an intended victim, as was the case in *Tarasoff,* the court ruled that the therapeutic relationship gives rise to an affirmative duty to benefit third persons, including the therapist's initiating whatever precautions are necessary to protect potential victims of the patient. The duty arises when the therapist knows or should know that dangerous propensities of the patient create an unreasonable risk of harm to others. Further discussion of these cases may be found in Vande-Creek and Knapp (1989), Woody and Woody (1988), and Woody (1984, 1988a, 1988b).

Confidentiality of Records

Some states, but not all, have explicit privileged communication for educational interactions or records, perhaps only if the school psychologist is licensed (not just certified) (Fischer & Sorenson, 1985). It should be noted, however, that a statute can always be challenged in a particular case; that is, an attorney can argue why, for example, confidentiality should not apply to information possessed by an educator. Even if a statute seems to grant confidentiality or privileged communication, other statutes (e.g., mandatory reporting of child abuse) or common law (e.g., reporting dangerousness) may provide the basis for judicial discretion to order production of the information or records. Moreover, each statute applies only to its jurisdiction (i.e., a particular state), and statutes are commonly and often amended.

Incidentally, the notion that "one way to preserve confidentiality is to keep no records" is foolish. In keeping with the next section on professional liability, records serve two purposes: to complement quality assurance for the client (e.g., sending records of an initial intervention to a second practitioner to benefit follow-up services to the client) and to provide the creator of the records with protection in the event that an ethical, regulatory (certification or licensure), or malpractice complaint is filed by a disgruntled client. Further, some jurisdictions have laws that require the keeping of records (Roach, Chernoff, & Esley, 1985); that is, keeping no records could prove to be negligence.

Releasing Confidential Information to Parents

A major problem arises when a student does not want his or her parents to receive information from a school psychologist. Most commonly, a school board policy will address this issue; law on the matter is often ambiguous. In one situation, a state attorney asserted that a licensing law prevented a psychologist from accepting parental rights to confidential information. The teenager, as a client of a licensed psychologist (who worked in the school), could enjoy the privileged communication afforded by the licensing law, as opposed to other law that supported a parent

could access the records of an unemanicpated minor son or daughter.

Although that particular situation was resolved amicably, it could have led to litigation, with no preordained outcome. That is, there was a conflict of laws, and supremacy would have had to be decided by a court. Rightly or wrongly, Fischer and Sorenson (1985) advise, "In the absence of policy requiring disclosure to parents, a counselor has no obligation to breach the confidentiality of communications with counselees even if parents request it" (p. 26). This might be logical at the onset, but the prudent school psychologist should pursue legal counsel as to whether or not there are any applicable laws in the jurisdiction. When adequately informed of the legal parameters, the school psychologist can then set about to resolve the conflict between the parent and student by a therapeutic strategy.

Exceptions to Privileged Communication

Returning to confidentiality in general, it should be obvious that confidentiality is never absolute, even if elevated to privileged communication by statute. Fischer and Sorenson (1985) indicate that a student may lose privileged communication in three situations:

> (1) child-custody cases in which either parent challenges the mental fitness of the other or where the therapist/counselor has reasonable suspicion of child abuse, (2) any case in which client/counselee introduces his or her mental condition as a relevant factor in the case, and (3) cases in which the client/counselee makes statements to a therapist/counselor in a course of psychiatric examination ordered by the court, after being told that the communication would not be privileged. (p. 25)

Since exceptions to confidentiality or privileged communications are seldom, if ever, clear-cut and legal controversy could occur, it is essential, once again, that the school provide legal counsel to the school psychologist. Exceptions are determined by the law of the jurisdiction (e.g., the above three exceptions from Fischer and Sorenson might not always be applicable).

PROFESSIONAL LIABILITY

It is understatement to assert that legal complaints against all human services professionals have increased dramatically and substantially (see Woody, 1988a, for details on malpractice crisis). School psychologists are no exception. Since the mid-1970s, there has been increasing scrutiny applied to and accountability demanded of school psychologists. To be a school psychologist, there are many standards that are intended to assure that school psychological services achieve a minimal level of quality. Whenever there is a perception that a school psychologist has possibly breached a standard, the accountability system accepts a complaint. Complaints may be classified as ethical, regulatory (certification or licensure), or malpractice. A single allegedly wrongful act could result in complaint to any or all of these three accountability sources.

Professional Self-Regulation by Ethics

Self-regulation by the discipline is an important threshold source of accountability. Hall (1987) points to three self-regulatory sources: (1) Ethical Principles for Psychologists (APA, 1981a, 1990), which Hall says "apply to all pyschologists" and "constitute the standards in the profession with the longest history" (p. 11); (2) General Guidelines for Providers of Psychological Services (APA, 1987a), which Hall describes as "the basic policy statement which 'governs psychological service functions offered by psychologists, regardless of their specialty, setting, or form or remuneration' " (p. 11); and (3) Specialty Guidelines for the Delivery of Services by (in this instance) School Psychologists (APA, 1981b), which Hall indicates "provide information 'about particular services available from the several specialties in professional psychology' for those who voluntarily wish to be designated as specialists" (p. 11).

Also within the realm of professional self-regulation, Claiborn (1982) identifies seven sources: standards for providers; ethical codes; professional standards review committees (PSRC, which are sponsored by state associations); third-party-payer quality assurance (QA) and utilization review (UR) efforts; state licensing/certification boards; the *National Register of Health Service Providers in Psychology;* and diplomate status (e.g., from the American Board of Professional Psychology). Hall warns, "However, like all 'minimal level' screening mechanisms, there is no ongoing procedure to detect incompetence; there is also little empirical evidence that the selection criteria actually related to competence" (p. 155). The National Association of School Psychologists seeks enforcement of standards with and regulation of its members through its Principles for Professional Ethics (1984a) and Standards for the Provision of School Psychological Services (1984b).

It should be pointed out that, except for state licensing/certification boards (which, since they are governmental agencies, Claiborn incorrectly terms a "self-regulation" source), the sources of professional self-regulation do not exercise law per se, and they are, therefore, essentially voluntary. That is, a practitioner can, by design, avoid any authority that they might possess. Also, the potential for a legal action against a professional association's self-regulatory attempts has led to increasing reluctance to pursue ethical investigations (APA, 1987b). The conclusion seems to be:

> (a) there is no evidence of increased endorsement of professional self-regulation, (b) there is a specter of malpractice hovering over all psychology practices, and (c) there is a diminution of charitable immunity and a proliferation of lawsuits against nonprofit organizations (because of lawsuits against the school system; one school board resigned en masse and requested that the system be placed in receivership!). (Woody, 1989, p. 80)

Governmental Regulation by Certification and Licensure

There are many legislative sources that, directly or indirectly, regulate the practice of school psychology; not the least, of course, would be PL

94-142, PL 99-457, and PL 101-476. Since school psychologists are primarily employed by public schools, state legislation, with rules and regulations, for general and special education are applicable to school psychology practice. School psychologists with a license from the state for private practice must answer, even if they are also employed by a school system, to the state certification/licensure board.

The state department that regulates educational employees or private practitioners will have a complaint system, one that is intended to assure the school psychologist with equal protection and due process (and other rights) but foremost to safeguard public safety and welfare. For example, some states require that if there is a disciplinary action taken within a particular school, the case must be communicated to a state-level review source within the department of education. Commonly, this state-level source may take further action, including (but not limited to) notifying a state licensing board which may, in turn, initiate additional disciplinary proceedings.

Although professional self-regulation by a discipline or professional association is voluntary and can be minimized or escaped, the school psychologist should be aware that working within a school system under certification or engaging in private practice under licensure carries a duty to submit to the demands for accountability from the legally authorized governmental unit. Since these sources give highest priority to protecting the public, it is important to accept that any complaint will be within an adversarial framework, which necessitates a vigorous defense (best achieved, no doubt, by having astute legal counsel; see Woody, 1988b, for protective strategies).

Afterall, a disciplinary action by a governmental regulatory agency will potentially be a lifelong blemish on the professional's record, and recision of his or her certification or licensure could result in direct or indirect banishment from employment as a school psychologist (and possibly other human service roles as well). In some ways, a complaint to a state regulatory source may create a greater threat of long-lasting effects than a malpractice suit (since the latter might be covered by malpractice insurance, including the cost of an attorney, whereas a regulatory complaint would not likely be eligible for insurance coverage).

Legal Action for Malpractice

Being a care-giving professional, the concomitant accountability opens the courtroom door to any person who believes that he or she has suffered damage as a result of the practitioner. By definition, *malpractice* means that there has been bad service, but there is usually ambiguity about what is "good" versus "bad" service. Under public policy, any controversy can only be resolved by the parties, be it through a negotiated settlement or a decision for a judge or jury. (*Note:* Whether the trier-of-fact will be a judge or a jury will be determined by the nature of the case and the laws of the jurisdiction.) Malpractice is multifaceted:

> *Malpractice is the failure to fulfill the requisite standard of care.* Malpractice can occur by *omission* (what should have been done, but was not done) or *commission* (doing something that should not have been done). In either case, the act is not subject to a malpractice legal action unless it satisfies the elements of negligence, namely that there was a duty which was breached and which caused injury to a person to whom the duty was owed, and damages can be used to remedy the tortious infringement on the injured person's rights. (Woody, 1988a, pp. 2–3)

There are many reasons why a school psychologist could be sued: the reasons are referred to as "causes of action." A few of them are malicious infliction of emotional distress, libel, assault and battery, breach of confidentiality or privileged communication (e.g., unauthorized release of information), misrepresentation of competency, sexual misconduct or impropriety, improper administrative handling, misdiagnosis, incorrect treatment, violation of civil rights, bodily injury, failure to cure, failure to refer, failure to warn of dangerousness or prevent violence resulting in bodily injury to self or others, improper termination, undue influence, and the list goes on (see Bersharov, 1985, Hogan, 1979, Trent, 1978, Woody, 1988a, 1988b).

Fischer and Sorenson (1985) indicate that malpractice for school personnel most likely involve "prescribing or administering drugs, giving birth control advice, giving abortion-related advice, making statements that might be defamatory, assisting in searches of students' lockers, and violating the privacy of records" (p. 50); and they provide a useful analytic review of cases involving school personnel. Hopkins and Anderson (1985) discuss school-related malpractice in cases involving individual counseling, group counseling, crisis intervention, birth control, abortion, prescribing and administering drugs and treatment, illegal search, defamation, invasion of privacy ("derogatory information is communicated to a third party who has no need or privilege to receive it," p. 61) or administering a test without informed consent, and breach of contract (implied or explicit, such as, perhaps, what the school psychologist commits to advocate for the individualized education program). Work as an attorney leads the senior author to believe that school psychologists will, compared to a principal or teacher, have an expanded list of causes of action, due to their psychological, clinical, and authoritative roles.

Immunity

At one time, school personnel were accorded a degree of immunity from personal liability; indeed, the school system itself used to have highly restricted or no liability. Public policy justified this immunity by the fact that the services were governmental and nonprofit, intended to benefit society. Woody (1989) warns that school psychologists cannot "be complacent by virtue of being employed in the schools—a lawsuit can move from the courthouse to the schoolhouse" (p. 80). Suffice it to say that immunity is no longer granted, except under the most rarest of circumstances. Increasingly, liability seems to extend

from persons providing intervention services to those acting as policy makers, albeit the latter can sometimes successfully void liability by their remoteness from the direct events.

Standard of Care

The cornerstone of a malpractice action is an alleged breach of the standard of care. The standard of care is not a specific document or even a set of clear-cut principles. By public policy, any professional "is required not only to exercise reasonable care in what they do, but also to possess a standard minimum of special knowledge and ability" (Prosser, 1971, p. 161). The professional's conduct, by omission or commission, must be reasonable and prudent.

For school psychologists who seek to be on the cutting edge, there is no legal solace from the fact that "professional school psychologists are encouraged to develop innovative theories and procedures and to provide appropriate theoretical and/or empirical support for their innovations" (APA, 1981b). The legal test requires that there be proof of adherence to an acceptable school or theory. ("A 'school' must be a recognized one with definite principles, and it must be the line of thought of at least a respectable minority of the profession," Prosser, 1971, p. 163.)

Stated differently, professional zeal cannot overcome a duty to assure safeguards and quality care for the recipients of services. It is not enough that the relevant discipline does or does not do something; professional conduct must always pass through a public policy filter. By legal theory, an entire discipline could be negligent, such as not taking adequate safeguarding precautions or performing a procedure for which the benefits outweigh its cost and invasiveness.

The various sources of standards promulgated by professional associations (e.g., APA, 1981a, 1981b, 1987a, 1990; NASP, 1984a, 1984b) provide important definition for the standard of care, but—even if taken together—they do not assuredly comprise a conclusive legal benchmark. Certainly the school psychologist's acceptance and compliance with these organizational proclamations will offer a constructive channel, but for safe steerage, it must parallel the direction of the law. Unfortunately, graduate training programs often erroneously elevate disciplinary preferences to unjustified lofty heights and fail to prepare the trainees for an awareness and knowledge of substantive legal principles.

The standard of care that will apply to alleged malpractice by a school psychologist will consider the disciplinary ideas—indeed, if not too self-serving for the benefit of the discipline, the preferences of the discipline will be weighted heavily. Nonetheless, there will always be the need to reconcile the disciplinary standards with the legal standard that emerges from public policy and the law.

SERVING AS AN EXPERT WITNESS

By nature, a legal dispute produces controversy. A politically oriented institution (like a school) and the people within it (like board members and administrators) do not like controversy—primarily because controversy can breed questions of competency of the guardianship. The outcome could be negative public opinion and, often in short order, a lessening of political attractiveness and power. These principles of institutionalization have pragmatic impact on the school psychologist who, voluntarily (by advocacy) or involuntarily (by subpoena) enters into a legal fray as an expert witness. The school system, through its board members and administrators, will likely be prone to look askance at the school psychologist's providing expert testimony, notwithstanding his or her seeking to fulfill the public policy requirement that faces every citizen and most certainly every professional: contributing to the legal system.

Beyond political motives, reservations about participation in legal disputes (e.g., a dispute between parents over who will have custody of a child with whom the school psychologist has been working) is understandable from a risk management vantage point. It is well known that in domestic disputes, there is never an easy an-

swer. When talking about child custody disputes, judges often comment, in effect, "If I can make a ruling that leads to both parents' leaving the courtroom sensing that each has won a little and lost a little, justice has been served."

Ego defense mechanisms and the peerless penetration into the human psyche that are associated with any legal dispute over a child may lead both parents to be looking for redress for the failure to achieve a 100 percent victory. For defensive or neurotic purposes, the "lost a little" may balloon into "lost a lot," and a complaint may be filed about the perceived (albeit unjustified) source of the loss. Ethical, regulatory, and malpractice complaints are often predicted on allegations that, *but for* the faulty psychological assessment and testimony provided by the professional, the complainant would have received custody, avoided truncated litigation and extra attorney fees, and/or not suffered mental duress and other compensable personal injuries.

Stated simply, serving as an expert witness is another one of those double-edged swords that cut wide swaths through professionalism. On one hand, public policy essentially commands that all professionals, including school psychologists, provide unreserved service to the legal system; and when the welfare of children is at stake, this command is directly issued to all school personnel, especially school psychologists. On the other hand, providing expert testimony imposes close scrutiny on the professional's quality of conduct, and any perceived flaw may be the basis of a complaint.

Being an Advocate versus a Behavioral Scientist

Part of the "double-edged" problem is advocacy. Philosophically, there should be unfettered advocacy of the rights and best interests of the child. Unfortunately, advocacy, especially if it can be construed as "apostolic zeal," can be fuel for the litigious flame. In keeping with the concept of the standard of care, public policy gives little or no credence, and virtually no legal sanctity, to advocacy from expert witnesses. Public policy demands that professionalism be driven by behavioral science, with emphasis on objective and scholarly information. This may be another instance where the Ivory Tower notions about the practice of school psychology involving advocacy are abruptly rebuffed by the real world controlled by needs, expectations, and requirements of consumers, public policy, and law.

Entering the Legal Arena

The school psychologist may be drawn into a wide array of legal problems involving the children and youths served in the school. Types of cases requiring expert testimony from a school psychologist could include (among others) delinquent or criminal behavior, termination of parental rights (e.g., for neglect or abuse), foster placement, adoption, personal injury or wrongful death (e.g., a child injured or killed in an accident), discrimination or other civil rights violations, child custody, and child abuse. Crespi (1990) describes the issues associated with school psychologists working in forensic psychology.

Regardless of the type of case, the school psychologist is required to maintain professional standards, which may be different for the legal arena than for the school services. For example, an attorney might attempt to extract testimony for which the school psychologist has no predetermined standard (e.g., research or data to support a viewpoint) and, even with an appropriate objection from the opposing legal counsel, the judge will order that the opinion be expressed. This is the sort of situation that leads Anderten, Staulcup, and Grisso (1980) to say that "many ethical pitfalls may await psychologists who participate as expert witnesses in the legal process" (p. 764). Relatedly, Rogers (1987) laments, "Clinicians who provide forensic services are faced with singularly difficult ethical issues with little assistance from available ethical guidelines" (p. 159).

There is a multitude of courtroom scenarios

that could create an ethical dilemma for and a possible breach of the standard of care, albeit unintentional, by the school psychologist. Risk management undergirds that the school system should provide legal counsel and malpractice insurance coverage to the school psychologist who must enter into legal proceedings as an expert witness.

Although courts will normally strain to uphold the professional, all testimony will be subject to impeachment. That is, the entry into a legal proceeding is likely to encounter an unfriendly reception from one or more people whose interests or preferences are not compatible with the testimony being offered by the school psychologist. Ziskin and Faust (1989) suggest two avenues for opposing expert testimony from mental health professionals:

> One is to challenge both the level and the quality of expertise within these disciplines; another is to question the conduct of the evaluation, including the experts' errors of omission or commission and those conclusions that are unwarranted by the supporting data or by the state of knowledge. (p. 45)

As might be assumed, cross-examination will surely be an aggressive attempt to disprove competency as an expert and discredit the findings and opinions. It can be a devastating attack to the professional ego.

Understandably, some school psychologists quickly join with their school system's board members and administrators in wanting to avoid involvement in legal cases. It seems probable that reticence leads to selective perception. For example, Wilson and Gettinger (1989) found that "school psychologists were more likely to report physical or sexual abuse than neglect or emotional abuse; they were also more likely to report abuse occurring at the present time than in the past" (p. 98).

Under mandatory reporting law, there may be doubt about the practitioner with a reasonable basis for any abuse or neglect selectively referring some but not other cases. Slater (1988) says,

"The clearest duty of the school psychologist, because it is mandated by law, is to report any suspected case of abuse to the appropriate authorities" (p. 1). Here, it could be argued that Slater's "any suspected case" translates into "every suspected case" that fits the legal (not psychological) interpretations of the jurisdiction.

Wilson and Gettinger (1989) speculate that school psychologists may be deterred from reporting because they sense "social services do not have the necessary resources to investigate all types of reportable abuse and neglect, and therefore must focus on only the most heinous cases" (p. 100). Although that may be a viable partial explanation, it also seems possible that school psychologists are reluctant to report any case that is not clear and definite, thereby, consciously or unconsciously avoiding controversy, liability, and involvement in legal proceedings.

Guidelines for Being an Expert Witness

It is inappropriate for this book to cover assessment methods for child custody or abuse cases or other legal disputes involving children. However, basic guidelines for entering into child-oriented legal disputes are certainly in order:

1. Keep all conduct, by omission or commission, consonant with the prevailing, mainline standard of care of the applicable professional discipline.
2. The school psychologist should have an academic understanding of the psychological issues that are to be dealt with in the legal proceedings.
3. Any assessment method or intervention strategy used must meet measurement or theoretical standards (take no shortcuts).
4. Personal reports must be evaluated for veracity, reliability, and validity. Note that testimony by children, such as in child custody and abuse cases, cannot be automatically or unquestionably accepted. (See Haugaard, 1988, for a useful discussion about children's competency to testify.) Children may be prone to be honest, but they come under strong influence from others in legal proceedings.
5. Provide testimony about only those factors specified by law; the issues should be delineated prior to the testimony (or the writing of a report that will be used in a legal proceeding).
6. Safeguard against personal bias; avoid undue countertransference.
7. Maintain objectivity; do not advocate. Function as an applied behavioral scientist.
8. Never issue an opinion without adequate and complete data; make only scientifically based statements.
9. Beware of and resist attempts by attorneys (or occasionally a judge) to induce testimony beyond professional standards.
10. Do not try to turn legal proceedings into therapeutic encounters. Remember that the sole purpose for the involvement of an expert is to provide information to the trier-of-fact.
11. Educate the parties (parents), attorney(s), judge, and jury to the acceptable use of psychoeducational data; correct misunderstandings and faulty expectations.
12. Present facts and descriptions, not conclusions.
13. Avoid opinions about the ultimate legal issue (e.g., guilty or innocent, who gets custody, did abuse occur?), especially when there is no research-base for the opinion. Public policy supports that the expert can provide information and testify, but the ultimate legal question must be answered by the trier-of-fact (judge or jury).
14. Do not hesitate to apply accepted standards to the testimony provided by other experts. It is an essential service to public policy and the judicial process for an expert to academically critique the testimony provided by other experts.
15. Have personal legal counsel available for determining all responses (e.g., communications to attorneys, releasing records), reviewing all materials, and monitoring all

interactions (e.g., depositions, courtroom testimony).

16. Be wary of incurring liability through participation in a legal proceeding.

(See Meyer, Landis, and Hays, 1988, and Woody, 1984, for additional information on providing expert testimony.)

In this day and age, there is no question that school psychology occurs within a legal framework. As presented, legal influences come from a myriad of sources, such as federal and state legislation, case or common law, and professional position statements. It is foolhardy to attempt to practice school psychology without a definite understanding of the interface between the law and the discipline, and to make day-to-day decisions without legal counsel being readily available.

SUMMARY

Professional standards for school psychology must adhere to legal prescriptions and proscriptions, as relevant to state-level administrative agencies, school administrations, classroom teachers, and psychoeducational personnel. School psychologists must be acquainted with law and education—the nature of criminal and civil law, statutory and common (case) law, jurisdiction, and the rules of civil and criminal procedure.

Given the necessity of participating in legal proceedings involving children and their families, school psychologists must be prepared to deal with cross-examination and impeachment, and stay within the proper confines for expert testimony. Federal and state legislation dictates educational programming for handicapped children. It is essential that each individualized education program and/or individualized family service plan be appropriate and that the family's educational and privacy rights be honored.

Considerable litigation has occurred, which provides interpretations for policies and practices. Confidentiality and privileged communication are particularly important, which means that educational records and information must be protected. Public policy has, however, created exceptions, such as the duty to warn (e.g., in child abuse or violent situations). Failure to meet the standard of care, as defined legally, triggers professional liability or malpractice actions. Regarding standard of care, governmental control, especially through licensure and certification by state agencies, is increasing.

REFERENCES

American Psychological Association. (1981a). Ethical principles for psychologists. *American Psychologist, 36*(6), 633–638.

American Psychological Association. (1981b). Specialty guidelines for the delivery of services by school psychologists. *American Psychologist, 36*(6), 670–681.

American Psychological Association. (1987a). General guidelines for providers of psychological services. *American Psychologist, 42,* 712–723.

American Psychological Association. (1987b). Report of the Ethics Committee: 1986. *American Psychologist, 42,* 730–734.

American Psychological Association. (1990). Ethical principles of psychologists. *American Psychologist, 45*(3), 390–395.

Anderson, J. E. (1979). *Public policy-making: Deci-sions and their implementation* (2nd ed.). New York: Holt, Rinehart and Winston.

Anderten, P., Staulcup, V., & Grisso, T. (1980). On being ethical in legal places. *Professional Psychology, 11*(5), 764–773.

Ballinger, P. (1986). Untitled memorandum. Washington, DC: United States Department of Education, September 17, 1986.

Bersoff, D. N. (1980). *Larry P. v. Riles:* Legal perspective. *School Psychology Review, 9,* 112–122.

Bersoff, D. N. (1983). Regarding psychologists testily: The legal regulation of psychological assessment. In C. J. Scheirer & B. L. Hammonds (Eds.), *Psychology and the law. Volume 2* (pp. 37–88). Washington, DC: American Psychological Association.

Besharov, D. J. (1985). *The vulnerable social worker:*

Liability for serving children and families. Silver Spring, MD: National Association of Social Workers.

Carpignano, J. (1987). Problems in the practice of responsible school psychology. *School Psychologist, 41*(4), 1–4.

Claiborn, W. L. (1982). The problem of professional incompetence. *Professional Psychology, 13,* 153–158.

Cleary, E. W. (Ed.). (1972). *McCormick's handbook on the law of evidence* (2nd ed.). St. Paul, MN: West.

Crespi, T. D. (1990). School psychologists in forensic pathology: Converging and diverging issues. *Professional Psychology, 21*(2), 83–87.

Dewey, J. (1922). *Human nature and conduct.* New York: Howard Holt & Company [Carlton House] (also see Modern Library Edition, 1930).

Downey, W. S., Jr. (1989). The Education of the Handicapped Act. *Florida Bar Journal, 63*(7), 58–61.

Fischer, L., & Sorenson, G. P. (1985). *School law for counselors, psychologists, and social workers.* New York: Longman.

Gallant, C. B. (1982). *Mediation in special education disputes.* Silver Spring, MD: National Association of Social Workers.

Hall, J. E. (1987). Standards for the individual practitioner—A moving target. *Register Report, 13,* 11–12.

Haugaard, J. J. (1988). Judicial determination of children's competency to testify: Should it be abandoned? *Professional Psychology 19*(1), 102–107.

Hobbs, N. (1964). Mental health's third revolution. *American Journal of Orthopsychiatry, 34,* 822–833.

Hogan, D. B. (1979). *The regulation of psychotherapists. Volume III. A review of malpractice suits in the United States.* Cambridge, MA: Ballinger.

Hopkins, B. R., & Anderson, B. S. (1985). *The counselor and the law.* Alexandria, VA: American Association for Counseling and Development.

Jensen, A. R. (1980). *Bias in mental testing.* New York: The Free Press.

Kionka, E. J. (1977). *Torts: Injuries to persons and property.* St. Paul, MN: West.

Martin, R. (1979). *Educating handicapped children: The legal mandate.* Champaign, IL: Research Press.

Meisels, S. J. (1989). Meeting the mandate of Public Law 99-457: Early childhood intervention in the nineties. *American Journal of Orthopsychiatry, 59*(3), 451–460.

Meyer, R. G., Landis, E. R., & Hays, J. R. (1988). *Law for the psychotherapist.* New York: W. W. Norton.

National Association of School Psychologists. (1984a). Principles for professional ethics. In *Professional Conduct Manual* (pp. 3–17). Stratford, CT: Author.

National Association of School Psychologists. (1984b). Standards for provision of school psychological services. In *Professional Conduct Manual* (pp. 19–33). Stratford, CT: Author.

Palagi, R. J., & Springer, J. R. (1984). Personal injury law. In R. H. Woody (Ed.), *The law and the practice of human services* (pp. 155–198). San Francisco: Jossey-Bass.

Prosser, W. L. (1971). *Handbook of the law of torts* (4th ed.). St. Paul, MN: West.

Roach, W. H., Jr., Chernoff, S. N., & Esley, C. L. (1985). *Medical records and the law.* Rockville, MD: Aspen.

Rogers, R. (1987). Ethical dilemmas in forensic evaluations. *Behavioral Sciences & the Law, 5*(2), 149–160.

Saks, M. J. (1989). Legal policy analysis and evaluation. *American Psychologist, 44*(8), 1110–1117.

Schroeder, S. R., Schroeder, C. S., & Landesman, S. (1987). Psychological services in educational settings to persons with mental retardation. *American Psychologist, 42*(8), 805–808.

Sido, K. R., & King, P. R. (1989). Litigation involving students with handicaps. *Trial, 8,* 56–60.

Slater, B. R. (1988). School psychologists and abused children. *School Psychologist, 42*(5), 3–4.

Slovenko, R. (1973). *Psychiatry and law.* Boston: Little, Brown.

Sticks, R. S. (1984). Rights of handicapped children to an education. In R. H. Woody (Ed.), *The law and the practice of human services* (pp. 341–372). San Francisco: Jossey-Bass.

Trent, C. L. (1978). Psychiatric malpractice and its problems: An overview. In W. E. Barton & C. J. Sanborn (Eds.), *Law and the mental health professions* (pp. 101–117). New York: International Universities Press.

VandeCreek, L., & Knapp, S. (1989). *Tarasoff and beyond: Legal and clinical considerations in the treatment of life-endangering patients.* Sarasota, FL: Professional Resource Exchange.

Wigmore, J. H. (1940). *Evidence* (3rd ed.). (10 vols.)

Boston: Little, Brown, 1940. (Originally published in 1913; vol. 3 rev. 1970, vol. 4 rev. 1972, by J. H. Chadbourn.)

Wilson, C. A., & Gettinger, M. (1989). Determinants of child-abuse reporting among Wisconsin school psychologists. *Professional School Psychology* 4(2), 91–102.

Woody, J. D., & Woody, R. H. (1988). Public policy in life-threatening situations. *Journal of Marital and Family Therapy, 14*(2), 133–137.

Woody, R. H. (1984). Professional responsibilities and liabilities. In R. H. Woody (Ed.), *The law and the practice of human services* (pp. 373–401). San Francisco: Jossey-Bass.

Woody, R. H. (1988a). *Fifty ways to avoid malpractice: A guidebook for mental health professionals.* Sarasota, FL: Professional Resource Exchange.

Woody, R. H. (1988b). *Protecting your mental health practice: How to minimize legal and financial risk.* San Francisco: Jossey-Bass.

Woody, R. H. (1989). Public policy, ethics, government, and law. *Professional School Psychology, 4*(1), 75–83.

Woody, R. H., & Mitchell, R. E. (1984). Understanding the legal system and legal research. In R. H. Woody (Ed.), *The law and the practice of human services* (pp. 1–38). San Francisco: Jossey-Bass.

Woody, R. H., Woody, J. D., & Greenberg, D. B. (1991). Case management for the individualized family service plan under Public Law 99-457. *American Journal of Family Therapy, 19*(1), 67–76.

Woody, R. H., Yeager, M., & Woody, J. D. (1990). Appropriate education for handicapped children: Introducing family therapy to school-based decision making. *American Journal of Family Therapy, 18*(2), 189–196.

Ziskin, J., & Faust, D. (1989). Psychiatric and psychological evidence in child custody cases. *Trial, 25*(8), 44–49.

APPENDIX A: The American Psychological Association's (1990) Report of the Association: Ethical Principles of Psychologists *(Amended June 2, 1989)*

Preamble

Psychologists respect the dignity and worth of the individual and strive for the preservation and protection of fundamental human rights. They are committed to increasing knowledge of human behavior and of people's understanding of themselves and others and to the utilization of such knowledge for the promotion of human welfare. While pursuing these objectives, they make every effort to protect the welfare of those who seek their services and of the research participants that may be the object of study. They use their skills only for purposes consistent with these values and do not knowingly permit their misuse by others. While demanding for themselves freedom of inquiry and communication, psychologists accept the responsibility this freedom requires: competence, objectivity in the application of skills, and concern for the best interests of clients, colleagues, students, research participants, and society. In the pursuit of these ideals, psychologists subscribe to principles in the following areas: 1. Responsibility, 2. Competence, 3. Moral and Legal Standards, 4. Public Statements, 5. Confidentiality, 6. Welfare of the Consumer, 7. Professional Relationships, 8. Assessment Techniques, 9. Research With Human Participants, and 10. Care and Use of Animals.

Acceptance of membership in the American Psychological Association commits the member to adherence to these principles.

Psychologists cooperate with duly constituted committees of the American Psychological Association, in particular, the Committee on Scientific and Professional Ethics and Conduct, by responding to inquiries promptly and completely. Members also respond promptly and completely to inquiries from duly constituted state association ethics committees and professional standards review committees.

Principle 1: Responsibility

In providing services, psychologists maintain the highest standards of their profession. They accept responsibility for the consequences of their acts and make every effort to ensure that their services are used appropriately.

a. As scientists, psychologists accept responsibility for the selection of their research topics and the methods used in investigation, analysis, and reporting. They plan their research in ways to minimize the possibility that their findings will be misleading. They provide thorough discussion of the limitations of their data, especially where their work touches on social policy or might be construed to the detriment of persons in specific age, sex, ethnic, socioeconomic, or other social groups. In publishing reports of their work, they never suppress disconfirming data, and they acknowledge the existence of alternative hypotheses and explanations of their findings. Psychologists take credit only for work they have actually done.

b. Psychologists clarify in advance with all appropriate persons and agencies the expectations for sharing and utilizing research data. They avoid relationships that may limit their objectivity or create a conflict of interest. Interference with the milieu in which data are collected is kept to a minimum.

c. Psychologists have the responsibility to attempt to prevent distortion, misuse, or suppression of psychological findings by the institution or agency of which they are employees.

d. As members of governmental or other organizational bodies, psychologists remain accountable as individuals to the highest standards of their profession.

e. As teachers, psychologists recognize their primary obligation to help others acquire knowledge and skill. They maintain high standards of scholarship by presenting psychological information objectively, fully, and accurately.

f. As practitioners, psychologists know that they bear a heavy social responsibility because their recommendations and professional actions may alter the lives of others. They are alert to personal, social, organizational, financial, or political situations and pressures that might lead to misuse of their influence.

Principle 2: Competence

The maintenance of high standards of competence is a responsibility shared by all psychologists in the interest of the public and the profession as a whole. Psychologists recognize the boundaries of their competence and the limitations of their techniques. They only provide services and only use techniques for which they are qualified by training and experience. In those areas in which recognized standards do not yet exist, psychologists take what-

Source: Ethical principles of psychologists. *American Psychologist, 45*(3), 390–395. Copyright 1990 by the American Psychological Association. Reprinted by permission.

ever precautions are necessary to protect the welfare of their clients. They maintain knowledge of current scientific and professional information related to the services they render.

a. Psychologists accurately represent their competence, education, training, and experience. They claim as evidence of educational qualifications only those degrees obtained from institutions acceptable under the Bylaws and Rules of Council of the American Psychological Association.

b. As teachers, psychologists perform their duties on the basis of careful preparation so that their instruction is accurate, current, and scholarly.

c. Psychologists recognize the need for continuing education and are open to new procedures and changes in expectations and values over time.

d. Psychologists recognize differences among people, such as those that may be associated with age, sex, socioeconomic, and ethnic backgrounds. When necessary, they obtain training, experience, or counsel to assure competent service or research relating to such persons.

e. Psychologists responsible for decisions involving individuals or policies based on test results have an understanding of psychological or educational measurement, validation problems, and test research.

f. Psychologists recognize that personal problems and conflicts may interfere with professional effectiveness. Accordingly, they refrain from undertaking any activity in which their personal problems are likely to lead to

---

This version of the *Ethical Principles of Psychologists* was adopted by the American Psychological Association's Board of Directors on June 2, 1989. On that date, the Board of Directors rescinded several sections of the Ethical Principles that had been adopted by the APA Council of Representatives on January 24, 1981. Inquiries concerning the substance or interpretation of the *Ethical Principles of Psychologists* should be addressed to the Administrative Director, Office of Ethics, American Psychological Association, 1200 Seventeenth Street, N.W., Washington, DC 20036.

These Ethical Principles apply to psychologists, to students of psychology, and to others who do work of a psychological nature under the supervision of a psychologist. They are intended for the guidance of nonmembers of the Association who are engaged in psychological research or practice.

The Ethical Principles have previously been published as follows:
American Psychological Association. (1953). *Ethical Standards of Psychologists,* Washington, DC.
American Psychological Association. (1958). Standards of ethical behavior for psychologists. *American Psychologist, 13,* 268–271.
American Psychological Association. (1959). Ethical standards of psychologists. *American Psychologist, 14,* 279–282.
American Psychological Association. (1963). Ethical standards of psychologists. *American Psychologist, 18,* 56–60.
American Psychological Association. (1968). Ethical standards of psychologists. *American Psychologist, 23,* 357–361.
American Psychological Association. (1977, March). Ethical standards of psychologists. *The APA Monitor,* pp. 22–23.
American Psychological Association. (1979). *Ethical Standards of Psychologists,* Washington, DC: Author.
American Psychological Association. (1981). Ethical principles of psychologists. *American Psychologist, 36,* 633–638.
Request copies of the *Ethical Principles of Psychologists* from the APA Order Department, P.O. Box 2710, Hyattsville, MD 20784; or phone (703) 247-7705.

inadequate performance or harm to a client, colleague, student, or research participant. If engaged in such activity when they become aware of their personal problems, they seek competent professional assistance to determine whether they should suspend, terminate, or limit the scope of their professional and/or scientific activities.

Principle 3: Moral and Legal Standards

Psychologists' moral and ethical standards of behavior are a personal matter to the same degree as they are for any other citizen, except as these may compromise the fulfillment of their professional responsibilities or reduce the public trust in psychology and psychologists. Regarding their own behavior, psychologists are sensitive to prevailing community standards and to the possible impact that conformity to or deviation from these standards may have upon the quality of their performance as psychologists. Psychologists are also aware of the possible impact of their public behavior upon the ability of colleagues to perform their professional duties.

a. As teachers, psychologists are aware of the fact that their personal values may affect the selection and presentation of instructional materials. When dealing with topics that may give offense, they recognize and respect the diverse attitudes that students may have toward such materials.

b. As employees or employers, psychologists do not engage in or condone practices that are inhumane or that result in illegal or unjustifiable actions. Such practices include, but are not limited to, those based on considerations of race, handicap, age, gender, sexual preference, religion, or national origin in hiring, promotion, or training.

c. In their professional roles, psychologists avoid any action that will violate or diminish the legal and civil rights of clients or of others who may be affected by their actions.

d. As practitioners and researchers, psychologists act in accord with Association standards and guidelines related to practice and to the conduct of research with human beings and animals. In the ordinary course of events, psychologists adhere to relevant governmental laws and institutional regulations. When federal, state, provincial, organizational, or institutional laws, regulations, or practices are in conflict with Association standards and guidelines, psychologists make known their commitment to Association standards and guidelines and, wherever possible, work toward a resolution of the conflict. Both practitioners and researchers are concerned with the development of such legal and quasi-legal regulations as best serve the public interest, and they work toward changing existing regulations that are not beneficial to the public interest.

Principle 4: Public Statements

Public statements, announcements of services, advertising, and promotional activities of psychologists serve the purpose of helping the public make informed judgments and choices. Psychologists represent accurately and objectively their professional qualifications, affiliations, and functions, as well as those of the institutions or organizations with which they or the statements may be associated. In public statements providing psychological information or professional opinions or providing information about the availability of psychological products, publications, and services, psychologists base their statements on scientifically acceptable psychological findings and techniques with full recognition of the limits and uncertainties of such evidence.

a. When announcing or advertising professional services, psychologists may list the following information to describe the provider and services provided: name, highest relevant academic degree earned from a regionally accredited institution, date, type, and level of certification or licensure, diplomate status, APA membership status, address, telephone number, office hours, a brief listing of the type of psychological services offered, an appropriate presentation of fee information, foreign languages spoken, and policy with regard to third-party payments. Additional relevant or important consumer information may be included if not prohibited by other sections of these Ethical Principles.

b. In announcing or advertising the availability of psychological products, publications, or services, psychologists do not present their affiliation with any organization in a manner that falsely implies sponsorship or certification by that organization. In particular and for example, psychologists do not state APA membership or fellow status in a way to suggest that such status implies specialized professional competence or qualifications. Public statements include, but are not limited to, communication by means of periodical, book, list, directory, television, radio, or motion picture. They do not contain (i) a false, fraudulent, misleading, deceptive, or unfair statement; (ii) a misinterpretation of fact or a statement likely to mislead or deceive because in context it makes only a partial disclosure of relevant facts; (iii) a statement intended or likely to create false or unjustified expectations of favorable results.

c. Psychologists do not compensate or give anything of value to a representative of the press, radio, television, or other communication medium in anticipation of or in return for professional publicity in a news item. A paid advertisement must be identified as such, unless it is apparent from the context that it is a paid advertisement. If communicated to the public by use of radio or television, an advertisement is prerecorded and approved for broadcast by the psychologist, and a recording of the actual transmission is retained by the psychologist.

d. Announcements or advertisements of "personal growth groups," clinics, and agencies give a clear statement of purpose and a clear description of the experiences to be provided. The education, training, and experience of the staff members are appropriately specified.

e. Psychologists associated with the development or promotion of psychological devices, books, or other products offered for commercial sale make reasonable efforts to ensure that announcements and advertisements

are presented in a professional, scientifically acceptable, and factually informative manner.

f. Psychologists do not participate for personal gain in commercial announcements or advertisements recommending to the public the purchase or use of proprietary or single-source products or services when that participation is based solely upon their identification as psychologists.

g. Psychologists present the science of psychology and offer their services, products, and publications fairly and accurately, avoiding misrepresentation through sensationalism, exaggeration, or superficiality. Psychologists are guided by the primary obligation to aid the public in developing informed judgments, opinions, and choices.

h. As teachers, psychologists ensure that statements in catalogs and course outlines are accurate and not misleading, particularly in terms of subject matter to be covered, bases for evaluating progress, and the nature of course experiences. Announcements, brochures, or advertisements describing workshops, seminars, or other educational programs accurately describe the audience for which the program is intended as well as eligibility requirements, educational objectives, and nature of the materials to be covered. These announcements also accurately represent the education, training, and experience of the psychologists presenting the programs and any fees involved.

i. Public announcements or advertisements soliciting research participants in which clinical services or other professional services are offered as an inducement make clear the nature of the services as well as the costs and other obligations to be accepted by participants in the research.

j. A psychologist accepts the obligation to correct others who represent the psychologist's professional qualifications, or associations with products or services, in a manner incompatible with these guidelines.

k. Individual diagnostic and therapeutic services are provided only in the context of a professional psychological relationship. When personal advice is given by means of public lectures or demonstrations, newspaper or magazine articles, radio or television programs, mail, or similar media, the psychologist utilizes the most current relevant data and exercises the highest level of professional judgment.

l. Products that are described or presented by means of public lectures or demonstrations, newspaper or magazine articles, radio or television programs, or similar media meet the same recognized standards as exist for products used in the context of a professional relationship.

Principle 5: Confidentiality

Psychologists have a primary obligation to respect the confidentiality of information obtained from persons in the course of their work as psychologists. They reveal such information to others only with the consent of the person or the person's legal representative, except in those unusual circumstances in which not to do so would result in clear danger to the person or to others. Where appropriate, psy-

chologists inform their clients of the legal limits of confidentiality.

a. Information obtained in clinical or consulting relationships, or evaluative data concerning children, students, employees, and others, is discussed only for professional purposes and only with persons clearly concerned with the case. Written and oral reports present only data germane to the purposes of the evaluation, and every effort is made to avoid undue invasion of privacy.

b. Psychologists who present personal information obtained during the course of professional work in writings, lectures, or other public forums either obtain adequate prior consent to do so or adequately disguise all identifying information.

c. Psychologists make provisions for maintaining confidentiality in the storage and disposal of records.

d. When working with minors or other persons who are unable to give voluntary, informed consent, psychologists take special care to protect these persons' best interests.

Principle 6: Welfare of the Consumer

Psychologists respect the integrity and protect the welfare of the people and groups with whom they work. When conflicts of interest arise between clients and psychologists' employing institutions, psychologists clarify the nature and direction of their loyalties and responsibilities and keep all parties informed of their commitments. Psychologists fully inform consumers as to the purpose and nature of an evaluative, treatment, educational, or training procedure, and they freely acknowledge that clients, students, or participants in research have freedom of choice with regard to participation.

a. Psychologists are continually cognizant of their own needs and of their potentially influential position vis-à-vis persons such as clients, students, and subordinates. They avoid exploiting the trust and dependency of such persons. Psychologists make every effort to avoid dual relationships that could impair their professional judgment or increase the risk of exploitation. Examples of such dual relationships include, but are not limited to, research with and treatment of employees, students, supervisees, close friends, or relatives. Sexual intimacies with clients are unethical.

b. When a psychologist agrees to provide services to a client at the request of a third party, the psychologist assumes the responsibility of clarifying the nature of the relationships to all parties concerned.

c. Where the demands of an organization require psychologists to violate these Ethical Principles, psychologists clarify the nature of the conflict between the demands and these principles. They inform all parties of psychologists' ethical responsibilities and take appropriate action.

d. Psychologists make advance financial arrangements that safeguard the best interests of and are clearly understood by their clients. They contribute a portion of their services to work for which they receive little or no financial return.

e. Psychologists terminate a clinical or consulting relationship when it is reasonably clear that the consumer is not benefiting from it. They offer to help the consumer locate alternative sources of assistance.

Principle 7: Professional Relationships

Psychologists act with due regard for the needs, special competencies, and obligations of their colleagues in psychology and other professions. They respect the prerogatives and obligations of the institutions or organizations with which these other colleagues are associated.

a. Psychologists understand the areas of competence of related professions. They make full use of all the professional, technical, and administrative resources that serve the best interests of consumers. The absence of formal relationships with other professional workers does not relieve psychologists of the responsibility of securing for their clients the best possible professional service, nor does it relieve them of the obligation to exercise foresight, diligence, and tact in obtaining the complementary or alternative assistance needed by clients.

b. Psychologists know and take into account the traditions and practices of other professional groups with whom they work and cooperate fully with such groups. If a psychologist is contacted by a person who is already receiving similar services from another professional, the psychologist carefully considers that professional relationship and proceeds with caution and sensitivity to the therapeutic issues as well as the client's welfare. The psychologist discusses these issues with the client so as to minimize the risk of confusion and conflict.

c. Psychologists who employ or supervise other professionals or professionals in training accept the obligation to facilitate the further professional development of these individuals. They provide appropriate working conditions, timely evaluations, constructive consultation, and experience opportunities.

d. Psychologists do not exploit their professional relationships with clients, supervisees, students, employees, or research participants sexually or otherwise. Psychologists do not condone or engage in sexual harassment. Sexual harassment is defined as deliberate or repeated comments, gestures, or physical contacts of a sexual nature that are unwanted by the recipient.

e. In conducting research in institutions or organizations, psychologists secure appropriate authorization to conduct such research. They are aware of their obligations to future research workers and ensure that host institutions receive adequate information about the research and proper acknowledgment of their contributions.

f. Publication credit is assigned to those who have contributed to a publication in proportion to their professional contributions. Major contributions of a professional character made by several persons to a common project are recognized by joint authorship, with the individual who made the principal contribution listed first. Minor contributions of a professional character and extensive clerical or similar nonprofessional assistance may be acknowledged in footnotes or in an introductory statement. Acknowledgment through specific citations is made for unpublished as well as published material that has directly influenced the research or writing. Psychologists who compile and edit material of others for publication publish the material in the name of the originating group, if appropriate, with their own name appearing as chairperson or editor. All contributors are to be acknowledged and named.

g. When psychologists know of an ethical violation by another psychologist, and it seems appropriate, they informally attempt to resolve the issue by bringing the behavior to the attention of the psychologist. If the misconduct is of a minor nature and/or appears to be due to lack of sensitivity, knowledge, or experience, such an informal solution is usually appropriate. Such informal corrective efforts are made with sensitivity to any rights to confidentiality involved. If the violation does not seem amenable to an informal solution, or is of a more serious nature, psychologists bring it to the attention of the appropriate local, state, and/or national committee on professional ethics and conduct.

Principle 8: Assessment Techniques

In the development, publication, and utilization of psychological assessment techniques, psychologists make every effort to promote the welfare and best interests of the client. They guard against the misuse of assessment results. They respect the client's right to know the results, the interpretations made, and the bases for their conclusions and recommendations. Psychologists make every effort to maintain the security of tests and other assessment techniques within limits of legal mandates. They strive to ensure the appropriate use of assessment techniques by others.

a. In using assessment techniques, psychologists respect the right of clients to have full explanations of the nature and purpose of the techniques in language the clients can understand, unless an explicit exception to this right has been agreed upon in advance. When the explanations are to be provided by others, psychologists establish procedures for ensuring the adequacy of these explanations.

b. Psychologists responsible for the development and standardization of psychological tests and other assessment techniques utilize established scientific procedures and observe the relevant APA standards.

c. In reporting assessment results, psychologists indicate any reservations that exist regarding validity or reliability because of the circumstances of the assessment or the inappropriateness of the norms for the person tested. Psychologists strive to ensure that the results of assessments and their interpretations are not misused by others.

d. Psychologists recognize that assessment results may become obsolete. They make every effort to avoid and prevent the misuse of obsolete measures.

e. Psychologists offering scoring and interpretation services are able to produce appropriate evidence for the validity of the programs and procedures used in arriving

at interpretations. The public offering of an automated interpretation service is considered a professional-to-professional consultation. Psychologists make every effort to avoid misuse of assessment reports.

f. Psychologists do not encourage or promote the use of psychological assessment techniques by inappropriately trained or otherwise unqualified persons through teaching, sponsorship, or supervision.

Principle 9: Research With Human Participants

The decision to undertake research rests upon a considered judgment by the individual psychologist about how best to contribute to psychological science and human welfare. Having made the decision to conduct research, the psychologist considers alternative directions in which research energies and resources might be invested. On the basis of this consideration, the psychologist carries out the investigation with respect and concern for the dignity and welfare of the people who participate and with cognizance of federal and state regulations and professional standards governing the conduct of research with human participants.

a. In planning a study, the investigator has the responsibility to make a careful evaluation of its ethical acceptability. To the extent that the weighing of scientific and human values suggests a compromise of any principle, the investigator incurs a correspondingly serious obligation to seek ethical advice and to observe stringent safeguards to protect the rights of human participants.

b. Considering whether a participant in a planned study will be a "subject at risk" or a "subject at minimal risk," according to recognized standards, is of primary ethical concern to the investigator.

c. The investigator always retains the responsibility for ensuring ethical practice in research. The investigator is also responsible for the ethical treatment of research participants by collaborators, assistants, students, and employees, all of whom, however, incur similar obligations.

d. Except in minimal-risk research, the investigator establishes a clear and fair agreement with research participants, prior to their participation, that clarifies the obligations and responsibilities of each. The investigator has the obligation to honor all promises and commitments included in that agreement. The investigator informs the participants of all aspects of the research that might reasonably be expected to influence willingness to participate and explains all other aspects of the research about which the participants inquire. Failure to make full disclosure prior to obtaining informed consent requires additional safeguards to protect the welfare and dignity of the research participants. Research with children or with participants who have impairments that would limit understanding and/or communication requires special safeguarding procedures.

e. Methodological requirements of a study may make the use of concealment or deception necessary. Before conducting such a study, the investigator has a special responsibility to (i) determine whether the use of such techniques is justified by the study's prospective scientific, educational, or applied value; (ii) determine whether alternative procedures are available that do not use concealment or deception; and (iii) ensure that the participants are provided with sufficient explanation as soon as possible.

f. The investigator respects the individual's freedom to decline to participate in or to withdraw from the research at any time. The obligation to protect this freedom requires careful thought and consideration when the investigator is in a position of authority or influence over the participant. Such positions of authority include, but are not limited to, situations in which research participation is required as part of employment or in which the participant is a student, client, or employee of the investigator.

g. The investigator protects the participant from physical and mental discomfort, harm, and danger that may arise from research procedures. If risks of such consequences exist, the investigator informs the participant of that fact. Research procedures likely to cause serious or lasting harm to a participant are not used unless the failure to use these procedures might expose the participant to risk of greater harm, or unless the research has great potential benefit and fully informed and voluntary consent is obtained from each participant. The participant should be informed of procedures for contacting the investigator within a reasonable time period following participation should stress, potential harm, or related questions or concerns arise.

h. After the data are collected, the investigator provides the participant with information about the nature of the study and attempts to remove any misconceptions that may have arisen. Where scientific or humane values justify delaying or withholding this information, the investigator incurs a special responsibility to monitor the research and to ensure that there are no damaging consequences for the participant.

i. Where research procedures result in undesirable consequences for the individual participant, the investigator has the responsibility to detect and remove or correct these consequences, including long-term effects.

j. Information obtained about a research participant during the course of an investigation is confidential unless otherwise agreed upon in advance. When the possibility exists that others may obtain access to such information, this possibility, together with the plans for protecting confidentiality, is explained to the participant as part of the procedure for obtaining informed consent.

Principle 10: Care and Use of Animals

An investigator of animal behavior strives to advance understanding of basic behavioral principles and/or to contribute to the improvement of human health and welfare. In seeking these ends, the investigator ensures the welfare of animals and treats them humanely. Laws and regulations notwithstanding, an animal's immediate protection depends upon the scientist's own conscience.

a. The acquisition, care, use, and disposal of all animals are in compliance with current federal, state or provincial, and local laws and regulations.

b. A psychologist trained in research methods and experienced in the care of laboratory animals closely supervises all procedures involving animals and is responsible for ensuring appropriate consideration of their comfort, health, and humane treatment.

c. Psychologists ensure that all individuals using animals under their supervision have received explicit instruction in experimental methods and in the care, maintenance, and handling of the species being used. Responsibilities and activities of individuals participating in a research project are consistent with their respective competencies.

d. Psychologists make every effort to minimize discomfort, illness, and pain of animals. A procedure subjecting animals to pain, stress, or privation is used only when an alternative procedure is unavailable and the goal is justified by its prospective scientific, educational, or applied value. Surgical procedures are performed under appropriate anesthesia; techniques to avoid infection and minimize pain are followed during and after surgery.

e. When it is appropriate that the animal's life be terminated, it is done rapidly and painlessly.

APPENDIX B: The American Psychological Association's (1987) General Guidelines for Providers of Psychological Services Board of Professional Affairs, Committee on Professional Standards

Preamble

A set of practices and implicitly recognized principles of conduct evolves over the history of every profession. Such principles guide the relationships of the members of the profession to their users, to each other, and to the community of which both professionals and users are members. Making such guiding principles and practices explicit is a sign of the profession's maturity and serves the best interests of the profession, its users, and the community at large.

Because psychology is a continually evolving science and profession, guidelines for practice are living documents that require periodic review and revision. The *General Guidelines for Providers of Psychological Services*[1,2] represents an important milestone in the evolutionary development of professional psychology.

These General Guidelines are a set of aspirational statements for psychologists that encourage continual improvement in the quality of practice and service. Some of these General Guidelines have been derived from specific APA Ethical Principles (APA, 1981a).[3] Providers of psychological services have the same responsibility to uphold these specific General Guidelines as they would the corresponding Ethical Principles. The language of the other General Guidelines must at all times be interpreted in light of their aspirational intent.

These General Guidelines are general in nature and, as such, are intended for use by all providers of psychological services; they are supplemented by the *Specialty Guidelines for the Delivery of Services by Clinical (Counseling, Industrial/Organizational, and School) Psychologists* (APA, 1981b).

Introduction

This version of the *General Guidelines* is the second revision of the principles originally adopted by the American Psychological Association on September 4, 1974, and first revised in 1977.[4] The *General Guidelines* are intended to improve the quality, effectiveness, and accessibility of psychological services.

Since 1970, the American Psychological Association has worked to develop and codify a uniform set of guidelines for psychological practice that would serve the respective needs of users, providers, third-party purchasers, and other sanctioners of psychological services. In addition, the APA has established a Committee on Professional Standards, which is charged with keeping the General Guidelines responsive to the needs of these groups and with upgrading and extending them as the profession and science of psychology continue to develop knowledge, improved methods, and additional modes of psychological service. These General Guidelines have been established by organized psychology as a means of self-regulation in the public interest.

When providing any of the covered psychological service functions at any time and in any setting, whether public or private, profit or nonprofit, any persons representing themselves as psychologists are expected, where feasible, to observe these General Guidelines of practice to promote the best interests and welfare of the users of such services. Functions and activities related to the teaching of psychology, the writing or editing of scholarly or scientific manuscripts, and the conduct of scientific research do not fall within the purview of the present *General Guidelines*.[5]

Underlying Principles

Six basic principles have guided the development of these General Guidelines:

1. These General Guidelines apply to psychological service functions offered by psychologists, regardless of their specialty, of the setting, or of the form of remuneration given to them. Professional psychology has a uniform set of guidelines just as it has a common code of ethics (APA, 1981a). These General Guidelines apply equally to individual practitioners and to those who work in a group practice, an institutional agency, or another organizational setting.

2. Guidelines describe levels of quality for covered psychological services that providers strive to attain, regardless of the nature of the users, purchasers, or sanctioners of such covered services.

3. Those people who provide psychological services

These General Guidelines were revised by the Committee on Professional Standards (COPS) in consultation with the Board of Professional Affairs (BPA) and providers of psychological services from throughout the American Psychological Association (APA). The assistance of APA staff is gratefully acknowledged. The names of members and staff who supported this effort are included in Footnote 4. This document was approved by the APA Council of Representatives in February 1987.

Comments or questions on these General Guidelines should be addressed to the Committee on Professional Standards, American Psychological Association, 1200 Seventeenth Street, NW, Washington, DC 20036.

meet acceptable levels of education, training, and experience that are consistent and appropriate to the functions they perform. The final responsibility and accountability for defining qualifications and supervision requirements for service rest with a professional psychologist[6] (see Definitions).

4. Guidelines do not constrain psychologists from employing new methods (see Guideline 1.8) or from making flexible use of support personnel in staffing the delivery of services. The General Guidelines illuminate potential weaknesses in the delivery of psychological services and point to their correction. Some settings may require additional guidelines for specific areas of service delivery than those herein proposed. There is no intent to diminish the scope or quality of psychological services that exceed these General Guidelines. Systematically applied, these General Guidelines serve to establish desirable levels of psychological service. They serve to establish a more effective and consistent basis for evaluating the performance of individual service providers, and they serve to guide the organizing of psychological service units in human service settings.

5. It is recognized that there are significant differences among the established fields of professional psychology in regard to education and training, technical methodology, user populations served, and methods and settings of service delivery. The *Specialty Guidelines for the Delivery of Services* (APA, 1981b) provides acknowledgment of these differences while conforming to the guiding principles delineated by the General Guidelines.

6. These General Guidelines have been developed with the understanding that psychological services must be planned and implemented so that they are sensitive to factors related to life in a pluralistic society such as age, gender, affectional orientation, culture, and ethnicity.

Implications of Guidelines

The General Guidelines presented here have broad implications both for members of the public who use psychological services and for providers of such services.

1. The Guidelines furnish a basis for a mutual understanding between providers and users. Further, they facilitate improved quality of services and more effective evaluation of these services and their outcomes.

2. The Guidelines are an important step toward greater uniformity in legislative and regulatory actions involving providers of psychological services, and provide a model for the development of accreditation procedures for service facilities.

3. The Guidelines give specific content to the profession's concept of ethical practice as reflected in the APA *Ethical Principles of Psychologists* (1981a).

4. The Guidelines have significant impact on training models for both professional and support personnel in psychology.

5. Guidelines for the provision of psychological services influence what is considered desirable organizational structure, budgeting, and staffing patterns in these facilities.

Definitions

Providers of Psychological Services

This term subsumes two categories of providers of psychological services. The two categories are as follows:

A. Professional psychologists. Psychologists have a doctoral degree in psychology from an organized, sequential program in a regionally accredited university or professional school.[6,7,8] Specific definitions of professional psychologists by each of the recognized specialties are provided in the *Specialty Guidelines for the Delivery of Services* (APA, 1981b).

B. Other persons who provide psychological services. Qualifications and supervision for these persons are commensurate with their responsibilities and are further delineated in these policies[9] and in the *Specialty Guidelines for the Delivery of Services.*

Psychological Services

This term refers to one or more of the following:[10]

A. Evaluation, diagnosis,[11] and assessment of the functioning of individuals, groups, and organizations.

B. Interventions, preventive and ameliorative, that facilitate the functioning of individuals, groups, and organizations.[12]

C. Consultation relating to A and B.

D. Program development services in the areas of A, B, and C.[13]

E. Administration and supervision of psychological services.[14]

F. Evaluation of all psychological services.

Psychological Service Unit

This is the functional unit through which psychological services are provided:

A. A psychological service unit is a unit that provides predominantly psychological services and is composed of one or more professional psychologists and support staff.

B. A psychological service unit may operate as a functional or geographic component of a larger governmental, educational, correctional, health, training, industrial, or commercial organizational unit, or as an independent professional service unit.[15]

C. A psychological service unit may take the form of one or more psychologists providing professional services in a multidisciplinary setting.

D. A psychological service unit also may be an individual or group of individuals in a private practice or a psychological consulting firm.

Users

Users include the following:

A. Direct users or recipients of psychological services.

B. Public and private institutions, facilities, or organizations receiving psychological services.

Sanctioners

Sanctioners include the following:

A. Direct users or recipients of psychological services.

B. Public and private institutions, facilities, or organizations receiving psychological services.

C. Any other individual, group, organization, institution, or governing body having legitimate interaction with a psychologist functioning in a professional capacity.

General Guideline 1: Providers

1.1 Each psychological service unit offering psychological services has available at least one professional psychologist and as many more professional psychologists as are necessary to assure the quality of services offered.[16]

ILLUSTRATIVE STATEMENT:[17] The intent of this General Guideline is that one or more providers of psychological services in any psychological service unit meet the levels of training and experience of professional psychologists as specified in the preceding definitions.[18] When a professional psychologist is not available on a full-time basis, the facility retains the services of one or more professional psychologists on a regular part-time basis to supervise the psychological services provided. The psychologist who is so retained has authority and participates sufficiently to enable him or her to assess the needs for services, to review the content of services provided, and to assume professional responsibility and accountability for them.

1.2 Providers of psychological services who do not meet the requirements for professional psychologists are supervised, directed, and evaluated by a professional psychologist to the extent required by the tasks assigned (see Definitions and the *Specialty Guidelines for the Delivery of Services,* APA, 1981b). Tasks assigned to these providers are in keeping with their demonstrated areas of competence. The level and extent of supervision may vary from task to task, as long as the professional psychologist retains a close relationship that is sufficient to meet this General Guideline. In situations in which those providers work in a fair, autonomous fashion, they maintain an appropriate level of consultation and supervisory support from a professional psychologist. (See Ethical Principles 2, 7c, and 8f.)

ILLUSTRATIVE STATEMENT: For example, in health care settings, support personnel may be assigned varying levels of responsibility for providing designated functions within their demonstrated areas of competence. Support personnel are considered to be responsible for their functions and behavior when assisting in the provision of psychological services and are accountable to a professional psychologist. Ultimate professional responsibility and accountability for the services provided require that the supervisor review reports and test protocols and review and discuss intervention plans, strategies, and outcomes. In these settings, the nature and extent of supervision is determined by the professional psychologist to assure the adequacy of psychological services provided.

To facilitate the effectiveness of the psychological service unit, the nature of the supervisory relationship is clearly and explicitly communicated to support personnel, preferably in writing. Such communications describe and delineate the duties of the employees, such as the range and type of services to be provided. The limits of independent action and decision making are defined. Descriptions of responsibilities specify the means by which employees will contact the professional psychologist in the event of emergency or crisis situations.

1.3 Wherever a psychological service unit exists, a professional psychologist is responsible for planning, directing, and reviewing the provision of psychological services.

ILLUSTRATIVE STATEMENT: The psychologist who directs or coordinates the unit maintains an ongoing or periodic review of the adequacy of services and plans in accordance with the results of such evaluation. This psychologist coordinates the activities of the psychological service unit with other professional, administrative, and technical groups, both within and outside the facility. This psychologist, who may be the director, chief, or coordinator of the psychological service unit, has related responsibilities including, but not limited to, recruiting qualified staff, directing training and research activities of the service, maintaining a high level of professional and ethical practice, and assuring that staff members function only within the areas of their competence.

To facilitate the effectiveness of services by increasing the level of staff sensitivity and professional skills, the psychologist who is designated as director participates in the selection of professional and support personnel whose qualifications include sensitivity and consideration for the language, cultural and experiential background, affectional orientation, ethnic identification, age, and gender of the users, and whose professional skills are directly relevant to the needs and characteristics of these users. Additionally, the director ensures that professional and support personnel do not provide services in any manner that is discriminatory or exploitative to users.

In other institutional and organizational settings, psychologists may be administratively responsible to individuals from disciplines other than psychology. In these instances, the psychologist should seek to sensitize the administrator to the need to allow participation of the psychologist in planning, directing, and reviewing the provision of psychological services.

1.4 When functioning within an organizational setting, professional psychologists seek, whenever appropriate and feasible, to bring their education, training, experience, and skills to bear upon the goals of the organization by participating in the planning and development of overall operations. (See Ethical Principle 1d.)

ILLUSTRATIVE STATEMENT: One way psychologists maintain high professional standards is by being active representatives on boards and committees concerned with service delivery and overall operation of their facility. These activities may include but are not limited to active participation as voting and as office-holding members, on the governance staff as well as on executive, planning, and evaluation boards and committees.

1.5 All providers of psychological services attempt to maintain and apply current knowledge of scientific and professional developments that are directly related to the services they render. This includes knowledge relating to special populations (such as ethnic or other minorities) that may compose a part of their practice. (See Ethical Principles 2, 2c, and 2d.)

ILLUSTRATIVE STATEMENT: Methods through which knowledge of scientific and professional developments may be gained include, but are not limited to, continuing education, attendance at workshops, participation in staff development programs, formal and informal on-the-job training, and reading scientific and professional publications. All providers have access to reference material related to the provision of psychological services. All providers are prepared to show evidence periodically that they are staying abreast of and utilizing current knowledge and practices.

1.6 Professional psychologists limit their practice, including supervision, to their demonstrated areas of professional competence. Special proficiency supervision of psychologists may be provided by professionals from other disciplines whose competence in the given area has been demonstrated by previous education, training, and experience. (See Ethical Principles 2 and 2d.)

ILLUSTRATIVE STATEMENT: Psychological services are offered in accordance with the providers' areas of competence as defined by verifiable education, training, and experience. Before offering professional services beyond the range of their experience and usual practice (e.g., providing services to culturally/linguistically diverse populations), psychologists strive to obtain pertinent knowledge through such means as education, training, reading, and appropriate professional consultation.

1.7 Psychologists who change or add a specialty meet the same requirements with respect to subject matter and professional skills that apply to doctoral education, training, and experience in the new specialty.[19]

ILLUSTRATIVE STATEMENT: Retraining psychologists to qualify them for a change in specialty must be under the auspices of a program in a regionally accredited university or professional school that offers the doctoral degree in that specialty. Such education and training are individualized, due credit being given for relevant coursework or requirements that have previously been satisfied. Merely taking an internship or acquiring experience in a practicum setting or in an employment setting is not considered adequate preparation for becoming a clinical, counseling, industrial/organizational, or school psychologist. Fulfillment of such an individualized training program is attested to by official certification by the supervising department or professional school indicating the successful completion of educational preparation in the

particular specialty. Specific requirements for retraining in each of the recognized specialties are detailed in the *Specialty Guidelines for the Delivery of Services* (APA, 1981b).

1.8 Psychologists are encouraged to develop and/or apply and evaluate innovative theories and procedures, to provide appropriate theoretical or empirical support for their innovations, and to disseminate their results to others. (See Ethical Principles 2 and 2c.)

ILLUSTRATIVE STATEMENT: A profession rooted in a science continually explores, studies, conducts, and evaluates applications of theories and procedures with a view toward developing, verifying, and documenting new and improved ways of serving users.

General Guideline 2: Programs

2.1 Composition and organization of a psychological service unit

> **2.1.1** The composition and programs of a psychological service unit strive to be responsive to the needs of the people and settings served.

ILLUSTRATIVE STATEMENT: A psychological service unit is structured to facilitate effective and economical delivery of services. For example, a psychological service unit serving a predominantly low-income or ethnic minority group has a staffing pattern and service program adapted to the linguistic, experiential, attitudinal, and financial characteristics of the user population.

> **2.1.2** A psychological service unit strives to include sufficient numbers of professional psychologists and support personnel to achieve its goals, objectives, and purposes.

ILLUSTRATIVE STATEMENT: The workload, diversity of the psychological services required, and the specific goals and objectives of the setting determine the numbers and qualifications of professional psychologists and support personnel in the psychological service unit. Where shortages in personnel exist, so that psychological services cannot be rendered in a professional manner, the director of the psychological service unit initiates action to modify appropriately the specific goals, objectives, and timetables of the service. If necessary, the director appropriately modifies the scope or workload of the unit to maintain the quality of the services and, at the same time, makes continued efforts to devise alternative systems for delivery of services.

2.2 Policies

> **2.2.1** A written description of roles, objectives, and scope of services is developed by multi-provider psychological service units as well as by psychological service units that are a component of an organization, unless the unit has a specific alternative approach. The written description or alternative ap-

proach is reviewed annually and is available to the staff of the unit and to users and sanctioners upon request.

ILLUSTRATIVE STATEMENT: The psychological service unit reviews its objectives and scope of services annually and makes revisions as necessary to ensure that the psychological services offered are consistent with staff competencies and current psychological knowledge and practice. This statement is discussed with staff, reviewed by the appropriate administrator, and distributed to users and sanctioners upon request and whenever appropriate. Psychologists strive to be aware of management theories and practices that will aid in the delivery of psychological services.

> **2.2.2** Providers of psychological services avoid any action that will violate or diminish the legal and civil rights of users or of others who may be affected by their actions.[20] (See Ethical Principles 3b, 3c, 5, 6, and 9.)

ILLUSTRATIVE STATEMENT: Providers of psychological services are continually sensitive to the issue of confidentiality of information; they strive to be sensitive to the potential impact of their decisions and recommendations, and to other matters pertaining to individual, legal, and civil rights. Providers of psychological services strive to be aware of issues such as self-incrimination in judicial proceedings, involuntary commitment to hospitals, protection of minors, protection of legal incompetents, discriminatory practices in employment selection procedures, recommendations for special education provisions, information relative to adverse personnel actions in the armed services, and adjudication of domestic relations disputes in divorce and custodial proceedings. Providers of psychological services are encouraged to make themselves available to local committees, review boards, and similar advisory groups established to safeguard the human, civil, and legal rights of service users.

> **2.2.3** Providers of psychological services are familiar with and abide by the American Psychological Association's *Ethical Principles of Psychologists* (1981a), *Specialty Guidelines for the Delivery of Services* (1981b), *Standards for Educational and Psychological Testing* (1985), *Ethical Principles in the Conduct of Research with Human Participants* (1982), *Guidelines for Computer-Based Tests and Interpretations* (1986), "Guidelines for Psychologists Conducting Growth Groups" (1973), and other APA policy statements relevant to guidelines for professional services issued by the Association.[21] (See Ethical Principle 3d.)

ILLUSTRATIVE STATEMENT: Psychological service units have available a copy of each of these documents, and providers maintain current knowledge of relevant APA guidelines and principles.

> **2.2.4** Providers of psychological services seek to conform to relevant statutes established by federal, state, and local governments. At times psychologists may seek to challenge legal constraints that they reasonably and honestly believe unduly infringe on the rights of their users or on the right of psychologists to practice their profession; however, any such

challenges should conform to appropriate legal procedures. (See Ethical Principle 3d.)

ILLUSTRATIVE STATEMENT: All providers of psychological services seek to be familiar with and practice in conformity with relevant statutes that relate directly to the practice of psychology. They also endeavor to be informed about governmental agency regulations that have the force of law and that relate to the delivery of psychological services (e.g., evaluation for disability retirement or for special education placements). In addition, all providers seek to be aware that federal agencies such as the Veterans Administration, the Department of Education, and the Department of Health and Human Services have policy statements regarding psychological services. Providers of psychological services attempt to be familiar with other statutes and regulations, including those addressed to the civil and legal rights of users (e.g., those promulgated by the federal Equal Employment Opportunity Commission) that are pertinent to their scope of practice.

> **2.2.5** In recognizing the matrix of personal and societal problems, providers make available, when appropriate, information regarding additional human services, such as specialized psychological services, legal aid societies, social services, employment agencies, health resources, and educational and recreational facilities. (See Ethical Principle 7a.)

ILLUSTRATIVE STATEMENT: Psychologists and support personnel are sensitive to the broader context of human needs. They refer to such resources and are encouraged, when appropriate, to intervene actively on behalf of the users. Providers make appropriate use of other professional, research, technical, and administrative resources whenever these serve the best interests of the users, and they establish and maintain cooperative or collaborative arrangements with such other resources as are required to meet the needs of users.

> **2.2.6** In the best interest of the users, providers of psychological services endeavor to consult and collaborate with professional colleagues in the planning and delivery of services when such consultation is deemed appropriate. (See Ethical Principles 7 and 7a.)

ILLUSTRATIVE STATEMENT: Psychologists recognize the areas of special competence of other psychologists and of other professionals for consultation and referral purposes.

2.3 Procedures

> **2.3.1** Each psychological service unit is guided by a set of procedural guidelines for the delivery of psychological services.

ILLUSTRATIVE STATEMENT: Depending on the nature of the setting, and whenever feasible, providers are prepared to provide a statement of procedural guidelines in oral and/or written form that can be understood by users as well as sanctioners. This statement may describe the current methods, forms, procedures, and techniques being used to achieve the objectives and goals for psychological services.

This statement is communicated to staff and, when appropriate, to users and sanctioners. The psychological service unit provides for the annual review of its procedures for the delivery of psychological services.

2.3.2 Psychologists develop plans for psychological services appropriate to the problems presented by the users.

ILLUSTRATIVE STATEMENT: Ideally, a plan for intervention or consultation is in written form and serves as a basis for accountability. Regardless of the type of setting or users involved, a plan that describes the psychological services indicated and the manner in which they will be provided is developed and agreed upon by the providers and users.[22] A psychologist who provides services as one member of a collaborative effort participates in the development and implementation of the overall service plan and provides for its periodic review.

2.3.3 There is a mutually acceptable understanding between a provider and a user or that user's responsible agent regarding the delivery of service. (See Ethical Principles 6 and 6b.)

ILLUSTRATIVE STATEMENT: A psychologist discusses the plan for the provision of psychological services with the user, noting procedures that will be used and respective responsibilities of provider and user. This interaction is repeated whenever major changes occur in the plan for service. This understanding may be oral or written, but in any event, the psychologist documents the nature of the understanding.[23]

2.3.4 Professional psychologists clarify early on to users and sanctioners the exact fee structure or financial arrangements and payment schedule when providing services for a fee. (See Ethical Principle 6d.)

ILLUSTRATIVE STATEMENT: Psychologists inform users of their payment policies and of their willingness to assist users in obtaining reimbursement. Those who accept reimbursement from a third party are acquainted with the appropriate statutes and regulations, instruct their users on proper procedures for submitting claims, and inform them of limits on confidentiality of claims information, in accordance with pertinent statutes.

2.3.5 Accurate, current, and pertinent records of essential psychological services are maintained.

ILLUSTRATIVE STATEMENT: At a minimum, records kept of psychological services should include identifying data, dates of services, and types of services, and where appropriate, may include a record of significant actions taken.[24] Providers make all reasonable efforts to record essential information concerning psychological services within a reasonable time of their completion.

2.3.6 Each psychological service unit follows an established policy for the retention and disposition of records.[25] (See Ethical Principle 5c.)

ILLUSTRATIVE STATEMENT: Such a policy conforms to government statutes and regulations, or to organizational or institutional regulations, policies, or practices where such are applicable.

2.3.7 Psychologists establish and maintain a system that protects the confidentiality of their users' records. (See Ethical Principles 5, 5a, 5c, and 5d.)[26]

ILLUSTRATIVE STATEMENT: Psychologists establish and maintain the confidentiality of information about the users of services, whether obtained by themselves or by those they supervise. If directed otherwise by statute, by regulations with the force of law, or by court order, psychologists seek a resolution that is both ethically and legally feasible and appropriate; for example, psychologists might request in camera (judge's chambers) hearings when they are required by the court to produce records. All people who are supervised by psychologists, including nonprofessional personnel and students, and who have access to records of psychological services are also expected to maintain this confidentiality of information. Psychologists do not release confidential information, except with the written consent of the user involved, or of his or her legal representative, guardian, or other holder of the privilege on behalf of the user, and only after being assured by whatever means may be required that the user has been assisted in understanding the implications of the release. Even after the consent has been obtained for release, psychologists clearly identify such information as confidential for the recipient of the information.

Users are informed in advance of any limits in the setting for maintaining the confidentiality of psychological information. For instance, psychologists in hospital settings inform their patients that psychological information in a patient's clinical record may be available to other hospital personnel without the patient's written consent. Similar limitations on confidentiality of psychological information may be present in certain school, industrial, business, government, or military settings or in instances where the user has waived confidentiality for purposes of third-party payment. When the user's intention to waive confidentiality is judged by a professional psychologist to be contrary to the user's best interest or to be in conflict with that person's legal or civil rights, it is the responsibility of the psychologist to discuss the implications of releasing the psychological information and to assist the user in limiting disclosure by specifying the nature of the information, the recipients, and the time period during which the release is in effect, recognizing, however, that the ultimate decision concerning release of information is that of the user. Providers of psychological services are sensitive to both the benefits and the possible misuse of information regarding individuals that is stored in computerized data banks. Providers take necessary measures to ensure that such information is used in a socially responsible manner.

Users have the right to information in their agency

records and to be informed as to any regulations that govern the release of such information. However, the records are the property of the psychologist or of the facility in which the psychologist works and are, therefore, under the control of the psychologist or of the facility. Users have the right to examine such psychological records. Preferably such examination should be in the presence of a psychologist who judges how best to explain the material in a meaningful and useful manner.

In school settings, parents have the legal right to examine such psychological records, preferably in the presence of a psychologist. In the event that a family moves to another school system, the parents have the legal right to examine a copy of such records from the former school in the new school setting. In either circumstance, the rationale for allowing parents to examine such records is to assure that parents are not in a disadvantaged position if they choose to challenge a school's decision regarding the child. Disclosure of such psychological information in the records from a former school is conducted under secure conditions; such records have been transmitted to the new school to a psychologist under whose supervision the records may be examined. Psychologists and the institutions in which they work have written policy regarding the storage and access of pupils' records. Parents are informed of the results of a psychological assessment of their child in a form most meaningful and useful to the parents.

Raw psychological data (e.g., test protocols, therapy or interview notes, or questionnaire returns) in which a user is identified are ordinarily released only with the written consent of the user or of the user's legal representative, and are released only to a person recognized by the psychologist as competent to interpret the data. Any use made of psychological reports, records, or data for research or training purposes is consistent with this General Guideline. Additionally, providers of psychological services comply with statutory confidentiality requirements and with those embodied in the *Ethical Principles of Psychologists* (APA, 1981a).

2.3.8 Providers of psychological services do not use privileged information received in the course of their work for competitive advantage or personal gain. (See Ethical Principle 5.)

ILLUSTRATIVE STATEMENT: Providers of psychological services often obtain privileged information through their work with users, or while reviewing the proposals of competing practitioners or agencies. Such information may include but not be limited to users' or user associates' business interests, or the interests of competing colleagues or practitioners. When providers acquire such information and it is protected by applicable law or through agreement, it is held confidential and shall not be used for competitive advantage. Further, information that is potentially harmful to users or their associates, or to professional colleagues, should not be used for personal advantage.

2.4 Environment

2.4.1 Providers of psychological services promote the development of a physical, organizational, and social environment in the service setting that facilitates optimal human functioning.

ILLUSTRATIVE STATEMENT: As providers of services, professional psychologists are concerned with the environment of their service unit, especially as it affects the quality of service, but also as it impinges on human functioning in the larger unit of an organization when the service unit is included in such a larger context. Attention is given to the comfort and, where relevant, to the privacy of providers and users. Federal, state, and local requirements for safety, health, and sanitation are observed. Physical arrangements and organizational policies and procedures are conducive to the human dignity, self-respect, and optimal functioning of users and to the effective delivery of service. The atmosphere in which psychological services are rendered is appropriate to the service and to the users, whether in an office, clinic, school, college, university, industrial setting, or other organizational or institutional setting.

General Guideline 3: Accountability

3.1 The promotion of human welfare is the primary principle guiding the professional activities of all members of the psychological service unit. (See Preamble of Ethical Principles.)

ILLUSTRATIVE STATEMENT: Providers of psychological services are expected to interact with users in a manner that is considerate, effective, economical, and humane; to be mindful of their accountability to the sanctioners of psychological services and to the general public; and to see that appropriate steps are taken to protect the confidentiality of the service relationship.

The psychological service unit does not withhold services to a potential user on the basis of that user's national or ethnic origin, religion, gender, affectional orientation, or age; nor does it provide services in a discriminatory or exploitative fashion. However, this does not preclude psychologists from serving agencies whose publicly declared policy restricts users to membership of a particular religious, ethnic, or other specified group, as long as that policy does not constitute unlawful discrimination.[27] Professional psychologists who find that psychological services are being provided in a manner that is discriminatory or exploitative of users or that is contrary to these General Guidelines or to government statutes or regulations take appropriate corrective actions, which may include the refusal to provide services. When conflicts of interest arise, psychologists are guided in the resolution of differences by the principles set forth in the *Ethical Principles of Psychologists* (APA, 1981a).

Recognition is given to the following considerations in regard to the withholding of services: (1) the professional right of psychologists to limit their practice to a specific category of users with whom they have achieved demonstrated competence (e.g., individuals, families, groups, ethnic minorities, or organizations); (2) the right and responsibility of psychologists to withhold an assessment procedure when not validly applicable; (3) the right and responsibility of psychologists to withhold services in specific instances in which their own limitations or user characteristics might impair the quality of the services; (4) the obligation of psychologists to seek to ameliorate through peer review, consultation, therapeutic procedures, or other procedures those factors that inhibit the provision of services to particular individuals, families, groups, ethnic minorities, or organizations; and (5) the obligation of psychologists who withhold services to assist the users in obtaining services from another source.

3.2 Psychologists pursue their activities as members of the independent, autonomous profession of psychology.

ILLUSTRATIVE STATEMENT: Psychologists, as members of an independent profession, are responsible both to the public and to their peers through established review mechanisms. Psychologists are aware of the implications of their activities for the profession as a whole. They seek to eliminate discriminatory practices instituted for self-serving purposes that are not in the interest of the users (e.g., arbitrary requirements for referral and supervision or sign-off by another profession). They are cognizant of their responsibilities for the development of the profession. They participate where possible in the training and career development of students and other providers, participate as appropriate in the training of support personnel or other professionals, and integrate their contributions within the structure established for delivering psychological services. They facilitate the development of and participate in professional standards review mechanisms and seek to work with other professionals in a cooperative manner for the good of the users and for the benefit of the general public.

Psychologists recognize that it is their responsibility to keep supervisors, administrators, and other agency personnel informed of APA guidelines, principles, standards, policies, and other criteria related to their professional functioning. This information is imparted at times that are appropriate in the individual setting. This may include statements of policy procedures, disclaimers, and so forth. Psychologists are responsible for defining and developing their profession, consistent with the general canons of science and with the public welfare.[28]

3.3 There are periodic, systematic, and effective evaluations of psychological services.

ILLUSTRATIVE STATEMENT: When the psychological service unit is a component of a larger organization, regular assessment of progress in achieving goals is provided in the service delivery plan. Such evaluation could include consideration of the effectiveness of psychological services relative to costs in terms of time, money, and the availability of professional and support personnel. Evaluation of the psychological service delivery system could be con-ducted both internally and, when possible, under independent auspices. Descriptions of therapeutic procedures and other services as well as outcome measures should be as detailed as possible. This evaluation might include an assessment of effectiveness (to determine what the service accomplished), costs, continuity (to ensure that the services are appropriately linked to other human services), availability (to determine appropriate levels and distribution of services and personnel), accessibility (to ensure that the services are barrier-free to users), and adequacy (to determine whether the services meet the identified needs of users). In such evaluations, care is taken to maintain confidentiality of records and privacy of users. It is highly desirable that there be a periodic reexamination of review mechanisms to ensure that these attempts at public safeguards are effective and cost-efficient and do not place unnecessary encumbrances on providers or unnecessary additional expenses on users or sanctioners for services rendered.

3.4 Professional psychologists are accountable for all aspects of the services they provide and are appropriately responsive to those people who are concerned with these services.

ILLUSTRATIVE STATEMENT: Depending upon the settings, accurate and full information is made available to prospective individual or organizational users regarding the qualifications of providers, the nature and extent of services offered, and, where appropriate, financial costs and potential risks. In recognizing their responsibilities to users, sanctioners, third-party purchasers, and other providers, wherever appropriate and consistent with the users' legal rights and privileged communications, professional psychologists make available information about initiation, continuation, modification, termination, and evaluation of psychological services and provide counsel to users regarding their decisions about such issues.

3.5 In the public interest, professional psychologists may wish to provide some services to individuals or organizations for little or no financial return. (See Ethical Principle 6d.)

ILLUSTRATIVE STATEMENT: Professional psychologists are encouraged to contribute a portion of their services and work for which they receive little or no financial return, according to the *Ethical Principles of Psychologists* (APA, 1981a), and to encourage those they supervise to perform services on a similar basis.

FOOTNOTES

[1] The footnotes to these General Guidelines represent an attempt to provide a coherent context of other policy statements of the APA regarding professional practice. The General Guidelines extend these previous policy statements where necessary to reflect current concerns of the public and of the profession.

[2] Note that the title and emphasis of these General Guidelines have been changed from the 1977 version of the *Standards for Providers of Psychological Services*. This has been done to reflect the development and adoption of the *Specialty Guidelines for the Delivery of Services* by the APA in 1980. The profession continues to grow in a variety of areas

in which specific guidelines are not yet necessary. These General Guidelines are intended to support practitioners in these areas.

As stated later in the Preamble, the General Guidelines are aspirational in nature. The change in title is meant to signify that the professional practice of psychology is constantly changing. No collection of principles can adequately direct these changes, and there is no intent to limit future development even though this collection represents the consensus of the profession at this time.

[3] The Ethical Principles from which the General Guidelines have been derived are noted in parentheses at the end of the corresponding General Guidelines.

[4] Early in 1970, acting at the direction of the APA's Council of Representatives, the Board of Professional Affairs (BPA) appointed a task force composed of practicing psychologists with specialized knowledge in at least one of every major class of human service facility and with experience relevant to the setting of standards. The task force's charge was to develop a set of standards for psychological practice. Soon thereafter, partial support for this activity was obtained through a grant from the National Institute of Mental Health (NIMH Grant MH 21696).

The task force promptly established liaison with national groups already active in setting and accrediting standards. It was therefore able to influence two groups of the Joint Commission on Accreditation of Hospitals (JCAH), the Accreditation Council for Facilities for the Mentally Retarded (JCAH, 1971) and the Accreditation Council for Psychiatric Facilities (JCAH, 1972), in their adoption of certain basic principles and in their wording of their standards for psychological services. It also contributed substantially to the "constitutionally required minimum standards for adequate treatment of the mentally ill" ordered by the U.S. District Court in Alabama in the case of *Wyatt v. Stickney* (1972). In concert with other APA committees, the task force also represented the APA in national-level deliberations with government groups and insurance carriers that defined the qualifications necessary for psychologists involved in providing health services.

These interim outcomes involved influence by the APA on actions by groups of nonpsychologists that directly affected the manner in which psychological services were employed, particularly in health and rehabilitation settings. However, these measures did not relieve the Association from exercising its responsibility to speak out directly and authoritatively on what standards for psychological practice should be throughout a broad range of human service settings.

In September 1974, after more than four years of study and broad consultations, the task force completed the APA's first edition of the *Standards for Providers of Psychological Services* (1974). The task of collecting, analyzing, and synthesizing reactions to the original Standards fell to two successive committees. They were charged similarly to review and revise the Standards and to suggest means to implement them, including their acceptance by relevant government and private accreditation groups. The dedicated work of the psychologists who served on both of those committees is gratefully acknowledged. Also recognized with thanks are the several hundred comments received from scores of interested persons representing professional, academic, and scientific psychology; from consumer groups; from administrators of facilities; and from others.

Members of the Task Force on Standards for Service Facilities, which submitted the original Standards in September 1974, were Milton L. Blum, Jacqueline C. Bouhoutsos, Jerry H. Clark, Harold A. Edgerton, Marian D. Hall, Durand F. Jacobs (1972–1974 Chair), Floyd H. Martinez, John E. Muthard, Asher R. Pacht, William D. Pierce, Sue A. Warren, and Alfred M. Wellner (1970–1971 Chair). Staff liaisons from the APA Office of Professional Affairs were John J. McMillan (1970–1971), Gottlieb Simon (1971–1973), and Arthur Centor (1973–1974).

In January 1975, the APA Council of Representatives created the original Committee on Standards for Providers of Psychological Services. The Committee was charged with updating and revising the Standards adopted in September 1974. Members of the Committee were Jacqueline C. Bouhoutsos, Leon Hall, Marian D. Hall, Mary Henle, Durand F. Jacobs (Chair), Abel Ossorio, and Wayne Sorenson. The task force liaison was Jerry H. Clark, and the APA Central Office liaison was Arthur Centor.

In January 1976, the Council modified its charge to the Committee to review the Standards and to recommend revisions needed to reflect the varying needs of only those psychologists engaged in the activities

of clinical psychology, counseling psychology, industrial/organizational psychology, and school psychology. The Committee was reconstituted with one member representing each of the four applied activities, plus one member representing institutional practice and one representing the public interest. Members were Jules Barron (later replaced by Morris Goodman), clinical; Barbara A. Kirk (later replaced by Milton Schwebel), counseling; Virginia Schein (later replaced by Frank Friedlander), industrial/organizational; Durand F. Jacobs (Chair), institutional practice; M. Brewster Smith (later replaced by Pearl Mayo Dansby), public interest; Marian D. Hall (later replaced by Jack I. Bardon and Nadine M. Lambert), school. Arthur Centor and Richard Kilburg were the APA Central Office liaisons. The revised *Standards for Providers of Psychological Services* was approved by the APA Council of Representatives in January 1977 (APA, 1977).

In January 1980, the APA Council of Representatives instructed the Board of Professional Affairs to amend the 1977 Standards in keeping with the principles enunciated by the Council in connection with its action approving the four sets of *Specialty Guidelines for the Delivery of Services* (APA, 1981b). The BPA referred the task of revising the 1977 Standards to the newly created Committee on Professional Standards, composed of Juanita Braddock, public member; Judy E. Hall, experimental/mental retardation; Nadine M. Lambert, school; David Mills (Chair, January–April 1981), clinical/counseling; Milton Schwebel, counseling; Gilfred Tanabe (1980 Chair), clinical; and Murphy Thomas (Chair, May–December 1981), clinical. Subsequent members of the Committee on Professional Standards included William Chestnut, counseling; Lorraine D. Eyde, industrial/ organizational; Morris Goodman (1982–1983 Chair), clinical; John H. Jackson, school; Caroline Miller, public member; William Schofield (1984 Chair), clinical; and Barbara Wand, social. These past members of the Committee on Professional Standards were responsible for completing the 1984 revision of the Standards. Central Office staff assistance was provided by Richard Kilburg and Joy Burke (1980), Sharon Shueman and Pam Juhl (1980–1982), Jutta N. Hagner (1982–1984), and Patricia J. Aletky (1982–1985).

The 1985 draft revision was prepared by Committee on Professional Standards members Susan Robbins Berger, school; LaMaurice Gardner, clinical; Jo-Ida Hansen, counseling; Marlene Muse, public member; Lyle Schoenfeldt, industrial/organizational; William Schofield (1985 Chair), clinical; and Barbara Wand (1985 Vice-Chair), social. Central Office staff assistance was provided by Patricia J. Aletky, Patricia Brown, and Rizalina Mendiola. Between March 1985 and June 1985, a BPA work group on the Standards (composed of John H. Jackson, Chair; Morris Goodman; and William Schofield) reviewed and modified the 1985 draft revision. Central Office staff assistance was provided by Patricia J. Aletky, Patricia Brown, and Rizalina Mendiola.

In November 1985, BPA approved a revised effort that involved Committee on Professional Standards members and work groups representing each of the recognized specialties. The Committee on Professional Standards members participating were Lyle Schoenfeldt (1986 Chair), industrial/organizational; Susan Robbins Berger (1986 Vice-Chair), school; LaMaurice Gardner, clinical; Jo-Ida Hansen, counseling; Richard Kilburg, clinical; and Alan Malyon, clinical. Work group participants, by specialty area and Division, were as follows: Clinical: Robert Weitz (Division 12); Patricia Hannigan and Gerald Koocher (Division 29); Donna Copeland, Marlene Eisen, and Billie S. Strauss (Division 30); Arthur Bodin (Divisions 31, 38, 39, 42, 43); Ronald Kurz (Division 38); and Florence Kaslow (Divisions 41 and 43); Counseling: Ricki Bander, John Corrigan, Thomas Dowd, David Fago, and Milton Schwebel (Division 17); Industrial/Organizational: Hannah R. Hirsh and Manuel London (Division 14); School: Judith Alpert, John H. Jackson, and Ralph D. Wenger (Division 16); and Milton Shore (Division 37). Central Office assistance was provided by Pam Juhl, Sheila Lane Forsyth, Russell Newman, and Mary Lisa Debraggio.

[5] These General Guidelines are designed to be consistent with existing APA policies. One APA policy governing this issue is the 1987 Model Act for State Licensure of Psychologists, prepared by a subcommittee of APA's Committee on Professional Practice and adopted by the APA Council of Representatives in February 1987.

[6] People who met the following criteria on or before the date of adoption of the original Standards on September 4, 1974, shall also be considered professional psychologists: (a) a master's degree in a program

primarily psychological in content from a regionally accredited university or professional school; (b) appropriate education, training, and experience in the area of service offered; (c) a license or certificate in the state in which they practice, conferred by a state board of psychological examiners; or, in the absence of statutory regulation, the endorsement of the state psychological association through voluntary certification; or, for practice in primary and secondary schools, a state department of education certificate as a school psychologist provided that the certificate required at least two graduate years. Wherever the term *psychologist* is used in these General Guidelines, it refers to *professional psychologist.*

Within the specialty of school psychology, those persons who met the following criteria on or before, but not beyond, January 31, 1985, are also recognized as professional school psychologists: (a) a master's or higher degree, requiring at least two years of full-time graduate study in school psychology, from a regionally accredited university or professional school; (b) at least three additional years of training and experience in school psychological services, including a minimum of 1,200 hours in school settings; and (c) a license or certificate conferred by a state board of psychological examiners or a state educational agency for practice in elementary or secondary schools.

[7] Some federal and state legislation uses the term *clinical psychologist* to identify a set of service providers that is not limited to clinical psychologists as defined by the APA in the *Specialty Guidelines for the Delivery of Services by Clinical Psychologists* (APA, 1981b). APA defines the term *clinical psychologist* in health service delivery legislation in a generic sense to include all qualified professional psychologists who provide relevant services. Intraprofessionally, as represented by its *Specialty Guidelines,* APA currently supports specific and meaningful differentiation in the education, training, and practices of the specialties of clinical psychology, counseling psychology, industrial/organizational psychology, and school psychology.

[8] This definition is similar to the recommended statutory language in the "Requirements for Licensure" section of the 1987 APA Model Act for State Licensure of Psychologists (APA, 1987b), a policy statement setting forth model state legislation affecting the practice of psychology and recognizing the doctorate as the minimum educational requirement for entry into professional practice as a psychologist:

Applicants for licensure shall possess a doctoral degree in psychology from an institution of higher education. The degree shall be obtained from a recognized program of graduate study in psychology as defined by the rules and regulations of the Board.

By 1995 applicants for licensure shall have completed a doctoral program in psychology that is accredited by the American Psychological Association (APA). In areas where no accreditation exists, applicants for licensure shall have completed a doctoral program in psychology that meets recognized acceptable professional standards as determined by the Board. When a new specialty of professional psychology is recognized as being within the accreditation scope of the APA, doctoral programs within that specialty will be afforded a transition period of eight years from their first class of students to the time of their accreditation. During that transition period, graduates of such programs may sit for licensure examination whether or not the program has been accredited. The same principle applies as well to new doctoral programs of specialties previously recognized within the scope of APA accreditation.

Applicants trained in institutions outside the United States shall meet requirements established by the Board. (APA, 1987b, p. 698)

In addition to the above educational requirements, the following experience requirements also appear in the 1987 APA Model Act for State Licensure of Psychologists:

For admission to the licensure examination, applicants shall demonstrate that they have completed two years of supervised professional experience, one year of which shall be postdoctoral. The criteria for appropriate supervision shall be in accordance with regulations to be promulgated by the Board. Postdoctoral experience shall be compatible with the knowledge and skills acquired during formal doctoral or postdoctoral education in accordance with professional requirements and relevant to the intended area of practice. Applicants shall be required to show evidence of good character, that is, that they have not been

convicted of a criminal offense that bears directly on the fitness of the individual to be licensed. (APA, 1987b, p. 698)

[9] With regard to the roles, responsibilities, and supervision process for other persons who provide psychological services, a professional psychologist should consider the following issues and suggestions:

(a) A professional psychologist is identified as the ethically responsible agent in all advertising, public announcements, and billings for supervised psychological services.

(b) A supervising psychologist reviews and is responsible for all reports prepared by the assistant.

(c) Professional psychologists set a reasonable limit on the number of assistants who are employed and supervised by a single supervisor.

(d) Professional psychologists must be sufficiently available to ensure adequate evaluation or assessment, intervention planning, direction, and consultation.

(e) Assistants provide services or carry out activities at the direction of the psychologist employer/supervisor who is responsible for those services or activities.

(f) Assistants work in reasonably close physical proximity to the supervising psychologist so as to have available regular and continuing supervision.

[10] As was noted in the opening section of the General Guidelines, functions and activities of psychologists relating to the teaching of psychology, the writing or editing of scholarly or scientific manuscripts, the conduct of scientific research, and the activities of members of other professions do not fall within the purview of the General Guidelines.

[11] For the purposes of these General Guidelines and consistent with the 1987 APA Model Act for State Licensure of Psychologists, the term *diagnosis* may include the diagnosis of mental, emotional, nervous, or behavioral disorders or conditions of individuals and groups by professionals trained to do so, such as clinical, counseling, school, rehabilitation, and health psychologists (see Footnote 13).

[12] Consistent with the 1987 APA Model Act for State Licensure of Psychologists, such interventions include, but are not limited to, psychotherapy and counseling (see Footnote 13), and other interventions may include vocational development, cognitive rehabilitation, process consultation, psychological skills training, techniques of health psychology, selection and placement of personnel, and organizational development.

Specific definitions of interventions by each of the recognized specialties are provided in the *Specialty Guidelines for the Delivery of Services* (APA, 1981b).

[13] These definitions should be compared to the 1987 APA Model Act for State Licensure of Psychologists (APA, 1987b, p. 697), which includes definitions of *psychologist* and *practice of psychology* as follows:

Psychologist: A person represents himself or herself to be a psychologist if that person uses any title or description of services incorporating the words *psychology, psychological,* or *psychologist,* or if he or she possesses expert qualification in any area of psychology or if that person offers to the public or renders to individuals or to groups of individuals services defined as the practice of psychology in this Act.

Practice of Psychology is defined as the observation, description, evaluation, interpretation, and modification of human behavior by the application of psychological principles, methods, and procedures, for the purpose of preventing or eliminating symptomatic, maladaptive, or undesired behavior and of enhancing interpersonal relationships, work and life adjustment, personal effectiveness, behavioral health, and mental health. The practice of psychology includes, but is not limited to, psychological testing and the evaluation or assessment of personal characteristics such as intelligence, personality, abilities, interests, aptitudes, and neuropsychological functioning; counseling, psychoanalysis, psychotherapy, hypnosis, biofeedback, and behavior analysis and therapy; diagnosis and treatment of mental and emotional disorder or disability, alcoholism and substance abuse, disorders of habit or conduct, as well as of the psychological aspects of physical illness, accident, injury or disability; and psychoeducational evaluation, therapy, remediation and consultation. Psychological services may be rendered to individuals, families, groups, and the public. The practice of psychology shall be construed within the meaning of this definition without regard to whether payment is received for services rendered. (See Section J for exemptions.)

[14] As indicated in the *Ethical Principles of Psychologists* (APA, 1981a), especially Principle 1 (Responsibility) and Principle 3 (Moral and Legal Guidelines), when functioning as an administrator or manager in an organization or unit that is not a psychological services unit, psychologists apply their knowledge, skills, and abilities in furtherance of the objectives of that organization while remaining aware of the requirements of their profession's ethics and guidelines.

[15] The relation of a psychological service unit to a larger facility or institution is also addressed indirectly in the APA *Guidelines for Conditions of Employment of Psychologists* (APA, 1987a), which emphasizes the roles, responsibilities, and prerogatives of the psychologist when he or she is employed by or provides services for another agency, institution, or business.

[16] At the time of the adoption of these General Guidelines, there were four state statutes that did not require a doctoral degree for unsupervised provision of psychological services. Therefore, the goal of having the highest level of training for psychological practitioners is not, at the current time, fully achievable. (See Footnote 18 and Guideline 2.2.4.)

In addition to the small minority of states that recognize nondoctoral psychologists as independent providers of psychological services, almost all states recognize nondoctoral school psychologists who meet the requisite education, training, and experience prescribed by state departments of education as independent practitioners within local, regional, and state school systems.

[17] These illustrative statements have been selected to clarify how these General Guidelines might be implemented or apply in particular situations, and/or the importance of particular implications of the General Guidelines. The APA recognizes that there may be a variety of implications of and methods for implementing a specific General Guideline depending on the situation in a given setting.

[18] This General Guideline reflects changes in the 1987 revision of the Model Act for State Licensure of Psychologists adopted by the APA Council of Representatives in February 1987 (APA, 1987b). Guideline 1.1 expresses the goal of the APA that psychological service units in all organizations have at least one professional psychologist available to assure the quality of services offered.

[19] This General Guideline follows closely the statement regarding "Policy on Training for Psychologists Wishing to Change Their Specialty" adopted by the APA Council of Representatives in January 1976 and revised by the Council in January 1982. Included therein is the implementing provision that "this policy statement shall be incorporated in the guidelines of the Committee on Accreditation so that appropriate sanctions can be brought to bear on university and internship training programs which violate [it]" (Conger, 1976, p. 424).

[20] See also *Ethical Principles in the Conduct of Research with Human Participants* (APA, 1982) and *Principles Concerning the Counseling and Therapy of Women* (APA, 1978).

[21] These documents are available from the American Psychological Association, 1200 Seventeenth Street, NW, Washington, DC 20036.

[22] Another example of a specific application of this principle is found in Guideline 2 in "Guidelines for Psychologists Conducting Growth Groups" (APA, 1973):

2. The following information should be made available in writing to all prospective participants:
(a) An explicit statement of the purpose of the group;
(b) Types of techniques that may be employed;
(c) The education, training, and experience of the leader or leaders;
(d) The fee and any additional expense that may be incurred;
(e) A statement as to whether or not a follow-up service is included in the fee;
(f) Goals of the group experience and techniques to be used;
(g) Amounts and kinds of responsibility to be assumed by the leader and by the participants. For example, (i) the degree to which a participant is free not to follow suggestions and prescriptions of the group leader and other group members; (ii) any restrictions on a participant's freedom to leave the group at any time; and
(h) Issues of confidentiality. (p. 933)

[23] When the user of the service is a child, it is desirable that both parent (or legal guardian) and child, to the extent possible, be involved in this understanding.

[24] Health care providers hold widely varying views about the wisdom of written records relating to the content of the psychotherapeutic relationship.

[25] In the absence of such, the policy is as follows:

1. Retain the full record intact for a specified period of time, if not in perpetuity. Some records need to be retained during the lifetime of an individual, either by the provider or by some other agency through arrangement by the provider. These records are necessary in special circumstances, such as in the case of handicapped individuals who need to comply with requests from the Social Security Administration for information on documented disabilities during their childhood years.
2. If a full record is not retained following completion of service delivery, a summary of the record is maintained for a specified period of time.
3. A record or the summary of a record may be disposed of only after a specified period of time following completion of planned services or the date of last contact, whichever comes later. (See the relevant sections of the *Specialty Guidelines for the Delivery of Services*, APA, 1981b, for specific retention and disposition guidelines. These are Guidelines 2.3.4 for clinical, counseling, and school psychologists.)

In the event of the death of or the incapacity of a psychologist in independent practice, special procedures are necessary to assure the continuity of active service to the user and the safeguarding of records in accordance with this Guideline. For this reason, with the approval of the affected user, it is appropriate for another psychologist, acting under the auspices of the Professional Standards Review Committee (PSRC) or the Ethics Committee of the state, where such a committee is available, to review the record with that user and recommend a course of action for continuing professional service, if needed. Depending on local circumstances, appropriate arrangements for record retention and disposal are also recommended by the reviewing psychologist. This General Guideline has been developed to address a variety of circumstances that may arise, often years after a set of psychological services has been completed. Increasingly, records are being utilized in forensic matters, for peer review, for investigation of ethical complaints, and in response to requests from users, other professionals, or other legitimate parties requiring accurate information about the exact dates, nature, course, and outcome of a set of psychological services.

[26] Support for the principle of privileged communication is found in the Model Act for State Licensure of Psychologists (APA, 1987b):

In judicial proceedings, whether civil, criminal, or juvenile; in legislative and administrative proceedings; and in proceedings preliminary and ancillary thereto, a patient or client, or his or her guardian or personal representative, may refuse to disclose or prevent the disclosure of confidential information, including information contained in administrative records, communicated to a psychologist licensed or otherwise authorized to practice psychology under the laws of this jurisdiction, or to persons reasonably believed by the patient or client to be so licensed, and their agents, for the purpose of diagnosis, evaluation, or treatment of any mental or emotional condition or disorder. In the absence of evidence to the contrary, the psychologist is presumed authorized to claim the privilege on the patient's or client's behalf.

This privilege may not be claimed by the patient or client, or on his or her behalf by authorized persons, in the following circumstances:
1. where abuse or harmful neglect of children, the elderly, or disabled or incompetent individuals is known or reasonably suspected;
2. where the validity of a will of a former patient or client is contested;
3. where such information is necessary for the psychologist to defend against a malpractice action brought by the patient or client;
4. where an immediate threat of physical violence against a readily identifiable victim is disclosed to the psychologist;
5. in the context of civil commitment proceedings, where an immediate threat of self-inflicted damage is disclosed to the psychologist;

6. where the patient or client, by alleging mental or emotional damages in litigation, puts his or her mental state at issue;

7. where the patient or client is examined pursuant to court order; or

8. in the context of investigations and hearings brought by the patient or client and conducted by the Board, where violations of this Act are at issue. (pp. 702–703)

Specific provisions for the maintenance of confidentiality are spelled out in each of the *Specialty Guidelines for the Delivery of Services* (APA, 1981b).

[27] Examples of such agencies are clinics for battered women, clinics for Spanish-speaking users, and clinics for members of a specific religious faith or church.

[28] The APA is prepared to provide appropriate assistance to responsible members who are subjected to unreasonable limitations upon their opportunities to function as practitioners, administrators, or consultants. The APA is prepared to cooperate with any responsible professional psychological organization in opposing any unreasonable limitations on the professional functions of the members of that organization. This insistence upon professional autonomy has been upheld over the years by the affirmative actions of the courts and of other public and private bodies in support of the right of psychologists to pursue those functions that they are trained and qualified to perform. Psychologists recognize that other professions and other groups will, from time to time, seek to define the roles and responsibilities of psychologists. The APA opposes such attempts.

REFERENCES

American Psychological Association. (1973). Guidelines for psychologists conducting growth groups. *American Psychologist, 28,* 933.

American Psychological Association. (1974). *Standards for providers of psychological services.* Washington, DC: Author.

American Psychological Association. (1977). Standards for providers of psychological services. *American Psychologist, 32,* 495–505.

American Psychological Association. (1978). Principles concerning the counseling and therapy of women. *Counseling Psychologist, 7*(4), 74–76.

American Psychological Association. (1981a). Ethical principles of psychologists. *American Psychologist, 36,* 633–638.

American Psychological Association. (1981b). Specialty guidelines for the delivery of services by clinical (counseling, industrial/organizational, and school) psychologists. *American Psychologist, 36,* 639–681.

American Psychological Association. (1982). *Ethical principles in the conduct of research with human participants.* Washington, DC: Author.

American Psychological Association. (1986). *Guidelines for computer-based tests and interpretations.* Washington, DC: Author.

American Psychological Association. (1987a). Guidelines for conditions of employment of psychologists. *American Psychologist, 42,* 724–729.

American Psychological Association. (1987b). Model act for state licensure of psychologists. *American Psychologist, 42,* 696–703.

Conger, J. J. (1976). Proceedings of the American Psychological Association, Incorporated, for the year 1975: Minutes of the annual meeting of the Council of Representatives. *American Psychologist, 31,* 406–434.

Joint Commission on Accreditation of Hospitals, Accreditation Council for Psychiatric Facilities. (1972). *Accreditation manual for psychiatric facilities: 1972.* Chicago, IL: Author.

Joint Commission on Accreditation of Hospitals, Accreditation Council for Facilities for the Mentally Retarded. (1971). *Standards for residential facilities for the mentally retarded.* Chicago, IL: Author.

Standards for educational and psychological testing. (1985). Washington, DC: American Psychological Association.

Wyatt v. Stickney, 325 F. Supp. (M.D. Ala. 1971), 334 F. Supp. 1341 (M.D. Ala.), 344 F. Supp. 373 (M.D. Ala. 1972), *aff'd sub nom.* Wyatt v. Aderholt, 503 F.2d 1305 (5th Cir. 1974).

APPENDIX C: The American Psychological Association's (1981) Specialty Guidelines for the Delivery of Services by School Psychologists

The Specialty Guidelines that follow are based on the generic *Standards for Providers of Psychological Services* originally adopted by the American Psychological Association (APA) in September 1974 and revised in January 1977 (APA, 1974b, 1977b). Together with the generic *Standards*, these Specialty Guidelines state the official policy of the Association regarding delivery of services by school psychologists. Admission to the practice of psychology is regulated by state statute. It is the position of the Association that licensing be based on generic, and not on specialty, qualifications. Specialty guidelines serve the additional purpose of providing potential users and other interested groups with essential information about particular services available from the several specialties in professional psychology.

Professional psychology specialties have evolved from generic practice in psychology and are supported by university training programs. There are now at least four recognized professional specialties—clinical, counseling, school, and industrial/organizational psychology.

The knowledge base in each of these specialty areas has increased, refining the state of the art to the point that a set of uniform specialty guidelines is now possible and desirable. The present Guidelines are intended to educate the public, the profession, and other interested parties regarding specialty professional practices. They are also intended to facilitate the continued systematic development of the profession.

The content of each Specialty Guideline reflects a consensus of university faculty and public and private practitioners regarding the knowledge base, services provided, problems addressed, and clients served.

Traditionally, all learned disciplines have treated the designation of specialty practice as a reflection of preparation in greater depth in a particular subject matter, together with a voluntary limiting of focus to a more restricted area of practice by the professional. Lack of specialty designation does not preclude general providers of psychological services from using the methods or dealing with the populations of any specialty, except insofar as psychologists voluntarily refrain from providing services they are not trained to render. It is the intent of these Guidelines, however, that after the grandparenting period, psychologists not put themselves forward as *specialists* in a given area of practice unless they meet the qualifications noted in the Guidelines (see Definitions). Therefore, these Guidelines are meant to apply only to those psychologists who wish to be designated as *school psychologists*. They do not apply to other psychologists.

These Guidelines represent the profession's best judgment of the conditions, credentials, and experience that contribute to competent professional practice. The APA strongly encourages, and plans to participate in, efforts to identify professional practitioner behaviors and job functions and to validate the relation between these and desired client outcomes. Thus, future revisions of these Guidelines will increasingly reflect the results of such efforts.

These Guidelines follow the format and, wherever applicable, the wording of the generic *Standards*.[1] (Note: Footnotes appear at the end of the Specialty Guidelines. See pp. 679–681.) The intent of these Guidelines is to improve the quality, effectiveness, and accessibility of psychological services. They are meant to provide guidance to providers, users and sanctioners regarding the best judgment of the profession on these matters. Although the Specialty Guidelines have been derived from and are consistent with the generic *Standards*, they may be used as a separate document. *Standards for Providers of Psychological Services* (APA, 1977b), however, shall remain the basic policy statement and shall take precedence where there are questions of interpretation.

Professional psychology in general and school psychology in particular have had a long and difficult history of attempts to establish criteria for determining guidelines for the delivery of services. In school psychology, state departments of education have traditionally had a strong influence on the content of programs required for certification and on minimum competency levels for practice, leading to wide variations in requirements among the many states. These national Guidelines will reduce confusion, clarify important dimensions of specialty practice, and provide a common basis for peer review of school psychologists' performance.

The Committee on Professional Standards established by the APA in January 1980 is charged with keeping the generic *Standards* and the Specialty Guidelines respon-

---

These Specialty Guidelines were prepared through the cooperative efforts of the APA Committee on Standards for Providers of Psychological Services (COSPOPS) and the APA Professional Affairs Committee of the Division of School Psychology (Division 16). Jack I. Bardon and Nadine M. Lambert served as the school psychology representatives of COSPOPS, and Arthur Centor and Richard Kilburg were the Central Office liaisons to the committee. Durand F. Jacobs served as chair of COSPOPS, and Walter B. Pryzwansky chaired the Division 16 committee. Drafts of the school psychology Guidelines were reviewed and commented on by members of the Executive Committee of Division 16, representatives of the National Association of School Psychologists, state departments of education, consultants in school psychology, and many professional school psychologists in training programs and in practice in the schools.

Source: Specialty guidelines for the delivery of services by school psychologists. *American Psychologist, 36*(6), 33–44 (or 670–681). Copyright 1981 by the American Psychological Association. Reprinted by permission.

sive to the needs of the public and the profession. It is also charged with continually reviewing, modifying, and extending them progressively as the profession and the science of psychology develop new knowledge, improved methods, and additional modes of psychological services.

The Specialty Guidelines for the Delivery of Services by School Psychologists have been established by the APA as a means of self-regulation to protect the public interest. They guide the specialty practice of school psychology by specifying important areas of quality assurance and performance that contribute to the goal of facilitating more effective human functioning.

Principles and Implications of the Specialty Guidelines

These Specialty Guidelines have emerged from and reaffirm the same basic principles that guided the development of the generic *Standards for Providers of Psychological Services* (APA, 1977b):

1. These Guidelines recognize that admission to the practice of school psychology is regulated by state statute.

2. It is the intention of the APA that the generic *Standards* provide appropriate guidelines for statutory licensing of psychologists. In addition, although it is the position of the APA that licensing be generic and not in specialty areas, these Specialty Guidelines in school psychology should provide an authoritative reference for use in credentialing specialty providers of school psychological services by such groups as divisions of the APA and state associations and by boards and agencies that find such criteria useful for quality assurance.

3. A uniform set of Specialty Guidelines governs school psychological service functions offered by school psychologists, regardless of setting or source of remuneration. All school psychologists in professional practice recognize and are responsive to a uniform set of Specialty Guidelines, just as they are guided by a common code of ethics.

4. School psychology Guidelines establish clearly articulated levels of training and experience that are consistent with, and appropriate to, the functions performed. School psychological services provided by persons who do not meet the APA qualifications for a professional school psychologist (see Definitions) are to be supervised by a professional school psychologist. Final responsibility and accountability for services provided rest with professional school psychologists.

5. A uniform set of Specialty Guidelines governs the quality of services to all users of school psychological services in both the private and the public sectors. Those receiving school psychological services are protected by the same kinds of safeguards, irrespective of sector; these include constitutional guarantees, statutory regulation, peer review, consultation, record review, and staff supervision.

6. These Guidelines, while assuring the user of the school psychologist's accountability for the nature and quality of services specified in this document, do not preclude the school psychologist from using new methods or developing innovative procedures for the delivery of school psychological services.

These Specialty Guidelines for school psychology have broad implications both for users of school psychological services and for providers of such services:

1. Guidelines for school psychological services provide a foundation for mutual understanding between provider and user and facilitate more effective evaluation of services provided and outcomes achieved.

2. Guidelines for school psychological services are essential for uniformity of regulation by state departments of education and other regulatory or legislative agencies concerned with the provision of school psychological services. In addition, they provide the basis for state approval of training programs and for the development of accreditation procedures for schools and other facilities providing school psychological services.

3. Guidelines give specific content to the profession's concept of ethical practice as it applies to the functions of school psychologists.

4. Guidelines for school psychological services have significant impact on tomorrow's education and training models for both professional and support personnel in school psychology.

5. Guidelines for the provision of school psychological services influence the determination of acceptable structure, budgeting, and staffing patterns in schools and other facilities using these services.

6. Guidelines for school psychological services require continual review and revision.

The Specialty Guidelines presented here are intended to improve the quality and the delivery of school psychological services by specifying criteria for key aspects of the service setting. Some school settings may require additional and/or more stringent criteria for specific areas of service delivery.

Systematically applied, these Guidelines serve to establish a more effective and consistent basis for evaluating the performance of individual service providers as well as to guide the organization of school psychological service units.

Definitions

Providers of school psychological services refers to two categories of persons who provide school psychological services:

A. Professional school psychologists.[2,3] Professional school psychologists have a doctoral degree from a regionally accredited university or professional school providing an organized, sequential school psychology program in a department of psychology in a university or college, in an appropriate department of a school of education or other similar administrative organization, or in a unit of a professional school. School psychology programs that are accredited by the American Psychological Association are recognized as meeting the definition of a school psychology program. School psychology programs that are not accredited by the American Psychological Association meet the definition of a school psychology program if they satisfy the following criteria:

1. The program is primarily psychological in nature and stands as a recognizable, coherent organizational entity within the institution.

2. The program provides an integrated, organized sequence of study.

3. The program has an identifiable body of students who are matriculated in that program for a degree.

4. There is a clear authority with primary responsibility for the core and specialty areas, whether or not the program cuts across administrative lines.

5. There is an identifiable psychology faculty, and a psychologist is responsible for the program.

Patterns of education and training in school psychology[4] are consistent with the functions to be performed and the services to be provided, in accordance with the ages, populations, and problems found in the various schools and other settings in which school psychologists are employed. The program of study includes a core of academic experience, both didactic and experiential, in basic areas of psychology, includes education related to the practice of the specialty, and provides training in assessment, intervention, consultation, research, program development, and supervision, with special emphasis on school-related problems or school settings.[5]

Professional school psychologists who wish to represent themselves as proficient in specific applications of school psychology that are not already part of their training are required to have further academic training and supervised experience in those areas of practice.

B. All other persons who offer school psychological services under the supervision of a school psychologist. Although there may be variations in the titles and job descriptions of such persons, they are not called school psychologists. Their functions may be indicated by use of the adjective *psychological* preceding the noun.

1. A *specialist in school psychology* has successfully completed at least 2 years of graduate education in school psychology and a training program that includes at least 1,000 hours of experience supervised by a professional school psychologist, of which at least 500 hours must be in school settings. A specialist in school psychology provides psychological services under the supervision of a professional school psychologist.[6]

2. Titles for others who provide school psychological services under the supervision of a professional school psychologist may include *school psychological examiner, school psychological technician, school psychological assistant, school psychometrist,* or *school psychometric assistant.*

School psychological services refers to one or more of the following services offered to clients involved in educational settings, from preschool through higher education, for the protection and promotion of mental health and the facilitation of learning:[7]

A. Psychological and psychoeducational evaluation and assessment of the school functioning of children and young persons. Procedures include screening, psychological and educational tests (particularly individual psychological tests of intellectual functioning, cognitive development, affective behavior, and neuropsychological status), interviews, observation, and behavioral evaluations, with explicit regard for the context and setting in which the professional judgments based on assessment, diagnosis, and evaluation will be used.

B. Interventions to facilitate the functioning of individuals or groups, with concern for how schooling influences and is influenced by their cognitive, conative, affective, and social development. Such interventions may include, but are not limited to, recommending, planning, and evaluating special education services; psychoeducational therapy; counseling; affective educational programs; and training programs to improve coping skills.[8]

C. Interventions to facilitate the educational services and child care functions of school personnel, parents, and community agencies. Such interventions may include, but are not limited to, in-service school personnel education programs, parent education programs, and parent counseling.

D. Consultation and collaboration with school personnel and/or parents concerning specific school-related problems of students and the professional problems of staff. Such services may include, but are not limited to, assistance with the planning of educational programs from a psychological perspective; consultation with teachers and other school personnel to enhance their understanding of the needs of particular pupils; modification of classroom instructional programs to facilitate children's learning; promotion of a positive climate for learning and teaching; assistance to parents to enable them to contribute to their children's development and school adjustment; and other staff development activities.

E. Program development services to individual schools, to school administrative systems, and to community agencies in such areas as needs assessment and evaluation of regular and special education programs; liaison with community, state, and federal agencies concerning the mental health and educational needs of children; coordination, administration, and planning of specialized educational programs; the generation, collection, organization, and dissemination of information from psychological research and theory to educate staff and parents.

F. Supervision of school psychological services (see Guideline 1.2, Interpretation).

A *school psychological service unit* is the functional unit through which school psychological services are provided; any such unit has at least one professional school psychologist associated with it:

A. Such a unit provides school psychological services to individuals, a school system, a district, a community agency, or a corporation, or to a consortium of school systems, districts, community agencies, or corporations that contract together to employ providers of school psychological services. A school psychological service unit is composed of one or more professional school psychologists and, in most instances, supporting psychological services staff.

B. A school psychological service unit may operate as an independent professional service to schools or as a functional component of an administrative organizational unit, such as a state department of education, a public or private school system, or a community mental health agency.

C. One or more professional school psychologists providing school psychological services in an interdisciplinary or a multidisciplinary setting constitute a school psychological service unit.

D. A school psychological service unit may also be one or more professional psychologists offering services in private practice, in a school psychological consulting firm, or in a college- or university-based facility or program that contracts to offer school psychological services to individuals, groups, school systems, districts, or corporations.

Users of school psychological services include:

A. Direct users or recipients of school psychological services, such as pupils, instructional and administrative school staff members, and parents.

B. Public and private institutions, facilities, or organizations receiving school psychological services, such as boards of education of public or private schools, mental health facilities, and other community agencies and educational institutions for handicapped or exceptional children.

C. Third-party purchasers—those who pay for the delivery of services but who are not the recipients of services.

D. Sanctioners—such as those who have a legitimate concern with the accessibility, timeliness, efficacy, and standards of quality attending the provision of school psychological services. Sanctioners may include members of the user's family, the court, the probation officer, the school administrator, the employer, the facility director, and so on. Sanctioners may also include various governmental, peer review, and accreditation bodies concerned with the assurance of quality.

Guideline 1
PROVIDERS

1.1 *Each school psychological service unit offering school psychological services has available at least one professional school psychologist and as many additional professional school psychologists and support personnel as are necessary to assure the adequacy and quality of services offered.*

INTERPRETATION: The intent of this Guideline is that one or more providers of psychological services in any school psychological service unit meet the levels of training and experience of the professional school psychologist specified in the preceding definitions.

When a professional school psychologist is not available on a full-time basis to provide school psychological services, the school district obtains the services of a professional school psychologist on a regular part-time basis. Yearly contracts are desirable to ensure continuity of services during a school year. The school psychologist so retained directs the psychological services, supervises the psychological services provided by support personnel, and participates sufficiently to be able to assess the need for services, review the content of services provided, and assume professional responsibility and accountability for them. A professional school psychologist supervises no more than the equivalent of 15 full-time specialists in school psychology and/or other school psychological personnel.

Districts that do not have easy access to professional school psychologists because of geographic considerations, or because professional school psychologists do not live or work in the area employ at least one full-time specialist in school psychology and as many more support personnel as are necessary to assure the adequacy and quality of services. The following strategies may be considered to acquire the necessary supervisory services from a professional school psychologist:

A. Employment by a county, region, consortium of schools, or state department of education of full-time supervisory personnel in school psychology who meet appropriate levels of training and experience, as specified in the definitions, to visit school districts regularly for supervision of psychological services staff.

B. Employment of professional school psychologists who engage in independent practice for the purpose of providing supervision to school district psychological services staff.

C. Arrangements with nearby school districts that employ professional school psychologists for part-time employment of such personnel on a contract basis specifically for the purpose of supervision as described in Guideline 1.

The school psychologist directing the school psychological service unit, whether on a full- or part-time basis, is responsible for determining and justifying appropriate ratios of school psychologists to users, to specialists in school psychology, and to support personnel, in order to ensure proper scope, accessibility, and quality of services provided in that setting. The school psychologist reports to the appropriate school district representatives any findings regarding the need to modify psychological services or staffing patterns to assure the adequacy and quality of services offered.

1.2 *Providers of school psychological services who do not meet the requirements for the professional school* *psychologist are supervised directly by a professional school psychologist who assumes professional responsibility and accountability for the services provided. The level and extent of supervision may vary from task to task so long as the supervising psychologist retains a sufficiently close supervisory relationship to meet this Guideline. Special proficiency training or supervision may be provided by a professional psychologist of another specialty or by a professional from another discipline whose competency in the given area has been demonstrated.*[9]

INTERPRETATION Professional responsibility and accountability for the services provided require that the supervisor review reports and test protocols; review and discuss intervention strategies, plans, and outcomes; maintain a comprehensive view of the school's procedures and special concerns; and have sufficient opportunity to discuss discrepancies among the views of the supervisor, the supervised, and other school personnel on any problem or issue. In order to meet this Guideline, an appropriate number of hours per week are devoted to direct face-to-face supervision of each full-time school psychological service staff member. In no event is this supervision less than one hour per week for each staff member. The more comprehensive the psychological services are, the more supervision is needed. A plan or formula for relating increasing amounts of supervisory time to the complexity of professional responsibilities is to be developed. The amount and nature of supervision is specified in writing to all parties concerned.

1.3 *Wherever a school psychological service unit exists, a professional school psychologist is responsible for planning, directing, and reviewing the provision of school psychological services.*

INTERPRETATION: A school psychologist coordinates the activities of the school psychological service unit with other professionals, administrators, and community groups, both within and outside the school. This school psychologist, who may be the director, coordinator, or supervisor of the school psychological service unit, has related responsibilities including, but not limited to, recruiting qualified staff, directing training and research activities of the service, maintaining a high level of professional and ethical practice, and ensuring that staff members function only within the areas of their competency.

To facilitate the effectiveness of services by raising the level of staff sensitivity and professional skills, the psychologist designated as director is responsible for participating in the selection of staff and support personnel whose qualifications are directly relevant to the needs and characteristics of the users served.

In the event that a professional school psychologist is employed by the school psychological service unit on a basis that affords him or her insufficient time to carry out full responsibility for coordinating or directing the unit, a specialist in school psychology is designated as

director or coordinator of the school psychological services and is supervised by a professional school psychologist employed on a part-time basis, for a minimum of 2 hours per week.

1.4 *When functioning as part of an organizational setting, professional school psychologists bring their backgrounds and skills to bear on the goals of the organization, whenever appropriate, by participating in the planning and development of overall services.*

INTERPRETATION: Professional school psychologists participate in the maintenance of high professional standards by serving as representatives on, or consultants to, committees and boards concerned with service delivery, especially when such committees deal with special education, pupil personnel services, mental health aspects of schooling, or other services that use or involve school psychological knowledge and skills.

As appropriate to the setting, school psychologists' activities may include active participation, as voting and as office-holding members, on the facility's executive, planning, and evaluation boards and committees.

1.5 *School psychologists maintain current knowledge of scientific and professional developments to preserve and enhance their professional competence.*

INTERPRETATION: Methods through which knowledge of scientific and professional developments may be gained include, but are not limited to, (a) the reading or preparation of scientific and professional publications and other materials, (b) attendance at workshops and presentations at meetings and conventions, (c) participation in on-the-job staff development programs, and (d) other forms of continuing education. The school psychologist and staff have available reference material and journals related to the provision of school psychological services. School psychologists are prepared to show evidence periodically that they are staying abreast of current knowledge in the field of school psychology and are also keeping their certification and licensing credentials up-to-date.

1.6 *School psychologists limit their practice to their demonstrated areas of professional competence.*

INTERPRETATION: School psychological services are offered in accordance with the providers' areas of competence as defined by verifiable training and experience. When extending services beyond the range of their usual practice, school psychologists obtain pertinent training or appropriate professional supervision. Such training or supervision is consistent with the extension of functions performed and services provided. An extension of services may involve a change in the theoretical orientation of the practitioner, in the techniques used, in the client age group (e.g., children, adolescents, or parents), or in the kinds of problems addressed (e.g., mental retardation, neurological impairment, learning disabilities, family relationships).

1.7 *Psychologists who wish to qualify as school psychologists meet the same requirements with respect to subject matter and professional skills that apply to doctoral training in school psychology.*[10]

INTERPRETATION: Education of psychologists to qualify them for specialty practice in school psychology is under the auspices of a department in a regionally accredited university or of a professional school that offers the doctoral degree in school psychology, through campus- and/or field-based arrangements. Such education is individualized, with due credit being given for relevant course work and other requirements that have previously been satisfied. In addition to the doctoral-level education specified above, appropriate doctoral-level training is required. An internship or experience in a school setting is not adequate preparation for becoming a school psychologist when prior education has not been in that area. Fulfillment of such an individualized training program is attested to by the awarding of a certificate by the supervising department or professional school that indicates the successful completion of preparation in school psychology.

1.8 *Professional school psychologists are encouraged to develop innovative theories and procedures and to provide appropriate theoretical and/or empirical support for their innovations.*

INTERPRETATION: A specialty of a profession rooted in science intends continually to explore, study, and conduct research with a view to developing and verifying new and improved methods of serving the school population in ways that can be documented.

Guideline 2
PROGRAMS

2.1 *Composition and organization of a school psychological service unit:*

2.1.1 *The composition and programs of a school psychological service unit are responsive to the needs of the school population that is served.*

INTERPRETATION: A school psychological service unit is structured so as to facilitate effective and economical delivery of services. For example, a school psychological service unit serving predominantly low-income, ethnic, or racial minority children has a staffing pattern and service programs that are adapted to the linguistic, experiential, and attitudinal characteristics of the users. Appropriate types of assessment materials and norm reference groups are utilized in the practice of school psychology.

2.1.2 *A description of the organization of the school psychological service unit and its lines of responsibility and accountability for the delivery of school psychological services is available in written form to instructional and administrative staff of the unit and to parents, students, and members of the community.*

INTERPRETATION: The description includes lines of responsibility, supervisory relationships, and the level and extent of accountability for each person who provides school psychological services.

2.1.3 *A school psychological service unit includes sufficient numbers of professional and support personnel to achieve its goals, objectives, and purposes.*

INTERPRETATION: A school psychological service unit includes one or more professional school psychologists, specialists in school psychology, and other psychological services support personnel. When a professional school psychologist is not available to provide services on a full- or part-time basis, the school psychological services are conducted by a specialist in school psychology, supervised by a professional school psychologist (see Guideline 1.2).

The work load and diversity of school psychological services required and the specific goals and objectives of the setting determine the numbers and qualifications of professional and support personnel in the school psychological service unit. For example, the extent to which services involve case study, direct intervention, and/or consultation will be significant in any service plan. Case study frequently involves teacher and/or parent conferences, observations of pupils, and a multi-assessment review, including student interviews. Similarly, the target populations for services affect the range of services that can be offered. One school psychologist, or one specialist in school psychology under supervision, for every 2,000 pupils is considered appropriate.[11]

Where shortages in personnel exist, so that school psychological services cannot be rendered in a professional manner, the director of the school psychological service unit informs the supervisor/administrator of the service about the implications of the shortage and initiates action to remedy the situation. When this fails, the director appropriately modifies the scope or work load of the unit to maintain the quality of services rendered.

2.2 *Policies:*

2.2.1 *When the school psychological service unit is composed of more than one person or is a component of a larger organization, a written statement of its objectives and scope of services is developed, maintained, and reviewed.*

INTERPRETATION: The school psychological service unit reviews its objectives and scope of services annually and revises them as necessary to ensure that the school psychological services offered are consistent with staff competencies and current psychological knowledge and practice. This statement is discussed with staff, reviewed by the appropriate administrators, distributed to instructional and administrative staff and school board members, and when appropriate, made available to parents, students, and members of the community upon request.

2.2.2 *All providers within a school psychological service unit support the legal and civil rights of the users.*[12]

INTERPRETATION: Providers of school psychological services safeguard the interests of school personnel, students, and parents with regard to personal, legal, and civil rights. They are continually sensitive to the issue of confidentiality of information, the short-term and long-term impacts of their decisions and recommendations, and other matters pertaining to individual, legal, and civil rights. Concerns regarding the safeguarding of individual rights of school personnel, students, and parents include, but are not limited to, due-process rights of parents and children, problems of self-incrimination in judicial proceedings, involuntary commitment to hospitals, child abuse, freedom of choice, protection of minors or legal incompetents, discriminatory practices in identification and placement, recommendations for special education provisions, and adjudication of domestic relations disputes in divorce and custodial proceedings. Providers of school psychological services take affirmative action by making themselves available to local committees, review boards, and similar advisory groups established to safeguard the human, civil, and legal rights of children and parents.

2.2.3 *All providers within a school psychological service unit are familiar with and adhere to the American Psychological Association's* Standards for Providers of Psychological Services, Ethical Principles of Psychologists, Standards for Educational and Psychological Tests, Ethical Principles in the Conduct of Research With Human Participants, *and other official policy statements relevant to standards for professional services issued by the Association.*

INTERPRETATION: A copy of each of these documents is maintained by providers of school psychological services and is available upon request to all school personnel and officials, parents, members of the community, and where applicable, students and other sanctioners.

2.2.4 *All providers within a school psychological service unit conform to relevant statutes established by federal, state, and local governments.*

INTERPRETATION: All providers of school psychological services are familiar with and conform to appropriate statutes regulating the practice of psychology. They also are informed about state department of education requirements and other agency regulations that have the force of law and that relate to the delivery of school psychological services (e.g., certification of, eligibility for, and placement in, special education programs). In addition, all providers are cognizant that federal agencies such as the Department of Education and the Department of Health and Human Services have policy statements regarding psychological services. Providers of school psychological services are familiar as well with other statutes and regulations, including those addressed to the civil and legal rights of users (e.g., Public Law 94-142, The Education for All Handicapped Children Act of 1975), that are pertinent to their scope of practice.

It is the responsibility of the American Psychological Association to maintain files of those federal policies, statutes, and regulations relating to this section and to assist its members in obtaining them. The state psychological associations, school psychological associations, and state licensing boards periodically publish and distribute appropriate state statutes and regulations.

2.2.5 *All providers within a school psychological service unit inform themselves about and use the network of human services in their communities in order to link users with relevant services and resources.*

INTERPRETATION: School psychologists and support staff are sensitive to the broader context of human needs. In recognizing the matrix of personal and societal problems, providers make available to clients information regarding human services such as legal aid societies, social services, health resources like mental health centers, private practitioners, and educational and recreational facilities. School psychological staff formulate and maintain a file of such resources for reference. The specific information provided is such that users can easily make contact with the services and freedom of choice can be honored. Providers of school psychological services refer to such community resources and, when indicated, actively intervene on behalf of the users. School psychologists seek opportunities to serve on boards of community agencies in order to represent the needs of the school population in the community.

2.2.6 *In the delivery of school psychological services, providers maintain a cooperative relationship with colleagues and co-workers in the best interest of the users.*

INTERPRETATION: School psychologists recognize the areas of special competence of other psychologists and of other professionals in the school and in the community for either consultation or referral purposes (e.g., school social workers, speech therapists, remedial reading teachers, special education teachers, pediatricians, neurologists, and public health nurses). Providers of school psychological services make appropriate use of other professional, research, technical, and administrative resources whenever these serve the best interests of the school staff, children, and parents and establish and maintain cooperative and/or collaborative arrangements with such other resources as required to meet the needs of users.

2.3 *Procedures:*

2.3.1 *A school psychological service unit follows a set of procedural guidelines for the delivery of school psychological services.*

INTERPRETATION: The school psychological service staff is prepared to provide a statement of procedural guidelines in written form in terms that can be understood by school staff, parents, school board members, interested members of the community, and when appropriate, students and other sanctioners. The statement describes the current methods, forms, case study and assessment procedures, estimated time lines, interventions, and evaluation techniques being used to achieve the objectives and goals for school psychological services.

This statement is communicated to school staff and personnel, school board members, parents, and when appropriate, students or other sanctioners through whatever means are feasible, including in-service activities, conferences, oral presentations, and dissemination of written materials.

The school psychological service unit provides for the annual review of its procedures for the delivery of school psychological services.

2.3.2 *Providers of school psychological services develop plans appropriate to the providers' professional practices and to the problems presented by the users. There is a mutually acceptable understanding between providers and school staff, parents, and students or responsible agents regarding the goals and the delivery of services.*

INTERPRETATION: The school psychological service unit notifies the school unit in writing of the plan that is adopted for use and resolves any points of difference. The plan includes written consent of guardians of students and, when appropriate, consent of students for the services provided. Similarly, the nature of the assessment tools that are to be used and the reasons for their inclusion are spelled out. The objectives of intervention(s) of a psychological nature as well as the procedures for implementing the intervention(s) are specified. An estimate of time is noted where appropriate. Parents and/or students are made aware of the various decisions that can be made as a result of the service(s), participate in accounting for decisions that are made, and are informed of how appeals may be instituted.

2.3.3 *Accurate, current, and pertinent documentation of essential school psychological services provided is maintained.*

INTERPRETATION: Records kept of psychological services may include, but are not limited to, identifying data, dates of services, names of providers of services, types of services, and significant actions taken. These records

are maintained separately from the child's cumulative record folder. Once a case study is completed and/or an intervention begun, records are reviewed and updated at least monthly.

2.3.4 *Each school psychological services unit follows an established record retention and disposition policy.*

INTERPRETATION: The policy on maintenance and review of psychological records (including the length of time that records not already part of school records are to be kept) is developed by the local school psychological service unit. This policy is consistent with existing federal and state statutes and regulations.

2.3.5 *Providers of school psychological services maintain a system to protect confidentiality of their records.*

INTERPRETATION: School psychologists are responsible for maintaining the confidentiality of information about users of services, from whatever source derived. All persons supervised by school psychologists, including nonprofessional personnel and students, who have access to records of psychological services maintain this confidentiality as a condition of employment. All appropriate staff receive training regarding the confidentiality of records.

Users are informed in advance of any limits for maintenance of confidentiality of psychological information. Procedures for obtaining informed consent are developed by the school psychological service unit. Written informed consent is obtained to conduct assessment or to carry out psychological intervention services. Informing users of the manner in which requests for information will be handled and of the school personnel who will share the results is part of the process of obtaining consent.

The school psychologist conforms to current laws and regulations with respect to the release of confidential information. As a general rule, however, the school psychologist does not release confidential information, except with the written consent of the parent or, where appropriate, the student directly involved or his or her legal representative. Even after consent for release has been obtained, the school psychologist clearly identifies such information as confidential to the recipient of the information. When there is a conflict with a statute, with regulations with the force of law, or with a court order, the school psychologist seeks a resolution to the conflict that is both ethically and legally feasible and appropriate.

Providers of school psychological services ensure that psychological reports which will become part of the school records are reviewed carefully so that confidentiality of pupils and parents is protected. When the guardian or student intends to waive confidentiality, the school psychologist discusses the implications of releasing psychological information and assists the user in limiting disclosure to only that information required by the present circumstance.

Raw psychological data (e.g., test protocols, counseling or interview notes, or questionnaires) in which a user is identified are released only with the written consent of the user or his or her legal representative, or by court order when such material is not covered by legal confidentiality, and are released only to a person recognized by the school psychologist as competent to use the data.

Any use made of psychological reports, records, or data for research or training purposes is consistent with this Guideline. Additionally, providers of school psychological services comply with statutory confidentiality requirements and those embodied in the American Psychological Association's *Ethical Principles of Psychologists* (APA, 1981).

Providers of school psychological services remain sensitive to both the benefits and the possible misuse of information regarding individuals that is stored in large computerized data banks. Providers use their influence to ensure that such information is managed in a socially responsible manner.

Guideline 3
ACCOUNTABILITY

3.1 *The promotion of human welfare is the primary principle guiding the professional activity of the school psychologist and the school psychological service unit.*

INTERPRETATION: School psychological services staff provide services to school staff members, students, and parents in a manner that is considerate and effective.

School psychologists make their services readily accessible to users in a manner that facilitates the users' freedom of choice. Parents, students, and other users are made aware that psychological services may be available through other public or private sources, and relevant information for exercising such options is provided upon request.

School psychologists are mindful of their accountability to the administration, to the school board, and to the general public, provided that appropriate steps are taken to protect the confidentiality of the service relationship. In the pursuit of their professional activities, they aid in the conservation of human, material, and financial resources.

The school psychological service unit does not withhold services to children or parents on the basis of the users' race, color, religion, gender, sexual orientation, age, or national origin. Recognition is given, however, to the following considerations: (a) the professional right of school psychologists, at the time of their employment, to state that they wish to limit their services to a specific category of users (e.g., elementary school children, exceptional children, adolescents), noting their reasons so

that employers can make decisions regarding their employment, assignment of their duties, and so on; (b) the right and responsibility of school psychologists to withhold an assessment procedure when not validly applicable; (c) the right and responsibility of school psychologists to withhold evaluative, psychotherapeutic, counseling, or other services in specific instances in which their own limitations or client characteristics might impair the effectiveness of the relationship; and (d) the obligation of school psychologists to seek to ameliorate through peer review, consultation, or other personal therapeutic procedures those factors that inhibit the provision of services to particular users. In such instances, it is incumbent on school psychologists to advise clients about appropriate alternative services. When appropriate services are not available, school psychologists inform the school district administration and/or other sanctioners of the unmet needs of clients. In all instances, school psychologists make available information, and provide opportunity to participate in decisions, concerning such issues as initiation, termination, continuation, modification, and evaluation of psychological services. These Guidelines are also made available upon request.

Accurate and full information is made available to prospective individual or organizational users regarding the qualifications of providers, the nature and extent of services offered, and where appropriate, the financial costs as well as the benefits and possible risks of the proposed services.

Professional school psychologists offering services for a fee inform users of their payment policies, if applicable, and of their willingness to assist in obtaining reimbursement when such services have been contracted for as an external resource.

3.2 *School psychologists pursue their activities as members of the independent, autonomous profession of psychology.*[13]

INTERPRETATION: School psychologists are aware of the implications of their activities for the profession of psychology as a whole. They seek to eliminate discriminatory practices instituted for self-serving purposes that are not in the interest of the users (e.g., arbitrary requirements for referral and supervision by another profession) and to discourage misuse of psychological concepts and tools (e.g., use of psychological instruments for special education placement by school personnel or others who lack relevant and adequate education and training). School psychologists are cognizant of their responsibilities for the development of the profession and for the improvement of schools. They participate where possible in the training and career development of students and other providers; they participate as appropriate in the training of school administrators, teachers, and paraprofessionals; and they integrate, and supervise the implementation of, their contributions within the structure established for delivering school psychological services. Where appropriate, they facilitate the development of, and participate in, professional standards review mechanisms.

School psychologists seek to work with other professionals in a cooperative manner for the good of the users and the benefit of the general public. School psychologists associated with special education or mental health teams or with multidisciplinary settings support the principle that members of each participating profession have equal rights and opportunities to share all privileges and responsibilities of full membership in the educational or human service activities or facilities and to administer service programs in their respective areas of competence. (Refer also to Guideline 2.2.5, Interpretation.)

3.3 *There are periodic, systematic, and effective evaluations of school psychological services.*

INTERPRETATION: When the psychological service unit representing school psychology is a component of a larger organization (e.g., school system, county or state regional district, state department of education), regular evaluation of progress in achieving goals is provided for in the service delivery plan, including consideration of the effectiveness of school psychological services relative to costs in terms of use of time and money and the availability of professional and support personnel.

Evaluation of the school psychological service delivery system is conducted internally and, when possible, under independent auspices as well. This evaluation includes an assessment of effectiveness (to determine what the service unit accomplished), efficiency (to determine the costs of providing the services), continuity (to ensure that the services are appropriately linked to other educational services), availability (to determine the appropriateness of staffing ratios), accessibility (to ensure that the services are readily available to members of the school population), and adequacy (to determine whether the services meet the identified needs of the school population).

It is highly desirable that there be a periodic reexamination of review mechanisms to ensure that these attempts at public safeguards are effective and cost efficient and do not place unnecessary encumbrances on the providers or impose unnecessary expenses on users or sanctioners for services rendered.

3.4 *School psychologists are accountable for all aspects of the services they provide and are responsive to those concerned with these services.*

INTERPRETATION: In recognizing their responsibilities to users, sanctioners, and other providers, and where appropriate and consistent with the users' legal rights and privileged communications, school psychologists make available information about, and provide opportunity to participate in, decisions concerning such issues as initiation, termination, continuation, modification, and evaluation of school psychological services.

Guideline 4
ENVIRONMENT

4.1 *Providers of psychological services promote development in the school setting of a physical, organizational, and social environment that facilitates optimal human functioning.*

INTERPRETATION: Federal, state, and local requirements for safety, health, and sanitation are observed.

As providers of services, school psychologists are concerned with the environment of their service units, especially as it affects the quality of service, but also as it impinges on human functioning in the school. Attention is given to the privacy and comfort of school staff, students, and parents. Parent and staff interviews are conducted in a professional atmosphere, with the option for private conferences available. Students are seen under conditions that maximize their privacy and enhance the possibility for meaningful intervention; for example, they should have the opportunity to leave their classroom inconspicuously and should be free from interruptions when meeting with the psychologist. Physical arrangements and organizational policies and procedures are conducive to the human dignity, self-respect, and optimal functioning of school staff, students, and parents and to the effective delivery of service.

FOOTNOTES

[1] The footnotes appended to these Specialty Guidelines represent an attempt to provide a coherent context of earlier APA policy statements and other documents regarding professional practice. The Guidelines extend these previous policy statements where necessary to reflect current concerns of the public and the profession.

[2] There are three categories of individuals who do not meet the definition of *professional school psychologist* but who can be considered professional school psychologists if they meet certain criteria.

The following two categories of professional psychologists who met the criteria indicated below on or before the adoption of these Specialty Guidelines on January 31, 1980, are considered professional school psychologists: Category 1—those who completed (a) a doctoral degree program primarily psychological in content, but not in school psychology, at a regionally accredited university or professional school and (b) 3 postdoctoral years of appropriate education, training, and experience in providing school psychological services as defined herein, including a minimum of 1,200 hours in school settings; Category 2—those who on or before September 4, 1974, (a) completed a master's degree from a program primarily psychological in content at a regionally accredited university or professional school and (b) held a license or certificate in the state in which they practiced, conferred by a state board of psychological examiners, or the endorsement of a state psychological association through voluntary certification, and who, in addition, prior to January 31, 1980, (c) obtained 5 post-master's years of appropriate education, training, and experience in providing school psychological services as defined herein, including a minimum of 2,400 hours in school settings.

After January 31, 1980, professional psychologists who wish

to be recognized as professional school psychologists are referred to Guideline 1.7.

The APA Council of Representatives passed a "Resolution on the Master's-Level Issue" in January 1977 containing the following statement, which influenced the development of a third category of professional school psychologists:

> The title "Professional Psychologist" has been used so widely and by persons with such a wide variety of training and experience that it does not provide the information the public deserves.
>
> As a consequence, the APA takes the position and makes it a part of its policy that the use of the title "Professional Psychologist," and its variations such as "Clinical Psychologist," "Counseling Psychologist," "School Psychologist," and "Industrial Psychologist" are reserved for those who have completed a Doctoral Training Program in Psychology in a university, college, or professional school of psychology that is APA or regionally accredited. In order to meet this standard, a transition period will be acknowledged for the use of the title "School Psychologist," so that ways may be sought to increase opportunities for doctoral training and to improve the level of educational codes pertaining to the title. (Conger, 1977, p. 426)

For the purpose of transition, then, there is still another category of persons who can be considered professional school psychologists for practice in elementary and secondary schools. Category 3 consists of persons who meet the following criteria on or before, but not beyond, January 31, 1985: (a) a master's or higher degree, requiring at least 2 years of full-time graduate study in school psychology, from a regionally accredited university or professional school; (b) at least 3 additional years of training and experience in school psychological services, including a minimum of 1,200 hours in school settings; and (c) a license or certificate conferred by a state board of psychological examiners or a state educational agency for practice in elementary or secondary schools.

Preparation equivalent to that described in Category 3 entitles an individual to use the title *professional school psychologist* in school practice, but it does not exempt the individual from meeting the requirements of licensure or other requirements for which a doctoral degree is prerequisite.

[3] A professional school psychologist who is licensed by a state or District of Columbia board of examiners of psychology for the independent practice of psychology and who has 2 years of supervised (or equivalent) experience in health services, of which at least 1 year is postdoctoral, may be listed as a "Health Service Provider in Psychology" in the *National Register of Health Service Providers in Psychology*:

> A Health Service Provider in Psychology is defined as a psychologist, certified/licensed at the independent practice level in his/her state, who is duly trained and experienced in the delivery of direct, preventive, assessment and therapeutic intervention services to individuals whose growth, adjustment, or functioning is actually impaired or is demonstrably at high risk of impairment. (Council for the National Register of Health Service Providers in Psychology, 1980, p. xi)

[4] The areas of knowledge and training that are a part of the educational program for all professional psychologists have been presented in two APA documents, *Education and Credentialing in Psychology II* (APA, 1977a) and *Criteria for Accreditation of Doctoral Training Programs and Internships in Professional Psychology* (APA, 1979). There is consistency in the presentation of core areas in the education and training of all professional psychologists. The description of education and training in these Guidelines is based primarily on the document *Education and Credentialing in Psychology II*. It is intended to indicate broad areas of required curriculum, with the ex-

pectation that training programs will undoubtedly want to interpret the specific content of these areas in different ways depending on the nature, philosophy, and intent of the programs.

[5] Although specialty education and training guidelines have not yet been developed and approved by APA, the following description of education and training components of school psychology programs represents a consensus regarding specialty training in school psychology at this time.

The *education* of school psychologists encompasses the equivalent of at least 3 years of full-time graduate academic study. While instructional formats and course titles may vary from program to program, each program has didactic and experiential instruction (a) in scientific and professional areas common to all professional psychology programs, such as ethics and standards, research design and methodology, statistics, and psychometric methods, and (b) in such substantive areas as the biological bases of behavior, the cognitive and affective bases of behavior, the social, cultural, ethnic, and sex role bases of behavior, and individual differences. Course work includes social and philosophical bases of education, curriculum theory and practice, etiology of learning and behavior disorders, exceptional children, and special education. Organization theory and administrative practice should also be included in the program. This list is not intended to dictate specific courses or a sequence of instruction. It is the responsibility of programs to determine how these areas are organized and presented to students. Variations in educational format are to be expected.

The *training* of school psychologists includes practicum and field experience in conjunction with the educational program. In addition, the program includes a supervised internship experience beyond practicum and field work, equivalent to at least 1 academic school year, but in no event fewer than 1,200 hours, in schools or in a combination of schools and community agencies and centers, with at least 600 hours of the internship in the school setting. An appropriate number of hours per week should be devoted to direct face-to-face supervision of each intern. In no event is there less than 1 hour per week of direct supervision. Overall professional supervision is provided by a professional school psychologist. However, supervision in specific procedures and techniques may be provided by others, with the agreement of the supervising professional psychologist and the supervisee. The training experiences provided and the competencies developed occur in settings in which there are opportunities to work with children, teachers, and parents and to supervise others providing psychological services to children.

[6] In order to implement these Specialty Guidelines, it will be necessary to determine in each state which non-doctoral-level school psychologists certified by the state department of education are eligible to be considered professional school psychologists for practice in elementary and secondary schools. A national register of all professional school psychologists and specialists in school psychology would be a useful and efficient means by which to inform the public of the available school psychological services personnel.

[7] Functions and activities of school psychologists relating to the teaching of psychology, the writing or editing of scholarly or scientific manuscripts, and the conduct of scientific research do not fall within the purview of these Guidelines.

[8] Nothing in these Guidelines precludes the school psychologist from being trained beyond the areas described herein (e.g., in psychotherapy for children, adolescents, and their families in relation to school-related functioning and problems) and, therefore, from providing services on the basis of this training to clients as appropriate.

[9] In some states, a supervisor's certificate is required in order to use the title *supervisor* in the public schools. Supervision of providers of psychological services by a professional school psy-

chologist does not mean that the school psychologist is thereby authorized or entitled to offer supervision to other school personnel. Supervision by the school psychologist is confined to those areas appropriate to his or her training and educational background and is viewed as part of the school psychologist's professional responsibilities and duties.

The following guideline for supervision has been written by the Executive Committee of the Division of School Psychology:

> In addition to being a professional school psychologist, the person who supervises school psychological services and/or school psychological personnel shall have the following qualifications: broad understanding of diagnostic assessment, consultation, programming, and other intervention strategies; skills in supervision; the ability to empathize with supervisees; and commitment to continuing education. The supervising school psychologist also shall have had the equivalent of at least 2 years of satisfactory full-time, on-the-job experience as a school psychologist practicing directly in the school or dealing with school-related problems in independent practice.

[10] This Guideline follows closely the statement regarding "Policy on Training for Psychologists Wishing to Change Their Specialty" adopted by the APA Council of Representatives in January 1976. Included therein was the implementing provision that "this policy statement shall be incorporated in the guidelines of the Committee on Accreditation so that appropriate sanctions can be brought to bear on university and internship training programs that violate [it]" (Conger, 1976, p. 424).

[11] Two surveys of school psychological practice provide a rationale for the specification of this Guideline (Farling & Hoedt, 1971; Kicklighter, 1976). The median ratios of psychologists to pupils were 1 to 9,000 in 1966 and 1 to 4,000 in 1974. Those responding to Kicklighter's survey projected that the ratio of psychologists to pupils would be 1 to 2,500 in 1980. These data were collected before the passage of Public Law 94-142, the Education for All Handicapped Children Act of 1975. The regulations for implementing this act require extensive identification, assessment, and evaluation services to children, and it is reasonable in 1981 to set an acceptable ratio of psychologists to pupils at 1 to 2,000.

[12] See also *Ethical Principles of Psychologists* (APA, 1981), especially Principles 5 (Confidentiality), 6 (Welfare of the Consumer), and 9 (Research With Human Participants), and *Ethical Principles in the Conduct of Research With Human Participants* (APA, 1973). Also, in 1978 Division 17 approved in principle a statement on "Principles for Counseling and Psychotherapy With Women," which was designed to protect the interests of female users of counseling psychological services.

[13] Support for the principle of the independence of psychology as a profession is found in the following:

> As a member of an autonomous profession, a psychologist rejects limitations upon his [or her] freedom of thought and action other than those imposed by his [or her] moral, legal, and social responsibilities. The Association is always prepared to provide appropriate assistance to any responsible member who becomes subjected to unreasonable limitations upon his [or her] opportunity to function as a practitioner, teacher, researcher, administrator, or consultant. The Association is always prepared to cooperate with any responsible profes-

sional organization in opposing any unreasonable limitations on the professional functions of the members of that organization.

> This insistence upon professional autonomy has been upheld over the years by the affirmative actions of the courts and other public and private bodies in support of the right of the psychologist—and other professionals—to pursue those functions for which he [or she] is trained and qualified to perform. (APA, 1968, p. 9)

> Organized psychology has the responsibility to define and develop its own profession, consistent with the general canons of science and with the public welfare.

> Psychologists recognize that other professions and other groups will, from time to time, seek to define the roles and responsibilities of psychologists. The APA opposes such developments on the same principle that it is opposed to the psychological profession taking positions which would define the work and scope of responsibility of other duly recognized professions. (APA, 1972, p. 333)

REFERENCES

American Psychological Association. *Psychology as a profession.* Washington, D.C.: Author, 1968.

American Psychological Association. Guidelines for conditions of employment of psychologists. *American Psychologist,* 1972, 27, 331–334.

American Psychological Association. *Ethical principles in the conduct of research with human participants.* Washington, D.C.: Author, 1973.

American Psychological Association. *Standards for educational and psychological tests.* Washington, D.C.: Author, 1974. (a)

American Psychological Association. *Standards for providers of psychological services.* Washington, D.C.: Author, 1974. (b)

American Psychological Association. *Education and credentialing in psychology II.* Report of a meeting, June 4–5, 1977. Washington, D.C.: Author, 1977. (a)

American Psychological Association. *Standards for providers of psychological services* (Rev. ed.). Washington, D.C.: Author, 1977. (b)

American Psychological Association. *Criteria for accreditation of doctoral training programs and internships in professional psychology.* Washington, D.C.: Author, 1979 (amended 1980).

American Psychological Association. *Ethical principles of psychologists* (Rev. ed.). Washington, D.C.: Author, 1981.

Conger, J. J. Proceedings of the American Psychological Association, Incorporated, for the year 1975: Minutes of the annual meeting of the Council of Representatives. *American Psychologist,* 1976, 31, 406–434.

Conger, J. J. Proceedings of the American Psychological Association, Incorporated, for the year 1976: Minutes of the annual meeting of the Council of Representatives. *American Psychologist,* 1977, 32, 408–438.

Council for the National Register of Health Service Providers in Psychology. *National register of health service providers in psychology.* Washington, D.C.: Author, 1980.

Farling, W. H., & Hoedt, K. C. *National survey of school psychologists.* Washington, D.C.: Department of Health, Education, and Welfare, 1971.

Kicklighter, R. H. School psychology in the U.S.: A quantitative survey. *Journal of School Psychology,* 1976, 14, 151–156.

APPENDIX D: The National Association of School Psychologists' (1984) Principles for Professional Ethics

I. INTRODUCTION

Standards for professional conduct, usually referred to as ethics, recognize the obligation of professional persons to provide services and to conduct themselves so as to place the highest esteem on human rights and individual dignity. A code of ethics is an additional professional technique which seeks to ensure that each person served will receive the highest quality of service. Even though ethical behavior involves interactions between the professional, the person served and employing institutions, responsibility for ethical conduct must rest with the professional.

School psychologists are a specialized segment within a larger group of professional psychologists. The school psychologist works in situations where circumstances may develop which are not clearly dealt with in other ethical guidelines. This possibility is heightened by intense concern for such issues as due process, protection of individual rights, record keeping, accountability and equal access to opportunity.

The most basic ethical principle is that of the responsibility to perform only those services for which that person has acquired a recognized level of competency. Recognition must be made of the uncertainties associated with delivery of psychological services in a situation where rights of the student, the parent, the school and society may conflict.

The intent of these guidelines is to supply clarification which will facilitate the delivery of high quality psychological services in the school or community. Thus they acknowledge the fluid and expanding functions of the school and community. In addition to these ethical standards, there is the ever present necessity to differentiate between legal mandate and ethical responsibility. The school psychologist is urged to become familiar with applicable legal requirements.

The ethical standards in this guide are organized into several sections representing the multifaceted concerns with which school psychologists must deal. The grouping arrangement is a matter of convenience, and principles discussed in one section may also apply to other areas and situations. The school psychologist should consult with other experienced psychologists and seek advice from the appropriate professional organization when a situation is encountered for which there is no clearly indicated course of action.

Source: Principles for professional ethics. In *Professional Conduct Manual* (pp. 4–17). Copyright 1984 by the National Association of School Psychologists. Reprinted by permission of the publisher.

II. PROFESSIONAL COMPETENCY

A) General

1. The school psychologist's role mandates a mastery of skills in both education and psychology. In the interest of children and adults served in both the public and private sector, school psychologists strive to maintain high standards of competence. School psychologists recognize the strengths, as well as limitations, of their training and experience, and only provide services in areas of competence. They must be professional in the on-going pursuit of knowledge, training and research with the welfare of children, families and other individuals in mind.

2. School psychologists offer only those services which are within their individual area of training and experience. Competence levels, education, training and experience are accurately represented to schools and clients in a professional manner. School psychologists do not use affiliations with other professional persons or with institutions to imply a level of professional competence which exceeds that which has actually been achieved.

3. School psychologists are aware of their limitations and enlist the assistance of other specialists in supervisory, consultative or referral roles as appropriate in providing services competently.

4. School psychologists recognize the need for continuing professional development and pursue opportunities to learn new procedures, become current with new research and technology, and advance with changes that benefit children and families.

5. School psychologists refrain from involvement in any activity in which their personal problems or conflicts may interfere with professional effectiveness. Competent professional assistance is sought to alleviate such problems and conflicts in professional relationships.

III) PROFESSIONAL RELATIONSHIPS AND RESPONSIBILITIES

A) General

1. School psychologists take responsibility for their actions in a multitude of areas of service, and in so doing, maintain the highest standards of their profession. They are committed to the application of professional expertise for promoting improvement in the quality of life available to the student, family, school, and community. This objective is pursued in ways that protect the dignity and rights of those served. School psychologists accept responsibility for the consequences of their acts and ensure that professional skills, position and influence are applied only for purposes which are consistent with these values.

2. School psychologists respect each person with whom they are working and deal justly and impartially with each regardless of his/her physical, mental, emotional, political, economic, social, cultural, racial or religious characteristics.

3. School psychologists apply influence, position and professional skills in ways that protect the dignity and rights of those served. They promote the improvement of the quality of education and of life in general when determining assessment, counseling and intervention.

4. School psychologists define the direction and the nature of personal loyalties, objectives and competencies, and advise and inform all persons concerned of these commitments.

5. School psychologists working in both public schools and private settings maintain professional relationships with students, parents, the school and community. They understand the importance of informing students/clients of all aspects of the potential professional relationship prior to beginning psychological services of any type. School psychologists recognize the need for parental involvement and the significant influence the parent has on the student/client's growth.

6. In a situation where there are divided or conflicting interests (as between parents, school, student, supervisor, trainer) school psychologists are responsible for attempting to work out a plan of action which protects the rights and encourages mutual benefit and protection of rights.

7. School psychologists do not exploit their professional relationships with students, employees,

clients or research participants sexually or otherwise. School psychologists do not engage in, nor condone, deliberate comments, gestures or physical contacts of a sexual nature.

B) Students

1. School psychologists are guided by an awareness of the intimate nature of the examination of personal aspects of an individual. School psychologists use an approach which reflects a humanistic concern for dignity and personal integrity.

2. School psychologists inform the student/client about important aspects of their relationship in a manner that is understood by the student. The explanation includes the uses to be made of information, persons who will receive specific information and possible implications of results.

3. School psychologists recognize the obligation to the student/client and respect the student's/client's right of choice to enter, or to participate, in services voluntarily.

4. School psychologists inform the student/client of the outcomes of assessment, counseling or other services. Contemplated changes in program, plans for further services and other pertinent information are discussed with the student as a result of services. An account of alternatives available to the student/client is included.

5. The student/client is informed by the school psychologist of those who will receive information regarding the services and the type of information that they will receive. The sharing of information is formulated to fit the age and maturity of the student/client and the nature of the information.

C) Parents

1. School psychologists confer with parents regarding assessment, counseling and intervention plans in language understandable to the parent. They strive to establish a set of alternatives and suggestions which match the values and skills of each parent.

2. School psychologists recognize the importance of parental support and seek to obtain this by assuring that there is direct parent contact prior to seeing the student/client. They secure continuing parental involvement by a frank and prompt reporting to the parent of findings and progress.

3. School psychologists continue to maintain contact with the parent even though the parent objects to having their child receive services. Alternatives are described which will enable the student to get needed help.

4. School psychologists discuss recommendations and plans for assisting the student/client with the parent. The discussion includes alternatives associated with each set of plans. The parents are advised as to sources of help available at school and in the community.

5. School psychologists inform parents of the nature of records made of parent conferences and evaluations of the student/client. Rights of confidentiality and content of reports are shared.

D) Service Delivery

1. School psychologists employed by school districts prepare by becoming knowledgeable of the organization, philosophy, goals, objectives and methodology of the school.

2. School psychologists recognize that a working understanding of the goals, processes and legal requirements of the educational system is essential for an effective relationship with the school.

3. Familiarization with organization, instructional materials and teaching strategies of the school are basic to enable school psychologists to contribute to the common objective of fostering maximum self development opportunities for each student/client.

4. School psychologists accept the responsibility of being members of the staff of those schools. They recognize the need to establish an integral role within the school system and familiarize themselves with the system and community.

E) Community

1. Although enjoying professional identity as a school psychologist, school psychologists are also citizens, thereby accepting the same responsibilities and duties expected of all members of society. School psychologists are free to pursue individual interests, except to the degree that these may compromise fulfillment of their professional responsibilities and have negative impact on the profession. Awareness of such impact guides public behavior.

2. As citizens, school psychologists may exercise their constitutional rights as the basis for procedures and practices designed to bring about social change. Such activities are conducted as involved citizens and not as representatives of school psychologists.

3. As employees or employers, in public or private domains, school psychologists do not engage in or condone practices based on race, handicap, age, gender, sexual preference, religion, or national origin.

4. School psychologists avoid any action that could violate or diminish civil and legal rights of clients.

5. School psychologists in public and private practice have the responsibility of adhering to federal, state and local laws and ordinances governing their practice. If such laws are in conflict with existing ethical guidelines, school psychologists proceed toward resolution of such conflict through positive, respected and legal channels.

F) Related Professions

1. School psychologists respect and understand the areas of competence of other professions. They work in full cooperation with other professional disciplines in a relationship based on mutual respect and recognition of the multidisciplinary service needed to meet the needs of students and clients. They recognize the role and obligation of the institution or agency with which other professionals are associated.

2. School psychologists recognize the areas of competence of related professions and other professionals in the field of school psychology. They encourage and support use of all the resources that best serve the interests of their students/clients. They are obligated to have prior knowledge of the competency and qualifications of a referral source. Professional services, as well as technical and administrative resources, are sought in the effort of providing the best possible professional service.

3. School psychologists working within the school system explain their professional competencies to other professionals including role descriptions, assignment of services, and the working relationships among varied professionals within the system.

4. School psychologists cooperate with other professionals and agencies with the rights and needs of their student/client in mind. If a student/client is receiving similar services from another professional, school psychologists assure coordination of services. Private practice school psychologists do not offer their own services to those already receiving services. As school psychologists working within the school system, a need to serve a student may arise as dictated by the student's special program. In this case, consultation with another professional serving the student takes place to assure coordination of services for the welfare of the student.

5. When school psychologists suspect the existence of detrimental or unethical practices, the appropriate professional organization is contacted for assistance and procedures established for questioning ethical practice are followed.

G) Other School Psychologists

1. School psychologists who employ, supervise and train other professionals accept the obligation of providing experiences to further their professional development. Appropriate working conditions, fair and timely evaluation and constructive consultation are provided.

2. School psychologists acting as supervisors to interns review and evaluate assessment results, conferences, counseling strategies, and documents. They assure the profession that training in the field is supervised adequately.

3. When school psychologists are aware of a possible ethical violation by another school psychologist, they attempt to resolve the issue on an informal level. If such informal efforts are not productive and a violation appears to be enacted, steps for filing an ethical complaint as outlined by the appropriate professional association are followed.

IV. PROFESSIONAL PRACTICES - PUBLIC SETTINGS

A) Advocacy

1. School psychologists consider the pupils/clients to be their primary responsibility and act as advocates of their rights and welfare. Course of action takes into account the rights of the student, rights of the parent, the responsibilities of the school personnel, and the expanding self-independence and mature status of the student.

2. School psychologists outline and interpret services to be provided. Their concern for protecting the interests and rights of students is communicated to the school administration and staff. Human advocacy is the number one priority.

B) Assessment and Intervention

1. School psychologists strive to maintain the highest standard of service by an objective collecting of appropriate data and information necessary to effectively work with students. In conducting a psychoeducational evaluation or counseling/consultation services, due consideration is given to individual integrity and individual differences. School psychologists recognize differences in age, sex, socioeconomic and ethnic backgrounds, and strive to select and use appropriate procedures, techniques and strategies relevant to such differences.

2. School psychologists insist on collecting relevant data for an evaluation that includes the use of valid and reliable instruments and techniques that are applicable and appropriate for the student.

3. School psychologists combine observations, background information, multi-disciplinary results and other pertinent data to present the most comprehensive and valid picture possible of the student. School psychologists utilize assessment, counseling procedures, consultation techniques and other intervention methods that are consistent with responsible practice, recent research and professional judgment.

4. School psychologists do not promote the use of psychoeducational assessment techniques by inappropriately trained or otherwise unqualified persons through teaching, sponsorship or supervision.

5. School psychologists develop interventions which are appropriate to the presenting problems of the referred student/client, and which are consistent with the data collected during the assessment of the referral situation.

6. The student/client is referred to another professional for services when a condition is identified which is outside the treatment competencies or scope of the school psychologist.

7. When transferring the intervention responsibility for a student/client to another professional, school psychologists ensure that all relevant and appropriate individuals, including the student/client when appropriate, are notified of the change and reasons for the change.

C) Use of Materials and Computers

1. School psychologists are responsible for maintaining security of psychological tests which might be rendered useless by revealing the underlying principles or specific content. Every attempt is made by school psychologists to protect test security and copyright restrictions.

2. Copyright laws are adhered to regarding reproduction of tests or any parts thereof. Permission is obtained from authors of noncopyrighted published instruments.

3. School psychologists who utilize student/client information in lectures or publications, either obtain prior consent in writing or remove all identifying data.

4. When publishing, school psychologists acknowledge the sources of their ideas and materials. Credit is given to those who have contributed.

5. School psychologists do not promote or encourage inappropriate use of computer-generated test analysis or reports.

6. School psychologists maintain full responsibility for computerized or any other technological services used by them for diagnostic, consultative or information management purposes. Such services, if used, should be regarded as tools to be used judiciously without abdication of any responsibility of the psychologist to the tool or to the people who make its operation possible.

7. In the utilization of technological data management services, school psychologists apply the same ethical standards for use, interpretation and maintenance of data as for any other information. They are assured that the computer programs are accurate in all areas of information produced prior to using the results.

D) School-Based Research and Evaluation

1. School psychologists continually assess the impact of any treatment/intervention/counseling plan and terminate or modify the plan when the data indicate that the plan is not achieving the desired goals.

2. In performing research, school psychologists accept responsibility for selection of topics, research methodology, subject selection, data gathering, analysis and reporting. In publishing reports of their research, they provide discussion of limitations of their data and acknowledge existence of disconfirming data, as well as alternate hypotheses and explanations of their findings.

E) Reporting Data and Conferencing Results

1. School psychologists ascertain that student/client information reaches responsible and authorized persons and is adequately interpreted for their use in helping the student/client. This involves establishing procedures which safeguard the personal and confidential interests of those concerned.

2. School psychologists communicate findings and recommendations in language readily understood by the school staff. These communications describe possible favorable and unfavorable consequences associated with the alternative proposals.

3. When reporting data which are to be representative of a student/client, school psychologists take the responsibility for preparing information that is written in terms that are understandable to all involved. It is made certain that information is in such form and style as to assure that the recipient of the report will be able to give maximum assistance to the individual. The emphasis is on the interpretations and recommendations rather than the simple passing along of test scores, and will include an appraisal of the degree of reliance and confidence which can be placed on the information.

4. School psychologists ensure the accuracy of their reports, letters and other written documents through reviewing and signing such.

5. School psychologists comply with all laws, regulations and policies pertaining to the adequate storage and disposal of records to maintain appropriate confidentiality of information.

V. PROFESSIONAL PRACTICES - PRIVATE SETTINGS

A) Relationship with School Districts

1. Many school psychologists are employed in both the public and private sectors, and in so doing, create a possible conflict of services if they do not adhere to standards of professional ethics. School psychologists operating in both sectors recognize the importance of separation of roles and the necessity of adherence to all ethical standards.

2. School psychologists engaged in employment in a public school setting and in private practice, may not accept a fee, or any other form of remuneration, for professional work with clients who are entitled to such service through the schools where the school psychologists are currently assigned.

3. School psychologists in private practice have an obligation to inform parents of free and/or mandated services available from the public school system before providing services for pay.

4. School psychologists engaged in employment in a public, as well as private, practice setting, maintain such practice outside the hours of contracted employment in their school district.

5. School psychologists engaged in private practice do not utilize tests, materials or services belonging to the school district without authorization.

6. School psychologists carefully evaluate the appropriateness of the use of public school

facilities for part-time private practice. Such use can be confusing to the client and may be criticized as improper. Before the facility is utilized, school psychologists enter into a rental agreement with the school district and clearly define limits of use to the district and the client.

B) Service Delivery

1. School psychologists clarify financial arrangements in advance of services to ensure to the best of their ability that they are clearly understood by the client. They neither give nor receive any remuneration for referring clients for professional services.

2. School psychologists in private practice adhere to the conditions of a contract with the school district, other agency, or individual until service thereunder has been performed, the contract has been terminated by mutual consent, or the contract has otherwise been legally terminated. They have responsibility to follow-up a completed contract to assure that conclusions are understood, interpreted and utilized effectively.

3. School psychologists in private practice guard against any misunderstanding occurring from recommendations, advice or information given a parent or child which a school may not be prepared to carry out, or which is in conflict with what the district is doing for the child. Such conflicts are not avoided where the best interests of those served require consideration of different opinion. Direct consultation between the school psychologist in private practice and the school psychologist assigned to the case at the school level may avoid confusing parents by resolving at the professional level any difference of interpretation of clinical data.

4. School psychologists provide individual diagnostic and therapeutic services only within the context of a professional psychological relationship. Personal diagnosis and therapy are not given by means of public lectures, newspaper columns, magazine articles, radio and television programs or mail. Any information shared through such media activities is general in nature and utilizes only current and relevant data and professional judgment.

C) Announcements/Advertising

1. Considerations of appropriate announcement of services, advertising and public media statements are necessary in the role of the school psychologist in private practice. Such activities are necessary in assisting the public to make appropriate and knowledgeable decisions and choices regarding services. Accurate representation of training, experience, services provided and affiliation are made by school psychologists. Public statements must be made on sound and accepted theory, research and practice.

2. Individual, agency or clinical listings in telephone directories are limited to the following: name/names, highest relevant degree, certification status, address, telephone number, brief identification of major areas of practice, office hours, appropriate fee information, foreign languages spoken, policy with regard to third party payments and license number.

3. Announcements of services by school psychologists in private practice, agency or clinic are made in a formal, professional manner limited to the same information as is included in a telephone listing. Clear statements of purposes with clear descriptions of the experiences to be provided are given. The education, training and experience of the staff members are appropriately specified.

4. School psychologists in private practice may utilize brochures in the announcement of services. The brochures may be sent to professional persons, schools, business firms, governmental agencies and other similar organizations.

5. Announcements and advertisements of the availability of publications, products and services for sale are presented in a professional, scientific and factual manner. Information may be communicated by means of periodical, book, list, directory, television, radio or motion picture and must not include any false, misleading or comparative statements.

6. School psychologists in private practice do not directly solicit clients for individual diagnosis or therapy.

7. School psychologists do not compensate in any manner a representative of the press, radio or television in return for personal professional publicity in a news item.

8. School psychologists do not participate for personal gain in commercial announcements or advertisements recommending to the public the purchase or use of products or services.

PROCEDURAL GUIDELINES FOR THE ADJUDICATION OF ETHICAL COMPLAINTS

SECTION I. **RESPONSIBILITY AND FUNCTION**

The Ethics and Professional Conduct Committee shall be responsible for developing and maintaining a clearly defined position of the Association regarding the ethical and professional conduct principles to be adhered to by its members. The major area of particular ethical concern to the Committee will be that of the protection and general well-being of individuals served by school psychologists, in schools and in private practice, and in institutions or agencies through which this service is rendered. The Committee is further charged to study and make recommendations to the Executive Board when it is alleged that a member has failed to follow the ethical principles of the Association.

Members of the Ethics and Professional Conduct Committee recognize that their role is an extremely important one, involving the rights of many individuals, the reputation of the profession and the careers of individual professionals. They bear a heavy responsibility because their recommendations may alter the lives of others. Therefore, they must be alert to personal, social, organizational, financial or political situations or pressures that might lead to misuse of their influence. The Ethics and Professional Conduct Committee shall assure the responsible use of all information obtained in the course of an inquiry or investigation. The objective with regard to the individual shall, whenever possible, be constructive and educative, rather than punitive in character.

The function of the Committee in investigating complaints of alleged ethical misconduct involves obtaining a thorough and impartial account of the behaviors or incidents in order to be able to evaluate the character of the behaviors in question. When responding to complaints, members of the Ethics and Professional Conduct Committee have the responsibility to consider the competency of the complainant, to act in an unbiased manner, to work expeditiously, and to safeguard the confidentiality of the Committee's activities. Committee members and their designees have the added responsibility to follow procedures which safeguard the rights of all individuals involved in the complaint process.

SECTION II. **SCOPE AND AUTHORITY**

The Ethics and Professional Conduct Committee shall address issues of ethical misconduct in an investigatory, advisory, educative and/or remedial role. What constitutes ethical misconduct shall be determined on the basis of the provisions of the NASP *Principles for Professional Ethics* and any published advisory opinions that from time to time are developed by the Ethics and Professional Conduct Committee. In applying the Principles, the authorized opinions of those charged by NASP with the administration and interpretation of the ethical principles shall be binding on all members and on the members of state associations affiliated with NASP.

When investigating and/or responding to a complaint or inquiry, the Ethics and Professional Conduct Committee shall conduct itself in a manner consistent with the Bylaws of the Association and with the NASP *Principles for Professional Ethics* and shall also be bound by these procedures. The Ethics and Professional Conduct Committee shall endeavor to settle cases informally, recommend disciplinary action when unethical conduct has occurred, report regularly to the Delegate Assembly on its activities and shall revise and amend (subject to ratification by the Delegate Assembly), the NASP Principles and these procedures in a timely manner. The Association may, at the recommendation of the Ethics and Professional Conduct Committee, and in accordance with the Bylaws of the Association, expel a NASP member.

When a complaint is received about a non-member, the Ethics and Professional Conduct Committee shall respond only in an advisory or educative fashion and shall have no authority to investigate the case or to discipline the individual in question. However, the Ethics and Professional Conduct Committee may cooperate with other agencies and associations who do have authority in the matter, by sharing relevant and factual information or by referring the complainant to a more appropriate resource.

Complaints that address concerns about professional standards, organizations, employers and the like, shall be referred to the Professional Standards and Employment Relations Committee. Nevertheless, it should be recognized that in situations where an individual psychologist is being coerced to behave unethically, he/she bears certain ethical responsibilities and to fail to take appropriate action, e.g., refusing to behave unethically, could eventuate changes of misconduct against the individual psychologist involved. However, as a rule, such "standards" concerns would not fall under the purview of this complaint process.

SECTION III. RECEIPT AND ACKNOWLEDGEMENT OF COMPLAINTS AND INQUIRIES

A. The Ethics and Professional Conduct Committee shall recognize and respond to all complaints and inquiries from any responsible individual or group of individuals in accordance with these procedures. The individual who petitions the Committee (hereinafter referred to as the *complainant)*, need not be a member of NASP or the affiliated state association. Anonymous letters and phone calls will not be recognized.

B. An oral complaint or inquiry may be formally handled, referred elsewhere when appropriate, or an Ethics and Professional Conduct Committee chairperson may request that the complaint be formally submitted in writing. Only written statements expressing the details of the alleged misconduct will be accepted for action. Such written statements shall be signed by the complainant and should state, in as much detail as practicable, the facts upon which the complaint is based. All the correspondence, records and activities of the Ethics and Professional Conduct Committee shall remain confidential.

C. Within 15 days of receipt of a written statement outlining the details of the alleged misconduct, the chairpersons of the Ethics and Professional Conduct Committee shall do the following:

1. Determine if the individual against whom the complaint is made (hereinafter referred to as the *respondent*), is a member of NASP. If the respondent is not a member of NASP, the complainant shall be so advised and when appropriate, referred to other agencies and/or associations who would have authority in the matter.

2. If the respondent is a member of NASP, the Ethics and Professional Conduct Committee chairpersons, with any advisory opinions deemed necessary, shall review the complaint. If it is determined that the alleged misconduct, even if true, would *not* constitute an actual violation of the NASP Principles, a chairperson shall notify the complainant.

3. If the information obtained from the complainant is insufficient to make a determination regarding the alleged misconduct, the chairpersons may send a written request to the complainant, asking for clarification and/or additional information as would be needed to make such a determination.

4. If it is determined that the alleged misconduct, if substantiated, would constitute an actual violation of the NASP Principles, the Ethics and Professional Conduct Committee chairpersons shall direct a letter to and advise the complainant that the allegation will be investigated by the Committee. The complainant shall be asked to sign a release, authorizing that his/her name be revealed to the respondent.

5. If the complainant refuses to permit his/her identity to be made known to the respondent, such refusal will serve as a basis for forfeiting the complaint process. (However, the Ethics and Professional Conduct Committee may proceed on its own volition when a member appears to have engaged in ethical misconduct that tends to injure the Association or to adversely affect its reputation, or that is clearly inconsistent with or destructive of the goals and objectives of the Association.)

SECTION IV. CONDUCT OF AN INFORMAL INQUIRY

A. Within 15 days of receipt of the signed release, the Ethics and Professional Conduct Committee shall inform the respondent, in writing, with the envelope marked "confidential," that a complaint has been filed against him/her. This letter shall describe the nature of the complaint, indicate the principle(s) which appear to have been violated, and request the respondent's cooperation in obtaining a full picture of the circumstances which led to the allegations. A copy of the NASP *Principles for Professional Ethics*, these procedures, and any pertinent advisory opinions of the Ethics and Professional Conduct Committee shall also be enclosed. Ordinarily, the respondent shall be informed of the name of the complainant, when written permission to do so has been obtained. (See Section III, C-5 above for exception.)

B. The respondent shall be asked to provide a written statement outlining his/her view of the situation in order that the Committee may be cognizant of all relevant aspects of the case.

C. Whenever possible, the Ethics and Professional Conduct Committee shall attempt to resolve differences privately and informally through further correspondence with all parties involved. An attempt shall be made to bring about an adjustment through mediative efforts in the interest of correcting a general situation or settling the particular issues between the parties involved.

D. If the respondent does not respond to the original inquiry within 30 days, a follow-up letter shall be sent to the respondent by registered or certified mail, marked "confidential," with a return receipt requested.

E. If the respondent refuses to reply to the Committee's inquiry or otherwise cooperate with the Committee, the Committee may continue its investigation, noting in the record the circumstances of the respondent's failure to cooperate. The Committee shall also inform the respondent that his/her lack of cooperation may result in action which could eventuate his/her being dropped from membership in the Association.

F. As a rule, if the complainant wishes to withdraw the complaint, the inquiry is terminated, except in extreme cases where the Committee feels the issues in the case are of such importance as to warrant completing the investigation in its own right and in the interest of the public welfare or the Association. (See Section III, C-5.)

G. The Association will not recognize a respondent's resignation from membership while there is a complaint pending before the Ethics and Professional Conduct Committee or before an ethics committee of a state association unless he/she submits an affidavit stating that:

  1. The resignation is free and voluntary;

  2. He/she is aware of a pending investigation into allegations of misconduct;

  3. He/she acknowledges that the material facts upon which the complaint is based are true; and

  4. He/she submits the resignation because he/she knows that if charges are predicated on the misconduct under investigation, he/she could not defend him/herself successfully against them.

H. Within 30 days of receipt of the written statement from the respondent, or (in the event the respondent fails to reply or otherwise cooperate), within 30 days of receipt of the return receipt requested from the second notification by the Committee (Section IV, D, E), the chairpersons through advice of the Committee, shall determine if a violation may have occurred, and if so, what principles have potentially been violated.

I. If, in the opinion of the Committee, the complaint has a basis in fact but is considered likely to be corrected without further action, the chairpersons shall so indicate in the record and shall so inform all parties involved.

J. If, in the opinion of the chairpersons, the issues raised by the complaint would, if true, constitute a violation of the principles, and if it appears that the complaint cannot be resolved by less formal means, the chairpersons shall, in coordination with the appropriate State Delegate, appoint two impartial NASP members from the state in which the respondent practices to form an Ad Hoc Committee, together with the chairpersons of the Ethics and Professional Conduct Committee. The purpose of this Ad Hoc Committee is to investigate the case, to evaluate the character of the behavior(s) in question and to make recommendations to the Ethics and Professional Conduct Committee for final disposition of the case.

K. The Ethics and Professional Conduct Committee chairpersons shall transmit to the members of the Ad Hoc Committee, by registered or certified mail, in envelopes marked "confidential," copies of the following:

  1. The original complaint or material;

  2. The letter to the respondent apprising him/her of the nature of the alleged violation;

3. The response from the respondent; and

4. Any such further facts related to the case as the chairpersons can assemble from sources of evident reliability.

L. The Ad Hoc Committee shall then determine whether:

1. The case shall be closed;

2. Further investigation by correspondence is indicated;

3. Further investigation by a Fact-Finding Committee is indicated (see Section VI);

4. The respondent and/or complainant shall be asked to appear before the Ad Hoc Committee; or

5. Some other action or a combination thereof shall be taken.

SECTION V. **RECOMMENDATIONS OF THE AD HOC COMMITTEE**

A. When the Ad Hoc Committee has obtained sufficient information with which to reach a decision, or, in any event, in not more than 60 days from the formation of the Ad Hoc Committee, the Ethics and Professional Conduct chairpersons shall request that the Ad Hoc Committee vote on the disposition of the case.

B. If, in the unanimous opinion of the Ad Hoc Committee members, a violation of the NASP Principles has occurred and if, in the opinion of the Ad Hoc Committee, the unethical behavior can be terminated by action of the Committee itself, one of the following recommendations shall be made:

1. The Ad Hoc Committee shall request, in writing, that the respondent take corrective measures to modify or stop certain activities or practices;

2. The Ad Hoc Committee shall, in writing, censure or reprimand the respondent;

3. The Ad Hoc Committee shall require that the respondent provide restitution to or apologize, in writing, to an individual, group of individuals, or organization harmed by the respondent's unethical conduct; or

4. The Ad Hoc Committee shall recommend that the respondent be placed under a period of probation of membership or surveillance under fixed terms agreed to by the respondent.

C. Within 5 days, the Ethics and Professional Conduct chairpersons shall inform the respondent of the Ad Hoc Committee's determination and recommendations. The respondent shall be notified that he/she may make a request for a hearing on the charges within 30 days from the receipt of a statement of the charges and the Committee's findings and recommendations. Such a request shall be in writing and directed to the President of the Association.

D. The Ethics and Professional Conduct Committee chairpersons shall draft a report, summarizing the findings and recommendations of the Ad Hoc Committee, copies of which shall be distributed to the two other Ad Hoc Committee members, the respondent and, at the Committee's discretion, the complainant. This report shall be transmitted in envelopes marked "confidential" in the case of the respondent, by registered or certified mail with a return receipt requested.

E. A summary report shall then be edited by the Ethics and Professional Conduct Committee chairpersons, ensuring the confidentiality of all persons involved is strictly maintained, for purposes of reporting to the Delegate Assembly at the next regularly scheduled meeting on the activities and recommendations of the Ethics and Professional Conduct Committee and its designees, e.g., any Ad Hoc Committee so convened in the interim.

F. The unanimous decision of the Ad Hoc Committee shall be binding on the Association unless overturned by the Hearing Committee, Executive Board or Delegate Assembly in accordance with the procedures outlined herein. (See Section VIII)

SECTION VI. **CONDUCT OF A FORMAL INVESTIGATION**

A. A formal investigation shall be undertaken if any one of the following circumstances prevails:

   1. The Ad Hoc Committee finds that it lacks sufficient data with which to proceed;

   2. The Ad Hoc Committee is unable to reach consensus;

   3. The recommendations of the Ad Hoc Committee do not lead to resolution of the problem; or

   4. The facts alleged in the complaint, if substantiated, would likely require action leading to termination of the respondent's membership in the Association.

B. When a formal investigation is warranted under these procedures, the Ethics and Professional Conduct chairpersons, in coordination with the President of the Association, shall appoint a Fact-Finding Committee, which shall appoint its own chairperson, to consist of not less than three nor more than five members of the Association for the specific purpose of more fully investigating the charges. No member previously involved in reviewing the case may continue on the Fact-Finding Committee. The Ethics and Professional Conduct Committee chairpersons shall serve on the Fact-Finding Committee in ex-officio status in order to apprise the Fact-Finding Committee of the procedures by which they are bound and to serve in an advisory capacity.

C. The Fact-Finding Committee shall be bound by the same procedures and timelines as outlined in Sections III and IV of these procedures. In addition, the Fact-Finding Committee may, at the discretion of the Executive Board, retain a legal advisor as counsel to the committee while investigating its case.

D. The respondent may seek advice from any individual, including an attorney or another member of the Association, for assistance in preparing and presenting documentary evidence requested by the Fact-Finding Committee.

SECTION VII. **RECOMMENDATIONS OF THE FACT-FINDING COMMITTEE**

A. If the formal investigation was convened following a decision by consensus of the Ad Hoc Committee, and if the Fact-Finding Committee unanimously concurs with the Ad Hoc Committee's findings and recommendations, all parties shall be so informed and this decision shall be binding on the Association unless overturned by the Hearing Committee, Executive Board or Delegate Assembly, in accordance with the procedures outlined herein.

B. If the case was not resolved at the Ad Hoc Committee level, the Fact-Finding Committee must announce its findings and recommendations within the prescribed timelines. The Fact-Finding Committee may exercise any of the recommendations open to the Ad Hoc Committee (Section V, B) and in addition may also recommend that the respondent's membership in the Association be terminated.

C. Should the Fact-Finding Committee so recommend, the chairpersons of the Ethics and Professional Conduct Committee must present the findings and recommendations of the Fact-Finding Committee to the NASP Executive Board and Delegate Assembly. A summary report shall be prepared, such that the confidentiality of all parties involved, i.e., identifying information of the informer, is strictly maintained. The case shall be reviewed in sufficient detail so as to allow the Executive Board and the Delegate Assembly members to vote to concur or overrule the decision of the Fact-Finding Committee.

D. In accordance with NASP Bylaws, cases involving a recommendation for expulsion from the Association by the Ethics and Professional Conduct Committee shall be confirmed by a 2/3 vote of the Executive Board, with a majority ratification by the Delegate Assembly.

E. At the discretion of the Executive Board and Delegate Assembly, the respondent may be allowed to voluntarily resign his/her membership in the Association.

F. Within five days, the Ethics and Professional Conduct Committee chairpersons shall inform the respondent of the decision of the Executive Board and Delegate Assembly in the same manner as provided in Section V, C of these procedures.

G. If the Executive Board and/or the Delegate Assembly do not concur with the Committee's recommendation for expulsion from membership, the case shall be remanded back to the Fact-Finding Committee for consideration of a lesser penalty.

SECTION VIII. **CONDUCT OF THE HEARING COMMITTEE**

A. Within 30 days of receipt of a statement of the charges against him/her and a statement of the Committee's findings and recommendations, the respondent has the right to request from the President of the Association a hearing on the charges. This right shall be considered waived if such request is not made, in writing, within the 30 day period.

B. If the respondent does request a hearing, the President shall select a panel of ten members of the Association, none of whom shall be members of the Ethics and Professional Conduct Committee or have had any prior connection with the case. From the panel, the respondent shall have 30 days in which to chose a Hearing Committee of five members. If he/she does not make a selection, the President shall choose the five members to comprise the Hearing Committee.

C. The President shall select a chairperson of the Hearing Committee who shall conduct the hearing and assure that the procedures are properly observed. There shall be no communication between the members of the Hearing Committee and the Ethics and Professional Conduct Committee or any of its representatives prior to the hearing itself.

D. A date for the hearing shall be set by the President with the concurrence of the respondent. In no event shall the hearing take place later than 90 days from the date of the respondent's request for a hearing.

E. At least 30 days prior to the hearing, the respondent and the Hearing Committee members shall be provided with copies of all documents to be presented and the names of all witnesses that will be offered by the Ethics and Professional Conduct Committee in support of the charges.

F. Presentation of the case against the respondent shall be the responsibility of the Ethics and Professional Conduct Committee or such others as the Ethics and Professional Conduct Committee has designated to investigate the complaint. Legal counsel for the Association may participate fully in the presentation of the case.

G. All evidence that is relevant and reliable, as determined by the chairperson of the Hearing Committee, shall be admissible. Evidence of mitigating circumstances may be presented by the respondent.

H. The respondent shall have the right to counsel, to present witnesses and documents and to cross-examine the witnesses offered by the Ethics and Professional Conduct Committee.

I. The hearing may be adjourned as necessary and the Ethics and Professional Conduct Committee may introduce rebuttal evidence.

J. In the interest of obtaining a full and accurate record of the hearing, a tape recorder or other transcription device may be used, at the discretion of the Hearing Committee and the respondent.

SECTION IX. **RECOMMENDATIONS OF THE HEARING COMMITTEE**

A. At the conclusion of the hearing, the Hearing Committee shall have 30 days in which to issue its report and recommendations.

B. If the Hearing Committee recommends that the respondent be dropped from membership or that the respondent be permitted to resign, the matter shall be referred to the Executive Board. A recommendation that the respondent be expelled or be allowed to resign must be made by 4 of the 5 committee members. Other disciplinary measures may be recommended by a simple majority and would be decided upon per individual case.

C. Only the disciplinary measures specified by the Ethics and Professional Conduct Committee in the formal statement of charges, or a lesser penalty, shall be recommended by the Hearing Committee. Although the Ethics and Professional Conduct Committee recommendations may be modified by the Hearing Committee, it may not increase the penalty recommended.

D. The Hearing Committee shall submit its report and recommendations simultaneously to the Executive Board and to the respondent.

E. The respondent shall have 15 days from receipt of the Hearing Committee's report in which to file a written statement with the Executive Board. The Ethics and Professional Conduct Committee shall then have 15 days in which to file a response.

F. After consideration of the record, the recommendation of the Hearing Committee and any statements that may be filed, the Executive Board shall adopt the recommendations of the Hearing Committee unless it determines that:

　　1. The NASP Principles and/or the procedures herein stated have been incorrectly applied;

　　2. The findings of fact of the Hearing Committee as stated in the report are not supported by the evidence; or

　　3. The procedures followed were in violation of the Bylaws of the Association.

G. The Ethics and Professional Conduct Committee shall inform the respondent and, at its discretion, may inform the complainant of any final action taken by the Executive Board. The Ethics and Professional Conduct Committee shall report to the Delegate Assembly at its next regularly scheduled meeting, in Executive Session, the names of those members who have been allowed to resign or who have been expelled from membership, and the ethical principle(s) involved.

H. The Ethics and Professional Conduct Committee shall report annually and in confidence to the Delegate Assembly and Executive Board, in Executive Session, the names of members who have been expelled from the Association and the ethical principle(s) involved.

I. In severe cases and when the welfare of the public is at stake, and when the Ethics and Professional Conduct Committee deems it necessary to maintain the principles of the Association and the profession, it may also notify affiliated state and regional associations and state and local licensing and certification boards of the final disposition of the case. Other interested parties may be notified of the final action when, in the opinion of the Ethics and Professional Conduct Committee, notification is necessary for the protection of the public.

REFERENCES

American Psychological Association, "Amendments in CSPEC's Rules and Procedures," as documented in the non-confidential minutes of CSPEC's Action Agenda, February 22-23, 1980.

American Psychological Association. *Ethical Standards of Psychologists*, Washington, D.C.: American Psychological Association, Inc., 1977.

American Psychological Association, "Rules and Procedures - Committee on Scientific and Professional Ethics and Conduct," *American Psychologist*, September, 1974, pp. 703-710.

Bersoff, D. N., "Review of CSPEC Rules and Procedures," American Psychological Association Memorandum, February 6, 1980.

Illinois Psychological Association, "Revised Procedural Guidelines for Ethics Committee," *Illinois Psychologist*. January-March, 1975, pp. 23-31.

Illinois School Psychologists Association, "Procedures for Handling Complaints of Alleged Violations of Ethical Principles," September, 1980.

National Association of School Psychologists, *Principles for Professional Ethics*, October, 1974.

National Association of School Psychologists, "Procedures for Handling of Complaints of Alleged Violations of Ethical Principles," October, 1974.

APPENDIX E: The National Association of School Psychologists' (1984) Standards for the Provision of School Psychological Services

1.0 Definitions

1.1 A *School Psychologist* is a professional psychologist who has met all requirements for credentialing as stipulated in the appropriate NASP standards. The credential is based upon the completion of a school psychology training program which meets the criteria specified in the NASP *Standards for Training and Field Placement Programs in School Psychology.*

1.2 A *Supervising School Psychologist* is a professional psychologist who has met all NASP requirements for credentialing, has completed three years of successful supervised experience as a school psychologist, and who has been designated by an employing agency as a supervisor responsible for school psychological services in the agency.

1.3 *Parent(s)*, as used in these *Standards*, includes both biological parent(s) and/or legal guardian(s).

2.0 Standards for Administrative Agencies

The purpose of this section of the standards is to provide guidance to federal and state administrative agencies in regard to administrative organization, laws, and regulations as they pertain to the provision of school psychological services.

2.1 Federal Level Administrative Agency

2.1.1 Organization

The federal education agency should employ a supervising school psychologist in order to accomplish the following objectives:

2.1.1.1 To provide professional leadership and assistance to the federal education agency, state education agencies, and the school psychology profession in regard to standards, policies, and procedures for program delivery, and for utilization, funding, education and training, and inservice education of school psychological services personnel.

2.1.1.2 To participate in the administration of federal programs providing funding for school psychological services in state, intermediate, and local education agencies, and for the education and training of school psychologists.

2.1.1.3 To encourage and assist in evaluation, research, and dissemination activities; to determine the effectiveness of school psychological education, training, and service programs; to determine needed changes; and to identify and communicate exemplary practices to training and service units.

2.1.1.4 To assure that consistent communication is established and maintained among professional organizations, federal, state, and local education agencies, and university training programs involved in providing and developing school psychological services.

2.1.2 Laws

2.1.2.1 The Congress of the United States should ensure that the rights of all parents and children are protected by the creation and modification of laws which provide for the services of school psychologists. These services include, but are not limited to, consultation, assessment, and intervention for individuals, groups, and systems. These services are available to all children, their families, and school personnel.

2.1.2.2 The Congress should ensure that school psychological services are provided in a free and appropriate manner to all children, their families, and school personnel in need of such services.

2.1.2.3 The Congress should ensure that federal laws recognize the appropriate involvement of school psychologists in educational programs and that adequate federal funding is made available for the education, training, services, and continuing professional development of school psychologists in order to guarantee appropriate and effective services.

2.1.2.4 The Congress should create no laws which effectively prohibit the credentialed school psychologist from the ethical and legal practice of his/her profession in the public or private sector, or which would be in violation of these standards.

Source: Standards for the provision of school psychological services. In *Professional Conduct Manual* (pp. 24–33). Copyright 1984 by the National Association of School Psychologists. Reprinted by permission of the publisher.

2.1.3 Regulations

2.1.3.1 All federal agencies should utilize the services of the federal educational agency school psychologist in developing and implementing regulations pursuant to all relevant federal laws.

2.1.3.2 All federal agencies should seek the advice and consultation of the National Association of School Psychologists prior to the adoption of regulations pursuant to any federal law which involves or should reasonably involve the profession of school psychology.

2.1.3.3 Federal agencies should promulgate regulations consistent with the principles set forth in these *Standards* and the NASP *Principles for Professional Ethics.*

2.2 State Level Administrative Agencies

2.2.1 Organization

Each state educational agency (SEA) should employ at least one full-time supervising school psychologist for each 500 (or fewer) school psychologists within the state. An equivalent ratio should be maintained if there are more than 500 school psychologists. It is recognized that this ratio may vary based upon administrative structures, available resources, and types of programs served. Appropriate objectives to be accomplished by the SEA school psychologist(s) include the following:

2.2.1.1 To provide professional leadership assistance to the SEA, local educational agencies, and the profession with regard to standards, policies, and procedures for school psychology program delivery.

2.2.1.2 To support the utilization, funding, education, training, and inservice education of school psychologists.

2.2.1.3 To participate in the administration of state and federal programs providing funding for school psychological services in intermediate and local educational agencies, and for the education and training of school psychologists.

2.2.1.4 To encourage and assist in evaluation, research, and dissemination activities to determine the effectiveness of school psychological education, training, and service programs; to determine needed changes; and to identify and communicate exemplary practices to training and service units.

2.2.1.5 To maintain communication with and assure the input of state school psychological associations into the policy making of the SEA.

2.2.1.6 To communicate with the federal education agency school psychologist to ensure recognition of state issues and to facilitate input into federal policy.

2.2.2 Laws

2.2.2.1 All state legislative bodies should ensure that the rights of parents and children are protected by the creation and modification of laws which provide for the services of school psychologists. These services include, but are not limited to, consultation for individuals, groups, and systems, assessment, and intervention. These services are available to all children, their families, and school personnel.

2.2.2.2 The state legislature should ensure that school psychological services are provided in a free and appropriate way to all children, their families, and school personnel in need of such services.

2.2.2.3 The state legislature should ensure that state laws recognize the appropriate involvement of school psychologists in educational programs.

2.2.2.4 The state legislature should ensure that adequate funding is made available for the education, training, services, and continuing professional development of school psychologists in order to guarantee appropriate and effective services.

2.2.2.5 The state legislature should ensure that state laws provide for the credentialing of school psychologists consistent with NASP standards.

2.2.2.6 The state legislature should create no laws which prohibit the school psychologist from the ethical and legal practice of his/her profession in the public or private sector, or that prevent the school psychologist from practicing in a manner consistent with these *Standards.*

2.2.2.7 The state legislature should ensure that there are sufficient numbers of adequately prepared and credentialed school psychologists to provide services consistent with these *Standards.* In most settings, this will require at least one full-time school psychologist for each 1,000 children served by the LEA, with a maximum of four schools served by one school psychologist. It is recognized that this ratio may vary based upon the needs of children served, the type of program served, available resources, distance between schools, and other unique characteristics.

2.2.3 Regulations

2.2.3.1 All state agencies should utilize the services of the SEA school psychologist(s) in developing and implementing administrative rules pursuant to all relevant state laws, federal laws, and regulations.

2.2.3.2 All state agencies should seek the advice and consultation of the state school psychologists' professional association prior to the adoption of rules pursuant to any state law, federal law, or regulation which involves or should reasonably involve the profession of school psychology.

2.2.3.3 All state education agencies should utilize the services of the SEA school psychologist(s) in the SEA review and approval of school psychology training programs.

2.2.3.4 All state education agencies should utilize the services of the SEA school psychologist(s) in developing and implementing administrative rules for credentialing school psychologists. Such rules shall be consistent with NASP *Standards for the Credentialing of School Psychologists*.

2.2.3.5 State education agencies should promulgate regulations consistent with the principles set forth in these *Standards* and the NASP *Principles for Professional Ethics*.

3.0 Standards for Employing Agencies

The purpose of these standards is to provide employing agencies with specific guidance regarding the organization, policies, and practices needed to assure the provision of adequate school psychological services.

3.1 Comprehensive Continuum of Services.

Employing agencies assure that school psychological services are provided in a coordinated, organized fashion, and are deployed in a manner which ensures the provision of a comprehensive continuum of services as outlined in Section 4.0 of these *Standards*. Such services are available to all students served by the agency and are available to an extent sufficient to meet the needs of the populations served.

3.2 Professional Evaluation, Supervision, and Development

3.2.1 Supervision.

Employing agencies assure that an effective program of supervision and evaluation of school psychological services exists. School psychologists are responsible for the overall development, implementation, and professional supervision of school psychological service programs, and are responsible for articulating those programs to others in the employing agency and to the agency's constituent groups.

3.2.2 Supervisor(s).

The school psychological services program is supervised by a designated school psychologist who meets the requirements for a supervising school psychologist (Section 1.2) and who demonstrates competencies needed for effective supervision.

3.2.3 Availability of Supervision.

Supervision is available to all school psychologists to an extent sufficient to ensure the provision of effective and accountable services (see Section 4.6 for specific requirements). In most cases, one supervising school psychologist should be employed for every ten school psychologists to be supervised (an equivalent ratio should be maintained for part-time supervisors). It is recognized that this ratio may vary based upon the type of program served, staff needs, and other unique characteristics.

3.2.4 Intern Supervision

A credentialed school psychologist meeting the requirements of a supervising school psychologist, with at least one year of experience at the employing agency, supervises no more than two school psychology interns at any given time (consistent with the NASP *Standards for Training and Field Placement Programs in School Psychology*).

3.2.5 Peer Review

After attaining independent practice status (see Section 4.5), school psychologists continue to receive appropriate supervision. The independent practitioner should also engage in peer review with other school psychologists. Peer review involves mutual assistance with self-examination of services and the development of plans to continue professional growth and development. Employing agencies assure that school psychologists are given appropriate time and support for peer review activities.

3.2.6 Accountability and Program Evaluation.
Employing agencies assure that school psychologists develop a coordinated plan for accountability and evaluation of all services provided in order to maintain and improve the effectiveness of services. Such plans include specific, measurable objectives pertaining to the planned effects of services on all relevant elements of the system. Evaluation and revision of these plans occurs on a regular basis.

3.2.7 Continuing Professional Development.
Employing agencies recognize that school psychologists are obligated to continue their professional training and development through participation in a recognized Continuing Professional Development (CPD) program (see Section 4.6). Employing agencies provide release time and financial support for such activities. They recognize documented continuing professional development activities in the evaluation and advancement of school psychologists. Private practitioners who contract to provide services are responsible for their own CPD program, and these activities should also be encouraged by employing agencies.

3.3 Conditions for Effective Service Delivery
In order to assure that employment conditions enable school psychologists to provide effective services, employing agencies adopt policies and practices ensuring that Sections 3.3.1 through 3.3.4 are met.

3.3.1 School psychologists are not subjected to administrative constraints which prevent them from providing services in full accordance with these *Standards* and the NASP *Principles for Professional Ethics*. When administrative policies conflict with these *Standards* or the NASP *Ethics*, the principles outlined in the *Standards* or *Ethics* take precedence in determining appropriate practices of the school psychologist.

3.3.2 School psychologists have appropriate input into the general policy making of the employing agency and the development of programs affecting the staff, students, and families they serve.

3.3.3 School psychologists have appropriate professional autonomy in determining the nature, extent, and duration of services they provide. Specific activities are defined within the profession, although school psychologists frequently collaborate and seek input from others in determining appropriate service delivery. Legal, ethical, and professional standards and guidelines are considered by the practitioner in making decisions regarding practice (see Section 4.4).

3.3.4 School psychologists have access to adequate clerical assistance, appropriate professional work materials, sufficient office and work space, and general working conditions that enhance the delivery of effective services. Included are test materials, access to a private telephone and office, secretarial services, therapeutic aids, professional literature (books, journals), and so forth.

3.4 Contractual Services
It is recognized that employing agencies may obtain school psychological services on a contractual basis in order to ensure the provision of adequate services to all children. However, each student within the educational system must be assured the full range of school psychological services necessary to maximize his/her success and adjustment in school. When an employing agency utilizes contractual services, the following standards are observed.

3.4.1 Contractual school psychological services encompass the same comprehensive continuum of services as that provided by regularly employed school psychologists. Overall, psychological services are not limited to any specific type of service and include opportunities for follow-up and continuing consultation appropriate to the needs of the student. Individual contracts for services may be limited as long as comprehensive services are provided overall.

3.4.2 Persons providing contractual psychological services are fully credentialed school psychologists as defined by these *Standards*. In specific instances, however, services by psychologists in other specialty areas (e.g., clinical, industrial/organizational) might be used to supplement school psychological services.

3.4.3 Contractual school psychological services are not to be utilized as a means to decrease the amount and quality of school psychological services provided by an employing agency. They may be used to augment programs but not to supplant them.

3.4.4. School psychologists providing contractual services are given appropriate access and information. They are familiar with the instructional resources of the employing agency to ensure that students they serve have the same opportunities as those served by regularly employed school psychologists.

3.4.5 Contractual school psychological services are provided in a manner which protects the due process rights of students and their parents as defined by state and federal laws and regulations.

3.4.6 Contracting for services is not to be used as a means to avoid legitimate employee rights, wages, or fringe benefits.

3.4.7 Psychologists providing contractual school psychological services provide those services in a manner consistent with these *Standards*, NASP *Principles for Professional Ethics*, and other relevant professional guidelines and standards.

3.5 Non-Biased Assessment and Program Planning

Employing agencies should adopt policies and practices in accordance with the following standards:

3.5.1 General Principles

3.5.1.1 School psychologists use assessment techniques to provide information which is helpful in maximizing student achievement and educational success.

3.5.1.2 School psychologists have autonomous decision-making responsibility (as defined in Section 4.4) to determine the type, nature, and extent of assessment techniques they use in student evaluation.

3.5.1.3 School psychologists have autonomy (as defined in Section 4.4) in determining the content and nature of reports.

3.5.1.4 School psychologists use assessment techniques and instruments which have established validity and reliability for the purposes and populations for which they are intended.

3.5.1.5 School psychologists use, develop, and encourage assessment practices which increase the likelihood of the development of effective educational interventions and follow-up.

3.5.2 Professional Involvement

3.5.2.1 A multidisciplinary team is involved in assessment, program decision-making, and evaluation. The team conducts periodic evaluations of its performance to ensure continued effectiveness.

3.5.2.2 The multidisciplinary team includes a fully trained and certified school psychologist.

3.5.2.3 The school psychologist communicates a minority position to all involved when in disagreement with the multidisciplinary team position.

3.5.3 Non-Biased Assessment Techniques

3.5.3.1 Assessment procedures and program recommendations are chosen to maximize the student's opportunities to be successful in the general culture, while respecting the student's ethnic background.

3.5.3.2 Multifaceted assessment batteries are used which include a focus on the student's strengths.

3.5.3.3 Communications are held in the client's dominant spoken language or alternative communication system. All student information is interpreted in the context of the student's socio-cultural background and the setting in which she/he is functioning.

3.5.3.4 Assessment techniques (including computerized techniques) are used only by personnel professionally trained in their use and in a manner consistent with these *Standards*.

3.5.3.5 School psychologists promote the development of objective, valid, and reliable assessment techniques.

3.5.3.6 Interpretation of assessment results is based upon empirically validated research.

3.5.4 Parent/Student Involvement

3.5.4.1 Informed written consent of parent(s) and/or student (if the student has reached the age of majority) is obtained before assessment and special program implementation.

3.5.4.2 The parent(s) and/or student is fully informed of all essential information considered and its relevancy to decision-making.

3.5.4.3 The parent(s) and/or student is invited to participate in decision-making meetings.

3.5.4.4 The parent(s) and/or student is routinely notified that an advocate can participate in conferences focusing on assessment results and program recommendations.

3.5.4.5 A record of meetings regarding assessment results and program recommendations is available to all directly concerned.

3.5.5 Educational Programming and Follow-Through

3.5.5.1 School psychologists are involved in determining options and revisions of educational programs to ensure that they are adaptive to the needs of students.

3.5.5.2 The contributions of diverse cultural backgrounds should be emphasized in educational programs.

3.5.5.3 School psychologists follow-up on the efficacy of their recommendations.

3.5.5.4 Student needs are given priority in determining educational programs.

3.5.5.5 Specific educational prescriptions result from the assessment team's actions.

3.5.5.6 Where a clear determination of the student's needs does not result from initial assessment, a diagnostic teaching program is offered as part of additional assessment procedures.

3.5.5.7 Regular, systematic review of the student's program is conducted and includes program modifications as necessary.

3.6 School Psychological Records

3.6.1 The employing agency's policy on student records is consistent with state and federal rules and laws, and ensures the protection of the confidentiality of the student and his/her family. The policy specifies the types of data developed by the school psychologist which are classified as school or pupil records.

3.6.2 Parents may inspect and review any personally identifiable data relating to their child which were collected, maintained, or used in his/her evaluation. Although test protocols are part of the student's record, school psychologists protect test security and observe copyright restrictions.

3.6.3 Access to psychological records is restricted to those permitted by law who have legitimate educational interest in the records.

3.6.4 School psychologists interpret school psychological records to non-psychologists who qualify for access.

3.6.5 School psychological records are only created and maintained when the information is necessary and relevant to legitimate educational program needs and when parents (or student if age of majority has been attained) have given their informed consent for the creation of such a record. This consent is based upon full knowledge of the purposes for which information is sought, and the personnel who will have access to it. The school psychologist assumes responsibility for assuring the accuracy and relevancy of the information recorded.

3.6.6 School psychological records are systematically reviewed, and when necessary purged, in keeping with relevant federal and state laws in order to protect children from decisions based on incorrect, misleading, or out-of-date information.

4.0 Standards for the Delivery of Comprehensive School Psychological Services

The purpose of these standards is to ensure the delivery of comprehensive services by school psychologists.

4.1 Organization of School Psychological Services

4.1.1 School psychological services are planned, organized, directed, and reviewed by school psychologists.

4.1.2 School psychologists participate in determining the recipients and the type of school psychological services offered.

4.1.3 The goals and objectives of school psychological services are available in written form.

4.1.4 A written set of procedural guidelines for the delivery of school psychological services is followed and made available upon request.

4.1.5 A clearly stated referral system is in writing and is communicated to parents, staff members, students, and other referral agents.

4.1.6 The organization of school psychological services is in written form and includes lines of responsibility, supervisory, and administrative relationships.

4.1.7 Where two or more school psychologists are employed, a coordinated system of school psychological services is in effect within that unit.

4.1.8 Units providing school psychological services include sufficient professional and support personnel to achieve their goals and objectives.

4.2 Relationship to Other Units and Professionals

4.2.1 The school psychological services unit is responsive to the needs of the population that it serves. Psychological services are periodically and systematically reviewed to ensure their conformity with the needs of the population served.

4.2.2 School psychologists establish and maintain relationships with other professionals (e.g., pediatricians, bilingual specialists, audiologists) who provide services to children and families. They collaborate with these professionals in prevention, assessment, and intervention efforts as necessary. They also cooperate with advocates representing children and their families.

4.2.3 Providers of school psychological services maintain a cooperative relationship with colleagues and co-workers in the best mutual interests of clients, in a manner consistent with the goals of the employing agency. Conflicts should be resolved in a professional manner.

4.2.4 School psychologists develop plans for the delivery of services in accordance with best professional practices.

4.2.5 School psychologists employed within a school setting coordinate the services of mental health providers from other agencies (such as community mental health centers, child guidance clinics, or private practitioners) to ensure a continuum of services.

4.2.6 School psychologists are knowledgeable about community agencies and resources. They provide liaison and consulting services to the community and agencies regarding psychological, mental health, and educational issues.

4.2.6.1 School psychologists communicate as needed with state and community agencies and professionals (e.g., child guidance clinics, community mental health centers, private practitioners) regarding services for children, families, and school personnel. They refer clients to these agencies and professionals as appropriate.

4.2.6.2 School psychologists are informed of and have the opportunity to participate in community agency staffings of cases involving their clients.

4.2.6.3 Community agency personnel are invited to participate in school system conferences concerning their clients (with written parental permission).

4.3 Comprehensive School Psychological Services Delivery

School psychologists provide a range of services to their clients. These consist of direct and indirect services which require involvement with the entire educational system: (a) the students, teachers, administrators, and other school personnel; (b) the families, surrogate caretakers, and other community and regional agencies, and resources which support the educational process; (c) the organizational, physical, temporal, and curricular variables which play major roles within the system; and (d) a variety of other factors which may be important on an individual basis.

The intent of these services is to promote mental health and facilitate learning. Comprehensive school psychological services are comprised of diverse activities. These activities complement one another and therefore are most accurately viewed as being integrated and coordinated rather than discrete services. However, for descriptive purposes, they will be listed and described separately. The following are the services that comprise the delivery system.

4.3.1 Consultation

4.3.1.1 School psychologists consult and collaborate with parents, school, and outside personnel regarding mental health, behavioral, and educational concerns.

4.3.1.2 School psychologists design and develop procedures for preventing disorders, promoting mental health and learning, and improving educational systems.

4.3.1.3 School psychologists provide inservice and other skill enhancement activities to school personnel, parents, and others in the community, regarding issues of human learning, development, and behavior.

4.3.1.4 School psychologists develop collaborative relationships with their clients and involve them in the assessment, intervention, and program evaluation procedures.

4.3.2 Psychological and Psychoeducational Assessment

4.3.2.1 School psychologists conduct multifactored psychological and psychoeducational assessments of children and youth as appropriate.

4.3.2.2 Psychological and psychoeducational assessments include consideration as appropriate of the areas of personal-social adjustment, intelligence-
scholastic aptitude, adaptive behavior, language and communication
skills, academic achievement, sensory and perceptual-motor functioning, environmental-cultural influences, and vocational development, aptitude, and interests.

4.3.2.3 School psychologists utilize formal instruments, procedures, and techniques. Interviews, observations, and behavioral evaluations are included
in these procedures.

4.3.2.4 When conducting psychological and psychoeducational assessments,
school psychologists have explicit regard for the context and setting in
which their assessments take place and will be used.

4.3.2.5 School psychologists adhere to the NASP resolutions regarding non-
biased assessment and programming for all students (see Section 3.5.3).
They also are familiar with and consider the *Standards for Educational
and Psychological Tests* (developed by APA, AERA, and NCME) in the
use of assessment techniques.

4.3.3 Interventions

4.3.3.1 School psychologists provide direct and indirect interventions to facilitate the functioning of individuals, groups, and/or organizations.

4.3.3.2 School psychologists design programs to enhance cognitive, affective,
social, and vocational development.

4.3.3.3 School psychologists facilitate the delivery of services by assisting those
who play major roles in the educational system (i.e., parents, school
personnel, community agencies). Such interventions consist of but are
not limited to: inservice training, organization development, parent counseling, program planning and evaluation, vocational development, and
parent education programs.

4.3.4 Supervision

School psychologists provide and/or engage in supervision and continuing professional development as specified in Sections 3.2 and 4.6.

4.3.5 Research

4.3.5.1 School psychologists design, conduct, report, and utilize the results of
research of a psychological and educational nature. All research conducted is in accordance with relevant ethical guidelines of the profession
(e.g., APA *Ethical Principles in the Conduct of Research with Human
Participants*).
Applied and/or basic research should be pursued, focusing on:
(a) Psychological functioning of human beings;
(b) Psychoeducational assessment tools and procedures;
(c) Educational programs and techniques applied to individual cases and
groups of various sizes;
(d) Educational processes;
(e) Social system interactions and organizational factors associated with
school communities; and
(f) Psychological treatments and techniques applied to individual cases
or groups.

4.3.5.2 School psychologists' involvement in research can range from support or
advisory services to having direct responsibility for one or more major
components of a research project. These components may include planning, data collecting, data analyzing, disseminating, and translating
research into practical applications within the school community.

4.3.6 Program Planning and Evaluation

4.3.6.1 School psychologists provide program planning and evaluation services
to assist in decision-making activities.

4.3.6.2 School psychologists serve on committees responsible for developing
and planning educational and educationally-related activities.

4.4 Autonomous Functioning

School psychologists have professional autonomy in determining the nature, scope, and
extent of their specific services. These activities are defined within the profession,
although school psychologists frequently collaborate with and seek input from others in
determining appropriate services delivery. Legal, ethical, and professional standards
and guidelines are considered by the practitioner in making decisions regarding prac-

tice. All practice is restricted to those areas in which the school psychologist has received formal training and supervised experience.

4.4.1 Professional Responsibility and Best Practices

Professional autonomy is associated with professional responsibility. The ultimate responsibility for providing appropriate comprehensive school psychological services rests with the individual practitioner.

While being cognizant of the fact that there often are not explicit guidelines to follow in providing comprehensive school psychological services, the individual practitioner has a responsibility to adhere to the best available and most appropriate standards of practice. There is no substitute for sensitive, sound, professional judgment in the determination of what constitutes best practice. Active involvement in supervision and other continuing professional development activities will assist the practitioner in adhering to best professional practices.

4.5 Independent Practice

A credentialed school psychologist who has completed a school psychology training program which meets the criteria specified in the NASP *Standards for Training and Field Placement Programs in School Psychology* and three years of satisfactory supervised experience is considered qualified for independent practice, regardless of work setting.

4.6 Continuing Professional Development

The practice of school psychology has and will continue to undergo significant changes as new knowledge and technological advances are introduced. The development of new intervention techniques, assessment procedures, computerized assistance, and so forth, will require that practitioners keep abreast of these innovations as well as obtain appropriate professional education and training in these areas. All school psychologists actively participate and engage in activities designed to continue, enhance, and upgrade their professional training and skills and to help ensure quality service provision. These efforts are documented by participation in the NASP or other formal Continuing Professional Development (CPD) programs, although they are not limited to such activities. Memberships in professional organizations, reading of professional journals and books, discussions of professional issues with colleagues, and so forth, are also an integral component of a school psychologist's overall CPD activities.

4.6.1 Participation in CPD activities and the maintenance of high professional standards and practice are continuing obligations of the school psychologist. These obligations are assumed when one initially engages in the practice of school psychology and should be required for continued credentialing.

4.6.2 School psychologists receive supervision by a supervising school psychologist for the first three years of full-time employment (or the equivalent) as a school psychologist. The supervisor shares professional responsibility and accountability for the services provided. While the level and extent of supervision may vary, the supervisor maintains a sufficiently close relationship to meet this standard. Individual face-to-face supervision is engaged in for a minimum of one hour per week or the equivalent (e.g., two hours bi-weekly). Standards for intern supervision are contained in the NASP *Standards for Training and Field Placement Programs in School Psychology.*

4.6.3 After completion of the first three years of supervision, all school psychologists continue to engage in supervision and/or peer review on a regular basis, and further their professional development by actively participating in CPD activities. The level and extent of these activities may vary depending on the needs, interests, and goals of the school psychologist, with more comprehensive service delivery requiring more extensive related professional exchanges. At a minimum, however, these activities are at the level required for successful participation in an appropriate CPD program.

4.6.4 School psychologists, who after three years no longer have supervision available, engage in peer review activities. These may include discussions of cases and professional issues designed to assist with problem solving, decision-making, and appropriate practice.

4.6.5 School psychologists readily seek additional consultation with supervisors, peers, or colleagues with particularly complex or difficult cases, and/or when expanding their services into new areas or those in which they infrequently practice (e.g., low incidence assessment).

4.7 Accountability

4.7.1 School psychologists perform their duties in an accountable manner by keeping records of these efforts, evaluating their effectiveness, and modifying their practices and/or expanding their services as needed.

4.7.2 School psychologists devise systems of accountability and outcome evaluation which aid in documenting the effectiveness of intervention efforts and other services they provide.

4.7.3 Within their service delivery plan, school psychologists include a regular evaluation of their progress in achieving goals. This evaluation should include consideration of the cost effectiveness of school psychological services in terms of time, money, and resources, as well as the availability of professional and support personnel. Evaluation of the school psychological delivery system is conducted internally, and when possible, externally as well (e.g., through state educational agency review, peer review). This evaluation includes an assessment of effectiveness, efficiency, continuity, availability, and adequacy of services.

4.7.4 School psychologists are accountable for their services. They should make information available about their services, and provide consumers with the opportunity to participate in decision-making concerning such issues as initiation, termination, continuation, modification, and evaluation of their services. Rights of the consumer should be taken into acount when performing these activities.

4.8 Private Practice

4.8.1 School psychologists practicing in the private sector provide comprehensive services and adhere to the same standards and guidelines as those providing services in the public sector.

4.8.2 School psychologists document that they have formal training, supervised experience, licensure and/or certification, and demonstrated competence, in any areas of service they intend to deliver to clients within the private sector. They also have a responsibility to actively engage in CPD activities.

4.8.3 School psychologists in private practice adhere to the NASP *Principles for Professional Ethics*, and practice only within their areas of competence. If the services needed by clients fall outside the school psychologist's areas of competence, they are referred elsewhere for assistance.

4.8.4 It is the responsibility of the school psychologist engaging in private practice to inform the client that school psychological services are available without charge from the client's local school district.

4.8.5 School psychologists do not provide services on a private basis to students residing within their employing district who would be eligible to receive the services without charge. This includes students who are attending non-public schools located in the district.

4.8.6 School psychologists offering school psychological services in the private sector ensure that, prior to the commencement of treatment/services, the client fully understands any and all fees associated with the services, and any potential financial assistance that may be available (i.e., third-party reimbursement).

4.8.7 Parents must be informed by the school psychologist that if a private school psychological evaluation is to be completed, this evaluation constitutes only one portion of a multidisciplinary team evaluation. Private services must be equally comprehensive to those described in Section 4.3.

4.8.8 School psychologists in private practice provide and maintain written records in a manner consistent with Section 3.6.

4.9 Professional Ethics and Guidelines

Each school psychologist practices in full accordance with the NASP *Principles for Professional Ethics*, and these *Standards*.

INDEX

ABOUT THE AUTHORS

Robert Henley Woody is Professor of Psychology and Director of School Psychology Training at the University of Nebraska at Omaha. He received a Doctor of Philosophy degree from Michigan State University, a Doctor of Science degree from the University of Pittsburgh, and a Juris Doctor degree from Creighton University.

Joseph C. LaVoie is a Professor of Psychology at the University of Nebraska at Omaha. He received a Doctor of Philosophy degree from the University of Wisconsin.

Susan Epps is an Associate Professor of Pediatrics at the University of Nebraska Medical Center and a staff psychologist at Meyer Rehabilitation Institute and University Hospital. She received a Doctor of Philosophy degree from the University of Minnesota.